THE DEVELOPMENT OF ENGLISH DRAMA IN THE LATE SEVENTEENTH CENTURY

THE DEVELOPMENT OF
ENGLISH DRAMA
IN THE LATE
SEVENTEENTH CENTURY

Robert D. Hume

Clarendon Press · Oxford
1976

Oxford University Press, Ely House, London W.1

GLASGOW NEW YORK TORONTO MELBOURNE WELLINGTON
CAPE TOWN IBADAN NAIROBI DAR ES SALAAM LUSAKA ADDIS ABABA
DELHI BOMBAY CALCUTTA MADRAS KARACHI DACCA
KUALA LUMPUR SINGAPORE HONG KONG TOKYO

ISBN 0 19 812063 X

Printed in Great Britain by
Butler & Tanner Ltd, Frome and London

for
A. H. Scouten

PREFACE

My aim in this book is to bring a new perspective to the study of 'Restoration' drama. I want both to consider what types of plays appeared in the 1660–1710 period, and to see how they changed in the course of half a century. This drama has benefited from much good scholarship over the past half-century. We have had several important general surveys, from Nicoll's *History* (1923) to James Sutherland's more critically perceptive account in his volume of the Oxford History of English Literature (1969). Source studies have been numerous, and continue to prove fruitful. Close analyses of a few plays and playwrights—especially those by Dobrée, Fujimura, Underwood, Holland, and Zimbardo—have greatly added to our appreciation of some of the high points of this drama. Studies of such elements as love and honour, raillery, and the 'gay couple' have brought important themes and generic characteristics to our attention. What seems singularly lacking in this scholarship is any real sense of what defines this period in dramatic history, and how the plays change over a span of nearly two generations. Critics still commonly think of Restoration drama as comprising 'comedy of manners' and 'heroic plays', without pausing to reflect that the major heroic plays are produced during a very short time while the plays of Wycherley and Congreve (which we so casually lump together) are actually separated by twenty years of rapid shifts in theatrical fashion. All too often critics concentrate on a very small number of plays while ignoring drastic changes from decade to decade or relying on misleading clichés about the rise of 'sentimental' comedy. My hope is to define these changes more precisely by examining a large number of plays with special attention to chronological sequence.

This study is both ambitious and modest. The treatment of the plays is anything but comprehensive: rather, my endeavour has been to analyse a single facet of the subject—the development of English drama over roughly half a century. My subject is really theatrical fashion. With regret, I have had to refrain from following up questions of sources and influences. Similarly, I have largely avoided discussion of Renaissance plays on the Restoration stage—the subject of a recent book by Gunnar Sorelius. By no means can this study claim to be a 'history'; I have not tried to provide a full descriptive account of plays or playwrights. Nor is this a 'critical study'. Rather, it is a historical prolegomenon to future critical studies. I start with no comprehensive theory of the evolution involved, and I conclude with none. My postulate is that the drama of this period is vastly varied and complex in type, and further that the different types change and interact on an almost season-by-season basis. My hope is simply to display these types and their changes as clearly as possible, taking full advantage of the information recently made available in *The London Stage, 1660–1800*.

Only a tiny number of 'Restoration' plays are often read or discussed: this study is meant to help provide a more solid background and context against which to view not only those few works, but also the many others well worth attention. Useful though 'readings' of a few major plays have been, they are often seriously vitiated by ignorance of historical context and indifference to theatre history. As I will try to show, plays from this period closely reflect fads and fashion in a small, highly competitive theatrical world which is constantly being buffeted by political and social change. Some few plays remain more than topical ephemera, but to view even those few entirely without reference to the context from which they came can yield very curious readings. Certain parts of this study will inevitably prove controversial. My sense of the over-all shift encompassed by this survey—from court-oriented 'Carolean' drama to a new phase, here designated 'Augustan'—seems to me fundamentally sound, whatever one may think of the terms in which the change is defined. But both my readings of particular works and my ways of reading the plays contradict a great deal of opinion and methodology now widely accepted. I hope, however, that even where subsequent critics dissent from my particular judgements, they will find useful the sense of context and year-by-year change I have endeavoured to supply.

Necessarily, I have had to discuss a great many forgotten

plays, although I have tried not to neglect the works in which critics will be most interested. The obscure has not been heaped up for its own sake—rather the reverse, for a great deal has been silently digested and suppressed. As a basis for this study I read all of the preserved plays believed to have been publicly performed in London during the period from 1660 to 1710—including the five hundred 'new' plays which are my subject. In what I present here, anonymous and unperformed plays, pageants, and the like get short shrift. Similarly, comment has been kept to a minimum on translations and little-altered adaptations, except when they seemed especially significant or indicative of trends in taste. Even so, much space is devoted to the markedly obscure, and I have deliberately avoided undue highlighting of well-known plays. Some critics may find distasteful my placing Wycherley and Congreve in the company of such writers as Durfey and Ravenscroft. The point of doing so is not to imply that no more is to be found in the former than in the latter. And not for a moment would I deny the helpfulness of close readings of the best plays. But I think that to insist on analysing the famous writers and plays in isolation is a mistake: much may be learned by viewing them as they originally appeared— variably successful in the midst of a prolific, unstable, and rapidly changing theatre world. The reader who feels that I do not do justice to the most famous plays and writers should realize that I am not trying to.

Except for a few specialists, not many critics have been able to feel much enthusiasm for most of the plays I discuss. Restoration drama has long suffered detraction, both overt and implicit: even among its most distinguished students, few seem truly to have delighted in it. Here Montague Summers deserves a place of honour, whatever his failings in other respects. Critics remain astonishingly defensive about the masterpieces of this period. Even to those not worried by the idiotic squabble over morality these plays usually seem insufficiently serious or profound. Anyone who brings expectations based on Shakespeare to this drama will indeed find it trivial, gross, and dull. I propose no defence or justification. If many scholars see little to enjoy in these plays, I do not imagine that my pleading would change their minds. Like most of the good things in life—Shakespeare and unblended malt whisky included—Restoration plays are an acquired taste. Both the comedy and the serious drama are primarily theatre of entertainment—and entertainment, moreover, designed to appeal to contemporary popular taste. If one is content to take this drama as it is, and cultivate an appreciation of its forms, one will find many plays which are quite delightful.

Cornell University
June 1974

ACKNOWLEDGEMENTS

The author gratefully acknowledges permission to use material in altered form from the following copyright works:

'Reading and Misreading *The Man of Mode*': Robert D. Hume; from *Criticism*, vol. xiv, no. 1 (Winter 1972), pp. 1–11; by kind permission of the Wayne State University Press.

'Theory of Comedy in the Restoration': Robert D. Hume; from *Modern Philology*, vol. lxx, no. 4 (May 1973), © University of Chicago Press, 1973; by kind permission of the University of Chicago Press.

'Diversity and Development in Restoration Comedy 1660–1679': Robert D. Hume; from *Eighteenth-Century Studies*, vol. v, no. 3 (Spring 1972), pp. 365–97, ©1972 by The Regents of the University of California; by kind permission of The Regents.

'Formal Intention in *The Brothers* and *The Squire of Alsatia*': Robert D. Hume; from *English Language Notes*, vi (1969), pp. 176–84; by kind permission of the editor.

The author would also like to thank: Harold F. Brooks, Maurice Johnson, Shirley Strum Kenny, Judith Milhous, David B. Morris and John Harold Wilson for encouragement, criticism, and advice.

CONTENTS

Contents

A Note on Dates, Texts, and Bibliography

DATES of plays are those of first performance (not publication) unless otherwise specified. Days and months are Old Style, but following the practice of *The London Stage* the new year is considered to begin 1 January. Dates are normally taken from *The London Stage*. Where they differ, the grounds for the change will be explained in the *Supplement* volume to that work being prepared by A. H. Scouten and myself.

Texts are, of course, a vexed matter. Many of these plays have not been edited or reprinted in modern times. In such cases I have used first editions, or microfilms of them. Some plays are now available in facsimile. Where a good modern edition exists, I have used it—for example, the Weales *Wycherley*, the Davis *Congreve*, the Kenny *Steele*, and volumes VIII, IX, and X of the 'California' *Dryden*. Reluctantly, I have also quoted the Nonesuch *Vanbrugh* and *Farquhar*, and Montague Summers's *Behn*, *Shadwell*, and (where necessary) *Dryden*. For my purposes the texts are adequate, and they have the virtue of being widely available. Plays are quoted and page numbers given without identification in the text. The edition used is specified in the Index of Plays.

Hoping to keep scholarly clutter to a minimum, I have tried to be severe in limiting documentation. With some hesitation, I decided not to append a bibliography of secondary sources consulted. I hope that full credit has been given wherever due, but in all probability there will be some omissions, and I tender my apologies to any critic, living or dead, thus unintentionally slighted.

Works Frequently Cited

Downes	John Downes. *Roscius Anglicanus* (London, 1708).
Genest	John Genest. *Some Account of the English Stage from the Restoration in 1660 to 1830*, 10 vols. (Bath, 1832).
The London Stage	*The London Stage 1660–1800*, 11 vols. (Carbondale, Ill., 1960–8). Part 1, ed. William Van Lennep, with a Critical Introduction by Emmett L. Avery and Arthur H. Scouten (1965). Part 2, ed. Emmett L. Avery (1960).
Nicoll	Allardyce Nicoll. *A History of English Drama 1660–1900*, revised edition, 6 vols. (Cambridge, 1952–9).
J. H. Smith	John Harrington Smith. *The Gay Couple in Restoration Comedy* (Cambridge, Mass., 1948).

PART I

THE DRAMATIC TYPES IN THEORY AND PRACTICE

CHAPTER I

WHAT IS 'RESTORATION' DRAMA?

WHAT do we mean by the term 'Restoration' drama? The question may seem to smack of triviality or love of quibbling, yet its implications, fully pursued, take us into very significant problems. What period do we mean? Twenty years, forty years, seventy-seven years? Is there a case for recognizing a number of periods and sub-periods? I am going to argue against a broad application of the designation 'Restoration'; instead, I favour viewing the development of English drama between 1660 and 1710 as a single long movement comprising some fairly distinct phases. With the period defined, we will want to know what playwrights are included. Do we mean to discuss five plays or five hundred? Several books supposedly on Restoration drama deal with three writers and their eleven plays; others cover six or eight writers. To explain who is covered and why seems only fair: the critic owes his readers a clear explanation of what defines the period or group he is analysing, how its parts cohere or relate to each other, and, more generally, just what sort of subject he thinks he is dealing with and why.

I. CHRONOLOGICAL DIVISIONS AND SUBDIVISIONS

Critics almost never worry about precisely what period is designated by the term 'Restoration' drama. Very often the question disappears in the phrase 'Restoration and Eighteenth-Century Drama', the transition being considered slightly untidy but not terribly important. But since the phrase is usually taken to supply some kind of characterization, one can fairly ask what is being described. Like 'Neoclassicism', the term 'Restoration' should not be applied unthinkingly. Literally, of course, it refers to the re-establishment of the monarchy in 1660. No great amount of drama concerns or coincides with this event. Most commonly, the term is meant to include the years 1660–1700, but extension is often made to 1707, or even 1737.

The 1660–1700 concept has the virtue of tidiness. The theatres reopen in 1660, after an eighteen-year hiatus imposed by the Commonwealth; a drama appears reflecting (we are told) the dissolute court of Charles II; it evolves in Darwinian fashion to its culmination in *The Way of the World;* the 'failure' of that play in 1700 brings the period to an end. *Love's Last Shift* appears in 1696; Vanbrugh's 'answer' in *The Relapse* comes out later the same year; Jeremy Collier's blast in 1698 paves the way for Congreve's failure in 1700 and the appearance of Steele's first play in 1701. Many critics have felt that this sequence constitutes a very tidy shift from Restoration to sentimental comedy. That Farquhar should do most of his work after 1700 is unfortunate, but perhaps he can be dismissed as not entirely in Congreve's camp. Allardyce Nicoll ends the first volume of his *History* in 1700, pleased that the break is so neat. Most critics have a weakness for convenient divisions. There is nothing greatly wrong with the notion of a 1660–1700 period, save first that no real break appears at the end of this time, and second that it leads to an unwarrantable assumption of homogeneity.

Signs of 'post-1700' drama are quite apparent by the early 1690s, and with Farquhar active until 1707 one finds signs of turmoil and conflict in the theatre over a period of about twenty years. I do not want to go into this in detail here—the whole second half of this book is devoted to a full analysis of such matters. But I find the idea that there was any sharp break hard to justify—especially a break which turns out to come right in the middle of a great theatrical uproar. Those critics whose notion of the period includes Farquhar have several good points in their favour. First, there is no major dramatist in this tradition who comes immediately afterward: hence there is no sudden truncation. Second, the uproar of the late 1690s has died down, leaving the theatre in a rather quiescent state. Third, reflecting this condition, the second company again collapses, and as of 1708 there is only one struggling company, not minded to be experimental—a state of affairs signalling the end of an era. Only after the Hanoverian succession in 1714 does the theatre really come to life again.

Behind both the 1660–1700 and 1660–1707 concepts lies the notion that something unique develops during the reign of

Charles II, which carries on for a while, but, deprived of patronage and its old coterie audience, dwindles, flickers gloriously, and peters out around the end of the century. Possibly such a construct takes too narrow a view. The simplistic idea that 'sentimental' quickly replaces 'Restoration' drama may blind us to the complexity of the connections between the old and the new during the 1690s. Most early eighteenth-century drama can quite properly be viewed as an outgrowth of late seventeenth-century developments. Until the Licensing Act of 1737 English drama does develop in a natural (if erratic) way, unimpeded by deliberate interference. Tremendous changes occur between 1675 and 1735, but if one wants, in the fashion of John Loftis, to trace the reflections of society in the theatre, the developments make good sense.[1] In my view, the changes are too great to be comprised within a single, meaningful period: nonetheless, the time between the reopening of the theatres in 1660 and the government's interference with them in 1737 can usefully be considered as a unit of one sort in English theatre history. Although I do not agree with Loftis that the term 'Restoration' can properly be applied to it—even informally—I see perfect good sense in publishing a series of plays from the period thus conceived.[2] Even though I do not propose to cover so broad a span, it is useful to recollect that we do not positively have to think in terms of short, discrete units of time.

Having considered three possible late terminations for the dramatic period under consideration, we might turn to some earlier ones. 'Restoration', with its reference to the Stuart monarchy, could logically be taken to signify 1660–88 (the Glorious Revolution), or even just the reign of Charles II (1660–85). Would this make sense for dramatic history? I think so. I will be arguing in detail later that the 1680s constitute a great watershed, making almost as considerable a break as the Commonwealth period before or the Licensing Act to come. The awkwardness of stopping with 1685 or 1688 is that Congreve, Vanbrugh, and Farquhar are then left out,

---

[1] *Comedy and Society from Congreve to Fielding* (Stanford, Calif., 1959).

[2] See Loftis's Introduction to each volume of the Regents Restoration Drama Series (1965–), of which he is general editor, for a defence of the application of 'Restoration' to the entire period 1660–1737.

and these men do genuinely represent a continuation of the dramatic tradition of the 1670s. I want to argue though that we can very well study these post-Carolean[1] writers as an integral part of a tradition, but that they should be seen as a revival and continuation of the earlier developments. Restoration drama proper is basically Carolean drama; the distinctive productions of the late 1660s and the 1670s are on the wane by the end of the seventies, and the political upheaval of the Popish Plot scare, followed by Charles's death, spells an end to a brief but glorious era. The revival of the Carolean tradition in the 1690s under Dryden's sponsorship is essentially a separate matter, and one entangled with a new wave in drama.

Thus far we have been concerned solely with terminal dates, but why is 1660 sacred as a beginning? The public theatres are reopened, true enough. But a case could be made for 1656, when Davenant privately produced Part I of *The Siege of Rhodes*. More important, one can ask whether the break in theatrical production imposed by the Commonwealth was really all that important. The idea that new concepts of staging were born *ex nihilo* in May 1660 has long been discredited.[2] Similarly, the sorts of plays written in the first years of the Carolean period bear a very great resemblance to the 'Caroline' productions of the late 1630s. This resemblance should be no surprise, for the two patent theatres were being run by a pair of middle-aged Caroline playwrights. Alfred Harbage has gone so far as to argue at length that there is really no significant break at all in theatrical tradition between 1642 and 1660.[3] I do not entirely agree with Harbage's insistence upon 'the natural progression from dramatic types familiar before 1642 toward the two most conspicuous types of the Restoration–Drydenesque heroic tragedy and Etheregean

---

[1] Because of the penchant of Kings of England for passing on the same names, the drama of King Charles I's reign has already taken the adjective 'Caroline'. Personally, I would be glad to describe drama in the reign of Charles II as 'Restoration', but since the broader usage of that term is probably irreversible, I prefer to avoid it most of the time, and so have adopted the variant *Carolean*, used by some British scholars two generations ago, but not common since. Certainly drama in the time of Charles II is quite as distinctive as that now dubbed Elizabethan, Jacobean, Caroline, or Georgian.

[2] See Leslie Hotson, *The Commonwealth and Restoration Stage* (Cambridge, Mass., 1928).

[3] *Cavalier Drama* (New York, 1936). The following quotation is from p. 255.

social comedy': post-1660 innovations do seem to me markedly to alter the directions of the drama. But Harbage's perspective is interesting and useful. Refusing to acknowledge the supposedly sharp break in 1660, he treats most of the drama of the 1660s—including heroic tragedy—as a continuation of the Caroline Cavalier tradition. The dates covered by his study are 1626–69. As I will suggest in detail in Chapter 6, only a number of years after the reopening of the theatres in 1660 does a distinctively Carolean drama start to appear. Consequently a case could be advanced for saying that Restoration drama proper—if there is such a thing—consists of the productions between about 1667 and 1680.

Despite the importance of recognizing the Caroline carry-over, 1660 remains a useful date from which to begin. For although new productions are mostly in the older style for a number of seasons, the innovations and alterations attendant on the re-establishment of public theatres soon encouraged experimentation. In brief, the important factors are the creation of a patent monopoly; the introduction of actresses; new designs for playhouses; a rapid increase in the use of scenery and machines; and growing emphasis on music and dance.[1] The result is the fairly quick appearance of new fashions in drama. The years 1660–5 see clear signs of the new directions. Then the theatres were closed for nearly a year and a half on account of plague, and thereafter one finds not post-Caroline experiments but the exuberant flowering of 'Restoration'—or more properly, Carolean—drama. What precisely happens between 1668 and 1680 will be the subject of extensive investigation in Chapter 7. Here it suffices to say that in this brief span of a dozen years we will find a greater theatrical vitality than was again achieved for many years—only the 1730s can come close to matching it, and they produced nothing like as many great plays. The false dawn of the 1690s gave way to chaos and theatrical prostitution as the two companies resorted to singers, dancers, jugglers, and tumbling acts in a desperate struggle to stay in business during the first years of the eighteenth century. The 1670s had seen the great plays of Dryden, Shadwell, Etherege, Wycherley, Behn, Lee, and most of those of Otway—a flowering to be emulated but

[1] For a convenient summary, see the Introduction to Part I of *The London Stage*.

not matched by Congreve, Southerne, Vanbrugh, and Farquhar. The great importance of differentiating the drama of the nineties from that of the seventies has only recently been recognized,[1] and to insist on the importance of this division is one of my major points.

Some signs of confusion, decline, and disarray are already evident by the late 1670s, but the Carolean boom was brought to a quick and untimely end by the uproar of the Popish Plot in 1678. A number of fine political plays do appear in the years 1680–5, but basically the theatres were in very poor shape, and the end of the era is signalled by the collapse of the King's Company and the formation of the United Company in 1682. Naturally a reduction in the number of new plays resulted. The death of Charles in 1685 was another blow, for it removed an active and interested patron. During James's brief and troubled reign the monarch was too preoccupied to lend much support. To say, as writers tend to, that England was 'politically settled' after the Revolution of 1688[2] is to belittle through hindsight the tensions of a very strained and unstable situation. Not sentiment but profound uncertainty made a large number of nobles and government functionaries keep in touch with the Pretender for many years. Nonetheless, London was comparatively much calmer after 1688, and theatrical activity picks up again. However, the conditions of the seventies were not to be recaptured. The close connection between the theatre and the Stuart monarchy had almost vanished: King William had none of his predecessors' interest in English plays, and Queen Mary died in 1694. Anne in turn refused to close the theatres, but she had no real interest in them.

The changing audience has long been a cliché: the court circle of the seventies died off, and its place had to be filled by wooing a new, bourgeois audience which objected to smut and demanded moral edification. This explanation is a little too neat: certainly some rather racy plays did well in the late nineties. Yet the audience *was* changing. Shadwell, always

[1] See particularly A. H. Scouten, 'Notes Toward a History of Restoration Comedy', *Philological Quarterly*, xlv (1966), 62–70.

[2] My example is from a fine essay by Roger Sharrock, 'Modes of Satire', in *Restoration Theatre*, ed. John Russell Brown and Bernard Harris, Stratford-Upon-Avon Studies, 6 (London, 1965), p. 116.

sensitive to taste and fashion, obviously recognized this. In his prologue to *The Squire of Alsatia* (1688), his first play in seven years, he tells the audience 'Our Poet found your gentle Fathers kind', and says he hopes to please the new generation as well. Significantly, he then proceeds to stress his avoidance of the bawdy.

What one finds in the early nineties is the existence of two modes side by side. Shadwell heralds the new 'Augustan' mode, while Southerne and Congreve attempt to revive and carry on the Carolean comedy. Tragedy in this period is largely marking time with imitations of the post-heroic modes of the early eighties; the move toward pathos is well under way. But no kind of drama was really flourishing, and despite the re-establishment of a second company in 1695, the theatre was in a precarious condition. Collier's attack in 1698 hurt, but it was a symptom of and an addition to extant problems, not the cause of them. By 1708, when the second company again succumbed, the modes developed in the 1670s were played out. But by no means were the newer modes healthy. To suppose that 'Restoration' comedy was driven off the boards by 'senti- mental' comedy is a mistake. Neither was consistently doing well.

For my purposes—tracing developments from the reopening of the theatres through the decay, disappearance, and trans- formation of the types which developed—1710 is a good terminal date. 1700 is too soon; 1707 or 1708, marking the death of Farquhar and the closing of the second theatre, would be perfectly reasonable; 1714, when the Hanoverian accession brought relative stability and the second company revived again, could be taken as a logical terminal point. A year or two either way is not important. In truth there are no very precisely defined periods in dramatic history. From one point of view, 1625–69 is a useful unit to consider. Carolean drama (1660–85) should very definitely be seen as a cohesive unit. The years 1688–1708, though less characterizable, do constitute a sort of drawn-out turning point. A critic interested in the plays of the 1720s might well want to start his survey in 1688 for comedy, perhaps ten years earlier for tragedy. The history of drama, closely considered, is infuriatingly untidy. Nonetheless, I am going to argue in Chapter 10 that in the decade preceding 1710

the remnants of the Carolean play types are assimilated into a
new 'Augustan' synthesis, one whose dramatic and ideological
bases are so decisively different that the resulting drama cannot
properly be lumped together with that produced in the reign
of Charles II.

Out of this sketchy survey several points emerge. First,
English drama in the half-century following 1660 is no
monolith. Initially there remains a strong Caroline residue, and
later seventeenth-century forms give way to Augustan ones
only gradually and confusingly over a twenty-year period:
roughly 1688–1708 for comedy, 1680–1700 for tragedy. Second,
periods of great activity happen to be followed by sloughs of
despond. This pattern is no law of nature; rather, it is largely
the result of political upheaval. During the 1680s the succession
crisis seriously damages the theatre; during the years 1707–14
political struggles, a costly war, and another succession crisis
again interfere—this time with a theatre already enfeebled by
various causes. These slackenings in theatrical activity mark
turning points. Third, the plays of the 1690s should not casually
be grouped with those of the 1670s. To designate all of them as
'Restoration' drama is both misleading and, in an elementary
terminological sense, inaccurate. Most of the plays of the nineties do not really represent a development of the modes of the
seventies. Proof of these points will occupy much of the second
part of this book.

The period 1660–1710 does make a kind of unit, not self-
contained but internally cohesive, even though it comprises
some very disparate sorts of plays. The phrase 'late seventeenth
century' is meant to indicate, non-controversially, that I
intend to trace the emergence of a Carolean drama and also to
survey its aftermath. The latter task takes me through most of
the first decade of the eighteenth century, and necessitates some
account of the growth of rival modes as the end of the seventeenth century approaches.

II. THE CONCEPT OF DEVELOPMENT

To speak of Carolean drama is precise in one sense, misleading
in another. The term implies—as 'Restoration drama' does—
that the plays of the period exhibit a unity, uniformity, and
cohesiveness which somehow makes them a special, self-con-

tained group. Considered in comparison with Jacobean or early Georgian (1760–80) plays, Carolean comedies and tragedies do seem to be of a special type; considered by themselves, they seem altogether lacking in uniformity. Failure to perceive differences is most often the fault of the beholder, and though to many readers the plays of the later seventeenth century seem essentially interchangeable, so to other observers do Chinamen, Italian Renaissance paintings, and the piano concertos of Mozart. Even within the Carolean period there is a considerable diversity of plays.

'Restoration drama', in its usual sense an even more unwieldy grouping than Carolean, is very often thought of as a quintessence best exemplified in *The Way of the World,* and highly characteristic of the period from 1660 to 1700. Such a view is pernicious on two counts. It distracts our attention from the changes within the period, and limits our attention to a tiny number of plays—a limitation which has the dual disadvantage of casting many fine works into outer darkness, and blinding us to major differences between the few plays which remain. In truth, even *The Country-Wife* and *The Plain-Dealer* are so very different from *The Way of the World* in tone, characters, outlook, comic devices, language, and plot, that the customary grouping of Wycherley, Etherege, and Congreve can be achieved only with patent evasiveness or laborious excuses. Fujimura, in an important and influential book, defines an 'aesthetics of wit comedy' with reference to these three writers only, but to do so he has to give a peculiarly incomplete view of Wycherley.[1] *The Way of the World* is arguably a quintessence of perhaps half a dozen plays scattered over a period of more than thirty years. To trace a lineal evolution involving these plays alone seems a highly questionable procedure: writers do not work in a vacuum, oblivious to all but a few perfect models.

Those critics who are aware of the extreme rarity of 'comedies of manners' commonly justify their attention to this one strand with an appeal (tacit or overt) to quality. Thus Nicoll, admitting that 'Restoration comedy is by no means a thing wholly of the manners style', asserts that 'the manners style was in point of fact too high to be attained by all the playwrights of the age,

[1] Thomas H. Fujimura, *The Restoration Comedy of Wit* (Princeton, 1952).

who chose rather the humbler paths of pure Jonsonian imitation.'[1] This hierarchical view is little better than the reductive
idea of a quintessence. To place 'comedy of manners', whatever that may be, at the top of the heap is to see all plays as
insignificant which are not contributing to the growth of the
form toward its 'culmination' in Congreve. Thus Nicoll finds
merit in Dryden's *The Wild Gallant* (1663) because he thinks it
'a step in the direction of Etherege', who is himself a welcome
step toward Congreve.

Two sorts of fallacy need to be disposed of. Most critics
continue to say or assume that, as Anne Righter puts it,
'Etherege . . . charted the basic dimensions of Restoration
comedy in *She Wou'd if She Cou'd*.[2] But actually, 'Restoration
comedy' so conceived is only a tiny and atypical part of the
whole. Critics who want to make this sort of assertion need to
tell us precisely what plays are supposed to be part of this
tradition and how they follow from each other. Criticism of
the 'quintessence' school suffers from its concern with what
the plays are supposed to be evolving *toward*. H. H. R. Love
rightly takes to task 'the school of commentators descending
from Allardyce Nicoll' for whom 'the only question that needs
to be asked of a writer of Restoration comedy is by how much
he failed to write *The Way of the World*'.[3] Is the final cause of
Etherege and Wycherley really to assist in preparing for
Congreve?

Second, far too little attention has been paid to the sheer
magnitude of the late seventeenth-century period. Writing
nearly three centuries later, we can think of the 'Restoration'
as a brief, discrete era. Actually, the period surveyed here is
a full half-century; a quarter-century separates the major
Carolean plays from the principal plays of Congreve, Vanbrugh,
and Farquhar; seventeen years separate the last plays of
Wycherley and Etherege from the first play of Congreve. And
since five years is often a long time in terms of theatrical trends,
we should anticipate some rather drastic changes in the course
of even a fraction of these fifty years. In fact, one could say

[1] Nicoll, I. 194.

[2] 'William Wycherley', in *Restoration Theatre*, p. 71.

[3] Review of the Regents Restoration Drama Series, *Journal of the Australasian
Universities Language and Literature Association*, xxvii (1967), 106–8.

that politically, socially, and theatrically, 1710 was little closer to 1660 than 1970 was to 1920. In 1660 the monarchy was restored, following eighteen years of cataclysm—bloody civil war, the beheading of a king, numerous exilings, and much seizure and redistribution of property. The Restoration was not universally acclaimed, and the cavaliers never felt wholly secure. The frustrating wars of the 1660s and 1670s were followed by the horrors of the Popish Plot. The attendant succession crisis brought the country to the verge of another civil war; the accession of a Catholic king in 1685 led to Monmouth's invasion, and three years later to the successful overthrow of the Stuart monarchy. Its partial re-establishment, first under William and Mary (1688–1702) and then under Anne (1702–14), was far from secure: the most powerful monarch in Europe supported the claims of the Pretender. England was in the throes of semi-permanent and very costly war after the accession of William: by 1710 anti-war sentiment had reached the point of frenzy, and despite Marlborough's prestige, the Whig 'junto' fell that year, placing the settlement of 1688 in jeopardy. In short, turmoil was the order of the day, and changes in and threats to the whole social and governmental establishment were quite as immediate and drastic as those in our own century.

In looking for explanations of the many and major changes in the drama, one can well afford to consider extrinsic and non-literary causes. The old cliché about the rise of a new, bourgeois audience around the end of the century has some truth in it, but it is only part of a larger pattern. To put complex matters very simply, one can say that seventeenth-century drama had come to rely heavily on support from the court, and when it was substantially deprived of that support, the theatres were in serious trouble.

Turning from one sort of problem in periodization to another, we should inquire how a period is best characterized. Should the critic select what he considers the best works? the most popular ones? 'typical' ones? Perhaps the 'best' should be contrasted with the typically popular? Unfortunately, a great many critics have been quite content to ignore all but a tiny minority of the relevant playwrights. For example, a recent book by Virginia Ogden Birdsall, entitled *Wild Civility: The*

English Comic Spirit on the Restoration Stage,[1] consists of close
analyses of eleven plays by three authors. Are we to gather
that 'The English Comic Spirit' (whatever that may be)
appears exclusively or quintessentially in the work of three
writers during the later seventeenth century? Some critics are
willing to add Vanbrugh and Farquhar to the big three;
occasionally Dryden and even Shadwell are noticed.[2] Writers
on tragedy have been less inclined to be quite so exclusive,
perhaps because little serious drama of this period is highly
regarded.

To claim to characterize a period by analysing three to
seven writers selected on the ground that posterity remembers
them seems arbitrary and unsound. To raise this objection is
not to deny the utility of analyses of single authors or types.
Of course one can ask whether there really are distinct types.
Rhymed heroic drama would be one, but comedy of manners
has proved a tenuous concept; so has comedy of humours. Is
Fujimura's comedy of wit really a special and distinguishable
mode? I think not. The difficulties are apparent in Nicoll's
study: after making elaborate distinctions for comedy he
admits, rather sadly, that 'none of these seven separate schools
can be wholly dissociated from another, and most often we see
merely general mixtures of two or three of them more or less
successfully welded together.'[3] As far as I can determine,
writers had very little sense of distinct genres and sub-genres. I
find myself quite incapable of deciding whether a given play
should be called comedy of wit, comedy of humours, comedy
of manners, or something else. Tragedy is worse. For the
historian's purposes, isolating a group of five plays, eleven
plays, or twenty-five plays makes little sense, for who is to
say what necessity binds the group together? The critic may
juxtapose what plays he pleases, letting mutual illumination
justify his choices. The historian of literature has no business
taking isolated examples in chronological order and assuming
that by laying them side by side he is proving something about
a progression. Indeed, almost any statement about progression
tends to be rash, especially if it is postulated on the supposition

---

[1] (Bloomington, 1970).

[2] For example, in Bonamy Dobrée's pioneering and long-influential *Restoration
Comedy* (Oxford, 1924).   [3] Nicoll, I. 195.

that because A precedes B, A has some determinative effect on B. Why should it?

English plays—unfortunately for literary historians—are not laboratory mice. One does not beget another. From one to the next there need be no advance; indeed, there need be no relationship between the two at all. We may often see, or think we see, a relationship, but proving it in any but the most wishful and impressionistic way may be impossible. Students raised on the literary history implicit in survey courses come unthinkingly to believe in tidy, necessary, forward movement. Etherege exists to mould Congreve's form; Defoe helps establish the realism and individuality in the novel which will make Richardson possible. The whole obnoxious notion of pre-Romanticism is a perfect instance of misplaced Darwinian faith. There early materials are viewed as the prelude to what people are really interested in. Here the Carolean drama is similarly seen largely as a prelude leading toward triumph (*The Way of the World*) and collapse (the onset of sentimental drama).[1] To take this view is to rationalize after the event. No one would wish to deny the fact of 'influence' where its effects are demonstrable. But even when clearly established, the relation between influence and creation remains problematic. Could Joyce not have written *Ulysses* if he had never read Dujardin and Svevo? Would *The Way of the World* have gone unwritten had Etherege never lived? One doubts it.

If the usual notions of 'development' are simplistic nonsense, some justification for writing a book about it is in order. Development can, I believe, be a useful concept. Indeed, to seek to explain change is a natural human instinct. Change we can chronicle (in 1950 we had aeroplanes; in 1850 trains; in

---

[1] Carolean drama can also be viewed as degenerate Renaissance drama. One of 'Restoration' drama's problems has been that many of the writers who helped establish common views of the subject came to it from Shakespeare and the earlier period, and could see the later works only in terms of decay. This disparaging view still surfaces occasionally, as in Cyrus Hoy's assertion that Restoration drama represents 'the final working out of tendencies present in English drama for at least half a century prior to 1660' ('The Effect of the Restoration on Drama', *Tennessee Studies in Literature*, vi (1961), 85–91). Hoy goes on to say that 'the decay had begun during the Jacobean and Caroline periods, and the Restoration merely confirmed it.' I would reply, first, that Hoy seems oblivious to the importance of Restoration theatrical innovations; second, that his assumptions—amounting to a myth of triumph and decay—preclude any real appreciation of this drama.

1750 neither), but to say *why* it comes about is much more difficult. In his *Life of Plutarch* (1683) Dryden distinguishes between '*annals*' and '*history* properly so called'. Annals are 'naked history; or the plain relation of matter of fact, according to the succession of time, divested of all the other ornaments. The springs and motives of actions are not here sought, unless they offer themselves, and are open to every man's discernment.' History proper seeks to explain these springs and motives of actions. Part II of this book is a fifty-year survey in which the sequence is examined (closely in itself and with reference to outside events) in search of the springs and motives of change.

In some way not easy to pin down, the plays of 1668 make a markedly different impression than do those of 1703. Critics once assumed that we can usefully talk about how we get from one group to the other, but now seem far less sure about it. One cannot well perform such a feat for the novel. Who can 'explain' the progression from Fielding to Austen to Dickens to Joyce to Burgess? One cannot even say why Sterne writes as he does, following Richardson, Fielding, and Smollett. Can one do any better with the drama? Over all, perhaps not much; but the limited period considered here is another matter. The historian of late seventeenth-century drama in England begins with the enormous advantage of a 'closed system'. There are only two playhouses (sometimes one), and to get his work performed, a writer had to satisfy one of two managers. The composition of the London audience, and changes in it, remain disputed matters, but we do know that it was tiny—a few thousand people in total, with a core of regular theatre-goers numbering only a few hundred. And by the standards of the nineteenth- and twentieth-century novel-reading public, or the potential London or New York theatre audience today, the Carolean audience was comparatively homogeneous in taste. Today Norman Mailer and the Reverend Billy Graham both attract capacity audiences all over the world, but they appeal to essentially distinct groups. Restoration playwrights, on the other hand, had no way to attract special, separate, and distinct followings. A novelist or poet, especially today, can write for the select few, can be as eccentric or esoteric as he wishes, and can sneer at or ignore 'popular' culture. A playwright whose work is deeply offensive to most of the current audience can still do very well in an experimental theatre setting. Consequently, in the modern theatre, developments which really have no relation to each other can exist side by side; they often reflect the tastes of entirely separate audiences, and will prove a sure puzzle to anyone trying to find tidy evolution in a genre.

No such problem besets the historian of late seventeenth-century drama. The closed system forced writers to be responsive to popular taste. Dryden could heartily damn the taste of the multitude (or indulge in a pose of doing so), but if he wanted to prosper, he had at least to trim his sails to the wind. Fickle breezes of fashion and sudden gusts of fad were of enormous importance to any Restoration playwright who wanted to eat. Even the well-to-do writers tried for hits, and almost all of the professional writers were exquisitely sensitive to what was currently successful. Hence they imitated each other, plagiarized, adapted, and burlesqued each other's works. The two houses competed hotly, vying to outdo each other in whatever had caught the audience's fancy at the moment. Only a few new plays could be mounted each year; most of the writers were living in London, and they could easily see all the new plays. Long waits between composition and production were unusual for established playwrights; hence trends could develop quickly. This short response time and the small number of plays in each new season are a great advantage to the historian, who can identify new movements quickly and easily. The rise of sex comedy during the 1670s, for example, can be traced very precisely. To suppose that a sort of biological evolution occurs from season to season is to make stupid use of a misleading metaphor. What one really sees is a very great *interaction* among plays and playwrights. In each successive season, recently popular types, devices, plots, characters, and titles appear in new combinations and permutations.

Given this theatrical situation, one cannot properly select a few plays as typical, or extract isolated examples and read a progression into them. Etherege's second and third plays, for example, make their appearance in wholly different worlds. What proved popular in 1676 would have been found impudent and unacceptable in 1668. So rapid a change is unsurprising: musical shows exhibiting nudity in the late 1960s could not have been staged ten years earlier, and would not then have attracted the bourgeois audience they later did, even had the police allowed the shows to remain open. Close readers of Etherege's plays seem puzzled by the immense differences in tone, technique, and morality exhibited in *She wou'd if she cou'd* and *The Man of Mode*, but the explanation is clear. Etherege stayed up to date, and his later play reflects eight years of rapid change, including the appearance of a whole new sub-genre: sex comedy. What happened in the 1670s is in many ways analogous to the developments of the 1960s: capitalizing on audience titillation, writers pushed ever further in sex, innuendo, and sexual deviation.

My procedure in tracing 'development' will be to look for trends in a large number of plays over fairly short spans of time. Only very rough classifications need be made. To define and employ rigid groupings would be self-defeating. One can, however, usually make some distinctions on the basis of such points as the play's purpose, style, characters, tone, setting, and type of plot. The next four chapters will offer an extended analysis of the play types in this period: in practice, one often does best simply to note similarities and disparities. An intrigue comedy such as *The Rover* is not much like a humours comedy such as *The Sullen Lovers*. The centre of interest in the plots is wholly different. 'Low' London city comedy (*The Cheats*) is utterly removed in tone and characters from *précieuse* tragi-comedy (*The Generall*). 'Spanish romance' is a distinctive mode with an important vogue in the early 1660s; later it is mixed with 'low' humour and loses its distinctive quality. In some plays one finds several popular modes loosely joined—in *The Comical Revenge*, for instance, the pseudo-heroic, upper-class social comedy, gulling comedy, and farce jostle together.

Most accounts of dramatic history in this period proceed from an assumption about the outline of developments: Restoration drama is supplanted by sentimental drama. Starting with this theory of the history, critics can easily find examples to 'prove' it. Here my procedure is the opposite: starting with an annal of taste in dramatic modes, I will try to see what over-all patterns appear, where the few well-known plays fit, and how one can account for evident changes. I have no concern with arriving at triumph in the perfection of comedy of manners, or catastrophe in the supposed advent of sentimental drama. What I trace will not show 'development' in any neat, tidy, and sophisticated sense. But the results should not suffer from a prejudicial pre-selection. And since my primary aim is to show *how* the drama changed, rather than *why*, my concern is with relatively factual matters.

The justification for this kind of developmental overview is threefold. First, the forty- to fifty-year span involved is not homogeneous, and examination should show that the period is properly conceived as comprising a number of fairly clear-cut subdivisions. Second, the closeness of the survey will demonstrate that even within quite restricted periods of time, very diverse kinds of comedy and tragedy are popular—thus refuting common notions about stereotyped Restoration dramatic forms. Third, following the trends in new plays closely year by year, one finds surprisingly logical patterns of interaction, combination, and permutation in the common types. A major reason for this close-knit effect and counter-effect lies in the nature of the playhouse system and its audience.

III. THE THEATRES, THE AUDIENCE, AND THE NATURE OF THE PLAYS

Reading and writing three centuries later—and reading rather than seeing—we can easily lose sight of the degree to which these plays are the product of highly particular sets of theatrical, social, and political circumstances. To a reader in the North Room of the British Museum, a battered quarto from 1681 looks much like one from 1675, and indeed plays from those two years will usually have a good many conventional elements in common. But to the practising dramatist, 1675 and 1681 were worlds apart. However briefly, we must try to recapture some sense of the *theatrical* context.

The limitation to two patent theatres is important for many reasons. Two theatres seem to have been the maximum London could support until after the Hanoverian accession. But the patents gave considerable power to Davenant and Killigrew, and thus influenced the directions Carolean drama was to take. To try to imagine what would have happened with different patentees, or with no patent restrictions at all, is not entirely idle. Probably developments would not have been greatly different anyway, given the availability of veteran actors and the necessity of finding a large number of old plays to serve as the basis for the repertory. Not until the 1663-4 season was a substantial number of new plays offered. But the presence of a pair of Caroline Court playwrights as managers (both happy to mount their own works) must have helped ensure the Caroline–Carolean continuity which Harbage urges. The mad scramble for power in 1659 and 1660, the subsequent fencing between Davenant and Killigrew, and their joint sparring with Sir Henry Herbert (who was determined to maintain all possible power as censor) are well described elsewhere.[1] The upshot was that Killigrew emerged in possession of the more experienced actors, and with exclusive rights to perform a large number of popular plays. Davenant was left with a collection of beginners and a desperate repertory problem: his company had permanent rights to only two plays—*The Changeling* and *The Bondman*.[2] He was forced to beg for temporary permission to perform half a dozen others just to get through the 1660-1 season. In December 1660 the Lord Chamberlain did grant Davenant exclusive rights to his own ten plays, to nine of Shakespeare's, and to a couple of others. However, by the terms of the grant Davenant was legally required to 'reform' (i.e. alter and modernize) all of these plays but his own. Freehafer makes a vital but previously unnoticed point: Davenant *had* to 'improve' Shakespeare's plays, whether he wanted to or not, while Killigrew was free to perform others unaltered. This observation sheds an interesting light on the many twentieth-century denunciations of Davenant for his adaptations.

In short, while Killigrew inherited what was essentially a

---

[1] See the Introduction to Part I of *The London Stage*. The fullest account of the appearance of the two companies is given by John Freehafer, 'The Formation of the London Patent Companies in 1660', *Theatre Notebook*, xx (1965), 6-30, to whose work I am indebted here.

[2] Killigrew's company was a descendant of the 'old' Caroline King's Company, and so had the rights to its plays. The troupe was actually a going concern under Mohun's direction when Killigrew took it over. Davenant inherited most of Rhodes's company, a pick-up group inferior even to that run by George Jolly under special licence during the first year after the Restoration. Davenant and Killigrew then made common cause to cheat Jolly out of his licence, as Freehafer puts it.

going concern, Davenant had to start almost from scratch. The situation set up a classic type of competition: a conservative, established concern matched against a struggling, upstart outfit which was forced to be innovative in order to survive. Killigrew actually had less say in the King's Company than he would have liked: Mohun, Hart, and Lacy (veteran actors, major shareholders, and the King's personal favourites) retained a great deal of power. Davenant, on the other hand, quickly took command of the Duke's Company, gained an ascendency over its fledgling actors, and had the great luck to acquire the young Betterton. Davenant was also a really brilliant impresario, just the man to get the best out of an inexperienced troupe, and full of plans for experiments. He had been putting on proto-opera privately since 1656, and his interest in introducing changeable scenery into the public theatre went back at least to 1639.[1] At that time Davenant had obtained a patent authorizing construction of a new theatre of exceptional size, specifically for the purpose of accommodating action, music, scenery, and dancing. The project met with objections from such public theatre writers as Brome, who feared this invasion of Court-drama technique; opposition imposed delay, and 1642 saw the closing of the theatres. But Davenant had the germ of the ideas which led him to equip and open a theatre designed to accommodate changeable scenery in 1661, and to employ music, dance, and scenes to the full thereafter. The King's Company was forced to follow suit, and when it opened its new theatre in 1663, scenery was provided for. A good many developments in the next twenty years can be traced to increasingly elaborate staging and heated competition between the two companies. Even after Davenant's death in 1668 the Duke's Company maintained its pattern: the enormously successful 1674 version of *The Tempest* is a good example of its work, and Shadwell proved his skill in exploiting fancy scenes, music, and machines in such works as *Psyche* (1675) and *The Lancashire Witches* (1681). But we should not forget that the very rapid rise of these elements in the Carolean drama was partly due to Davenant's personal

---

[1] For the details of the following information, see John Freehafer, 'Brome, Suckling, and Davenant's Theater Project of 1639', *Texas Studies in Literature and Language*, x (1968), 367–83.

inclinations, and partly to the necessity of his competing against a much more experienced and established group.

This spirited Carolean competition had great and largely beneficial influence on the kinds of plays produced and the directions drama was to take. Conversely, at the end of the century, after the Lincoln's Inn Fields breakaway restored competition, this became bitterly destructive. Betterton, his company floundering, resorted to the expedient of interpolating singers, dancers, vaulting acts, and the like between acts of the plays. The Drury Lane company responded with jugglers and tumblers, as well as more singers and dancers: the resulting pattern of distracting entr'actes and afterpieces is a symptom of serious trouble in the legitimate theatre.

What should be emphasized, however, is the intense and direct competition between the two theatrical companies. Reading a play here and a play there, and very probably not even knowing which house put it on, we get a very inadequate sense of the circumstances in which late seventeenth-century drama flourished. Experienced writers almost invariably wrote specifically for one company or the other; consequently, they knew precisely what actors would be available and for what sort of roles. When one house did well, the other might try to steal its thunder (in Dennis's phrase) by imitation, or produce a novelty as a counter-attraction, or mock the success. Responding to the Duke's Company's innovations, the King's Company followed suit with scenery; put on Spanish romances as a counter to Davenant's success with that mode; and fought back against operatic spectaculars with snide prologues and travesties—for example, Duffett's *Mock-Tempest* (1674) and *Psyche Debauch'd* (1675). By now we find it hard to appreciate just how vigorous the competition was. But when one company had a hit, the other suffered and retaliated. Writing on 4 July 1661, Pepys notes that he had seen Killigrew's tragicomedy *Claracilla* 'well acted' by the King's Company, adding, 'But strange to see this house, that use to be so thronged, now empty since the opera begun.'[1] Davenant had opened his new theatre in June and mounted *The Siege of Rhodes* with fancy scenery: obviously Killigrew's business was suffering, and he

---

[1] *The Diary of Samuel Pepys*, ed. Robert Latham and William Matthews, 11 vols. (London, 1970–), II. 132.

soon had to fight fire with fire. Throughout the period both companies cheerfully stole, imitated, parodied, and combined the elements of recent successes. This sort of interaction is half the history of the theatre in this period.

The obvious intensity of the competition for audience favour naturally raises questions about the nature of that audience. That the total potential theatre-going audience was quite small is one of the few points on which much agreement has been reached. Conjectural figures are of little importance for my purposes, but one can get a sense of the limited number of play-goers from the rapid turnover of plays. Performance records are maddeningly incomplete until about 1705, but *The London Stage* gives a clear enough picture. Ten consecutive performances constituted a smash hit; for many years Tuke's *Adventures of Five Hours* (1663) may well have held a record with thirteen. Ravenscroft's *The Citizen Turn'd Gentleman* (1672) ran nine nights initially and claimed thirty performances in its first few months—a staggering success. From what records we have, we might conjecture that most new plays were lucky to have a good audience for three or four nights consecutively, and a play that was run (intermittently) more than eight or ten times had to draw a lot of repeat attenders. Unlike the present New York or London theatre, there was little hope of more than a week's steady run for any play, since the theatres could not draw on a steady stream of visitors and the large, generally untapped reserve of occasional play-goers which exists today in major cities.[1] Plainly this situation was conducive to a high turnover in repertory, the production of a relatively large number of new plays, and concomitantly rapid changes in fashion.

Naturally critics have been anxious to discover the composition, character, and tastes of this all-important audience.

---

[1] The small potential audience, as critics have always said, is partly the result of high prices. Admission ran between 1*s*. and 4*s*., and many merchants who had the money also had moral objections to play-going. No neat formula will give an equivalency in modern money. Pepys's plaints and fits of conscience about the expense of regular attendance have sometimes led to the assumption that the theatre was accessible only to the well-to-do. But just as a student today can attend the opera five times a week by skimping on everything else, so, I suspect, a young man-about-town, a law-student, or a clerk might have contrived to attend the theatre regularly in 1675.

Many of the critical misunderstandings about Restoration drama have stemmed from misconceptions about the audience and its demands. Macaulay and Beljame in the last century contributed greatly to the incredible myth that playwrights had to pander to an audience consisting almost entirely of vicious debauchees. Such a view is still current: thus K. M. P. Burton asserts that 'the theatre suffered from being a royal monopoly, patronized by a very limited audience . . . [the main part of which] consisted of courtiers, hangers-on and prostitutes.'[1] D. R. M. Wilkinson takes essentially this view in treating Restoration comedy as an expression of the sterile and effete conventions of a dissolute society.[2] But is this picture of the courtly audience true? Reliable sociological evidence is hard to come by three hundred years after the fact, but enough has been uncovered to discredit the courtly audience supposition very thoroughly.

The best treatment of the subject to date, written in a highly contentious style, but not the less sound for that, is Harold Love's.[3] Love starts from an excellent point: such critics as John Wain suppose that the whole object of Restoration comedy is to show the courtly audience that it is 'wittier, handsomer and more successful' than its 'anti-type' the cit.[4] But as Love points out: (a) not many comedies actually abuse the cits; (b) one that does so spectacularly, Ravenscroft's *The London Cuckolds* (1681), is known to have been a special favourite *with the cits*; (c) the regularity and ferocity with which fops, gallants, and whores are attacked in prologues, epilogues, and plays suggests either that they were written not *for* but *against* the audience, or that these classes were simply well-defined minorities within the audience.

In a heated reply to Love, A. S. Bear maintains that the audience was indeed an 'elite', a 'coterie' hostile to the bulk of English society. Love correctly replies that the many criticisms of aristocratic taste and behaviour cited by Bear almost all come from sources later than 1695 (Blackmore, Collier, Addison, Steele, and Dennis), while he himself had been

---

[1] *Restoration Literature* (London, 1958), p. 63.

[2] *The Comedy of Habit* (Leiden, 1964).

[3] 'The Myth of the Restoration Audience', *Komos*, vol. i, no. 2 (1967), pp. 49–56.

[4] 'Restoration Comedy and its Modern Critics', *Essays in Criticism*, vi (1956), 367–85.

primarily concerned with an earlier period. No one, I think, would deny the increasing importance of the bourgeois component in the audience after 1688, a subject well treated by John Loftis.[1] What one sees here again is the non-homogeneous nature of the so-called 1660–1700 period. The heyday of the Carolean Court circle vanished forever with the Popish Plot: to suppose that Congreve and Farquhar, who were small children at that time, wrote for a Court audience is ridiculous.

If there was any time at which the Court circle dominated the theatres, it was during the 1660s, when strenuous puritan objections to the playhouses reopening would have discouraged many merchants from attending. Supposedly the theatres were a prime reason for God's visitation of plague and fire on London. Two interesting points can be made, however. First, the plays of the sixties are not very dissolute. So ultra-chaste a play as Tuke's *Adventures of Five Hours* appears to have been a great favourite with the Court group. The smuttier plays appear in the mid-1670s and the 1690s—long after the cit element had made major inroads. If the courtiers were a collection of vicious beasts, why did they flock to see Tuke? Second, from a very early date one can find Pepys complaining about the number of 'citizens' in the audience (for example, 27 December 1662). By 1 January 1668 we find him reflecting that he had seen 'a mighty company of citizens, 'prentices, and others; and it makes me observe, that when I begun first to be able to bestow a play on myself, I do not remember that I saw so many by half of the ordinary 'prentices and mean people in the pit at 2s. 6d. as now'. Writing of *Tu Quoque*, the previous twelfth of September, Pepys had called it 'a very silly play', adding grumpily, 'but it will please the citizens'. From this sort of evidence, sketchy though it is, we may conclude that an increasing number of plebeians were attending the theatre by the end of the 1660s.

From Pepys one can also learn a surprising amount about just who was at the theatre. Emmett L. Avery, making a close study of those names and classes mentioned in the *Diary* (which

---

[1] A. S. Bear, 'Criticism and Social Change: The Case of Restoration Drama', *Komos*, vol. ii, no. 1 (n.d.), pp. 23–31; Harold Love, 'Bear's Case Laid Open: Or, A Timely Warning to Literary Sociologists', *Komos*, vol. ii, no. 2 (n.d.), pp. 72–80; John Loftis, *Comedy and Society*.

covers the 1660s only, of course), concludes that 'on the whole, it appears that the audience contained persons of all ranks and classes, of many professions, and of a wide range of interests in the drama.'[1] Even in the 1660s, then, the notion of an elite, coterie audience seems untenable. Yet one must remember that the regular theatre-goers, though a surprisingly heterogeneous group, had more homogeneous tastes than might be expected. The entire audience seems to have enjoyed everything from farcical knockabout to heroic rant. One must also bear in mind that this relative homogeneity in taste is not a static concept: tastes often changed quite quickly.

The underlying shifts in audience composition remain hard to gauge. Pierre Danchin, in a study based on prologues and epilogues, has offered three main conclusions.[2] (1) The audience became increasingly boisterous and unruly between 1660 and 1700. This is probably true. By our standards the audience was rowdy, but instances of genuinely riotous behaviour were always fairly rare, and called forth special comment when they occurred. One might add that to find the more 'courtly' audience better behaved than the later more 'bourgeois' audience is interesting. Pepys exhibits no qualms about his wife's attending the theatre alone, and Avery notes that many parents were in the habit of taking their children. (2) The audience can be analysed into component parts: royalty, quality, gallants, citizens, whores. I suspect this analysis to be fallacious, since it is based on prologues and epilogues, and their exaggerated rhetoric need not reflect all parts of the audience equally. (3) The 1671–2 season marks an important swing toward citizen taste. The quality was off at the wars, and such prologues as Crowne's for *Charles VIII* and Dryden's for *Marriage A-la-Mode* suggest the necessity of having suddenly to please a rather different audience. I think this case may be exaggerated—after all the quality soon came back— but the trend in drama could certainly have been influenced significantly by the temporary phenomenon to which Danchin calls attention.

---

[1] 'The Restoration Audience', *Philological Quarterly*, xlv (1966), 54–61.

[2] 'Le Public des théatres londoniens à l'époque de la Restauration d'après les prologues et les épilogues', *Dramaturgie et Société*, ed. Jean Jacquot, 2 vols. (Paris, 1968), II. 847–88.

Even within the Carolean period considerable changes seem to have taken place in audience composition. Far greater ones are in evidence by the end of the 1680s. The shift does not take place overnight and is hard to pin down sociologically, but the results are plain enough in terms of objections to character-istically Carolean comedy and the gradual emergence of 'exemplary' comedy and pathetic tragedy. The former term (as opposed to 'sentimental') is proposed by John Harrington Smith in an important article on the changing taste in the last years of the century.[1]

What one must conclude from recent work, however fragmentary and contradictory, is simply that a courtly coterie audience is, at least, an exaggeration, and probably mostly a myth. Highly coloured accounts of duels, drunken brawls, and whores are not untrue, but alone they give a rather misleading impression. One of the best of such popular descriptions is John Harold Wilson's,[2] but his suppositions about the 'coterie' are questionable, and his account of the nature of the drama seems to me misleading. When Wilson asserts that the audience 'wanted to see itself pictured on the stage, not as it really was, but as it liked to think of itself—as the finest product of modern civilization, brilliant, witty, cultured, and refined'—he is really thinking about only a tiny handful of plays, Etherege's *The Man of Mode* for instance. A large majority of comedies, early and late, are anything but brilliant, witty, cultured, and refined. The wit versus cit division is not especially common; more important still, one can find few plays in which the hero–wit is actually a courtier. This simple truth is extremely awkward for the theory that comedy displays an idealized picture of the beau-monde. Just try to make a list of plays that do—it will be short.

To deny the dominance of a courtly coterie is not to deny its influence, or that of the king. James Sutherland points out that never again in England was a monarch to be a boon companion of several major authors (Buckingham, Rochester, Dorset, Sedley); others (Dryden, Wycherley, Crowne, and Durfey) knew Charles II personally and followed his literary

---

[1] 'Shadwell, the Ladies, and the Change in Comedy', *Modern Philology*, xlvi (1948), 22–33.

[2] *A Preface to Restoration Drama* (1965; rpt. Cambridge, Mass., 1968), Chapter 4.

suggestions.[1] Charles's intervention demonstrably exerted a profound influence in helping establish the rhymed heroic drama, while his patronage of Durfey had a marked effect on comedy in the 1670s. The playhouses were a Stuart recreation (in two, or even three senses), and deprived of that close personal interest, so apparent in the Carolean period, they were in trouble. Perhaps it is more than wholly coincidence that the mounting revival of the theatres in the 1690s starts to fade not long after the death of Queen Mary in December 1694. The second theatre reopened the following spring and scored a great hit with *Love for Love*, but with Mary's death there was no longer a royal patron prepared to take any significant interest in the theatre.

In conclusion, I think one can say with fair assurance that there never was a genuinely *dominant* court coterie, even though Court patronage was important; that the composition of the audience altered by the end of the 1660s, and changed greatly by the 1690s; that a successful writer had to please a fair fraction of a rather small total potential audience; and that this group was socially varied (*vide* Pepys) and quite prepared to enjoy very disparate sorts of plays. Since the two theatres are demonstrably offering similar fare to a single audience for which they compete (rather than attracting separate and distinct coteries), that audience *must* have been able to like plays as dissimilar as *The Conquest of Granada*, *The Rehearsal*, *The Citizen Turn'd Gentleman*, and *Marriage A-la-Mode*, all of which were popular at about the same time.

In this introductory chapter, I have tried briefly to give some sense of the period with which I am concerned—*in toto* and in its parts; to indicate some of the extra-literary forces which influence the plays; and to justify studying them in terms of 'development'. It is well to conclude with a cautionary point about the kind of drama with which we are dealing. I have tried to make plain its highly circumstantial character: the plays reflect theatrical, political, and social conditions, a point easy to forget when reading the texts in isolation. Another factor easily forgotten or ignored is the attitude of the audience

---

[1] 'The Impact of Charles II on Restoration Literature', *Restoration and Eighteenth-Century Literature: Essays in Honor of Alan Dugald McKillop*, ed. Carroll Camden (Chicago, 1963), pp. 251–63.

toward these plays. The drama of this period was *popular entertainment*, not for the masses (it being both expensive and ungodly), but for a relatively small group of Londoners for whom the plays provided a frequent diversion. Although for some theatre-going was apparently a special event, occasioned by a *première* or a holiday season, for a lot of regulars to wander in of an afternoon was commonplace—very often people would simply look in at each playhouse to see what was on.[1] Even Pepys is sometimes unclear about what he has seen, and often on who wrote it.[2] Titles were put up on playbills and announced at the end of a play for the next day—not always accurately.

Premières and other unusual occasions would draw antici-patory crowds long before curtain-time: Pepys testifies to the throngs which crowded in to see such long-awaited plays as *She wou'd if she cou'd* and *The Mulberry-Garden*. On a day-to-day basis, though, many people seem to have looked in at the theatres much as one might now turn on a television when bored and flip from channel to channel. One may or may not settle down to watch a programme, and if one does, the title may or may not register; in either case one is unlikely to notice the credits.[3] We now think of these plays as literary productions of particular authors; indeed, compared to the Elizabethans, the Carolean audience is moving in that direction, but by our standards the authors often retain a surprising degree of anonymity. Most plays were published with the author's name, and authorship was often widely known, but apparently no play was advertised by author until the very end of the century.[4]

The casual adaptations, translations, and pure plagiarism

---

[1] The admission system was such that one could get in for a while (an act or so) without paying. See *The London Stage*, Part 1, pp. lxx–lxxiv.

[2] Thus for 13 January 1669 he writes, 'to the King's playhouse, and there saw, I think, "The Maiden Queene" ', when in fact he appears to have seen *Catiline*.

[3] The habits of the infuriating James Brydges, who always names the people he talked with but almost never the play he saw, are an excellent illustration. See Lucyle Hook, 'James Brydges Drops in at the Theater', *Huntington Library Quarterly*, viii (1945), 306–11.

[4] Writing to Mrs. Steward, 4 March 1699, Dryden remarks: 'This Day was playd a reviv'd Comedy of Mr Congreve's calld the Double Dealer, which was never very takeing; in the play bill was printed,—Written by Mr Congreve; with Severall Expressions omitted: What kind of Expressions those were you may easily ghess; if you have seen the Monday's Gazette, wherein is the King's Order, for the refor-mation of the Stage: but the printing an Authours name, in a Play bill, is a new

common in the late seventeenth century are a world away from our notions of original composition. A playwright who worked today the way Dryden did would be sued from all sides and hooted out of the theatre. Attitudes were changing; pride in originality was developing: Langbaine's savaging of 'thefts and plagiaries' in *An Account of the English Dramatick Poets* (1691) is symptomatic of the shift. But the bulk of late seventeenth-century drama remains essentially casual entertainment, the equivalent of everyday television fare. As with television, some writers were serious and ambitious, but all who hoped to succeed commercially had to adapt to the entertainment demands of the theatre. Dryden is a prime example of this pressure: he almost always writes to please himself, but he is not working in a vacuum and he is always acutely aware of audience taste.

'Restoration' drama has long been criticized for frivolity, vapid superficiality, and worse. Some recent critics have tried to rescue it by making claims for profundity and high serious-ness. Dale Underwood sees Etherege as a philosopher; Rose Zimbardo treats Wycherley as a serious satirist; Anne T. Barbeau makes Dryden out to be a profound political theorist. These interpretations will be assessed in detail later. In a nutshell, though, I do not think that they are helpful: such claims just make the plays look weaker. 'Restoration' plays are full of social and political commentary, and bits of the philosophy of the time are recognizable enough, but almost without exception they aim more at entertainment than at deep meaning. The plays are often acute, pointed, pathetic, or satiric—but very seldom do they probe character deeply or present ideas which are essentially more than commonplaces.

As I write this, I have a horrid vision of every profundity-zealot for years to come triumphantly seizing on what I have been saying here, to 'show' that no one understands and appreciates these plays, before going on to 'prove' the serious-ness, complexity, profundity, and high moral worth of what-

---

manner of proceeding, at least in England.' *The Letters of John Dryden*, ed. Charles E. Ward (Durham, N.C., 1942), no. 59. If Dryden is right, using the author's name as bait is a device first tried by Betterton, and the innovation is probably just one more symptom of the desperate trouble in which the Lincoln's Inn Fields company found itself near the end of the century.

ever play he may be in the process of resurrecting. My point is
most decidedly not to belittle plays for which I have great
affection, and for whose art I entertain great respect. But
making exaggerated and untenable claims for a work does it no
service. Matthew Arnold notwithstanding, the value of a work
of literature does not vary in direct proportion to the quantity
and quality of its 'ideas'. These late seventeenth-century plays
are highly conventional, imitative, and repetitive; they are
also extremely effective and enjoyable entertainment. That is
what they were written for. Some are outstanding in art and
skill, but all bear the imprint of a highly circumstantial context,
and we will read them the better for recognizing that fact.

CHAPTER 2

THEORIES OF COMEDY

THE numerous late seventeenth-century pronouncements on comedy have never proved notably helpful in reading the plays of the time. Critic after critic tells us that comedy must instruct and please by 'holding the glass' to a society in need of satiric correction—and faced with such platitudes, modern readers have tended to look elsewhere for help. Indeed, literary theory in this period appears in scraps, and recent studies of it have generally consisted either of dismal lists of puzzling clichés, or of heaps of evidence piled up to support preconceptions.[1] If, however, we can get beyond the platitudes and consider more practical issues, we will find information of real value for reading Carolean and post-Carolean comedies. And in the light of recent disagreements about the very nature of 'Restoration comedy' and how we should respond to it this seems a worthwhile endeavour.

The difficulties must not be minimized. The relevant documents are scattered, occasional, and often partisan. A strong case can be made for the charge that late seventeenth-century writers pay lip service to inherited moral platitudes which they disregard in practice. Puritan outcry about the reopening of the theatres induced a defensive attitude from the start, and the largest body of contemporary comment on the nature and function of comedy appears at the very end of the century in the form of answers to Jeremy Collier. The resultant piety is certainly suspect, and we cannot, in any case, uncritically group the pronouncements of the 1690s with those of the 1660s. Another problem is simply the immense diversity of the works labelled 'a comedy' in this period. Anyone who has read more than the few well-known plays is aware that our assumptions

---

[1] For an example of each, see Edwin E. Williams, 'Dr. James Drake and Restoration Theory of Comedy', *Review of English Studies*, xv (1939), 180–91; and Sarup Singh, *The Theory of Drama in the Restoration Period* (Bombay, 1963), Chapter 8.

about generic distinctions can be very misleading. Sarup
Singh's work suffers badly from his assuming that all other
sorts of comedy are merely secondary or contributory to the
'comedy of manners'. His procedure in this respect is a common
one, but it supposes that the critic is entitled to isolate what he
likes best and then build a theoretical foundation to support it.
Such favouritism and over-simplification should be avoided.
These playwrights do not work to a tidy formula, and the
modern critic must expect to find a continuing state of confusion and change in both theory and plays. Indeed, it quickly
becomes evident that beyond the level of a few clichés, there is
no such thing as a standard 'theory of comedy' in this period.
Nor will we find a set of discrete competing theories, or a clear-
cut transition from a satire-oriented Carolean formula to a
subsequent 'sentimental' one. My aim then is merely to map
some of the fundamental disagreements and divergences of
opinion about the subjects, structures, component devices, and
proper effect of comedy.

I. THE CLICHÉS: COMEDY OF MANNERS AND COMEDY OF HUMOURS

Certain ideas about comedy are so widespread in this period
that a minimum of examples will suffice. Thus on the issue of
moral utility, Congreve and the now despised Blackmore are in
perfect accord. 'Comedy (says *Aristotle*) is an Imitation of the
worst sort of People . . . in respect to their Manners. . . . They
must be exposed after a ridiculous manner: For Men are to be
laugh'd out of their Vices in Comedy.'[1] 'The business of
Comedy [is] to render Vice ridiculous, to expose it to publick
Derision and Contempt, and to make Men asham'd of Vile
and Sordid Actions.'[2] Practically everyone says the same thing
at one time or another—including Flecknoe, Dryden, Shadwell,
Aphra Behn, Farquhar, and Dennis. However, some long-
standing moral objections to the plays involved cast doubt on
the completeness of their moral uplift. Dryden, for example,
insisted indignantly in his preface that *Mr. Limberham* (1678)—

---

[1] William Congreve, *Amendments of Mr. Collier's False and Imperfect Citations* (London, 1698), pp. 7–8.

[2] Sir Richard Blackmore, 'Preface to *Prince Arthur*', in *Critical Essays of the Seventeenth Century*, ed. J. E. Spingarn, 3 vols. (Oxford, 1908–9), III. 228.

a roaring, dirty farce—was 'an honest Satyre'. We may well
wonder just how many other moral claims are equally questionable. Unfortunately, claims for the moral effect of comedy
possessed an almost sacred status, and whatever writers may
have thought of them, they went almost entirely unchallenged.
Dryden could say that he aimed primarily to please, secondarily
to instruct (though he was attacked for it), and there are
isolated gibes at 'reformers'.[1] But only in Mrs. Behn's preface
to *The Dutch Lover* (1673), I believe, is there a harsh, reasoned,
full-scale denial of moral instruction in comedy:

> . . . in my judgement the increasing number of our latter Plays have
> not done much more towards the amending of men's Morals, or
> their Wit, than hath the frequent Preaching, which this last age
> hath been pester'd with, (indeed without all Controversie they have
> done less harm) nor can I once imagine what temptation anyone
> can have to expect it from them; for sure I am no Play was ever
> writ with that design. If you consider Tragedy, you'll find their
> best of Characters unlikely patterns for a wise man to pursue. . . .
> And as for Comedie, the finest folks you meet with there are still
> unfitter for your imitation, for though within a leaf or two of the
> Prologue, you are told that they are people of Wit, good Humour,
> good Manners, and all that: yet if the Authors did not kindly add
> their proper names, you'd never know them by their Characters. . . .
> Even those persons that were meant to be the ingenious Censors of
> the Play, have either prov'd the most debauch'd, or most unwittie
> people in the Company: nor is this error very lamentable, since as I
> take it Comedie was never meant, either for a converting or a con-
> forming Ordinance: In short, I think a Play the best divertisement
> that wise men have: but I do also think them nothing so [important
> as those (?)], who do discourse as formallie about the rules of it, as if
> 'twere the grand affair of humane life. This being my opinion of
> Plays, I studied only to make this as entertaining as I could.[2]

Edwin Williams is thoroughly upset by this brutal denunciation
of claims for the moral utility of drama, and he hastens to
dismiss the passage as 'ironic'.[3] In fairness one must point out
that in the dedication of *The Lucky Chance* (1687)—a cheerful

---

[1] For example, early in the period John Lacy mocks preaching in plays in his
prologue to *The Dumb Lady* (*c.* 1669)—but he was an actor-farcewright who
announced in another prologue that he wrote 'To you that laugh aloud with wide-
mouth'd grace,/To see *Jack Pudding's* Custard thrown in's face'. And in 1698 there
is a flurry of jeers and mockery in response to Collier—for example, in Jo Hayns's
epilogue to *Love and a Bottle*.   [2] *Works*, I. 222–3.   [3] Williams, p. 183.

farce—Mrs. Behn states that plays 'are secret Instructions to the People, in things that 'tis impossible to insinuate into them any other Way. . . . 'Tis Example alone that inspires Morality, and best establishes Vertue.'[1] Nonetheless, Mrs. Behn's earlier blast at the supposed moral function of comedy seems to describe prevailing practice a good deal better than the moral commonplaces Williams pulls out of James Drake. The formula runs something like this:

The business of comedy is to recommend virtue and discountenance vice. Its effectiveness depends on a realistic copying of the characters and manners of the time, though personal satire is not allowable. The characters should be neither vicious nor admirable. The author aims to rouse scorn rather than indignation, and an intellectual rather than an emotional response.

I have chosen to paraphrase Drake here, partly because Williams emphasizes his complete 'orthodoxy' and urges that we 'accept him as a spokesman of the period'[2]—which a number of recent critics have done. Two questions arise: does this theory tell us much about contemporary practice, and does it really represent a restrictive theoretical orthodoxy? I think the answer to both is No. Are such successes as *The Adventures of Five Hours*, *Sir Martin Mar-all*, *The Citizen Turn'd Gentleman*, *The Spanish Fryar*, *Love for Love*, and *The Recruiting Officer* written to such a formula? Clearly not, and neither are the plays we now rate higher. Even where Drake's description does fit, it does not seem comfortably to get at the plays' essential nature, much less to allow for their differences. Within this supposedly orthodox formula there are actually a number of controversial issues: realism; debauched versus virtuous characters; personal attack; the nature of comic 'effect'—all of which will require exploration here. I think it best to start, however, with an examination of an influential attempt at categorization of comedies of the period from 1660 to 1700.

Although the extent of the diversity of the contemporary comic theory has gone almost unrecognized, critics have long

---

[1] *Works*, III. 183.

[2] Williams, p. 190. Williams works from Drake's *The Antient and Modern Stages survey'd. Or, Mr. Collier's View of the Immorality and Profaneness of the English Stage Set in a True Light* (London, 1699). As the title makes amply plain, Drake's book has little to do with Restoration drama properly conceived.

been worried by the small number of the 'wit' comedies which
are generally taken to characterize comic drama in this period.
Allardyce Nicoll rightly notes that several sorts of comedy
coexist: he rather awkwardly identifies them as (1) Jonsonian;
(2) intrigue; (3) Dryden; (4) manners; (5) farce; (6) sentiment.[1]
Plainly such a division is a counsel of despair: the categories
have incongruous bases; Dryden was neither *sui generis* nor
consistent; many Jonsonian plays have 'intrigue' plots, so do
many farces, and so does *The Plain-Dealer*—which is a comedy
of manners according to most critics, a satire or a wit comedy
according to others. Such a system of categorization obscures
as much as it clarifies the playwrights' aims and methods.

The commonest way of differentiating *methods* has been to
extract from contemporary arguments a basic opposition between wit and manners comedy on the one hand, and comedy
of humours on the other. The crisp but not unfriendly exchanges
between Dryden and Shadwell (1668–71) are often quoted.
They are worth examining again, however, because their
import is often misunderstood. In his preface to *An Evening's
Love* (1671) Dryden speaks of the importance of 'our refining
the Courtship, Raillery, and Conversation of Playes', announces his 'disgust of low Comedy' and its 'ill nature in the
observation of . . . follies' of 'the vulgar'. Dryden finds Jonson
strong on judgement but short on wit, and emphasizes his
preference for 'more of the *Urbana, venusta, salsa, faceta*' in place
of 'the natural imitation of folly'.[2] Shadwell too snarls vigorously
at farce, but he speaks strongly in favour of the Jonsonian
method—what Dryden calls 'natural imitation of folly'—which
stresses humour and judgement rather than wit or refinement.
And Shadwell says bluntly that 'My design was . . . to repre-
hend some of the Vices and Follies of the Age, which I take
to be the most proper, and most useful way of writing Comedy',
going on to object to Dryden's emphasis on 'delight' rather
than 'instruction' in the 'Defence of an Essay of Dramatique
Poesie' (1668).[3]

Supposedly we can see here the basis of a fundamental

---

[1] Nicoll, I. 193–201. A more satisfactory, if rough and unpretentious division is
offered by John Harold Wilson in his *Preface to Restoration Drama*: farce, burlesque,
intrigue, humour, satire, wit, tears.

[2] *Works*, X. 202–6.   [3] Preface to *The Humorists*.

division between the low, crudely instructive 'comedy of humours', and the gay, witty, refined 'comedy of manners'. Actually, the issues involved seem a good deal more complicated. For one thing, both men's positions prove temporary. Shadwell's first two original comedies are quite atypical of his work as a whole, and though he talks about Jonson and humours for the rest of his life, one cannot fully trust this terminology, which he also uses to describe his proto-exemplary plays after 1688. Indeed, within a year of the preface to *The Humorists*, he had written *Epsom-Wells*, a play which seems to fall half-way between Wycherley's *Love in a Wood* and *The Country-Wife*. And in *Epsom* Shadwell promptly proceeds to employ the witty and 'indecent' lead characters of whom he had complained so bitterly in his first two prefaces.[1]

Turning to Dryden's part in the exchange one is faced with an awkward truth: his comments are being pressed into service for lack of any theoretical statement from Etherege or Wycherley. This expedient would seem more satisfactory if Dryden had written or were ever to write the sort of wit or manners comedy he is alleged to be advocating. Actually, *Secret Love* and *Marriage A-la-Mode* are as close as he comes to fulfilling his prescriptions here—a pair of semi-heroic, double-plot plays, set abroad, and a far cry from *The Man of Mode* or *The Country-Wife*. Dryden does see a fundamental distinction between comedy of wit and comedy of humour:

the chief end of it [comedy] is divertisement and delight. . . . For the business of the Poet is to make you laugh: when he writes humour he makes folly ridiculous; *when wit, he moves you, if not always to laughter, yet to a pleasure that is more noble.*[2]

As I shall suggest in detail later, what Dryden seems to have in mind is not a division between two sorts of satiric correction, but rather a distinction between comedy regarded as the vehicle of corrective satire and comedy conceived as an almost exemplary display of social grace and witty refinement. Some

---

[1] 'In the *Playes* which have been wrote of late, there is no such thing as perfect Character, but the two chief persons are most commonly a Swearing, Drinking, Whoring, Ruffian for a Lover, and an impudent ill-bred *tomrig* for a Mistress, and these are the fine People of the *Play* . . . their chief Subject is bawdy, and profaneness.' Preface to *The Sullen Lovers*; cf. the preface to *The Royal Shepherdess*.

[2] Preface to *An Evening's Love*, *Works*, X. 209 (italics added).

critics have chosen to regard the plays of Etherege, Wycherley, and Congreve as such displays, but some impressive evidence to the contrary has been assembled in recent years.[1] Wycherley is now often regarded as a hard-hitting satirist or a savagely funny sceptic, and—in his reply to Collier at least—Congreve sounds much more like Shadwell than like Dryden.

One is left to conclude that this supposedly neat and tidy debate on wit versus humour leads straight to total confusion. No short cut is available: to make sense even just of Carolean pronouncements on the nature of comedy, one must start by looking at areas of debate and disagreement on more practical matters.

II. SATIRIZED AND EXEMPLARY CHARACTERS

Perhaps the most crucial issue boils down to this: is even Carolean comedy entirely a comedy of *ridicule*? Despite the amount of lip service paid to this idea, the answer is No, and herein lies the key to much critical difficulty. Late seventeenth-century playwrights are very far from practising what they usually preach, and by no means do they always preach ortho-dox 'classical' doctrine.

A long-standard construct for the development of comedy in the 1660–1710 period goes something like this. Restoration comedy proper (i.e. wit or manners comedy) has its basis in Jonsonian low life and satire, but is leavened with Fletcherian wit and refinement to suit the more courtly nature of the age.[2] As the century draws to an end, this witty and satiric comedy is supplanted by sentimental (or more precisely, 'exemplary') comedy in which the lead characters are held up for admiration and emulation rather than ridiculed. And although exemplary theory appears even at the outset of the period (note that Mrs. Behn is busy rejecting it in 1673), while satiric theory is never obliterated, this change is real. Between 1650 and 1750 there is indubitably an over-all shift in the dominant concept of humour: Hobbesian ridicule is largely supplanted by

[1] See especially Charles O. McDonald, 'Restoration Comedy as Drama of Satire: An Investigation into Seventeenth Century Aesthetics', *Studies in Philology*, lxi (1964), 522–44.

[2] Such a construct has some support in Carolean criticism. For example, Dryden specifically advocates this combination in his 'Defence of the Epilogue' to Part II of *The Conquest of Granada* (1672).

benevolent sympathy,[1] and the effect on the drama is obvious. We may note, however, that the 'benevolist' creator of Parson Adams was perfectly capable of harsh satire in his plays, and we may wonder whether Congreve, apostle of the satiric function of comedy, did not slip in some almost exemplary characters.[2] At any rate, much seems to turn on a determination of what sort of response or responses a late seventeenth-century writer hoped his characters would elicit from the audience.

According to standard critical dogma, the essence of comedy is ridicule. Thus Dryden announces (in 1668, we may notice) that admiration is the essence of tragedy, satire of comedy.[3] To find that this idea is the mainstay of the conservative Dennis's view is no surprise. 'Comedy . . . must please by the *Ridiculum*'; 'Ridicule [is] that which distinguishes Comedy from every other kind of Poetry.'[4] In an epistle attached to Durfey's *The Marriage-Hater Match'd*, Charles Gildon asserts that the whole object of comedy is satire 'design'd to correct Vice, and Folly, by exposing them'. Shadwell similarly excuses his including 'ill Wives' in a play on the grounds that by exposing them to contempt, he is upholding faithful marriage.[5] An anonymous writer makes the point more generally: 'Comedy is a Representation of common Conversation; and its Design is to represent things Natural; to shew the Faults of Particular Men in order to correct the Faults of the Publick, and to amend the People thro' a fear of being expos'd.'[6]

[1] See Stuart M. Tave, *The Amiable Humorist: A Study in the Comic Theory and Criticism of the Eighteenth and Early Nineteenth Centuries* (Chicago, 1960).

[2] Whether Jean Gagen ('Congreve's Mirabell and the Ideal of the Gentleman', *PMLA*, lxxix (1964), 422–7) is correct in believing Mirabell to be an exemplary character has been warmly debated. I disagree. But the very fact that serious debate is possible shows how blurry the satiric/exemplary division can be.

[3] 'A Defence of an Essay of Dramatique Poesie', *Works*, IX. 11.

[4] Quotations are from *The Critical Works of John Dennis*, ed. Edward Niles Hooker, 2 vols. (Baltimore, 1939, 1943), I. 224, and II. 261. Criticizing Steele's attempt to elicit 'a Joy too exquisite for Laughter', Dennis says angrily that this shows that 'he knows nothing of the Nature of Comedy' (II. 259). If Dennis's argument is accepted, Dryden is vulnerable to the same charge.

[5] Epilogue to *Epsom-Wells* (1672).

[6] *A Letter to A. H. Esq; Concerning the Stage* (London, 1698), p. 15. 'Particular Men' here means single instances, not recognizable individuals from London society. Critics throughout this period are unanimous in denouncing 'personal' satire. Nonetheless, there was plenty of it, *The Rehearsal* and Shadwell's *The Sullen Lovers* being particularly notorious instances. In the light of *Mr. Limberham*, and his

In theory, then, the aim and method of comedy are extremely simple. But what if the audience did not recognize the ridicule? Throughout the whole period there is a persistent unease about the attractiveness of debauched lead characters. Writing in 1694 James Wright repeats in almost the same words Shadwell's complaint of 1668:

the Common Parts and Characters in our Modern Comedies, are two young Debauchees whom the Author calls Men of Wit and Pleasure, and sometimes Men of Wit and Sense . . . these two Sparks are mightily addicted to Whoring and Drinking. The Bottle and the Miss . . . make their *Summum Bonum*.[1]

Blackmore says precisely the same thing the next year in his preface to *Prince Arthur*. Replying to Collier's like charge three years later, the author of *A Letter to A. H.* loads his examples:

After all, my Lord *Foppington* was never design'd to teach People to speak or act like him; nor was it intended that the Ladies shou'd be byass'd by the Example of *Berinthia* to turn Coquetts. These and the like Characters in other Plays, are not propos'd as a Direction for the *Gallant Man*, or the *Vertuous Lady*; but that seeing how such Persons behave themselves on the Stage, that they may not make the like Figure in the World: but if any body shou'd rather be in love than terrified by these Examples, 'tis their Fault, and not the Poets.[2]

Foppington is a safe enough instance, as Sir Fopling Flutter would be. But what about, say, Dorimant and Harriet? A distinguished modern critic states unequivocally that they are 'admirable from the point of view of Restoration Society',[3] and if he does not see ridicule here, perhaps Collier and others can be forgiven the same view.

The Man of Mode is thus a convenient illustrative case. In the *Spectator*, 65 (1711), Steele angrily attacks this supposed 'pattern of genteel comedy' on the grounds that:

a fine gentleman should be honest in his actions, and refined in his language. Instead of this, our hero, in this piece, is a direct knave in

---

political poems, Dryden's denunciations of personal satire are no more convincing than his many pious condemnations of smut.

[1] *Country Conversations* (London, 1694), pp. 4–5. For Shadwell's comment, see n. 1, p. 37, above.   [2] *A Letter to A. H.*, pp. 11–12.

[3] John Harold Wilson, *The Court Wits of the Restoration* (1948; rpt. New York, 1967), p. 164.

his designs, and a clown in his language. . . . This whole celebrated piece is a perfect contradiction to good manners, good sense, and common honesty . . . there is nothing in it but what is built upon the ruin of virtue and innocence. . . . I allow it to be nature, but it is nature in its utmost corruption and degeneracy.

Dennis replies a decade later:

How little do they know of the Nature of true Comedy, who believe that its proper Business is to set us Patterns for Imitation: For all such Patterns are serious Things, and Laughter is the Life, and the very Soul of Comedy. 'Tis its proper Business to expose Persons to our View, whose Views we may shun, and whose Follies we may despise; and by shewing us what is done upon the Comick Stage, to shew us what ought never to be done upon the Stage of the World.[1]

And Dorimant, he maintains, was neither meant nor taken as an admirable figure.

Here we see very clearly the difference between the traditional, ridicule-oriented view of comedy, and the newer, 'exemplary' notion. According to Dennis, Steele misunderstands the nature of comedy, and so responds inappropriately to a comic character. But the confusion is not solely in the eye of the beholder. Dorimant may be mildly satirized, but he remains a glamorous and successful character, and to find him actually instructive would not be easy. Using Dennis as his principal source, Charles McDonald argues forcefully that there are *no* heroes in 'Restoration comedy'; that even 'Truewits' are not sympathetic; that Restoration comedy (however he may understand that phrase) concerns 'low' characters and teaches by negative example. For him, Steele is simply a-historical, and Dennis gives us a true picture of comedy as it was understood in the court of Charles II. Unfortunately for his argument, it is easy to show that moral charges similar to those of Steele were being made very early. Thus in 1671 Dryden complains:

'Tis charg'd upon me that I make debauch'd persons . . . my Protagonists, or the chief persons of the *Drama*; and that I make them happy in the conclusion of my Play; against the Law of Comedy, which is to reward virtue and punish vice. I answer first, that I know no such law to have been constantly observ'd in Comedy. . . . But,

---

[1] 'A Defence of Sir Fopling Flutter' (1722), in *Critical Works*, II. 245.

lest any man should think that I write this to make libertinism
amiable . . . I must farther declare . . . that we make not vicious
persons happy, but only as heaven makes sinners so: that is by
reclaiming them first from vice. For so 'tis to be suppos'd they are,
when they resolve to marry. . . .[1]

Unconvincing fifth-act repentances were a commonplace long
before the time of *Love's Last Shift* (1696). But plainly someone
was complaining strenuously enough about the appearance
of 'debauched' protagonists for Dryden, even in 1671, to feel
compelled to defend himself—and he does not do so, we should
note, on satiric grounds.

To suppose that any clear divide can be established between
satiric and exemplary comedy is plainly erroneous. Attitudes
toward protagonists vary widely. Dennis, a real reactionary,
supposes them all ridiculed. Steele, the other extreme, wants
them to be exemplary. Dryden believes that imperfect characters
can properly be made happy and prosperous. Over the period
as a whole, there is clearly an increased tendency to see the
lead character as the 'hero'. We find Congreve objecting to the
terminology and the idea behind it in his preface to *The
Double-Dealer* (1694). By no means though is the 'hero' notion a
late development. Consider Cowley's defence of his *Cutter of
Coleman-Street* (pub. 1663):

others . . . were angry that the person whom I made a true Gentleman, and one both of considerable Quality and Sufferings in the
Royal party, should not have a fair and noble Character throughout.
. . . This is a refined exception, such as I little foresaw. . . . The
truth is, I did not intend the Character of a *Hero*, one of exemplary
virtue, and as *Homer* often terms such men, Unblameable, but an
ordinary jovial Gentleman. . . . If you be to choose parts for a
Comedy out of any noble or elevated rank of persons, the most
proper for that work are the worst of that kind. Comedy is humble
of her Nature. . . . If I had designed here the celebration of the
Virtues of our Friends, I would have made the Scene nobler. . . .
They should have stood in Odes, and Tragedies, and Epique Poems.
(Preface)

Here, at the very outset of the period, Cowley is arguing that
heroes are not proper to comedy. But if there were not objections to imperfect characters, why bother? True, the objection

[1] *Works*, X. 208–10.

in this instance is more political than aesthetic, but the claim is that a cavalier should be *admirable*, not that he has no place in a comedy. Similarly John Wilson, writing in 1663, states that 'Comedy, either is, or should be, the true Picture of Vertue, or Vice; yet so drawn, as to shew a man how to follow the one, and avoid the other.'[1] Thus even in the reign of Charles II there is no clear-cut agreement on the nature of characters in comedy.

Thus far I have been concerned with contradictions in the case for a uniformly satiric theory of comedy. I think, however, it can be shown that very different sorts of comedy are actively championed. If one stops to think about the orthodox theory upheld by Dennis, it should be obvious that the formula works pretty well for Jonsonian comedy, but can have little applicability to Shakespearean romance. Equally, this limitation must hold good for much late seventeenth-century comedy as well, for 'love' is one of the major interests of all sorts of drama in this period. Dryden says of Jonson:

let us not think him a perfect pattern of imitation; except it be in his humour: for love, which is the foundation of all comedies in other languages, is scarcely mentioned in any of his plays. . . . The poets of this age will be more wary than to imitate the meanness of his persons. Gentlemen will now be entertained with the follies of each other.[2]

Here Dryden does suggest that the 'follies' of gentlemen are the subject of comedy, but in the same essay we can see clear evidence that he is not thinking primarily of ridiculing gentlemen. He argues at length the advantages of contemporary over Elizabethan comedy, basing his stand on the 'gallantry', 'civility', and polished 'conversation' which the Carolean playwright derives from court and King, noting that 'the desire of imitating so great a pattern' has profoundly affected English high society. Obviously Dryden does not mean to

---

[1] 'The Author, To The Reader', *The Cheats*, ed. Milton C. Nahm (Oxford, 1935), p. 237.

[2] 'Defence of the Epilogue', in *Of Dramatic Poesy and Other Critical Essays*, ed. George Watson, 2 vols. (London, 1962), I. 182. Shadwell disagrees (*Works*, I. 185); Dennis says that '*Shakespear* had little Love in the very best of his Plays, and *Johnson* less in his . . . he was so sensible, that the *Ridiculum* was the chief thing in Comedy, that he has always in his chief Comedies joyn'd his Love with Humour, and so made it ridiculous' (*Critical Works*, I. 285).

ridicule this 'refined' society in comedy. He never entirely abandons his conviction, expressed late in life, that 'the characters of comedy and tragedy . . . are never to be made perfect',[1] but both in his heroic dramas and in several of the comedies he wrote at about the same time the principal characters seem to be largely admirable, if not actually patterns for imitation.[2]

With this point in mind, the dangers of preconceived generic distinctions should be evident, but they are worth spelling out further. Modern critics have generally conceived 'Restoration comedy' and heroic drama as contradictory extremes, but to study their connections as well as their differences can be instructive. The immediate antecedents of Dryden's famous heroic plays (*The Indian Emperour*, 1665; *Tyrannick Love*, 1669; *The Conquest of Granada*, 1670–1) are disparate, but they include Orrery's plays (a cross-breed between French drama and Caroline romantic tragicomedy) and Spanish romance. The latter form—before it is debased with comic additions—is called comedy or tragicomedy, and presents rigidly decorous lead characters who are plainly meant to be exemplary models of propriety. Dryden's *The Rival Ladies* (1664) is an imitation of the generic prototype, Tuke's *Adventures of Five Hours* (1663). The pattern makes a clear appearance in the top plot of Etherege's *The Comical Revenge* (1664), which takes place in heroic couplets and revolves on moral dilemmas of love and honour; an obvious echo appears in Wycherley's imitative *Love in a Wood* (1670), though no longer in verse. What all this tells us is simply that *in the 1660s it was perfectly possible to have exemplary, even heroic, characters in a work regarded as a comedy*. Writing around January 1671 Mrs. Evelyn praises *The Conquest of Granada* as 'a play so full of ideas that the most refined romance I ever read is not to compare with it; love is made so pure, and valour so nice, that one would imagine it designed for an Utopia rather than our stage.' Though delighted by Dryden's ability 'to feign such exact virtue', Mrs. Evelyn is dubious about his departure from 'the strict law of

---

[1] 'A Parallel of Poetry and Painting' (1695), *Critical Essays*, II. 184.

[2] For an account of Dryden's preference for admiration over ridicule in comedy, see Frank Harper Moore, *The Nobler Pleasure: Dryden's Comedy in Theory and Practice* (Chapel Hill, N.C., 1963).

comedy'—the unities. But plainly she did not think of comedy solely in terms of ridicule of low or foolish characters. Neither did James Wright, who (writing nearly a quarter of a century later) says angrily that 'we seldom or never see a Character of True Worth, Integrity, and Honour, in any of these Comedies. . . . The Debauchee is always the fine Gentleman.' He goes on to say that in older plays—the most recent he names are those of Davenant and Dryden—there *are* virtuous characters who are true gentlemen, witty rather than lewd, 'But now . . . the *Utile* seems wholly lost and forgotten, and the *Dulce* is become Pall'd, Corrupted, and Sowr.'[1]

Exemplary characters are not a post-Carolean development; rather, in the early period they belong largely in the province of heroic and pseudo-heroic drama. By no means though is the pseudo-heroic excluded from the province of comedy. We have noted its presence in early Etherege and Wycherley, and we find it in the mature Dryden. *Marriage A-la-Mode* is called simply 'A Comedy' on the title-page, although the principal plot is heroic in kind. This is no accident: Dryden is making a deliberate attempt to 'raise' comedy by emphasizing the 'admiration' he had once considered proper to tragedy. Ironic as we now find his dedication to Rochester, Dryden was plainly proud of the courtly air of his play:

if there be any thing in this Play, wherein I have rais'd my self beyond the ordinary lowness of my Comedies, I ought wholly to acknowledge it to the favour, of being admitted into your Lordship's Conversation. . . . The best Comick Writers of our Age, will joyn with me to acknowledge, that they have copy'd the Gallantries of Courts, the Delicacy of Expression, and the Decencies of Behaviour, from your Lordship.

In the epilogue Dryden argues that he leads the audience 'to Reformation', but differentiates his method from both 'dull Morals, gravely writ', and from the procedure of 'Some stabbing Wits, to bloudy Satyr bent', who 'Would lay the Scene at home, of Husbands tell,/For Wenches, taking up their Wives i' th' Mell'.

Dryden's play should be seen as part of a deliberate attempt

---

[1] Wright, pp. 8, 16–17. The preceding quotation from Mrs. Evelyn is from *The Diary and Correspondence of John Evelyn*, ed. William Bray, 4 vols. (London, 1863), IV. 25.

to raise the social tone of comedy, an attempt which is a conscious reaction against the increasing incursions of farce after 1670. (On this reaction see Chapter 7, below.) The bitter protests of both Dryden and Shadwell in 1671 against this 'French' invasion have already been noted, but Dryden is worth quoting further.

Most of those Comedies, which have been lately written, have been ally'd too much to Farce: and this must of necessity fall out till we forbear the translation of *French Plays*: for their Poets wanting judgement to make, or to maintain true characters, strive to cover their defects with ridiculous Figures and Grimaces. While I say this I accuse my self as well as others: and this very play would rise up in judgment against me. . . . [1]

Here Dryden is plainly proposing the sort of 'heightened' comedy he was soon to attempt in *Marriage A-la-Mode* and *The Assignation* (1672).

A very similar case is advanced in a much neglected but important pair of prefaces by his brother-in-law, Edward Howard, who argues at length for a strong heroic admixture in comedy. He says that 'mixt Plays' are 'sutable to the English Stage', and defends the ascription tragicomedy on the grounds that it is 'somewhat below the denomination of their Heroicks to call them simply Comedies (which as they are corruptly understood, imply, little more then scurrility and laughter, though of far greater dignity, if rightly apply'd)'. He aims at a 'Heroick mixture'.

As the chief end of Comedy is improvement of manners, so the mirth arising thence, is to entertain our passions, and affections with delight proper thereunto; wherefore to make laughter the chiefest end of Comedy, is to impair its more superiour esteem, since what is ridiculous, is not therefore Comedy.

Howard says that 'a Clown . . . shewn in a Ladies Gown, or a Scaramuchio' are merely instances of 'vulgar folly'. Farce he detests, though he finds

no reason to call Comedy low, though consisting of mean characters . . . if by the skill and wit of the Writer, the characters of vulgar men

---

[1] Preface to *An Evening's Love*, *Works*, X. 204.

are made worth the observation of the greatest. . . . Notwithstanding *I would not be thought averse from such a choice of persons in Comedy, as are most fit to character the most generous instruction of manners.*[1]

In short, Howard is prepared to put exemplary characters in a 'comedy'.

Surveying the whole question of response to the characters in late seventeenth-century 'comedies', a number of conclusions emerge. First, the bulk of the contemporary critical theory is postulated on the traditional view that comedy works by ridiculing low characters. Second, as 'love' becomes a central interest, and the social level of the characters rises, a confusion of different responses is the natural result. 'Romantic' comedy does not work by ridicule; rather, the audience is encouraged to sympathize with the lead characters and rejoice in their success. Certainly late seventeenth-century comedy does very often employ a romantic plot formula, and though it can be used without eliciting much sympathy (in the Plautine fashion), satiric impact does tend to be blurred if we are following the progress of young lovers to a happy resolution—just as the presentation of upper-class characters tends to yield a confusion of response, especially when stress is laid on their genuine gentility. Collier objects to any satire on the gentry; Dennis replies vigorously that a foolish or corrupted Lord is a fair and useful satiric target.[2] Nobles and knights are indeed often satirized. Nonetheless, as the social level of the lead characters rises from the low life of orthodox comic theory to the social level of the bulk of the audience and above it, the old sense of innate superiority obviously diminishes.

The structural formula common to an enormous number of these comedies involves a young man winning a lady (and often fortune) against the wishes of parents and her other suitors. But vastly different responses to 'hero' and 'heroine' may be evoked in this stock plot. We may despise them; or take a casual interest from a superior vantage point; or identify strongly with the interests of characters who are 'like us'; or we may be made to look up to the characters as exemplary models. The resulting plays—all based on the same formula— will be as different as Ionesco's *Jack; or The Submission*, Plautus's

[1] Preface to *The Womens Conquest* (1671) (italics added).
[2] *The Usefulness of the Stage* (1698), in *Critical Works*, I. 181–2.

Rudens, Shakespeare's *As You Like It,* and Steele's *The Conscious Lovers.*[1] The diversity of characters in some seventeenth-century plays covers the full range of this spectrum, and the characters in many plays cover a good deal of it. Carolean playwrights uphold exemplary characters both in theory and in practice, and to assume with McDonald that there are no 'heroes' in 'Restoration comedy' is simply erroneous.[2] But to suppose with Fujimura that there is a sharp dividing line between satirized Witwouds and admirable Truewits is almost equally mistaken, for as McDonald does show, many a Truewit is made fun of. Horner is a witty, successful figure whose schemes we support, but he is scarcely admirable.

The characters of both Carolean and post-Carolean comedy run the gamut from contemptible to admirable. This diversity is perfectly obvious in practice, and despite the preponderance of emphasis on satire of 'low' characters, warrant for it in contemporary theory is easy to find, as I have shown. One cannot, therefore, rely on platitudes about exposing the follies of the age as an accurate index to the nature of the comedies actually produced—the platitudes rest, after all, on assumptions about audience response to character which are demonstrably false in practice.

III. REALISM AND THE 'PARTS' OF A COMEDY

The survey just concluded was addressed to recent debates on the nature of late seventeenth-century comedy and the audience response it was designed to elicit. The results tell strongly against any theory which claims consistent or monolithic purposes for this drama. Hence we must turn from authors' lip

---

[1] For a fuller discussion of differentiation by type of response to character, see my essay, 'Some Problems in the Theory of Comedy', *Journal of Aesthetics and Art Criticism,* xxxi (1972), 87–100.

[2] McDonald dismisses Shadwell, Steele, and Collier together as 'naively moralistic', and suggests that their emphasis on positive example 'indicates a major confusion of epic and comic theories made by no discriminating writer on comedy in the period. . . . All the major writers insist . . . following the classical line, that comedy deals with "low characters," and, hence, no contamination of theories was possible' (p. 534). One has only to look at Dryden, in theory and practice, to see that this is inaccurate. Congreve preached satire in response to Collier, but whether he consistently practised it is open to question. The first plays of both Etherege and Wycherley contain pseudo-heroic characters who are taken seriously. How many 'major writers' are left?

service about moral aims and the 'object' of comedy to consider
more specific commentary on how a comedy is to be put
together. We have already asked what is to be imitated in
comedy: the answer is any kind of character from the contemptible to the admirable. We have now to ask *how* the
characters are to be imitated, and what kind of structure is to be
erected for their presentation. Two major issues are involved:
(1) realism, and (2) emphasis on 'action' versus emphasis on
'character' or 'discourse'—which involves a concomitant
squabble about the 'parts' of a comic work. Both are crucial
questions, but the first is the proper starting point. Most
contemporary commentary on comedy turns on a prescriptive
realism; in investigating claims and counter-claims the further
problem of differentiating comedy from tragedy and farce
necessarily arises.

The claims for realism are both ubiquitous and misleading.
The apparent suggestion that 'Restoration' playwrights put
the real life of the time on stage has been accepted by an
astonishing number of later critics, and has given rise to moral
blasts at both theatre and audience. In point of fact, though,
realism is a hotly debated subject, and it does not mean quite
what one would think.[1]

The commonplaces are entirely familiar. Wycherley's Plain
Dealer announces to the audience in a prologue that the
author 'Displays you, as you are'. References to mirrors are
legion—as in Sir Car Scroope's prologue for *The Man of Mode*
('Since each is fond of his own ugly Face,/Why shou'd you,
when we hold it, break the Glass?'), or William Burnaby's
painting metaphor in the prologue to *The Modish Husband*
(1702):

> Thus for your Pictures while you gravely sit,
> Like Ill-bred Painters, we our Colours fit,
> To make you scorn the Native lines that strike ye,
> And justly hate the Piece for being like ye.

[1] One of the most sensible accounts of the alleged realism is given in a pair of
seldom-quoted notes by Elmer Edgar Stoll, 'The *Beau Monde* at the Restoration',
Modern Language Notes, xlix (1934), 425–32, and 'The "Real Society" in Restoration
Comedy: Hymeneal Pretenses', ibid., lviii (1943), 175–81. I quite agree with his
conclusion that what we find 'is not the image of the *beau monde* but an entertainment to its taste'.

In similar terms John Stafford writes:

> In Comedy your little Selves you meet,
> 'Tis *Covent-Garden* drawn in *Bridges-street*:
> Smile on our Author then, if he has shown
> A jolly Nut-brown Bastard of your own.
> Ah! Happy you, with Ease and with Delight,
> Who act those Follies, Poets toil to Write!
> (Epilogue to Southerne's
> *The Disappointment*, 1684)

The prologue to Vanbrugh's *The Provok'd Wife* (1697) announces that:

> 'tis the Intent and Business of the Stage,
> To Copy out the Follies of the Age;
> To hold to every Man a Faithful Glass,
> And shew him of what Species he's an Ass.

Dennis is a veritable catalogue of demands for realism and probability in comedy. 'Comedy is drawing after the Life . . . a Comick Poet is obliged to Copy the Age to which he writes.' '*Rapin* tells us with a great deal of Judgment, *That Comedy is as it ought to be, when an Audience is apt to imagine, that instead of being in the Pit and Boxes, they are in some Assembly of the Neighbourhood.*' 'All our true Comedies are but Copies of the foolish or vicious Originals of the Age.'[1]

Despite the number and weight of such pronouncements, they are extremely suspect. That people would be entertained (or instructed) by a reproduction of their own daily life seems highly improbable. Still less may we suppose that *The Country-Wife*, *The Plain-Dealer*, *The Man of Mode*, or *The Way of the World* would have been taken as such by the audience. To do so would be as silly as to suppose that a modern television audience finds its daily life mirrored in situation comedies and serial melodramas. One obvious index to the anti-realistic nature of late seventeenth-century comedy is the freedom authors have to make their plots turn on legal impossibilities. Marriage is one of the commonest themes and plot centres in this drama, yet a large number of the tricked or faked marriages (and occasional

---

[1] *Critical Works*, I. 290; II. 248, 312. Cf. especially, I. 285, 293; II. 243, 263, 336–7. For a long list of similar pronouncements from other critics, see Hooker's notes, I. 477–8.

divorces) are perfectly impossible according to the law of the time.[1] This is true throughout the period. A few of the many plays which rely on legal impossibilities are *Cutter of Coleman-Street* (1661), *Sir Martin Mar-all* (1667), *The Virtuoso* (1676), *Sir Courtly Nice* (1685), *Sir Anthony Love* (1690), *The Old Batchelour* (1693), *Love for Love* (1695), and *The Beaux Stratagem* (1707). If the comedies of this period were realistic in most other respects, one might expect some outcry about legal impossibilities, but I am aware of none. Personally, I suspect that the 'displays you as you are' rhetoric—a speciality of prologues and epilogues—is a roundabout flattery of an audience which liked to imagine that it was a little more rakish than it actually was. Real rakes were presumably indifferent to dramatic satire, but there seems ample evidence that, then as now, an audience could enjoy being a bit shocked—hence the rapid rise of sex comedy during the 1670s.

Probably 'realism' has been overstressed partly as a result of confusion about 'natural imitation'. According to the most common view, tragedy exalts nature while comedy leaves it as it is.[2] Dryden describes tragedy as 'Nature wrought up to an higher pitch . . . exalted above the level of common converse'.[3] According to the traditional view maintained by Dennis, comedy copies only the low, while Dryden prefers the 'mixed way'—but they agree that comedy is to be like life, while tragedy is lifted to a higher plane. From this perspective, realism often need mean no more than a mid-point between tragedy and farce.

Comedy consists, though of low persons, yet of natural actions, and characters; I mean such humours, adventures, and designes, as are to be found and met with in the world. Farce, on the other side, consists of forc'd humours, and unnatural events. Comedy presents us with the imperfections of humane nature: Farce entertains us with what is monstruous and chimerical. The one causes laughter in those who can judge of men and manners, by the lively representation of

---

[1] For lists of such instances, see Gellert Spencer Alleman, *Matrimonial Law and the Materials of Restoration Comedy* (Wallingford, Pa., 1942).

[2] For example, 'The Spirit of Tragedy shou'd always soar; Nature is not to be directly copy'd as in Comedy.' *A Comparison Between the Two Stages* (anonymous; 1702), ed. Staring B. Wells (Princeton, N.J., 1942), p. 60.

[3] *Of Dramatick Poesie*, in *Works*, XVII, ed. Samuel Holt Monk *et al.* (Berkeley, Calif., 1971), p. 74.

their folly or corruption; the other produces the same effect in those who can judge of neither, and that only by its extravagances.[1]

Peter Motteux (writing in the *Gentleman's Journal*, May 1692) makes a similar differentiation, commending comedy for its resemblance to ordinary life, criticizing tragedy as too elevated from the ordinary, and objecting to farce as an 'unnatural' exaggeration of the 'humane Follies' which are the subject of comedy. To take this distinction too seriously would be unwise, for there is plenty of farce to be found in the plays of Dryden, Shadwell, Wycherley, Etherege, and Congreve. But the idea is basically plain: tragedy inflates its characters above life; comedy presents both high and low characters in semi-probable situations; farce entertains with knockabout and improbable buffoons.

Edward Howard makes a good point, though, when he says that 'extravagancies' are not merely the province of farce, but appear in the inflated characters of tragedy and can properly be employed in comedy. With a good deal of insight, Howard argues that satire does not consist simply in realistic portrayal, but 'must be highly Hyperbolical'—noting that Ben Jonson presents 'very many characters of no being amongst men, as in his *Devil's an Ass*, *Cinthio's Revels*, and others'—and he goes on to cite Morose as a clear instance of hyperbole.[2] The more common view is clearly put by Laurence Echard, who criticizes Plautus for having 'strain'd his *Characters* to an extravagant pitch', adding that 'With these sort of *Characters* many of our modern *Comedies* abound, which makes 'em too much degenerate into *Farce*.'[3] But as far as practice goes, Edward Howard is right: characters like Sir Fopling Flutter are plainly hyperbolical.

Farquhar offers an interesting commentary on the whole problem of realism. He heatedly condemns 'unnaturalness' in contemporary comedy, but he does not believe in 'verisimilitude' or the 'rules' commonly adduced in its support.

The Poet does not impose Contradictions upon you, because he has told you no Lie; for that only is a Lie which is related with some

---

[1] Preface to *An Evening's Love, Works*, X. 203. Dryden is referring here only to what he calls 'low comedy'.

[2] Prefaces to *The Womens Conquest* and *The Six days Adventure* (1671).

[3] Preface to *Plautus's Comedies* (1694).

fallacious Intention that you should believe it for a Truth; now the
Poet expects no more that you should believe the Plot of his Play,
than old *Æsop* design'd the World shou'd think his *Eagle* and *Lyon*
talk'd like you and I. . . . If you are so inveterate against improbabilities, you must never come near the Play-House at all; for
there are several Improbabilities, nay, Impossibilities, that all
the Criticisms in Nature cannot correct; as for instance; In the part
of *Alexander* the Great . . . we must suppose that we see that great
Conquerour. . . . Yet the whole Audience at the same time knows
that this is Mr. *Betterton*, who is strutting upon the Stage, and tearing
his Lungs for a Livelihood. And that the same Person shou'd be Mr.
Betterton, and *Alexander* the Great, at the same time, is somewhat
like an Impossibility, in my Mind.[1]

Farquhar goes still further in arguing that comedy instructs
not by verisimilitude, but in the fashion of a beast fable.

The Nature of Comedy . . . bears so great a Resemblance to the
Philosophical *Mythology* of the Ancients, that old *Æsop* must wear
the Bays as the first and original Author. . . . Comedy is no more at
present than a *well-fram'd Tale handsomly told, as an agreeable Vehicle
for Counsel or Reproof*. . . . Where shou'd we seek for a Foundation, but
in *Æsop's* symbolical way of moralizing upon Tales and Fables,
with this difference, That his Stories were shorter than ours: He had
his Tyrant *Lyon*, his Statesman *Fox*, his Beau *Magpy*, his coward
Hare, his Bravo *Ass*, and his Buffoon *Ape*, with all the Characters that
crowd our Stages every Day. . . . *Utile Dulci* was his Motto . . . and
as he would improve Men by the Policy of Beasts, so we endeavour
to reform Brutes with the Examples of Men.[2]

A comparison with the symbolization of human traits in
Aesop's beasts seems to me as accurate and meaningful a
description of late seventeenth-century satiric technique as the
usual mirror metaphor. Interestingly, Farquhar's comparison
to Aesop is anticipated in Edward Howard's preface and
epilogue to *The Six days Adventure*. Speaking in favour of
hyperbolical characters, Howard points to Ovid and Aesop as
parallel ventures, and argues that the plays of the Restoration
are really no more realistic. The epilogue adds: 'Great *Æsop*
did by Fools the Wise direct,/Allow our Author's hear the same
effect . . . [he] hopes the Moral is above the Jest.'

In sum, the common call for realism is in many ways

---

[1] 'Discourse upon Comedy', *The Complete Works of George Farquhar*, ed. Charles
Stonehill, 2 vols. (1930; rpt. New York, 1967), II. 340–1.   [2] *Works*, II. 336.

misleading. Not only can counter-blasts be found, but in
practice realism seems to mean simply a negative middle
ground: lead characters are neither exaggeratedly silly (as in
farce) nor 'heightened' as for tragedy, and the action is to
consist neither of mere knockabout nor of great events.
Obviously writers were very far from limited by such prescriptions, as we can see from Dryden's *Marriage A-la-Mode* at
the one extreme and his *Mr. Limberham* at the other.[1]

Allowing, then, that realism is no reliable common denomi-
nator in either theory or practice, one can turn with more
confidence to an issue which, though related, is vastly less
discussed—the relative claims of 'action' and 'discourse'. Both
are commonly linked with 'verisimilitude', and a healthy sense
of the elasticity of that concept is useful here.

E.N. Hooker notes, without elaboration, that 'there
appeared in the criticism of comedy [during the late seventeenth
century] certain forces tending to modify, if not to destroy,
the traditional pattern of Aristotelian formalism.'[2] This seems
to me an over-simplification, since Aristotelian formalism was
never very securely established before the Restoration, and
later in the eighteenth century there was a great boom in the
mode Farquhar so resolutely mocks. Indubitably, though, there
was during the 1660–1710 period a continuing argument over
whether plot should be the pre-eminent element in a comedy.[3]

Dennis naturally insists that wit and humour should be
subordinated to design.[4] In taking plot as the principal element
in drama he is of a mind with Rymer, and both of them with
Ben Jonson.[5] This Aristotelian outlook is flatly controverted
by Dryden:

... consider what is the work of a Poet, and what the Graces of a
Poem: The Story is the least part of either: I mean the foundation
of it, before it is modell'd by the art of him who writes it; who formes

---

[1] For a sensible reconsideration of the subject, see John Loftis, 'The Limits of
Historical Veracity in Neoclassical Drama', *England in the Restoration and Early
Eighteenth Century*, ed. H. T. Swedenberg, Jr. (Berkeley, Calif., 1972), pp. 27–50.
See also David S. Berkeley, 'Some Notes on Probability in Restoration Drama',
Notes and Queries, cc (1955), 237–9, 342–4.   [2] Dennis, *Critical Works*, I. 515 nn.
[3] See Peter Seary, 'Language versus Design in Drama: A Background to the
Pope–Theobald Controversy', *University of Toronto Quarterly*, xlii (1972), 40–63.
[4] For example, *Critical Works*, I. 281.
[5] 'The parts of a Comedie are the same with a *Tragedie*.' *Timber*, in Spingarn, I. 58.

it with more care, by exposing only the beautiful parts of it to view, than a skilful Lapidary sets a Jewel. On this foundation of the Story the Characters are rais'd. . . .[1]

This division is more than semantic: it helps clarify, for example, the considerable differences between Shadwell and his idol Jonson, especially in the former's earlier plays. In his preface to *The Sullen Lovers* (1668) Shadwell says:

the want of design in the Play has been objected against me: which fault . . . I dare not absolutely deny: I conceive . . . that no man ought to expect such Intrigues in the little actions of Comedy, as are requir'd in Playes of a higher Nature: but in Playes of Humour . . . there is yet less design to be expected.

Shadwell later takes more trouble with design, and his bustling plots are adequately managed, but character almost always remains pre-eminent. Farquhar sharply satirizes the champions of plot in his 'Discourse upon Comedy', and Vanbrugh announces that both 'entertainment' and 'Moral' rest 'much more in the Characters and the Dialogue, than in the Business and the Event'.[2] Farquhar certainly would not go that far; but when he sets out to consider the means and end of comedy, he notes the vast variety of 'Humours' in the character of the English, and uses this as a justification for more than one plot— that is, he will employ a double plot in order to include a greater variety of characters. Thus character (or humour) plays a major role in shaping the work.[3] But even late in the period, plot has strong defenders. Echard says flatly that '*Comedy* consists more in *Action* than *Discourse*', and gives preference to Plautus over Terence on that basis. Similarly William Burnaby, in an essay on dramatic criticism (1701), states that:

In *Comedy*, *Action* is absolutely necessary, as well as in *Tragedy*; and whatever is contrary to that, is to have no Place in either. In Comedy also the chief Thing is the Fable, or Plot; the Excellence of which is to bring in such Characters and Incidents, as may naturally produce *Humour*. There will yet be room enough for *Wit*; but that Comick

---

[1] Preface to *An Evening's Love*, *Works*, X. 212. Cf. Rymer, who announces that '*Fable* or *Plot*' is 'the *Soul* of a *Tragedy*', without which 'there is no talking of Beauties'. *The Critical Works of Thomas Rymer*, ed. Curt A. Zimansky (New Haven, Conn., 1956), p. 18.   [2] *A Short Vindication of the Relapse* (London, 1698), p. 57.   [3] *Works*, II. 337–8.

Poet, that makes *Wit*, and (what we call) *Dialogue*, his chief Aim, ought to write nothing but Dialogues, for he can never obtain the Name of a Dramatick Writer, with the best Judges.[1]

This division of opinion may reflect the decline of 'instruction' as a primary goal. Though Dennis held in later life that 'Tragedy instructs chiefly by its Design, Comedy instructs by its Characters', Hooker is correct in saying that 'the function of instruction was generally associated with fable, or plot': thus increasing emphasis on characters tended to go along with a primary concern for entertainment.[2] This need not be the case: Steele's *The Conscious Lovers* is character-oriented, while Mrs. Behn's racy intrigue comedies are not. The association may in part be related to 'poetic justice'. An instructive play was often reckoned one in which the 'design' left good characters rewarded and bad punished. Collier is very insistent about this, and most subsequent critics found it prudent to agree. Thus an anonymous author complains about Sable in Steele's *The Funeral* (1701) because he 'goes off unpunish'd, contrary to the Law of *Comedy*'.[3] Addison's devastating attack on the whole concept of poetic justice in the *Spectator*, 40 (1711), is a complete reversal of widely acknowledged doctrine. As we have seen, even Dryden, a believer in 'character' and 'discourse' who had the nerve to admit that he wrote principally to delight, had hedged and prevaricated when charged with making 'vicious persons happy'.

IV. METHODS: PLOT, SATIRE, HUMOUR, WIT, AND EXAMPLE

Two points should now be plain. First, despite widespread lip service to 'realism', even unto Dennis's lengths, in practice *verisimilitude* is one thing, *naturalness* (as opposed to the imitation practised in tragedy and farce) another. Second, the marked differences between the action-centred comedy (*The Rover*) and the talk-centred (*The Man of Mode*) actually reflect quite different concepts of the nature of a comedy. In its extreme form, the division boils down to this: do the characters exist to carry out the action, or is the action contrived to display the

---

[1] *The Dramatic Works of William Burnaby*, ed. F. E. Budd (London, 1931), Appendix B, p. 459.   [2] Dennis, *Critical Works*, II. 245; cf. notes on I. 486 and 515.
[3] *A Comparison Between the Two Stages*, p. 83.

characters? Some writers—Farquhar for example—really cannot be pigeon-holed one way or the other. But since, as we have seen, the discourse versus design question was hotly debated around the end of the seventeenth century, an awareness of the two concepts is useful in considering the sorts of responses that dramatists sought to elicit from the audience.

However one may characterize the split (discourse–design, or character–plot), it may seem all too reminiscent of the chicken–egg paradox. Obviously all plays short of *The Bald Soprano* have both plot and characters. The differentiation is best understood in terms of the Aristotelian concept of the 'parts' of a poem. Dryden defines the parts of a 'tragic or heroic' poem as (1) *fable*; (2) *order* of plot elements; (3) *manners* of the characters; (4) *thoughts* expressing the manners; (5) *words* expressing the thoughts.[1] A crucial distinction must be made between the sequence of these 'parts' in composition, versus the relative emphasis they are given in the resulting play. In his criticism Dryden was in the habit of moving sequentially from consideration of plot, to characters, to manners, to thoughts, to words.[2] This does not mean, however, that Dryden follows the Aristotelians in rating these elements in descending order of importance. (Rymer does so; cf. Dryden's 'Heads of an Answer to Rymer'.) Certainly Dryden must have written his plays in this sequence: thus he says in a letter to Walsh that he has 'plotted' the whole of a play '& written two Acts of it'.[3] It would be hard to write a play without plotting it first. But in a fair number of late seventeenth-century plays, plot seems to me distinctly secondary in importance to character. *The Man of Mode* is a prime example. Or—to take a non-controversial illustration—many of Molière's plays (for example, *Tartuffe*, *L'Avare*, *Le Bourgeois Gentilhomme*) have perfectly standard plots with young lovers achieving marriage and money, but what we remember and care about is the humours characters.

Although I have taken this account of the 'parts' of drama from a discussion of tragedy, a generally plot-oriented writer

[1] 'Heads of an Answer to Rymer' (1677), *Works*, XVII. 190.
[2] Farquhar follows the same sequence in his 'Discourse upon Comedy'. For a fuller discussion of Dryden's valuation of the 'parts' of a work, see my essay, 'Dryden on Creation: "Imagination" in the Later Criticism', *Review of English Studies*, n.s. xxi (1970), 295–314.   [3] *Letters*, no. 24.

like Dennis would consider it equally applicable to comedy,
and moreover would, like Rymer, view it as a hierarchical
construct with the various elements appearing in descending
order of importance. Dryden (who is character- and discourse-
oriented even in tragedy and epic) would certainly not. We see
on the one side a concept of comedy in which the basis is a plot
—in theory at least contrived to serve the ends of poetic
justice. On the other, we have more of a problem. Supposing
that the various elements can in practice be variably emphasized, at least three basic possibilities emerge: plot- or action-
oriented comedy; character-oriented comedy; thought- and
word-oriented comedy.[1] Recognizing this three-way division
should clarify a point on which seventeenth-century theorists
are decidedly hazy. Heretofore, I have categorized discourse-
and character-oriented plays together in opposition to the plot-
oriented. No very clear warrant can be found in contemporary
theory for separating them. But the difference is essentially that
between comedy of humour and comedy of wit. Shadwell, no
plot-monger, did not care for 'slight Plays' whose basis was 'a little
tattle sort of Conversation'.[2] In essence this is the distaste of a
character-oriented writer for the products of those interested
primarily in verbal wit. Obviously a variety of combinations
and permutations are possible. Thus Durfey announces in his
preface to *Love for Money*, 'I don't overload my Plays with Wit.
Plot and Humour are my Province.'

Supposing then that either character or discourse can be the
prime element in comedy, we want to know how the dramatists
conceived the varying potentialities of the form. Evidence is
scanty, but highly suggestive. If the primary concern is not a
'design' calculated to bring about poetic justice, presumably
moral ends will have to be achieved by direct ridicule of
persons. But 'ridicule' can be of very different sorts. In an
essay published in 1677 Dryden says that:

comedy is both excellently instructive, and extremely pleasant:
satire lashes vice into reformation, and humour represents folly so
as to render it ridiculous. Many of our present writers are eminent

---

[1] A very similar case is argued by R. S. Crane in his well-known distinction
between plots of action, plots of character, and plots of thought in 'The Concept of
Plot and the Plot of *Tom Jones*', *Critics and Criticism*, ed. Crane (Chicago, 1952),
pp. 620–1.   [2] Dedication of *The Virtuoso* (1676).

in both these kinds; and particularly the author of the *Plain Dealer*, whom I am proud to call my friend, has obliged all honest and virtuous men by one of the most bold, most general, and most useful satires which has ever been presented on the English theatre.[1]

Note especially the phrase 'in both these kinds'. Here Dryden suggests that *a distinction must be made between real satire and the humorous representation of folly*. The one involves a more serious moral aim; the other is essentially good humoured, even if satiric. This distinction appears clearly enough in practice in the obvious differences of tone between *The Plain-Dealer* and *The Man of Mode*.

The concept behind this differentiation is made even clearer in an observation of Shadwell's in his dedication of *The Virtuoso*. 'I have endeavoured, in this Play, at Humour, Wit, and Satyr, which are the three things (however I may have fallen short in my attempt) which your Grace has often told me are the life of a Comedy.' Two years later in the dedication of *A True Widow* he repeats this suggestion that 'Wit, Humour, and Satyr' are the basic elements which constitute a comedy. Humour, Shadwell argues in the former dedication, does not consist of 'fantastick, extravagant Dress', nor 'affectation of some *French* words', nor 'unnatural Farce Fools', nor natural imperfections; rather it is the 'Artificial folly' of those who 'with great Art and Industry' make themselves cranks or coxcombs. In the prologue Shadwell adds:

> In the last Comedy some Wits were shown;
> In this are Fools that much infest the Town. . . .
>
> He's sure in Wit he cann't excel the rest,
> He'd but be thought to write a Fool the best.

Again, the distinction between humour and satire is worth noting, since the two are often equated. The separation of humour and wit is more expected. 'The last Comedy', I believe, refers to *The Man of Mode*, which was the last new comedy staged by the Duke's Company. If so, Shadwell is surely right: Etherege's play does emphasize wit and conversation more than humour or satire, while *The Virtuoso*, which emphasizes the latter two elements, is less heavily weighted toward serious satire than, say, *The Plain-Dealer*.

[1] 'Apology for Heroic Poetry and Poetic License', *Critical Essays*, I. 199.

These three plays have a good deal in common. Staged the same year, they are all part of the mid-1670s boom in sex comedy; all have often been treated as comedy of manners; all concern relatively upper-class characters; all have a considerable satiric element; all are praised by such later critics as Dennis as true, moral comedy. Nonetheless, the three leave very different impressions, for in tone they differ markedly. To suggest that one is comedy of wit, one comedy of humour, and one comedy of satire would be a ridiculous exaggeration. As Shadwell recognizes, each play is a combination of the three elements: what changes is the relative emphasis on them which each play reflects.

Writing in 1695 Congreve makes some of the same points:

Wit is often mistaken for Humour. . . . But there is a great Difference between a Comedy, wherein there are many things *Humorously*, as they call it, which is *Pleasantly* spoken; and one, where there are several Characters of *Humour* . . . which naturally arise from the different Constitutions, Complexions, and Dispositions of Men. . . . As *Wit*, so, its opposite, *Folly, is sometimes mistaken for Humour.*[1]

Sounding very much like Shadwell, Congreve goes on to object to 'Farce fools', ridiculous dress, and satire on 'Natural Deformities'; he differs in feeling that affectation (though usable) is not really humour, but he had apparently altered his opinion by the time of the dedication of *The Way of the World*. There he stresses both ridicule of affectation and the virtues of genteel conversation, thanking the Earl of Mountague for 'the Honour of your Lordship's Conversation'—which should recall Dryden's thanks to Rochester. In the following prologue he announces that the play has some plot, some humour, no farce, and 'Satire, he thinks, you ought not to expect,/For so Reform'd a Town, who dares Correct?' As Congreve thus announces, the play rather evenly balances the elements that late seventeenth-century playwrights juggle. It is discourse- rather than plot-oriented, but not so lacking in plot as *The Man of Mode*; genteel, witty conversation is stressed, but several humours characters are prominent; satire (though ironically denied) is an important part of the play, though not so obtrusively as in *The Double-Dealer*.

[1] Letter to Dennis, 10 July 1695 ('Concerning Humour in Comedy'). *William Congreve: Letters and Documents*, ed. John C. Hodges (New York, 1964), pp. 177–8.

Thus the comic dramatist could find in the inexact and ill-sorted parlance of the time a considerable number of options, and was by no means confined to a single clear-cut formula or even to a selection of them. He could build his play around plot, character, and discourse combined as he pleased, and was then free to emphasize satire, humour in characters, and wit in whatever degrees and combinations he found attractive. This point seems so obvious in practice that I am embarrassed to have to insist on it at such length, but the assumption of monolithic aims, purposes, and methods for all writers of true 'Restoration' comedies by such critics as McDonald demands correction.

To the common Carolean formula—*satire, humour, wit*—must be added a fourth element—*example*. Roughly speaking, example constitutes a parallel to satire, serving however to elicit the opposite response. In comedies with English settings, example is largely a post-Carolean phenomenon. The whole vexed question of 'sentimental' comedy will be taken up later. But we can fairly say that characters who serve as moral examples are increasingly introduced between 1688 and 1710 into plays which otherwise do preserve what John Loftis defines as the 'Restoration Stereotypes'.[1] From Belfond jun. in Shadwell's *The Squire of Alsatia* (1688) to Bevil jun. in *The Conscious Lovers* (1722) is a considerable jump: we can scarcely imagine Steele's hero seducing a virtuous girl in the course of the play, and then paying her off in a gentlemanly way in order to marry a wealthier one. But both men are explicitly presented as admirable. 'The Fine Gentleman'—as Steele once thought of titling his last play—is increasingly a common figure in comedy; virtuous females are even more frequent. In essence they represent the characters 'of True Worth, Integrity, and Honour' demanded by James Wright in 1694 (quoted above): in the Carolean period, such characters generally appear in romantic comedy or tragicomedy set abroad, but more and more they become frequent in plain English-set comedies. By the time of Taverner's *The Maid the Mistress* (1708), Mrs. Centlivre's *The Man's Bewitch'd* (1709), and Charles Shadwell's *The Fair Quaker of Deal* (1710) they are a commonplace. By no means though should we suppose that

[1] See Chapter 3 of Loftis, *Comedy and Society*.

example and satire are mutually exclusive, any more than are humour and wit. Steele's first play, *The Funeral*, has a good deal of example in the person of the abused son, Lord Hardy, and in the final noble speeches of Lord Brumpton. The play also savagely satirizes undertakers and the class of widows represented by Lady Brumpton. Steele's preface emphasizes his employment of ridicule and satire; in his later *Apology* (1714) Steele notes that though the play is 'full of incidents that move Laughter' it makes 'Virtue and Vice appear just as they ought to do'.[1] Here example and satire are more or less equally balanced.

Surveying the ground covered in this chapter, I think one must acknowledge the considerable variety of possibilities open to the writer of comedies in the period 1660–1710. He could evoke anything between contempt and admiration for the lead characters; emphasize plot, character, or discourse; and work with radically different balances of wit, humour, satire, and example. The result in practice is a collection of works whose radical diversity has given modern readers a good deal of trouble. Not even the most capacious of pigeon-holes will accommodate more than a limited selection of these comedies. Looking back, there is always a great temptation to codify, clarify, and organize; our predilection for Etherege, Wycherley, Congreve, and a few others has made us group them together, both isolating them and ignoring their differences to an unhealthy degree. The 'aesthetics of wit comedy' deduced by Fujimura, and the 'drama of satire' postulated by McDonald are radically incomplete views of a complicated whole. That two such well-argued constructs should be so contradictory should remind us to beware of all-inclusive statements about this drama. Spanish romance, intrigue comedy of Aphra Behn's sort, the high comedy championed by Dryden, comedy variously emphasizing wit, humour, satire, and example—all find ample warrant in contemporary critical theory. An awareness of the immense variety of options open to the writers of late seventeenth-century comedy should make us more sympathetic and sensitive to both their subtle differences and their drastic divergencies.

---

[1] *Tracts and Pamphlets by Richard Steele*, ed. Rae Blanchard (Baltimore, 1944), p. 339.

CHAPTER 3

THE NATURE OF THE COMIC DRAMA

A GOOD many attempts to characterize Restoration comedy have been produced in the last sixty years. Amidst the welter of contradictory opinion, the basic puzzle remains: what sorts of plays are these? We need to determine what subjects the plays have, how the dramatists utilize their materials, and toward what ends. As a beginning, we can usefully do two things: survey recent characterizations, and analyse some key plays. We will find that although the comedies are quite formulaic, there are too many variables to allow rigorous classification. Nonetheless, we can readily identify the basic modes favoured during any given part of the period. The dramatists ring a wide variety of changes on these types, and the results, when considered all together, look like chaos. But by returning to elementary questions and attending to chronology, the Gordian knot can be circumvented, if not cut or untied.

I. RECENT CHARACTERIZATIONS

Critical discussion of late seventeenth-century comedy has continued to be plagued by the ghost of Macaulay. This assertion may seem peculiar: few twentieth-century critics since Archer have expressed moral outrage about these plays. But the history of recent criticism is a kind of comic-opera sequel to earlier misunderstandings.[1] Macaulay presumed that the comedies reproduced the life of a sodomite court for a pack of degenerate courtiers to drool over. The natural rebuttal was the claim that (as Lamb had already said) the world of the comedies was artificial and unreal—and hence of no moral significance whatever. The ethereal drawing-room descriptions

---

[1] See Irène Simon, 'Restoration Comedy and the Critics', *Revue des langues vivantes*, xxix (1963), 397–430, and Andrew Bear, 'Restoration Comedy and the Provok'd Critic', *Restoration Literature: Critical Approaches*, ed. Harold Love (London, 1972), pp. 1–26.

are a corollary. What is fragile, precious, witty, and artificial can scarcely be brutal, coarse, and nastily realistic. Palmer and his followers (Dobrée, Perry, Lynch) defended the plays against moral objections by downplaying content in favour of form and style. L. C. Knights produced a very effective answer to these devotees of genteel art-for-art's-sake artificiality. Knights accepted their account of the comedy, but objected that such formalized exercises were trivial and dull. In short, he demanded a meaningful content as well as a polished form.[1] Since his essay, critics have laboriously claimed a variety of subjects and aims as the grounds of serious worth in Restoration comedy.

A brief survey of the stages of this unfortunate sequence gives some idea of the origin of common conceptions of Restoration comedy. Writing in 1913 and 1914, trying to remove the moral odium which clung to the plays, John Palmer argued that as a 'holiday from the sublime and beautiful, from the coarse and the real' they should be considered a 'strange country' and judged only 'according to the laws of imagination'.[2] Here we are back to Cloud-cuckoo-land. According to this theory, one must enjoy the 'artificial' trifling of the form, not attend seriously to the content. In the later book, Palmer speaks of

the comedy of manners . . . holding the reality of life away, or letting it appear only as an unruffled thing of attitudes. Life is here made up of exquisite demeanour. Its comedy grows from the incongruity of human passion with its cool, dispassionate and studied expression. Laughter . . . ripples forth in ironic contemplation. . . . We are no longer men; we are wits and a peruke. We are no longer women; we are ladies of the tea-table.[3]

Frigid, frivolous, artificial, vapid, drawing-room comedy—these are the terms Palmer's description calls to mind. The school of critics he spawned was a disaster for this drama. To say that it is 'a sublimation of the trivial, turning to fine art the accidents and trappings of life', or that 'the comedy of manners is life in terms of a muffin'[4] certainly suggests that the

---

[1] 'Restoration Comedy: The Reality and the Myth', *Explorations* (London, 1946), pp. 131–49. (Originally published in *Scrutiny* in 1937.)

[2] John Palmer, *Comedy* (London, n.d. [1914]), pp. 32–5; *The Comedy of Manners* (London, 1913), pp. 29, 292–3.   [3] *Comedy*, pp. 32–3.   [4] Ibid., pp. 33–5.

whole subject is of little importance. H.T.E. Perry says solemnly that this comedy is necessarily 'a superficial literature',[1] and one gathers from this sort of description that it must be thoroughly namby-pamby as well. A curious reversal of Macaulay!

For many of the older critics, the question of *point* seems hardly to have arisen. George Sherburn expresses a common view when he says that the comedy is 'hard, cynical, and immoral', but concerned with 'manners rather than morals'. Etherege, he says, 'transcribed life, but he lacked philosophy. To him life was a frivolous game.' Wycherley is at least granted 'imaginative and intellectual conviction' for sordid exposés.[2] John Harold Wilson, writing of plays by the 'wits', says that 'since their own particular society was obviously well-ordered, they discussed no problems.'[3] Nicoll, in his long-standard *History*, puzzles over the 'peculiar, intangible sort of thing' which is the comedy of manners. After saying that it 'depends rather on an atmosphere which cannot be precisely analysed', he hazards an account of 'the true characteristics of the species':

In the main, we may say, the invariable elements of the comedy of manners are the presence of at least one pair of witty lovers, the woman as emancipated as the man, their dialogue free and graceful, an air of refined cynicism over the whole production, the plot of less consequence than the wit, an absence of crude realism, a total lack of any emotion whatsoever.[4]

Could we find even half a dozen plays which arguably exhibit all of these 'invariable' elements? I doubt it. Nicoll obviously has *The Man of Mode* and *The Way of the World* in mind; how he contrives to discuss Wycherley's plays as comedies of manners is hard to see. Naturally he finds Wycherley unsatisfactory. With complete accuracy Nicoll complains that 'there is almost something of Shadwell in Wycherley's work.' This is indeed a disaster if one demands that comedy be 'wholly intellectual and passionless'.[5] For Nicoll too the best of these comedies consist of bloodless trifling.

[1] *The Comic Spirit in Restoration Drama* (New Haven, Conn., 1925), p. 131.

[2] *A Literary History of England*, ed. Albert C. Baugh, 4 vols. (New York, 1948), III. 763, 767, 769.   [3] *The Court Wits of the Restoration*, p. 172.

[4] Nicoll, I. 196–7.   [5] Ibid., 238, 199.

For a good many critics, the point of the comedy is to display manners, and this is essentially an end in itself. Kathleen M. Lynch, in a learned book, accepts Palmer's views and proceeds to trace artificiality and social refinement in a large number of the plays. Perhaps because of her obsessive concern with social refinement and artificial *précieuse* form and convention, she sees the plays largely as expressions of true and false fashion, believes the later comedy to follow a pattern established by Etherege, and even asserts that 'by 1676 the dramatic mode of Restoration comedy of manners had become so authoritative that all comic dramatists felt the pressure of its unwritten laws.' In this view, the point of all the comedies (not merely the few) is to present good and bad manners for the delectation of the audience: we are to laugh at fools and pretenders to fashion, and smile ironically at the foibles and affectations of the genuinely fashionable.[1] The point of doing so (if any) is not an issue which concerns Miss Lynch. Taking a slightly different position, Wilson says that the comedy 'presented libertines and Truewits to be admired [a disputed claim], and moralists and would-be wits to be laughed at as contemptible and ridiculous. It ran the gamut from broad, vulgar farce . . . to the comedy of wit.' The latter, he tells us, 'was written for a drawing-room society—the *beau monde*—not for those who expected comedy to provide a serious criticism of life'.[2] John Harrington Smith takes a similar position:

the typical writers of Restoration comedy had aimed at humorously reflecting and criticizing the actual social scene. For the most part they had accepted the moral code actually operative in their day and been content to permit it to express itself in their plays. Only Wycherley and Southerne can be said to have been outraged by it (though neither Congreve nor Vanbrugh was insensible of its faults).[3]

This seems to me a very fair statement.

Smith's assessment does not, however, make much of a rebuttal to L. C. Knights's loud complaint that the comedies are 'trivial, gross, and dull'. That late seventeenth-century comedies display manners is clearly true. However, such

---

[1] *The Social Mode of Restoration Comedy* (1926; rpt. New York, 1965), *passim*, but esp. pp. 6–7, 174, 182.

[2] *A Preface to Restoration Drama*, pp. 129, 168.

[3] J. H. Smith, p. 224.

critics as Knights and John Wain[1] reply by saying, yes, but *what for?* Very naturally, a number of recent critics have responded by trying to show that in or beneath the manners one can find a serious point to these comedies.

Fujimura developed his interpretation in reaction against the delightful-but-aimless school. Dobrée, perhaps the best of the art-for-art's-sake critics, can say:

> we feel that no values count, that there are no rules of conduct, hardly laws of nature. Certainly no appeal, however indirect, is made to our critical or moral faculties. . . . We are permitted to play with life, which becomes a charming harlequinade without being farce. It is all spontaneous and free, rapid and exhilarating; the least emotion, an appeal to common sense, and the joyous illusion is gone.[2]

Fujimura rightly objects that such a view entirely neglects the malice, lust, and coarse realism of the plays: oddly enough, he is then capable of turning around and asserting that 'wit comedy introduces us to a harmonious, graceful, and free world where the playful judgment can be exercised.'[3] How harmonious, graceful, and free is the world of *The Plain-Dealer?* But Fujimura's basic endeavour is to demonstrate the presence of a substantial intellectual and moral basis for 'Restoration comedy of wit'—a small group of plays, we discover. He gives a lengthy and learned definition of 'wit' (making it vastly broader than repartee) and argues that the comedies present not 'the bright, shimmering image of aristocratic manners' but 'the wit, and the naturalistic and skeptical temper' which reflect 'the troubled intellectual life of the times'. In Fujimura's view, the plays present 'a meaningful world where a definite order prevails and definite values exist': in essence, we identify with Truewits as they outwit Witwouds and Witlesses, while appreciating (if not necessarily accepting) 'the witty apprehension of life'. This outlook is, he asserts, not merely vapid pleasure-seeking, but should please us with its 'fine sense of proportion, of moderation, good taste, and naturalness implicit in the ideal of decorum'.[4] As a description of Etherege this seems to me quite helpful; Congreve it fits uncomfortably;

---

[1] 'Restoration Comedy and its Modern Critics' (cited in Chapter 1, p. 24, above).

[2] See Bonamy Dobrée, *Restoration Comedy*, pp. 13–14. See also *Comedies by William Congreve*, ed. Dobrée (London, 1925).

[3] Fujimura, pp. 8, 72.   [4] Ibid., pp. 56–7, 64, 65, 62–3.

Wycherley and others scarcely at all. But the importance of Fujimura's work is its attempt to see the comedies as an expression of contemporary intellectual issues and outlooks. The attempt may be imperfect, but we have to be grateful for it. No longer are the comedies part of Cloud-cuckoo-land. Probably Fujimura accepts too literally the supposed ideal of 'photographic realism', but since his book appeared, critics have been willing to consider the comedies as more than aimless trifles.

Dale Underwood goes considerably further. He starts by undertaking to refute the commonplaces, of which he gives a very clear account. The reader will have heard, he says,

that these dramatists created a verbally brilliant yet essentially casual, topical, and uncomplicated body of plays; that they were concerned solely with the surface manners of a small and specialized segment of Restoration society; that the manners were characterized by witty cynicism and sexual promiscuity; that the plays, like the society, were largely divorced from the central problems and pre-occupations of their age; and that they have little or nothing to say concerning the perennial problems of man.[1]

He then produces a brilliant account of the 'libertine' or 'sceptical' tradition in seventeenth-century thought, and proceeds to read Etherege's plays in the light of it. Underwood demonstrates one thing beyond a doubt: a critic *can* find solid intellectual substance in contemporary thought, and he can show numerous parallels to the situations and sentiments of the comic drama. This answers Knights with a vengeance: far from being trivial, Etherege 'made the comedy of manners the expression of man's mind and wit ambiguously groping among the abstractions by which he had thought to order his world' (p. 161).

What Underwood does for Etherege, Rose A. Zimbardo attempts for Wycherley, though from a different angle. Her book has the very great virtue of not grouping Etherege, Wycherley, and Congreve together: Mrs. Zimbardo considers Etherege a philosopher, Wycherley a serious satirist in a more or less distinct tradition, and Congreve 'well on his way to

[1] Dale Underwood, *Etherege and the Seventeenth-Century Comedy of Manners* (New Haven, Conn., 1957), p. 3.

sentimental comedy'.[1] The first two, at least, she takes seriously. *'Etherege's central concern is to reproduce in drama the philosophical ambivalence that marks seventeenth-century thought'* [italics added]. And she quotes with approval Underwood's assertion that the 'controlling concern' for all the major late seventeenth-century comedies is 'the quest for reality'.[2]

A less radical position is taken by Norman Holland. He finds that the plays embody a basic conflict between 'manners' (social conventions) and anti-social 'natural' desires. In essence the works then stand as explorations of the problem of the individual making ethical and social adaptations to the demands of society. This account makes Holland's position seem more abstract than it is: he is primarily concerned with close readings. In practice, he finds a *right-way* versus *wrong-way* dichotomy appearing in the plays; even so, Holland believes that, over all, these comedies 'question' rather than 'affirm'.[3]

Two other recent critics deserve mention. Charles O. McDonald, in an article discussed in the previous chapter, claims that all major Restoration comedy (an entity he leaves undefined) is serious satire. This would indeed give it a genuine purpose: I doubt, however, that many plays would stand up to such a view. Another writer, Virginia Ogden Birdsall, suggests that the comedies are celebrations of sex and the life spirit in rebellion against a restrictive morality.[4] Plainly there is some truth to this: Mrs. Birdsall is extending a position partially implicit in the work of Fujimura and Underwood. Indeed, Guy Montgomery long ago suggested a similar reading, proposing that the comedies are a questioning of old morals, much as the new science was a questioning of inherited dogma.[5] But I do think Mrs. Birdsall may be going rather too far. She is talking about only eleven plays—and Holland has observed (correctly) that all eleven require the 'reform' of the hero.[6] Her belief in Horner's excellence I find hard to accept. Amusingly enough, she sees the plays in precisely opposite

[1] *Wycherley's Drama* (New Haven, Conn., 1965), Chapter 1; quotation from p. 13.

[2] Zimbardo, p. 4; Underwood, p. 49.

[3] Norman N. Holland, *The First Modern Comedies* (Cambridge, Mass., 1959), esp. pp. 4, 114, 224, 233-4.

[4] *Wild Civility*, Chapter 1.

[5] 'The Challenge of Restoration Comedy', *University of California Publications in English* i (Berkeley, Calif., 1929), 133–51.   [6] Holland, p. 203.

terms to those of McDonald or Holland: where they find serious attack or questioning, she sees serious affirmation!

In seeking to discover the truth—if that can ever be found—about the nature of the comedies, it seems to me helpful to ask first what plays we are discussing, and second what are their *subjects*?

The first question has already been discussed at length in Chapter 1. Most characterizations of Restoration comedy are inadequate or misleading because they are based on a handful of writers or works by no means typical of the period. Few critics have been as knowledgeable and honest as Nicoll, who warns us that 'the chief things to remember about the development of the comedy of manners are, that it was not the principal fare of the theatres from 1664 to 1700, and that it was not even distinctively of the Restoration age at all.'[1] As for the second question, the common answer is that the subject of these comedies is 'artificial manners'. 'B' in T. S. Eliot's 'A Dialogue on Dramatic Poetry' says that 'Restoration comedy is a comedy of social manners. . . . It laughs at the members of a society who transgress its laws.'[2] A second answer, mostly out of favour with the comedy's defenders, is the obvious—intrigues, cuckolds, fornication, disease, drunkenness, cowardly buffoons, and the like. A third answer might be summed up (unsympathetically) as 'philosophic abstractions'. Fujimura, Underwood, and Zimbardo move rather far in this direction. It would be injustice not to acknowledge the excellence of the close readings by Holland and Birdsall, but even they, in their anxiety to rescue the comedies from belittlers, exaggerate the importance of what turn out to be secondary and subsidiary elements—when such elements are present at all. To get away from the aimless-artificiality reading is a welcome departure, but we must not lose sight of the plays themselves. Plainly some of them, especially those by the court wits, do reflect serious intellectual and social issues of the time. But is this what they are *about*?

Among recent critics who have defended these plays, I believe that only three have come out bluntly against 'intel-

[1] Nicoll, I. 194–5, 247.
[2] *Selected Essays*, 2nd edn. (New York, 1950), pp. 40–1.

lectual' readings. Clifford Leech suggests 'that the majority of Restoration comedies were more or less haphazard assemblies of diverting or striking situations, facile jests and contradictory stock sentiments'.[1] This statement is meant to apply to a very large number of works, and of course it does not do justice to the art of the best comedies. But even the famous few prominently display stock situations, characters, and sentiments, and to ignore that fact is irresponsible. I am very much in agreement with James Sutherland's assessment:

Defenders have not been wanting in recent years; and the comedy of Dryden, Etherege, Wycherley, and Congreve (few modern critics seem to be familiar with any other) is now seen as offering a serious and consistent criticism of contemporary life, embodying an attitude of philosophical libertinism, and submitting inadequate moral attitudes and social customs to the ridicule or contempt of satire. So far has this moral and intellectual rehabilitation proceeded that it has now perhaps overshot the mark.[2]

If one can stop fretting about profundity and important issues, and simply look at the obvious features of any given group of comedies, the plain, sane views of such critics as Smith, Wilson Leech, and Sutherland have much to recommend them.

What are these comedies about? Stock characters and situations. The young lovers who bring off an outwitting plot, the heavy fathers, the fops, fools, hectors, country innocents, hapless Frenchmen, cuckolds, old husbands with young wives, lecherous old men, religious hypocrites, social pretenders, young wastrels, witty girls, young men of wit and little money, bawds and whores, long-suffering, stupid, or tricky servants, hapless tradesmen—these are the people of the comedies. The same plots are used again and again: the young man wins his

[1] 'Restoration Comedy: The Earlier Phase', *Essays in Criticism*, i (1951), 165–84; quotation from p. 169.

[2] *English Literature of the Late Seventeenth Century* (Oxford, 1969), pp. 152–3. In an important book published since this chapter was first written, Harriett Hawkins has argued forcefully that Restoration comedies are about people, not ideas or ethical abstractions, and that they present the complexities and ambiguities of human experience rather than a simple white-or-black picture of what man should or should not be (*Likenesses of Truth in Elizabethan and Restoration Drama* (Oxford, 1972)). Dealing with only the greatest of the Restoration comedies, she overemphasizes their originality and individuality, but her basic arguments seem very convincing, especially her objections to the easy judgements of 'the moralistic school' as represented by Aubrey Williams in this period.

girl, and usually reforms in the process; fortune is won; adulterous copulation is achieved, without discovery—or the consequences are evaded. The same perils of discovery are run in comedy after comedy. The wanton wives, young libertines, jealous husbands, and witty young ladies produce highly repetitive patterns of events and situations.

But what is fascinating and challenging is the great disparity in the results. When we ask what these comedies are like, we find that plays with much the same subjects and components have entirely different tone and effect. The principal object of critical characterization is not to limit arbitrarily, or to categorize, but to explore the great variety of results in comedy— results which run from the quasi-heroic to the farcical.

II. EIGHT KEY CASES

The best way to see what the comedies are actually like is to look at some. The eight analysed here have been selected for their diversity in type, authorship, and date. All were exceptionally successful, several of them for an unusually long time. They are arranged here in a rough order of descending seriousness, from exemplary romance to farce. These analyses are presented without reference to context (which is dealt with in Part II of this book), but readers should realize that both major modes and chronological change are represented in this choice of plays. The city intrigue comedy and Spanish romance popular in the 1660s are illustrated in Howard's *The Committee* and Tuke's *The Adventures of Five Hours* respectively. The 'wit comedy' so dear to critics appears in Etherege's *The Man of Mode*; the social sex comedy of the sort developed in the seventies in Wycherley's *The Country-Wife*. The popular farce despised by Carolean critics is represented by Ravenscroft's *The Citizen Turn'd Gentleman*. Congreve's *Love for Love* is included as a sample of the 'hard' Carolean comedy in the 1690s— tinged with a new 'humane' outlook then developing. Shadwell's *The Squire of Alsatia* is a quasi-exemplary reform comedy, an important prototype for the didactic branch of Augustan comedy. Mrs. Centlivre's *The Busie Body* shows us city intrigue comedy in its laundered Augustan form. My object in each discussion is to provide a brief, straightforward account of the materials, devices, and tone as a means of approaching a

difficult but crucial question: what kind of audience response
was desired?

The Adventures of Five Hours: Spanish Romance

Sir Samuel Tuke's only play, first performed 8 January 1663,
had a splendid initial run (thirteen nights), and remained
popular for some time. The piece is heavily reliant on a Spanish
source: as Tuke says in the 1671 preface, 'the *Plot* needs no
Apology; it was taken out of *Dom Pedro Calderon* . . . recommended to me by *His Sacred Majesty* [i.e. Charles II], as an
Excellent Design' (3–4). Pepys raves over the play. Of the
première he wrote, with his customary exuberant superlatives,
'the play, in one word, is the best, for the variety and the most
excellent continuance of the plot to the very end, that ever I
saw or think ever shall. And all possible, not only to be done
in that time, but in most other respects very admittible and
without one word of ribaldry.' Praise of the unities and moral
purity has perhaps seemed uninviting to recent critics. Worse
yet, on 20 August 1666 Pepys notes that he was reading
Othello, 'which I ever heretofore esteemed a mighty good play;
but having so lately read *The Adventures of five hours*, it seems a
mean thing.' This curious judgement has both damaged
Pepys's credit as a critic and left scholars wary of Tuke's play.
Evelyn's view is juster: 'the plot was incomparable, but the
language stiffe & formall.' Even the carping Langbaine calls it
'One of the best Plays now extant, for Oeconomy and Contrivance'.[1] Among modern scholars only Summers voices more
than tepid approval, calling the play 'a very important, a very
interesting, and, I think we may truly claim, a very excellent
drama'.[2] I concur, and cannot imagine how the work acquired
its reputation for deadly dullness. Not only is the piece of great
significance historically, but it is thoroughly entertaining.

Whether *The Adventures* should be treated as a comedy may
be questioned. Both the 1663 and the 1671 title-pages dub the
piece 'A Tragi-Comedy'. Its serious tone, love and honour
dilemmas, and occasional couplet passages may seem to take

---

[1] Evelyn, *Diary* for 8 January 1663. Gerard Langbaine, *An Account of the English
Dramatick Poets*, 2 vols., Introduction by John Loftis (1691; rpt. Los Angeles, 1971),
II. 505.

[2] Introduction to the van Thal edition, p. xxx. See also John Loftis, *The Spanish
Plays of Neoclassical England* (New Haven, Conn., 1973), pp. 71–9.

the play a long way toward heroic drama. However, the entirely domestic setting and concerns, the amusing servants, the lack of rant, and the romantic-comedy structure with double wedding in prospect at the end greatly limit the resemblance to heroic plays to come. The top plot in Etherege's *The Comical Revenge* a year later is a useful comparison: that too involves love and honour problems, brings protagonists into serious danger, and all of it takes place in couplets. In truth, Spanish romance, of which *The Adventures* is the greatest embodiment, influences both comic and serious drama, but the greater relevance is to comedy, and such later Spanish romances as *The Carnival*, *Flora's Vagaries*, and *Tarugo's Wiles* are undeniably comedies.

The plot Tuke borrowed, despite its reputation for formidable complexity, is a fine one. Its basic pattern is an ordinary comedy scheme: two men love two girls, and the couples arrive at the point of marriage despite ferocious opposition by one girl's brother (who stands *in loco parentis*) and assorted complications. Five of the six main characters are announcedly exemplary—Porcia and Octavio, Camilla and Antonio, and Camilla's brother Carlos. Porcia's brother–guardian Henrique, the blocking character, is described in the *dramatis personae* as 'Cholerick, Jealous, Revengeful', but nonetheless turns out to be essentially honourable. His fierce enmity to Octavio is well motivated: Henrique mistakenly believes Octavio to be a favoured rival for Camilla, and Octavio has accidentally killed Henrique's friend Pedro in a night-time scuffle. Thus for once opposition to marriage in a comedy has a real and serious cause, a pleasant change from the usual parental cantankerousness.

The action moves excitingly fast. A great deal turns on darkness, disguise, and confusion of identity. Such things are the stuff of comedy, despite the exalted seriousness and moral rectitude of the lead characters. Contretemps in a garden (54–5), the girl's flight with her suitor, and the mistake which re-deposits her in her brother's house, are routine comedy turns. The serious debate on honour and justice (61–3) is not. Nor in an English setting (here the scene is Seville) would we expect to find such elaborate exaltation of personal honour. The climax in the fifth act involves a particularly famous set of

honour-motivated reversals by Antonio. He has sworn as a
friend to protect Octavio, but he believes Octavio to have
tried to steal his fiancée. (Antonio was engaged to Porcia
without having seen her, and now believes Camilla to be
Porcia.) So Antonio is awkwardly situated. His prime desire
in life is to kill Octavio, but he cannot stand idly by and watch
Henrique do so.

> . . . it must ne'r be said,
> That Passion could deturn *Antonio*
> From the strict Rules of Honour; Sir, I tell you
> Nothing can make me violate my first
> Engagement. (121–2)

So Antonio rescues Octavio from Henrique, and having got
him alone announces his intention

> To kill thee now my self; having perform'd
> What my Engagement did exact from me
> In your defence 'gainst others; my Love now
> Requires its Dues, as Honour has had his. (123)

As the two of them are fighting, Henrique breaks in the door, but
as he 'makes at *Octavio*', '*Antonio* turns to *Octavio's* side', saying:

> Nay, then my Honour you invade anew,
> And by assaulting him, revive in me
> My Pre-engagements to protect and serve him
> Against all others. (125)

Henrique inquires testily 'Were you not doing, all you could,
to kill him?' only to receive the reply:

> *Henrique*, 'tis true, but finding in my Breast
> An equal strife 'twixt Honour and Revenge,
> I do in just compliance with them both
> Preserve him from your Sword, to fall by mine.

Carlos, struck with admiration, then exclaims 'Brave Man,
how nicely he does Honour weigh!' This honour-mongering is
much exaggerated, even ridiculous, but it does have a certain
lunatic nobility. The code is not merely Almanzoresque: the
importance of the gentleman's duelling code is seriously
maintained everywhere in Carolean comedy. Interestingly,
Molière, at just about this time, makes utterly serious use of
the same device in order to illustrate a character's nobility
(*Don Juan*, Act III).

In strong contrast to such heroics, and to the formidably serious, moral, and exemplary sets of lovers, are the comical servants. Octavio's Diego in particular becomes a byword (turning up in Dryden's *Of Dramatick Poesie*, for instance). His banter with Porcia's maid Flora leads finally to a third marriage—arranged with deliberately ostentatious literary contrivance. With serious affairs happily wound up, Flora notes that "twould make a fine Plot for a Play', Diego rejoins, 'Faith, *Flora*, I should have the worst of that;/For by the Laws of *Comedy*, 'twould be/My Lot to marry you'. Whereupon Octavio puts in 'Well thought on', and that is that.

Right through the play Diego draws laughs, both for his cowardice and for his quips. Lawyers, he notes, 'sell their Breath: Much dearer than you Souldiers do your Blood' (37). Having been roundly berated for cowardice and told that only his base blood has saved his life, Diego says with relief, 'Why then a thousand Thanks to my Base Blood/For saving my Good Flesh' (75). Told 'Be not afraid', he snaps 'You had as good command me not to breathe' (53). When Octavio is frantic to get over a wall and into a fight, he exclaims 'this Tree may help me/To climb o'r; if not, I'll flie t'him'. Diego comments: 'You may do so; your sprightly Love has Wings,/And's ever Fledge; 'tis molting time with mine; . . . Here I will sit, and out of danger's reach/Expect the Issue' (55). Caught by his master's enemies, Diego groans 'Whoever has but the least grain of Wit,/Would never serve a *Lover Militant*' (88). By no means are the lovers' heroics immune from satirical commentary. When Octavio rapturously receives a letter from Porcia, Diego explains:

> This is some Missive from the *Heroine*.
> If it ends not in Fighting I'l be hang'd;
> It is the Method of their dear *Romances*,
> And Persons of their Ranck make love by Book.
> Curse on th' Inventor of the damn'd devise
> Of Painting words, and speaking to our Eyes!
> Had I a hundred Daughters, by this Light,
> Not one of 'em should ever Read or Write. (49)

This sentiment would have pleased the father in Colman's *Polly Honeycombe* just a century later.

By no means, though, does such commentary significantly
undercut the heroic–exemplary side of the play. Tuke is not
trying to debunk love and honour. Rather, like Etherege, he
can see two sides to a matter and appreciate both. A little
ironic scepticism by no means spoils our pleasure in high-
blown flummery. Tuke is no fuddled Quixote, believing im-
plicitly (and expecting us to) in pseudo-heroic fantasy. With
him we enjoy it and admire it, but Diego's observations help
maintain our sense of perspective. The extent to which Diego is
allowed to comment on the main characters is worth emphasizing, since he is normally considered merely a device for trivial
comic relief.

The play really has only one plot line, into which are
worked the affairs of both couples and the servants. This
makes for difficulties in tidy summarization, since each
character is entangled with all the others. Nonetheless the
story is perfectly easy to follow, and works up an eminently
satisfying tension. The oppositions and complications rise
naturally out of circumstances and temperament; hence we
never feel that the plot revolves on artificially contrived
difficulties. The retention of Calderón's focus on the last few
hours of a lengthy story helps give a sense of stepping into a
real action *in medias res*, though the contrived and stilted way
the girls provide background for each other (and us) during
Act I is to be regretted. The characterizations are remarkably
good, given the limitations of exemplary behaviour. Plainly
Tuke was proud of his job here. In the 1671 preface to the
revised edition he says that 'though it be unusual, I have in a
distinct *Column*, prefix'd the several *Characters* of the most
eminent *Persons* in the *Play*; that being acquainted with them
at his first setting out, he [the reader] may the better judge
how they are carried on in the whole *Composition*.' Antonio has
a markedly more heroic cast than Octavio, though both are
Valiant Cavaliers. Camilla is clearly more outgoing than
Porcia, though both are severely virtuous. Carlos's good
nature and good sense are well contrasted at several points
to Henrique's touchy, suspicious impetuosity.

Beyond a doubt, Tuke was quite self-conscious about the
sort of play he had produced. 'The *English* Stage ne'r had so
New a Play' he boasts in the first prologue (1663 edition),

commenting on the Spanish source and his adherence to the unities. By 1671 he had become aware of his unusual moral rectitude. 'Our Late Poets', he complains, make 'Bawdery' their chief concern, 'As if they writ onely to th' Vizard-Masks'. His pride in his '*Innocent Piece*' is evident, though he archly mocks himself as one who 'in this brave Licentious Age' dares 'bring his musty *Morals* on the Stage!' Why, he exclaims, 'such another modest *Play* would blast/Our new *Stage*', for ' 'Tis whisper'd i' the Pit,/This may be Common Sense, but 'tis not Wit.' Tuke labours to 'bring dull Vertue into Reputation'— and does so in rousing fashion. The fast pace, the sword-play, and the humour make palatable but do not disguise the overtly didactic intentions and exemplary method of the playwright. Plays, he tells us, are '*Moral Pictures*' whose 'chiefest Perfections consist in the Force and Congruity of *Passions* and *Humors*, which are the Features and Complexion of our Minds'.[1] Sir Richard Steele would no doubt have deplored the sword-play and the exaltation of the heroic code. But for purity, psychological acuity, humour, exemplary method, and sustained tension he has more than a match in Sir Samuel Tuke.

The Squire of Alsatia: Reform Comedy

This late play of Shadwell's was an extraordinary success. It ran for thirteen nights uninterrupted when premièred in 1688, and was long popular, holding the stage for some eighty years. Downes informs us that 'The Poet receiv'd for his third Day in the House in *Drury-Lane* at single Prizes [i.e. ordinary prices, not raised as on some special occasions] 130*l*. which was the greatest Receipt they ever had at that House at single Prizes.'[2] Plainly the audience liked the work: our job now is to see wherein lay its appeal.[3]

The basis of the play—a contrast of town and country educations—is taken from Terence's *Adelphi* (*The Brothers*). This fact was noted by Langbaine, who correctly dismisses the

---

[1] Quotations are from the 1671 preface and epilogue.

[2] *Roscius Anglicanus*, p. 41.

[3] Ronald Berman ('The Values of Shadwell's *Squire of Alsatia*', *ELH*, xxxix (1972), 375–86) finds the play a celebration of 'Whig' and a sharp debunking of 'Tory' ideology. While I agree with this account of Shadwell's outlook, I doubt whether the play was taken so politically: it scored its initial triumph in May 1688, with James II and his court forming part of the audience.

idea of interposition from the French (i.e. Molière's *L'École des maris*), and adds 'no Comedy has found better success than this, since the Restauration of the Theatre.'[1] Shadwell fills out Terence's spare, simple story immensely. The result really consists of a juxtaposition of three trains of interest. (1) A comparison of the two father-figures and their systems of education. (2) The country-bred elder brother, a gull fallen into the hands of sharps, bullies, and cheats. (3) The town-bred younger brother, whose career we follow in two separate plot lines. We see him both in his relations with two mistresses (one current, one ex) and in the process of contracting a wealthy marriage—for which he makes an exemplary moral reform. As an adjunct to this last plot line, we follow briefly the tribulations of his wife-to-be and her cousin.

The foolishly confident gull in the midst of London low life had long been a favourite subject for comedy. Even more common is the daughter or ward (or often, as here, both) designed for an unwelcome marriage by an overbearing father or guardian. The girl's outwitting him in order to marry the dashing young man-about-town—who promises to abandon his tom-cat ways—was one of the commonest bases for a comedy. (We will see it looming large in *The Busie Body*.) The gallant's relations with past mistresses, and perhaps with a new one, are again standard fare, as in *The Man of Mode*. James Howard's *All Mistaken* presents half a dozen ex-mistresses, all complete with bastards. Shadwell's hero has a mere one.

What is decidedly unusual in Shadwell's play is the markedly didactic central design and the playwright's pointed insistence on it throughout the play. Shadwell's didacticism goes well beyond the commonplace pledge of constancy given by the gallant. David S. Berkeley lists about a dozen actual 'rakes' who undergo such a conversion in plays prior to this one,[2] and he ignores such characters as Wildblood and Bellamy in *An Evening's Love*, whom Dryden felt compelled to defend as 'suppos'd' to be fully reclaimed from vice when they win their ladies. Despite the presence of many familiar elements in Shadwell's play, we may find reason to be uncomfortable about

---

[1] Langbaine, II. 450.

[2] 'The Penitent Rake in Restoration Comedy', *Modern Philology*, xlix (1952), 223–33. The dates run from 1664 to 1687.

it. John Harrington Smith considers the work a key step in a transition into pure and 'exemplary' comedy, and its hero, he says, 'becomes [an 'example'] at play's end by virtue of his reclamation from rakish courses'.[1] Is Belfond jun. indeed an example of what a gentleman should be? Shadwell certainly says so. But Allardyce Nicoll, not without reason, finds the play 'hopelessly and permeatingly vulgar, brutal and immoral', adding 'the strangeness of it all is that Shadwell imagined he had before him a moral purpose.' For Nicoll, the hero remains at the end 'as heartless, as cruel and as cynical as he was before'.[2] Plainly Nicoll imports some a-historical prejudices, but the play does present a curious mixture of elements.

Few of these comedies are much illuminated by comparison with their sources, but this is one instance where the comparison is helpful in defining the nature of the play's impact and seeing the dramatic possibilities of the basic situation. Terence shows that both educations have bad effects, but he presents a steady contrast between the farcical cock-sureness and arrogance of the country father and the liberal, kindly tolerance of the town father. The audience naturally supports the latter, whose policy seems abundantly borne out by results in the course of the play. But just as we are preparing to applaud the tidy, if predictable ending, Terence completely undercuts our commitment, showing that what we have taken as wise benevolence is really quite as much weakness, indulgence, and extravagance. The outcome is a compromise on both sides, but the severe country principles are largely sustained. With consummate skill Terence achieves a reversal of our initial judgements, and sends us away chastened by the realization that our reactions have been too thoughtless and facile.

The Squire offers a straightforward contrast between the cloddish country family and the refined town one. Sir William Belfond is rigid, morose, covetous, clownish, and obstinate ('Dramatis Personae'); he is a farcical figure, wildly changeable and brutally insensible to the individuality of his son or his possible preferences in a wife. 'What's matter whether he like her, or no? Is it not enough for him, that I do? Is a Son, a Boy, a Jackanapes, to have a will of his own?' (IV. 253). In complete

---

[1] 'Shadwell, the Ladies, and the Change in Comedy'.
[2] Nicoll, I. 198, 200.

contrast to his brother, Sir Edward is kind, tolerant, understanding, 'well read in good Books' and 'possessed with all
Gentlemanlike qualities'. Similarly, Belfond sen. is rustic,
swinish, lewd, vicious, and obstinate, while his brother is
'instructed in all the Liberal Sciences, and in all Gentlemanlike
Education', 'a man of Honour and of excellent disposition',
though 'Somewhat given to Women'.

In the first act the audience is shown immediately that Sir
William is grossly deceived in thinking Belfond sen. virtuous;
we wonder then whether Sir Edward is just as deceived in
Belfond jun. The central conflict of the play is clearly established when the two 'fathers' debate the efficacy of their
educational systems (219–20). Sir Edward insists that Belfond
jun. 'conceals nothing from me', holding that 'Rigour makes
nothing but Hypocrites', and the act concludes as he suggests
that they go to see Belfond jun. 'I'll lay my life you'll find
him perusing some good Author; he ever spends his whole
morning in study.' Sir William replies: 'no doubt but we shall
find him perusing of some Whore or other, instead of a Book.'

Act II opens with Belfond jun. just getting out of bed with
Lucia and trying to convince her that she was quite right to
yield to his seduction (222–3). He has to hide her in a closet
when his singing-master comes. A little later we learn from
his friend Truman that Belfond jun. is trying to woo a lady;
Truman observes the signs of amorous activity, and his sarcastic
comment ('You are a sincere honest Lover indeed') is more
telling than Belfond jun.'s excuse: 'we may talk of mighty
matters; of our Honesty and Morality; but a young Fellow
carries that about him that will make him a Knave now and
then in spite of his Teeth. . . . Oh if I can but prevail upon my
little pretty Churchwoman, I am resolv'd to conform to her for
ever' (226). Belfond jun.'s praise of Truman's setting of
Horace's 'The Pure Soul' (Ode 22) is presumably meant to
show that at heart he is a serious and moral young man, but
under the circumstances it is hard to avoid being distracted by
the apparently unconscious irony of his sententiousness (225).

Upon the appearance of his uncle and father, Belfond jun.
is forced to hide a second mistress (Mrs. Termagant) in the
closet, and when the two women fight he is ingloriously
exposed, although he tries to convince his father that Lucia

'was never here before; she brought me Linnen from the *Exchange*' (230). Though this may be literally true, it is not the whole truth, and it is said with intent to deceive; one can hardly see how any intelligent man could say, as Sir Edward does shortly thereafter, that he 'never took him in a Lye since he could speak' (240).

At this point the audience might suppose, with considerable justice, that Shadwell was offering it a biting satire on the educational pretensions of *both* father-figures. But not so. Shadwell follows the exposure scene with a debate on education in which Sir Edward extols the virtues of a classical education, music, study of the law, the grand tour, and military service (231–2). Sir William pooh-poohs it all, saying that his son 'Knows his seasons of Plowing, Sowing, Harrowing, laying fallow: Understands all sorts of Manure. . . .' By the standards of late seventeenth-century England it seems inconceivable that Shadwell meant his objections to be anything but ridiculous.

As the play progresses, Shadwell continues to extol the virtues of Belfond jun., and, by comparison with his block-headed brother he is indeed a paragon. At the end of the play he rescues his father and brother from the Alsatian cheats and receives the plaudits of all. Sir William admits his disappointment in his educational system, concluding 'Brother, I look upon you as a true Friend, that would not insult upon my Folly and Presumption, and confess you are nearer to the right than I' (271). Shadwell ends the play unequivocally enough:

Sir Edward: Come Brother, now who has been in the right, you or I?
Sir William: You have: Prithee do not triumph.
Belfond Junior: Farewell for ever all the Vices of the Age.
    There is no peace but in a Virtuous Life,
    Nor lasting Joy but in a tender Wife.
Sir Edward: You, that would breed your Children well, by Kindness
 and Liberality endear 'em to you: And teach 'em by Example.
    Severity spoils ten, for one it mends:
    If you'd not have your Sons desire your ends,
    By Gentleness and Bounty make those Sons your
      Friends.

What are we to make of this? Between the town and country products there is, indeed, no serious comparison. But Shadwell

claims an ideality for Sir Edward's liberal town education
which seems excessive in view of Belfond jun.'s little weaknesses.
He coolly and calculatingly seduces a 'nice' girl of respectable
middle-class background and then casts her off; the reparation
which his gentlemanly uncle makes is to pay her handsomely
(£1,500). Belfond jun. tells her 'It is with some Convulsions I
am torn from you; but I must Marry I cannot help it' (275).
This is completely untrue: he is doing precisely as he pleases.
And, excusing it as a white lie, he swears to Lucia's innocence,
which makes slightly peculiar his uncle's decision to pay her
anyway (275–6). Belfond jun.'s treatment of Mrs. Termagant
is mitigated for the audience by her violence and his sweet
reasonableness in continuing to support an ex-mistress (by
whom he has a 3-year-old bastard). It still seems unlikely,
though, that he is as blameless as he swears in order to convince
the wealthy Isabella to marry him (269–70). But Mrs. Termagant too is paid off, and Belfond jun. is left with all the odour
of sanctity that money can buy. Even supposing that women
who yield when they should not are, by the code of the time,
not deserving of our concern, this does not wholly excuse
Belfond jun.'s womanizing, or make his lies more acceptable.
Even in Act IV he is still busy sweet-talking Lucia, making her
half-promises which he has no intention of keeping; he salves
such conscience as he possesses by telling himself that he 'will
better her condition' (251–2).

We are left to assume with J. H. Smith that the love of a
good woman purifies the once errant Belfond jun.[1]

Isabella: How can I be secure you will not fall to your old courses
agen?

Belfond Junior: I have been so sincere in my Confessions, you may
trust me; but I call Heav'n to witness, I will hereafter be entirely
yours. I look on Marriage as the most solemn Vow a Man can
make; and 'tis by consequence, the basest Perjury to break
it. (279)

Thus we are to suppose that a humane and liberal upbringing
makes Belfond jun. receptive to the influence of virtue.

Roman comedy is scarcely known for its warmth and
humanity, but by comparison *The Brothers* seems a remarkably

[1] A similar reading is given by Michael W. Alssid, *Thomas Shadwell* (New York,
1967), pp. 137–46.

humane play. Consider the treatment of the seduced girl.
Aeschinus marries the penniless Pamphila, and his father and
uncle are deeply ashamed of his having seduced her. Belfond
jun. is not so much as reproached for having debauched the
equally respectable Lucia; his uncle simply pays off her family.
While this is undoubtedly better than turning her onto the
streets, it is not an action which bespeaks much of the human
warmth which Terence finds a redeeming feature in Aeschinus.
In *The Squire*, even for the humane Sir Edward, wealth is the
principal factor in marital eligibility, and Lucia's attorney
father does not have enough of it.

In terms of technical skill, *The Brothers* is the better play.
Though more complex, less black and white, it is never
ambiguous: Terence induces a false commitment to one point
of view, reaffirms it, and then demolishes it, demanding a
complete reversal and reorientation on the part of the audience.
In *The Squire* Shadwell fails to provide any compromise or
alternative for the town education he begins by praising. His
viewpoint remains constant: we do wonder for a while whether
Belfond jun. too is being satirized, but by comparison to his
brother he is so relatively admirable that the possibility must
be dismissed. In essence Shadwell takes the bulk of Terence's
play at face value, and glorifies the town education as, in fact,
actually ideal. He is then forced to make his conclusion conform to his thesis, and so announces a reformation in Belfond
jun. which has little basis in what we have seen of his character
and actions. He is certainly not a Tom Jones, educated by
experience; nor is he really a *penitent* rake, since he callously
abandons Lucia and is rewarded with a wealthy wife, to whom
he *says* he will be faithful. Perfunctory reform is nothing new.
Do we really believe that Etherege's Dorimant will never
chase another skirt? What is different and surprising in
Shadwell's play is the fervour of his serious claims for the town
education. Belfond jun. is shown up just enough for him to fail
to make a fully convincing exemplary figure: Shadwell's
slightly haphazard satire makes for awkward contradictions of
of his high educational ideal. Nicoll's extreme disgust with this
play is basically a reaction against the loud claim that Belfond
jun. is the model of a fine gentleman.

The Squire actually exhibits a peculiar transitional combination of techniques and characters, and rests uneasily between the courtiers' morality of its story and the exemplary–didactic method of Steele. Actual seductions during the course of a play were extremely common in the 1670s, but became rare during the nineties. Had Shadwell simply left out the educational debate and the fifth-act moralizing, the tone of the play would seem largely appropriate to the later seventies. In a sense, Shadwell is anticipating the exemplary method of Steele, but he applies it to incongruous material. One cannot conceive a Steele hero seducing and abandoning a virtuous girl. As Act II makes clear, the materials of the play have the potentialities for a biting satire on *both* systems of education, but Shadwell largely foregoes his opportunities. His placid acceptance of Belfond jun.'s moral code in a play so markedly didactic now seems peculiar, but I can find no evidence to show that the original audience was disturbed. I find it odder, given the combination of didactic claims and seduction, that no protest seems to have been made about performances a few years later.

Whatever objections may be raised against the play's imperfect didacticism, one must grant its very great theatrical effectiveness. The brilliantly vivid scenes of London low life and the use of its cant language take the play out of the realm of the literary formulas it relies on.[1] The boisterous tavern scenes in Alsatia and the sword-play make for rollicking vigour, and Shadwell contrives some highly effective situations—especially the unmasking of Belfond jun. in Act II, an event not in the interests of didactic clarity. The unusually large cast makes for tremendous variety and bustle; the misplaced confidence of the country father, and his son's folly are beautifully strung out. Rapid pace, high spirits, and plenty of variety all contribute to a thoroughly entertaining play.

Our final reactions are for the most part clearly dictated. For the Alsatia cheats and Mrs. Termagant we are to feel only amusement and contempt. Sir William and Belfond sen. come off little better, but are allowed apologies and good resolutions for the future at the end. Lucia and her father have our condescending good will, but are beneath serious regard.

---

[1] Shadwell even includes a glossary—e.g. '*Coale, Ready, Rhino, Darby*. Ready money.' '*Hog*. A Shilling.' '*To lugg out*. To draw a Sword.' '*Smoaky*. Jealous.' (201).

The heiresses are the usual stock types: likeable and strictly virtuous. Finally Sir Edward, Belfond jun., and his friend Truman stand not only as fine gentlemen, but as exemplary models of decency and probity.

Shadwell makes full use of conventional plot lines and characters. Thus we find the bully (Hackum), the cheat (Cheatly), the wealthy, knavish puritan pretender to piety (Scrapeall), the country servant (Lolpoop), the French valet (La Mar), the 'precise Governess' (Ruth), the cast mistress (Mrs. Termagant), and assorted whores. With these characters present, no heavy tone of piety dampens the play, despite the moralizing. Racy colloquial prose helps, but the seduction notwithstanding suggestive wit is not employed. Shadwell says in the prologue that 'Baudy the nicest Ladies need not fear,/The quickest fancy shall extract none here'—and he is correct. In this respect, the play is markedly pure. With the lack of bawdy, the didactic central design, and five professedly exemplary lead characters, *The Squire of Alsatia* is very obviously an attempt to alter the type and tone of the comedies whose elements it freely utilizes.

The Man of Mode: Wit Comedy

Modern critics have almost all agreed that Etherege's last play is one of the greatest late seventeenth-century comedies, but no consensus at all has been reached on what kind of play it really is. How are we to respond to it? The quarrel goes back at least as far as Dennis and Steele. To Steele's charge that the play 'is a perfect contradiction to good manners, good sense, and common honesty' Dennis replies that in presenting 'a young Courtier, haughty, vain, and prone to Anger, amorous, false, and inconstant', Etherege had never imagined that anyone would take this 'Hero' (Steele's term) as a 'Pattern for Imitation'.[1] Twentieth-century critics have generally followed this line of debate either by elaborating Dennis's contention that the work is a hard-hitting satire, or by trying to refute Steele by denying that morals have a significant part in the play.[2] The basic issue is simple: is Dorimant meant to be

---

[1] *Spectator*, 65 and Dennis, *Critical Works*, II. 241–50. On this quarrel, see Chapter 2, Section II, above.

[2] Charles O. McDonald's well-known essay is the best example of the satiric view. Bonamy Dobrée's is the best-known anti-moralistic reading. He argues that

admired? This is a nasty question; little wonder that Holland and Underwood squirm and equivocate. But since *The Man of Mode* is often taken as a key illustrative case, some clear answers about how we should respond to it seem especially desirable.

An obvious characteristic of *The Man of Mode* is its slight action and emphasis on display of character. Within the almost static plot we find four centres of interest: (1) Fopling, who has no necessary connection with any other part of the play. (2) Dorimant's affairs with Loveit and Bellinda. (3) The courtship of Dorimant and Harriet. (4) The marriage of Young Bellair and Emilia. For these last two, Lady Woodvil, Old Bellair, and Lady Townley provide some slight interconnections, but the parental opposition is utterly *pro forma*: Old Bellair gives in to his son's marriage and accepts his own disappointment with hardly a murmur, while Harriet's mother is so charmed by Dorimant (posing as 'Mr. Courtage') that she drops her objections to him. Seldom has the course of true love run so smooth. Indeed, the story is incredibly thin, and its pieces are only loosely patched together. Not only is Fopling irrelevant to the action, but the Young Bellair–Emilia plot has little real connection to the two plots involving Dorimant, which in turn are almost independent of each other. Obviously, to read the results in terms of Northrop Frye's archetypal 'movement from adversity to prosperity' will radically distort the play: where does Fopling fit? Is there really any change? Should we have sympathy for Dorimant, and rejoice in his apparently successful courtship?

Plainly our reading of the play rests on the way we respond to the various characters, particularly Dorimant. We see him casting off and tormenting Mrs. Loveit, seducing Bellinda, and then falling for and courting Harriet. According to Underwood, he suffers a conflict between 'passion' and libertine, Machiavellian 'reason': the result (in Holland's terms) is his removal from the affairs of the 'low plot' to the 'heavenly' realm of true feeling and love. In short, says Holland, 'the play is nothing more nor less than the old sentimental story of the rake reformed, indeed redeemed, by the love of a good woman.' But having put himself well out on a limb,

---

Etherege's plays 'are pure works of art directed to no end but themselves', 'not animated by any moral stimulus'. *Restoration Comedy*, p. 60.

Holland hastens to qualify his position: 'At least that *would* be the basic form of the action, were it not so variously under-cut by irony.' Here is the rub: in the final scene Dorimant agrees to go to the country to court Harriet, but simultaneously he is trying to set up another assignation with Bellinda ('we must meet agen') and assuring Loveit that he is courting Harriet only 'to repair the ruines of my estate that needs it'. Perhaps then, as Underwood speculates, his courtship of Harriet is simply one more Machiavellian scheme. The following exchange can be quoted in support of such a view:

Young Bellair: You had best not think of Mrs. *Harriet* too much, without Church security, there's no taking up there.
Dorimant: I may fall into the Snare too. But—
    The wise will find a difference in our Fate,
    You wed a Woman, I a good Estate. (II. 263)

Actually, this cynicism may be partly self-justification, for his friends are quite ready to tease him, as a passage just before this one shows:

Dorimant: What's your business?
Medley: Ma-tri-mony, an't like you.
Dorimant: It does not, Sir.
Young Bellair: It may in time, *Dorimant*; what think you of Mrs. *Harriet*?

Earlier we have seen him struggle, at first against falling for Harriet, later against letting her realize that he has done so: 'she has left a pleasing Image of her self behind that wanders in my Soul—it must not settle there' (237); 'I love her, and dare not let her know it, I fear sh'as an ascendant o're me and may revenge the wrongs I have done her sex. . . . I have took the infection from her, and feel the disease now spreading in me' (249). In short, Dorimant's passion seems genuine, how-ever economically advantageous.

Although a great deal is said by critics about the 'brutality' of Dorimant's treatment of his mistresses, they generally agree that by seventeenth-century standards the women deserve no sympathy. Loveit's transports of rage show a contemptible lack of self-control, while Bellinda's failure to learn from her friend's experience ('Had you seen him use Mrs. *Loveit* as I have done, you wou'd never endure him more', she says—226) makes her fall inexcusable. Why should we pity her when she has deliberately and knowingly let herself in for it? Harriet, by contrast, is ruthlessly self-controlled: 'I feel as great a change within; but he shall never know it' (235), she says—and unlike Dorimant, she is able to keep her word. Harriet's character is a matter of some confusion. Clifford Leech calls her 'a creature of delight', which may be true, but she is no romantic heroine in the fashion of Shakespeare's Rosalind. Summers is as close to the truth when he calls her 'a perfectly callous little baggage with a vile tongue'. She is beautiful, witty, and self-willed, capable of bending her mother to her wishes (V. ii), an expert at social games—note the spectacular dissimulation scene with Young Bellair (III. i)—and capable of perfectly gratuitous insults to Mrs. Loveit: 'Mr. *Dorimant* has been your God Almighty long enough, 'tis time to think of another', followed by the sneering advice that she take to a nunnery (286). Dorimant is scarcely redeemed by the love of a good woman; rather, the great lady-killer here meets his match in a woman cold and tough enough to get him where she wants him. To make Harriet out as a spotless romantic heroine is either to insist on a staggeringly improbable reformation in Dorimant, or to see her caught in a degrading and potentially disastrous association. Neither seems to be the case.

Plainly our reading turns on our response to the characters, but problems of historical perspective intrude: presumably the Carolean audience applied its own standards, and these may differ from ours. The crux of the matter is this: did the original audience view the play as a representation of real life, or as a comic distortion of it, or as Cloud-cuckoo-land? Did they regard it in a serious moral light? Consider the possibilities. There are two conceivable grounds for the claim that the play has no moral or social significance: either a dirty-minded court audience loved every bit of the smut (Macaulay's assumption), or the audience made no connection whatever between art and life (Dobrée's view). The first supposition is at odds with theatre history. Courtiers are most prominent in the 1660s, but many of the plays then most popular (like Tuke's) were quite moral. Even Etherege's second play, *She wou'd if she cou'd* (1668), though full of references to sex, very decorously prevents any of them from coming to anything. The rise of sex comedy is a phenomenon of the 1670s: the first real comedy of sex and cuckoldry is probably Betterton's *The Amorous Widow* (*c.* 1670), which was produced, we should recall, at a time when Pepys was complaining about the growing number of cits in the audience. During the 1670s increasingly blatant indecency is used for shock value, culminating in plays like Dryden's *Mr. Limberham* (1678). Abundant contemporary references tell us that the audience—or a good part of it—was shocked by these plays. Like film makers today, playwrights were seeing just how far they could go, and I suspect that the contemporary audience enjoyed the titillation without actually approving of what it saw. The playwrights' protestations about satire are a little too loud: they claim to be edifying by negative example, which smacks of justification for showing what the audience enjoyed but did not really approve of: 'satire' was the Carolean equivalent of 'redeeming social importance'. Wycherley suggests in *The Plain-Dealer* (Act II) that audience objections to the 'china' scene in *The Country-Wife* were hypocritical, but obviously there *were* objections. Despite the fad for sex comedy in the mid-seventies we cannot suppose that the audience approved wholeheartedly of what it saw.

The alternative, that no connection was seen between the world of the play and reality, is harder to dismiss outright. Despite prologue rhetoric, the plays are clearly not realistic. Conversely, the London setting of a majority of the comedies, and the extensive contemporary references, make it difficult to ignore all of the implicit commentary on the times. In the case of *The Man of Mode* we may get some sense of the contemporary response by reflecting on play-goers' speculation about who was who. Dennis remarks of Dorimant 'that it was unanimously agreed, that he had in him several of the Qualities of *Wilmot* Earl of *Rochester*', and further that 'they who were acquainted with the late Sir *Fleetwood Shepherd*, know very well, that not a little of that Gentleman's Character is to be found in Medley.' Sir Fopling, Dryden's disclaimer in the epilogue notwithstanding, has often been identified with Beau Hewitt. None of these identifications is exact, and the last one appears wrong; Dennis himself is cautious about the extent of the portraiture. But 'personation' had been a common and controversial tactic in the preceding decade,[1] and the audience might well look for reference to high society in a play by a court wit. I greatly doubt whether the characters in the play were written as recognizable portraits. But the work could well have been viewed, rightly or wrongly, as an *à clef* composition, a picture of high and scandalous society.[2] Similarly today books and magazines about film stars are read by outsiders as a revelation of what 'really goes on' in a special and glamorous world. Sometimes we may clearly recognize a given actress or playboy, more often we may merely speculate. Probably a majority of the readers of such stuff do not 'approve' of what goes on, but therein lies half the fun. Etherege and his friends represent only a small but influential minority in the Carolean audience; for the majority, the world of *The Man of Mode* was far from a reflection of daily life. Even for the select few, I believe John Harold Wilson is accurate in saying that the

idealized portraits are recognizable as the patterns of mannered, aristocratic society. Here is no question of realism; Etherege seized upon and embodied in his play not the real, day by day life of Whitehall, but the life which Whitehall was pleased to imagine it led. Individual items may be factual, but the total picture is a comic illusion.[3]

Does such a view lend credence to the Cloud-cuckoo-land theory or one of its modern variants? I think not. McDonald has assembled impressive evidence that the Carolean audience did bring moral standards to the theatre, and that a dramatist could more or less count on their being applied. Dennis tells

---

[1] For example, in Shadwell's *The Sullen Lovers*, the suppressed Howard–Buckingham *Country Gentleman*, and *The Rehearsal*. Arthur Sherbo has argued persuasively against the identification of Fopling with Beau Hewitt, *Notes and Queries*, cxciv (1949), 296–303.

[2] Speculation was wild and inaccurate. See Brett-Smith, I. xxiv–xxv. Peter Killigrew wrote to his sister three days after the *première* that 'generall opinion will have Sr Fopling to be Mr. Villers, Ld Grandisons eldest son. Mr. Batterton under the name of Dorimant means the Duke of Monmouth & his intrigue with Moll Kirke, Mrs. Needham, & Lady Harriott Wentworth.' Unpublished letter quoted in Joseph Spence, *Anecdotes*, ed. James M. Osborn, 2 vols. (Oxford, 1966), II. 638 (Appendix to no. 678).

[3] *The Court Wits*, p. 164. This is a valuable corrective to H. F. B. Brett-Smith's influential Introduction to his edition of Etherege (1927), in which he maintained, misleadingly, that Etherege was 'concerned to give an exact picture of fashionable life', and to show 'nature as nature was to be seen in the London of 1676' (I. lxx, lxxxiii).

us, at any rate, that theatre-goers in the time of Charles II knew enough not to take the characters in comedy as 'Patterns for Imitation'. Probably there was occasional confusion, especially when the social level of the characters rose beyond a certain point. Ben Jonson does not satirize high society, and the likes of Subtle, Face, and Dol Common are short on glamour. But when Dryden and others try to raise the social tone of comedy, the results blur Aristotle's neat distinction between comedy and tragedy, for the lead characters become witty, refined, and glamorous, even if morally imperfect. Hence it is no surprise to find Dryden complaining that critics are mistakenly associating authors with their characters: 'The Wits they describe, are the Fops we banish: for Blasphemy and Atheism, if they were neither Sin nor Ill Manners, are Subjects so very common, and worn so Thredbare, that people who have sence avoid them, for fear of being suspected to have none' (Dedication of *The Assignation*, 1673). All in all, given the semblances of realism in the comedies, and the obvious sensitivity of the authors to complaints about immorality and bawdiness, I think that the Cloud-cuckoo-land theory is hard to take seriously. At least part of the audience *must* have taken a moral view.

A number of recent critics, particularly Underwood, have complained about *The Man of Mode*'s lack of 'an adequate set of values' by which to judge the world of the play. Similarly Holland throws up his hands: 'it is difficult to say what, if anything, Etherege wants us to take seriously.' From this point of view, Etherege is suffering from a sort of Hobbesian *Weltschmerz* in which nothing counts but a 'meaningless social game'. These critics make a plausible case, but they base it on negative evidence, the absence of positive moral standards. And if this absence is simply a convention resting on the supposition that the audience would supply a reasonable ethical norm, then their case collapses. Aimlessness is one extreme; serious purpose another. McDonald's argument that this play (in particular) is a satire is essentially an extrapolation from Dennis's assertion (in 1722) that in 1676 everyone knew that such characters were not to be taken as examples. Dennis may well be correct, but McDonald's extension seems questionable.

Consider the possibilities of his reading. Supposing the play to be a serious social satire, designed to render its characters ridiculous or contemptible, we might inquire just what the moral of this edifying fable is supposed to be. Presumably we are to learn (1) that you should not dress like a French fop and parade like a peacock; (2) that a young woman should not sleep with a man to whom she is not married; and (3) that if you debauch enough young ladies, you will ultimately be rewarded with one who is wittier, prettier, and, above all, wealthier.

As a serious satirist, Etherege has some shortcomings. Dorimant is too glamorous and too successful to serve as a very effective negative example. Presumably Loveit and Bellinda are properly cautionary figures, but Harriet is too good a schemer to stand comfortably as a spotless redeemer. However, Fopling is the real problem. If we assume that he is seriously ridiculed, we must accept the corollary—that Etherege was so inexpert a satirist as to apply a cannon to a sitting duck. Sir Fopling's French affectations are ridiculous, but he is so extravagant that he is a figure of fun, not the object of serious attack. His good humour and his lack of involvement in matters of importance (cf. Sir Novelty Fashion/Lord Foppington) make him entertaining rather than contemptible or revolting. Set against the insouciant light-heartedness of Etherege's presentation of Sir Fopling is Dorimant's much-commented-on cruelty. His pleasure in deliberately tormenting the luckless Loveit is decidedly unattractive, however contemptible she may be. He glories in his own sadism. Though he has cast Loveit off he determines to revenge her attempt to make him jealous, for as he tells Medley, 'my reputation lyes at stake there' (263). Brutal is the word for his announcement to Loveit that he has come 'To give you joy of your growing infamy' (270). As before, we come back to the basic problem: how should we react? To ignore all questions of ethics and values seems difficult; to find a moral and consistently serious satire seems impossible.

Consider again the basic elements of the play. Fopling occupies a place out of all proportion to his part in the action, and yet, as the popularity of the sub-title (*Sir Fopling Flutter*) suggests, the audience particularly delighted in him. The other

characters make a game of 'showing' him off for their amusement; plainly the audience too should enjoy his good-humoured
foppery. The Young Bellair–Emilia strand is a thin and rather
flavourless version of a common Carolean romantic love story.
The Harcourt–Alithea plot occupies a similar place in *The
Country-Wife*. I would not go so far as to say that in either case
the couple is a 'high moral norm' for the play, but we are glad
enough to see these characters succeed, and we are not much
bothered by their shortcomings. Neither of course do we view
these conventional lovers with the attention, delight, and empathy
we accord some of Shakespeare's romantic couples, especially
his heroines. Within the world of *The Man of Mode* certain
categorizations are easy. (1) We approve of Young Bellair and
Emilia, even if we do not take them seriously. (2) Old Bellair
and Mrs. Woodvil are good-humouredly satirized for their
crotchets and old-fashioned views, but both are basically
good-hearted. Medley and Lady Townley, the confidants,
exist on much the same plane of mild satire and condescending
approval. (3) Mrs. Loveit is brutally derided; we should have
little but contempt for her. Fopling, though not attacked in the
same way, similarly elicits no approval or respect.

Dorimant, Harriet, and Bellinda are more problematical
cases. Wilson says flatly that all three are 'admirable from the
point of view of Restoration society'. I cannot agree. Bellinda
especially cannot properly be grouped with Harriet and
Emilia as a 'jillflirt': she, after all, stupidly succumbs to
Dorimant's blandishments, going into the affair with her eyes
open and the example of Mrs. Loveit to warn her. Once
hooked, she does not thrash about and make herself ridiculous,
as Loveit does, but the two of them share the contemptible
position of cast mistress. Harriet, whose self-control is perfect,
plainly demands much more respect, as does Emilia. Critics
sometimes hold against Emilia Dorimant's comment that he
can have no hope of success with her until she is married
('She's a discreet Maid, and I believe nothing can corrupt her
but a Husband'—202), but this reflects his cynicism more than
her 'easiness'. Brilliant though Harriet is, she is a bit too tough
to be quite the 'creature of delight' Shakespeare's romantic
heroines are. And our response to her must be largely a function
of our response to Dorimant, since she falls for him.

Dorimant is undeniably glamorous. Like Rochester, Dennis tells us, he has wit, spirit, an amorous temper, charm for women, an agreeable manner of chiding servants, and a love of Waller; he is also guilty of falsehood and inconstancy. Both men command from us a combination of fascination and disapproval. In the first half of *The Man of Mode* Dorimant is the archetypal Don Juan. Critics, especially Underwood, have emphasized 'a Hobbesian aggressiveness, competitiveness, and drive for power and "glory"; a Machiavellian dissembling and cunning; a satanic pride, vanity, and malice; ... an egoistic assertion of self through the control of others' (p. 73). All very true—but what happens? The mighty lady-killer meets his match, *succumbs to love*, and is tamed by a woman even tougher and more self-controlled than he. This is extremely funny, and we should not be blinded to that fact by Dorimant's rationalizations. He says he is after money; he continues to intrigue with women; but, as we have seen, he admits that he loves Harriet. And, unlike his mistresses, she sees through him, recognizes his affectations (III. iii), and can cut off his cant with a sardonic retort.

Dorimant: I will renounce all the joys I have in friendship and in
    Wine, sacrifice to you all the interest I have in other Women——
Harriet: Hold—Though I wish you devout, I would not have you
    turn Fanatick. (278–9)

This is no romantic match, and unless (against all evidence) we are to consider Harriet a blinded fool, we must suppose that she knows what she is getting in Dorimant and wants it. So we either pity her folly or class her as one who can out-Dorimant the devil himself. I incline to the latter.

I take Dorimant to be glamorous but reprehensible. The common comparison with Horner is inexact but instructive. To some degree we enjoy both men's power, just as we do with Jonson's rogues. Outside the context of the play we disapprove of both, though Dorimant is harder to look down on than most 'rogue heroes'. But while Horner victimizes no one, Dorimant, were it not for his succumbing to Harriet, would seem a distinctly brutal figure. As it is, our fascinated disapproval is tempered with amusement.

What kind of play is *The Man of Mode*? It mingles a number of elements—straight romantic lovers, a fantastic fop, some elderly humours characters, and a high-life rake who finally meets his match. Little happens: the whole concoction is a piece of cream-puffery, an entertaining display of wit and character spiced with a touch of scandal in high life. Harriet's triumph sharply undercuts any revelling in the powers of a Machiavellian rake, but though the play seems satiric, it is scarcely a serious satire. Most of the characters are to some degree mocked (Dorimant as much as his fellow man of mode, Fopling), but Etherege amuses us with fine raillery, he does not lecture us with a devastating critique in the fashion of Wycherley. Of course Etherege belonged to this world as few Carolean playwrights did: three months after the *première* of this play he and Rochester were involved in a scandalous brawl with the Watch.

Recent critics have been endeavouring to prove that late seventeenth-century comedy is great literature by claiming for it a profundity and philosophical relevance it does not usually possess. *The Man of Mode* has been a favourite proving ground. Rose Zimbardo amplifies Underwood in claiming that 'Etherege's central concern', here and elsewhere, is to display a philosophical ambivalence reflecting an unresolvable conflict between passion and reason. The reader who now comes to the play well versed in the intellectual history of the age will be able to see a good bit of it reflected fragmentarily in the play. Nonetheless, to say that even commonplaces are given any systematic exposition would be a great exaggeration. I consider *The Man of Mode* an excellent play, but I suspect that Etherege's 'central concern' was to display his own wit. I see no reason to claim high seriousness, satiric or otherwise for the play: surely we can enjoy it without the excuse of 'philosophical' justification. Etherege gives us some pleasantly tart views of his characters, but the play has little of substance to say by way of either moral or philosophical paradox. The results are more for our delectation than our instruction. I am sceptical about sentimental or manners-oriented interpretations: as Davies says, 'it is an uncompromisingly tough and realistic play'—one which (in Jocelyn Powell's words) leaves us 'floating between laughter and indignation'.[1] We cannot

[1] See Paul C. Davies, 'The State of Nature and the State of War: A Reconsideration of *The Man of Mode*', *University of Toronto Quarterly*, xxxix (1969), 53–62;

reasonably suppose that the audience was immoral or amoral, but the Carolean dramatists' claims to instruction are largely a ramp, and we need to recognize a play like *The Man of Mode* for what it is—a delightfully satiric entertainment.

The Country-Wife: Sex Comedy

Wycherley's third play (1675) presents problems quite similar to those posed by *The Man of Mode*. Coming at about the same time, both plays are part of the sex-boom; both have provoked drastically divergent interpretations; and in each case central interpretative questions remain problematical.

The spread of critical opinion on *The Country-Wife* is almost ludicrous, even ignoring those who are morally outraged. According to John Palmer, it is 'the most perfect farce in English dramatic literature—a whirlwind of inspired buffoonery. . . . All questions of motive and moral value disappear.' At another extreme, Bonamy Dobrée speaks of Wycherley's 'deep pessimism . . . the *saeva indignatio* of Swift', his 'strange revulsions against the society in which he now lived', evidenced in 'a savage snarl'. For Dobrée, Horner is a 'grim, nightmare figure', and the play as a whole shows Wycherley facing down the utter vileness of his world with bitter laughter. For Virginia Ogden Birdsall, the play is a kind of manifesto on the virtues of sexual liberation, and Horner, as representative of the 'élan vital' and 'the life force triumphant' she sees as 'a wholly positive and creative comic hero . . . squarely on the side of health, of freedom, and . . . of honesty'.[1] All three readings are carried out with some skill and plausibility, as are half a dozen others of varying purport.

Faced with such chaos, one has to return to basic questions. Is there an identifiable topic or subject in this play, and if so, what is it? For Palmer no subject need appear. Dobrée sees 'the sex question'—left decorously unspecific—as central. Mrs. Birdsall believes that 'Wycherley's central thematic concern'

Jocelyn Powell, 'George Etherege and the Form of a Comedy', *Restoration Theatre*, ed. Brown and Harris, pp. 43–69. For recent sentimental and manners-oriented readings see respectively Ronald Berman, 'The Comic Passions of *The Man of Mode*', *Studies in English Literature*, x (1970), 459–68; and John G. Hayman, 'Dorimant and the Comedy of a Man of Mode', *Modern Language Quarterly*, xxx (1969), 183–97.

[1] Palmer, *Comedy of Manners*, p. 128; Dobrée, *Restoration Comedy*, pp. 78, 80, 94, 95, 102; Birdsall, pp. 136, 156.

is 'the whole question of repression or tyranny as opposed to freedom in marital relationships'. H. T. E. Perry says that the play is conceived and presented as a satire on jealousy; Kenneth Muir feels that the main thrust of the satire is against 'female hypocrisy'; R. Edgley finds no serious criticism of sexual morality, but sees the subject of the play as exposure of 'folly'. David M. Vieth and William Freedman suggest from different vantage points that the 'subject' is the nature of masculinity.[1] Holland, Fujimura, and Zimbardo, in different ways, believe the play presents a right-way/wrong-way dichotomy of social ethics—so of course does Mrs. Birdsall, but she explicitly disagrees about what the 'right way' is (p. 147). Plainly we are beginning to slip from subject to object: a topic and the author's aims in introducing it are different matters. But if we want to pin down the author's apparent aim in *The Country-Wife*, plainly we must know the theme or subject, if such a thing is identifiable.

Even in a play we feel fairly certain of comprehending, to identify a central theme or topic is no simple matter. I think most of us would hesitate to assign such a subject to *As You Like It* (psychic benefits of a pastoral setting?), *The School for Scandal* (goodness of heart rewarded?), or *Arms and the Man* (the silliness of romantic ideals?). The third suggestion is the least foolish; but to see Shaw's play as no more than an illustration of that proposition is as partial and unsatisfactory as to call *The Country-Wife* a lecture on the pettiness of jealousy, as Perry does. Edgley has argued this matter with skill, asking if alchemy and the behaviour of the vulgar are the 'main interests' of *The Alchemist*. But I think that he overstrains his case by seeking to make 'folly' the centre of *The Country-Wife*. Why should the play have an identifiable central theme? That Wycherley does possess a didactic bent is clearly true, and is well demonstrated by Vernon. As Peter Malekin observes, though 'the action is farcical and the characters are Hogarthian caricatures' they are used 'to disclose what lies behind the

---

[1] Birdsall, p. 138; Perry, pp. 43, 45; Kenneth Muir, *The Comedy of Manners* (London, 1970), p. 76; Edgley, 'The Object of Literary Criticism', *Essays in Criticism*, xiv (1964), 221–36, esp. 233; Vieth, 'Wycherley's *The Country Wife*: An Anatomy of Masculinity', *Papers on Language and Literature*, ii (1966), 335–50; Freedman, 'Impotence and Self-Destruction in *The Country Wife*', *English Studies*, liii (1972), 421–31.

façade of society's pretences'.[1] But one can admire Wycherley's cutting social and psychological observations without agreeing that he is writing treatises. To write 'critical' comedy—and I agree that Wycherley does—need not imply a systematic ethical didacticism. Like Etherege, Wycherley is capable of casting a very cold analytic eye on London society, but neither writer seems seriously to envision any alternative. This should make us chary of easy assumptions about the 'satiric' nature of their comedies.

Nonetheless, by a great many accounts, *The Country-Wife* is a 'satire'. Even Fujimura, who is commendably cautious about exaggerating this side of Wycherley, admits that his contemporaries saw him as a satirist. Langbaine's account ends with a quotation from Evelyn: 'As long as Men are false, and Women vain,/ . . . /In pointed Satyr *Wycherley* shall Reign.'[2] And as satire is attack, and attack must have an object, we should be able to identify the subject and target of the play—Q.E.D. So say a number of critics. Must the target be specific, however, or may it be quite general—behaviour in a given social class? Mrs. Zimbardo, an advocate of the satire theory, opts for the former, asserting that 'the play opens, as satire must, with a declaration of the thesis to be argued. The vice in question is lust'—especially, she says, lust cloaked with hypocrisy (pp. 154–6). Mrs. Birdsall, of course, comes up with an almost opposite view. *The Country-Wife* is an odd sort of satire on lust, since Horner, the principal exemplar, succeeds gloriously in his designs. If the *plot* were to be 'instructive', Horner ought to catch the pox from Lady Fidget and find himself impotent. In the absence of such unambiguous morality in the play, Mrs. Zimbardo has to make a more complicated argument: in essence, she says that Horner is made to appear unattractive. But do we really find him disgusting and contemptible because he 'degenerates into mean knavery when at last he sacrifices Alithea's true honor to the preservation of his false disguise' (p. 161)? This supposes that we really care about Alithea, and take her and Harcourt seriously as a 'satiric

---

[1] P. F. Vernon, *William Wycherley* (London, 1965). Peter Malekin, 'Wycherley's Dramatic Skills and the Interpretation of *The Country-Wife*', *Durham University Journal*, n.s. xxxi (1969), 32–40.

[2] Fujimura, pp. 117–19; Langbaine, II. 515.

antithesis'. This proposition will have to be examined more fully.

Supposing that *The Country-Wife* is a satire in some sense, the critic wants to know what is being attacked (lust? hypocrisy? affectation? jealousy?) and who is being satirized. Pinchwife, Sparkish, Sir Jaspar, and the three honourable ladies are without doubt thoroughly ridiculed. But is Horner? And do Harcourt and Alithea stand as serious positive norms? A number of analytic schemes have been applied to the characters of the play. Fujimura naturally uses his Truewit/ Witwoud/Witless categorization, which puts Horner in a fairly attractive role. For Fujimura, he is neither 'nightmare figure' nor 'joyous' hedonist; rather, he is a Truewit who carries out a witty intrigue successfully and in the process exposes the affectations and follies of the others. Fujimura comes close to making Horner the spokesman for Wycherley's own outlook.[1] Granting some similarities, how attractive does Horner appear by the play's end? If we admire him, how do we feel about Harcourt? A second way of looking at the characters is Edgley's analysis of eight characters split into three groups of three (Horner appearing twice), each consisting of two men and a woman. In each instance a fool yields his woman to the other man. Thus Sir Jaspar presses his wife on Horner; Pinchwife brings Margery to Horner; and Sparkish loses Alithea to Harcourt. Within these parallel situations we find contrasts of wit and folly, honesty and hypocrisy, naturalness and artificiality.[2] According to Edgley, we prefer the truth and honour of the active Harcourt to the dissimulation and passivity of Horner. Here, of course, he relies on a positive response to Harcourt to temper our view of Horner.

Such a view has attracted a good deal of support. Anne Righter says that 'two young lovers (Alithea and Harcourt) stand in the centre of the play . . . it is by their standard that Wycherley intends the other characters, including Horner, to be judged.' But she has to admit, glumly, that 'the trouble with *The Country Wife* is, that although the centre of the comedy clearly lies with Alithea and Harcourt, Wycherley cannot really bring himself to believe in them.' Or perhaps the critic is in error here? Muir more cautiously holds that the young

[1] Fujimura, pp. 139, 145.   [2] Edgley, pp. 234–5.

lovers are a 'hint' at the true 'standards' of judgement.[1] The best-known statement of this view is Holland's right-way/wrong-way thesis. In his view, deception is wrong, honesty right, but within 'the social framework of pretense' the honesty must be sophisticated, unlike Margery's. This reading is extremely plausible and quite satisfying, but is it right? Holland gives us fine words about a couple who 'realize the importance of an aim that goes beyond the merely social and answers one's inner nature' (p. 83). However, I wonder how many spectators really feel this way about Harcourt and Alithea, any more than about Young Bellair and Emilia? Holland claims that Harcourt is 'idealized' on the grounds that his 'ineffectual schemes are definitely not typical of the hero of a Restoration comedy' (p. 84). On the contrary, I would say that such frustration of schemes (and hare-brained schemes) are extremely typical for the male romantic lead in Carolean comedies. Four acts of bafflement and miscarriage is the norm —as for Wycherley's own Gerrard in *The Gentleman Dancing-Master*. What is unusual in the Harcourt–Alithea relationship is her block-headed loyalty to an obnoxious fool. This has been held against her ideality, as has her joining the chorus in Horner's illegitimate defence in Act V ('Come Brother, your Wife is yet innocent you see. . . .')—which Muir excuses as sympathy for Margery.

But no matter. If Harcourt and Alithea are supposed to represent a high moral norm in the play and make us view Horner with disapprobation, then Wycherley made a mess of things. For in practice one is benevolently indifferent to the couple during the play and scarcely remembers them in it afterwards. The moral eye of the beholder may convert them into standards of moral judgement, but in the play we are given little ground for seeing the pair in more than conventional two-dimensional perspective. Harcourt is the usual good fellow and honest friend of the hero; Alithea is a much less routine figure, but we see her mostly as stubbornly foolish. If the vapid Harcourt was supposed to be a standard of measurement, then the ideal is betrayed by its feeble presentation. Far more probably, I believe, the Harcourt–Alithea–Sparkish plot line is included for necessary fullness and variety. Wycherley

[1] Righter, pp. 77–9; Muir, pp. 78–9.

uses it to ridicule a pretender to wit, to introduce such farcical tricks as those in the impersonated-parson episode, and to get what mileage he can out of a routine boy-gets-girl story. What makes it better than, for example, the treatment of the Young Bellair and Emilia story, is his changing the nature of the obstacle, making it internal to the woman rather than parental.

One is left to return to the central question: is Horner satirized or somehow denigrated? Since we could postulate a negative reaction based on extrinsic audience assumptions (in the fashion of McDonald on Etherege) regardless of what happens in the play, no definitive answer is possible. Nonetheless, since the whole play really turns on this point, the problem cannot be ignored. The possibilities are limited. With Anne Righter we can consider Horner 'wholly negative' and 'an agent of destruction'; with Mrs. Birdsall we can view him as a positive and creative comic hero. Arguably, we should seek a middle position. What are the grounds for either of the extreme views? Within the play, we are given very little direct appraisal of Horner. In what remains the most sensible and helpful study of Wycherley's satire, T. W. Craik makes a telling point: 'actions do not speak for themselves in Wycherley; if he disapproves, he tells us so.'[1] This is true: Horner derides practically everyone, but is never himself directly attacked. Critics often compare our response to him with our response to Volpone: at first we sympathize with the trickster, but turn against him when we see the good attacked. But does Horner ever actually damage anyone worth caring about? Indeed, he is largely a passive figure, used by the hypocritical women. And unlike Volpone, Horner succeeds, escapes retribution, and goes off triumphant. Presumably Wycherley could have brought Horner's affairs to a Jonsonian crash had he wished. Perhaps the audience is supposed to despise him on sight, but the play itself does little to render him foolish. Dobrée feels that Horner gets only 'a sorry enjoyment from his success' (p. 94); I must agree with Craik, however, that though Horner may be a glutton rather than a connoisseur, he relishes his successes and the audience is glad to see them. Had we really been turned against him, would we not want him exposed? But the nature

---

[1] 'Some Aspects of Satire in Wycherley's Plays', *English Studies*, xli (1960), 168–79. Neither Zimbardo nor Birdsall ever mentions this important essay.

of our support is sharply qualified. Gerald Weales astutely observes that no doubt 'the hidden *Playboy* reader in all of us is bound to identify with his sexual triumphs . . . [but] his seductions become merely mechanical. He is more like a chain smoker than a great lover.'[1] Here perhaps is the crux. We are glad enough to see Horner succeed, but we cannot identify very seriously with his endeavours. His triumphs are attained in a world both he and we despise. Perhaps *he* is happy with Lady Fidget *et al.*, but they are not made very attractive to *us*, except as sexual objects of the grossest sort. We may well tend to identify with the glamorous, potent Dorimant. Do we really envy Horner his sordid little *coups*? Even Margery shows up rather badly in this play: country ignorance seldom comes out well by the sophisticated town standards of Carolean comedy, and Margery is made to appear more silly than lovable. In the world of fools and hypocrites in which he lives, Horner is welcome to his triumph. We do not, however, take it very seriously.

Should *The Country-Wife* be considered 'a satire'? I am not persuaded that the play is substantially a sermon against hypocrisy, jealousy, or lust. Clearly a majority of the characters are savagely ridiculed. Margery is foolish and ignorant; Pinchwife is contemptible in every way; Sir Jaspar is an obnoxious fool; the ladies prating of their 'dear honour' draw only scorn. No doubt then the play contains a great deal of satire. We should note, however, that the objects of all the ridicule are no more than grotesque exaggerations of the commonplace butts of Carolean comedy. The violently but ineffectually jealous husband, the stupidly complacent husband, the hypocritical and lustful wives, the country innocent—all are comic stereotypes. To say that Wycherley, vastly more than Etherege, presents a degraded and often disgusting view of man and society is perfectly accurate. To call him a serious satirist is probably an exaggeration, for he never goes beyond exposing the obvious to contempt and ridicule. Never, as in Swift, is the audience made to identify itself with what is attacked. The satire is often highly amusing; almost never are its criticisms genuinely serious and thought-provoking in the fashion of Molière.

[1] Introduction to *The Complete Plays of William Wycherley*, p. xii.

The result in *The Country-Wife* is an immensely enjoyable play in which we take almost nothing seriously. Palmer exaggerates in saying that all questions of motive and moral value disappear: hypocrisy, affectation, and dissimulation enter too strongly to be ignored. Inspired buffoonery, though, is a fair description. Perhaps that phrase does less than justice to the ugliness and nasty quality often present in the play. But the critic may tend to forget just how much is plain farce. The gross character exaggerations are characteristic of farce, more than of comedy. Pinchwife is super-jealous, Sir Jaspar and Sparkish super-blind, Margery ultra-innocent, the ladies blatantly and exuberantly hypocritical. Margery dressed as her brother, Harcourt rigged out as a parson, the switched letters, the china scene, the substitution of Margery for Alithea, and the final resolution are all extraordinarily improbable and more the stuff of high farce than romantic comedy or serious satire. Delightfully bawdy and funny *The Country-Wife* is; profound it is not, and only a prude, a hypocrite, or a stuffy academician would have it otherwise.

Love for Love: Sentiment-Tinged Romance

Congreve's penultimate comedy (1695) was indubitably a great success, and long remained so. Looking at the play's modern critics, we find the usual muddle. There are few outright contradictions in the criticism, but if anything the disagreements are the more baffling for this lack of sharply focused issues. As frequently happens with these late seventeenth-century plays, critics read their own preoccupations into a text whose point (if any) is not unmistakably clear. For Aubrey Williams the play is a demonstration of God's providence operating in the world. For Fujimura it is given its 'substance' by the wit of the lead couple. For Mrs. Birdsall the work is a consideration of a 'central question': can 'naturalness' or 'honesty' exist in so inhuman, unnatural, and dishonest a world?[1] Every man to his own Rorschach, says Gerald Weales concerning Wycherley. But given the results, can we see what Congreve was trying to do?

[1] Aubrey Williams, 'The "Utmost Tryal" of Virtue and Congreve's *Love for Love*', *Tennessee Studies in Literature*, xvii (1972), 1–18, and 'Poetical Justice, The Contrivances of Providence, and the Works of William Congreve', *ELH*, xxxv (1968), 540–65; Fujimura, pp. 176–83; Birdsall, Chapter 9, esp. p. 215.

Certain extraneous considerations probably affected the writing of the play. Congreve's great success with *The Old Batchelour* (1693) had been followed by a very cool reception for *The Double-Dealer* at the end of the same year. He was working under the patronage of Dryden and Southerne, and was being touted as the man who could combine the 'Courtship' of Etherege with the 'Satire, Wit, and Strength of Manly Witcherly', as Dryden put it in 'To My Dear Friend Mr. Congreve' (1694). *The Double-Dealer* had been essentially a deliberate attempt at a more polished version of Wycherley; thus baulked, Congreve made far more concession to popular taste and the theatrical climate the next time. By no means do I want to imply that *Love for Love* is not the better play; clearly it is. The critic should realize, however, that the later play is built (like Congreve's first) out of tried and true devices, and hence is well calculated for popular appeal.

The prologue contains a fairly explicit analysis: whether we should altogether believe it may be disputed.

> We hope there's something that may please each Taste,
> And tho' of Homely Fare we make the Feast,
> Yet you will find variety at least.
> There's Humour, which for chearful Friends we got,
> And for the thinking Party there's a Plot.
> We've something too, to gratifie ill Nature,
> (If there be any here) and that is Satire.
> Tho Satire scarce dares grin, 'tis grown so mild;
> Or only shews its Teeth, as if it smil'd.

Congreve promptly goes on to claim that he is the first writer since Wycherley who has 'dar'd to lash this Crying Age'. Few critics have felt that the play accords with this claim to be carrying on a tradition of serious satire. Dobrée is almost alone in doing so, and he oddly finds it a failed satire because 'overweighty'. Clifford Leech's observation that Congreve, however wittily critical, usually lacks the 'animus' of the serious satirist seems to me an apter comment.[1] We can certainly grant Congreve's own analysis that humours characters loom large in the play, and further that so does 'plot'—in this case principally a distinctly romantic outwitting plot. The 'satire' (as

---

[1] Dobrée, pp. 132–8; Leech, 'Congreve and the Century's End', *Philological Quarterly*, xli (1962), 275–93.

distinct from simple ridicule of the humours characters)
consists basically of direct negative commentary on almost the
whole social context of the action. Novak correctly notes that
Congreve here 'clearly conceives of satire in terms of direct
invective'.[1] Scandal is employed as a kind of official, cynical,
plain-dealing railer. So to a lesser extent is the servant, Jeremy.
Valentine, when 'mad', announces 'I am Truth', and delivers
a few blunt observations.[2]

Given its component parts, *Love for Love* is a verbally polished
cross between Fletcher and Jonson. Resemblances in the
romantic plot to Fletcher's *The Elder Brother* and *The Scornful
Lady* have been remarked by critics. No special Jonson source
is drawn upon, but the use of extravagant humours to characterize several individuals, especially Foresight, is to employ a
technique which was recognized as Jonson's speciality.[3] The
result is an enormously lively play which is not romantic
comedy, nor hard-hitting satire, nor humours comedy. The
prominence of all these elements explains some of the disparate critical reactions. Mrs. Zimbardo, wanting satire, is
offended by the suspiciously 'sentimental' bent of the romantic
plot. Those who would like a strong romantic affirmation are
bothered because the ending seems almost cavalier and hence
'unconvincing'. A reading which concentrates on only one of
the major component elements will invariably distort the play
by its lop-sidedness.

The lines of action are beautifully interwoven: unlike many
of these plays, *Love for Love* does not comprise a pattern of
different actions balanced against each other. The central
plot line (the romantic plot) is a relatively unusual twist to the
usual stand-by: Valentine must secure his endangered inheritance against the opposition of his father in order to win
his lady, Angelica. He must also win her consent, which he
obtains only at the very end. The direct competition between

---

[1] Maximillian E. Novak, *William Congreve* (New York, 1971), pp. 108–9.

[2] For example, 'I am Truth. 'Tis hard I cannot get a Livelyhood amongst you. I
have been sworn out of *Westminster-Hall* . . .' (280); 'Prayers will be said in empty
Churches, at the usual Hours. Yet you will see such Zealous Faces behind Counters,
as if Religion were to be sold in every Shop' (289).

[3] Kathleen Lynch (p. 192) sees possible borrowing in Foresight from Mopus in
Wilson's *Cheats* and Lump in Shadwell's *A True Widow*—both avowedly Jonsonian
plays. The precise sources, if any, really make no difference.

father and son for the same woman is a common device (cf. the Bellairs and Emilia). Valentine has been a wastrel and rake. During the play, however, he is almost entirely generous, sensible, and attractive.[1] Congreve gets good comic mileage out of Valentine's predicaments. The scene in which he tries to put off Trapland (who wants a loan repaid) with good fellowship is well borrowed from Molière. The mad scene amusingly frustrates Sir Sampson, since if insane, Valentine cannot legally fulfil his written promise to sign away his inheritance to his younger brother. Despite his schemes, Valentine can do no more than stall; the happy ending is achieved by Angelica, who gulls the hard-hearted father into believing she will marry him, and so gains control of the crucial papers. The audience is sufficiently badly disposed toward Sir Sampson for it to be able thoroughly to relish his ill-founded gloating over his forthcoming marriage.

This account, like most others, overstresses the romantic plot. During the play, much of our attention is occupied with other matters. Briefly, these are (1) a cuckolding action: Scandal successfully seduces Mrs. Foresight, an action perfectly agreeable to us, in light of our view of Mr. Foresight. (2) A trick marriage: Tattle is duped into marrying Mrs. Frail (Mrs. Foresight's sister), believing that she is Angelica disguised. (3) Satire on an astrological pretender: Foresight's intervention in others' business is pleasantly ridiculous; the Molière-originated scene in which Scandal convinces him he is sick makes a good prelude to the adultery. (4) The introduction of a country innocent, Foresight's daughter Prue, allows Tattle's hilarious instruction of her in town ways and a near-seduction. Prue is laughed at for her total lack of sophistication; she also makes an effective foil against which to show up the hypocritical dissimulation of her town-bred elders.

All four of these interests are hoary devices. All of them

---

[1] Mrs. Birdsall (p. 214) contrasts his 'genuine concern and affection' when he gives money for one of his bastards with Sir Sampson's harsh treatment of his legitimate elder son. But her rhapsody over his generosity omits all mention of his comment on the woman to Scandal: 'Pox on her . . . a thoughtless two handed Whore, she knows my Condition well enough, and might have overlaid the Child a Fortnight ago' (221). At best, this is a rather graceless joke. On the coarse sensibility thus revealed, see George Parfitt, 'The Case Against Congreve', *William Congreve*, ed. Brian Morris (London, 1972), pp. 21–38.

would be perfectly in place in *The Country-Wife*. Probably we should note that Congreve is careful to keep his male romantic lead out of the cuckolding plot, and to frustrate the seduction of the innocent: 1695 is not 1675. The most prominent of the non-romantic elements has not even yet been mentioned: Valentine's younger brother, Sailor Ben, who, his father admits, wants 'a little Polishing' (262). His nautical jargon is funny in itself, as is his complete innocence of the ways of the London world.

It's but a folly to lie: For to speak one thing, and to think just the contrary way; is as it were, to look one way, and to row another. Now, for my part d'ee see, I'm for carrying things above Board, I'm not for keeping any thing under Hatches,—so that if you ben't as willing as I, say so a God's name, there's no harm done. (263)

This bluff honesty, and Ben's independent spirit, are attractive in a way, and serve beautifully to show up the tortuous hypocrisies and deceitful schemes of the more polished characters. Unfortunately, Ben is almost pathetically vulnerable to dissimulation, and luck alone saves him from falling prey to Mrs. Frail's schemes. We laugh *at* him; by no means could he be taken as a model; yet nonetheless our response is largely positive.

Even allowing for the heavy reliance on stock characters, *Love for Love* seems a thoughtful play. Just how much intellectual substance does it really possess? Norman Holland's brilliant analysis claims a good deal. Holland sees the essence of the work as a contrast of types of 'knowledge' and social adjustment. 'Presocial' characters (Prue and Ben) are set against people representing ordinary social standards, and both groups are set against Valentine and Angelica, 'suprasocial' characters who can escape the trivialities and dishonesties of society to a better personal world. The bulk of the play, so conceived, traces the 'education' of Valentine, who must be brought to realize that there is a higher reality, that he must abandon all pretences and accept the 'religion of love' which wins him Angelica (note her name) in the final scene. According to Holland's reading, 'the ethic of Etherege is gone.' 'Knowledge' is no longer just what allows the 'hero to succeed in a corrupt and foolish society'. Rather, knowledge becomes the means to a 'larger freedom', in which 'the hero retreats from the social world of deception and illusion to a personal haven of psychological truth and emotional sincerity'.[1]

Whether one accepts such a reading depends on how seriously one takes the ending. When Valentine makes a noble renunciation, thinking to please Angelica, she is touched by his devotion, now proved, and exclaims 'Generous *Valentine*!' and goes on: 'Had I the World to give you, it cou'd not make me worthy of so generous and faithful a Passion: Here's my Hand, my Heart was always yours, and struggl'd very hard to make this utmost Tryal of your Virtue.' Valentine replies in pseudo-religious terms: 'Between Pleasure and Amazement, I am lost—But on my Knees I take the Blessing' (312). Scandal then praises Angelica for having 'done Exemplary Justice, in punishing an inhumane Father, and rewarding a Faithful Lover'. Her 'Third good Work', he continues, is having 'converted' Scandal himself to belief in women's good sense.

This ending is most pleasant. It is produced, though, more with the air of a conjurer pulling a rabbit from a hat than with the serious feeling of high romantic comedy. The audience, having been long aware of Angelica's true feelings, sees it coming and relishes Valentine's unawareness of the truth. I agree with Clifford Leech in finding the final sentiments exaggerated and unnecessary. Critics can speak of a 'miracle of love'; Williams can tout 'Providential justice'. Actually, what brings off the happy ending is the skilful dissimulation—or call it blatant lying and dishonesty—of Angelica, who deliberately pays court to Sir Sampson, invites and accepts a proposal of marriage, and so gains control of the crucial papers. What is so marvellously providential about this? The sort of 'contrivance' involved can be found in any of fifty intrigue comedies from the period.[2]

---

[1] Holland, Chapter 14; quotation from p. 174.

[2] Like the Reverend Jeremy Collier, Aubrey Williams draws some astonishing allegorical conclusions from the word 'Providence'. (Cf. Collier, *A Short View of the Immorality and Profaneness of the English Stage* (London, 1698), pp. 84–5.) In his *Short Vindication* Vanbrugh replies to Collier: 'Every body knows the word Providence in Common Discourse goes for Fortune. If it be answer'd, Let it go for what it will, it is in strictness God Almighty; I answer again, That if you go to strictness, Fortune is God Almighty as much as Providence, and yet no one ever thought it Blasphemy to say, Fortune's blind, or Fortune favours Fools: And the reason why it is not thought so, is because 'tis known it is not meant so.' (*Works*, I. 201.)

Much the best reading of the play is Novak's. He calls it a 'beautiful, satisfying fairy tale which Congreve serves as a delightful feast', and I think this assessment is just right. The whole play is a ragout of popular devices: tricked marriage, attempted seduction, extravagant humours characters, inheritance achieved by trick, foolish beau, *ingénue*, country (here sea-going) innocent, witty heroine, love game, and blatant dissimulation. The devices and social world are basically those of Carolean sex comedy, but the handling is different. J. H. Smith finds the play 'a mixture' of the old elements and the new sentiment.[1] Certainly the romantic element is stronger than in late Wycherley or Etherege. The fairy-tale quality is marked at the end. Sir Sampson stomps off and simply disappears; scarcely any disposition is made of all the other characters. They have served their purpose, and having entertained, can be ignored. We are given two pages of lovers' chat to make us feel good, and the rest of the world simply vanishes. The substance of the play is highly derivative; the satire (both explicit and implicit) consists of routine hits at the usual obvious targets. Against this background we are given a purer, gayer romantic plot than was usual. I am not convinced that we should take it much more seriously than we do the rest of the play: we can very well delight in the fairy tale without attaching metaphysical significance to it.

To say that *Love for Love* is 'about' a particular theme or problem is to distort it. As Novak says, 'it would be doing violence to Congreve's art to suggest that it was a play of ideas, but it is one of contrasts and paradoxes.' Several kinds of 'honesty' are introduced in Ben, the plain-dealing Scandal, and the gradually educated Valentine. Tattle is explicitly balanced against Scandal, Prue against Mrs. Foresight. Valentine is allowed his reward only after he has been driven first to feign madness and then to what Scandal finds real madness in offering to give up everything in Act V. *Love for Love* is set up as a kind of fortune-hunting play in which inheritance is all-important. Penelope Gilliatt said sarcastically, writing of a recent performance, that *Love for Loot* would be an apter title. There is a good deal of truth in the observation.

---

[1] J. H. Smith, pp. 156–8. Cf. the romantic reading by Charles Lyons, 'Congreve's Miracle of Love', *Criticism*, vi (1964), 331–48.

What are we to think when Congreve chooses to give the loot (and lady) to the man who has just renounced both? Is this ending sentimental slush, as Leech and Zimbardo complain? Or is it a transcendental romantic affirmation, as Holland and Lyons think? Or is it perhaps just a delicious joke?

The Committee: City Intrigue Comedy

Sir Robert Howard's most successful comedy (1662) is one of those works which gets a few commendatory sentences in literary histories but has never attracted serious attention. Indeed, the only genuine critical discussion known to me is in A. H. Scouten's soon to be published contribution to the Methuen *History of English Drama*, to which I am indebted.[1] Howard is now remembered mostly for an unfortunate critical dispute with his brother-in-law Dryden, but his literary obscurity should not be allowed to detract from the excellence of this play. As Summers might say, it is a capital comedy which well deserved the popularity which kept it on the stage to the time of Sir Walter Scott. This record is the more astonishing in that *The Committee* is an extremely topical play, much of it being devoted to savage satire on the recently deposed puritans. Like some other exceptionally popular comedies (*The Citizen Turn'd Gentleman*, *The Busie Body*) Howard's play is so simple as to present no critical problems. The meaning is obvious; the proper responses to the characters are clear beyond argument. We can, however, profitably analyse the play's appeal.

The Committee is built around a bitter and irreconcilable conflict between puritans and cavaliers. The time is the late 1650s, the scene London. The title refers, of course, to Cromwell's notorious sequestration committee. Two royalist colonels, in danger of losing their estates, succeed in outwitting the committee, and in the process win heiresses. Thus the play contrasts black and white, vicious hypocritical puritan scoundrels versus noble, attractive, high-minded gentlemen. Irrelevant to the central conflict is a third element of equal importance to the play—Colonel Careless's Irish servant Teague (or Teg). By rights, perhaps, the work should

[1] A sympathetic description of the play is given in H. J. Oliver's biography, *Sir Robert Howard* (Durham, N.C., 1963), Chapter 4, and Montague Summers gives an enthusiastic appreciation in *The Playhouse of Pepys* (London, 1935), pp. 170–3.

fall apart, since the satire and central plot lines are entirely predictable, and the jolly but irrelevant bungling servant might not seem adequate compensation. In fact though, the excellence of the execution makes the clichéd elements magnificently effective.

Satire on puritans had been a comic stand-by for more than half a century; that Howard's could be both so savage and so delightfully funny is quite a surprise. The characters are vivid and well individualized, even such committee-men as the slippery Nehemiah Catch and the ponderous Jonathan Headstrong. Mr. Day, the chairman, a scheming, whining pig; his loutish, stupid, self-satisfied son Abel; and his pompous clerk Obadiah are marvellously drawn; but all take a back seat to Mrs. Day, a woman whose brains, ruthlessness, and domination over her husband Lady Macbeth would be proud to salute. Summers compares this crew with Dickens's minor characters, and the suggestion is apt. With great economy of space Howard gives all these people a gritty and sordid reality which is very striking indeed. Especially effective is the way he sets off their complete unscrupulousness and rapacity with an intimate picture of the Days' married life. Mr. Day is utterly under his wife's thumb, and tries to placate her with constant endearments, especially the incongruous pet name 'Duck' ('Nay, good duck, no chiding now, But to your councel'), which is so often reiterated that it starts to get a laugh all by itself. The committee's completely outrageous way of transacting its business is depicted early and briefly (90), and after that Howard wisely avoids labouring the obvious.

Colonels Careless and Blunt are less vivid characters. Basically, they are noble royalists who serve as foils for the puritans and can be rewarded with the two girls, Arbella and Ruth. The latter turns out to be Anne, not the daughter of the Days, as is pretended, but the daughter and heiress of Sir Basil Throughgood. This discovery of parentage and inheritance, which might have seemed an awful cliché, Howard makes something of a joke of throughout, by saying over and over, in essence, 'such a girl just *couldn't* be the Days' child—no, no, that's impossible'—and sure enough, she is not. Ruth herself teases her lover Careless about her alleged parentage, letting Howard both use the cliché and mock it.

The romantic plot is taken fairly seriously, but Howard does not let it become saccharine. The girls are attractive and spirited, the men true gentlemen. Nonetheless their love at first sight is archly mocked when Howard goes out of his way to assure the audience that there will be no mix-up about who loves whom. And a beautiful example of comic deflation occurs in Act V when Careless is about to escape from jail via a rope ladder. He sees Ruth at the bottom of the wall, and exclaims magniloquently, 'I'le leap into thy arms',— only to have her reply tartly, 'So you may break your neck' (126). And when (arrived at ground level) he asks to kiss her hand, she teases him: 'Pish, there's a dirty Glove upon't' (127). Despite this playfulness, both love affairs are presented in a plain, simple, and entirely moral way: there is no 'love game' here. Ruth tells Careless, 'I have try'd you fully; You are noble, and I hope you love me; be ever firm to Virtuous principles' (126); Arbella tells the bashful Blunt, 'I'le save you the labour of Courtship, which Shou'd be too tedious to all plain and honest natures: It is enough I know you love me' (130). The result is an attractive and seriously received romantic love plot, held in balance against the satiric plot line.

Yet excellent as the rest of the play is, its glory is Teg. A long series of commentators down to Sir Walter Scott testify to the role's attractions. The great John Lacy first took the part: Evelyn says that he acted it 'to admiration', and Pepys, though he found the play 'merry but indifferent', calls Lacy's Teg 'beyond imagination'.[1] The role offers considerable possibilities, mixing touching goodness of heart with a natural simplicity and ignorance calculated to produce comic catastrophes. Withal, Teg is not merely ineffectual, foolish, or contemptible. Blunderers, sometimes well-meaning ones, were especially popular in comedies throughout the period: *Sir Martin Mar-all* and *The Busie Body* are good examples of plays which employ one prominently. Teg is unusual in being a very early example of a simple character at whom we laugh, but sympathetically, since we really like him. This attitude is made explicit early in the play.

Col. Blunt: I am pleased yet, with the poor fellows mistaken kindness;
I dare warrant him honest to the best of his understanding.

[1] Evelyn, *Diary*, 27 November 1662; Pepys, *Diary*, 12 June 1663.

Col. Careless: This fellow I prophesie will bring me into many
troubles by his mistakes. . . . Yet his simple honesty prevails with
me, I cannot part with him. (86)

The kindly feelings of the Colonels carry over to the audience,
and we never feel for Teg the contempt usually elicited by
foolish servants and French valets. When he 'takes' the
'Covenant' for his master by stealing a pamphlet called 'The
Solemn League and Covenant' from a bookseller (84), or
gloriously and unintentionally insults Mrs. Day into a fury
(100), we cannot help loving the fellow. The splendid scene in
which Teg, obeying orders, succeeds in getting the pompous
clerk Obadiah uproariously drunk is a well-deserved triumph,
which concludes with Obadiah singing cavalier songs damning
puritan committees (114–15). Told to get the clerk out of the
way a second time, Teg cannot repeat his trick—Obadiah
refuses to drink—so Teg ties him into a halter at knife-point,
and proudly leads him on stage at the end of the play. Unhappily, the Irish dialect, the zaniness, the human warmth of
the character are mere shadows on the printed page: one gets
only a hint of why the role was a favourite vehicle for actors,
from Lacy and Leigh to Macklin, Jack Johnstone, and John
Moody late in the eighteenth century.

Scouten makes the important point that we can see in this
play a conflict visible in a great many later comedies. The
cavaliers—not the aristocracy, but the upper middle class—
are pitted against puritan upstarts, 'this new Gentry' (71) as
an under-tipped coachman bitterly calls them here. The lines
of social and economic conflict so clearly drawn in this play
are often blurred and twisted later, especially in the post-
Carolean period, but outcroppings of them are legion. We
seldom find the actual confrontation of Cavalier and Round-
head,[1] but the feeling surfaces as man of fashion versus cit, and
in consistently unpleasant pictures of merchants, puritans,
aldermen, and the like. Later the conflict has largely social
overtones: here it is blatantly economic. The puritans are
trying to steal the cavaliers' estates, and to cheat cavalier

---

[1] Two examples are Sedley's *The Mulberry-Garden*, which makes only peripheral
use of it, and Mrs. Behn's *The Roundheads* (1681), an adaptation of Tatham's *The
Rump* made to capitalize on anti-puritan feeling during the Popish Plot.

heiresses out of their money. All the hostilities of long-exiled and still frightened cavaliers are packed here into a really nasty picture of the puritan animal. Mr. Day makes a contemptible pose of piety: he is actually a double-crosser, a liar, and a wencher. When he drops his keys, enabling the girls to steal his papers, they discover that he has had a bastard and tried to force another of his mistresses to get an abortion against her will. Mrs. Day is silenced at the end of the play by the threat of exposure as a forger.

Despite the presence of some attractive and essentially exemplary characters in the play, the view of human nature which emerges over all is distinctly cold and sceptical. No sunny resolution is allowed—and rightly, for no resolution of the conflicts is possible. The cavaliers acquire compromising evidence, forcing the puritans to give in, but they do not recant. Scouten observes that Howard avoids a sweeping reversal. Poetic justice could have been achieved by *deus ex machina* with the return of the king, a trick used by Sedley in *The Mulberry-Garden*. Howard does conclude with advice to Day: 'if you will have good luck in every thing, Turn Cavalier, and cry, God bless the King.' This sentiment aside, the hostilities at the end of the play are precisely what they were at the beginning. Colonel Careless and his 'old Kitchen-stuff-acquaintance' Mrs. Day are not about to adjust their differences. No more than Careless can Howard forgive the social pretensions and new status of a woman who 'was my Father's Kitchen-maid, and in Time of yore called *Gillian*' (95–6). The brilliant scene with which the play opens has Mrs. Day and Blunt (with others) as fellow-passengers in a stagecoach, and mordantly exposes her in two pages as a gross and obnoxious bore. The delicate punchline of a long story of hers about another coach ride is praise of the gentlemanly Mayor of Redding, who 'Held his Hat for the Girle to ease her Stomach in' (73).

For all its harsh ridicule and minimal resolution, *The Committee* is a brisk and breezy play, and a remarkably good-humoured one. Its political satire is more an expression of contempt and ill will than anything else: writing in 1662 Howard is attacking abuses of the past, not satirizing present wrongs. Prominent though the anti-puritan portions are, they do not swamp the play, as its longevity on the stage attests. Teague does a great deal to make the piece pleasant rather than bitter. The balance of elements works out well: contemptible low characters, attractive and eminently decent romantic couples, and a laughable, lovable innocent. The play does not read well, save for the idlest kind of amusement. It gives the critic no problem to grapple with, and nothing to explicate which is not obvious to any knowledgeable reader. The conflict it embodies is made black and white. But the critic needs to remember the play's long success and comprehend the reasons for it. The fast action, the sprinkling of attractive characters, and the gritty vividness of the unattractive ones add up to a highly effective theatrical vehicle.

The Busie Body: Augustan Intrigue Comedy

Mrs. Centlivre's *The Busie Body* (1709) started out as a great success and continued so, remaining popular well into the nineteenth century. It is an ultra-formulaic play, utterly representative in materials and tone of early eighteenth-century utilization of stock materials from the late seventeenth century.

The cast of characters is quite small, and is organized into two neat and parallel plot lines. (1) Sir George Airy (a wealthy young man) loves Miranda, whose old guardian, Sir Francis Gripe, designs to marry her himself. (2) Charles (Sir Francis's son and Airy's friend) loves Isabinda, whose father, Sir Jealous Traffick, wishes to marry her to a Spaniard (who does not appear). Three servants are employed, of whom only Patch, Isabinda's maid, has more than walk-on importance. The two plot lines are joined principally by means of the bungling but well-meant interference of Marplot, another ward of Sir Francis. Our attention is divided between the schemes of the lovers in the boy-gets-girl plots, the father-figures' foolishness, and Marplot's blunders.

Much of the play's substance is lifted from Jonson's *The Devil is an Ass*, and from either Molière's *L'Étourdi*, or from the Newcastle–Dryden adaptation of it, *Sir Martin Mar-all*, or both. Mrs. Centlivre's results with this material make an effective vehicle for a theatrical romp, but no one has ever found much literary value in it. Dobrée calls the play 'an empty comedy of intrigue, without any reality of emotion whatsoever'.[1] This judgement seems excessively harsh: Marplot has struck some readers as a highly engaging character,[2] and Sir Francis Gripe's passion for his ward Miranda (and her response to it) seems to me very effectively if unattractively drawn. Indubitably, though, most critics have felt that the basis of the play was its use of intrigue, Nicoll going so far as to call it 'one of the masterpieces' of the 'comedy of intrigue'.[3] What, specifically, does this description mean?

Basically, *The Busie Body* consists of long series of schemes for each plot. Sir George must woo Miranda under her guardian's nose, and she must persuade that guardian to settle her money on her before he has married her himself. Similarly, Charles must marry Isabinda without her forfeiting her fortune; and as an added complication, he has no money, since his father has by trickery retained the modest fortune his uncle willed to Charles. Stratagems are called for—the more frequently because between Marplot's insatiable curiosity and his willing assistance, a large number of the best-laid plans go thoroughly agley. Much of the fun of the comedy lies in our waiting to see what will go wrong next. Let a letter be sent and the maid is sure to drop it in her master's way (43–5). Let Charles enter his beloved's house disguised as her Spanish fiancé and Marplot is sure to turn up on the doorstep, full of curiosity, to let the cat out of the bag without realizing what he is doing (66–7). Let Miranda contrive to send her guardian off to Epsom 'under pretence that a Brother Usurer of his, is to make him his Executor'—and he will be back in a trice at a highly inconvenient moment, having encountered the gentleman hale and hearty a few streets away (52–3, 59).

Actually, though schemes loom large in the play, it relies much less on rapid action, sword-play, and suspense of outcome than does a play like Mrs. Behn's *The Rover* (1677), or even *The Adventures of Five Hours*. The relaxed tone and lack of melodramatic action leave the audience in no doubt at all

---

[1] Bonamy Dobrée, *English Literature in the Early Eighteenth Century* (Oxford, 1959), p. 236.

[2] Particularly F. W. Bateson, *English Comic Drama 1700–1750* (1929; rpt. New York, 1963), pp. 69–71. Bateson calls Marplot 'one of the most attractive of literature's simpletons'.

[3] Nicoll, II. 167.

about the eventual outcome; one simply cannot find much excuse for feeling suspense here. What really occupies and entertains the audience is not intrigue *per se*, but a veritable catalogue of comic devices and formulas.

The girl who must outwit her guardian is a commonplace, and the Airy–Miranda plot is largely a routine development of the type. Sir George pays court to her by giving Sir Francis £100 to let him approach her in his presence: the result is an entertaining dumb scene (partly from Jonson) in which the lovers accomplish what they need to while leaving the guardian unsuspicious. On another occasion (10–13) the couple (with the lady masked) engage in a witty encounter. Sir George, unaware of her identity, plays the dashing philanderer ('No Child, a Dish of Chocolate in the Morning never spoils my Dinner; the other Lady, I design a set Meal.'), but Miranda persuades him to turn his back for a moment and sneaks away. Pretty feeble philandering! The dumb scene wrings fine irony out of the guardian's fatuous complacency about his ward's affections. Mrs. Centlivre is clever enough to use an unusual twist on a hoary device: instead of having Miranda convey a letter by pretending to hand one back, Mrs. Centlivre makes the refusal of the letter genuine, but lets Sir George turn the incident to advantage (22–3). Miranda's making an appointment with her suitor by telling Marplot to warn him off (38) is another standard trick (especially well used in Otway's *The Souldiers Fortune*, for example). Two unexpectedly quick returns of the guardian (54, 59) are very much the stuff of routine comic fuss and consternation. What is unusual about this plot development is the relationship between Miranda and Sir Francis Gripe. His drooling fondness for her is very effectively conveyed. 'Thou dear little Rogue, let me buss thee . . . .Nay, adod, I will, *Chargee*, so muzle, and tuzle, and hug thee; I will, I faith, I will. (*Hugging and Kissing her.*)' (34). The necessity of convincing him that he is the man she really adores produces a series of nauseatingly effective scenes of endearment between *Guardee* and *Chargee* which positively set our teeth on edge, without being serious enough to upset us.

The second plot line is even more formulaic. Sir Jealous Traffick's Spanish humour for sequestering his daughter until he can marry her to a Spaniard she has never seen (nor has he) is an old stand-by. His fit over her showing herself on a balcony (24) is typical of the jealous mania many writers make sport of—for example, Crowne with Belguard in *Sir Courtly Nice*. Spanish sequestration was of course a commonplace in Spanish romances: the handling here is more reminiscent of the use of the theme in Wycherley's *The Gentleman Dancing-Master*. In *The Busie Body* the jealousy is so pleasantly exaggerated that it becomes almost purely a joke. When Sir Jealous returns unexpectedly (Marplot fuels his suspicions), Charles thinks of standard remedies: 'can you shut me into no Cupboard, Ram me into no Chest?' The maid replies, 'Impossible, Sir, he Searches every Hole in the House' (31). The loss of a letter, and Sir Jealous's surprising Charles in the house (48) are pretty well predictable, but handled with entertaining fuss and panache. The trick which finally works is one of the oldest in the bag: Charles disguises himself as the Spanish suitor, Seignor Diego Babinetto. Sir Jealous enters, '*dragging in* Isabinda', and abuses the 'perverse Slut' when she objects to the marriage—another formulaic confrontation, carried out here with ironic gusto. Once apprised of the trick, Isabinda is 'all Obedience', Sir Jealous is delighted ('Ha! then thou art my Child agen'), and the marriage proceeds, though, thanks to Marplot, it has to be completed while Sir George Airy holds off Sir Jealous at swordpoint (61–9).

The Busie Body's basis in schemes and frustrations is nowhere more apparent than at the end of the play. Having brought off both marriages, Mrs. Centlivre is content to stop with the merest pretence at a comic resolution. When Sir Francis discovers Miranda's marriage, he is completely unforgiving, snarls 'Confound you all!', and vanishes (70–1). He has already announced that his son 'shall starve first' when asked to settle his estate, but is foiled when he learns that Miranda has stolen papers which prove Charles's right to his uncle's estate—a plot device well used in *The Committee* and many other plays. But the complete lack of reconciliation is unusual. As a rule foiled fathers yield to the inevitable, with resignation if not always with grace. By way of contrast, Sir Jealous does an instantaneous and highly improbable about turn and winds up leading a dance. Having played an exaggeratedly heavy father for four and three-quarter acts, he learns of his daughter's marriage to

Charles, pauses long enough to laugh at Sir Francis's frustrations, and says, 'Come, young Man, seeing thou hast outwitted me, take her, and Bless you both' (71). The only justification given for this complete reversal of character is his bland assertion that 'I always lov'd Precaution, and took care to avoid Dangers. But when a thing was past, I ever had Philosophy to be easie.' Some such recantations are more believable, Old Bellair's in *The Man of Mode* for example. This one is as thoroughly improbable as the father's at the end of Sheridan's comic opera *The Duenna*.

The audience does not, I think, ever get much concerned with the characters. The four lovers are too characterless to elicit more than indifferent good will; the father-figures are too silly to seem really threatening, and we take them as *pro forma* blocking devices. The one character who is more than papier-mâché is Marplot. Oddly enough, both plot lines could easily have been contrived without him, yet he is the most memorable part of the play. His frantic curiosity, good heart, and weakness of intellect make an engaging combination. As Bateson comments, he is absurd, but not contemptible. Like the good soldier Schweik, Marplot is the man to deliver a *billet-doux* to the lady's husband, but he bears subsequent blows and reproaches with aplomb, and we love him anyway, knowing that he has done his best. His character is little developed: we simply watch him produce blunder after blunder. I find him too silly to be really likeable in the fashion of Schweik or Teague, but I have no doubt that a clever actor could make him quite appealing on stage. Apparently Mr. Pack did well enough to encourage a sequel (*Mar-plot*, December 1710), but it lacks the charm of the original.

Certain features of *The Busie Body* betray its period. Nothing approaching bawdy appears, and though sentiment is played down, bits of it slip in. Miranda is quite cautious, and when she pauses to 'reason a little', reviews Sir George coolly. She likes him, believes in his love, and has 'inquir'd into his Character' with satisfactory results (51). When she frets about the seriousness of elopement, her maid reassures her:

O fear not, Madam, you'll find your account in Sir *George Airy*; it is impossible a Man of Sense shou'd use a Woman ill, indued with Beauty, Wit and Fortune. It must be the Lady's fault, if

she does not wear the unfashionable Name of Wife easie, when
nothing but Complaisance and good Humour is requisite on either
side to make them happy. (58)

Such sentiments would be appropriate in Steele, but not in
Etherege, Dryden, Southerne, or Congreve. Nonetheless,
The Busie Body is clearly a laughing and non-exemplary
comedy. Jess Byrd calls it amusing but inoffensive.[1] However,
I would differ from Byrd when he calls the play 'realistic';
I see it rather as fanciful and farcical. What does 'realistic'
mean when applied to this mixed bag of theatrical clichés?
Basically, Mrs. Centlivre aims to amuse, but decorously.[2]

Despite the decorum, we find no didacticism here at all.
Not one of the characters is viewed in exemplary fashion.
Mrs. Centlivre's concern is to breathe life into standard
devices, and as even Dobrée grudgingly admits, she has a flair
for it. An example is her brilliant use of Marplot in the 'monkey'
scene (54–6). Miranda has to hide Sir George behind the
chimney board; Sir Francis enters (with Marplot) peeling an
orange. Tidily inclined, he is about to put the peel in the fire-
place. Miranda has to stop him with the plea that she has shut
up a young monkey there. Marplot is frantic to see it, and is
restrained with great difficulty. Naturally he takes the first
opportunity to investigate, and ... All this is good clean
farcical fun. Mrs. Centlivre knows how to wring comic suspense
and laughter out of predictable situations. Whether there is
really any more intrigue here than in *The Country-Wife* or fifty
other variously designated comedies I doubt.

The Citizen Turn'd Gentleman: 'French' Farce

Ravenscroft's first play (1672) has attracted almost no critical
analysis. Such neglect is quite comprehensible, since the play
presents no significant interpretative problems and no one has
found many virtues in it. Nor is this merely the opinion of
posterity, for the major Carolean playwrights are unanimous
in damning the work (see Chapter 7, below). Notwithstanding
the loud chorus of sneers, Ravenscroft's play was a vast success

[1] Introduction to the Augustan Reprint Society facsimile edition (1949).

[2] She was no theorist, but two epistles in a collection give a fair indication of
her views: 'the main design of Comedy is to make us laugh', she says, and cites
Farquhar's plays as amusing but 'virtuous'. (Abel Boyer, ed., *Letters of Wit,
Politicks, and Morality* (London, 1701), pp. 361–4.)

(probably the extent of the success roused most of the opposition), and hence we can well be curious about the reasons for its popularity. What was the attraction in this hash of debased Molière?

The substance of the play comes straight out of *Le Bourgeois Gentilhomme*, with additions from *M. de Pourceaugnac*.[1] As one would expect, Ravenscroft felt compelled to fill out the characteristically thin French plot line with a gulling story about a country knight, Sir Simon Softhead. The scene is naturally changed to London, but little in the work is made really English—perhaps a significant point, in the light of the considerable part of the play which might be classified as social satire. The critic has to wonder, though, just what Ravenscroft's attitude toward his creation was, and how seriously he entertained any purpose beyond that of producing a delectable piece of entertainment. He affects scorn for the play: thus the prologue spoken at the Middle Temple announces that 'A fortnights sickness did this Play produce;/His sickness was the Bawd unto his Muse', and the regular prologue contains pointed sneers at current taste for low comedies, for 'Playes of Rhyme and Noyse with wond'rous show', and especially for plays of just this sort: 'when the translating vein is past,/. . you must not expect new Plays so fast,/Then Wit and sence will come into request.' This passage is highly reminiscent of Ravenscroft's commendatory verses for Edward Howard's *The Six days Adventure*, published the previous year. In both cases, Ravenscroft's professed opinions seem markedly at odds with his practice. Two other features of the two prologues and the epilogues are noteworthy. The first is Ravenscroft's insistence on his social background. 'From the Court party we hope no success,/Our Author is not one of the Nobless,/. . . Nor is he one you call a Town-Gallant', the epilogue says, perhaps ruefully, perhaps cleverly. The Middle Temple prologue announces that the author 'is one of you'. The second point of note, a related one, is Ravenscroft's emphasis on his play's purity in the epilogue. 'Ladies, our Author trusts in you', he pleads, dubbing himself 'A sober man'; and going on to lament that 'modesty's not much approv'd . . . And is of late so out of

[1] See John Wilcox, *The Relation of Molière to Restoration Comedy* (1938; rpt. New York, 1964), pp. 131–3.

fashion grown', he fears that with even women now debauched, he will have to follow suit. This moral appeal 'to the Ladies' in 1672 is not commented on by J. H. Smith, but is just the sort of thing which, coming twenty years later, he catalogues as heralding the advent of Steele. Indeed, *The Citizen Turn'd Gentleman* is a markedly chaste play. If this was Ravenscroft's bent, he was born twenty years too soon. In any case, he adapted himself to his audience, and in *The London Cuckolds* nine years later he produced one of the most blithely indecent of the Carolean comedies.

Ravenscroft cheerfully caters to audience taste. He never takes much trouble with his plays: they are outstandingly unoriginal even for their age, and noticeably careless in minor details of construction and characterization. Withal, Ravenscroft has excellent theatrical sense, and however crude his artistry, his results are very good fun.[1] More than that, they give us an excellent idea of what the Carolean audience liked to see. For many favourite schemes and devices *The Citizen Turn'd Gentleman* displays clear and unadorned archetypes. Its basic elements can be summarized as follows. (1) Gulling comedy, always a popular type and here forming the essence of both plots. (2) The theme of pretension. This is a key item in a large number of Carolean comedies, and is here put in exceptionally obvious form. (3) Plain farce: numerous laughable episodes have no more necessary connection to the plot than does a custard-pie episode in an old silent film. (4) Extensive use of disguise. Another standard device, disguise can be used to further intrigue, or as here, can serve mostly to further the opportunities for farce. (5) Spectacle. This element is the hardest to judge from the printed page, but very probably the visual impact of Act V was a major factor in the play's success.

In a technical sense, *The Citizen Turn'd Gentleman* presents the oft-repeated pattern of two boy-gets-girl plots. Here, however, the complete vacuity of the romantic characters and

---

[1] Critics often comment on Wycherley's deliberate reminders to the audience that what it sees is the author's artificial contrivance. Ravenscroft too plays such games. He comments on the final plot turn that it is 'fitter for a Comedy' than a romance (107), and deliberately withholds information from the audience with the excuse, as Cleverwit says to Lucia, that 'you shall as in Comedies have the divertisement of the surprise' (12).

the emphasis on other matters make love and marriage a minor and *pro forma* interest. Young Jorden will get Marina, and Mr. Cleverwit will win Lucia, but these plot lines merely serve as formal motivations for all the tricks and disguises. Mr. Jorden ('Formerly a Citizen, but now sets up for a Gentleman') and Sir Simon Softhead ('A Country Knight') are wide-open targets for satiric deflation: most of our delight in the play follows from watching the schemes that are practised on them. Trickmore and Cureal are intriguers *par excellence*, and with Mr. Cleverwit they provide a merry stream of plots and tricks. Some of the pranks are as schoolboyish as stealing clothes while a man is fencing (13–15), or locking Sir Simon in a trick chair to give him a 'doctor's' examination (42–3). Others are more subtle. For example, Cleverwit claims Sir Simon's acquaintance (without foundation), and the deftly handled interplay between assured cheat and puzzled gull is delicious (23–4).

Gulling comedy and the theme of pretension go beautifully together, as many Carolean dramatists well knew. Ben Jonson had used this combination superbly in *The Alchemist* and *Volpone*. In Ravenscroft's play the pretensions expose the two main gulls to ridicule, but both are so preposterous that we enjoy the ludicrousness of their folly more than we take it as a statement of serious satire. That the original audience did not take all the satire on social pretension very seriously is suggested in Downes's report that the critics found this 'a Foolish Play'. The biting edge of Molière's ridicule is indeed gone, but Ravenscroft gets highly diverting results out of his material. We enjoy Jorden's pleasure in 'Doctor' Cureal, who 'does me the honour to let me lend him a sum of money now and then . . . and does it so Courtly and Gentleman like' (27); we savour his inept courtship of Marina, attempting 'love Ala mode, to act like a Gentleman, Ala negligence' (37), or his happy acceptance of Trickmore's explanation that Jorden's father was not a mercer but a gentleman with 'great skill in silks' (73–4). As in Molière's play, Jorden is duped to greater and greater degrees. From giving money to those he believes can get him a knighthood he moves to higher things, and is finally induced to sign away his whole estate and turn Mahometan in order to be dubbed a 'Mamamouchi', highest of Turkish nobles. From the awkward posturing as a 'gentleman' learning French, dancing, and fencing in the opening scene, Jorden moves to the outlandish dress and inflated pretensions of a great Turkish Lord—and then the bubble bursts. Here Ravenscroft departs entirely from Molière, who ends his play with Jorden un-deceived, leaving the rest to the imagination. Probably Molière was wise, since his Jorden, however foolish, is sufficiently humanized for his discomfiture to seem unpleasant. Ravens-croft's Jorden elicits less concern, and the demolition of his dreams is skilfully done. The Turkish chimera having been exposed, Jorden is greatly afraid that he will have to accept 'a pittiful Knighthood' after all—and then that delusion too is destroyed (106). But young Jorden's return of half his father's estate (107) makes a generous and acceptable solution all around. The imposition of a final moral (some fools need 'Experience, and not precept') is ham-handed, but over all the utilization and adaptation of Molière's would-be gentleman is competent and amusing.

The Softhead plot is cruder, and the two plots are messily stitched together. The country knight is here a plain farce fool, and squirting him liberally with 'Glister' (i.e. enema medicine) was the sort of thing calculated to draw sneers from Dryden. But it *is* funny. Indeed the whole play, staged with verve, would be hilarious. The luckless knight is trapped in a trick chair, squirted with glister, forced to disguise himself as a woman, and then made to pay off a 'constable' (Cureal in yet another disguise) for a non-existent 'rescue', and finally married off to a princess—who turns out to be Betty Trickmore, a lady's maid. Hoary devices here abound, but like a rapid-paced silent film the comedy piles on the expected so thick and fast that the audience is caught up in the flood and carried along. The trick marriage with the fake heiress, father and son courting the same young woman, the French valet with an atrocious accent are all commonplaces. The French accent had already been worked hard by Etherege, Lacy, James Howard, and Wycherley, but Ravenscroft gets good mileage out of it. The valet Jaques teaches Jorden lists of words, so he can give the impression he knows the language. Simple stuff, no doubt, but it offers a good actor some opportunities.

Despite the tacked-on moral, the whole play is good-humoured, and Ravenscroft exhibits a cheerful disregard for consistency, which he willingly sacrifices for the sake of a good line. Thus, when Jorden announces his determination to marry Lucia to a knight and she protests, he thunders, 'If you anger me, I'l make you a Dutchess, a Countess at least' (9–10). Similarly, Cleverwit asks if Softhead is a knight; Jorden says yes; and Cleverwit asks if 'He is a fool too?': Jorden replies sagely, 'A little shallow . . ., but that is a blot in many a Knights Escutcheon' (11). Sir Simon is given to *sententiae*: 'Plain dealing is a Jewel' (23) he announces gravely. The interaction of the two gulls (largely of Ravenscroft's own contriving) is amusingly handled. Jorden wants his daughter to grab a title while she can, so brushes aside Cureal's report that Sir Simon will not be much of a breeder, having received inexpert medical attention following a trip to France (52). But Sir Simon is led to believe that Lucia is a loose woman, and he wisely declines to buy 'a pigg in a poke' (64). The pride of the two gulls in their canniness and skill in affairs is well done.

Disguise and impersonation are favourite Carolean devices, and *The Citizen Turn'd Gentleman* employs them extensively. Cureal plays the king's physician and a constable; Betty Trickmore is paraded as 'a German Princess'; Sir Simon is forced to disguise himself as a woman; Cleverwit plays the Grand Turk (with full retinue). A critic so inclined could interpret the whole play as a didactic exercise in appearance and reality, a lesson in the blindness which pretensions induce. To the exegetically minded, a lesson can be extracted from anything, but only a pretty determined moralist would see anything more than a merry romp in this play.

Social pretensions, appearance and reality, and so forth set aside, *The Citizen Turn'd Gentleman* remains a very simple play with little literary merit. Especially in comparison with its sources, it seems a trivial thing. Such a judgement is both fair and unfair. This is not a play for reading: what one can read is no more than the bare bones for a frolic. Take the scenario for a Buster Keaton film, or the script for one of W. C. Fields's or the Marx Brothers' films—and how much literary merit would one find? The appeal of the finished product would hardly appear at all. Critics are accustomed to pay lip service to the gap between text and production in drama, but nonetheless tend to see a play as literature. By this standard, *The Citizen Turn'd Gentleman* deserves its total lack of critical attention. But view it as bare bones, as a vehicle, and suddenly one can conceive it as a thoroughly enjoyable evening's entertainment.

Even more than most farces, this play depends on spectacle. Act V is a real *tour de force*, and the popularity of the Turkish scenes is evidenced in Ravenscroft's retitling the play *Mama-mouchi* (1675 quarto); this was apparently what the audience really loved. The idea is striking: go through four acts in a very plain, English bourgeois setting, and then introduce into the middle of it the most spectacular near-eastern costumes that the theatre could afford for heroic drama. The Turkish mumbo-jumbo, nonsense words, initiation rites, and ceremonial prancing about come to life not at all on the printed page, but are just the sort of thing to which an audience in the right mood can abandon itself. The rest of the play is pretty ordinary French-cum-Carolean farce, but the Act V extravaganza makes a fine dizzy ending.

The critic–reader, looking for Significant Form and Meaning, too easily forgets the possibility of delight in plain scrappy trivia. Pepys's readiness to be charmed by an isolated jig, song, scene, character, or shapely female leg should remind us not to rely wholly on literary judgements of popular theatrical entertainments. By literary-critical rights, *The Citizen Turn'd Gentleman* ought to be a document of coterie contempt for bourgeois social pretensions, but it is nothing of the sort. Ravenscroft produced a hodge-podge of foolery which could be brought to life on stage. Current fashion is to puff the literary skills of a few authors from this time while ignoring or belittling the rest. But I must admit that if I wanted an evening's fun, I would far rather see a spirited production of *The Citizen Turn'd Gentleman* than any performance imaginable of Wycherley's *Gentleman Dancing-Master* (1672). Not surprisingly, this was the verdict of the Carolean audience too.

III. ELEMENTS, VARIABLES, AND THE PLAY TYPES

I have devoted so much space to a few specific analyses for two reasons. First, because I will need examples on which to draw for the present summation, and do not wish to present the appearance of pulling rabbits out of a hat. Second, because

Part II of this book will allow for only very summary descriptions and analyses of a great many plays, and I want to illustrate fully here my fashion of reading them. A return to broader issues brings us to the question how, if at all, we are going to divide, classify, and differentiate between a large number of plays. We need no fancy terms to tell us that *The Adventures of Five Hours* is very different from *The Citizen Turn'd Gentleman*. But almost all critics have felt a need for some sort of groupings.

The basic questions remain. What is this drama like? What is it about? Basically, one must start by accepting the idea of a wide-ranging and untidy genre. If neat groupings existed they would have been recognized long ago. Our proper aim is not to recover a set of non-existent lost types into which all plays might neatly fall, but rather to find terminology and concepts which can help us keep track of a large and kaleidoscopically variable collection of comedies.

The Formulas

Carolean and post-Carolean comedy is formulaic in the extreme. Any real understanding of this drama must begin with this fact. Unfortunately, it has proved exceedingly embarrassing to most students of the subject. But to admit that the plays are about stock characters and situations, and that their structural patterns are few in number, should not be taken as denigration. Haydn is a formulaic composer. There are two excellent reasons for systematically familiarizing ourselves with the formulas. First, the best plays achieve many of their effects by stretching them. Second, an appreciation of the common formulas and character types will actually help show how diverse late seventeenth-century comedies are. Even specialists seem to have remarkably little sense of the points on which one comedy differs from the next. Most of the comedies are built around a plot formula: as in any period, a great number of the plays rely on a boy-gets-girl recipe. Usually more than one formula will be employed, allowing for two or more contrasting lines of action.

Common Plot Formulas

(1) Marriage is the object of schemes and action. The commonest of the formulas is the simplest: male and female outwit blocking characters and make marriage possible. Often

this involves gaining money (*Committee*; *Busie Body*), but some-times not (Young Bellair and Emilia in *Man of Mode*; *An Evening's Love*). Common variants include the man winning the woman over (Harcourt and Alithea in *Country-Wife*; *Love for Love*), or the woman taming the man (*Man of Mode*).

(2) Cuckolding or fornication is the object. Most commonly, male pursues female (Horner in *Country-Wife*; *The London Cuckolds*), but occasionally an amorous, often older woman is the pursuer (*She wou'd if she cou'd*; *The Amorous Widow*), or an ineffectual male, usually a henpecked husband, is a comic pursuer (Sir Oliver Cockwood in *She wou'd*).

(3) Gulling is the object. Usually we do not really want the schemes to succeed, but enjoy all the plots and counter-plots before knavery is exposed (*The Cheats*; the Sir Nicholas Cully plot in *The Comical Revenge*; the Belfond sen. plot in *The Squire of Alsatia*). Occasionally we do favour success, especially when the gulling is at least technically in support of a marriage plot, as in *The Citizen Turn'd Gentleman*.

(4) A marriage in disrepair motivates the actions. Basically there are three possibilities: the couple comes to a parting of ways (the Sullens in *The Beaux Stratagem*); the situation is left unresolved (*The Provok'd Wife*); a reconciliation is effected (*Love's Last Shift*).

Obviously these action patterns (like the character types analysed below) could readily be found in most languages and periods. They simply help to establish some basic categories: the tone and ambience of the four types tend to differ consider-ably.

Rather few plays have a major centre of action not essentially belonging to one of these patterns. Manly in *The Plain-Dealer* is one. As in that case, most of the exceptions are related to characters introduced principally to display their virtues or vices. Sir Positive At-all (in *The Sullen Lovers*) is gulled, but is not introduced primarily to serve as a gull—he is a personal attack on Sir Robert Howard. Sir Fopling Flutter can scarcely be said to participate in a plot line in any way. Lord Hardy (in *The Funeral*) is rewarded with Lady Sharlot, but only incidentally so—he is introduced basically to be virtuous. In such instances plot line almost vanishes, or exists only to show off character. Occasionally a plot line will be aborted, as in

Durfey's *The Richmond Heiress*, where a marriage plot is broken off to make a moral point. Good writers often manage to ring striking changes on standard formulas. Thus, for example, Southerne presents us a *female* rakehell in *Sir Anthony Love*. In farces, plot often serves merely to occasion slapstick; in certain comedies plots nominally concerned with marriage, sex, or gulling really exist for their political import—as in *City Politiques* or *The Lancashire Witches*.

Despite such necessary qualifications, one can fairly say that when a dramatist in this period set out to construct a comedy, he would almost invariably select two or three of the basic action patterns with which to build. The lack of variety between most of these plays is striking: comedies of all ages tend to fall into the boy-gets-girl story, but one certainly sees less restricted and repetitive use of the formula in, say, comedies of Shakespeare, Jonson, Fletcher, and others around the beginning of the century.

Similarly, the characters employed are mostly drawn from a list of types and get fitted together in highly predictable ways. The types are these.

Male Characters

(1) The male lead, and

(2) His friend. The coupling is deliberate. Dorimant and Young Bellair (*Man of Mode*), Horner and Harcourt (*Country-Wife*), Valentine and Scandal (*Love for Love*), Belfond jun. and Truman (*Squire of Alsatia*), Sir George Airy and Charles (*Busie Body*), Don Henrique and Don Carlos (*Adventures of Five Hours*), Young Jorden and Cleverwit (*Citizen Turn'd Gentleman*), Colonels Careless and Blunt (*Committee*) are all paired in this fashion. Very often both wind up married; sometimes only the lead male does (Valentine), occasionally only the friend (Harcourt).

(3) The would-be friend, occasionally just a rival (Sir Novelty Fashion in *Love's Last Shift*), who is commonly witwoud butt, fop, or coward. (Sparkish in *The Country-Wife*, Sir Fopling in *The Man of Mode*, Tattle in *Love for Love*.)

(4) The heavy father. This character is usually the blocking figure who creates the problem which necessitates action in the comedy—opposition to marriage, refusal to give needed money. Jorden (*Citizen Turn'd Gentleman*), Sir William Belfond (*Squire*

of Alsatia), Don Henrique—actually a brother playing a father's role (*Adventures*), Old Bellair (*Man of Mode*), Sir Sampson Legend (*Love for Love*), Sir Jealous Traffick (*Busie Body*).

(5) The dolt or gull. Abel Day (*Committee*), Belfond sen. (*Squire*).

(6) The humour-butt. Generally less purely a 'dupe' figure than the preceding type. Obadiah (*Committee*), Sir Simon Softhead (*Citizen*), Pinchwife and Sir Jaspar Fidget (*Country-Wife*), Foresight and Ben (*Love for Love*)—the latter less of a butt than usual.

(7) The trickster. Often a helper to the romantic lead, but not always (cf. Cheatly in *Squire*). Cureal and Trickmore (*Citizen*), Jeremy (*Love for Love*)—this last a 'bright servant'.

(8) The foolish servant. Teg (*Committee*) is a lovable bungler. Jaques (*Citizen*) and La Mar (*Squire*) are French valets, a popular subtype. Lolpoop (*Squire*) is a country simpleton. Diego (*Committee*) becomes a byword and prototype for the cowardly, amorous, amusing servant.

(9) Professional types: lawyer, parson, doctor. Usually a bit part. Quack (*Country-Wife*), Parson (*Squire*), Trapland and Buckram (*Love for Love*). Tradesmen and Justices of the Peace occasionally turn up in this sort of role.

(10) The hypocrite. The pious puritan fraud is an especially popular form; the type is often combined with no. 4 (heavy father) or no. 6 (humour-butt). Scrapeall (*Squire*) is an instance of the former combination, Mr. Day (*Committee*) is another; Alderman Gripe (*Love in a Wood*) is an example of the latter combination.

(11) The Hector or Bully. A bit part (Hackum in *Squire*).

(12) The lapsed or discontented husband. Loveless (*Love's Last Shift*), Sir John Brute (*The Provok'd Wife*), Sir Oliver Cockwood (*She wou'd*).

Female Characters

(1) The romantic lead, and

(2) Her friend and confidante. A solitary female (Angelica in *Love for Love*) is a rarity. Ruth and Arbella (*Committee*), Marina and Lucia (*Citizen*), Isabella and Teresia (*Squire*), Harriet and Emilia (*Man of Mode*), Miranda and Isabinda (*Busie Body*), Porcia and Camilla (*Adventures*). *The Country-Wife*

is unusual, but even there Alithea and Margery are closely associated.

(3) The scheming maid. Betty Trickmore (*Citizen*), Lucy (*Country-Wife*), Patch and Scentwell (*Busie Body*).

(4) The heavy mother or strict governess. Mrs. Day (*Committee*), Ruth (*Squire*), Mrs. Woodvil (*Man of Mode*)—the last an ineffectual specimen of the type.

(5) The mistress. Lucia (*Squire*), Bellinda (*Man of Mode*).

(6) The cast mistress. Mrs. Termagant (*Squire*), Mrs. Loveit (*Man of Mode*).

(7) The whore. Mrs. Hackum *et al.* (*Squire*), Moll (mentioned in *Man of Mode*).

(8) The amorous, usually older woman. Lady Fidget *et al.* (*Country-Wife*), Mrs. Foresight (*Love for Love*), Lady Cockwood (*She wou'd*), Lady Laycock (*The Amorous Widow*). Often this character is ludicrously conceited, almost a female fop, for example Lady Fancyfull in *The Provok'd Wife*.

(9) The *ingénue*. Margery Pinchwife (*Country-Wife*), Prue (*Love for Love*).

(10) The abused wife. Amanda in *Love's Last Shift*, Lady Brute in *The Provok'd Wife*, Mrs. Sullen in *The Beaux Stratagem*, Mrs. Friendall in *The Wives Excuse*.

Subdivisions and finer distinctions could easily be made, but in this list one can find the basic type for an overwhelming number of the characters in late seventeenth-century comedy. A given play may use no more than seven or eight of the character types (*The Busie Body*) or almost all of them may be employed (*The Squire of Alsatia*). Ten or a dozen is the norm. One must of course remember that there is tremendous latitude for variation in the presentation of each type. Thus the male lead may range from any of several sorts of rake,[1] to scoundrel (Goodvile in *Friendship in Fashion*), to attractive trickster, to penitent prodigal, to exemplary gentleman.

Most of the plays turn on the exploits of the male lead, who is commonly an amiable young man in quest of a wife. Only

---

[1] For a useful distinction between types of rake, see Robert Jordan, 'The Extravagant Rake in Restoration Comedy', *Restoration Literature*, ed. Harold Love, pp. 69–90. Cf. the a-historical but stimulating speculations by John Traugott, 'The Rake's Progress from Court to Comedy: A Study in Comic Form', *Studies in English Literature*, vi (1966), 381–407.

occasionally will a husband occupy this spot. *The Country-Wife* makes trickster Horner the male lead; his friend Harcourt, however, pursues the more usual romantic and marital concerns. The 'friend' is almost ubiquitous. He may vary from an equal personage who goes through a parallel courtship (Col. Blunt) to a distinctly secondary figure (Martin in *The Gentleman Dancing-Master*), but a hero's friend there almost certainly will be. Sometimes there are two of them: Harcourt and Dorilant in *The Country-Wife*; Young Bellair and Medley in *The Man of Mode*. The commonest pattern is to marry off both male lead and friend, though either may be spared. Even in plays with a major marital discord plot, that line of action is mixed with more standard ones. The bulk of *Love's Last Shift* is devoted to a routine romance action: the Worthy Brothers win Hillaria and Narcissa despite the father-figure (Sir Will. Wisewoud) and a fop-rival (Sir Novelty Fashion). Vanbrugh's plot in *The Provok'd Wife* is quite unusual: Constant, the male romantic lead, loves the abused wife and is left frustrated; his friend Heartfree does marry the second female, Bellinda, despite the machinations of her rival, amorous Lady Fancyfull. Like Farquhar with the Sullens in *The Beaux Stratagem*, both writers graft the marital discord plot onto a basically conventional structure.

Naturally the heroine has *her* friend and confidante—often admirably suited to the second male. (If there is no friend, a scheming maid is usually introduced.) The characterization of a female lead is a function of two key points: (a) is she prominent and active, or in the background as an object? (b) Is she a witty jillflirt or a serious moralist?

A romance plot demands opposition to the romance. This is provided by the heavy father (or mother), often aided and abetted by a strict governess (for example, Ruth in *The Squire of Alsatia*). Both roles invite a doubling of types. Thus the mother can be an amorous old woman (*She wou'd*); the heavy father is frequently a humour-butt (Foresight in *Love for Love*) or hypocrite and pious fraud (Scrapeall in *The Squire*).

In its simplest form, the marriage plot demands only these few individuals. Wycherley's *The Gentleman Dancing-Master* is a good example. Male lead Gerrard wins Hippolita against the opposition of her father, a man of exaggerated Spanish humour, and her aunt, who plays strict governess. Apart from the scheming lady's maid, Prue, the only other character of signifi-cance is the rival suitor, a butt with a preposterous French humour. Quite justly, this play has the reputation of being a bit thin: there is not quite enough activity to fill up five acts. The need for fullness and variety dictates a sub-plot in most of the comedies, most often a parallel romantic plot for the second male and female. Thus *The Busie Body*, very similar to Wycherley's play in many respects, moves back and forth between two parallel romantic plots, and never seems to repeat itself or strain to fill space.

If the two romantic lines are run as one plot (as in *The Squire of Alsatia* or *She wou'd*), or if there is only one, variety must be sought elsewhere. In the former case a large group of characters is deployed and an elaborate gulling plot intro-duced; in the latter, the antics of an amorous older woman contrast with the four-person romantic plot. Variety is frequently managed by displaying ridiculous characters on the fringes of the main plot. Marplot[1] and Teg function this way. The would-be friend, witwoud, or fop, is another such 'filler'. If such a figure is much involved in the plot, he will serve as a rival to be triumphed over, and perhaps as surrogate father-figure, as in *The Relapse*. Quite often, the fop is remarkably peripheral, as are many of the gulls, humour-butts, and cowardly servants. Only in rare cases will a humour-butt become the central character and principal interest, as in *The Citizen Turn'd Gentleman*.

To the critic raised on modern views of inspiration and organicism, the idea that these plays were cold-bloodedly concocted and constructed will seem peculiar, probably wrong, and certainly derogatory. It is, however, accurate. The ex-tremely derivative nature of most of the stories, characters, and situations is a clear indication of the way the authors worked. Read Langbaine, Summers's introductions, and Nicoll's long lists of sources and adaptations. Few of these plays are 'original compositions' in the sense most of us conceive literary original-ity. And the sense of filling up a play, deliberately working up a second plot line for that purpose, may seem odd, remote,

---

[1] Marplot is technically a second friend, albeit a humorous butt. He is employed, however, essentially in the capacity usually filled by the loyal but foolish servant.

and over-calculating. Nonetheless, these were the habits of the comic dramatists. Why do Molière adaptations almost without exception each draw on two or more of the French plays? Simply to achieve the fullness considered proper. The same prejudice is revealed in the ubiquitous underplot in tragedy. Dryden comments many times on the awkward necessity of contriving 'variety' for an audience accustomed to it.[1] Without injustice, then, we may assume that an author would quite deliberately set out to achieve variety, and would very often do so by borrowing plots from two older or foreign plays and interweaving them a bit. Such was then the way of the dramatist.

The Variables

Identifying standard formulas and character types helps to define the differences between the remarkably disparate comedies of this period. Roughly speaking, each comedy is characterized by its main plot line. Thus we find marriage comedy (*The Busie Body*); cuckolding comedy (*The Country-Wife*); gulling comedy (*The Cheats*); marital discord comedy (*The Provok'd Wife*). In the case of *The Busie Body* the two plot lines are of the same type. Quite often though, the subsidiary plot (or plots) will differ. Thus *The Country-Wife* emphasizes cuckoldry, but has a marriage plot in Harcourt and Alithea; *The Squire of Alsatia* has a prominent gulling plot. Obviously the character of the play is affected by the nature of the combination and the prominence of the subsidiary parts. Tragicomedy of the two-plot sort is yet another possibility. *Marriage A-la-Mode* combines a pseudo-serious heroic drama plot with one of ordinary comic marital discord; *All Mistaken* adds a fizzy and *risqué* courtship story to one of courtly intrigue. The possibilities for combination of plot types alone give rise to a multiplicity of results.

Some of the best comedies of the period derive freshness from working unusual twists into their plot formulas. Thus *The Country-Wife* is abnormal in two ways. The male lead is a trickster. And the secondary romance plot relies not on external, parental opposition, but on the woman's stubborn blindness

[1] For example in the preface to *Oedipus* (1679).

as an obstacle. *The Plain-Dealer* is even more atypical, importing a melodramatic tragicomedy plot (usually found only in foreign-set comedies) into a London setting, making Olivia and 'bosome friend' Vernish villainous cheats, and running an almost unique second plot—a romance story line in which the hero's true friend Freeman succeeds in blackmailing a widow out of half her money without even having to marry her. Impecunious-male-wins-coy-widow is an old stand-by from the time of *The English Mounsieur* and *The Comical Revenge*, but getting money without widow is a new turn. In *Marriage A-la-Mode* the prominence of a marital discord plot was at the time (1671) quite an innovation.[1] Valentine's predicament, with both father and girl in *Love for Love*, would be hard to find full precedent for. Originality can be found in these comedies, but it is largely originality within a set of basic formulas.

Not only plot patterns and characters are formulaic, but so to a large degree are comic devices, situations, and scenes. Gerald Weales, writing of Wycherley, speaks perceptively of the way in which exchanges between characters 'are as set as vaudeville comic turns'. Such predictability is very natural, given stereotyped characters and stories. A devotee of *Punch* or *New Yorker* cartoons knows how many of them are variations on some particular, and implausible, situations. The tiny desert island, Noah's Ark, the Garden of Eden, and knight rescuing damsel from dragon—all reasonably remote from most of the magazine's readers—recur regularly. So do more commonplace archetypes—boss and secretary, bar scenes, husband returning home late at night to face his irate wife. In both cases, part of our pleasure is in seeing a change rung on the predictable—if it is. Like such cartoons, or films of the Keystone Cops sort, comedies of this period play with clichés. No lengthy catalogue of examples seems necessary, but to identify a few from the plays just discussed may be illuminating.

In Act I of *The Country-Wife* Hero and Friend banter wittily, much of the time with a would-be Friend. The witty and

---

[1] The second plot in *Marriage A-la-Mode* is not really 'about' marital incompatibility. Rather, it suggests that men are so vain and selfish that they will give up a sure sexual conquest for fear that another man will poach on their present property.

wordly-wise exchanges (with or without the third party) are an Act I routine.[1] Similar exchanges between the female leads are a parallel commonplace—or lacking that, mistress–maid exchanges on marriage (Act III of *The Country-Wife*; cf. *The Busie Body*). The mock marriage (as in *The Country-Wife*) or masked marriage is so frequent as to occupy much of a learned book by G. S. Alleman—though its frequency in the social life of the period must have been little more than the intrusion of desert islands into the lives of *Punch* readers. Letters—switched, lost, misdirected—are a routine device, and a clever writer, like Mrs. Centlivre, could ring a neat change on the usual formulas, as she does twice in *The Busie Body*. Mistaken identity, masking, and disguises are ubiquitous: Margery acting as substitute for her 'brother' and for Alithea; Dorimant posing as Mr. Courtage; Harcourt playing Parson; Charles dressing up as a Spaniard (*The Busie Body*); Cureal's and Betty Trickmore's multiple roles (*The Citizen Turn'd Gentleman*). Females in male dress (Margery in *The Country-Wife*) are a favourite, for showing off legs, for allowing a special mode of lovers' banter, and for getting the woman into scrapes, such as having to fight a duel. Dryden's *The Rival Ladies* has a particularly fine specimen of this device. Shadwell uses such a conceit in *The Woman-Captain*, and one supposes that Betterton did so in *The Woman Made a Justice* (1670; not printed). Fidelia in *The Plain-Dealer* is a famous instance.

The love game studied with such attention by John Harrington Smith, itself an elaborate cliché, contains a number of parts, each of which is a special and recognized entity. Two of particular note are the 'proviso scene' (with its greatest embodiment in *The Way of the World*), and the initial encounter, often in a street, with the *badinage* which fires mutual attraction. Triangle situations are a natural for either romance or marital discord plots, and we find plenty of them. Father and son may vie for the same girl (the Bellairs, Sir Sampson and Valentine Legend, the Jordens), a guardian may wish to marry his ward (*Sir Salomon*; Sir Francis Gripe in *The Busie Body*), or the girl's

---

[1] On wit and language in the major comedies see particularly Fujimura and two articles by C. D. Cecil, 'Raillery in Restoration Comedy', *Huntington Library Quarterly*, xxix (1966), 147–59, and ' "Une Espèce d'éloquence abrégée": The Idealized Speech of Restoration Comedy', *Études anglaises*, xix (1966), 15–25.

father may force an unwelcome suitor on her[1]—a tremendously popular device, and one with some relevance to audience reality. In a marital discord play the natural resolution is unavailable, unless as in *The Beaux Stratagem* the playwright is ready to flout the realities of the divorce laws. Whatever the nature of the triangle, the tensions, hostilities, and schemes it gives rise to are a major feature of many plays. In this respect *The Country-Wife* is a good archetype, with its triple triangle, each giving a variant of the same story—an undeserving male loses his woman to another man. The foolish suitor and the old husband are stock elements in triangles: almost invariably we will side against them in the predictable outwitting plot, whether the object is marriage or fornication. The stratagems and mishaps along the way are highly predictable. Meetings in gardens, disguise as singing-master, rendezvous in coffee-houses, the unexpected appearance of husband or father, hiding under tables and in closets, scuffle and sword-play in the dark—such are the turns we anticipate, whether with Tuke's seriousness, Mrs. Behn's cowboys-and-indians fervour, or Mrs. Centlivre's joking high spirits. Everywhere we look, the archetypal devices and scenes appear. Master–servant relations are a fruitful ground, and one capable of considerable variation. The wiles of the clever servant (*Sir Martin Mar-all*), the banter between servant and master (Jeremy and Valentine in *Love for Love*), the well-meaning incompetent (Teg), and the likeable coward (Tuke's Diego) are all recognized norms with which the writer can play. The fourth was especially popular, Davenant going so far as to build (or adapt) a whole play on the idea, *The Man's the Master* (1668).

The point to all this discussion is very simple. Almost any relationship, any conflict, any character, any scene, any reference (from French customs to astrology) can be fitted into a whole tradition of such relationships, conflicts, characters, scenes, and references. And writers and audience were very much aware of the fact. Jokes about the staler clichés make this clear. To hit on a new twist, as in *The Country-Wife* or *Love's Last Shift*, took genius or great good luck.

---

[1] Examples are the second plot in *The Busie Body*, *The Gentleman Dancing-Master*, Young Bellair and Harriet in *The Man of Mode*, Tuke's *Adventures*, *The Committee*, *The Citizen Turn'd Gentleman*, and *The Squire of Alsatia*.

Some indication of the possible variables in comedy has already been given in the discussion of their constituent elements. These variables are almost innumerable, but the crucial ones can be summed up under four headings: (1) plot centre and type. Is a play romance, cuckoldry, gulling, or marital discord based? Does the plot emphasize action, character, or discourse? (2) The setting. Is it English or foreign, and is the social level high or low? (3) The attitude evoked toward lead characters. (4) The method stressed, or the nature of the combination of comic methods—action, satire, wit, humour, example, farce.

The nature of the main plot usually has a strong determinative effect on the play's character. An action leading to marriage gives one sort of atmosphere, one leading to fornication another, bitter marital discord a third. The results can be as far apart as the joyous freshness of *The Recruiting Officer*, the raucous bestiality of *Mr. Limberham*, the gritty bitterness of *The Wives Excuse* or the second plot in *The Atheist*. Such variation is largely inherent in the subject matter: whether we are taken up almost wholly by events, or allowed to concentrate on the persons involved makes a further difference. The breathless rapid-fire action of *The Cheats* or *Sir Patient Fancy* could not easily be mistaken for the almost reflective pace and procedure of *The Man of Mode* or *The Sullen Lovers*. Action is the principal component in most plots. However, its predominance should not blind us to the possible alternatives.

Setting has been a neglected crux. The common impression that drawing-room comedy involves aristocratic characters is far from the truth. Some very significant comedies are not set in England at all.[1] And the number of plays which transact most of their business in drawing-room conversation is extremely small. Save for obvious instances from Etherege and Congreve, one would have to struggle to find any examples. What about social level? Surprisingly few plays turn out to deal with aristocratic society. Lords and knights are frequently introduced only to be ridiculed; a fair number of the knights are actually puritan merchant figures (Sir Francis Gripe in *The Busie Body*), or 'knighted by *Oliver*' (Sir Nicholas Cully in

---

[1] *The Adventures of Five Hours, Marriage A-la-Mode, An Evening's Love,* and *The Spanish Fryar* are instances.

The Comical Revenge), and yet more are obnoxious father-figures (Sir Sampson Legend in *Love for Love*). The male romantic lead is quite unlikely to be titled or well-to-do. The social level of the majority of the principal characters is upper middle class. Our young men and their girls are the offspring of country gentry, modestly well-to-do families, not of Lords and high government functionaries. *The Man of Mode* has the reputation of being a particularly upper-class play; yet the one knight in it is the greatest fool in the work; Dorimant is respectably born but has wasted his inheritance; Harriet is of similar birth; the Bellairs are no aristocrats. Critics seldom note that the Woodvils are living in an orange-woman's rooming house.

Statistics in very rough form may be useful. Of 85 comedies (1661–1709) chosen for success, notoriety, influence, or historical significance, 15 have foreign settings, a small but not a negligible proportion. The foreign-set plays include some important Dryden comedies and the early, influential Spanish romances. They have a strong courtly element: almost as many have genuinely aristocratic characters as have merely middle- and upper-middle-class ones. None of the foreign-set comedies concentrates on low characters. Of the 70 set in England only half a dozen take place clearly and entirely out of London—two of those being very late Farquhar plays. Of the London comedies I count 7 dealing with low characters, and another 7 whose characters as a group seem to verge on the aristocratic—both surprisingly low figures. This leaves 50 basically middle-class London comedies.

Such categorizations are obviously extremely crude. What counts as aristocratic? How does one classify well-to-do puritan aldermen? Most plays have a considerable social spread: what determines our classification? Nonetheless, some basic and useful points are clear. We have to reckon with a significant foreign component, and one with courtly tendencies. A solid majority of the comedies deal with minor gentry and the upper middle class in London, though 'country' comedies, 'low life' comedies, and 'high life' comedies add up to a respectable 20, nearly a quarter of the total. The differences between these types scarcely need underlining. The social tone of a low city comedy like *The Cheats* is a world away from the refined town air of *The Man of Mode*, the country crudities of *The Old Troop*, the more bourgeois country world of *The Recruiting Officer*, the semi-genteel Spanish world in *The Amorous Old-woman*, or the aristocratic *Marriage A-la-Mode*. These are six rather different works, and the setting plays a major part in the variation.

The third major variable, the attitude evoked toward the lead characters, is a crucial matter, and one fraught with difficulties. Are we to 'approve' of Horner? of Dorimant? If we are to debate the usual designations (satiric, exemplary, sentimental) with any confidence, this crux cannot be evaded. Many of the plays contain characters who are savagely ridiculed and humiliated. Almost invariably, they are stock butts—sex-mad older women, jealous old husbands, fops, cowards, puritans. However, the mere presence of such goats does not make a play a satire. More to the point is our response to the male and female leads, except when their roles are played down. Such is the case with *The Committee*: we thoroughly approve of the lead couples, but the result is not on balance a romantic comedy, for other elements loom too large.

The possibilities for reaction to character are basically admiring, *pro, con.*, indifferent, and unsettled or mixed. One can create a romance plot which would elicit any of these responses. In practice, our response usually ranges from benevolently indifferent (*Gentleman Dancing-Master*) to very much *pro* (*Love for Love*). Cuckoldry and gulling comedies are likely to draw negative reactions (*Limberham, Friendship in Fashion*); marital discord plays often produce mixed or confused reactions (*The Provok'd Wife*; *Sir Harry Wildair*). The point really need not be belaboured. *The Twin-Rivals* is essentially a more disturbing play than *The Relapse* because of the sorts of characters employed and the seriousness with which we respond to them. Our thorough contempt for all the characters in *Limberham* or *A Fond Husband* gives these plays a debasement and frivolity to which *The Country-Wife* (on which they were modelled) does not descend. In Wycherley's play, as in *The Man of Mode*, our reactions are more ambivalent. Some of the best comedies tend to elicit mixed responses to their characters, just as they tend not to rely exclusively on action plots. But ambiguity *per se* is no index to quality. *The Lancashire Witches* and *The Squire of Alsatia*, two highly enjoyable plays, are badly marred by Shadwell's slovenly vagueness. In short, though, one can say that the sort of response the lead characters elicit is often the key point in differentiating plays with otherwise similar actions and methods.

Like reactions to character, 'method' (the last major variable) was discussed in the last chapter and so only brief reiteration is necessary. Plays which give marked prominence to one method or another will seem quite different in kind. *Epsom-Wells* emphasizes satire; *The Man of Mode* wit; *The Sullen Lovers* humour; *The Funeral* example; *Sir Patient Fancy* farce. Each employs other methods in varying degrees, but the characteristic feel of each play is greatly affected by the dramatist's choice of a predominant method.

Comedies of this period are as variable in 'method' as in constituent elements. That there are no simple groups to be described is perfectly obvious. At best the critic can hope to locate the combinations popular at any given time. This I will try to do in Part II, fully enough so that myriad variations, changes, and exceptions can be considered. Here I want only to indicate the grounds on which such analysis can be based, and to take up some matters of terminology.

The idea that even just Carolean comedy is a 'drama of satire' is wrong; to say that it gives way to 'sentimental' or 'exemplary' comedy around 1700 is almost as inaccurate. After 1688 playwrights frequently groan about satire going out of fashion and bewail the loss of the good old days.[1] Actually, the Carolean period produces few really satiric comedies. By my count, something like 15 per cent of the comedies dating from between 1660 and 1685 have a large enough proportion of satire to be classified primarily by its presence. This would include such plays as *The Rump*, *The Committee* (borderline), *The Cheats*, *The Rehearsal* (literary rather than social satire), Duffett's burlesques (likewise literary), Wycherley's last two plays (with doubts), *Limberham* (with more doubts), and *City Politiques*. Similarly, the number of plays after 1685 which have a prominent exemplary element is remarkably small. Shadwell's last plays, and Steele's, do so. By about 1710 with a

---

[1] For example, the prologue to *Love for Love*, Rowe's epilogue to *The Biter* (1704), Johnson's prologue to *The Generous Husband* (1711).

writer like Taverner the method is definitely gaining. But the famous example is *The Conscious Lovers* (1722), and one notices without surprise that J. H. Smith's illustrations of 'exemplary' comedy tend to be very late—1711, 1717, 1719, 1730, 1744.

To include Cibber in the exemplary school would be preposterous. *Love's Last Shift* capitalizes on bathos, but it does not give us models for imitation in the manner of *The Conscious Lovers*. Assumptions about goodness of heart become more frequent after 1688, but as many earlier cases of the 'penitent rake' show, the idea was not new. A vaguer concept than 'sentimental comedy' would not be easy to find.[1] Common notions about good or perfectable characters, a moral design, and excessive appeal to pity and the emotions have been shown to be thoroughly muddled and foolish by Arthur Sherbo, who is able to demonstrate that many plays commonly termed 'sentimental' fail to meet these criteria, while others which do fit (including Fletcher's *The Custom of the Country*!) have nothing to do with the usual ideas about the type.[2] The lesson is simple: to discuss 'sentimental' drama as an independent entity in the period 1660–1710 is to give further currency to nonsense. To use the term with reference to the French *comédie larmoyante* and its influence in England in the 1760s is another matter.

Undeniably the tone of comedy begins to change in the 1690s as a new mode rises to challenge the Carolean forms. Shirley Kenny has defined the resulting synthesis as 'humane comedy',[3] a term I have adopted to describe the whole new trend which eventuates in the norms of 'Augustan' comedy. Its writers tend to be benevolists, and a strong didactic element frequently produces 'reform' plots and even overtly exemplary models. One can fairly say that 'satire' plays a larger part in the plays of the Carolean period, 'example', a growing role in the plays produced during its twenty-five-year aftermath. As

[1] For a detailed consideration of problems concerned with definitions of 'sentimental' comedy and its alleged dominance in the eighteenth century, see my 'Goldsmith and Sheridan and the Supposed Revolution of "Laughing" Against "Sentimental" Comedy', in *Studies in Change and Revolution: Aspects of English Intellectual History 1640–1800*, ed. Paul J. Korshin (Menston, 1972), pp. 237–76.

[2] *English Sentimental Drama* (East Lansing, Mich., 1957).

[3] 'Humane Comedy', forthcoming in *English Dramatic Comedy from Congreve to Sheridan: A Collection of Critical Essays*, ed. Albert Wertheim and Philip Wikelund.

Chapter 10 will show, however, even by 1710 'example' is not remotely close to dominating prevalent comic methods. One can see a move in that direction, and a good deal of eighteenth-century comedy does become quasi-exemplary, but a very considerable quantity of laughing and outright satiric comedy is yet to come—including *The Beggar's Opera* and Fielding. Consequently I am unhappy with the tidiness of J. H. Smith's concept of the transition to exemplary comedy. The balance is slowly shifting in that direction, but no more than that, by 1710. Throughout the whole period playwrights have a far more varied set of options than most critics have supposed existed.

The Problem of Meaning

Saying that the plays are about stock situations and characters returns us to the critical broils of Section I. I have been asked (indignantly) by champions of this drama how I can suggest that people read these plays if I find 'nothing in them'. But what exactly should we want to find in them? I read all of them for pleasure and some few of them for their provocative rendering of human experience. Heavy reliance on formulas should not be equated with triviality—and is not in painting, music, and architecture. A formula or stock device may be used imitatively or mechanically; it may also be invested with significant contextual meaning. The sex comedy boom of the 1670s is a perfect example. 'Sex' may serve crudely as a titillative subject (as in Durfey's *A Fond Husband* or Behn's *Sir Patient Fancy*); it may also become an instrument by which the conflict of man's natural desires with society's conventions is illustrated (as in *The Country-Wife*). Nothing prevents simultaneous use of a theme as subject and instrument—as Dryden uses sex in *Marriage A-la-Mode*. But serious import in a play should never be confused with philosophical disquisition. And one must never forget that these works were popular entertainment, and, like the films of today, some are serious and meaningful, many are routine fare. Two questions can be raised: why study the routine fare, and wherein lies the meaning?

The lesser plays need to be studied for an appreciation of the formulaic devices on which the best plays too draw so heavily. Secondarily, they can be read for pleasure, because to anyone who has cultivated the taste, they are entertaining. The problem of 'meaning' is more difficult. When critics of the old school say that the comedies present no problems, no philosophy, no serious values, they are simply wrong. But when post-Knights critics argue that the plays are 'about' philosophical and ethical abstractions, they grossly exaggerate their case. Against this tendency to isolate thematic subjects I would argue first that the demand for profundity is misguided, and second that where serious meaning exists, the critics misunderstand its nature.

How valid is the demand for serious import? Is this the only ground on which the comedy's worth can be defended? I cannot think so. Gilbert and Sullivan remain widely loved, but not because the British navy is mocked in *Pinafore* and satire on the Victorian aesthetes is discernible in *Patience*. Are Ben Jonson's comedies good because they usually have an obvious moral? Who feels that Charlie Chaplin's films are trivial and dull because they lack Significant Themes? Those which do have them—*The Great Dictator* and *Monsieur Verdoux*—have been much criticized; if they are still great films, it is not because of the themes. Marx Brothers films offer an even better parallel. They really are a haphazard assembly of diverting situations, intrigue, facile jest, and contradictory stock sentiments. Serious young lovers, sentimental songs, melodrama, double entendre, farcical mistakes, and plain slapstick are jumbled together in a diverting *mélange*. The mixture in the great majority of these comedies is much the same: they were the equivalent light entertainment of an earlier generation. In both cases one will find 'Comic Truth' as well as sheer entertainment. One will also find contemporary issues, in flashes at least.

Theme-mongering is a pernicious and misguided business. Happily, a few critics seem now to be realizing its dangers.[1] A philosophical disquisition is 'about' abstract concepts; a play is a direct presentation of characters and their actions. I know of no way to prove that a given play is *not* 'about' or 'founded on' a 'quest for reality'—whatever that means. One

[1] See particularly Richard Levin, 'Some Second Thoughts on Central Themes', *Modern Language Review*, lxvii (1972), 1–10, who explodes the practice for English Renaissance plays. His strictures are equally applicable to this period.

can find serious themes implicit in almost anything. The whole problem of good and evil is implicit in every Victorian melo-drama, and one cannot rebut the man who insists that he sees the essence of all Kant, Nietzsche, and Schopenhauer in it. How can you stop a man from importing King Charles's head if that is what he is reminded of? Somehow one must keep things in perspective. These comedies are not (a) literal reproductions of contemporary life; (b) unreal evocations of Cloud-cuckoo-land; or (c) philosophical disquisitions.[1]

The subjects of these comedies are perhaps so self-evident as to be uninteresting to the critic. Taking play after play, the famous ones included, what one finds is simply that stock characters and situations are used over and over and over. In a given play one may well find fragments of philosophy and science, or social problems, or political satire mixed in. Examples are Otway's *Friendship in Fashion* (libertine philosophy and social code), Shadwell's *The Virtuoso* (new science), Crowne's *City Politiques* (Titus Oates *et al.*). And many of Mrs. Behn's plays deal quite seriously with the position of women in marriage, especially 'the misery of enforced marriage'. Such commentary is seldom central to the play, or at all profound. Those critics who have sensitized us to the presence of contem-porary issues in the plays have performed a valuable service; nonetheless, such issues seem to me almost invariably secondary in the over-all impact of any given play. *The Man of Mode* has been an especially popular hunting ground for the philosophi-cally inclined. But as we see the play, or reflect back on it, do we think first and foremost of its 'philosophical ambivalence' (Zimbardo's phrase)? Or do we recollect the vivid characters, the frothy tone of quip and banter, the overt foolery?

The kind of 'background' meaning or significance that Underwood studies does not explain the meaning of the play, but rather tells us something we need to know in order to appreciate it. There is a great deal of 'meaning' in *The Man of Mode*. But the play is not 'about' the libertine tradition; rather, the libertine tradition contributes to the ambience of

[1] Nor are they ethical *exempla*, as Ben Ross Schneider, Jr. has recently maintained in *The Ethos of Restoration Comedy* (Urbana, Ill., 1971). For an account of his errors in facts, method, and conclusions, see my review, *Philological Quarterly*, li (1972), 631–2, and those by Harriett Hawkins, *Review of English Studies*, n.s. xxiii (1972), 209–11, and Anne Barton, *Yearbook of English Studies*, iii (1973), 291–4.

the play, just as the pastoral tradition contributes to the ambience of *As You Like It*. However, to define *As You Like It*'s relation to the pastoral is not to explain its 'meaning', but rather to help establish its context. Similarly *Hamlet* draws heavily on, but is not limited to, a revenge tragedy genre. Contextual study must not be confused with interpretation. We will understand both *The Man of Mode* and its milieu better for Underwood's explication of the background—which is not to say that Etherege was a philosopher, or that his motive in composing was philosophical. James Sutherland is absolutely correct when he says that in the play Etherege succeeds 'in expressing an attitude to life . . . [developed] from seventeenth-century libertinism'.[1] Its meaning is communicated as a vivid sense of experience, not as an abstract proposition. And this is true excellence, true significance, *in drama*. We will find it in *Marriage A-la-Mode*, in *The Country-Wife* and *The Plain-Dealer*, in *Friendship in Fashion*, in *The Princess of Cleve*, in *The Way of the World*, and in many other plays. Such at least is my opinion, but the proof is in the plays, and each reader will decide for himself. I suspect, however, that few will find much philosophy in these plays beyond commonplaces—unless of course the object is to 'prove' seriousness and profundity. Why should serious 'themes' form the basis of a comedy? Shaw frequently has them, but he is often at his most tedious when they are most prominent. To insist on translating seventeenth-century comedies into bloodlessly abstract thematic propositions is a peculiar and unhappy enterprise. If you want philosophy, then read philosophy. The value of the plays, beyond entertainment, lies (as Sutherland suggests) in their vivid communication of complex and not wholly happy attitudes toward life. And they are designed to provide an experience, not a proposition for analytic dissection.

Thus by no means am I suggesting that all late seventeenth-century comedy is frivolous. One may legitimately distinguish between (1) philosophical or idea-oriented comedy of the sort produced by Shaw; (2) *critical* comedy, or 'serio-comedy', in which ideas and attitudes are important, but are not allowed to outweigh action, character, and comic entertainment; and (3) popular comedy, in which immediate consumption is the

[1] Sutherland, p. 106.

entire point—no further reflection is sought, and it would not be repaid. I would place most of Shakespeare's comedies in the second group—and, without claiming an equality for them, many of the comedies of Dryden, Etherege, Wycherley, Southerne, Congreve, Vanbrugh, and Farquhar as well. Their kinship to the majority of late seventeenth-century comedies, pot-boilers in the popular comedy mode, should not detract from their greater depth and significance. The best of them occupy a sane middle ground between Cloud-cuckoo-land and the Deep Profound. Two final points about seriousness in comedy are in order. First, when such writers as Shadwell, Steele, and Centlivre attempt to write comedies of ideas, the results are usually rather dismal. Second, the audience evidently viewed a tragedy or a heroic play with rather different expectations than they viewed a comedy. Generic expectation would not, I think, have led people to anticipate systematic exposition of ideas in a comedy, except in the form of moralizing and exemplary didacticism.

At the outset of this chapter I posed a crucial question: what is the comedy *like*? What is it *about*? The formulaic subject matter has been described. Likewise the great diversity in the tone and character of the plays has been shown and in some measure accounted for. As for what the plays are like, perhaps I may be permitted one sweeping generalization of my own. With most scholars, these comedies suffer from a damning reputation for precious artificiality, a reading mistakenly developed sixty years ago as a defence against misguided charges of smutty realism. But in truth what is most widely characteristic of late seventeenth-century comedies is rousing action, slapstick, *risqué* wit, and above all a boisterous *energy* which is greatly invigorating.

CHAPTER 4

THEORIES OF SERIOUS DRAMA

'RESTORATION theory of tragedy'—the title I am obviously avoiding here—is a vexed subject indeed. Most of the modern critics who have investigated the matter have arrived at fairly derogatory assessments of the so-called 'neoclassic' concept of tragedy, concluding that writers in this period fail to comprehend the very basis of genuine tragedy. And given the heavy emphasis seventeenth-century writers place on poetic justice, one must grant the evident—that they were not thinking of 'tragedy' as we now understand it. Given further that the plays these writers produced are now very much a cultivated taste at best, any exploration of the subject properly begins with the reopening of some very basic questions. How did the late seventeenth-century writers conceive of tragedy? What did they think it should *do*? We need an inventory of the subjects, methods of imitation, and types of effect considered proper to whatever set of modes of non-comic drama we may find championed. That the plays themselves have little appeal for modern taste is all the more reason for trying to comprehend what the writers thought they wanted to produce.

Certain difficulties are evident. One difficulty is how to define the proper scope of the investigation. Critics usually view the rhymed heroic plays of the 1660s and 1670s as a separate and special group, followed by a brief emergence of 'real' tragedy in the blank-verse plays of the later seventies. The pathetic 'she-tragedy' is commonly treated as a third stage, leading into dramatic degeneracy. Thus Eric Rothstein, in his *Restoration Tragedy*, omits all the rhymed plays and stops short of Rowe, making the heart of his subject late Dryden, Lee, Banks, and Otway. This is a valid grouping, but my purposes require a broader focus: I will expound the nature of these subdivisions, but I am looking also for common ground among superficially disparate types. A second problem is simply lack of germane evidence. Especially before the 1690s, English criticism is scattered, derivative, and often seems to be un-related to or to contradict the dramatists' actual practice. The critic is then tempted to turn to later English writers, or to the seventeenth-century French critics from whom their English contemporaries borrow literary theory so freely. Either source yields a gratifying amount of material, but whether it represents an accurate picture of English practitioners' views in the 1670s is much to be doubted. To use the French material is right, but it must be done with caution. By the nineties one has Dennis, a magnificent compendium conveniently indexed by Hooker. However, one must beware of citing Dennis uncritically as a source of orthodox opinion—a few recent scholars seem conveniently to have forgotten that some of Dennis's contem-poraries differed with him on occasion. Yet another difficulty is the tendency of the English writers to parrot pseudo-Aristotelian platitudes which they misunderstand or misapply.

Withal, what emerges from a survey of late seventeenth-century concepts of non-comic drama, despite some large areas of superficial agreement, is the realization that these concepts vary quite considerably from one to the next, and further, that the assumptions which underlie the whole ill-sorted group are so far from our notion of tragedy that to apply the term or make the comparisons it invites can only confuse and mislead us. Misguided these writers may have been (by our lights), but they were not incompetent.

I. CONCEPTS OF 'TRAGEDY': SUBJECT, FABLE, AND EFFECT

Late seventeenth-century *definitions* of tragedy display remark-ably few open contradictions. However messy the practice, theoretical clichés are neat enough. Dryden claims that:

A true definition of Tragedy [will show that] it is to reform Manners by delightful Representation of Human Life in great Persons, by way of Dialogue. . . . Not only Pity and Terror are to be mov'd as the only Means to bring us to Virtue, but generally Love to Virtue, and Hatred to Vice, by shewing the Rewards of one, and Punish-ments of the other; at least by rendring Virtue always amiable, though it be shown unfortunate; and Vice detestable, tho' it be shown Triumphant.[1]

---

[1] 'Heads of an Answer to Rymer' (1677), *Works*, XVII. 186.

On another occasion he supplies a fuller account drawn from authority.

Tragedy is thus defined by Aristotle . . . 'tis an imitation of one entire, great, and probable action; not told, but represented; which, by moving in us fear and pity, is conducive to the purging of those two passions in our minds. . . . I hasten to the end or scope of tragedy, which is, to rectify or purge our passions, fear and pity.[1]

These definitions are typical in several respects—the complacent citation of authority in the second, the assumption of an essential didactic function, the idea of an exalted subject matter, and especially the concern with the response evoked in the spectator. As Rothstein observes, these writers to an astonishing degree define genre solely in terms of effects—one might rather say supposed effects—wrought upon the audience.[2] Dennis can assert that 'Tragedy, according to *Aristotle*, is the imitation of an Important Action',[3] while insisting on the primacy of plot; but he remains much concerned with the moral impression conveyed by that action.

We tend to think of tragedy in terms of a pattern of action, a fall from prosperity to adversity which is the opposite of the usual pattern of comedy. Dryden's contemporaries tend instead to conceive it in terms of subject matter. Edward Howard calls it simply 'the representation of highest passions, and actions'.[4] And as we gather in Dryden's careful distinction —virtue is *either* to be rewarded or made 'amiable, though it be shown unfortunate'—no catastrophe is presupposed. This point is especially clearly made by d'Aubignac, writing in 1659.

[Greek] Tragedy represented the Life of Princes and great People full of disquiets, suspicions, troubles, rebellions, wars, murders, and all sorts of violent passions, and mighty adventures. . . . Many people have thought that the word *Tragical* never signifi'd any thing but some sad, bloody Event; and that a Drammatick Poem could not be call'd a *Tragedy*, if the *Catastrophe* did not contain the death of the chief persons in the Play; but they are mistaken, that word, in its true signification, meaning nothing else but a *Magnificent*,

---

[1] 'The Grounds of Criticism in Tragedy', *Critical Essays*, I. 243–5.
[2] *Restoration Tragedy* (Madison, Wis., 1967), p. 113.
[3] *Critical Works*, I. 31.
[4] Preface to *The Womens Conquest* (1671).

serious, grave Poem, conformable to the Agitations and sudden turns of the fortune of great people.[1]

A tragedy, then, is a dramatic imitation of an *action*—one which may end in 'joy' as well as in 'blood', d'Aubignac goes on to say, 'provided still the Adventures be of Illustrious persons'.

The object behind such an imitation, the critics universally agree, is its moral import. The author is to display what will have a beneficial influence. Thus Dryden, even when jotting notes to himself, says flatly that 'the Punishment of Vice, and Reward of Virtue, are the most Adequate ends of Tragedy, because most conducing to good Example of Life' ('Heads', XVII. 191). Especially after 1688, critics become very fierce indeed about the centrality of the moral. Speaking of Bevill Higgons's *The Generous Conquerour* (1701), an anonymous writer says:

I can't imagine what Moral the Poet can draw from such a Plot: This is the principal Business of the Play, and therefore shou'd give the Moral; tho' he makes the other [i.e. the sub-plot] do it, which ought not to be: The only Moral that can arise from this Story is, to advise us how we trust our Children with Nurses; a very edifying Doctrine![2]

Such moral-mongering was Rymer's method: grant his premiss (as all critics then did), and his conclusions follow as surely as night succeeds day. His sarcastic summation on *Othello* is perfectly sound, given his assumptions.

The Moral, sure, of this Fable is very instructive. 1. First, This may be a caution to all Maidens of Quality how, without their Parents consent, they run away with Blackamoors. . . . Secondly, This may be a warning to all good Wives, that they look well to their Linnen. Thirdly, This may be a lesson to Husbands, that before their Jealousie be Tragical, the proofs may be Mathematical.[3]

Dennis systematizes the same view when he asks if there is 'any thing like a generall morall in the *Hamlett*, the *Othello*, the

---

[1] François Hédelin, Abbé d'Aubignac, *The Whole Art of the Stage*, trans., anon. (London, 1684), Book 4, p. 140. References to this influential, semi-official French handbook are to the first English translation. (Books 3 and 4 are separately paginated from 1 and 2.)

[2] *A Comparison Between the Two Stages*, p. 67.   [3] *Critical Works*, p. 132.

Mackbeth, the *King Lear*, or the *Julius Caesar* in all which the good and Bad perish promiscuously?' He demands poetic justice—a term actually coined by Rymer—and hence insists that 'the very Foundation of a Tragedy . . . is a Fable'— that is, a fable with appropriate rewards and punishments for good and bad characters.[1] The rationale for this demand is religious. 'I conceive, that every Tragedy, ought to be a very Solemn Lecture, inculcating a particular Providence, and shewing it plainly protecting the Good, and chastizing the Bad . . . if it is otherwise, it is either an empty Amusement, or a scandalous and pernicious Libel upon the Government of the World.'[2] Blackmore and Collier come very close to Dennis. Blackmore's preface to *Prince Arthur* (1695) suggests that the representation of the characters'

Impious or their Generous Actions, and the different Event that attended them, was to deter Men from Vice and Impiety, and encourage them to be Generous and Virtuous, by shewing them the Vengeance that at last overtook the one, and the Rewards and Praises that crown'd the other. The End of Comedy was the same, but pursu'd in another way. . . . Tragedy design'd to Scare Men, Comedy to Laugh them out of their Vices.[3]

Collier draws the same parallel between tragedy and comedy, but stresses even more the corrective rather than the exemplary function.[4]

Whether tragedy is to provide a *Model* or a *Warning*, or a combination with distributive justice, was far from clear to these critics. Thus on one occasion Dryden can say: 'In Tragedy, where the Actions and Persons are great, and the crimes horrid, the laws of justice are more strictly to be observ'd [than in comedy]: and examples of punishment to be made to deterre mankind from the pursuit of vice' (preface to *An Evening's Love*). Here we have the Warning school of thought. At other times Dryden insists that 'admiration' is the principal 'delight' of tragedy, implying a Model theory—we are to admire the excellences of noble characters.[5] In retrospect, we

---

[1] *Critical Works*, II. 286.   [2] *Critical Works*, I. 200.   [3] Spingarn, III. 228.
[4] *A Short View of the Immorality and Profaneness of the English Stage*, pp. 156–7.
[5] 'A Defence of an Essay of Dramatique Poesie', *Works*, IX. 11; *Of Dramatick Poesie*, *Works*, XVII. 74. The preface to *Tyrannick Love* (1670), discussed below, gives an overtly exemplary view of the function of tragedy.

find Warning associated with tragedy, Model with what we would now call heroic drama, but so tidy a split does not even begin to appear in the critical terminology and categories of the late seventeenth century. The whole business is complicated by a disturbing vagueness about the connections between play and spectator: the process by which the play is supposed to affect spectators remains unclear. On the same page as a heated demand for emphasis on fable and poetic justice, Dennis can remark: 'I find by Experience, that I am no farther pleas'd nor instructed by any Tragedy, than as it excites Passion in me.'[1] This idea, that *arousing emotion* is the immediate aim of every writer of tragedy, is widespread. Dryden has Lisideius cite Aristotle to the effect that 'The end of Tragedies or serious Playes . . . is to beget admiration, compassion, or concernment' (*Works*, XVII. 35). His own agreement is implicit in his use of the point in defending English plays in the 'Heads': though 'the Plays of the Ancients are more correctly Plotted, ours are more beautifully written; and if we can raise Passions as high on worse Foundations, it shows our Genius in Tragedy is greater' (*Works*, XVII. 189).

Dryden is of course replying here to Rymer's denunciation of English irregularity in plot and poetic justice. Working outward from this dispute, Eric Rothstein divides concepts of tragedy in this period into two groups, *fabulist* and *affective*. Rymer considers that our admiration for God's dispensation of justice in a moral fable is central to the proper impact of tragedy; Dryden concerns himself with an evocation of feeling which he regards as ethically beneficial. This distinction seems much tidier than it is: affective critics almost unanimously uphold poetic justice or some variation thereof, and even so determined a fabulist as Dennis loudly asserts the claims for exciting passion, as we have just seen. Within this tangle are several key concepts in need of clarification: fable, poetic justice, the affective 'ends', and purgation.

The concept of fable is confused by universal agreement on its primacy—but primacy can mean two things. Rymer says, 'I have chiefly consider'd the *Fable* or *Plot*, which all conclude to be the *Soul* of a *Tragedy*'; he explains elsewhere that the other three 'parts' of drama (characters, thoughts, expression)

---

[1] *Critical Works*, I. 200.

are necessarily built upon, added to, the foundation of plot.[1] Dennis takes the same view in the preface to *Iphigenia* (1700). Both are concerned that tragedy should display an edifying providential justice. As Rymer observes of Desdemona's death, 'What instruction can we make out of this Catastrophe? Or whither must our reflection lead us? Is not this to envenome and sour our spirits, to make us repine and grumble at Providence; and the Government of the World? If this be our end, what boots it to be Vertuous?'[2] Dryden's view of poetic justice is centred not upon the internal design of the work, but upon the spectator's reaction. Speaking of Fletcher's Rollo he says, 'Poetique Justice is not neglected neither, for we stab him in our Minds for every Offence which he commits; and the point which the Poet is to gain upon the Audience, is not so much in the Death of an Offender, as the raising an Horror of his Crimes' ('Heads', XVII. 189). But Dryden's real difference of opinion comes in his insistence that the primacy of Fable is merely temporal: one must start writing with the Fable, but the effect of the piece, he maintains, depends more on the sequentially secondary parts of the execution of a design for which Fable is merely the foundation.

The Fable is not the greatest Master-Piece of a Tragedy, tho' it be the Foundation of it. . . . *Aristotle* places the Fable first; not *quoad dignitatem, sed quoad fundamentum* [not on account of its dignity (meaning importance), but on account of its priority]; for a Fable never so Movingly contriv'd, to those Ends of his, Pity and Terror, will operate nothing on our Affections, except the Characters, Manners, Thoughts and Words are suitable. ('Heads', XVII. 185)

Thus Dryden is basically *affective* in his outlook, or so Kirsch, Rothstein, and I have maintained.[3] Nonetheless, Dryden's concessions to the importance of design and poetic justice are sufficient to have misled at least one recent critic quite badly. Anne T. Barbeau actually claims that 'Dryden's chief norm

---

[1] *Critical Works*, pp. 18, 131.   [2] *Critical Works*, p. 161.

[3] Arthur C. Kirsch, *Dryden's Heroic Drama* (Princeton, N.J., 1965), Chapter 1 ('His preference for the writing over the plotting of plays was profound and unalterable'—p. 28); Rothstein, Chapter 1; Robert D. Hume, *Dryden's Criticism* (Ithaca, N.Y., 1970), Chapters 4 and 6. I have discussed Dryden's sense of the subsidiary importance of plot in more detail in 'Dryden on Creation: "Imagination" in the Later Criticism'.

for drama is exactitude and wholeness of design', and that 'it is in the design of the plays that the instruction lies . . . the dramatist shows the "laws of justice" at work in the plot, by dealing out rewards to the virtuous and punishments to the rest.'[1]

The confusing way in which seventeenth-century critics mix fabulist and affective criteria is well illustrated by William Burnaby.

In *Tragedy* we must remember that the End is to move *Terror* and *Pity*, by that motion to *purge* those two Passions. . . . It is a vulgar Error that has mightily obtain'd among our half Criticks, to value a *Tragedy* for what they call the *Language* and *Wit*. . . . But *Aristotle*, the best, if not only *Critick*, measures a Poet's Merit chiefly by the *Fable*. . . . The *Fable*, indeed, is the true Place of *Imitation*.[2]

Burnaby demands plot—but in aid of rousing emotion. Like Rymer, he brandishes Aristotle, who happens to be the *fons et origo* of the whole affective position! Similarly Rapin—whose *Reflections* on the *Poetics* were widely read in England in Rymer's translation—confusingly mingles an assertion of the centrality of moral fable with a primary concern for affective import.[3]

Demands for the primacy of fable and poetic justice are closely intertwined, but the first need not imply the second. Burnaby's heated denunciation of emphasis on character and language does not lead to an appeal for poetic justice. Conversely, practically all critics pay lip service to the concept of poetic justice, regardless of their position on fable. Thus Dryden says in the preface to *Don Sebastian* (1690) that to kill his protagonist off would be wrong, 'for the Learned Mr. *Rymer* has well observ'd, that in all punishments we are to regulate our selves by Poetical justice; and according to those measures an involuntary sin deserves not death.' E. N. Hooker gives a catalogue of opinion on poetic justice: in essence, everyone until Addison claimed to believe in it after a fashion. Addison's denunciation of the whole concept in the *Spectator*,

---

[1] *The Intellectual Design of John Dryden's Heroic Plays* (New Haven, Conn., 1970), pp. 149–50, 155–6.

[2] *The Dramatic Works of William Burnaby*, Appendix B, p. 457. The essay is reprinted from Abel Boyer's collection of *Letters of Wit, Politicks and Morality* (1701).

[3] René Rapin, *Reflections on Aristotle's Treatise of Poesie*, trans. Thomas Rymer (London, 1674), pp. 31, 103.

40 (1711), evoked a heated reply by Dennis—an interesting controversy which really falls outside our subject here.[1] Scarcely anyone would have disagreed with d'Aubignac's position:

> One of the chiefest, and indeed the most indispensible Rule of Drammatick Poems, is, that in them Virtues always ought to be rewarded, or at least commended, in spight of all the Injuries of Fortune; and that likewise Vices be always punished, or at least detested with Horrour, though they triumph upon the Stage for that time. (Book I, p. 5)

Even according to conservatives like Burnaby and Dennis, the writer's object was to induce an emotional response. One wants then to inquire (1) what emotions were to be roused; (2) how they were to be roused; and (3) why they were supposed to be roused. The types of effect sought will be the principal subject of Section III, but a brief survey is in order here. Aristotle is generally cited as saying that tragedy evokes pity and terror. That 'modern' tragedies should do so is a seventeenth-century commonplace: whether other emotions are legitimate is hotly debated. Dryden argues strongly for 'love' as an alternative in the 'Heads', but backs down in the 'Grounds'. Rapin admits that modern French tragedy is by no means limited to the evocation of pity and terror, but he has great misgivings about the employment of love.[2] Concepts which especially interest Dryden (apart from love) are admiration and concernment. The former conveys Dryden's sense of our delight in the greatness of the virtuous hero, and is obviously related to his sense of exemplary potentialities. The latter has been interpreted by Baxter Hathaway as an esoteric replacement for tragic fear; however, as E. N. Hooker observes, all the term means to Dryden is that the audience must identify with the characters and share sympathetically their emotions. Dryden uses the term to indicate *anxiety*, sometimes comprising compassion and fear, often representing fear alone.[3]

---

[1] Dennis, *Critical Works*, II. 18–22. See Hooker's notes to Dennis, II. 435–40, and Clarence C. Green, *The Neo-Classic Theory of Tragedy in England During the Eighteenth Century* (Cambridge, Mass., 1934), Chapter 6.

[2] *Reflections*, trans. Rymer, pp. 110–12.

[3] See Baxter Hathaway, 'John Dryden and the Function of Tragedy', *PMLA*, lviii (1943), 665–73; cf. review by Edward Niles Hooker, *Philological Quarterly*, xxiii

Fear of what, and pity for whom? These are legitimate questions, which I hope to answer in Section III. For the moment, suffice it that these feelings, arguably along with admiration, love, joy, and indignation, were to be roused. How this was to be done is a point on which the critics are singularly vague. One assumption seems almost universal: a skilful imitation would rouse the spectator. Critics then felt free to discuss the technicalities of rules and the regulations imposed by authorities without devoting further concern to the processes and mechanisms by which the spectator was affected and then responded. In a way, this blank is not surprising. We are looking at *legislative* criticism, that concerned with how an author should write. *Explanatory* or appreciative criticism, that written with audience or reader in mind, was in its infancy: not until Addison do we find serious speculation about the processes of literary response. But given the extent to which late seventeenth-century concepts of tragedy rely on affective assumptions, the critical blank is a revealing embarrassment.

All the falderal about 'rules' and imitation really rests on unexamined assumptions about the nature of audience response. All of d'Aubignac's agonies over the niceties of unbroken scenes and the unities of place, time, and action rest on a fatuous concept of realism. And the English writers seem largely to have sensed this. Despite some unease and lip service on the matter, English critics are remarkably negative about the rules. The myth of neoclassical rigidity is still current; nonetheless, Clarence Green is accurate in saying that 'the great majority, for one reason or another, were hostile to the unities.'[1] Rymer and Dennis insist fanatically that improbability and irregularity, especially in the fable, destroy audience response—but as Dryden notes in the 'Heads', an appeal to practice tells us otherwise.

The muddiness of the great rhyme controversy tells us how vague were the writers' ideas about audience response. The serious plays of the time are not remarkable for tidy moral fables; writers wanted to rouse emotion; and as one gathers from plays of the period, the object was attempted more with

---

(1944), 162–3. A convenient list of Dryden's uses of these terms appears in H. James Jensen's *A Glossary of John Dryden's Critical Terms* (Minneapolis, Minn., 1969).

[1] Green, p. 194, and Chapter 9, *passim*.

characters and language than with fable. (Little critical justification for rant can be found in contemporary criticism, but it is prominent in practice.) Thus, as in comedy, we find disagreement about the proper valuation of the 'parts' of drama. (See Chapter 2, Section IV, above.) As we have seen, Dryden argues in the 'Heads' that a fable is merely a foundation which can do little by itself: the power of the play resides in the characters, thoughts, and language. He may well be justifying his own interests and preferences, but his emphasis on language here is one of the few accurate critical reflections of contemporary practice. He concludes, glad to be able to cite authority:

Rapin attributes more to the *Dictio*, that is, to the Words and Discourses of a Tragedy, than *Aristotle* has done, who places them in the last Rank of Beauties; perhaps only last in Order, because they are the last Product of the Design. . . .

Rapin's Words are Remarkable:

'Tis not the admirable Intrigue, the surprizing Events, and extraordinary Incidents that make the Beauty of a Tragedy, 'tis the Discourses, when they are Natural and Passionate.

So are *Shakespear*'s. (*Works*, XVII. 192–3)[1]

The slightly cryptic reference to Shakespeare should remind us that Dryden realized what Dennis grudgingly admits in his *Essay on the Genius and Writings of Shakespear* (1712): 'He had so fine a Talent for touching the Passions, and they are so lively in him, and so truly in Nature, that they often touch us more without their due Preparations, than those of other Tragick Poets, who have all the Beauty of Design and all the Advantage of Incidents' (*Critical Works*, II. 4). One finds over all less emphasis on character and language by these critics than one would anticipate from practice, but here as in the quibblings over fable we can see implicit distinctions which are evident enough in contemporary plays.

Supposing that one wanted to rouse passion, and succeeded in doing so, what use did one make of it? Rothstein rightly distinguishes between *evocative* and *purgative* uses. Dryden serves to illustrate both critical positions. In the 'Heads' he speaks of 'those Ends of Tragedy which *Aristotle* and he [Rymer] propose, namely, to cause Terror and Pity' (XVII. 185). To *cause* pity

[1] Dryden is quoting the *Reflections*, trans. Rymer, p. 116.

and terror—period. To evoke them is regarded as an end
in itself.

More commonly, critics allow themselves a cautiously vague
invocation of purgation. Dryden is exceptionally specific in the
'Grounds', in a passage mostly borrowed from Rapin's
Reflections.

To instruct delightfully is the general end of all poetry. . . . To
purge the passions by example is . . . the particular instruction
which belongs to tragedy. Rapin, a judicious critic, has observed
from Aristotle that pride and want of commiseration are the most
predominant vices in mankind; therefore, to cure us of these two,
the inventors of tragedy have chosen to work upon two other passions, which are fear and pity. We are wrought to fear by their
setting before our eyes some terrible example of misfortune, which
happened to persons of the highest quality; for such an action
demonstrates to us that no condition is privileged from the turns
of fortune; this must of necessity cause terror in us, and consequently
abate our pride. But when we see that the most virtuous, as well as
the greatest, are not exempt from such misfortunes, that consideration moves pity in us, and insensibly works us to be helpful to, and
tender over, the distressed. (*Critical Essays*, I. 245)[1]

This passage represents Dryden at his most conservative:
normally he accepts positive as well as negative example, and
a prosperous as well as an unhappy ending. Most critics are
quite as vague on purgation as Burnaby (quoted earlier). The
author of 'An Essay at a Vindication of Love in Tragedies,
against Rapin and Mr. Rymer' takes a fairly common stand:
the end of tragedy is to rectify the passions—that is, to calm
them by giving them a thorough work-out. The dramatist's
principal aim is to move as much terror and compassion as
possible, and Love (which needs as much purging as pity or
fear) is conducive to that end, especially since it inspires noble
thoughts, and so dilates rather than contracts the soul.[2] This is

---

[1] Cf. Rapin, trans. Rymer, pp. 103–4. '*Tragedy* is a *publick Lecture* . . . [which]
teaches the *mind* by the sense, and rectifies the passions, by the passions themselves,
in calming by their emotion the troubles they excite in the heart. The Philosopher
had observ'd two important faults in man to be regulated, *pride*, and *hardness of
heart*, and he found for both Vices a cure in *Tragedy*. For it makes man modest, by
representing the great *masters of the earth humbled*; and it makes him tender and
merciful, by shewing him on the Theatre the strange accidents of life, and the
unforeseen disgraces to which the most important persons are subject.'

[2] *Miscellaneous Letters and Essays*, ed. Charles Gildon (London, 1694), pp. 161–6.
Authorship uncertain.

typical in its quantitative assumption that the more emotion roused the better, and in supposing that the arousal itself is psychologically beneficial and self-correcting. Even where more than mere evocation is specified, the playwright need do only the same thing: purgation, in brief, is left to look after itself.

This investigation of concepts of tragedy and its function has perhaps clarified certain basic issues, but a great deal remains highly problematical. Tragedy was considered basically in terms of its subject matter, regardless of the ending. On its moral and didactic functions there is remarkably little disagreement. The supposed split between fabulist and affective theories, as Rothstein himself admits, exists more in our hindsight than in seventeenth-century criticism or drama, for 'critics whose general attitude toward tragedy was consistent managed to maintain both of them.'[1] In truth, we have found that both poetic justice (the fabulist *raison d'être*) and the desirability of exercising the passions for their own sake (the affective premiss) are professed by essentially every critic.[2] Despite all this agreement in cliché, certain grounds for variance have appeared. The *purpose* may be agreed, but both in subjects and in the approved methods of imitating those subjects we will find differences of opinion. Even more striking are disagreements about *what* emotions are to be roused by the presentation—an issue basic to major divergencies in dramatic practice.

II. SUBJECTS AND METHODS OF IMITATION

Variations in the subjects of serious drama turn on several issues, particularly social level and *intérêt d'état*, action versus passion as principal topic, the demand for a 'historical' basis, and a division of opinion on perfect versus imperfect characters in drama.

Serious plays, we have gathered, represent the fortunes of illustrious persons. But how illustrious? The prominence of *intérêt d'état* is a key point, as one can tell in comparing *Aureng-Zebe*, *Secret Love*, *Venice Preserv'd*, and *The Orphan*. For Rymer,

[1] Rothstein, pp. 22–3.

[2] Even Rymer, the most determined fabulist, allows that the fable is to evoke 'pitty and terror' and grants the object of '*purging* of the *passions*', though he is frank in his greater concern for making the audience observe the 'harmony and beauty of Providence' (*Critical Works*, pp. 67, 75).

tragedy can function as a school for princes, though basically it does so by holding up an ideal for them to follow.[1] The remoteness of such a representation from the majority of viewers was occasionally seen as a didactic disadvantage. Shadwell, admittedly an interested party, maintains that 'Comedy [is] more useful than Tragedy; because the Vices and Follies in *Courts* (as they are too tender to be touch'd) so they concern but a few; whereas the Cheats, Villanies, and trouble-some Follies, in the common conversation of the World, are of concernment to all the Body of Mankind.'[2] This realization seems gradually to have taken hold around the end of the century: critics have long remarked what seems to be a shift toward the domestic in Otway. Even so, Rowe legitimately claims to be breaking with tradition as he announces in the prologue to *The Fair Penitent* (1703):

> Long has the Fate of Kings and Empires been
> The common Bus'ness of the Tragick Scene,
> As if Misfortune made the Throne her Seat,
> And none cou'd be unhappy but the Great.
> . . . .
> Stories like these with Wonder we may hear,
> But far remote, and in a higher Sphere,
> We ne'er can pity what we ne'er can share.
> . . . .
> Therefore an humbler Theme our Author chose,
> A melancholy Tale of private Woes:
> No Princes here lost Royalty bemoan,
> But you shall meet with Sorrows like your own.

This position is expounded by Steele in the *Tatler*, 172, where he argues that 'our fortunes are too humble to be concerned' about the 'unhappy catastrophes' of princes and 'persons who act in high spheres'. Consequently, says Steele, 'it would be of great use (if anybody could hit it) to lay before the world such adventures as befall persons not exalted above the common level.' When he claims that 'ordinary' men find that 'nothing can relate to them that does not happen to such as live and look like themselves', he is directly contradicting a venerable cliché. That the audience could be deeply concerned only about a man of high station, and would be edified by observing

---

[1] *Critical Works*, pp. 17, 42, 222n.   [2] Preface to *The Humorists* (1671).

him, was a proposition which long went unquestioned. The only real point of controversy about such subjects is just how glorified, magnified, and idealized the hero should be. Until the end of the century, tragedy remains the province of the quality: catastrophe tragedy and heroic plays present princes and generals.[1]

Technically, serious drama is an imitation of a single *action*; in practice, the characters, passions, and language of high life loom large in the representation, as Dryden insists. Even Dennis, the great upholder of imitation of a unified action, can remark that 'violent Passions . . . are the Subjects of Tragedy' (II. 248). Commenting on possible subjects, d'Aubignac analyses three sorts, founded respectively upon noble passions, intricate plot, and extraordinary spectacle. He finds that the plot-oriented play palls on second acquaintance, and so finds emphasis on passion preferable, though naturally he believes the best play will be 'mixt or compound'.[2] But as usual the prominence of passion is evident. What passions were appropriate to the nobility is disputed. 'Love' in particular is a bafflingly complicated matter, and one which as a critical concept has been little studied.[3] Plainly we must distinguish sharply between (1) love as a subject of plots and an emotion felt by the characters, and (2) love as a response to be elicited from the audience. Confusing the two is made easy because Dryden did so. Up to and in the 'Heads' Dryden somehow manages to equate the emotions roused in the audience with those feigned by the actors. Copying from Rapin, he clarifies matters in the 'Grounds', but until then Dryden assumes that if the hero feels 'love', so will the audience. Plainly he had devoted remarkably little thought to manipulating audience response.

Here we are concerned with love as a subject. (Love as a response, considered in the next section, is badly named: it really seems to signify an admiring and generous concernment.)

[1] A conservative like the author of *A Comparison Between the Two Stages*, writing in 1702, could admire Otway's command of the 'Passions', but was bothered by the 'humility and vulgarity of Expression' of characters to whom that vulgarity was appropriate (pp. 97, 101).

[2] D'Aubignac, Book 2, pp. 64, 68-9.

[3] For example it does not appear in Jensen's *Glossary*, although Dryden uses the term repeatedly and significantly.

Should the hero be in love? On this point the critics differ hotly. French drama was full of love, to Rapin's dismay. English heroic drama is equally love-laden, the agonies and dilemmas of the hero torn between the claims of love and honour being one of its principal subjects. 'Love and Valour ought to be the Subject', says Dryden in his 'Essay of Heroique Playes' (1672), which serves as preface to *The Conquest of Granada*. A large number of playwrights agreed with him, and despite the decline of the heroic play, as late as 1694 we find 'An Essay at a Vindication of Love in Tragedies, against Rapin and Mr. Rymer' in Gildon's *Miscellaneous Letters* (described above). But did love unman the hero in a contemptible way? Rymer commends the Greeks for avoiding love-dilemmas: 'Nor did their Love come whining on the Stage to Effeminate the Majesty of their Tragedy.'[1] Dennis agrees, objecting to Pope's showing Agamemnon 'talking as like an Amorous Milksop, as the whining Hero of a Modern Fustian Tragedy'.[2] The author of *A Comparison* approves Rymer's dictum that 'in Tragedy all Kings are presumptive Heroes', adding that 'there ought to be nothing in their Character but Majesty, Terror, Courage, and Resolution.'[3] St. Evremond, widely read in the 1680s and 1690s in English translation, finds love inimical to heroic grandeur: 'let not its [i.e. love's] greatest Favourers believe, that the chief Design of Tragedy, is to excite a Tenderness in our Hearts. In Subjects truly Heroick, a true Greatness of Soul ought to be preserved above all things.' Courage 'softened by Tears and Sighs', he goes on to say, is 'an indecent sight'.[4] Orrery and the young Dryden seem to have found the sight not indecent but fascinating. Twenty years later Dryden has changed his mind, saying that 'Love and Honour (the mistaken Topicks of Tragedy) were quite worn out' (preface to *Don Sebastian*). But whether the spectacle of the Hero suffering the pangs of love was moving or contemptible the critics could not agree.

Turning to the third crux, the call for a 'historical basis', we find an elaborately rationalized compromise. Writers com-

---

[1] *Critical Works*, p. 117.

[2] 'Remarks on Pope's Homer', *Critical Works*, II. 151.

[3] *A Comparison*, p. 64.

[4] 'A Discourse upon the *Grand Alexander*', in *The Works of Mr de St. Evremont*, trans. anon., 2 vols. (London, 1700), I. 198–9.

monly claim the virtues of truth and plausibility by trumpeting
the historical basis of their plots. Thus Settle says 'his Muse/
Had History and Truth for her Excuse' (epilogue to *The
Conquest of China*, 1676); Mary Pix announces her reliance on
'solid History' in the prologue to *Ibrahim* (1696). As Aristotle
says (*Poetics* IX. 6), what has actually happened is more
readily believed than fiction. But to be too 'strictly ty'd up to
the Truth' can be awkward, says Rymer.[1] There are two
reasons for this. A play which records actual events usually
fails to limit itself to a single, unified action, as a good tragedy
must. Dryden has Lisideius criticize Shakespeare's history
plays on this ground, and later does so in his own person.
Dennis makes the same points forty years later.[2] The second
objection to 'bare Historical' plays (Dennis's term) is that
actual history may include what is neither decorous nor poetically just. As Rymer complains, 'in History, the same *end*
happen[s] to the *righteous* and to the *unjust, vertue* often opprest,
and *wickedness* on the Throne'—which is 'a scandal to the
Divine Providence'. And since 'a *Poet* must of necessity see *justice*
exactly administered, if he intended to please', the ancients
found 'that *History*, grosly taken, was neither proper to *instruct*,
nor apt to *please*, and therefore they would not trust History
for their examples, but refin'd upon the History.'[3]

As Dryden puts the point, 'I have neither wholly follow'd
the truth of the History, nor altogether left it: but have taken
all the liberty of a Poet, to adde, alter, or diminish, as I thought
might best conduce to the beautifying of my work; it being not
the business of a Poet to represent Historical truth, but probability.'[4] This is the usual compromise: 'history' will provide
a foundation, but must be tidied up and improved upon.
Consequently the use of history often seems perverse. As Curt
Zimansky dryly remarks, this desire to raise admiration leads
to 'strange history', and often to unrecognizable history.[5]
Remarkably little sense of historicity appears in the English
plays, and even the critics do not pick up French concern
about it until the end of the century. For example, St. Evremond

---

[1] Preface to Rapin, *Critical Works*, p. 8.
[2] Dryden, *Works*, XVII. 36; *Critical Essays*, I. 172, 243; Dennis, *Critical Works*,
II. 5–6.   [3] *Critical Works*, pp. 22–3.
[4] Dedication of *The Indian Emperour*.   [5] Rymer, *Critical Works*, p. 221 n.

says: 'They that undertake to represent some Heroe of ancient Times, should examine the Genius of the Nation to which he belonged, the Time in which he lived, and particularly his own. A Writer ought to describe a King of *Asia* otherwise than a *Roman* Consul.'[1] Dryden is aware of cultural changes,[2] but his interest in historicity seems to stop at accurate representation of the 'known character' of individuals 'as we have them delivered to us by relation or history'; 'it is not a poet's choice to make Ulysses choleric, or Achilles patient, because Homer has described 'em quite otherwise.'[3]

Writers tend to turn to distant history—distant in place or time—to avoid unwelcome restrictions. Thus we see a lot of the Incas, Moguls, and American Indians. Relentless travelogue is mocked by Shadwell (epilogue to *The Miser*, 1672), and more seriously questioned by Rymer and others, partly on patriotic grounds. Rymer's *Edgar* (1677; unacted) he calls 'an *Heroick Tragedy*', written 'to extoll the *English* Monarchy'. Years later, setting up a model from Aeschylus, he comments: 'Were a Tragedy after this Model to be drawn for our Stage, *Greece* and *Persia* are too far from us: The Scene must be laid nearer home.'[4] Granted the outline then proposed for *The Invincible Armado* is uninviting; nonetheless the concepts behind it possess some merit.

Perfect and imperfect characters, like history, occasion debate on the necessity of maintaining poetic decorum. The critics generally disapprove of perfect characters in drama. Edward Howard calls them unnatural and unconvincing, and calls for heroes haughty, rash, or violent in love; but he stipulates against genuinely evil characters (preface to *The Womens Conquest*). Mulgrave tells us the same thing.

> Reject that vulgar error which appears
> So fair, of making perfect characters;
> There's no such thing in Nature, and you'l draw
> A faultless Monster which the world ne're saw;
> Some faults must be, that his misfortunes drew,
> But such as may deserve compassion too.[5]

---

[1] *Works*, I. 191.   [2] See my *Dryden's Criticism*, Chapter 3.
[3] *Critical Essays*, I. 249.
[4] Advertisement to *Edgar, Critical Works*, p. 77; *A Short View of Tragedy* (1693), in *Critical Works*, pp. 89–93.   [5] *An Essay upon Poetry* (1682), Spingarn, II. 293.

This is the usual middle-of-the-road position. Pressure toward faultless protagonists comes from two sources: decorumites and those with an exemplary bent. Rymer says, 'We are to presume the greatest vertues, where we find the highest of rewards; and though it is not necessary that all *Heroes* should be Kings, yet undoubtedly all crown'd heads by *Poetical right* are *Heroes*' (*Critical Works*, p. 42). Dennis elaborates, in a passage which illustrates the difficulties posed by history:

if a Poet is to draw a King . . . [and] if History has given that King or that Captain, any shamefull Frailty, or low Vice, which are unworthy of the Majesty of the one, and of the high Command of the other; the Poet is oblig'd to conceal that Frailty, and to dissemble that Vice. He is not indeed to give them the Excellence which is oppos'd to the Frailty, or the Virtue which is contrary to the Vice, with which they are attainted by History: Because that would be manifestly to destroy the Resemblance. (*Critical Works*, I. 73)

The more impressive call for exemplary characters is from Dryden, though he later backs down. In his heroic period he persistently presents and defends 'patterns' and characters who come close to that category. Thus he defends minor lapses in some characters in *Secret Love* by saying, 'it was as much as I design'd, to show one great and absolute pattern of honour in my Poem, which I did in the Person of the Queen' (preface). The dedication of *The Indian Emperour* defends his attempt to 'instruct . . . by drawing goodness in the most perfect and alluring shape of Nature'. St. Catharine in *Tyrannick Love* he calls a pattern of piety, and he frets over critics' denial that Almanzor is a 'perfect pattern of Heroick vertue', replying that he did not want to divest him of all 'humane passions and frailties'. By *Aureng-Zebe* (1675) he has backed down, claiming only to show 'a practicable Virtue, mix'd with the frailties and imperfections of humane life'.[1] He soon goes further: 'All reasonable men have long since concluded, That the Heroe of the Poem ought not to be a character of perfect Virtue, for, then, he could not without injustice, be made unhappy; nor yet altogether wicked, because he could not then be pitied.'[2] This became Dryden's settled position: we have seen him shift from the heroic to a more conventionally tragic formulation.

[1] Preface to *Tyrannick Love*; 'Of Heroique Playes'; dedication of *Aureng-Zebe*.
[2] Preface to *All for Love*. Cf. *Critical Essays*, II. 184.

In sum, we find the theorists remarkably vague about the spread of possibilities open to the playwright. In bits and pieces, justification for tragedy as either positive or negative example appears, and so (more commonly) does the concept of exercising the passions with concern for a flawed but attractive hero. Two further general points need to be made. First, most writers plainly feel that profound sympathy for a deeply flawed character is out of the question. Rymer goes so far as to say that 'no shadow of sense can be pretended for bringing any wicked persons on the Stage'; Dennis finds essentially evil characters 'too scandalous for any Tragedy'; even Dryden agrees that villains should be no more 'wicked' than 'necessity requires'.[1] (Of course a negative example, such as Nero, may be wicked.) The second general point is simply that, regardless of whether the protagonist is near perfect or markedly flawed, most writers do aim to elicit for him either outright admiration, or compassionate admiration. The idea of celebrating greatness, even a greatness destroyed by an internal flaw (as in *All for Love*), is more common than a dwelling upon evil. Villain tragedy can easily be found (e.g. Porter's *The Villain*, 1662; Lee's *Nero*, 1674; Otway's *Alcibiades*, 1675; Settle's *The Female Prelate*, 1680; Mrs. Manley's *The Royal Mischief*, 1696), and critical warrant for it exists, but it remains secondary in both theory and practice. Exalted subject matter, suitably admired, breeds expressions of heroism, and, later, evocations of pathos.[2]

How best to present the subject matter appropriate to serious drama was as hotly disputed a question as the choice of the subject matter itself. The grand pother over unities and French rules need little concern us.[3] The crux here is a dispute over *raised* versus *natural* imitation, a matter which takes us into quarrels about decorum and rhyme.

Dryden gives us the cliché: 'I never heard of any other

[1] Rymer, *Critical Works*, p. 67; Dennis, *Critical Works*, II. 53; Dryden, *Critical Essays*, I. 248.

[2] Eugene M. Waith, *Ideas of Greatness: Heroic Drama in England* (New York, 1971), pp. 3, 169.

[3] Sarup Singh, in *The Theory of Drama in the Restoration Period*, Chapters 1–4 and 7, summarizes opinions on these remarkably sterile matters. Basically, the rules served as a convenient stick with which to belabour opponents, and as authority behind which to hide. If I underplay them here, it is in the hope of reducing excessive attention to a peripheral subject.

foundation of Dramatique Poesie than the imitation of Nature' ('Defence of an Essay', *Works*, IX. 13). But what does imitation of nature signify? In a survey of Dryden's uses of the concept, Mary Thale finds that 'nature' can mean observed or 'particular' reality; or *la belle nature*, things as they *should* be; or what consistently pleases; or *heightened* reality.[1] Writers generally agree that the subject matter of serious drama should be exalted, and that representation of it ought to be 'selective' in order to preserve unity of action and decorum. As d'Aubignac puts the point:

[poets] are no Historians; they take out of Story so much as serves their turn, and change the rest; . . . The Stage therefore does not present things as they have been, but as they ought to be; for the Poet must in the Subject he takes reform every thing that is not accommodated to the Rules of his Art. (Book II, p. 65)

At the turn of the century Rowe was announcing his intention to 'shew you Men and Women as they are' (prologue to *The Fair Penitent*), but even then support for *la belle nature* remains strong. Thus Dennis says that 'to follow Nature . . . is not to draw after particular Men, who are but Copies and imperfect Copies of the great universal Pattern' (I. 418). Few would have questioned the assertion that 'The Spirit of Tragedy shou'd always soar; Nature is not to be directly copy'd as in Comedy: Every Person in't shou'd wear the Buskin, and talk above the common level.'[2]

But how far above the level of common converse and credible action was tragedy to soar? One view is represented by Rymer: for all his belief in decorum, his insistence on factual probability is ferocious. Contrarily, the young Dryden, defending his use of 'spirits' in *Tyrannick Love*, says that 'Heroick Representations . . . are not limited, but with the extremest bounds of what is credible' (preface). Dryden's desire, ghosts aside, is to do more than represent nature purged of its flaws in particulars; he wants rather to present nature exalted above the ordinary not merely by correction but by active inflation.

[1] 'Dryden's Critical Vocabulary: The Imitation of Nature', *Papers on Language and Literature*, ii (1966), 315–26. For a detailed survey of the evolution of Dryden's views on imitation in drama, see my *Dryden's Criticism*, Chapter 6.

[2] *A Comparison*, p. 60.

A serious Play . . . is indeed the representation of Nature, but 'tis Nature wrought up to an higher pitch. The Plot, the Characters, the Wit, the Passions, the Descriptions, are all exalted above the level of common converse, as high as the imagination of the Poet can carry them, with proportion to verisimility. (*Of Dramatick Poesie, Works*, XVII. 74)

Dryden is determined, indeed, to escape the limitations imposed by reference to ordinary reality. Hence 'Prose is not to be us'd in serious Plays, . . . because it is too near the nature of converse: there may be too great a likeness.' 'An Heroick Poet is not ty'd to a bare representation of what is true, or exceeding probable.' We see here the philosophy behind the heroic play. Obviously its practice was liable to abuse, especially in the use of language to convey exaltation. Dryden himself subsequently backs down, angrily condemning Settle's *The Empress of Morocco* (1673) as 'a Rapsody of non-sense', and admitting in 1681 that 'some Verses of my own *Maximin* and *Almanzor* . . . cry, Vengeance upon me for their Extravagance.'[1]

The differing opinions on imitation, and the confusing swirls and eddies of the debate, are neatly summed up in Dryden's *Essay of Dramatick Poesie* (pub. 1668).[2] The first and third of the debates, usually thought of as Ancients versus Moderns, and blank verse against rhyme, actually concern different parts of the same question—whether Crites's demands for near-literal representation are justified. The second debate (ostensibly French versus English) is postulated on Lisideius's premiss that imitation need *not* be literal: the speakers argue over how much literal restriction need remain. When Crites objects to the use of rhyme, suggesting that it makes the author's imitation of nature unnatural, Neander replies that rhyme helps 'exalt' a play above the level of common converse, which is desirable, since 'A Play . . . to be like Nature, is to be set above it' (XVII. 75). As in this debate, one finds in contemporary criticism support for literalism; for decorum-mania; for representation of *la belle nature*; and for heroic

---

[1] *Works*, IX. 6; 'Of Heroique Playes'; *Works*, XVII. 83; Dedication of *The Spanish Fryar*.

[2] For this reading of the *Essay*, see Dean T. Mace, 'Dryden's Dialogue on Drama', *Journal of the Warburg and Courtauld Institute*, xxv (1962), 87–112, and my *Dryden's Criticism*, Chapter 6.

puffery. One cannot categorize actual plays so neatly, but these are recognizable tendencies.

The concept of decorum has acquired negative connotations, and indeed some remarkable fatuities were propounded on its behalf. Some famous examples are from Rymer, who presumes all kings to be heroes and doubts that a king can be 'accessary to a crime', asserts that 'no woman is to kill a man', and triumphantly concludes that 'Poetical decency will not suffer death to be dealt to each other by such persons, whom the Laws of Duel allow not to enter the lists together' (*Critical Works*, pp. 42, 65). Happily for patriotism, he allows that 'a private *English Heroe* might overcome a King of some Rival Nation'.

But 'decorum' properly understood means two things: (1) appropriately selective representation of a serious subject; and (2) a *style* fitting to that subject. Reviewing 'the Indecencies of an Heroick Poem', Hobbes thus objects both to imputing inappropriate vices to 'great persons', and to the use of language too humble for a court.[1] Hobbes finds vice tolerable in tragedy, but a writer like Dryden (bent on heroic representation) does not agree. Even Dryden can occasionally succumb to the doctrine of subject-decorum, as when he says that 'according to the Laws of the *Drama* . . . *Sebastian* shou'd no more be seen upon the Throne' (preface to *Don Sebastian*). A more telling appeal to decorum is Edward Howard's criticism of 'Scenes, Machins, Habits, Jiggs, and Dances' in 'serious Plays', where, he says, they distract us from the 'Heroick foundation' (preface to *The Womens Conquest*). Most often though, decorum concerns language. A 'raised' style is thought appropriate to the exalted subject matter of serious drama. 'A Poet ought to be careful in his Words', claims an anonymous critic, for 'without a flowing hansome Stile' the whole work, however well contrived, loses its force and appears 'ragged and deform'd'. The same writer is quite typical in proceeding to examine many lines and phrases. One of his speakers says of a passage ''tis low but 'tis natural', only to be rebuked: ''Tis low, therefore 'tis unnatural in Tragedy.' Both thought and expression must be appropriately sublime, not 'too near the level of Conversation'.[2]

---

[1] 'Answer to Davenant', Spingarn, II. 64.
[2] *A Comparison*, pp. 46–7, 48, 74, 98, 100.

Obviously the great rhyme controversy is related to this
set of propositions demanding sublime language for noble
subject matter. The arguments are dreary, over-familiar, and
mostly uninstructive. Following Davenant, Orrery, and the
French, Dryden champions rhyme; Rymer (*Edgar* notwithstanding), the Howards, Shadwell, Buckingham, Richard
Leigh, and a host of others debunk it. The exchanges between
Dryden and Robert Howard have as much substance as any.
Howard finds rhyme preferable in a poem but 'unnatural' in
a play. Dryden replies that a serious play *should* be raised above
the natural, a process greatly aided by the dignity of rhyme—
and then the contestants grow heated.[1]

Allardyce Nicoll dismisses the squabble and the whole
issue as 'of very little account', pointing out that plays which
express heroic ideals are by no means always in rhyme (a
point well developed by Waith); nor are rhymed plays always
heroic, though most of the acted ones tend that way.[2] Arthur
Kirsch, replying, denies that rhyme is 'an adventitious feature',
arguing that for Dryden 'rhyme and figurative expression
were at the heart of heroic drama.'[3] The reason for this
connection is simple: Dryden is looking for a means to heroic
elevation in drama, and he thinks he has what he needs in
rhyme. The oft-quoted, much maligned claim by Dryden in
'Of Heroique Playes' that 'an Heroick Play ought to be an
imitation, in little of an Heroick Poem'—that is, of the epic—
may well be as misleading historically as recent critics have
maintained. Plainly Dryden does draw heavily on Jacobean
and Caroline drama, and on Corneille; hence his references
in 'Of Heroique Playes' to Homer, Virgil, Ariosto, Tasso, and
Spenser may be misconstrued. But Dryden's obvious inclination
to urge the epic analogy on us is an accurate key to the affective
terms in which he was thinking. In the period 1665–72 he
wants to elicit with plays the 'admiration' considered proper
to epic, and so he sets about constructing a theoretical basis for
his inclinations.

Lisideius's definition of a play, which Dryden later claims

---

[1] See Howard's preface to *Four New Plays* (1665); Dryden's *Of Dramatick Poesie*;
Howard's preface to *The Duke of Lerma* (1668); and Dryden's 'Defence of an Essay
of Dramatique Poesie' (1668).   [2] Nicoll, I. 100–2.

[3] Kirsch, p. 22. Since Kirsch and Rothstein (Chapter 2) describe and discuss
these broils in full, I see no need to do so here.

as his own, is set up to evade generic distinctions. 'A Play ought to be, *A just and lively Image of Humane Nature, representing its Passions and Humours, and the Changes of Fortune to which it is subject; for the Delight and Instruction of Mankind*.'[1] Crites instantly objects that this definition is '*a genere & fine*'—is not restricted to drama. Neander is to exploit this loophole. Comparing epic and tragedy he finds that if the heroic elevation of rhyme is suitable to the one, it must be allowed in the other, for

> there is a great affinity between them as may easily be discover'd in that definition of a Play which *Lisideius* gave us. The Genus of them is the same, a just and lively Image of humane nature, in its Actions, Passions, and traverses of Fortune: so is the end, namely for the delight and benefit of Mankind. The Characters and Persons are still the same, *viz.* the greatest of both sorts. (XVII. 75)

Tragedy employs dialogue, while epic uses narration, but both to be 'like Nature' must 'be set above it; as Statues which are plac'd on high are made greater then the life.'

Both the writing and the performance of rhymed plays fell off drastically after 1677. The craze of the earlier period is partly just a fad (Robert Howard succumbed, 'not to appear singular' he says in the preface to *Four New Plays*). But more than that, the use of rhyme reflects an endeavour at 'raised imitation', as Dryden clearly says. To rhyme or not to rhyme was in itself a matter of no great import; its relation to the imitation controversy and the effects designed is altogether more significant.

III. THE EFFECTS SOUGHT AND THE RESULTANT TYPES

What makes tragedy—especially catastrophe tragedy—pleasurable? This question greatly exercised eighteenth-century critics, and is significant, if less prominent, in the thinking of their predecessors. The attractiveness of heroic grandeur is easy to accept, but the fascination of the painful and repellent is less readily comprehended. Dryden, comparing poetry and painting, explains pleasure as admiration for a better-than-life picture:

> both these arts . . . are not only true imitations of nature, but of the best nature, of that which is wrought up to a nobler pitch. They

[1] *Works*, XVII. 15, cf. IX. 14.

present us with images more perfect than the life in any individual; and we have the pleasure to see all the scattered beauties of nature united by a happy chemistry, without its deformities or faults. They are imitations of the passions which always move, and therefore consequently please; for without motion there can be no delight, which cannot be considered but as an active passion. When we view these elevated ideas of nature, the result of that view is admiration, which is always the cause of pleasure. (*Critical Essays*, II. 194)

Rymer, citing Aristotle, provides the broader explanation that skilful imitation is pleasing in itself, regardless of subject: the ancients knew 'that many things naturally unpleasant to the World in *themselves*, yet gave *delight* when well *imitated*' (*Critical Works*, p. 23). Understandably, fuller explanations were sought. Three basic answers found favour. (1) Self-interest is gratified in watching another man suffer. (2) There is pleasure in the sense of one's benevolence in pitying another man's distress. (3) Emotional agitation is pleasurable in itself.[1]

The personal safety of the spectator is described by Lucretius in Book II of *De rerum natura:* 'Pleasant it is . . . to look upon another laboring in distress: not that you take delight in any man's ill fortune, but because you are pleased beholding from what miseries you yourself are free.' Hobbes, tougher-minded, finds essentially that self-love is gratified by our reflection on our own safety ('Of Human Nature'). In direct contradiction of the Hobbesian view, the benevolist or sympathetic school holds that innate generosity rather than innate self-love dictates a pleasurable response to intuitively natural pity. In full-dress form, this theory is a mid-eighteenth-century phenomenon visible in Burke, Hugh Blair, and Kames. One really sees only its beginnings in Rowe, though its assumptions were codified quite early by Shaftesbury, and are incipiently present earlier yet, as in Dryden's view (adapted from Rapin) that the sight of virtue unfortunate 'moves pity in us, and insensibly works us to be helpful to, and tender over, the distressed, which is the noblest and most god-like of moral virtues' (*Critical Essays*, I. 245).

---

[1] The ensuing discussion draws freely on three well-known articles: Baxter Hathaway, 'The Lucretian "Return Upon Ourselves" in Eighteenth-Century Theories of Tragedy', *PMLA*, lxii (1947), 672–89; Earl R. Wasserman, 'The Pleasures of Tragedy', *ELH*, xiv (1947), 283–307; and A. O. Aldridge, 'The Pleasures of Pity', *ELH*, xvi (1949), 76–87.

These audience-oriented speculations are largely irrelevant. Of the former in particular one may ask if ever a dramatist wrote with such a response in view. And the benevolist theory becomes important only in the eighteenth century. By far the commonest seventeenth-century explanation of response to tragedy is the simplest of the group—that emotional agitation is pleasant in itself. Wasserman expounds the Cartesian basis for this theory: pleasure arises from physical stimulation of the animal spirits. Rapin picks this up:

> that pleasure which *Tragedy* may yield . . . consists in the agitation of the Soul mov'd by the passions. . . . When the Soul is shaken, by motions so natural and so humane, all the impressions it feels, become delightful; its trouble pleases, and the emotion it finds, is a kind of charm to it, which does cast it into a sweet and profound meditation.[1]

With minor variations, we have seen this position maintained by Dryden in his call for raising passions as high as possible; in Dennis;[2] in the critic who contributed to Gildon's *Miscellaneous Letters*; and elsewhere. Though more elaborate rationalizations for tragic pleasure were later to be developed, during the period 1660–1710 most writers subscribe to the idea that the playwright's object was to *rouse emotion*—the more the better. Whether the purpose is merely evocative,[3] or technically purgative[4] makes no difference, since purgation is presumed to be an involuntary process entirely intrinsic to the spectator. Tragedies will naturally then vary with the types and mixtures of emotions roused.

Contemplating the types of subject we have seen proposed, one sees a whole spectrum of inherent possibilities.

(1) Virtue may be rewarded: the positive exemplary drama (*The Conquest of Granada*).

(2) Virtue may be shown amiable though unfortunate—

---

[1] *Reflections*, trans. Rymer, pp. 105–6.

[2] For example, *Critical Works*, I. 150 ('Pleasure is owing to Passion'), 264, 338. At times Dennis can also take the Hobbesian view, e.g. I. 165, 361.

[3] Of Mrs. Pix's *Ibrahim*, Gildon says it 'never fail'd to bring Tears into the Eyes of the Audience . . . which is the true End of Tragedy.' *The Lives and Characters of the English Dramatick Poets* (London, 1699), p. 111.

[4] In *The Usefulness of the Stage* (1698) Dennis hypothesizes that when the passions have risen past a certain point, reason automatically intervenes to purge and moderate them (*Critical Works*, I. 150).

also essentially exemplary drama, though with a pathetic tendency (St. Catharine in *Tyrannick Love*; *Cleomenes*).

(3) A 'mixed' character, virtuous but flawed, may survive happily (*The Mourning Bride*) or fail to do so (Shadwell's *Timon*).

(4) Vice may be shown temporarily ascendant but detestable; almost invariably, though, it is finally punished— negative exemplary drama (Crowne's *Thyestes*; Dryden and Lee's *The Duke of Guise*).

We almost never find at any one point in contemporary criticism an evident awareness of this whole set of possibilities. Critics tend to talk about one or two of them in a remarkably myopic way. For example, Dryden can state that fear is roused by an example of misfortune, pity by the realization that even the great are subject to misfortune (*Critical Essays*, I. 245), a formulation which by no means exhausts the possibilities of even types 2 and 3. In the 'Heads', however, we get some sense of the whole spectrum of possible responses—and by implication the relevant subjects—when Dryden champions love, pity, terror, joy, and indignation. Joy is appropriate to virtue rewarded, indignation to virtue unfortunate and vice ascendant. For virtue depressed, or the mixed character in danger, we will feel a mixture of fear, pity, and love—Dryden often terms such mixtures admiration and concernment, as we saw in Section I. To *admire* virtue with no doubt of the outcome; to feel a compassionate and admiring *concernment* for virtue or near-virtue in danger; and to *detest* vice, are radically different sorts of response. All have good critical warrant.

Traditional critical doctrine, often cited in this period, holds 'tragedy' to concern the fall of a good but imperfect man. This assumption that tragedy focuses on the flawed or erring protagonist appears in Dryden's assertion that:

The Pity which the Poet is to Labour for, is for the Criminal, not for those, or him, whom he has murder'd, or who have been the Occasion of the Tragedy: The Terror is likewise in the Punishment of the same Criminal, who if he be represented too great an Offender, will not be pitied; if altogether Innocent, his Punishment will be unjust. (*Works*, XVII. 192)

The limited view here should not blind us to some important distinctions. *Victim-* and *victimizer*-oriented tragedy are very different things. Given the allowability of either prosperous or catastrophic endings, we find still more possibilities. Exemplary, or *pattern* characters with a happy ending are not really allowed for in the victim and victimizer categories. The virtuous character as victim is likely to yield pity rather than admiration: as the century goes on, pathos and pity are increasingly stressed, and thus innocent sufferers like Otway's Belvidera are employed to affect the audience. In the victimizer category we are on more familiar ground: the possibilities are basically villain tragedy or 'high' tragedy—the self-destruction of the good man with a flaw.

So much of the contemporary criticism borrows from Continental essays postulated on the good but imperfect man as protagonist that we may pay too little attention to occasional calls for *pattern* characters. '*The End* of all is to shew *Virtue in Triumph*. The noblest thoughts make the strongest impression', says Rymer (*Critical Works*, p. 111). Dryden's claims in the preface to *Tyrannick Love* (1670) may be exaggerated, but are revealing.

Far be it from me, to compare the use of Dramatique Poesie with that of Divinity: I only maintain, against the Enemies of the Stage, that patterns of piety, decently represented, and equally removed from the extremes of Superstition and Prophaneness, may be of excellent use to second the Precepts of our Religion. By the Harmony of words we elevate the mind to a sense of Devotion, as our solemn Musick, which is inarticulate Poesie, does in Churches; and by the lively images of piety, adorned by action, through the senses allure the Soul: which while it is charmed in a silent joy of what it sees and hears, is struck at the same time with a secret veneration of things Celestial, and is wound up insensibly into the practice of that which it admires.

He goes on to reply to critics who complained of Maximin's blasphemy by pointing out that 'there is as much of Art, and as near an imitation of Nature, in a *Lazare* as in a *Venus*'; that Maximin is a heathen; that the doings of the wicked are recorded in Holy Scriptures, and hence that 'due use' may be made of them in drama; and that this due use of the part of Maximin, 'against which these holy Criticks so much declaim', was a deliberate contrast with 'the Character of S. *Catharine*'. Here we have a perfect instance of virtue amiable but unfortunate, vice detestable though temporarily triumphant.

The varieties of serious drama are best understood by following the practice of the time and referring to the effects sought. Subject and plot structure cannot be ignored but are secondary: the quarrels we have surveyed concerning appropriate subjects and type of imitation can usually be referred to the emotions aimed at. Pity and terror taken jointly are almost invariably acknowledged as appropriate objects. Disagreements centre on admiration, love, and pity by itself.

Admiration was of course a sixteenth-century invention of Minturno's. The concept took root, was exploited by Corneille, and became a commonplace, as in Eugenius's statement that 'the objects of a Tragedy' are 'to stir up a pleasing admiration and concernment' (*Works*, XVII. 30). Or as St. Evremond holds, 'We ought in Tragedy, before all things whatever, to look after a Greatness of Soul well expressed, which excites in us a tender Admiration.' Such 'good Examples' conduce to 'the agreeable Sentiments of Love and Admiration . . . discreetly interwoven with a rectified Fear and Pity'.[1] Note here the usual muddled reference to rectified fear and pity, and especially the approval of love as a *response*. Corneille stresses admiration for *grandeur d'âme* (among other things), but St. Evremond is contemptuous of love as a *subject*. At any rate, we see here the common idea that fear and pity can coexist with admiration. In practice, as modern critics have observed, admiration tends to replace, or drive out, the other emotions. The result is commonly a celebration of heroic grandeur with the audience duly inspired to wonder at and be in awe of the hero. Quite quickly in England there are objections. In his preface to *The Roman Empress* (1671) William Joyner denounces 'gingling Antitheses of Love and Honor' and admiration as inconsistent with the 'chief intent of Tragedy', which is 'to raise Terror and Compassion'. The sense that admiration and couplets belong to the epic genre, not tragedy, is evident in Nevil Payne's assertion that he has written 'A Tragedy, and not Heroick Verse'.[2]

---

[1] 'Of Dramatic Poetry', *Works*, II. 60.

[2] Epilogue to *The Fatal Jealousie* (1673). A similar distinction is envisioned by Dennis, who finds admiration suitable to the celebration of a hero, but inconsistent with the basis and purpose of tragedy—'the Imitation of an Action which excites Compassion and Terror' (*Critical Works*, II. 47).

When admiration supplants the other passions, the result is no longer tragedy in the usual sense. Similarly, when pity becomes the principal object the opposite occurs: the results, instead of being inflated into the heroic, sink beneath the proper level of tragedy. St. Evremond feels only disgust at such works.[1] Dennis grudgingly admits that 'perhaps it is not absolutely true, that the Sufferings of those, who are Sovereignly Vertuous, cannot excite Compassion.' But to take such a subject, he believes, is to 'have mistaken Horrour for Terrour and Pity' (I, 21). Or, as Colley Cibber flippantly observes in the prologue to *Perolla and Izadora* (1706), he has 'neglected . . . tho' much in fashion,/To murther Innocence to move Compassion'. Cibber's sardonic view is substantially accurate: when pathos becomes the predominant object, the means to it generally involve distressed innocence—only disputably an appropriate subject for tragedy.

Following Singh and others one might take the simplistic view that admiration breeds the heroic drama *circa* 1670, while pity (in excess) yields the pathetic drama of *circa* 1700. The two may seem at opposite extremes, antithetical to each other. Indeed, chronologically their heydays are divided by what critics persist in miscalling a vogue for pseudo-Shakespearean tragedy. But in fact, pity and even tears are by no means necessarily inimical to the admiration elicited by heroic drama: quite on the contrary, they can at times serve as proof of noble sympathy and magnanimity deserving admiration. Precisely how then do admiration and pity coexist?[2]

My answer rests on some necessary distinctions concerning pity, taken here as a response, not a subject (it serves as both). (1) We can weep for characters because we are sorry for them. This would be an appropriate response to *The Orphan*. (2) We may pity a hero for his misfortunes while simultaneously admiring the strength and nobility with which he endures. This view is expounded by Corneille in his 'Discours de la Tragédie'. (3) Intense pity may actually be moved by the

---

[1] See 'To an Author, who asked my Opinion of a Play, where the Heroine does nothing but Lament her self', *Works*, I. 329.

[2] Eugene M. Waith has addressed precisely this point in a Clark Library seminar, published as 'Tears of Magnanimity in Otway and Racine,' *French and English Drama of the Seventeenth Century* (Los Angeles, Calif., 1972), pp. 1–22. I am indebted to his excellent discussion.

greatness to which the characters rise in adversity, rather than by the adversity itself.

In the first instance we have purely pathetic drama, a form which is indeed at the opposite extreme from the heroic. In the second we see the kind of mixed response appropriate to traditional 'high' tragedy, though the pity is still the result of our being sorry about the characters' situation. In the third case this is no longer true: our pity and tears are not an expression of our being sorry for the characters, but our acknowledgement of greatness and goodness tested to the utmost. Pity is no longer really a satisfactory term for this response, which is in no way condescending or regretful. Pity in this highest sense is a compound of love and concernment, and it coexists very naturally with admiration: where greatness is unfortunate, the two almost converge.

Confusions here are natural. Pity = Tears = Pathetic drama is a common equation. Yet Otway can say with pride in his preface to *Don Carlos* (1676) that his 'Heroick Play . . . never fail'd to draw Tears from the Eyes of the Auditors, I mean those whose Souls were capable of so Noble a pleasure'. At times what is admirable moves pity; at others the capacity for pity is itself regarded as admirable. Pity, we have seen Dryden say, 'is the noblest and most god-like of moral virtues' (*Critical Essays*, I. 245). When we see a character shed 'tears of magnanimity' we have proof of his nobility; naturally we are glad to be made to feel noble ourselves.

One cannot then make neat equations between admiration and the heroic, pity and the pathetic, and so forth. The various minglings are legion. Thus Rowe in a famous passage grants that 'Terror and Pity are laid down for the Ends of Tragedy' by Aristotle, and offers the opinion that the audience 'should be struck with Terror in several parts of the Play, but always Conclude and go away with Pity, a sort of regret proceeding from good nature'.[1] Here pity is regretful and condescending: we are simply sorry for the wretched characters. As Rowe notes, such a feeling 'tho' an uneasiness is not always disagreeable'; we might say, a bit unsympathetically, that we are content to bask in our own 'tenderness or humanity', and the pathetic drama panders to this feeling.

[1] Dedication of *The Ambitious Step-mother* (1701).

Surveying the major variable factors allowed by contemporary criticism, we find no shortage: subject; action versus passion; happy or sad ending; raised or natural imitation; a whole spectrum of combinations and permutations of the possible responses to be sought. A very rough sorting into the common groups brings, in fact, no surprises: the heroic play, high tragedy, villain tragedy, pathetic tragedy. To these groups, already discussed, must be added at least two more types: so-called tragicomedy, or heroic comedy; and the two-plot tragicomedy. Both require some elucidation.

If tragedy (a picture of noble characters) could end prosperously, and comedy could depict the gentry, the two would quite naturally converge—and did so. *The Adventures of Five Hours* (1663) is called tragicomedy on its title-page, and is clearly in most respects an entirely serious drama; yet it is the beginning of what comes out as a comic sub-genre. Mrs. Behn's *The Forc'd Marriage* (1670) might be called tragicomedy or serio-drama, but belongs to a type which the author rapidly developed toward the purely comic. The heroic play has deep roots in Fletcherian tragicomedy, and with its customary happy ending often technically conforms to Fletcher's definition: tragicomedy is a play without deaths, 'which is inough to make it no tragedie, yet brings some neere it, which is inough to make it no comedie'.[1] The attempt championed by Dryden around 1670 to raise the social tone and seriousness of comedy badly blurs an already nebulous set of distinctions. There is even some French backing and authority for such a move. In the *Discours du poème dramatique*, Corneille notes that the many current plays which deal with exalted characters in a thoroughly decorous way but run them into no serious peril might better be dubbed *comédies heroiques*, rather than (meaninglessly) comedies or tragedies.

The terminological muddle is quite unresolvable. Happy-ending plays which are not heroic in subject and mode of imitation are usually tossed into the holdall of tragicomedy—though not always. (*Elvira*, a very serious play, is called 'A Comedy'.) The term is so vague as to be undesirable in this context.[2] We have nothing to meet the case. Romance,

---

[1] Preface to *The Faithful Shepherdess* (1609).
[2] See Karl S. Guthke, *Modern Tragicomedy* (New York, 1966).

melodrama, and heroic comedy all have about as much bearing as tragicomedy. The promiscuous application of 'tragedy' is quite unfortunate, especially in the largely modern monstrosity, 'heroic tragedy'. This unhappy phrase seems to find its principal authority in the title-page of Rymer's *Edgar*, 'An Heroick Tragedy'—a play which happens to end prosperously. Langbaine does refer to 'Tragedy . . . writ in Heroick Verse',[1] but Dryden and most of his contemporaries speak simply of 'heroic plays', a much less misleading description.

Double plot plays are commonly described, then and now, as tragicomedies. Not all such are so described: *Marriage A-la-Mode* is 'A Comedy'; Southerne's *Oroonoko* is 'A Tragedy'. In these cases the designation seems to reflect the happy and sad endings, respectively, of the main actions. Southerne cautiously calls *The Fatal Marriage* just 'A Play'. The whole question of sub-plots and double plots is untidy. English tragedy customarily required a sub-plot, a second line of action. Discussing his and Lee's adaptation of *Oedipus* (1679), Dryden comments on the difficulty of working in such diversity: 'The conduct of our Stage is much more difficult. . . . Custom likewise has obtain'd, that we must form an under-plot of second Persons, which must be depending on the first' (preface). The common call for 'variety' is the motive here. Practically all critics agree that the sub-plot is tolerable as long as it is related to ('depending on') and properly subordinate to the main one. Even the arch-conservative d'Aubignac approves 'a Play with two Walks', provided that the 'Second Stories be so incorporated into the chief Subject, that they cannot be separated from it', while remaining 'subordinate to it' (Book 2, pp. 94–6). In practice, however, two things tend to happen: connection and subordination sometimes diminish to a vanishing point, and very often the second story is overtly comic. The latter is anathema to d'Aubignac, who approves tragicomedy, meaning a play with a sub-plot, only if 'there is nothing at all Comical, all is grave and heroick' (Book 4, p. 145).

When connection vanishes and comedy enters, the result is a 'hip-hop' play, a stitching together of apparently disparate story lines. As Congreve says in his brilliant epilogue to Southerne's *Oroonoko* (1695):

1 Langbaine, I. 174.

We weep, and laugh, joyn mirth and grief together,
Like Rain and Sunshine mixt, in *April* Weather.
Your different tasts divide our *Poet's* Cares;
One foot the Sock, t'other the Buskins wears:
Thus, while he strives to please, he's forc'd to do't,
Like *Volscius*, hip-hop, in a single Boot.[1]

Critical objections to comic and tragic parts in the same play
are repeated *ad nauseam*, as in Milton's preface to *Samson
Agonistes* (1671), and Robert Howard's preface to *Four New
Plays*: 'mingling and interweaving Mirth and Sadness through
the whole Course' of a play confuses the audience by rousing
conflicting emotions which must cancel each other out.[2]
Dryden has Neander reply by denying that 'compassion and
mirth in the same subject destroy each other'; he defends the
contrast as realistic and conducive to a pleasing variety, and
concludes that it is 'a more pleasant way of writing for the
Stage' than any other known (*Works*, XVII. 46). In old age
Dryden recants, orthodoxly condemning multi-plot plays as
'wholly Gothic' and objecting to 'an unnatural mingle' of
mirth and gravity (*Critical Essays*, II. 202). Playwrights were
conscious of audience pressure for variety. Thus Dryden in the
dedication of *The Spanish Fryar* (1681) announces that he
decided 'to tack two Plays together; and to break a rule for
the pleasure of variety. The truth is, the Audience are grown
weary of continu'd melancholy Scenes: and I dare venture to
prophesie, that few Tragedies except those in Verse shall
succeed in this Age, if they are not lighten'd with a course of
mirth.' Is the double plot tragedy–comedy simply a triumph
of commerce over art and principle? In the same preface
Dryden claims to have 'us'd the best of my endeavour, in the
management of two Plots, so very different from each other,
that it was not perhaps the Tallent of every Writer, to have
made them of a piece'. I would give a good deal to know
exactly what Dryden meant by 'of a piece'.

Serious plays which are not heroic, high, villain, or pathetic
tragedy include 'tragicomedy' of at least three drastically

---

[1] 'Volscius' refers to the famous take-off of James Howard's *English Mounsieur* in *The Rehearsal*.

[2] Cf. Edward Phillips's acid reference to 'that *Linsie-woolsie* intermixture of *Comic* mirth with Tragic seriousness' now 'so frequently in use'. Preface to *Theatrum Poetarum* (1675), Spingarn, II. 270.

different and divergent types: (1) prosperous-ending plays; (2) works with a substantial mixture of serious and comic elements, usually in interwoven plot lines; and (3) split plot plays. For the third type, the 'hip-hop' variety, almost no critical justification exists save brazen appeals to variety. Yet in practice, some of these works exhibit remarkably subtle thematic contrasts and parallels. Despite their apparent schizophrenia, they are very much 'of a piece' when closely inspected.[1] The extreme untidiness of the 'tragicomedy' category is unhelpful, but the sorts of plays it comprises must certainly be treated as serious drama.

Indeed the relation of 'tragedy' to other forms is not nearly as tidy as reference to orthodox doctrine might suggest.

> Comedy (whose Province was humor and ridiculous matter only) was to represent things worse then the truth. History was to describe the truth, but Tragedy was to invent things better then the truth. Like good Painters they must design their Images like the Life, but yet better and more beautiful then the Life.[2]

This theory is beautifully neat, and intensely respectable, but in practice none of the generic boundaries really hold in this period. Some writers, especially Dryden, were anxious to exploit the 'great affinity' between tragedy and epic. The tendency to meld the two appears clearly already in Hobbes's account of the 'three sorts of Poesy':

> The Heroique Poem narrative ... is called an *Epique Poem*. The Heroique Poem Dramatique is *Tragedy*. The Scommatique Narrative is *Satyre*, Dramatique is *Comedy*. The Pastorall narrative is called simply *Pastorall*, anciently *Bucolique*; the same Dramatique, *Pastorall Comedy*. The Figure therefore of an Epique Poem and of a Tragedy ought to be the same, for they differ no more but in that they are pronounced by one or many Persons.[3]

On the one hand the drive toward epic produces a distinctive heroic drama; on the other, the popularity of the various tragicomedy forms and an inclination toward *comédie heroique*

---

[1] See, for example, Eric Rothstein's analysis of *Oroonoko*, *Restoration Tragedy*, pp. 146–7. For a useful survey of the potentialities of the multiple plot as it was exploited earlier in the century, see Richard Levin, *The Multiple Plot in English Renaissance Drama* (Chicago, 1971).

[2] Rymer, *Critical Works*, pp. 31–2.

[3] 'Answer to Davenant', Spingarn, II. 55. 'Scommatic' means gibing or scoffing.

produce an extensive body of serious plays which are by any usual concept non-tragic. Both the heroic and the tragicomic plays are 'elevated by passions or high concernments',[1] but their claim to 'tragedy' status is a function of subject matter, and says nothing about the pattern of action they present. Despite the predominance of traditional (and often simply derivative) criticism stressing pity and fear and the fall of the flawed but good protagonist, serious drama in practice is far more varied, and at least in bits and pieces and hints, we can see the justifications established for the other types. Late seventeenth-century critics tend to conceive genre in affective terms. Returning to the basic question, one asks: what does 'tragedy' *do*? The answer was simple: rouse emotion. What emotion? A writer had his choice. Admiration, love, terror, pity, joy, and indignation were all possibilities. Deployed singly or together they offer an almost infinite variety of emphases and combinations which add up in practice to several very disparate sorts of serious drama.

[1]Dryden, *Works*, XVII. 61.

CHAPTER 5

THE VARIETIES OF SERIOUS DRAMA

THE serious plays suffer less than do the comedies from a bewildering welter of violent critical disagreements. In attempting to convey the nature of the plays, and in particular to insist upon the considerable spread of possibilities in form and effect open to the playwright, I should perhaps beg indulgence for again thumping the tub of diversity. To a distressing number of specialists, however, as to most of those less informed, late seventeenth-century drama has seemed 'positively schizophrenic', hopelessly split between two 'implacably opposed forms, Restoration comedy and tragedy'.[1] But just as *The Way of the World* is no essence for all comedy, *The Conquest of Granada* is no essence for all heroic drama, and certainly not for the majority of serious plays. Some illustration of the most common types is then in order: they range from the straight heroic and villain tragedy, to high tragedy, the pathetic, the various sorts of 'tragicomedy', the operatic spectacular, and the plays which turn on history and politics. Fairly short accounts of single plays should suffice. Interpretative disagreements here are straightforward; some, however, are basic and unresolved—largely those concerning the heroic plays. Are the best of these works frivolous and empty, or are they profound intellectual disquisitions? Are they escapist fantasy or important social and political commentary? Are they self-satiric by design, or serious assertions of what they avowedly preach?

I. TWO CRUXES: INTELLECTUAL DESIGN AND SATIRE

Two general questions have worried students of the heroic plays. First, why did the audience like this drama? Second, are these plays what they seem? The first obviously turns on the second; dissatisfaction with the apparent character of the serious plays has led to critical revaluations suggesting that

---

[1] My example is from Anne Righter's witty and useful essay, 'Heroic Tragedy', in *Restoration Theatre*, ed. Brown and Harris, pp. 135–57.

traditional views have missed profundities or satiric complexities which both excuse and explain a taste for this drama. The possibilities are interesting: but can such a case really be made?

The rant and bombast, exotic settings and fancy scenery, poetic justice and orthodox moralizing common in some types of serious drama have usually repelled modern critics. Even Dryden, complains Clifford Leech, wrote 'only plays in which orthodox belief provided the framework and heroes were held up for imitation'—a depressing contrast to the searing agonies of Jacobean tragedy.[1] Considering the 'tragedy' more broadly, Anne Righter finds it 'less serious' than contemporary comedy; 'essentially frivolous'; and suggests that employment of 'the traditional accoutrements of Tragedy . . . bestowed the illusion of form upon a great emptiness'.[2] Such complaints represent majority opinion. We should note though that two separate grounds for condemnation are commonly and invalidly conjoined: one can grant the absence of the Shakespearean or Jacobean tragic outlook without necessarily implying triviality or intellectual vacuity. 'Orthodox' Dryden may be in many respects, but then so are Hooker and Milton, and who accuses them of triviality and vacuity? To look for 'the tragic sense' in this drama is a waste of time; to ask how serious and substantial the plays are is another matter entirely.

Are heroic plays the empty hodge-podges of rant and show for which they are often taken? D. W. Jefferson, for example, states flatly that '*Aurengzebe*, and the other works of the rhymed heroic play type, have no serious content.'[3] Naturally the proprietary vested interest of specialists has produced a series of justifications and excuses, especially for Dryden. One group has regarded the plays as subtle studies in anti-naturalistic concepts of heroic love and honour[4]—issues undeniably present, but which have seemed indescribably tedious and trivial

[1] 'Restoration Tragedy: A Reconsideration', *Durham University Journal*, n.s. xi (1950), 106–15.

[2] 'Heroic Tragedy', p. 135.

[3] ' "All, all of a piece throughout": Thoughts on Dryden's Dramatic Poetry', *Restoration Theatre*, p. 165.

[4] See especially Scott C. Osborn, 'Heroical Love in Dryden's Heroic Drama', *PMLA*, lxxiii (1958), 480–90; and Jean Gagen, 'Love and Honor in Dryden's Heroic Plays', *PMLA*, lxxvii (1962), 208–20.

to most readers. Another school of thought considers the plays explorations of heroism in a basically psychological sense.[1] This view is accurate, and covers a larger part of the plays than the straight love and honour interpretation—but to defend the plays as psychological studies invites comparison with other character-oriented drama, including Shakespeare, Webster, and Ford. In truth, if the heroic plays were designed as exercises in character analysis, they are second rate and worse, for most of the heroes, even Dryden's, are artificial, simplistic, and, as people, quite uninteresting. Can a better argument for these plays—or some of them—be made?

Anne T. Barbeau has recently claimed at length that 'beneath the surface of a conventional plot' and love story, Dryden produces 'plays of ideas', 'essentially concerned with man's proper role in the state'. 'Characters in these works are without nuances or ambiguity but are simply the best or most efficient means of expressing certain concepts.' Coupled with outstandingly clear analyses of the internal designs of five of Dryden's plays, this interpretation has some attractions. To abandon strained critical fascination with the *précieuse* elements is welcome. To admit that Dryden's characters 'generally represent only fragments of a whole man' saves defending the psychological profundity of what will not stand comparison with Jacobean drama.[2] The suggestion that we have gone looking for subjects and import that may be found elsewhere but not here, and so missed the real nature of the plays, might explain a lot. As argued by Barbeau, however, the case seems both exaggerated and one-sided.[3] Is it true that 'Dryden's audience welcomed his lucid, low-keyed, dispassionate disquisitions on man as a moral and political creature' (p. 11)? The heroic plays were popular, but who, then or now, has

---

[1] Much the best such study is Arthur C. Kirsch's *Dryden's Heroic Drama*. See also John Winterbottom, 'The Development of the Hero in Dryden's Tragedies', *Journal of English and Germanic Philology*, lii (1953), 161–73, who sees 'a movement away from the hero as social iconoclast toward the hero as embodiment of a social ideal'; and Selma Assir Zebouni's unreliable *Dryden: A Study in Heroic Characterization* (Baton Rouge, La., 1965).

[2] *The Intellectual Design of John Dryden's Heroic Plays*, esp. pp. 2, 3, 4, 5, 8, 11.

[3] Barbeau's book has stimulated vigorous but not hostile criticism in some very pointed reviews. See A. H. Scouten, *Philological Quarterly*, l (1971), 422–3; Eric Rothstein, *Journal of English and Germanic Philology*, lxx (1971), 157–61; George Falle, *Eighteenth-Century Studies*, v (1972), 480–4.

found them low-keyed and dispassionate? To call Dryden a Shavian dramatist (p. 9) suggests, and is explicitly meant to suggest, that his plays are first and foremost philosophical and political disquisitions. One would seldom suspect, reading Barbeau's analyses, that she is discussing plays. Reading contemporary diaries, letters, and criticism one finds constant reference to extravagant language and fabulous scenery, plenty of comments on super-heroes, *précieuse* sentiment, morality, and verse form—but very little on the intellectual import of the plays. The extreme dearth of such commentary (Barbeau cites none) suggests that people did not think of plays in this way.

Entirely to ignore spectacle, rant, and the obvious subjects of the plays is misguided. As Scouten observes, Buckingham did not write *The Rehearsal* because he disliked Dryden's moral philosophy. Barbeau is prepared to dismiss the 'surface' of Dryden's plays as merely 'a disguise rather than an indication of what the play is really about' (p. 21). Why Dryden should employ such disguise we are not told; whether other plays and playwrights exhibit the same intellectual aims is never discussed. But the unsatisfactoriness of Barbeau's position as she has left it must not obscure the virtues of her ideas. Is there perhaps a substratum of political and moral philosophy in Dryden's plays?

The question can be resolved only by reference to the plays themselves. Here I am concerned only with the theoretical viability of the proposition and its possible implications. Prima facie, the idea is at least plausible, once removed from Barbeau's strident exaggerations, exclusions, and dismissal of previous critics. Dryden's feelings about monarchy, authority, public and private morals were strong, as the 1680s were to prove. Intellectually, religiously, and politically he is now seen to be vastly more consistent and of a piece than earlier critics realized: it would be odd indeed if such convictions were not deeply embodied in the heroic plays, given their 'surface' subjects. Dryden's conservative view of monarchical authority emerges clearly enough, as do the lessons at the end of each play: the exciting criminals fall, and the exemplary characters are rewarded. Exemplary need not mean perfect; as with Almanzor, a balance must be struck between internal impulse and external authority. Contrariwise, an Ozmyn must find the same balance, but starting from the opposite extreme—undue dependence on authority. Much of the internal design of Dryden's heroic plays concerns contrasts of various characters with reference to the demands of the state.

Several questions seem apposite. Do other playwrights entertain such intellectual purposes? Are the ideas conveyed more than utter commonplaces? Why is the *sentence* so buried in *solas*? The first question is easily answered—they do, though not invariably so. For the second, one may ask if viable stage plays are the place for profound and original philosophy. What comes across from Dryden, Orrery, or Lee is intellectually suggestive, but is seldom systematic philosophy. And for the third, rejecting Barbeau's desire to find formal treatises, we may say that to ignore the obvious surface is as stupid as ignoring the obvious substance. But *is* the substance obvious? Perhaps not in the ways that modern readers expect.

John Wallace has recently called in doubt some basic assumptions about the way seventeenth-century readers and audiences were expected to respond to works with what he calls a 'historical' basis.[1] We are, he suggests, both 'too cautious' in exploring the historical relevance of a work, and 'too quick' to seize on merely topical 'allegories'. We tend to misread historically founded works because we ignore the capacity for extrapolation—the drawing of precepts, parallels, and explanations—that Dryden took for granted in his audience. This thesis is decidedly helpful. The assumption of an exegetical cast of mind could well explain the apparent haziness and subordination of the intellectual elements Barbeau inflates to undue prominence. One is left finally to try to give due attention to both surface and substance. The suggestion that they can be separate is obnoxious to modern critics, raised to venerate dogma about the indivisibility of form and content. But if Wallace's suggestions hold even partly true, critics will have to reinvestigate the kind of import and seriousness possessed by heroic drama. At present the charge of vacuity must at worst be regarded as not proven.

The extravagant surface, though, has been an embarrassment to most friendly critics. One obvious way out is to deny

---

[1] John M. Wallace, 'Dryden and History: A Problem in Allegorical Reading', *ELH*, xxxvi (1969), 265–90. Cf. my review, *Philological Quarterly*, xlix (1970), 374.

that all of it is meant seriously. Are the plays self-satiric? D. W. Jefferson argues that Dryden's 'treatment of heroism carries extravagance to the point of absurdity'; that this 'comic' effect is 'the result of a conscious artistic purpose'.[1] Some disentanglement is needed here. Again, is just Dryden involved? And how prominent is self-satire even in his plays? The idea that they were written as self-deflating pieces of puffery is absurd. If they had been so viewed, why was *The Rehearsal* written and why are there so many sneering remarks about heroic drivel from people like Shadwell? Conceivably Dryden could have put out what he knew was bad enough to please (as he later suggests he actually did), but even Jefferson admits that Dryden 'never confessed to any other than a serious and, indeed, orthodox attitude to his subject-matter'. Jefferson's position is usually misrepresented by hostile critics: he specifically rejects the idea that Dryden was writing self-burlesque and insists on the seriousness of the heroic elements, though his saying that 'Dryden deliberately used heroic melodrama as a playground for his powers of wit and rhetoric' invites misconstruction. Though the self-burlesque theory is preposterous (and has never been seriously proposed), one may fairly say that Jefferson and even Bruce King exaggerate the prominence and prevalence of the 'comic' elements. Like Barbeau, however, they have performed a valuable service in bringing unduly neglected parts of the plays to our attention. Indubitably there are some comic spots—Maximin's address to the shopkeeper gods (*Tyrannick Love*, V. i), or Almanzor in love (*Conquest of Granada*, Part 1, III), for example. Like Nell Gwyn's famous epilogue for *Tyrannick Love*, such passages plainly seem meant to be funny.

Does such comic interposition debase the heroic elements? I think not. Rather, it offers welcome contrast, complexity, and irony. At least two recent critics have been willing to accept such a combination, and both cite Colley Cibber's well-known comment on the point. Of Morat in *Aureng-Zebe* Cibber observes:

There are in this fierce Character so many Sentiments of avow'd Barbarity, Insolence, and Vain-glory, that they blaze even to a

---

[1] 'The Significance of Dryden's Heroic Plays', *Proceedings of the Leeds Philosophies, and Literary Society*, v (1940), 125–39. The position is developed at length by his follower, Bruce King, in *Dryden's Major Plays* (Edinburgh, 1966).

ludicrous Lustre, and doubtless the Poet intended those to make his Spectators laugh, while they admir'd them; but *Booth* thought it depreciated the Dignity of Tragedy to raise a Smile, in any part of it, and therefore cover'd these kind of Sentiments with a scrupulous Coldness. . . .[1]

Note particularly the conviction that the spectators could *laugh, while they admir'd.* Cibber goes on to discuss other instances of this phenomenon, especially in Shakespeare, and to record Addison's acceptance of such a reaction in *Cato.* On this evidence, and that remarked by such text-oriented critics as Jefferson and King, we cannot possibly call the heroic plays dead serious and humourless. To say this by no means implies that the plays are frivolous, or predominantly satiric. Their use of ironic exaggeration shows up their lack of 'tragic intensity', which is disconcerting—but that is quite another matter. The extreme position taken by Jefferson and King is perhaps no worse than the usual desperately over-solemn readings. Happily, critics are beginning to see that satiric and ironic complexities can coexist comfortably with substantially serious heroic displays.[2]

II. THE COMMON TYPES

The disputes just surveyed pertain largely to the heroic drama and especially to Dryden. The accounts which follow are an attempt to give capsule descriptions of all the major types of the serious drama, mostly without reference to chronology. That there are eight types is entirely coincidental: no parallel to the analyses of comedies in Chapter 3 is intended. The situations are not analogous: there readings of single, often overlapping plays were at issue; here the subject is differing types in a much broader sense.

Ideas of Greatness: The 'Heroic' Play

How cohesive is 'heroic drama'? Plainly this depends on your definition. Is a prosperous ending necessary? If so, what

---

[1] *An Apology for the Life of Colley Cibber,* ed. B. R. S. Fone (Ann Arbor, Mich., 1968), p. 72.

[2] See Robert S. Newman, 'Irony and the Problem of Tone in Dryden's *Aureng-Zebe*', *Studies in English Literature,* x (1970), 439–58; and Eugene M. Waith, *Ideas of Greatness,* pp. 214–16.

is Orrery's *Mustapha*? Is a villain-centred play truly heroic? I would say no—not unless a character of virtue figures prominently in contrast, as in *Tyrannick Love*. Does opera count?—and if not, do we ignore *The Siege of Rhodes*? Is rhyme a *sine qua non*? A play like *The Mourning Bride*, in blank verse, falls somewhere between prosperous-ending tragicomedy and the full-blown heroic. Such questions seem to me paramount. A great deal of critical attention has been expended on sources and influences—most of it profitless. The whole unhappy business need not be reviewed yet again. One can admit the influence of Beaumont and Fletcher while still acknowledging the excellent work of such critics as Arthur Kirsch and Harold Brooks in showing us the importance of Corneille as a model. But here I am concerned simply with play types.

Hostile critics imply that one lot of jingling bombast is much like the next. At the other extreme, critics have tried to define discrete 'schools'. Thus Nicoll establishes three groups: Drydenesque rant and battle; Orrerian history plays; and quasi-French displays of 'calm, precision, and artificiality'.[1] This division leaves me uncomfortable: even in *Henry the Fifth* Orrery's ideas of history are extremely loose, while the French or 'neoclassical' group seems to consist of insufficiently inflated oddments like Caryll's *The English Princess* and Shipman's *Henry III of France*. Neither in theory nor in practice can I find evidence for such differentiations. One looks then for common ground and for points of variance.

The defining element in the heroic play broadly conceived is the titanic protagonist. In Waith's words, the object is a 'celebration of greatness, where the conflicts of tragedy are replaced by ritual exaltation'. In practice, the

principal characters pursue energetically some ideal which stretches human capacities to the utmost, whether the ideal is impossibly remote and therefore self-destructive, like that of Coriolanus, or attainable, like that of Caesar in *The False One*; whether self-centred, like that of Tamburlaine, or beneficial to all, like that of Henry V; perverted, like those of the villain heroes, or thoroughly noble, like those of the *chevaliers sans peur et sans reproche* who, early and late, appear in the most romantic plays. The energy of their quest is an

---

[1] Nicoll, I. 116.

affirmation of the ideal, finding its natural dramatic expression in an elevated and extravagant rhetoric which we call heroic rant.[1]

But whether a play should be categorized as heroic depends on how central the 'idea of greatness' is. Where evil in one predominant character is stressed, I think we have a rather different kind of play, as in Lee's *Nero*. The presence of a comic plot (as in *Secret Love*) changes the character and impact of the whole. Where the principal action of the play shows the fall of the glorified hero, the pattern of high tragedy predominates over heroic exaltation, as in *All for Love* (a play Waith finds substantially heroic). The presence of overtly political elements can similarly shift attention from the heroic, as in *The Duke of Guise*.

Heroic characterization is clearly the key element, though not always an overriding and defining one. But supposing it predominant, what are the possible variables? The elements generally commented upon are rant and emotion; psychology; scenery; verse disputation; and moral design. None is a *sine qua non*; all are generally present to some extent. Nonetheless, early experiments show surprising variation.

Dryden acknowledges Davenant's *Siege of Rhodes* (1656 in its original form) as the first step, and so it is, though critics sometimes classify it separately as an opera. Davenant's dedication of the 1663 quarto discusses '*heroique Plays*'; declares the subject to be '*Ideas* of Greatness and Vertue'; commends Corneille; and defines his play's object to be 'heightening the Characters of Valour, Temperance, Natural Justice, and complacency to Government'. Dryden could have used the same words. The import of *The Siege* is complicated by its different versions (1656, 1661). Dent, however, argues persuasively that 'it was originally written not as an opera but as a play', then cut and made musical to evade government objections to plays.[2] Thus the work was probably written in heroic couplets, mangled, and then mostly restored. Its features seem striking: Christian–pagan conflict in a siege; love and heroism stressed; scenery exploited as much as possible. Rutland House imposed technical

---

[1] Waith, pp. 3, 169. I am uncomfortable about the inclusion of villain heroes as defining presences.

[2] Edward J. Dent, *Foundations of English Opera* (1928; rpt. New York, 1965), Chapters 3 and 4. Quotation from p. 65. Dent's very full analysis is excellent.

limitations, but even just using back flats (in 1656) Davenant was able to manage five spectacular scenes: Rhodes at peace; the city besieged; Solyman the Magnificent's pavilion and throne; the castle he has built on Mount Philermus; and finally the scene of the general assault. The scenes do not change, even when the action jumps to Sicily. Given a working theatre in 1661, Davenant was glad to introduce appropriate quick scene changes with sliding flats. His desire for spectacle is obvious. The language is noble but fairly plain; psychology is simple and strictly functional—love, honour, and Alphonso's irrational jealousy of his wife, the brave and virtuous Ianthe. The heart of the play lies (as Davenant suggests in the 1656 preface) in 'Heroical' representation of 'the Characters of Vertue in the shapes of Valor and conjugal Love'. Characters, language, and sentiments are less hoity-toity than in Caroline *précieuse* drama, but this is what the author of *Love and Honour* (1634) has half an eye on.

Orrery's *The Generall* (written 1661; staged 1664) makes an interesting contrast. As W. S. Clark proves, it was written without knowledge of changeable scenery.[1] Three plays later, with *The Black Prince* (1667), Orrery does finally start to localize his scenes sharply. The later works allow for fancy staging and spectacle, but Orrery's formula initially appears without regard for spectacle. Rhyme is conspicuous in that formula, and in Orrery's much quoted account of the play's genesis. Charles II

Commanded me, to write a Play for Him; . . . And therfore . . . I Presumed to lay at his majts Feet, a Trage-Comedi, All in Ten Feet verse, & Ryme. I writt it, in that manner . . . because I found his majty Relish'd rather, the French Fassion of Playes, then the English.[2]

The Generall is basically an inflated Caroline *précieuse* tragi-comedy. The inflation consists of rhyme; strict concentration on admiration for exalted characters (with no comic relief); provision of valour and refined sentiment; and almost endless

[1] *The Dramatic Works of Roger Boyle, Earl of Orrery*, 2 vols., ed. William Smith Clark, II (Cambridge, Mass., 1937), I. 28. Clark's excellent Critical and Historical Prefaces and notes are the best (almost the only) account of Orrery's plays, and I am indebted to them.

[2] *Dramatic Works*, I. 23.

philosophizing and argumentation. The subject of this disputation is naturally ethical problems posed by conflicts of love
and honour. In *Henry the Fifth*, *Mustapha*, and *The Black Prince*
pseudo-history is replaced by 'real' if wildly imaginative history;
the scenic element grows; crude verse and plain language
become more polished, complex, and intense. Orrery's bent,
however, is plain from the start. Action is suppressed, psychology
and moral design left simple, sentiment exalted but rant avoided:
emphasis is on super-subtle ethical calculus and what Clark
calls 'sophistical argument'. Orrery's plays tend to consist of
endless series of reports and static debates appropriate to the
chilly loftiness of tone he cultivates. A major exception is the
execution scene in *Mustapha* and what follows it: the violence
unleashed there is melodrama (as Clark complains), but for
once dramatically effective. In all, 'history' seems to me less the
defining element in these plays than super-*précieuse* sentiment
and versified ethical disputation. These features appear regularly in later heroic plays, but nowhere else in Carolean drama
are they so prominent.

The formula Dryden evolved (and explained in 'Of Heroique
Playes') is both intensely personal and highly influential. He
was an admirer and collaborator of Davenant's, and he addressed extravagant praise to Orrery in his dedication of *The
Rival Ladies* (1664), commenting especially on the possibilities
in 'Argumentation and Discourse' among 'great and noble'
persons. From the start, Dryden is disposed to exploit the
possibilities opened up by both men, but he adds his own concerns. Always fascinated by the epic mode, he argues 'That
an Heroick Play ought to be an imitation, in little of an
Heroick Poem: and consequently, that Love and Valour ought
to be the Subject of it'. Therein he aims to present 'to view'
'the highest patern of humane life'. Heroic characterization is
practised against a duly spectacular backdrop; verse disputation appears, but in smaller chunks. Dryden differs from
Orrery in wanting much more in the way of action, drums, and
trumpets, and in preferring the grandiose to the achingly
précieuse. He criticizes *The Siege of Rhodes* for want of 'design,
and variety of Characters', as well as for dull style. His curiously
naïve view that 'the Poet is . . . to endeavour an absolute
dominion over the minds of the Spectators' (i.e. 'to perswade

them, for the time, that what they behold on the *Theatre* is really perform'd') is widely quoted, but is not a good key to the nature of the experience Dryden contrives. Predictably, he is much concerned with language; as he inclines to the grandiose, the depiction of titanic passion leads him into rant. (Settle and Lee push this development on into the realm of rhapsodic nonsense, but Dryden should not be damned for their excesses.) Besides providing fancier language and more action than his predecessors, Dryden gives rather less simplistic psychological portraits. Such critics as Kirsch and Barbeau have been able to demonstrate a good deal of subtlety and complexity in Dryden's characters. As character studies, however, Dryden's plays certainly will not stand comparison with Jacobean tragedy, and too much must not be claimed for them in this respect. The special element that Dryden adds to his predecessors' formulae might be called a detailed moral design. Barbeau has treated this subject best, though her notion of 'intellectual design' seems excessively abstract. In his major heroic plays, *The Indian Emperour*, *Tyrannick Love*, and *The Conquest of Granada*, Dryden establishes a central cultural–religious contrast (Spaniards–Indians, Christian–pagan) and presents a picture of social decay and collapse. Simultaneously, he gives us a series of contrasting character studies. Thus in *The Indian Emperour* we watch the internal disintegration of the Indian state. Montezuma, the passion-ridden ruler, is contrasted with the conqueror Cortez, who increases his self-command during the play. Kirsch comments on how carefully Dryden balances Cortez's courtship of Cydaria against Montezuma's pursuit of Almeria. A similar antithesis is drawn between the brothers Guyomar and Odmar, the one duty-, the other love-oriented. From the play emerges a double picture of the exemplary hero: Cortez embodies passion ultimately bounded, while Guyomar's strict obedience is rendered active and responsible. This dual sense of the hero, passionate and correct, reappears in Almanzor and Ozmyn five years later. Like Corneille, Dryden is much interested in the conflict between internal will and external obligations, and he likes to set up the elaborate, almost schematic comparisons so well analysed by Barbeau.

To call the results 'intellectual' may be an overstatement. Dryden's political, social, and moral attitudes are readily deducible from the plays, but the quasi-allegorical 'design' is embedded in a totality in which language, character, and spectacle figure prominently. In this context, the design seems less an overt disquisition than an expression of outlook and an intuitive exploration of the heroic ethos. Dryden's contrasts are essays in definition: he is not content to present the cut and dried virtues sung by Davenant and Orrery. Waith shrewdly remarks that

Dryden's best plays have a dialectical structure which constantly aims at a definition of heroic values, while Lee's . . . are less schematic and less concerned with fine distinctions. They are lyrical celebrations of a kind of greatness which is frequently manifested in states of extreme emotion, whether pity, fury, fear or exaltation.[1]

As Waith's comment suggests, Lee has his own blend of the possible elements. Heroic exaltation remains, but here fed with supercharged emotions, exaggerated language, and abnormal psychology. The searing, choking intensity of Lee's heroic plays makes a startling contrast with Orrery's customary frozen calm. Yet both writers indubitably celebrate heroical greatness. Spectacular staging helped Lee at the box office, as it did Settle. But the element which makes Lee's plays what they are is the centrality of violent emotion and its expression in streams of words forced past the limits of sense. To categorize Lee with one of his predecessors would be futile. Dryden's success undoubtedly spurred on later writers, and Settle is an imitator, albeit a dismal one. Crowne's *The Destruction of Jerusalem* and Banks's *The Destruction of Troy* (both 1677) develop this tradition after a fashion.

Given the jingling rhymes, the bastard history, the tortuous intrigues, and the hordes of seemingly indistinguishable foreign character names, even the sympathetic reader is likely to find that one play blurs into the next. Actually, neither flavour nor formula is at all constant. Banks's pathos and Lee's rant and bloody endings are a long way from Dryden's practice. Even the political philosophy has occasioned confusion. Early attacks on Dryden[2] led to frequent interpretation of his heroes

---

[1] Waith, pp. 241–2.
[2] Notably by Richard Leigh, *The Censure of the Rota* (Oxford, 1673), who claims that Dryden's political and moral philosophy is taken 'from Mr. *Hobs*' (p. 19).

as glorifications of libertinism or of amoral Hobbesian power-mongering, a view which is ridiculous. Dryden does use Hobbesian ideas extensively—to characterize his *villains*.[1] Predictably, Dryden's position on rebellion is quite conservative: the power-seeker (Maximin, Morat) destroys himself; the hero who rebels against injustice (Almanzor, Porphyrius) is handled sympathetically, but not whole-heartedly endorsed. An almost opposite cliché, that heroic drama is simply divine-right propaganda, has an element of truth for Dryden, Davenant, and Orrery, but is flatly contradicted by Lee's work, much of which dwells on the tyranny of kings.[2] In short, when we speak of the heroic play (rhymed or not) we are referring to a phenomenon with a readily definable central idea, but, in other respects, with a great deal of room for divergence.

The Villain on Display: Horror Tragedy

Audience predilection for gore and horror has been underplayed by a lot of critics; Summers, Nicoll, J. H. Wilson, and Rothstein being honourable exceptions. This bent defies contemporary critical prescriptions and ill accords with later hypotheses about 'neoclassicism'. Considering the heritage of Jacobean blood-and-thunder melodrama, we might expect more than we find at the outset of the Carolean period: it flourishes from the mid-1670s on. Porter's highly successful *The Villain* (1662) is a rare early example. This rousing crowd-pleaser has fiendish intrigue by Malignii, attempted rape, and a very powerful mistaken-identity murder in which Beaupres kills his wife and Boutefeu (who is disguised as a friar). Jealousy, misapprehension, and highly plausible plots and quarrels give the play real dramatic power. But despite good character differentiation and genuinely affecting pathos in the deaths of Brisac, Charlotte, and Bellmont, the centre of the play remains Malignii—what one remembers is his evil power, unmasking, and death. For Samuel Sandford it was a fabulous role; as late as 1709 one finds in the *Tatler*, 134, comment on his

---

[1] A point decisively demonstrated by Louis Teeter, 'The Dramatic Use of Hobbes's Political Ideas', *ELH*, iii (1936), 140–69, and more particularly by John A. Winterbottom, 'The Place of Hobbesian Ideas in Dryden's Tragedies', *Journal of English and Germanic Philology*, lvii (1958), 665–83.

[2] A point elaborated by Frances Barbour, 'The Unconventional Heroic Plays of Nathaniel Lee', *University of Texas Studies in English*, (1940), pp. 109–16.

performance in the final torture scene, in which we hear
screams and then a door opens and we find 'Malignii *discover'd
peirc't with a stake*'.

A play like Lee's *The Tragedy of Nero* (1674) can be called
heroic, being a non-comic play mostly in couplets, but basically
it is a bloodbath. The virtuous Britannicus ('true Heire of
the Empire') and his wife Cyara are butchered, along with just
about everyone else. Nero and Poppea finally get wiped out,
the one simply a monster, the other (until a fifth-act repentance)
the sort of lustful villainess to become popular twenty years
later. By no standard save death toll is this anyone's 'tragedy':
we simply wallow in gross brutality (Nero: 'Villain, thou ly'st;
go pull his tongue out, haste; I'le see the roots on't'—I. 69), and
the trappings of the genre: sex, death, ghost, madness. Scraps
of the love-ethos appear (Nero: 'O mighty Love! 'Tis for thy
sake, I this disgrace endure'—68), but no love and honour
dilemmas of the usual heroic sort. The play might be con-
strued as a thinly veiled attack on the sexual debauchery of the
Carolean court (the dedication to Rochester notwithstanding),
but as Lee's recent editors note, it was apparently not taken
that way,[1] and so is perhaps a lesson in caution concerning
facile suppositions about topicality.

Otway's *Alcibiades* (1675) is another example of the couplet
bloodbath, though it indulges in more love and honour. A
vastly better play than *Nero*, it abounds in melodrama (Theramnes: 'But I'd forgot; beware of— [*Dyes*]' —I. 139); fancy
scenic effects (e.g. 'a darkn'd Tent', '*Elizium*', and 'A glorious
Temple . . . in the Ayr'—in the space of two pages, 157–8);
and all the usual trappings, including a ghost. Act V provides
excellent quick plot turns and suspense. But the villainous
schemes and slaughterhouse results override all else. Tissa-
phernes, the previous Spartan general, is simply a fiend—and
naturally hates Alcibiades. Theramnes, who displaced Alcibiades in Athens, is only a little better: he attempts to rape
Timandra, but has the grace to repent while dying. Deidamia,
villainous Queen of Sparta, lusts for Alcibiades and so kills
her husband (King Agris) with a dagger. Annoyed by Alcibiades's preference for Timandra, she forces her to take poison;
propositions him; and when refused, snarls: 'Go dotard in,

---

[1] *Works*, I. 22.

enjoy thy bride;/And know by me thy lov'd *Timandra* dy'd'
—as '*The* Scene *drawn discovers* Timandra *on a Couch in the midst
of her pains*' (163). The Queen and Alcibiades subsequently
stab themselves and expire severally. With only two secondary
and two strictly minor characters left alive out of the ten
specified parts, Otway has the Queen rise to speak an epilogue
mocking the whole bloody affair. This twist, like Lee's jesting
prologue for *Nero* (which was delivered by the comedian Jo
Hayns, who had no part), suggests once again the Carolean
audience's ability to laugh at what it revelled in.

Numerous other plays could be cited. Lee's *Caesar Borgia*
is one of the most shocking: three poisonings (with two deaths
on stage); five stranglings (all on stage); a death by sniffing
poisoned gloves; and finally a little boy, Borgia's son Seraphino, is led on stage to die, 'with his Eyes out, and Face cut'
(II. 141). After Borgia's own spectacular expiration, Machiavel
is left blandly to deliver a closing moral: 'No Power is safe, nor
no Religion good,/Whose Principles of growth are laid in
Blood.' Elkanah Settle's *The Female Prelate* (1680) gives us a
villainess *par excellence* (Pope Joanna Angelica) as part of anti-
Catholic propaganda. Another play related to the Popish
Plot is Lee's *The Massacre of Paris* (1679–81; banned until
1689), an orgy of poisoning and knifing of Huguenots: in the
final scene six Huguenot commanders 'standing with their
hands ty'd behind 'em' are shot by a firing squad, whereupon
'The Scene draws, and shews the Admiral's Body burning.'
Dryden's *Amboyna* (1672), Third Dutch War propaganda, includes a successful rape with the crucial part barely off stage
(IV. i) and dwells ghoulishly on a variety of tortures throughout
most of Act V. Mrs. Behn's *Abdelazer* (1676; a reworking of
Lust's Dominion, *c.* 1600), well analysed by J. H. Wilson, is a
non-political example of the blood and villainy mode. In the
1690s villain and especially villainess plays, replete with shock
tactics, enjoy a vogue. Banks's *Cyrus the Great* has a character
shredded by hooked-wheeled chariots: his lady lovingly re-
constructs the body on stage. Mrs. Manley's *The Royal Mischief*
has a man shot out of a cannon: we are told that his lady
bestowed 'burning Kisses' on every bit of the 'Horrid Pile' of
remains (46). Mrs. Pix has her heroine's hands sliced up by a
scimitar as a prelude to rape in *Ibrahim* (1696). Raped and

tortured women become an especially popular device. But as
one surveys these and other examples from minor dramatists,[1]
one must remember that the like can be found in Lee and
Dryden.

Except by way of negative examples, contemporary literary
theory has little justification for blood-and-torture villain
tragedy. But dramatists were quite ready to revel in fiendish
villains. Plays like Porter's, with its Iagoesque villain, can
be good character drama. Those which simply exploit the
devices are seldom effective. Powell ends *The Treacherous
Brothers* with Menaphon '*flung from* a Battlement *upon Spikes*' (61);
Settle's *The Conquest of China* displays a pile of 'Murdred
Women, some with Daggers in their Breasts, some thrust
through with Swords, some strangled, and others Poyson'd'
(60). The sixth engraving in *The Empress of Morocco* (opposite
page 70) shows four mutilated bodies hanging on hooks and
spikes in a dungeon, with the bones of previous victims on the
floor beneath them. Given the theory of the more response the
better, perhaps this is not surprising. Unlike Admiration and
Pity, Horror was uncanonical—but it too worked.

The Fall of the Hero: 'High' Tragedy

Insofar as the late seventeenth-century playwrights produce
tragedy proper, it mostly falls under this heading. The most
highly praised serious plays—*All for Love* and *Venice Preserv'd*
—are of this sort. If neither will stand direct comparison with
Shakespeare and Webster, perhaps the explanation lies in
Clifford Leech's observation that the tragic effect, in that
frame of reference, relies on a sense of pride in man's un-
availing but heroic struggle against implacable Fate. However, insistence on demonstrating the complete justice of
Heaven's decrees is an almost insuperable obstacle to eliciting
such a response. Anne Righter snidely and rightly remarks
that 'Restoration tragic heroes, faced with the spectacle of
virtue in distress, tend to take the heavens to task for temporary
mismanagement of the administration'.[2] This attitude is less
pervasive after the end of the Carolean period, and the vogue

---

[1] Rothstein, *Restoration Tragedy*, pp. 152–7, has a good short catalogue and
discussion.

[2] 'Heroic Tragedy', p. 144.

for happy endings can be exaggerated. A strong inclination toward poetic justice, however, tends to ensure that we see the fall of a *very* flawed character; or an emphasis on the machinations of a villain; or a move toward the pathetic.

Nahum Tate's version of *King Lear* (1681), in its own right a pleasant villain-intrigue melodrama, is a notorious example of the anti-tragic disposition: Lear is kept alive and Cordelia finally marries Edgar. If death or even just ruin are to be the protagonist's lot, there must be no mistake about his deserts, as one sees in Shadwell's handling of his adaptation of *Timon of Athens* (1678) or Dryden's of *Troilus and Cressida* the next year. In the latter, Troilus remains heroic, but his belief in Cressida's falseness and his subsequent behaviour require his eradication. When Dryden shows us heroic virtue destroyed in *Cleomenes* (1692), he does so specifically with the idea of 'moving Compassion', as the dedication tells us, though we are also to admire the hero's sublime stoicism.

Prominence for the villain is a characteristic of Henry Nevil Payne's *The Fatal Jealousie* (1673). This play might almost be classified as villain tragedy, so important is the vengeful Jasper (like Porter's Malignii, one of Sandford's roles). But the action is sufficiently dependent on Antonio's character to make the work rather different. Because Antonio's violent jealousy is a *donné* from the first line, the play is too much simply a presentation of successful machinations: we do not see Antonio make decisions or errors which destroy an initial state of happiness and security. The bloodbath element is stressed: all eleven of the named characters are dead by the end. Even so, Payne makes gore secondary to feeling, and Antonio is a well-drawn tragic protagonist. His feelings after wrongly killing his wife Cælia are affecting but not overdone. Critics have found both verbal reminiscences of and general parallels to *Othello*: the essential difference lies in Payne's reluctance to give Antonio the stature and virtues necessary for profound concernment.

All for Love (1677) gives us—in blank verse—an admirable but imperfect hero driven to heroic suicide. The ethics of love and honour loom large—here with heroical love triumphant. But despite fine verse, the play drags. One problem is the compression demanded by conformity to the unities: too little action and too much recapitulation kill suspense, and the current events Dryden contrives consist mostly of Antony's waverings. Three times in three rounds he is made to change his mind at others' behests, and when he exclaims to Octavia, 'I am vanquish'd: take me' (IV. 226), one cannot help feeling that he is vanquished rather frequently. The weakness of character is part of a larger problem: starting after Actium, Dryden has a protagonist already doomed by past decisions; the remaining question is how well he will die. Dryden shows us the fall itself, but not the processes which produced it; we never see Antony in his full stature as we do in Shakespeare. Lee's *The Rival Queens* the same year, despite fustian and wandering focus, does better in producing action from the flaws of an impressively effective hero. The rapid action is welcome: a fight, a ghost scene, Alexander the Great's triumphal entry, the two queens' quarrel, the killing of Clytus at a banquet, the murder of Queen Statira, and the poisoning of Alexander completely avoid the stasis of Dryden's play. The prominence of the two queens can seem distracting, but Stroup and Cooke are right in saying that their conflict, like the rest of the action, depends crucially on Alexander's character. His internal flaws and conflicts make the play a rarity for its time: a genuine tragedy of character not obviously predetermined from the start. Rant, spectacle, singing ghosts, and the paraphernalia of love and honour should not distract from this virtue.

Otway's much praised *Venice Preserv'd* (1682) is a peculiar work with its definite but limited political references, emphasis on pathos in Belvidera, and statureless protagonist. Jaffeir starts out as a doomed wastrel, and despite massive camouflage with love, honour, and the code of friendship, the problem remains. Nonetheless, the play is dramatically effective: its virtues lie in fine writing; vivid, accessible characters; and especially in skilful exploitation of practically every trick in the book: attempted rape of the innocent Belvidera; love and honour conflicts; rant ('Final destruction seize on all the world:/ Bend down, ye Heavens . . . Crush the Vile Globe into its first confusion. . . .' (II. 276)); a wild scaffold scene; bloody ghosts; Belvidera's insanity and death. The vividness of the characters allows Otway to get tremendous emotional response out of the melodramatic trappings often so dismal in lesser hands.

Jaffeir: *[Offers to stab her again]*
Belvidera: [Kneeling] Oh, mercy!
Jaffeir: Nay, no strugling.
Belvidera: [Leaps upon his neck and kisses him] Now then kill me. (268)

Whereupon Jaffeir *'throws away the dagger and embraces her'*.

To say that all these plays present poetic justice would be absurd. In various guises, however, the concept haunts late seventeenth-century tragedy. Unhappy endings are common enough, but all too often they are made acceptable in one of the fashions just described—the villain is made central; the protagonist suffers from a major flaw; or pathos is emphasized. The results are often good, but almost never do they escape the sense of rationalistic limitation of which Leech justly complains. Character is seldom uppermost even in this sub-type; genuine complexity of character is even rarer. (Lee's Alexander and Lucius Junius Brutus are two examples of success.) The catastrophe tends then to turn on accident and pathos (as in *The Orphan*), or evil and pathos, or on a flaw so great as to leave the audience feeling too-bad-but-serves-him-right.

The Musical Spectacular: 'English' Opera

This is an untidy sub-genre. Song and dance are staple elements in Carolean comedy; fancy staging and scenery are an important part of the heroic play. These elements, combining with the Stuart masque tradition, contribute to the origins of opera in England. *The Siege of Rhodes*, already discussed as a heroic play, is taken by Dent as the first opera. Yet only a few of the plays in this group could really be called opera: *King Arthur*, *Rinaldo and Armida*, and a few others—all productions of the 1690s. The earlier musicals, some of them immensely popular, are really hybrids, vehicles for stage display which are extrapolations from the masque (*Calisto*, *Albion and Albanius*), or from comedy (the 1674 *Tempest*) or tragicomedy (*Psyche*).

Songs in plays are occasionally functional in theme and situation (as in *Marriage A-la-Mode*), but are often not. Dances are usually, as in 1930s musicals, just interpolated entertainment. Convention, followed even in *The Country-Wife*, demanded a dance at the end of a comedy. Add dazzling scene shifts, and you have box-office appeal.[1] Davenant's version of *Macbeth* (1664) is a good example of the early Carolean spectacular.[2] About ten years later, a sudden upsurge in the specifically musical show occurs. At least two major factors are involved in this boom: the popularity of concerts and an awareness of French opera.

Roger North comments with astonishment that 'Musick shot up in to such request, as to croud out from the stage even comedy itself. . . . It had bin strange if they ['publik theaters'] had not observed this promiscuous tendency to musick, and not have taken it into their scenes and profited by it.'[3] North calls John Bannister's concerts 'the first attempt': from December 1672 on, *The London Stage* records a steady procession of his performances. North cites the Orfeo and Euridice masque in Settle's *The Empress of Morocco* (July 1673) as the beginning of a counter-attack.

By the 1673–4 season the playhouses were definitely feeling competition from foreign performers and 'opera'. Records of performances are maddeningly sketchy. On 5 January 1674 Evelyn notes 'I saw an Italian Opera in musique, the first that had been in England of this kind' (identity uncertain); a fancy 'Ballet et Musique' was put on at Court by French performers in February; Pierre Perrin's *Ariadne* ('An Opera, or Vocal Representation', according to the 1674 dual-language edition) was definitely played by March. That the fancy operatic reworking of the Dryden–Davenant *Tempest* appears in April does not seem wholly coincidental. Court taste for music and show is evident the following December, with the extraordinary preparations for Crowne's *Calisto*, usually dubbed, as in the Bulstrode Papers, 'a play & an opera'.[4] *Psyche* appears in February 1675.

From a contemporary letter, however, we know definitely

---

[1] Comments on these elements are legion in Pepys and from others, e.g. Baron von Schwerin's remark that 'because of the changing of the scenes', *The Tempest* 'was well worth seeing' (*Journal*, 4 June 1674: translation given in *The London Stage*, Part 1, p. 216).

[2] On which see Christopher Spencer, ed., *Davenant's 'Macbeth' from the Yale Manuscript* (New Haven, Conn., 1961).

[3] *Roger North on Music*, ed. John Wilson (London, 1959), pp. 302–7.

[4] For a very detailed account of *Calisto*, see Eleanore Boswell, *The Restoration Court Stage* (Cambridge, Mass., 1932).

that 'the long expected Opera of *Psyche*' (Downes) was at least on the drawing-board by August 1673.[1] At about this time Thomas Betterton visited Paris at Charles II's behest to study French stage decoration and machinery.[2] The Duke's Company retained its founder Davenant's innovative outlook, and after opening its fancy new theatre in Dorset Garden in November 1671, it was well equipped for spectaculars. *Psyche* itself is an adaptation of a French *tragedie-ballet* staged in 1671 with vast success in Paris, the work of Molière, Quinault, Lully, and Corneille. Betterton's first major effort in the new theatre seems to have been a revamped production of Davenant's *Macbeth* with 'new Cloath's, new Scenes, Machines, as flyings for the Witches; with all the Singing and Dancing'. Downes terms this mishmash 'in the nature of an Opera'.[3]

'Opera' proves a loose term. In the preface to *Albion and Albanius* (1685) Dryden offers a definition.

An *Opera* is a poetical Tale or Fiction, represented by Vocal and Instrumental Musick, adorn'd with Scenes, Machines, and Dancing. The suppos'd Persons of this musical Drama, are generally supernatural, as Gods and Goddesses, and Heroes. . . . The Subject therefore being extended beyond the Limits of Humane Nature, admits of that sort of marvellous and surprizing conduct, which is rejected in other Plays.

Later in the same preface he defines 'a Play Of the Nature of the Tempest' as 'a Tragedy mix'd with *Opera*; or a *Drama* Written in blank Verse, adorn'd with Scenes, Machines, Songs, and Dances'. The terminology is worth remarking, especially 'tragedy'.[4] In his preface to *Psyche*, Shadwell denigrates 'Plays of this kind', admitting that 'the great Design was to entertain the Town with variety of Musick, curious Dancing, splendid Scenes and Machines.' Nonetheless, he asserts that 'this is much more a Play' than his French source, and he is right.

---

[1] See *Letters to Sir Joseph Williamson*, ed. W. D. Christie, 2 vols., Camden Society (London, 1874), I. 180–1 (22 August 1673).

[2] See Robert W. Lowe, *Thomas Betterton* (1891; rpt. New York, 1972), p. 113.

[3] Downes, p. 33.

[4] One wonders which version of *The Tempest* Dryden had in mind: 1667 or 1674. Aline Mackenzie Taylor, in 'Dryden's "Enchanted Isle" and Shadwell's "Dominion"', *Essays in English Literature of the Classical Period*, ed. Daniel W. Patterson and Albrecht B. Strauss, *Studies in Philology* Extra Series, No. 4 (Chapel Hill, N.C., 1967), pp. 39–53, has argued that Dryden found the 1674 version violently offensive, but the evidence seems tenuous.

Music is used to heighten dramatic effect, but the lead characters never sing.

The 1674 *Tempest* is the best known of the musical spectaculars.[1] It benefits from some genuinely lovely music. The orchestra ('24 Violins, with the Harpsicals and Theorbo's which accompany the Voices') was double the usual size, according to Dent; an overture follows the prologue; singers were lent by the King for the first series of performances.[2] The initial stage direction indicates the special effects employed.

This Tempest (suppos'd to be rais'd by Magick) has many dreadful Objects in it, as several Spirits in horrid shapes flying down amongst the sailers, then rising and crossing in the Air. And when the Ship is sinking, the whole House is darken'd [i.e. to the limited extent possible], and a shower of Fire falls upon 'em. This is accompanied with Lightning, and several Claps of Thunder. (Shadwell, *Works*, II. 199)

As in the recent *Macbeth*, flying machines are given great play: Ariel's last speech is produced '*hovering in the Air*'. Trick effects, such as the vanishing bottles (249), are much in evidence. As the epilogues to the 1674 *Tempest* and *Psyche* complain, such displays were fearfully expensive to mount and hence quite a gamble.

Dryden's *Albion and Albanius* (1685), with music by Grabu, may seem a long way from such Broadway stuff. Essentially a super-masque, it is a thinly allegorical history of the Restoration, detailing the triumph of Stuart justice and order over anarchy and rebellion. But the libretto serves also as a vehicle for the spectacular. For example, '*Juno* appears in a Machine drawn by Peacocks . . . as it descends, it opens and discovers the Tail of the Peacock, which is so Large, that it almost fills the opening of the Stage' (V. 360). The 'Poetical Hell' of Act II recalls a similar scene in Act V of *Psyche*. Proteus is seized, 'and

---

[1] This is a reworking of the 1667 Dryden-Davenant adaptation of Shakespeare, apparently done by Shadwell (and Betterton?) with music by Matthew Lock, Pietro Reggio, and J. Hart, and dances arranged by Draghi. For a summary on the disputed authorship, see George Robert Guffey's Introduction to *After the Tempest* (Los Angeles, Calif., 1969). On the two adaptations see Hazelton Spencer, *Shakespeare Improved* (1927; rpt. New York, 1963), pp. 192–210.

[2] See Dent, pp. 139–44. Nicoll (I. 356) reprints the King's order to his musicians dated 16 May 1674.

changes himself into a Lyon, a Crocodile, a Dragon, and then
to his own shape again: He comes toward the front of the
Stage, and Sings' (376). Venus rises out of the sea in 'a great
Scallop-shell' (378). A figure representing Shaftesbury appears
'with Fiends Wings, and Snakes twisted round his Body: He is
incompast by several Phanatical Rebellious Heads, who suck
poyson from him, which runs out of a Tap in his Side' (380).

Somewhat closer to our notion of opera is the Dryden and
Purcell *King Arthur* (1691), a vast success. Dryden indulges
in an almost Spenserian siren scene; gives us an innocence-
scene reminiscent of his *Tempest* following the miraculous
restoration of Emmeline's sight; and then threatens her with
rape at the end of the act. Arthur and Oswald 'Fight with
Spunges in their Hands dipt in Blood' (VI. 281). The scenery
changes often and dazzlingly: '*Merlin* waves his Wand; the
Scene changes, and discovers the British Ocean in a Storm.
Æolus in a Cloud above [sings]' (283).

Withal, we do not have here opera of the Italian sort
which comes into vogue after 1705. Even Purcell's best known
'operas' contribute little sense of direction: *Dido and Aeneas*
was not written for professional production; *The Fairy-Queen* is
really only a set of masques interpolated into a mangled version
of *A Midsummer Night's Dream*. Several post-Carolean writers
make extensive use of music in quasi-operas, particularly
George Powell, Durfey, Settle, Motteux, Oldmixon, and Dennis,[1] but nothing like a genre really emerges. Whether used
frivolously, as in *Macbeth* or the 1674 *Tempest*, or in a piece
with more serious import (*Albion and Albanius, King Arthur*),
the devices of 'opera'—song, dance, spectacle, and machines—
are used for calculated box-office appeal. Enough works draw
heavily, even primarily, on such elements to constitute a sub-
group, but the musical spectacular definitely remains a miscellany form.

Split Plot and Mixed Plot Tragicomedy

The multi-plot play was an old and rich English tradition
developed by Shakespeare, Fletcher, Jonson, Middleton, Massinger, Ford, and Shirley, among others. The mingling of

---

[1] Their work is surveyed in Chapter 5 of Eugene Haun's *But Hark! More Harmony: The Libretti of Restoration Opera in English* (Ypsilanti, Mich., 1971).

serious and comic elements in a single play was at least as well established a custom. Neither practice finds much contemporary critical warrant: Dryden's Lisideius is orthodox in finding 'mirth and compassion . . . incompatible' and in proclaiming '*English* Tragi-comedie' 'absurd' (*Works*, XVII. 35). Neander disagrees, citing the virtues of 'variety' (XVII. 46), but such defences are rare. Nonetheless, both sorts of tragicomedy continued to flourish in the late seventeenth century.

Certain distinctions are necessary. At issue here are mixtures of serious and lighter elements, not second plot lines. In the preface to the Dryden–Lee adaptation of *Oedipus*, Dryden remarks that though they followed Sophocles 'as close as possibly we cou'd', a single line of action was not enough: 'Custom . . . has obtain'd, that we must form an under-plot of second Persons, which must be depending on the first.' Hence the main tragic action ends with Jocasta's suicide and Oedipus's defenestration, and into that story is woven a second dead serious tale—dealing with a heroical love conflict involving Eurydice, the noble prisoner Adrastus, and the scheming Creon, all of whom are killed. This underplot is neither split (i.e. radically dissociated from the main action) nor mixed (i.e. a comic addition to lighten the other). Two tragic actions could be encompassed in a single play, but almost invariably a split plot signals a serious–comic combination. Many serious plays will allow some 'mixture' of elements for variety (e.g. the Antonio–Aquilina scenes in *Venice Preserv'd*), but only where such material becomes quite substantial does the plot really become mixed. An example is Southerne's *The Fatal Marriage*: as Isabella, Mrs. Barry goes mad and commits suicide after accidentally commiting bigamy, but in the comic part of Victoria, Mrs. Bracegirdle is prominent for three acts. Southerne says in the Epistle Dedicatory, 'I have given you a little taste of Comedy with it, not from my own Opinion, but the present Humour of the Town', adding that he dropped the comedy as he approached 'the serious part'. A more typical, less skilful instance is Durfey's *The Injured Princess* (a 1682 adaptation of *Cymbeline*), a happy-ending tragicomedy in which the villain Shattillion confesses as he dies, Ursaces is prevented from suicide, and Eugenia forgives her husband for his treatment of her. Into this are mixed Cloten ('A Fool') and Jachimo ('A roaring drunken Lord, his Companion').

Occasionally the drastically mixed plot can be used to brilliant effect, as in Mrs. Behn's *The Widow Ranter: or, the History of Bacon in Virginia* (1689). General Bacon's heroical love for the Indian Princess Semernia, his accidental killing of her, and his suicide form a moving tragic action perfectly set off by two comic elements: satire on the corrupt and cowardly members of the governing council (who try to destroy Bacon), and a contrasting series of 'love' affairs: Hazard and Madam Surelove, Chrisante and Friendly, Mrs. Flirt and Parson Dunce, virtuous General Daring and the buxom Widow Ranter. As a mixture, the plot is a remarkably well-integrated three-level hierarchy touching equally on government and love.

To draw an absolute line between mixed and split plots is impossible, but the 'hip-hop' play is definitely a sub-type in its own right. Recent critics have proved decisively that at least some of these plays, schizophrenic though they seem, have well-worked-out thematic or formal parallelisms, and can claim subtly calculated artistic effects. Most play-goers may have recognized no more than pleasant variety, but from Dryden's prefaces Rothstein and King are easily able to prove that in his plays, at least, the subtleties were very much calculated. Thus in *The Spanish Fryar* (1680), well analysed by Bruce King, we have in the Torrismond–Queen–Bertran–Raymond plot a fairly schematic political fable about legitimacy, usurpation, and monarchical principle. In the comic plot, loosely connected in action but largely separate, the rake Lorenzo engages in a love affair with Gomez's wife Elvira and rebels against his father Alphonso, and so stands as an ironic contrast to the love and authority dilemmas of the serious plot. (The scoundrelly friar Dominic constitutes good topical anti-Catholic satire, but is, as King complains, thematically unnecessary.) Yet the purpose of the parallels is not parodic debunking; rather, the libertine ethic of Lorenzo serves as foil to exalt the code of the true heir, Torrismond. When Dryden claims in the dedication that never before has he made 'two Plots, so very different from each other' so perfectly 'of a piece', he is quite right. In theme and pattern the two plots have an astonishing number of parallels.

Such interconnections are often far less interesting. Etherege's first play, *The Comical Revenge* (1664), actually has four distinct levels of action: a quasi-heroic love and honour tale in couplets; Sir Frederick Frollick's courtship of the Widow Rich; a gulling plot involving the foolish Sir Nicholas Cully's search for a moneyed wife; and lastly the French valet Dufoy, a chaser of maids. (This last segment has not enough connected action to constitute a full plot line.) To find parallels in disguise, mistaken identity, friendship, sex and love, and deceit needs no Empson. But that these parallels make the play more than a slightly dizzying romp I do not see.

James Howard's *All Mistaken* balances a serious, emotional, happy-ending romantic tragicomedy against a roistering, scatological gay-couple farce that does not even end in marriage. Howard has some clever interconnecting touches. For example, the conceit that Amphelia swoons on the scaffold, recovers, and thinks herself beheaded and in heaven is mockingly anticipated early in the play when scapegrace Philidor, beset by nurses bearing six of his bastards, says despairingly 'I find I am in Hell, before I thought I shou'd' (9, 60). Similarly, Mirida's marvellous travesty of Davenant's celebrated tearjerking song, 'My Lodging it is on the cold ground', is followed three pages later by a return to the serious plot: the scene opens with the imprisoned 'Zoranzo and Amphelia *lyeing upon Straw together*' (54, 57). Howard seems mostly to have been amusing himself: the play has little sense of totality. Not much more could be said for Dryden's *Secret Love*, despite its vastly greater polish and gentility. Dryden contrives much fuller parallels in detail between his heroic and comic lines, but the over-all result is simply what Loftis calls it: a pleasant 'juxtaposition of love plots in different moods'.[1] A fuller and deeper relationship subsists between the apparently more disjunct plots of *Marriage A-la-Mode*. There the morality established as a norm for the comic plot serves as a useful contrast for that of the heroic line. Much the same can be said for Southerne's *Oroonoko*. There the husband-hunting comic plot may seem an odd bedfellow for a tragic plot ending in the death of the noble black slave-King Oroonoko and his Queen, Imoinda. But as Rothstein helpfully demonstrates, in both the everyday and the

[1] *Works*, IX. 335–6 nn. Loftis gives a good capsule account of the parallels.

heroic worlds Southerne develops themes of disguise, parentage, marriage; and the establishment of close moral parallels helps render Oroonoko's plight particularly clear and poignant.[1]

The late seventeenth-century predilection for mixed and sometimes split plots was plainly very strong. Good Renaissance precedent was easy to come by:[2] for example, Fletcher's *Rule a Wife and Have a Wife* and Shakespeare's *1 Henry IV* were especially popular plays in this period. Some split plots are indifferent, some ludicrous. *The Fatal Discovery* (anon., 1698) is a perfect case of parodic parallelism destroying tragic effect—not deliberately. But the split plot was a favourite form of Dryden's, and in his hands was capable of remarkable and highly effective complexity.[3] In *Don Sebastian*—well analysed by both Rothstein and King—he rises to heights which may justly be compared to good Shakespeare. That play may serve as a reminder that despite orthodox cries by the likes of Lisideius for 'uniformity and unity of design' (XVII. 37), in practice the demand for variety often carried the day—and such plays could be very good indeed.

Virtue Rewarded: The 'Pattern' Tragicomedy

The triumph of virtue is a commonplace in the serious drama, regardless of type. This 'tragicomic' pattern of action is to be found in anything from *The Tempest* (both versions), or *Marriage A-la-Mode* (a split plot play), to *The Conquest of Granada* (a heroic play). In such instances, another feature seems more central to the definition of the type of the play. Nonetheless, the classic *pattern* tragicomedy (as opposed to *split plot* or *mixed* tragicomedy) deserves recognition as a category in its own right. Noble characters are brought near death, but not to it. Barring obvious exceptions like *Oroonoko* and *The Fatal Marriage*, most split plot and mixed tragicomedies could be partially defined in this way. Whether a play like Durfey's *The Injured Princess*, with its slight comedy part and heavy emphasis on near-catastrophe, is better called mixed or pattern is an aimless question.

[1] Rothstein, *Restoration Tragedy*, pp. 146–7.

[2] For a full analysis of earlier uses of the multiple plot (both split and mixed), see Richard Levin, *The Multiple Plot in English Renaissance Drama*.

[3] His use of the form is analysed at length by Caroline Rodney, 'Dryden's Tragicomedy', unpub. diss. Cornell University, 1972.

Congreve's *The Mourning Bride* (1697) is an archetypal case of virtue rewarded in the classic tragicomedy pattern. In this instance the play has a definite heroic bent. Shadwell's *The Royal Shepherdess* (1669) has equally clear pastoral elements. This romance is simply an alteration of John Fountain's closet drama, *The Rewards of Virtue* (pub. 1661), and that title is a good clue to the play. Robert Howard's *The Surprisal* is a plain, effective, villainy-foiled tragicomedy. Edward Howard's 'Tragedy', *The Usurper*, was openly announced as a political play. In fact, the relevance to Charles's restoration is pretty indirect, and the action presented is straight reward of virtue and punishment of vice. The exiled King of Sicily, Cleander, regains his throne and marries Queen Timandra of Numidia; the vicious usurper Damocles kills his son Dionysius, and finally commits suicide. Cleander's loyal supporter Cleomenes is rewarded with the hand of his monarch's sister, Calanthe. Cleander, Dionysius, and Damocles (who tries to rape her) all covet Queen Timandra in the sort of love conflict so common in later heroic plays and romantic tragicomedies. But *The Usurper*, like *The Mourning Bride*, is flatly termed 'A Tragedy' on the title-page, though neither is a catastrophe play: uniform seriousness, not pattern of action, underlies the designation. Another play of this sort is the second version of Robert Howard's *The Vestal-Virgin*. Originally a violent bloodbath, it was rewritten, as the alternate ending explains, to be '*Acted the Comical way*': only the villainous Mutius is killed, though the lustful Sulpitius is dealt an admonitory wound.

Usually when a virtue-rewarded play is called a tragicomedy a secondary comical interest is implied—a mixed play. Thus in Edward Howard's excellent *The Change of Crownes* the complications of heroical love with a fortunate issue are lightened by Asinello, a country gentleman come to Court to buy a lucrative place. Similarly Mrs. Behn's *The Forc'd Marriage* has lighter moments in the amours of a cowardly fop, Falatius; the main action has the jealous Alcippus strangle his bride Erminia with a garter—but she revives, and the entangled love interests are eventually sorted out. The jumbled nature of the 'Tragi-Comedy' is well illustrated in Ravenscroft's *King Edgar and Alfreda* (1677). Lord Ethelwold and Edgar's Queen are rather cavalierly wiped out in a jealousy imbroglio in order to make possible their spouses' union. Even poetically 'better'd', the King's character is unattractive, but Alfreda's virtue (supposed to have a redeeming effect—Edgar agrees to endow a monastery) is appropriately rewarded. Variety here is achieved in two more love interests, one of them amusing. But Ravenscroft deliberately keeps his social tone high (unlike James Howard in *All Mistaken*): 'I have mix'd with it a run of Comedy, but not after the manner of our Old *Tragi-Comedies*, where one half of the *Play* are Heroes, and the other Mechanicks and Buffoons.' Here Alfreda's brother Aldernald wins the Princess Matilda; comedy enters in the 'Blunt Sea Captain' Durzo's successful wooing of the court lady Hillaria. Durzo's nautical terminology and humours are genuinely entertaining, but unlike Congreve's Ben, he is of the upper crust, and is finally appointed Admiral.

Not all prosperous-ending tragicomedies need centre on the reward of virtue. One of the finest serious plays of the period, Sir Robert Howard's *The Great Favourite* (usually known by its sub-title, *The Duke of Lerma*; 1668), reverses the formula and might better be called a case of disaster averted.[1] The failure of Lerma's power schemes (exciting in themselves) leads to the suicide and execution of his cohorts, and abandoned by his own brother, Lerma is summoned before Authority to receive what can only be a death sentence. There are few more thrilling scenes in all this drama, as Summers remarks, 'than when he appears not as a suppliant or guilty, but in all the pomp of pontifical state, clad in his sweeping scarlet robes, My Lord Cardinal, a sovran prince, whose sacred person the Grandees dare not touch nor molest'. This dazzling reversal comes as an utter surprise, though we realize as we see it that we have misunderstood a series of teasing hints. Lerma's virtuous daughter Maria is rewarded with marriage to the King, but the heart of the play is the escape of the villain. *The Duke of Lerma* is proof of the remarkable potentialities of 'untragic seriousness'; that the play is an isolated experiment is a great pity.[2]

---

[1] On problems of authorship and consequent neglect of the play see Chapter 6, below.

[2] The phrase is D. D. Arundell's, who reprinted the play in his *Dryden and Howard 1664–1668* (Cambridge, 1929). See also Summers's discussion, *The Playhouse of Pepys*, pp. 176–8.

Congreve's so-called tragedy, *The Mourning Bride*, is a schematically exact instance of virtue rewarded and vice punished. Political situation and love tangles are highly reminiscent of the plays of Edward Howard, with a bit of Drydenesque inflation. Almeria and Osmyn-Alphonso are duly united in prosperity; the usurper Manuel is mistakenly killed by his own favourite, Gonsalez, who subsequently expires of wounds while confessing 'the just Decrees of Heav'n' in destroying his schemes. The lustful captive Queen, Zara, poisons herself in the mistaken belief that the headless trunk of Manuel is Alphonso's. Under the same misapprehension Almeria is raising poison to her lips when Alphonso enters to bring about the happy ending. As Aubrey Williams has shown, *The Mourning Bride* is an explicit embodiment of poetic and overtly providential justice, just in the fashion touted by John Dennis.[1] Modern prejudices find the insistence on distributive justice in such melodramas forced and silly, but this was what contemporary criticism recommended, and the eighteenth-century audience loved it.

Virtue Distressed: Pathetic Tragedy

Great plays can make excellent use of pathos, as in *King Lear* and *Othello*. Children and female madness can work well toward that end, as in *Macbeth* and *Hamlet* respectively. But where such devices are overplayed, bathos results. Such is the charge commonly levelled against 'pathetic tragedy': its protagonists lack stature and the playwrights work too obviously on our sympathies. This is often true—but even so these works have a charm of their own. Their extreme emotionalism offers the sympathetic viewer an excuse for emotional self-indulgence. We usually think of pathetic tragedy in terms of suffering and death, even though the devices are prominently featured in such pattern tragicomedies as *The Forc'd Marriage*, *The Injured Princess*, and *The Mourning Bride*. And occasionally a pathetic play will end in prosperity: Boyer's version of *Iphigenia* does so, and Motteux's *Beauty in Distress* has a mostly happy ending. The pathetic trappings are likely to appear in any pattern tragicomedy, which *Iphigenia* is, but not to the extent of defining the play's type. Among the plays

---

[1] 'The "Just Decrees of Heav'n" and Congreve's *Mourning Bride*', in *Congreve Consider'd* (Los Angeles, Calif., 1971), pp. 1–22.

which are primarily pathetic, we may distinguish three common types: the history play, the bloodbath, and the weepy tragicomedy. A heavy female emphasis is evident in all three: hence the name applied to many of these works, 'she-tragedy'.

John Banks is the major developer of the historical she-tragedy. The subjects of *The Innocent Usurper* (the execution of Jane Gray), *The Island Queens* (the execution of Mary Queen of Scots), and *Vertue Betray'd: or, Anna Bullen* (the execution of Anne Boleyn) amply indicate Banks's *modus operandi*. His use of history had both advantages and disadvantages. A grounding in 'fact' was always welcome to these playwrights, especially when the whole foundation of the play was based on poetic non-justice. If the tale were 'true', no complaints could be raised about libelling providence. The drawback to history was the censor's sensitivity to political references and parallels: the execution of monarchs, especially female 'usurpers', became an increasingly touchy subject. Not surprisingly, *The Innocent Usurper* (pub. 1694) was never performed at all in this period. The less apposite *The Island Queens* (pub. 1684) was finally staged with alterations in 1704. Both are designed as noble tearjerkers. At the end of the former, the 'Scene draws, and discovers *Gilford* and the rest lying upon it beheaded' and the 'Curtain falls' as the virtuous and magnanimous Jane walks calmly toward the block. At the end of the latter, Queen Elizabeth unsuccessfully tries—seconds too late—to halt Mary's execution, having just received definitive proof of her innocence: hearing the news, Elizabeth 'Falls down on the Floor' in a frenzy of agony and remorse. The Anne Boleyn play casts Cardinal 'Woolsey' and Lady Elizabeth Blunt as a pair of fiendish persecutors of helpless innocents. Anna is tricked into marrying Henry VIII with the tale that her true love Piercy is faithless and has married someone else. Forged letters convince the King that Anna is guilty of incest with her brother Rochford, and despite young Princess Elizabeth's pleas ('Dear Father, will you save my Mother's life'—67), Anna is led to her execution, 'all in White'. Her farewell with Rochford has real power: Banks refrains from overblowing it, even when she forgives and blesses the King (72–5). Unlike those in the later two execution plays, the ending lacks simplicity. To the wounded Piercy enters 'a Gentleman with a Hanckerchief stain'd with the Queens Blood': Piercy kisses it, reopens his wound, and expires. We then learn that seeing the execution drove Lady Elizabeth Blunt mad, and she confessed. So Henry VIII orders Woolsey arrested, and the play ends with Henry's self-congratulation: '*A Prince can do no Ill!* . . . Heav'n n'ere made a King, but made him just.' How this got by the censor it is hard to see.

A less schematic play on a similar model is Mary Pix's *Queen Catharine: or, The Ruines of Love* (1698). The Queen is kept alive (and mercifully she merely wishes she had succumbed to madness), but her beloved Owen Tudor is stabbed by the Duke of Gloucester and dies before her eyes, and subsequently her ward Isabella dies a fine love-death. The play combines pathos and villain tragedy—and here the villains walk off unpunished. Mrs. Pix explains in the Epistle Dedicatory: 'I cou'd not, without a plain Contradiction to the History, punish the Instruments that made my Lovers unhappy'—but she pointedly reminds us what was to happen to Richard III on Bosworth field. History, she suggests, got around to poetic justice, albeit slowly.

In its bloodbath manifestations the pathetic play can encroach on villain–horror drama. In *The Injur'd Lovers* Mountfort kills off all six of his named characters. Sentiment has some play, as in a Steele-ish reconciliation of friends (29); even the wicked King can be moved by conscience (59). But the King rapes the virtuous Antelina (37). Thereafter Rheusanes kills his friend Dorenalus by mistake in the dark. Princess Oryala stabs herself in frustrated love. Antelina poisons the King's wine and they both drink it. (Told he is poisoned, the King says that this is just all the more reason for further sex in a hurry—67.) The King stabs Rheusanes and Antelina's wretched father Ghinotto, and everyone expires. Otway's *The Orphan* is a more fully pathetic play: it has no villain. 'Accident' breeds catastrophe. Polydore impersonates his brother Castalio to bed Monimia in the dark, not realizing that they have been secretly married. Monimia goes spectacularly mad and dies; Polydore provokes his baffled brother into giving him a fatal wound; Castalio stabs himself; and the family is suitably desolated. J. H. Wilson legitimately complains that Polydore is a cad, Castalio a fool: no reason is given for the marriage being secret, and the sexual substitution is a scoundrel's trick.[1] Nonetheless, in its searing language, display of broken friendship, madness, family wretchedness, and domestic-scale rant, *The Orphan* is an exciting play, and even a moving one. One cannot say quite as much for Rowe's famous *The Fair Penitent* (1703). Why the fair Calista (who knows what is what—39) ever yielded to the gay Lothario one cannot see: Rowe's explanation (5–6) carries little conviction. But working from that *donné*, the play is a good pathetic melodrama. Here again we find the fight between friends—who are reconciled when Altamont faints and Horatio thinks he has died (34, 50). The use of a room with a skull and Lothario's body on a bier (52) has a Gothic effectiveness. Sciolto presents his errant daughter with a dagger, and when she evinces willingness to use it exclaims 'Thou art my Daughter still' (56). He is then mortally wounded in a convenient fray. Three points seem noteworthy. First, Rowe pushes pathos hard, but strictly within the limits of poetic justice for Calista, who is guilty and therefore must die. Second, far more than Otway or Banks, Rowe accompanies pathos with overt and explicit didacticism.[2] Third, 'soft, complaining Rowe' works the chivalric code of friendship hard, but definitely favours an almost womanish sensibility. At the end Altamont faints, and Horatio says, 'The Storm of Grief bears hard upon his Youth,/And bends him like a drooping Flower to Earth.' Action and simile are both revealing.

Weepy tragicomedy can make full use of the devices of pathos. Abel Boyer's *Achilles: or Iphigenia in Aulis* (1700; basically a translation from Racine) has the heroine led off to be sacrificed, but averts the catastrophe. Motteux's *Beauty in Distress* (1698), technically 'A Tragedy', brings Placentia safely through threats of poisoning, stabbing, and rape to marry Fabiano. Vincentio yields his claim to her upon discovering that on account of baby-swapping she turns out to be his sister. Fabiano's father is so charmed by her virtue that he drops his violent opposition to the marriage and enthusiastically forwards it. The villain Ricardo does poison his fiancée, the Widow Laura, but he does so with mixed

---

[1] *Preface to Restoration Drama*, p. 111.

[2] This point is stressed by Frank J. Kearful, 'The Nature of Tragedy in Rowe's *The Fair Penitent*', *Papers on Language and Literature*, ii (1966), 351–60.

feelings (42), and when she subsequently stabs him, he ex-claims 'Strike, injur'd Goodness; strike again; I'll thank you' (54). She considers killing her children, to 'ease 'em', but they melt her resolve (57). Laura's death in wild torments is perhaps more dramatically exuberant than touching.

Throughout the pathetic drama both rape and incest appear regularly as threats and facts. Both devices can be used without excessive sentiment, as in *The Surprisal* and *Don Sebastian* respectively. J. H. Wilson complains that the latter is pathetic —and a weak play—because the catastrophe turns on accidental incest. But then so does Sophocles's *Oedipus*, and who calls that a weak or pathetic play? However, skilful use of such devices is not common.

In conclusion, a point so far ignored must be strongly em-phasized: the vogue and form of the pathetic play was greatly influenced by the availability of suitable actresses. Mrs. Barry played a lead role in all six of the plays discussed here, and the quarto tells us that she was scheduled to play in *The Innocent Usurper*. Her talent for noble wretchedness made her superb as Monimia, Anna Bullen, Laura, Calista, Queen Catharine, and Oryala. In the last four plays the female lead is double; in each instance beautiful Mrs. Bracegirdle took the contrasting role: Placentia, Lavinia, Isabella, Antelina. With these act-resses available, playwrights naturally followed the double lead pattern and pulled out the stops. The results mostly grate on modern critical sensibilities, but so do some of Schiller's greatest plays: the vogue was more than a passing aberration. One man's pathos is the next man's bathos.

History and Politics: 'Parallel' Plays

History and politics figure prominently in a large number of these plays, though they are the defining element in rather few. We have encountered an ostensibly historical basis in such plays as *Tyrannick Love*, *Nero*, *The Rival Queens*, *Albion and Albanius* (via transparent allegory), *The Duke of Lerma*, *Edgar and Alfreda*, *Anna Bullen*, and *Lucius Junius Brutus*. Nonetheless, no play in the period seems centrally and essentially historical in a defining way. Nicoll thinks of Orrery as a writer of historical heroic, but in *The History of Henry the Fifth* the main action (in-volving a love triangle of King Henry, Princess Katherine, and

Owen Tudor) is completely fictitious; *The Black Prince* has even less basis in fact. Neither play bears any resemblance to the Shakespearean chronicle play. Nor is either of them a dramatic analysis of a historical situation. Lee and Crowne furnish good examples of utilization of historical material. In Lee's *Sophonisba* and *Gloriana* Roman historians provide much of the substance, though Lee is not afraid to alter: in the latter Augustus Caesar is converted into the archetypal lustful tyrant so common in heroic plays. Lee's *Mithridates* is about as fictitious as Orrery's plays, and much the same is true of Crowne's *The History of Charles VIII of France* and *Regulus*. His *Darius* takes more from history, but the story serves largely as a vehicle for passion, sentiment, and ghosts. Like Tate's *The History of King Lear*, most such plays are only a little more truly historical than *The History of Tom Jones*. History is employed mostly as background and decoration for other dramatic types.

Politics are a different matter. The possible procedures in either comedy or tragedy are summarized by Virgil L. Jones: (1) parallel plays; (2) use of type characters; (3) personation; (4) miscellaneous commentary.[1] These methods may be used singly or in combinations. Relatively pure examples respectively are *The Duke of Guise*, *The Committee*, *The Rump*, and the 1667 *Tempest* (in the 'Commonwealth' sub-plot). The type-character anti-puritan satire was especially appropriate to comedy, and personal satire was fairly common,[2] though Aristophanic specificity is uncommon in both comedy and serious drama.

The substantially political serious plays seem to me to fall into three basic categories: those with obvious personal references (*The Loyal Brother*); the generalized warning (*The Misery of Civil-War*); and the parallel play (*The Generous Conquerour*). Nicoll observes further that political plays in this

---

[1] 'Methods of Satire in the Political Drama of the Restoration', *Journal of English and Germanic Philology*, xxi (1922), 662–9.

[2] Some examples: the Howard brothers in *The Sullen Lovers*; Sir William Coventry in the suppressed Robert Howard–Buckingham *The Country Gentleman*; Arlington in *The Rehearsal*; Titus Oates in *City Politiques*. Some authorities have held that Dryden was after Lauderdale in *Mr. Limberham*, but Susan Staves has shown that this is unlikely, 'Why Was Dryden's *Mr. Limberham* Banned? A Problem in Restoration Theatre History', *Restoration and 18th Century Theatre Research*, xiii (May 1974), 1–11.

period largely concern three distinct subjects: the Commonwealth and the Restoration; the Popish Plot; and the Glorious
Revolution.[1] The political import of *The Rump* or *City Politiques*
is impossible to miss. In the serious plays more obfuscation is
common. They rely on the audience being ready and able to
draw its own inferences freely, often from the midst of disguise
and contradiction. Parallel constructing was, as John Wallace
points out, one of the seventeenth century's favourite games—
and this is where it was played.

A good example of this mentality is the official reaction to
Tate's adaptation of *Richard II*. Refused a licence in December
1680, it was staged a month later under the wildly inappropriate title, *The Sicilian Usurper*. The result was an order
temporarily closing the theatre: plays about deposition were
touchy stuff. For the quarto Tate wrote a preface protesting
against the prohibition and complaining that he should not
be held 'accountable' for parallel-drawing. Admitting that
the play dealt with a 'dissolute' age and a 'corrupt' court
(sensitive matters themselves), he says: 'why a History of those
Times shou'd be supprest as a Libel upon Ours, is past my
Understanding. 'Tis sure the worst *Complement* that ever was
made to a Prince.' I myself cannot see more than thin and
strained political relevance in this lame adaptation—but to
suppose that this subject could be made to pass in the midst
of the Exclusion Crisis must require either disingenuousness
or plain stupidity. *Any* 'King' on stage could elicit extravagant
inferences. Thus Pepys records of *The Duke of Lerma*: 'the
play designed to reproach our King with his mistresses, that I
was troubled for it, and expected it should be interrupted. . . .
Its design I did not like of reproaching the King.'[2] One could
extrapolate such a design—and more besides, concerning English cabinet politics—from *The Duke of Lerma*: but was it
'meant'? Possibly. We simply cannot be certain.

At times character references seem beyond much dispute.
In Payne's *The Siege of Constantinople* the evil, intriguing Chancellor, busy objecting to the King's choice of allies on religious

---

[1] Allardyce Nicoll, 'Political Plays of the Restoration', *Modern Language Review*,
xvi (1921), 224–42. Much of what he discusses is anonymous, closet drama, or
unactable 'political dialogue'.
[2] Pepys, 20 February 1668.

grounds, is clearly an unflattering portrait of Shaftesbury. Thinking wishfully, Payne (later a ferociously loyal Jacobite who withstood torture heroically) leaves him 'Empal'd' amidst 'a great Number of Dead and Dying men' (87). Shaftesbury appears many times—most brilliantly as Antonio in *Venice Preserv'd*, where the savage scenes of sexual perversion constitute a famous and effective smear. That he appears also in that play as ringleader Renault has not disturbed critics, and should not: as with Gay's or Fielding's famous double portraits and split portraits the import is clear. In Southerne's *The Loyal Brother* Shaftesbury appears as Ismael, 'a Villanous favourite'. This play verges on the parallel category, for despite its love-triangle plot, the heavy emphasis on the virtue, nobility, and loyalty of the King's brother Tachmas definitely brings to mind the loyalist view of the Duke of York in 1682.

The general-warning play conveys propaganda of situation rather than person. Lee's fiercely anti-Catholic *The Massacre of Paris* (written *c.* 1679–81 and banned, but welcome on the stage in 1689) has no 'parallel' significance, but capitalizes on fears of a Catholic takeover. Dryden's *Amboyna* (1672) is nothing more than timely atrocity-mongering. Crowne's *The Misery of Civil-War* (1680), the first of his two adaptations from Shakespeare's *Henry VI* plays, is advertised as a warning: the prologue suggests that a country so involved in 'Religious Broyles' should reflect on the lessons of history. Through all the blood-and-thunder Crowne's view is uncompromisingly clear: 'A Monarch's Right is an unshaken Rock' (71). On a much less explicit level we can see Dryden's heroic plays in this category: they are not political treatises, but they do offer fertile ground for extrapolative readers. When Dryden wants to be particular politically, his intention is not easily mistaken.

The Duke of Guise (a collaboration with Lee) was banned in July 1682, but allowed to go forward the following November. In that period the King's victory had been consolidated.[1] Contemporary letters and newssheets suggest that the design of the play was entirely clear—to discredit Monmouth.[2] Such purpose the authors vigorously denied: the play 'was neither

---

[1] The tide had turned by late Autumn 1681. David Ogg calls June 1682 decisive in securing the King's position. *England in the Reign of Charles II*, 2nd edn. (Oxford, 1956), p. 636.   [2] See *The London Stage*, Part 1, p. 310.

a Libel, nor a Parallel of particular Persons', says the dedication. And Dryden saw fit to reply at long pamphlet length
to Shadwell's angry Whiggish plaint, *Some Reflections Upon
The Pretended Parallel In The Play Called The Duke of Guise*
(1683). Dryden's *Vindication* states that he had started the
play in 1660; that the parallel was 'betwixt the *Holy League*
plotted by the House of *Guise* . . . with the *Covenant* plotted by
the *Rebels* in the time of King *Charles* the *First*'; that the story
is genuine French history; that he personally always liked
Monmouth. All this *may* be perfectly true, but it is not the whole
story. Dryden's prologue starts: 'Our Play's a Parallel.' The
essence of the plot is this: a pack of noble scoundrels spouting
Shaftesburian doctrine demand the exclusion from succession
of the King's brother on religious grounds, insisting that he
substitute the popular Duke of Guise. The King refuses; a
crisis ensues; 'The Commons' try to force through an exclusion
bill; the King calls a special session of Parliament away from the
capital. Ultimately the King rides out the storm, and says at
the end:

> I'le wear
> The Fox no longer, but put on the Lyon. . . .
> . . . .
> Nought shall atone the Vows of speedy Justice,
> Till Fate to Ruine every Traytor brings,
> That dares the Vengeance of indulgent Kings. (V. 290)

Could the author of *Absalom and Achitophel* seriously imagine
that this would not instantly be taken as a reflection on Charles,
James, the Duke of Monmouth, the Exclusion Crisis, and the
famous Oxford Parliament of 1681? Dryden's *Vindication* confuses the issue well enough to have misled some critics.[1] The
weakness and indirection of Whig protests is no index to the
situation. What could they say? To show the connections in
detail was to prove the case against themselves, and could only
provoke an invitation to wear the shoe if it fitted.

A much less clear and consistent parallel play is Bevill
Higgons's *The Generous Conquerour* (*c.* December 1701). The

---

[1] See Summers, *Dramatic Works*, V. 212–13; and Charles H. Hinnant, 'The
Background of the Early Version of Dryden's *Duke of Guise*', *English Language Notes*,
vi (1968), 102–6. But cf. a reply by Lawrence L. Bachorik, ibid., x (1973), 208–12.

author's Jacobite sympathies were well known. One plot concerns a conspiracy to oust a legitimate king and establish a new royal line: reference to the events of 1688 cannot be missed. More centrally, Higgons has King Almerick make the son of the man he deposed his heir—thus proving himself the 'Generous Conqueror' Jacobites wished King William would be. The details of the play make quite impossible any systematic allegorical interpretation: too much is internally or externally contradictory—presumably deliberately so.[1] But behind the smoke screen Higgons's sympathies were and are obvious.

III. THE ATTRACTIONS OF OPERATIC EXTRAVAGANCE

The varieties of serious plays just outlined are anything but clear and distinct. *The Siege of Rhodes* is both heroic and musical; *The Fatal Jealousie* both villain- and fall-of-hero oriented. Split plot plays can reward virtue (*Marriage A-la-Mode*), and so can heroic plays (*The Conquest of Granada*) or pattern tragicomedy (*The Mourning Bride*). History and politics can be mixed into any other type. The categories are also unsatisfactory in depending on wholly different bases: subject, structural pattern, literary handling and devices. But these eight groupings do convey a fair sense of the full spread of dramatic practice.

Critical prescriptions and actual practice agree only imperfectly. Probably the strongest influence of contemporary theory appears in the widespread sense of the play as an exemplary construct—positive or negative. The obvious corollary, poetic justice, is not maintained in the pathetic plays, and is (happily) ignored in many others—for example, *The Rival Queens*, *Lucius Junius Brutus*, *Venice Preserv'd*, and most horror plays. But to a remarkable extent, fortune and misfortune are distributed as deserved. The playwrights' disinclination to focus on the self-caused fall of any but a markedly flawed hero is abundantly clear. The virtuous can succumb to the machinations of villainy, in which case we are invited to admire their nobility and fortitude.

---

[1] *The Generous Conquerour* is analysed at length in *A Comparison Between the Two Stages* (1702). An excellent analysis of its political import can be found in Staring B. Wells's notes to his 1942 edition (pp. 169–73).

To most later readers, these serious plays have seemed un-invitingly artificial, remote from 'reality', laboured, over-blown, stereotyped in plot and character. The plays have more complexity and intellectual content than was imagined twenty-five years ago—that much is plain even amidst the contradictions of recent studies. Nonetheless, the *appeal* of these plays has seemed incomprehensible to all but a few critics—and most of their explanations turn out to be mutually incompatible. Three theories are widely current: escapism, vicarious satisfaction of hunger for heroism, and pleasure in a debunking of Christian humanism.[1] All three concentrate on the heroic play, yet seem inadequate even for that. The first two, as Fujimura charges, are superficial and demonstrably inaccurate. His alternative is ingenious, but I can see little evidence that the original audience viewed the plays in this way. What then lay behind the plays' appeal? Probably the obvious: *spectacle* and *emotion*.

The sense of spectacle is almost entirely missing for the present-day critic.[2] The fabulous scenery and expensive costum-ing, the charming music, song, and dance all appeal to perdur-able tastes for travelogue, technicolour spectacular, and 'variety shows'—tastes satisfied today by gramophone records, maga-zines, films, and television. To the attractions of visual spectacle and aural charm must be added the special pleasures of ob-serving favourite actors in role after role. With the lead actors of a company involved in almost every production, the audience could get to know them extraordinarily well, and the immense appeal of Betterton, Hart, Mrs. Barry, and others has been documented again and again. Rymer complains, as Dryden later admits, that 'in a Playhouse every thing contributes to impose upon the judgment.'[3]

To cite 'emotion' as an attraction in these plays may seem odd: for twentieth-century readers, they seem emotionally thin and over-contrived, however supercharged. Here, at least,

[1] For the first, see Nicoll, I. 84. For the second, Bonamy Dobrée, *Restoration Tragedy* (Oxford, 1929), pp. 13, 16, 19–20, and Singh, p. 2. For the third, Thomas H. Fujimura, 'The Appeal of Dryden's Heroic Plays', *PMLA*, lxxv (1960), 37–45.

[2] For a splendid account of the true nature of the appeal of this drama, see Philip Parsons's recent essay, 'Restoration Tragedy as Total Theatre', *Restoration Literature*, ed. Harold Love, pp. 27–68.

[3] Dedication of *The Spanish Fryar*. Cf. Rymer, *Critical Works*, pp. 19, 74.

we can see what the original audiences saw, though without the advantage of acting: the barrier is a matter of conventions. Seventeenth-century serious drama is, even for scholarly readers, more inaccessible than nineteenth-century opera is for the majority of university students today. The attitudes involved make, I believe, a useful comparison. The heroic pomposities and 'philosophy' of Wagner, the oom-pah-pah blood-and-thunder of early Verdi, are entirely apposite. Psychology and intellectual substance can be discerned in these works, but both subject and handling appear thoroughly ludicrous to anyone not schooled to accept highly artificial conventions.[1] The twentieth-century enthusiast who finds (as I do) *Il Trovatore* and *Die Walküre* profoundly exciting and moving may wonder with baffled incomprehension how anyone could be deeply stirred by *The Rival Queens* or *Aureng-Zebe*; and yet the pleasure in both cases rests on the acceptance of conventions which are really quite similar. Thin and stereotyped characters, scenic spectacle, love and honour fatuities, and melodrama are the stuff of Italian opera. And the super-heroic heroes of Wagner, running about with horned hats on their heads, surely cannot seem less silly to the uninitiated than do the protagonists of heroic drama.

A large number of the serious plays of the late seventeenth century have the conventionalized and improbable subjects and extravagant, exuberant handling characteristic of later opera. If I may be indulged in a flight of fancy, I would compare Dryden to the schematic philosophizing of Wagner; Lee and Otway to the wild romps of early and middle Verdi; later Banks and Rowe to the likes of Leoncavallo's *Pagliacci* and Gounod's *Faust*; Settle, early Banks, and early Crowne to the lumbering extravaganzas of Meyerbeer. Exposure to the plays can, as I have myself discovered, breed an enjoyment very

---

[1] Lighting is a good example. Many scenes in these plays require 'total darkness', yet there was no way of fully darkening the stage: huge numbers of candles could not be quickly snuffed and relit, though some of them could be covered or removed. Yet an audience inured to the convention scarcely noticed it. Thus Pepys tells us (2 February 1669) 'it was pleasant to see Beeston come in with others, supposing it to be dark, and yet he [substituting for the injured Kynaston] is forced to read his part by the light of the candles: and this I observing to a gentleman that sat by me, he was mightily pleased therewith, and spread it up and down.'

similar to that of opera. As with Shakespeare or Noh-plays, liking depends on familiarity.

The opera parallel seems the sounder for having occurred to other observers. Rothstein points to *Aida* as an instance of the seventeenth-century cliché in later guise—'the conquering general soon disgraced, the Bracegirdle and Barry female leads, the royal oath', the death scene.[1] Leech calls Dryden's excitement 'operatic'. Dobrée speculates that Lee in particular might 'have been an operatic genius who mistook his medium', calling his plays appropriate to 'music of a pseudo-Wagnerian sort'.[2] Colley Cibber, disparaging the rant in *The Rival Queens*, draws a more contemporary parallel: 'When these flowing Numbers came from the Mouth of a *Betterton*, the Multitude no more desired Sense to them, than our musical *Connoisseurs* think it essential in the celebrate Airs of an *Italian* Opera.'[3] Commenting on this observation, Waith rightly notes that 'the triumph of sound over sense . . . is of a piece with the prominence of spectacle and song.'[4]

The standards and expectations we bring to 'Restoration tragedy' constitute an awkward barrier to understanding and enjoying it. Misconceptions engendered by the misnomer 'tragedy' are part of the difficulty. A related, more general problem lies in a difference in our concept of the basis of drama. Where we look to the intrinsic qualities of the work, the seventeenth-century writers tend to concern themselves with its affective qualities. A recent writer defines tragedy as comprising four elements: an act of shame or horror; the protagonist's consequent suffering; his tragic knowledge, generated by the suffering; and finally an affirmation of human life issuing from that knowledge.[5] Not only is this widely acclaimed formulation largely irrelevant to late seventeenth-century tragedy proper, but it reveals a theoretical disposition quite unsuited to affectively conceived drama. This is simply another way of putting Clifford Leech's case, cited earlier; the plays largely lack 'the tragic sense', and however fine the analytic net we cast, little will be found. The route into these plays is through the effects sought.

[1] Rothstein, *Restoration Tragedy*, p. 184.   [2] Dobrée, *Restoration Tragedy*, p. 118.
[3] *Apology*, p. 63.   [4] Waith, *Ideas of Greatness*, p. 241.
[5] Dorothea Krook, *Elements of Tragedy* (New Haven, Conn., 1969), Chapter 2.

Comparing the 'Restoration tragedy' he has analysed with the film of *Gone with the Wind*, Rothstein concludes that 'a work of art that depends on the creative emotions of the audience' quickly grows dated.[1] Undoubtedly he is right: the success of a primarily affective art form relies almost totally on an appreciation of its conventions which is usually short-lived. This is a matter of degree, since all works soon lose the advantage of their contemporary context. But the work which is primarily an account of its subject (as in the Krook hypothesis) will suffer less than that which is pre-eminently an address to its audience. The unhappy irony we are left with is the inaccessibility of what was a *popular* drama, one whose calculated appeal rested on elements of melodrama, heroic romance, violence, sex, pity, music, variety, and spectacle perennially popular to this day.

[1] Rothstein, *Restoration Tragedy*, p. 184.

PART II

THE DEVELOPMENT OF THE PLAY TYPES
1660–1710

CHAPTER 6

THE ESTABLISHMENT OF
CAROLEAN DRAMA 1660–1669

THE object of this chapter, and of the remainder of this book, is to investigate closely and chronologically the directions taken by English playwrights. My concern is basically with the kinds of new plays written at each stage in the half-century under consideration. Even a somewhat selective consideration involves about five hundred plays: necessarily then, theatre history and the productions of earlier English drama can receive only peripheral attention. For theatre history, one must turn to *The London Stage*; for an account of the fortunes of Renaissance drama in this period we have Sorelius's excellent study.[1] My focus will be on the way generic types appear, change, and interact—that is, on fad and fashion in the new plays. Where possible, the springs and motives of change will be sought, though we may have far greater confidence in the possibility of determining what happened than why it did so.

I. CONTINUITIES AND DISCONTINUITIES

How sharp is the break in tradition caused by the closing of the theatres between 1642 and 1660? Critics early in this century considered the discontinuity drastic; most recent scholars substantially accept Harbage's claim in *Cavalier Drama* that 'Restoration' drama grows naturally out of the Caroline drama. Few scholars now take seriously the once prevalent assumptions about pervasive and determinative French influence. But that there is a significant break and a conscious seeking of new directions after 1660 can easily be demonstrated.

[1] Gunnar Sorelius, '*The Giant Race Before the Flood*': *Pre-Restoration Drama on the Stage and in the Criticism of the Restoration* (Uppsala, 1966). For particular parts of the subject some earlier studies remain useful, especially John Harold Wilson's *The Influence of Beaumont and Fletcher on Restoration Drama* (Columbus, Ohio, 1928), Arthur Colby Sprague's *Beaumont and Fletcher on the Restoration Stage* (Cambridge, Mass., 1926), and Robert Gale Noyes's *Ben Jonson on the English Stage, 1660–1776* (Cambridge, Mass., 1935).

Neither the innovations nor the basic continuity in English drama should be scanted.

The presence of Davenant and Killigrew, Caroline courtiers and playwrights, at the head of the two companies during the 1660s obviously militated against sudden and drastic changes. So did the availability of a corps of veteran actors.[1] One might say that the old tradition dies with Hart and the King's Company at the end of the Carolean period. It must have been greatly diluted by attrition and addition in personnel, but even in the mid-seventies the acting style seems to have been markedly distinctive, as one can guess from Settle's abortive attempt to have *The Empress of Morocco* staged by the King's Company rather than by his parent Duke's Company, and from his subsequent remarks on Charles Hart. But the continuity runs deeper than managers, actors, and style: for three years essentially the entire repertory consisted of pre-Commonwealth plays, and those plays continue to loom large in the yearly performance figures (insofar as we have any) for the rest of the century. Since the veteran-based King's Company held the rights to most of these plays, they naturally became, in Sorelius's words, 'the custodians of the dramatic heritage'.[2] Entirely to abandon a tradition whose chief exemplars happen to form the basis of the current repertory would be difficult. To see, as we will, that the roots of the various Carolean modes are apparent in the older plays should come as no surprise. Heroic drama, wit comedy, mixed tragicomedy, London low comedy, and horror tragedy all have recognizable Jacobean and Caroline precedent. But as with the Darwinian descent of man, one must acknowledge the connections while still recognizing the differences. Man is not monkey and Dryden is not Fletcher.

The rise of literary criticism undoubtedly contributes to deliberate exploration of new walks. The 'Fletcher' plays were the largest single part of the Carolean repertory, but to Rymer they were 'of the Last Age', and Dryden obviously felt the same sense of distance. He could acknowledge their greatness, but saw abundant reason 'to attempt some other way'.[3] His snappish and niggling strictures in the 'Defence of the Epilogue'

---

[1] For details, see Hotson.   [2] Sorelius, p. 40.

[3] *An Essay of Dramatick Poesie, Works*, XVII. 73. See my *Dryden's Criticism*, pp. 89–101.

to Part 2 of *The Conquest of Granada* (1672) give a partial and extreme picture of the situation. Sorelius amply documents the widespread veneration for Shakespeare, Fletcher, and Jonson throughout the period. In the first decade after the Restoration one can scarcely overestimate the influence of Fletcher, an influence clearly on the wane by the time Dryden revised his *Essay of Dramatick Poesie* in 1684, when he downgraded Fletcher in comparison to Shakespeare. The early Carolean dramatists seem to have felt pulled between the genteel Fletcher tradition and the city comedy tradition headed by Ben Jonson.[1] One could even see Dryden's early split plot plays as an attempt to integrate the two types. A Fletcherean main plot is given a comic underplot equivalent to Jonsonian comedy but shorn of low-life characters. As this example suggests, admiration for Elizabethan and Jacobean writers coexists with a strong belief in the need for greater linguistic refinement and social decorum in plays. Pride in the great English heritage is qualified by doubts about 'how far we ought to imitate Shakespeare and Fletcher'.[2]

Despite such qualms and the natural desire to seek new ways, the older drama was extremely influential. Statistics help clarify its impact.[3] At least 175 pre-Commonwealth plays were revived between 1660 and 1700, about 40 of them in altered form only. (At least 18 were given both in original and modernized versions—e.g. *The Chances*.) Records of performances are maddeningly incomplete until after 1705, but until then the total number of known performances of old and new plays seems roughly equal. In the 1660s the old plays had a heavy preponderance; in the 1690s the opposite was true. Over all, far more new plays were written than old ones revived. I would endorse, however, Sorelius's hypothesis that about half of the stock plays (those revived regularly from year to year) were pre-Commonwealth works. Nonetheless, the replacement of old by new is in general easy to see. More than 90 per cent of the old plays ever revived had been played by 1670. And the proportion of adaptations to originals rises steadily each decade: starting at only about 10 per cent of the

[1] On the latter, see Brian Gibbons, *Jacobean City Comedy* (London, 1968).
[2] Dryden, *Critical Essays*, I. 246.
[3] See Sorelius, pp. 71–6; *The London Stage*, Part 1, pp. cxxvii–cxxx.

originals, the adaptations finally come to outnumber them in the nineties. In short, the old plays were popular and accessible as models, but gradually lost ground to the new. Given the small potential audience, we may wonder only that the supplantation was not faster.

The importance of pre-Commonwealth plays in the repertory, especially in the sixties, contributes heavily to continuity in tradition. We can safely conclude that 'uninterrupted' the course of English dramatic history would have been pretty much as it turned out anyway. As Harbage observes, 'Restoration' drama did not instantly assume full and final form when young Charles debarked from the *Naseby*.[1] The Commonwealth interruption did, however, produce a reshuffling and re-establishment which encouraged some experimentation and necessitated the recruitment of new actors and writers. The result is not a break in tradition so much as a fairly quick and definite turn in new directions.

In Part 1 of *The London Stage* Avery and Scouten point out five influential 'innovations and alterations' which bear on this turn. (1) The creation of the patent monopoly. Its importance is less in the monopoly—London could support no more theatres—than in the particular terms which matched Davenant's young, almost playless troupe against a set of established actors with exclusive rights to most of the standard repertory. Davenant could not compete directly on equal terms, but proved just the man to compete with innovation. (2) The introduction of women actors. Originally a move to promote decency by abolishing homosexual overtones, this change quickly bred overt heterosexual displays. The pleasures of viewing female legs in tight pants gradually gave way to more explicit titillation: the great sex comedy boom of the seventies is a direct result of the change. (3) New playhouse design. Relatively small indoor theatres and high prices combine with moral stigma to limit the popular appeal of Carolean drama. Though the idea of a homogeneous coterie has been much exaggerated, these plays are not equivalent to the popular drama of Shakespeare's day. (4) Increased use of scenery and machines. Emphasis on spectacle has a powerful effect by the early seventies. (5) More use of music and dancing, ultimately

[1] *Cavalier Drama*, pp. 1, 255.

in entr'actes. Over all, the upshot is considerable change in the character of English drama.

The roots are easily discerned, the changes real. Any discrimination of the Carolean modes of the 1670s must reckon with their quasi-Caroline foundations in the modes of the early sixties. As that phrase is meant to indicate, the plays of the 1660s, especially those written before 1665, do closely resemble the common Caroline types. The Caroline drama exhibits an almost schizophrenic split between the platonic, *précieuse* court drama fostered by Queen Henrietta Maria and the relatively low and realistic comedy of the popular theatre. Most of the early Carolean plays do seem outcroppings of the dominant Caroline types—serious court or romantic tragicomedy and comedy of London low life. The *précieuse* element is definitely carried over in both serious and comic drama: its conventions and clichés (sometimes mixed with contrasting 'libertine' themes) continue to appear throughout this period.[1]

Specific proofs of influence are hard to find. The supposed antecedents of 'Etheregean social comedy' are especially elusive. The plays we would expect to find influential, according to Harbage's theory of continuity—Shirley's *The Witty Fair One* (1628), *Hyde Park* (1632), *The Lady of Pleasure* (1635)—seem to have had no vogue on the Carolean stage. As Bernard Harris observes, this 'comparative neglect of Shirley's best social comedies by the Restoration audience is a sharp corrective to many easy assumptions about the essential continuity of social experience.'[2] The audience preference for Elizabethan and Jacobean rather than for the more recent Caroline plays, evident from the beginning of the sixties, suggests that Harbage overestimated the degree of social continuity between 1642 and 1660. In the serious drama we can see an even clearer gap between Carolean efforts and those of the earlier dramatists. Interminable arguments over the sources of heroic drama are

---

[1] Kathleen Lynch, in *The Social Mode of Restoration Comedy*, traces the *précieuse* element. See also C. D. Cecil, 'Libertine and *Précieux* Elements in Restoration Comedy', *Essays in Criticism*, ix (1959), 239–53; and David S. Berkeley, '*Préciosité* and the Restoration Comedy of Manners', *Huntington Library Quarterly*, xviii (1955), 109–28, and *The Précieuse, or Distressed Heroine, of Restoration Comedy* (Stillwater, Okla., 1959).

[2] 'The Dialect of those Fanatic Times', *Restoration Theatre*, ed. Brown and Harris, p. 21.

further testimony to the break. That the earliest Carolean plays should largely conform to previous types is entirely natural, especially with the old plays on the stage. Innovation comes quite quickly, however. Within five years several experimental forms have been tried: the serious musical (*The Siege of Rhodes*), topical political satire (*The Committee*), Spanish romance (*The Adventures of Five Hours*), and the rhymed heroic play (*The Indian Emperour*). The use of actresses quickly bred new turns in the witty-duel, gay-couple pattern later so common (*The English Mounsieur, The Comical Revenge, All Mistaken*).

Dryden, Etherege, and Wycherley did not spring full grown from the King's pocket: they were neither imported from France nor dreamed up *ex nihilo*. The Restoration in 1660 saw the revival and re-establishment of a theatrical tradition temporarily suppressed but far from extinct: a thirty-five-year break might have had a much more drastic effect. The circumstances after 1660 were sufficiently different to encourage more rapid changes than had occurred during the 1620s and 30s. The Caroline types revived but were quickly altered. The drama of the sixties is conveniently divided into two periods by the closing of the theatres from June 1665 to October 1666 on account of plague. Critics have usually paid little attention to plays from the earlier period; *The Comical Revenge* is often pointed out as a stepping stone toward the so-called comedy of manners, and Dryden's first plays are used as a point of reference, but most critics move quickly on toward the seventies. For the comic drama especially this is a mistake; it is to ignore crucial evidence about the modes which were firmly established before Etherege began to write and on which he and others clearly drew.

II. THE FIRST NEW PLAYS 1660–1665

Two obvious points can be passed over briefly. First, little new drama was produced for more than two years: only in the 1662–3 season do new plays start to appear regularly. Until then Davenant and Killigrew were busy organizing, consolidating, and stamping out competition. Performances by unlicensed actors persist until 1663. But if Pepys's account of the performance of Rowley's *All's Lost by Lust* on 23 March 1661 at the Red Bull (probably by George Jolly's company) is indicative, the competition was hopelessly weak. Second, initially there is a strong political element—basically anti-puritan satire.[1] This triumphal trampling upon the remains of the Commonwealth is unsurprising. Cowley capitalizes on such topical elements in his revision of *The Guardian* (1642) as *Cutter of Coleman-Street* (December 1661) by changing the time to 1658, letting the rogues Cutter and Worm pretend to be cavaliers, and pointing up his anti-puritan satire on Mistress Barebottle and her daughter Tabitha. The play is a multiple love intrigue with both semi-serious and satirical plot lines. Although popular well into the seventies, it has been little commented upon except for its topical references. Sir Robert Howard's *The Committee* (November 1662) is a splendidly vigorous combination of a love plot with satire on the sequestration committee and the hypocrisy of its members. (The play is analysed in detail in Chapter 3.) The machinations of the chairman and his wife supply the obstacle to true love, which neatly unites Howard's otherwise disparate centres of attention. Like *Cutter* the play deserved its long popularity, for the romantic plot and the escapades of the servant Teague make the play much more than a collection of mechanical hits at puritan villainy. Another play with extensive references to politics, though in a lower vein, is John Lacy's *The Old Troop* (acted by December 1664?), a farce which savages a 'Thieves-den governor' and Captain Tub-text (not to mention the two 'saints' he is found in bed with), but which also cuts freely at the plunderers among the King's forces. Lacy is careful to explain at the end that virtuous officers are putting a stop to such abuses. Of course incidental satire on puritans abounds throughout the period: Wycherley's Alderman Gripe and Dryden's Mrs. Saintly (in *Limberham*) are good examples. As a major interest, however, such satire is largely in abeyance between the mid-sixties and the time of the Popish Plot. Occasional parallel

---

[1] John Tatham's *The Rump*—a chronicle of political events between October 1659 and February 1660—is a savage lampoon of Lambert ('Bertlam'), Fleetwood ('Woodfleet'), Johnstone('Stoneware'), Whitelock('Lockwhit'), and other Commonwealth leaders. Virgil Joseph Scott, in 'A Reinterpretation of John Tatham's *The Rump: or the Mirrour of the Late Times*', *Philological Quarterly*, xxiv (1945), 114–18, argues persuasively that the play is actually a party satire written in February to eulogize General Monck. It is extremely vigorous, essentially plotless, and quite unlike later royalist satires.

plays appear, serious and comic. The Commonwealth sub-plot in the Dryden–Davenant *Tempest* (1667) is an example of the latter. Edward Howard's serious tragicomedy, *The Usurper* (January 1664), serves to illustrate the former (see Chapter 5, above). Behind the Italian names and setting Pepys had no trouble seeing Cromwell, Hugh Peter, Monck, and others—weirdly warped pictures, one must admit.

With *The Committee*, satire aside, Sir Robert Howard initiates a long popular pattern of light-hearted love intrigue set in London and involving a good deal of obvious (i.e. non-verbal) humour. Interestingly, Howard's first acted play, *The Surprisal* (April 1662), anticipates the other dominant mode in the early 1660s—serious, romantic intrigue comedy. H. J. Oliver has suggested connections with Fletcher, Ford, and Massinger.[1] The play is a high-flown melodrama; Oliver calls it 'uninteresting' and 'absurd', an excessively harsh judgement. The characters are pasteboard and the whole play unrealistic, but Howard contrives some striking scenes, especially Villerotto's beautifully drawn-out preparations to rape Emilia and Samira (IV. iii–V. ii). The play is seldom if ever associated with the coming vogue of Spanish romance, which is surprising, given its early date and its considerable resemblance to that mode in plot, characters, and handling. I see no evidence of actual influence on its successors, but the resemblance tells us something about audience taste.

The appearance of Sir Samuel Tuke's *The Adventures of Five Hours* (analysed in Chapter 3, above) in January 1663 marks the advent of Spanish romance. The Spanish influence in this decade is considerable, and has been studied in some detail.[2] Here I am concerned only with the dramatic type, which may be briefly characterized: a complex intrigue plot, set in Spain and involving Spanish cavaliers; utter moral propriety—everyone's honour is very important, the ladies are chaste beyond

---

[1] H. J. Oliver, *Sir Robert Howard*, Chapter 4.

[2] Montague Summers called attention to the subject in his Introduction to B. van Thal's edition of Tuke's *Adventures*. The importance of Spanish drama, especially to Dryden and Wycherley, has been fully argued by John Loftis in *The Spanish Plays of Neoclassical England*. But for a cautionary overview, see Patricia M. Seward, 'Was the English Restoration Theatre Significantly Influenced by Spanish Drama?', *Revue de littérature comparée*, xlvi (1972), 95–125. For a caveat on the use of the term 'Spanish romance', see Dryden, *Works*, X. 443–4 nn.

any possibility of reproach. Darkness and mistaken identity confuse matters, but all the love affairs are finally straightened out, and of course the unities are strictly observed. The noble characters are serious to the point of pomposity; comic relief is provided by the servants—in Tuke's play the coward Diego (who was to become a byword) and Flora. The chivalric code of behaviour leads to some ludicrous situations, as when Don Antonio, torn between inclination and honour, attacks Don Octavio one moment and the next is busy protecting him against Don Henrique. The fantastic success of *The Adventures* produced a spate of imitations. Chief among these are Dryden's second play, *The Rival Ladies* (May or June 1664),[1] and George Digby's *Elvira* (November 1664), which similarly rely on love and honour, mistaken identity, and nocturnal prowlings, all treated in an elevated tone. Dryden's play, dedicated to Orrery, contains some hints of self-burlesque, but pushes the form further toward the out-and-out heroic, especially in Don Gonsalvo's love and honour conflict. Digby (the Earl of Bristol) also wrote *'Tis Better than It Was* (*c*. July 1664—lost) and *Worse and Worse* (also lost); Pepys, who saw the latter on 20 July 1664, commented on its resemblance to Tuke's *Adventures*. All three were adaptations from 'Calderón'. Some other serious plays staged at about this time are Robert Stapylton's *The Slighted Maid* (February 1663) and *The Step-Mother* (October 1663), sprawling tragicomedies with intricate design, bungled psychology, and a few striking scenes; and 'Viscount Falkland's' *The Mariage Night* (October 1663), an indifferent, Websteresque, court–sex melodrama which is really too bloody to qualify as tragicomedy. Pepys's description is good: 'a kind of tragedy' (21 March 1667). All these testify to the popularity of serious intrigue plays.

Two Spanish romances deserve special mention: Richard Rhodes's *Flora's Vagaries* (*c*. November 1663) and Thomas Porter's *The Carnival* (Autumn? 1663). Rhodes's play is similar in outline to Howard's *Surprisal*. Porter's is full of virtue and love and honour dilemmas. But both are lively, bouncy plays

---

[1] On Dryden's indebtedness, see Allison Gaw, 'Tuke's *Adventures of Five Hours* in Relation to the "Spanish Plot" and to John Dryden', *Studies in English Drama*, ed. Gaw (University of Pennsylvania, 1917), pp. 1–61, and Dryden, *Works*, VIII. 264–75.

with a strong admixture of farce which is not restricted to the servants. Flora has to hide Alberto under a table; during the following card game her father complains about her letting the dog stay there—and so forth. Porter has Sancho (a witty servant) cut off half of Lorenzo's beard: for nearly a third of the play we wait uncomfortably for that gentleman to discover his loss. Even more suggestive of coming theatrical fashion is Sancho's disguising 'in a ridiculous French Dress' as the 'Brave Monsieur Kick-hose' (46). These humorous excursions are a considerable departure from Tuke's example: they foreshadow a major trend later in the decade toward a lighter form of romance.

If on the one hand we see serious romance deflated by comic additions, on the other we see it inflated into the full-blown heroic play. This is a tricky subject: perpetual argument rages over the origins of heroic drama. French romances, Beaumont and Fletcher, Caroline tragicomedy, and the epic all contribute—in what proportions no one agrees (and I do not think it much matters). Orrery's *The Generall* (September 1664) seems to have circulated in London as early as the spring of 1661. This work, a pumped-up Caroline tragicomedy written in rhyme on the French model, probably had some influence on Tuke's *Adventures* and Dryden's *Rival Ladies*.[1] Orrery's next plays, *Henry the Fifth* (August 1664) and *Mustapha* (April 1665), are more markedly French-influenced, and were by implication sharply criticized by Sir Robert Howard in his preface to *Four New Plays* (1665). Howard's preference was for more forward motion, psychology less freighted with the *précieuse*, and less sophistic disputation. *The Indian Queen* (January 1664) and *The Vestal-Virgin* (*c.* October 1664) are dead serious, full of heroic elevation, and move along much better than Orrery's plays.[2] These plays, along with Dryden's *Rival Ladies* (imitating Tuke and dedicated to Orrery), foreshadow the appearance of *The Indian Emperour* in April 1665, a play which takes the heroic form in the directions Dryden was later to pursue.

---

[1] For these points see Orrery's *Dramatic Works*, ed. Clark, I. 24, 31, 65–6.

[2] Dryden at least assisted Howard with the former play. I disagree with the California editors' summary dismissal of H. J. Oliver's case for Howard's authorship. *The Vestal-Virgin* in its first form is a bloody tragedy; revised with a happy ending it comes much closer to the intrigue mode Howard had explored in *The Surprisal* (see Chapter 5, above).

Returning to 1663 and 'low' comedy, we find a bumper crop. Dryden's *The Wild Gallant* (February 1663) has often been seized on as an important prototype, especially for its low and sexual humour and its relatively realistic London love plot. Mr. Loveby and the witty Constance seem more vivid than the typed figures in pseudo-Spanish melodrama. We must recall though that the play failed (crushed by Tuke's competition); it failed again in 1667 after revision; and the only form in which we possess the text is the revision. At best *The Wild Gallant* is indicative of a transition: much of the atmosphere, especially Lord Nonsuch's conviction that the devil has got him pregnant (Act IV), fairly reeks of Brome, but (at least in the 1667 revision) Constance seems to reflect an attempt at Fletcherian elevation.[1] No such endeavour marks John Wilson's *The Cheats* (March 1663). Nicoll attacks its 'incoherent brutality'—much too negative a view of an enjoyably boisterous, Middletonian city comedy. Alderman Whitebroth is blackmailed when he is caught copulating with Mrs. Double-Diligence; the Hectors Bilboe and Titere Tu are bawdy and boastful; the nonconformist Scruple and the astrologer–physician Mopus are well satirized. *The Cheats* is coarse (its blasphemies brought down the wrath of the censor) and old-fashioned, but it seems to have had a lasting popularity.[2]

Of the early comedies, however, James Howard's *The English Mounsieur* (July or earlier, 1663) is the most interesting. John Harrington Smith has called attention to this play as an important beginning in the 'gay couple' tradition, pointing out that Etherege's *Comical Revenge* is significantly indebted to it.[3] Smith is concerned with Welbred's courtship of Lady

---

[1] Alfred Harbage, 'Elizabethan–Restoration Palimpsest' *Modern Language Review*, xxxv (1940), 287–319, plausibly suggests that *The Wild Gallant* is simply 'an adaptation of a lost play by Brome' (p. 307). Moore (*The Nobler Pleasure*, pp. 15–22) gives a useful discussion of the disparate elements in the work. Ned Bliss Allen, *The Sources of John Dryden's Comedies* (Ann Arbor, Mich., 1935), Chapter 1, tries to explain away the disparities of type and style by hypothesizing that the 'Jonsonian' parts were written *c.* 1658.

[2] For a detailed account, especially of Herbert's censorship, see *John Wilson's The Cheats*, ed. Milton C. Nahm (Oxford, 1935). Langbaine and Edward Phillips admire the play; William Winstanley comments on its long-standing popularity in 1687. Had Middleton produced the same piece, I suspect it would be much better thought of now.

[3] J. H. Smith, pp. 48–53.

Wealthy; just as interesting is the anti-French satire in the Frenchlove–Vaine plot (an important anticipation of Wycherley's *Gentleman Dancing-Master* and Etherege's *Man of Mode*), and the delightful, subtle mockery of the elegant Comely. This gentleman falls passionately in love with a country lass, Elsba, but his eloquence gets him nowhere—the girl prefers the rustic William, and Comely finally yields with romantic graciousness, settling a hundred pounds a year on her for life. William's wooing is comic—'I find by the Comfashiousness of my heart, I could suck thy Eyes out of thy head, I could eat thy lips though I were not an hungard, I could lick thee all over as our Cow does her Calf' (56–7)—but it succeeds, and we are glad. The London setting, the genial tone, the combination of satire with love intrigues and a duel of wits all suggest popular comedy to come, despite some amateurish plot construction, especially at the outset. Howard's tone recalls Brome, but fumigated a bit. A more old-fashioned play in a somewhat similar vein is Killigrew's *The Parsons Wedding* (*c.* 1641; staged October 1664) which spends much more time attacking *précieuse* conventions (in the 'platonic' lovers, Constant and Sadd), but possesses a like blend of satire, horse-play, and love intrigue. Pepys called it 'a bawdy loose play', and so it is. Having the piece 'acted all by women' (Pepys, 5 and 11 October) added titillation to a work already well provided with it. The horse-play element becomes much more prominent in Lacy's *The Old Troop* (acted by December 1664?). Bawdy, satirical, and farcical, this play combines anti-French satire on Monsieur Raggou (a cook) with the schemes of the pregnant Dol Troop and attacks on the roundheads. The plot makes only occasional appearances, though from time to time we get snatches of a semi-serious romantic story involving the virtuous Biddy (disguised as a Cornet's boy) and the honest Tom Tell-troth. But as the prologue says, the play is fundamentally a rather crude farce.

Surveying the plays produced in these first few years, we can note some conclusions. Two sorts of plays, sharply differentiated, were popular: serious intrigue comedy, and low 'city' comedy with an English setting (and into which political satire was often mixed, as in *The Old Troop*, *The Committee*, and Cowley's *Cutter*). But these two types actually comprise disparate elements, and by 1665 are showing signs of developing in various directions. Serious comedy appears both inflated toward the heroic (as in *The Generall* and *The Indian Queen*), and also (despite its strong new Spanish admixture) lightened with humour, as in *The Carnival* and *Flora's Vagaries*. Tragedy as such in these years really appears only in Porter's *The Villain* (October 1662), a rousing and popular exercise in Jacobean blood-and-thunder. (See Chapter 5, above.) The London or city comedy shows at least three distinct strands: romantic plots similar to those in the lighter Spanish mode; gulling plots; and plain low farce.

We should probably not be surprised that the young George Etherege, seeking a sure-fire formula for his first play, hit on the expedient of combining four of the most popular distinguishable modes of the time. Critics tend to concentrate on only one part of *The Comical Revenge* (March 1664)— the humorous courtship between Sir Frederick Frollick and Widow Rich, a love duel of the sort on which Etherege focuses in his two later plays. Actually, this is merely the second-to-highest of four plot lines, differentiated according to social standing. (1) On the level of love and honour Etherege presents (in couplets) intrigues, sword-play, and fine sentiments ('Their blood's too good to grace such Villains Swords'—I. 53) in the fashion of Tuke,[1] that is, verging on the heroic. (2) The duel of wits between Sir Frederick and the Widow definitely resembles the main plot of Howard's *The English Mounsieur*. The successful love affair between witty, attractive couples was becoming common, as in the lighter Spanish romances and *The Committee*. (3) Sir Nicholas Cully ('Knighted by *Oliver*', we note) is duped by Palmer and Wheadle and tricked into marrying the whore Lucy—long a popular device. Similar gulling plots appear in *The English Mounsieur*, *The Cheats*, and *The Wild Gallant*. (4) Sir Frederick's French valet, Dufoy, is involved in a farcical plot with the Widow's maid, Betty. Here the satire on the French, and French pronunciation of English, again reminds us of *The English Mounsieur*, and the general level of the humour is typical of the low comedy discussed earlier. In short, Etherege has crammed into one play almost every popular

---

[1] There are some close resemblances, for example IV. iv, when we learn that Colonel Bruce has been imprisoned on a false charge of murder.

type and situation of the early Carolean theatre—a tribute to his acumen, if not to his originality. We should note especially, though, that a small part of the play, Dufoy's appearance in a sweating tub (IV. vii; the tub was part of the 'cure' for the *French* malady) was what greatly caught the audience's fancy—hence the sub-title by which the play was usually known, *Love in a Tub*. This fancy proved an earnest of taste to come.

By 1665, then, the Carolean modes are taking shape. Of some twenty-five significant new productions, almost a quarter are Spanish romance, and as many are London comedy. Five heroic plays have appeared; tragedy and tragicomedy together are about as numerous, but excepting *The Villain*, less successful. The plays of 'Viscount Falkland' and Stapylton, like those of William Killigrew, are backward-looking. William Killigrew's sprawling, sodden *Selindra* (March 1662), for example, is simply a Caroline romantic tragicomedy without the inflation and refinement of Orrery. For serious drama, the future lies in the heroic and in split tragicomedy. Comedy was to develop the light romantic plots and farce, without ever abandoning good old-fashioned gulling plots.

Support for the new forms and productions of new plays are divided with surprising evenness between the two companies. We might expect Davenant to have an edge here. The evidence suggests that Killigrew dragged his feet, but followed suit when necessary. Thus he follows the success of Tuke's *Adventures* (January 1663) with gayer Spanish romances (*The Carnival*, *Flora's Vagaries*) around the end of the year. When Davenant staged Orrery's *Henry the Fifth* in August 1664, Killigrew immediately followed suit in September with *The Generall*, though he had apparently been sitting on that play for nearly three years.[1] (On these plays, see Chapter 5, above.) Davenant's new Lincoln's Inn Fields theatre, opened in June 1661, hit the King's Company hard. People flocked to see the display of scenery, and liked it.[2] Killigrew had no choice but to construct new quarters to replace the Vere Street theatre he

[1] See Orrery, *Dramatic Works*, I. 102. *The Generall* had been acted in Dublin, 18 October 1662.

[2] Downes states (p. 34) that 'the first time the King was in a Publick Theatre' was to attend the opening of Davenant's new playhouse with Part I of *The Siege of Rhodes*. Attending 'A French Comedy' staged by a visiting troupe, 30 August 1661, Pepys sneers disgustedly at their poor scenery.

had remodelled out of Gibbons's Tennis Court. When the Theatre Royal in Bridges Street opened, 7 May 1663, Killigrew put on *The Humorous Lieutenant*, 'with scenes' as Pepys specifies. Three weeks later (28 May) Pepys found Killigrew's theatre 'so full they told us we could have no room', and so he had to go on to the 'Duke's house', where he saw Betterton play Hamlet. Scenes, machines, music, and dancing had a powerful box-office appeal. And there could be no end to the competition. Chancing 'to sit by Tom Killigrew' at *Bartholomew Fair* (2 August 1664) Pepys heard the manager boast (emptily, it turned out) that he planned to set up a Nursery, one able to mount four special 'operas' a year, 'where we shall have the best Scenes and Machines, the best Musique, and everything as Magnificent as is in Christendome; and to that end hath sent for voices and painters and other persons from Italy'. Notwithstanding Killigrew's retaliatory shifts and veteran actors, Pepys himself 'prefer[red] the other house before this infinitely' (13 January 1665). Performance records are too sketchy to tell us fully how directly the managers matched each other's offerings, but we may certainly deduce that they did so. A new play at one house could leave the other practically empty.[1] Is the appearance of both *Mustapha* and *The Indian Emperour* in April 1665 wholly coincidental? I doubt it.

In their playwrights the two houses came out about even. Davenant was more of an asset than Killigrew, but Sir Robert Howard was one of the major sharers in the King's Company, and all three Howards favoured Killigrew with their work in the early sixties, a significant advantage.[2] More important yet, their brother-in-law Dryden contracted himself to the King's Company. The Duke's Company never discovered so certain a meal ticket, though in Shadwell, later in the decade, they found a good one. Lazy Etherege produced only three plays in a dozen years for them. Orrery and Porter had plays staged by both houses. Actor John Lacy naturally wrote for the King's Company, to which he belonged. Single efforts (Tuke's *Adventures*, Sedley's *The Mulberry-Garden* in 1668) turn

---

[1] e.g. Pepys, 2 March 1661 and 7 March 1664.

[2] The fourth Howard, Henry, wrote only one play, *The United Kingdoms* (lost), staged *c.* 1661–2, auspices uncertain. From hits in *The Rehearsal*, one can guess that it was something like Edward's earlier plays.

up with equal frequency at both houses. We find less carryover of practising playwrights from the earlier period than might be expected. Shirley (d. 1666) wrote nothing new. Killigrew merely refurbished his old work. The Duke of Newcastle (no professional playwright) employed bright young men like Dryden and Shadwell to polish up his efforts.[1] Davenant put out a stream of adaptations, translations, and oddments, but no more original plays.[2] As an innovative manager his influence was great, but except for *The Siege of Rhodes* (analysed briefly in Chapter 5, above), his plays have little influence on the Carolean modes. Of the writers who are central in the period of Carolean glory, only Dryden and Etherege were active by 1665. That the Carolean directions should already be so clearly indicated by then is striking testimony to the influence of theatrical fashion on the playwrights of the time.

III. THE MODES COALESCE 1666–1669

The closing of the theatres in June 1665 temporarily interrupted production of the plays. Probably our principal loss was the first version of *The Rehearsal*, which was reputedly ready for production that month. We think of the work as a burlesque of the heroic play, which it was in the 1671 revision (printed 1672). But from the apparent remains of the original in the later version we can tell that such plays as *The English Mounsieur* and *The Slighted Maid* were equally the targets of Buckingham and his cohorts. Had we the 1665 form of the play, our view of the earlier drama would be much enhanced. Following the reopening of the theatres in October 1666 we find a straightforward continuation of the trends discernible by the end of 1664. Critics have often claimed or assumed that a

---

[1] *The Humorous Lovers* (1667), collaborating with Dryden, or Shadwell, or possibly old James Shirley. *Sir Martin Mar-all* (1667), with Dryden, an adaptation of works by Quinault and Molière. *The Triumphant Widow* (1674), with Shadwell, an adaption from his own MS. comic interlude, 1658.

[2] Principally *The Law Against Lovers* (1662), from *Measure for Measure* and *Much Ado*; *Macbeth* (1664); *The Rivals* (1664), from *The Two Noble Kinsmen*; *The Tempest* (1667), with Dryden; *The Man's the Master* (1668), translated from Scarron. *The Play-house to be Let* (*c.* August 1663) is a medley apparently concocted for the summer doldrums. Each act is a playlet: Act I is a kaleidoscopic introduction; II is from Molière; III and IV are Davenant's own entertainments from 1658, *The Cruelty of the Spaniards in Peru* and *I Sir Francis Drake*; V appears to be a burlesque of Katherine Philips's *Pompey* (1663), a translation from Corneille, possibly staged that spring in London. See *The London Stage*, Part 1, p. 64.

sudden jelling occurred in 1668; but we will see that this sudden change is largely mythical. The developments of the later sixties, in brief, are these. (1) Dryden and Orrery continue to exploit the heroic mode. (2) Low London comedy of various sorts becomes increasingly popular. (3) Pseudo-Spanish intrigue comedy continues its vogue, but in the light-hearted form of *The Carnival* and *Flora's Vagaries* rather than that of Tuke's serious *Adventures*. (4) Tragicomedy increases its popularity, especially in the split plot mode.

A change should be noted: the later sixties see a definite move toward the smut and profanity often considered typical of Carolean drama. Note the corollary: early Carolean drama is remarkably pure and clean, morally speaking. Alfred Harbage rightly insisted on this point forty years ago, and perhaps one day more critics will learn the lesson. As Harbage notes, 'the documents authorizing the revival of drama and licensing the companies were almost pietistic in tone',[1] and this sanctimoniousness was no mere hypocritical sham, as mistaken critics assume. The most popular plays in the early sixties were serious, romantic tragicomedies like Tuke's *Adventures*. Probably the smuttiest play of these years was *The Parsons Wedding*—a revision of a 1641 play. Signs of change appear in the lower plots of *The Comical Revenge* and *All Mistaken*, but we will find no upper-class comedy of cuckoldry. Most sex and sexual references appear at a low social level, as in *The Wild Gallant* (a failure) and *The Cheats*. Genteel smut is a development of the seventies: *The Country-Wife* (1675) could not possibly have been staged a decade earlier than it was. Some hint of audience opinion may be deduced from the King's Company's revival of Fletcher and Massinger's *The Custom of the Country* in January 1667. Richard Legh reported the work 'so damn'd bawdy that the Ladyes flung their peares and fruites at the Actors'; Pepys found it entirely unattractive. At the only other performance of which we have record, he reports 'the house mighty empty—more than ever I saw it'.[2] Perhaps the attempted revival is a sign of

---

[1] *Cavalier Drama*, p. 238.

[2] *The London Stage*, Part 1, p. 100. Pepys, 2 January and 1 August 1667. Dryden's claim (in the Preface to *Fables*) that 'there is more bawdry in one play of Fletcher's, called, *The Custom of the Country*, than in all ours together' is a considerable exaggeration—but the play is definitely gamey, and despite Fletcher's popularity, the audience of the sixties seems to have rejected the play completely.

times to come, but clearly it was premature. And we will do well to remember that the theatre was cleanest in the years when the court element was most dominant in the audience.

According to standard definitions, rhymed heroic drama flourished between 1664 (*The Indian Queen*) and 1675 (*Aureng-Zebe*), when Dryden grew weary of his long-loved mistress, rhyme. But the supposition that the later sixties see a systematic rise toward *The Conquest of Granada* (1670–1) has no foundation. Only four plays in these years are full-fledged heroic drama. Dryden's *Tyrannick Love* (1669) comes late, and will be discussed in Chapter 7. Orrery's *The Black Prince* (1667) and *Tryphon* (1668), though they initially attracted 'infinite full' houses, were simply, as Pepys complains, repetitions of a formula, and led nowhere. 'The contrivance . . . was almost the same that had been in his two former plays of "Henry the 5th" and "Mustapha", and the same points and turns of wit in both' (19 October 1667). At *Tryphon* Pepys reiterates his complaint, finding

the play, though admirable, yet no pleasure almost in it, because just the very same design, and words, and sense, and plot, as every one of his plays have, any one of which alone would be held admirable, whereas so many of the same design and fancy do but dull one another; and this, I perceive, is the sense of every body else, as well as myself, who therefore showed but little pleasure in it. (8 December 1668)

Pepys was dead right, and we can see why neither play (apparently) was ever revived, or had much influence. Probably Orrery himself realized that he was at a dead end: of *Guzman*, Pepys reports (16 April 1669), 'Shadwell, the poet . . . to my great wonder, do tell me that my Lord of [Orrery] did write this play, trying what he could do in comedy, since his heroique plays could do no more wonders.'

Until *Tyrannick Love*, the only other rhymed heroic play was John Caryll's rather neglected *The English Princess, or the Death of Richard III* (March 1667). One might call this pleasant and well-wrought play rhymed, but only half-blown heroic: 'nothing eminent in it', as Pepys remarks, though he liked it. The prologue accurately proclaims 'a plain English Treat of homely Fare', and disclaims Spanish novels, French romances, and foreign show. Noble display of love and honour is prominent, but the debates are curiously, and refreshingly, restrained (e.g. 25); characters throughout are surprisingly multifaceted, appealingly human, and for once grey rather than black or white. The grand scene at the end of Act IV, in which Betterton as Richard III appears 'distracted', 'walking in his Dream with a dagger in his hand, and surrounded by the Ghosts of those whom he had formerly killed', will stand comparison with Shakespeare's equivalent, in conception, though not in language (48). Richard's threat to Princess Elizabeth is too contrived (37, 42–3) and the happy ending a bit too certain. Withal, Caryll does a good job: Richard does not reach tragic heights, but the effect produces 'a most sad, melancholy' feeling, as Pepys found. Downes says that this play was admired and proved profitable, but it seems to have exerted no influence on what followed. I suspect that, rhyme notwithstanding, Caryll's play was seen more as a routine, serious tragicomedy (death of Richard III versus crowning of Henry VII) than as a heroic play. And that mode was not much in favour in the years which followed. Indeed, a distrust of the attractions of straight serious plays unhelped by verbal puffery and scenic splash may be deduced. Such plays are almost not to be found in these years, and one prominent example, Corneille's *Horace*, translated by Katherine Philips (the last act by poet John Denham) was roughly handled by the actors. The play had been performed at court (4 February 1668), but when tried by the King's Company in January 1669 it was not trusted to stand by itself. Pepys found it 'a silly tragedy; but Lacy hath made a farce of several dances— one between each act: . . . his words are but silly, and . . . as to the dances; only some Dutchmen come out of the mouth and tail of a Hamburgh sow.' One's imagination boggles, but the actors' opinion is clear. Audience preferences seem to be reflected in Pepys's commendation of Davenant's *Macbeth* as 'a most excellent play in all respects, but especially in divertisement, though it be a deep tragedy' (7 January 1667). The following 19 April he expresses delight in its 'variety of dancing and musique'. Almost the only non-heroic serious play of major import in the late sixties is Sir Robert Howard's *The Great Favourite; or The Duke of Lerma* (February 1668). This powerful and beautifully constructed drama (discussed briefly in Chapter 5, above) has gone almost without critical attention in recent years, probably because of Harbage's persuasive argument that it is a reworking of a lost play by John Ford.[1] The astonishing intensity and serious power of the play may thus be owing to Ford, but the virtue is there, and one can only regret that it seems to have had no influence on the directions tried by other dramatists. Neither tragedy nor the serious tragicomedy had much appeal in the later sixties. The rhymed spectacular is another matter: that mode was as yet sketchily defined and represented by few examples, but was very much in the air, as in the 1668 squabble between Dryden and Robert Howard. Davenant and Orrery were played out and no one else had come along; Dryden would in due course try to translate his earlier experiments and evolving theory into practice.

Reading many of these plays soon makes one fact evident: seventeenth-century playwrights did not work with sharp generic divisions in mind. The early heroic plays bear obvious resemblances to the serious (mostly Spanish) intrigue comedies then popular, and both owe a considerable debt to Caroline tragicomedy. *The Conquest of Granada* (1670–1) has moved a fair way from Mrs. Behn's *The Forc'd Marriage* (1670), a serious intrigue tragicomedy, but such double plot tragicomedies as *Secret Love* (1667) and *Marriage A-la-Mode* (1671) include plots definitely akin to the straight heroic. Rhyme is not everything, and generic distinctions are quite shaky here.

The double plot play is a striking instance, combining as it does a quasi-heroic story with the sort of witty-lovers plot which becomes a major feature of the 'wit' comedies of the seventies. These elements are supposedly akin to antithetical extremes; their harmonious and often effective combination was little noticed until recent years, partly because contemporary critics seldom defended the form except as a necessary concession to audience taste for 'variety'.[2] And indubitably the double plot form can allow an opportunist writer to exploit two popular modes at once. In these years, the most common combination is (1) a high plot which involves semi-heroic love

---

[1] 'Elizabethan–Restoration Palimpsest', pp. 297–304.
[2] See above, Chapter 4, Section III, and Chapter 5, Section II.

intrigue, skirts catastrophe, and ends happily, mixed with or set against (2) a low plot introducing witty lovers, or at least humorous diversion. Here some clarification is in order between the 'serious love intrigue' and the 'pseudo-heroic'. The former, as in *The Adventures of Five Hours*, *The Surprisal*, and *Elvira*, concerns private individuals, centres on a single house, and generally turns on parental or fraternal opposition or interference. The latter, as in *Secret Love*, *Marriage A-la-Mode*, *All Mistaken*, and *The Change of Crownes*, involves similar sorts of love complications among princes and nobility, thus bringing the national fortunes of piddling principalities into play. Both forms are full of love and honour, free of ribaldry (at least in the high plot), usually unrhymed, and tend to emphasize swordplay. The pseudo-heroic is a half-way point between the essentially private intrigue of the Spanish romance and the full inflation of the heroic play. In the fully heroic, *intérêt d'état* assumes major importance.

Secret Love (February 1667), a very popular play, is the first great example of the split plot mode. I have argued elsewhere, however, that James Howard's *All Mistaken; or The Mad Couple* was performed in the late spring of 1665, in which case it would be the prototype and have an important influence on the form of Dryden's play.[1] Howard combines an almost dead serious, *précieuse* upper plot in Caroline tragicomedy style[2] with a roistering, scatological humorous lovers low plot whose tone is reminiscent of *The Parsons Wedding*. The top plot is typical Italian principality stuff, well done, especially in the sensitive psychological handling of Arbatus and Artabella at the end of the play. The low plot is joyously and exuberantly coarse.[3] Its hero Philidor has several bastards, prominently displayed on stage, and is constantly pursued by half a dozen women whom he has seduced and abandoned. His gay-couple partner in boisterous practical joking, Mirida, tells her fat suitor Pinguister to lose weight (23–4). To do so he takes a potent purge and finds his bowels greatly loosened.

---

[1] See James Sutherland, 'The Date of James Howard's "All Mistaken, or The Mad Couple"', *Notes and Queries*, ccix (1964), 339–40; and my 'Dryden, James Howard, and the Date of *All Mistaken*', *Philological Quarterly*, li (1972), 422–9.

[2] It was modelled on Beaumont and Fletcher's *A King and No King* (1611; pub. 1619). See Wilson, *Influence of Beaumont and Fletcher*, pp. 68–9.

[3] Nicoll coldly dismisses it as 'wantonly vulgar' (I. 201).

Philidor:	S'death he runs like a *Duke*.	[he runs round
Mirida:	His stooles come very quickly upon him,	and somtimes
	One after another.	goes out to
Pinguister:	I must run with my Breeches in	untruss.]
	My hand, my Purge visits my Bumgut	
	So intollerable often. (33)	

This excremental theme is later repeated at greater length and in more graphic detail (51–2).

Dryden's *Secret Love*, presumably written while the theatres were closed, is usually considered particularly important both in the development of the split plot play and in helping establish a special type of anti-platonic lovers as protagonists in comedy. If my dating is correct, Dryden got both pattern and lovers from James Howard. In his hands, Howard's Caroline-style romantic plot,[1] terse, vigorous, and rant-free, becomes more fully heroic, while the crudities of the low plot are much refined. Dryden's Celadon and Florimell enchant us, like Beatrice and Benedick, with a love-banter in which antagonism does not hide true feeling. The attractions of a gay couple engaged in the love game were to be a major feature of later comedy: earlier examples (*The English Mounsieur*, *The Comical Revenge*) had featured attractive widows in the female part.

Dryden probably conceived his gay couple as a vehicle for Charles Hart and Nell Gwyn. Whatever the priority of the plays, the pair were reportedly superb in the roles of Philidor and Mirida as well as in those of Celadon and Florimell. They may also have helped inspire Buckingham's revisions to Fletcher's *The Chances* (February 1667), in which he strongly emphasizes a gay couple, Don John and 2 Constantia, and their anti-platonic banter. We know that Hart took the former part, and as Gwyn was in the play ('When *Nel* has danc'd her Jig'— epilogue), I would surmise that here too she was the second half of the gay couple, a possibility not raised by J. H. Smith. The gay and impudent wit in the repartee of all three couples is highly characteristic of comedies to come, especially in the attitude toward marriage. And I am convinced that we see here the particular talents of actors helping dictate policy to playwrights. At any rate, unless I am much mistaken, both of James Howard's extant plays are key items in the emergence of a

[1] The resemblance is noted by Harbage, *Cavalier Drama*, p. 245.

typically Carolean drama. They represent, I believe, an interim stage between the older kinds of Caroline plays initially imitated after 1660 and the newer sorts of plays that Dryden was a pioneer in establishing. In the witty London comedy, in double plot tragicomedy, and in the gay couple tradition James Howard's contributions are important.

Two more multi-interest plays deserve comment, especially Edward Howard's surprisingly neglected *The Change of Crownes* (April 1667). This play, suppressed personally by Charles II, was long believed lost. A MS. prompt copy was discovered and printed with an introduction by F. S. Boas in 1949. Why recent critics have not made much of it I do not understand. Pepys calls it 'the best that ever I saw at that house [i.e. put on by the King's Company], being a great play and serious; only Lacy did act the country-gentleman come up to Court, who do abuse the Court with all the imaginable wit and plainness about selling of places, and doing every thing for money. The play took very much.' Pepys's hyperbole may be discounted (the next night he 'never was more taken with a play' than with *The Silent Woman*), but Howard's work, stiff as the serious plot seems to modern taste, has considerable merit. Howard combines a taut, well-controlled high plot (Italian court politics and love complications) with a riotous satire on sellers of government posts and those who seek them. Asinello, the country gentleman in search of a sinecure, is a hilarious character: Howard deserves credit for giving the double plot form a new twist—political satire rather than witty lovers as the contrasting strand. Unfortunately the example did not inspire further experiment, for Charles II was *not* amused.

Another example in the multi-plot mode is Sedley's *The Mulberry-Garden* (May 1668). This play is almost always treated as an inferior version of *She wou'd if she cou'd* (February 1668). Both writers are 'court wits'; both satirize coxcombs and present witty men of fashion (Sedley's Wildish; Etherege's Courtall and Freeman); both employ a London setting. But to look only at these elements misrepresents Sedley's play, for its real source of inspiration is plainly not Etherege's second play but his first, *The Comical Revenge*. Sedley employs a very similar collection of sharply differentiated plots: Althea and

Diana are finally united with Eugenio and Philander (cavaliers in hiding—the time is spring 1660) in a heroic love-intrigue plot presented in rhymed couplets. Even the quintessential heroic device appears: Horatio fights to save his rival Eugenio (58). Set against this are the witty carryings-on of Victoria, Olivia, and Wildish—a rather thin plot; some satire on the fops; and a reminiscence of Etherege's gulling plot in which Sir Samuel Forecast is almost tricked into marrying a 'wealthy widow'. Only Etherege's servant plot is missing. Oddly enough, that portion of the play on which critics seize—the satire on the 'Witwoud' figures Estridge and Modish in a conflict with the 'Truewit' Wildish—is nowhere closely paralleled in Etherege's first two plays. Sedley's social satire does anticipate Wycherley, the later Etherege, and Congreve, but the closest parallel among his possible sources or inspirations is James Howard's Frenchlove and Vaine in *The English Mounsieur*. In its multi-strand construction, *The Mulberry-Garden* is a backward-looking play, despite its genteel London setting and its social satire.[1]

Turning to a related mode, the romantic intrigue comedy which was the most popular form in the early sixties, we again find heavy comic accretion, but here less separate from a high plot than in the split tragicomedies. The popularity of the form continues in the late sixties, but rigid propriety and decorum increasingly give way to massive doses of low humour. Digby's Donna Blanca in *Elvira* (1664) says nobly, 'I'de rather die, then have him think me Easie' (38), and Pepys comments admiringly of Tuke's *Adventures* (1663) that it is 'without one word of ribaldry': these chaste and serious works make a sharp contrast to the increasingly amusing, titillating romances later in the decade. The Dryden–Davenant *Tempest* (November 1667) transforms its original in a similar way. The addition of Hippolito ('one that never saw Woman') and Dorinda (a sister for Miranda) occasions some smutty humour, while the low plot is expanded into an anti-Commonwealth satire and the introduction of Caliban's sister Sycorax even gives it a sex

---

[1] For a sympathetic analysis with no attempt to excuse the play's scrappiness, see V. de Sola Pinto, *Sir Charles Sedley* (London, 1927), pp. 247–63. Yet another split plot play from about this time is Mrs. Frances Boothby's undistinguished *Marcelia* (early 1669?).

interest. Pepys notwithstanding ('the most innocent play that ever I saw'), the effect is to lower the tone of the original. Even so, the subtle use of a three-level hierarchy plot and some telling thematic interconnections make this adaptation far more than a prostituting of Shakespeare.

Two romantic comedies on the Spanish model with a lighter note are St. Serfe's *Tarugo's Wiles, or The Coffee House* (October 1667) and Davenant's Scarron adaptation, *The Man's the Master* (March 1668). Davenant's play includes a serious duel and plenty of sword-play, but the reversal of roles of Don John and his cowardly servant Jodelet makes for amusing situations, and Davenant is happy to add low verbal humour as well—'If I should kick him I could not hurt him. . . . We who have tender toes are ill provided for tough Bumms' (35). Pepys sums up very accurately: 'a translation out of French, and the plot Spanish, . . . the mirth was sorry, poor stuffe . . . fit for clownes' (26 March 1668). Most of the audience, however, liked clowns. St. Serfe's effort is more interesting. On a perfectly ordinary love and jealousy intrigue plot he hangs the antics of the tricky servant, Tarugo. Particularly in Act III, set in the 'Coffee House' of the sub-title, there is extended foolery and verbal joking perfectly unrelated to the plot. The setting remains technically Spanish—the assumptions of the high plot demand it—but much of the play could well be a London comedy of the type of *Sir Martin Mar-all* (August 1667), and this extension of a tendency we saw earlier in the 'Spanish' plays of Rhodes and Porter is symptomatic of a decisive shift away from the rigidly decorous love-intrigue play popular earlier. This type continues to appear in the double plot plays, but in the years 1666–70 we find it by itself only in Mrs. Behn's *The Forc'd Marriage* (1670), an old-fashioned work which was not much of a success.

Two more examples of this 'Spanish' type give us some further sense of the development of the mode. Dryden's *An Evening's Love* (June 1668), set in Madrid in Carnival time, turns on a rather thin intrigue in which Wildblood and Bellamy (*English* cavaliers) and one Don Lopez win the females they desire. Love and honour have pretty well vanished: instead we are entertained with a dirty prologue, lovers' chit-chat, and Bellamy's fumbling pretence at being an astrologer. The credulity of old Don Alonzo is hard to believe, and his conviction in Act V that Bellamy has raised spirits (one of which is suffering from sniffles) in the shape of his daughters is pure farce. As usual, Dryden knew precisely what he was about. 'I confess my chief endeavours are to delight the Age in which I live. If the humour of this, be for low Comedy, small Accidents, and Raillery, I will force my Genius to obey it.'[1] Three years later, in his preface to *An Evening's Love*, Dryden denigrates the play, and evidently this represented no change of mind. Within two weeks of the première, Pepys reports a visit to the publisher Herringman, who 'tells me Dryden do himself call it but a fifth-rate play' (22 June 1668). Pot-boiling farce or not, this jolly romp remained in the repertory for some twenty years. A more thoroughgoing farce is Orrery's *Guzman* (April 1669), another Spanish intrigue play with heavy reliance on the popular device of a mock-astrologer. The sword-play is mere buffoonery; the 'London' comic device of marrying gulls to ladies' maids appears here as mock marriage; Guzman's sublime assurance before a duel that the astrologer has made him invulnerable to bullets is representative of the farcical humour. *Guzman* is neatly put together, but the combination of sodden language and heavy-handed treatment of what should be gay knockabout undermines the play. Orrery's *Mr. Anthony* (December 1669) is constructed on exactly the same plan; probably the even greater complexity of its trivial intrigues contributed to its complete failure on the stage. The rapid degeneration of the Spanish intrigue mode is obvious. Its early concern with decorous love and honour vanishes, entirely subsumed into the heroic play. The increasing doses of humour injected after 1666 quickly demolish the special nature of the form. *Elvira* (1664) and *The Cheats* (1663) appear utterly distinct in type. Such plays as *Tarugo's Wiles* (1667) and *Guzman* do not seem much different from the London comedies of the same period.

The nature of this London comedy is not easy to summarize, and some account of its diversity must be attempted. The plays involved range from Lacy's *Sauny the Scot* (April 1667—an adaptation of *The Taming of the Shrew*) and John Caryll's *Sir Salomon* (a Molière adaptation) to Shadwell's *The Sullen Lovers*

---

[1] 'A Defence of an Essay of Dramatique Poesie' (1668), *Works*, IX. 7.

(May 1668) and *The Humorists* (December 1670). These last two deserve special notice: almost invariably dismissed as humours plays, doctrinaire imitations of Jonson, they are actually set apart by their vein of personal reference. Judged by the Jonsonian model Shadwell upholds in his preface, *The Sullen Lovers* is a bad play. The misanthropic Stanford and Emilia are contrasted to a pair of sprightly lovers, Lovel and Carolina, who are amused rather than upset by the foppery and nonsense of four fools. But there is little sense of structure or plot development; the plot is slight and all of Act I is given to mere display of character, while the misanthropy of the lead pair tends to pall on us well before Act V. But Pepys's report of his reaction indicates the play's real point. At first he finds it 'tedious' and lacking 'design'. But when word of the personal satire gets about, Pepys, in company with the rest of the audience, discovers much more to enjoy in the play. Sir Positive At-all is Sir Robert Howard; the poet Ninny his brother Edward; the 'loving Coxcombe Woodcock' is Lord St. John. Few critics seem to have known the contemporary figures and plays well enough to appreciate the excellence of Shadwell's caricatures, which are extremely unfair but beautifully pointed. Shadwell did unto the Howards as Dryden was to do unto him. Sir Robert Howard, the slightly cranky Crites of Dryden's *An Essay of Dramatick Poesie* (published this same year), is displayed as an insufferably arrogant bore who is finally married off to a pregnant prostitute. When Sir Positive discovers the truth he is made to conclude that it is all for the best: 'He's a wise man that marry's a harlot, he's on the surest side, who but an Ass would marry at uncertainty?' (I. 91). This sort of personal satire can be enormously effective, but quickly makes a play hopelessly dated. How many such references we miss is anyone's guess. There was some vogue for personal satire in the next decade: *The Rehearsal* (1671) is a prominent example. An incipient boom in personal satire in the late sixties was cut rather short by belligerent reactions. Possibly the boom was sparked off by the continuing success of *The Sullen Lovers*, to which a new topical scene was added during the summer of 1668.[1] In a play by Newcastle, *The*

---

[1] It appears in the Portland MS. but not in the printed quarto. See Richard Perkin, 'Shadwell's Poet Ninny: Additional Material in a Manuscript of *The Sullen Lovers*', *The Library*, 5th ser. xxvii (1972), 244–51.

Heiress (January 1669), Kynaston took off Sir Charles Sedley, for which he was 'exceedingly beaten with sticks' (Pepys, 1 February); the play was acted at least once more, with Beeston 'reading' Kynaston's part, but the piece has no further record of performance and was not printed.[1]

Less than a month later the King's Company got into another such imbroglio, only worse. This one has a clear political motivation. Into a play called *The Country Gentleman* by Sir Robert Howard, the Duke of Buckingham inserted a scene viciously ridiculing Sir William Coventry (a Commissioner of the Treasury) and Sir John Duncomb—an attack which was part of a systematic anti-Yorkist campaign. The circumstances under which this play was suppressed caused a major government scandal and cost Coventry his office in the Treasury. Coventry challenged Buckingham to fight, and told Pepys that 'he had told Tom Killigrew that he should tell his actors, whoever they were, that did offer any thing like representing him, that he would not complain to my Lord Chamberlain, which was too weak, nor get him beaten, as Sir Charles Sidley is said to do, but that he would cause his nose to be cut' (6 March 1669). Though the play was definitely prepared for production on 27 February, the King's intervention stopped both play and duel; the work was never printed, and only in 1973 was an MS. copy found and identified.[2]

Quite apart from the personal satire, the play is generically interesting. The title character, Sir Richard Plainbred, is a benevolent father and a satiric spokesman for the author—an exemplary model twenty years before Shadwell was to champion such figures. The plot revolves around his two daughters, wealthy heiresses sought by three pairs of men. The first set, Worthy and Lovetruth, are honourable country gentlemen of good means who win the ladies without any real difficulty. Their rivals are Vapor and Slander, two affected,

---

[1] Unless, as Harbage and Schoenbaum speculate, it was identical with *The Triumphant Widow*, staged in 1674 and printed in 1677. See *Annals of English Drama 975–1700*, 2nd edn. (London, 1964). However, the latter play lacks the scene 'in the dark' on which Pepys comments.

[2] See BM Add. MS. 36,916 f. 128; Oliver, *Howard*, pp. 167–8; and Arthur H. Scouten and Robert D. Hume, 'A Lost Restoration Comedy Found: "The Country Gentleman" by Sir Robert Howard and the Duke of Buckingham', *The Times Literary Supplement*, 28 September 1973.

Frenchified, cowardly fops; and two ponderously serious 'men of business', Sir Cautious Trouble-all and Sir Gravity Empty (i.e. Coventry and Duncomb). Two 'tricky servants' are introduced to keep the intrigues boiling: Trim is a barber and general factotum of the Plainbreds; Mistress Finicall Fart is their London landlady, an affected, ageing pretender to gentility who is much taken with the beaux. Over all, the play is light intrigue comedy—cheerful, lively, and full of brisk dialogue in keeping with the times. Short, rapid-fire speeches give the illusion of more motion than the plot really contains. Unlike *The Committee* and other more serious intrigue comedies, *The Country Gentleman* has no significant 'blocking figure': our attention fixes on the pranks of the heroines and the schemes of the tricksters, with no real concern for the outcome. The *badinage* is vigorous, though scarcely light in touch, reminding one more of Sedley than of Etherege. In the romantic couples we see Howard experimenting, in severely decorous form, with the gay-couple love game. Neither cuckolding nor extra-marital sex is ever an issue in the play. Howard does verge on a proviso-scene late in Act II, having his gentlemen promise thrift and fidelity for themselves, freedom and power within the marriage for the women ('your Commission shall not be taken from you after marriage, but always command in chief'). Midway through Act V the women are still talking down marriage, amusing themselves by playing a coquettish love game. But here it remains strictly a game: love and honourable marriage are upheld. Although Howard is no proposer of the libertine ethic, neither is he indulging in the old *précieuse* conventions. The vigour with which the heroines torment the beaux in Acts IV and V, purely for pleasure, and the impish mocking of the convention of killing female eyes at the end of Act III, place Howard very definitely between those two worlds. The anti-French satire, placed in a unique 'low' setting, makes an interesting comparison with James Howard's *The English Mounsieur*, Wycherley's *The Gentleman Dancing-Master*, and Dryden's *Marriage A-la-Mode*. The static setting of Howard's last comedy suggests an early instance of influence from contemporary French drama, and is consistent with Howard's critical essays and the position he is made to occupy as 'Crites' in Dryden's *Essay of Dramatick Poesie* a year earlier.

Howard's astonishing reversal of the usual town versus country clichés of 'Restoration comedy' may well be politically motivated. Sir Richard Plainbred is an upholder of the good old-fashioned English virtues of the sort Shadwell was to extol in *The Lancashire Witches* (1681). He is a great admirer of Queen Elizabeth (cf. Old Bellair in *The Man of Mode*) and country sports, and he loathes the crowded, polluted, dishonest city. Plain English cooking and ale are an absolute fetish with him. All this sounds as though he ought to be the subject of raillery and perhaps outright satire—but not so. The unusual ideological design of the play had, I suspect, ulterior motivations. Buckingham and his current supporters ('the Undertakers', including Sir Robert Howard) badly needed the support of the 'country party' in the Commons. Sir Richard Plainbred seems designed to placate this group, standing as an exemplar of the best of the breed. Of course almost everything he stands for (except Protestantism) was anathema to Buckingham's group, but presumably the flattery was good politics.

Probably the fate of Howard's play cooled enthusiasm for personal satire. At any rate, the story of this short-lived vogue is completed with Shadwell's second original play, *The Humorists*. At first glance, he appears to have put in more plot at the expense of personation, though character remains more prominent than plot. Actually, if the preface may be believed, the version we see was not what Shadwell had in mind: 'I was forced, after I had finish'd it, to blot out the main design of it; finding, that, contrary to my intention, it had given offence.'[1] Followed by a disavowal of 'personating particular men' this suggests that Shadwell failed to get away with it a second time, an impression sustained by the slightly patchy nature of the remains. Like his first play, this one is set in the London of the year of first performance, but in neither does the setting seem as central as in Shadwell's later plays: these first efforts are atypical both of Shadwell and of contemporary comedy.

Examining the London comedies of this period we find an astonishing number of adaptations, especially from Molière.

---

[1] I have examined the MS. of an earlier (and vastly different) version of *The Humorists* in the possession of the Duke of Portland, now on loan to the University of Nottingham library. I will refrain from commenting on the MS., since Mr. Richard Perkin of Leeds University is now editing it. His edition should prove of very great interest.

Indeed, excepting Shadwell's first plays—which do borrow hints from Molière—and *The Humorous Lovers* (March 1667), an old-fashioned play in which Shadwell may have assisted New-castle, all of these plays fit into this category. John Lacy followed the vein of his *Old Troop* in his *Sauny* (1667) and *The Dumb Lady, or the Farriar Made Physician* (acted by 1670). Drawing heavily on *Le Médecin malgré lui* (1666) this last play is far more tightly con-structed than Lacy's first: the romantic plot involving Olinda and Leander remains in view most of the time, unlike the Biddy–Tom Tell-Troth plot in the first play. 'Doctor' Drench is by turns henpecked, clever, and indecent—the last especially in his advances to the nurse. The play is excellent fun, but as John Wilcox says, the net effect of the adaptation is to coarsen the tone and remove the point of a cleverly satirical farce.[1] Putting 'Cow-itch' down another doctor's back is not the stuff of which comedy of manners is made. Many standard devices appear: the poltroonery of Squire Softhead, old Gernette's goatishness, a mock-marriage which turns out here to be real. Caryll's *Sir Salomon* (April or May 1670), much closer to its original, is a neatly wrought city-intrigue play whose bounce and bustle deserve the praise which Summers is almost alone in granting.[2] Wilcox notes with disgust that the real spirit of *L'École des femmes* (1662) is gone; but Caryll handles his plot well, individuates his characters, and makes the knockabout lively. As the prologue says, the play 'is but *Punchinello* drawn at length': nonetheless, the play retained a steady popularity for more than thirty years. In contrast to this skilful utilization of Molière, we should note Matthew Medbourne's feeble trans-lation of *Tartuffe* (Spring 1670) and Richard Flecknoe's wretched *Damoiselles a la Mode* (privately printed in 1667; performed by the King's Men in September 1668). On its second night Pepys describes the latter as 'a translation out of French by Dryden' (*caveat* attributor!), and reports its dismal failure: 'when they come to say it would be acted again to-morrow, both he that said it, Bees[t]on, and the pit fell a-laughing, there being this day not a quarter of the pit full' (15 September). Presumably Flecknoe lost his third-night takings.

Two plays of the London variety, both drawing on Molière,

---

[1] *The Relation of Molière to Restoration Comedy*, pp. 48–53.
[2] *Playhouse of Pepys*, pp. 372–4.

deserve special attention: *Sir Martin Mar-all* for its enormous popularity, and Betterton's *The Amorous Widow* for its supposed place in the 'comedy of manners'. *Sir Martin* (August 1667) was immensely successful and long remained so. We find frequent references to it throughout the seventies. Pepys's comment gives us some essentials:

To the Duke's playhouse, where we saw the new play acted yesterday, 'The Feign Innocence, or Sir Martin Marr-all'; a play made by my Lord Duke of Newcastle, but, as every body says, corrected by Dryden. It is the most entire piece of mirth, a complete farce from one end to the other, that certainly was ever writ. I never laughed so in all my life. I laughed till my head [ached] all the evening and night with the laughing.[1]

As Moore says, the play is 'comedy of folly', not 'comedy of wit'. The Covent Garden setting, the colloquial language, the farcical devices, and the play's roaring high spirits all combine to make it a riot. Sir Martin's cocksure belief in his wit makes him mar every scheme the clever Warner can concoct. His abortive pretence at playing the lute (V. i) long drew almost proverbial reference (as in Act I of *The Country-Wife*), and the 'Frolick of the Altitudes', which immobilizes Moody and Sir John while the necessary marriages are effected, is a ludicrous kind of *deus ex machina*. Warner and Millisent are clever but far from refined, while the sub-plot involving Lord Dartmouth, Lady Dupe, and the pregnant but unmarried Mrs. Christian is straightforwardly coarse rather than merely suggestive. Betterton's *Amorous Widow*, though far less impressive, has a similar tone at times. Lady Laycock's panting desire for Cuningham and Lovemore reminds us of Etherege's Lady Cockwood, but our attention is only intermittently drawn to this part of the plot. The disguising of Merryman as Viscount Sans-Terre, the antics of Clodpole, and especially the near-cuckolding and humiliation of the shopkeeper Barnaby Brittle rather overshadow the title situation. The romantic plot involving Cuningham and Philadelphia is very slight;

---

[1] Pepys's account of the authorship—primary responsibility to Newcastle, correction by Dryden—seems borne out by recent investigations. See *Works*, IX. 352–69, and F. H. Moore, 'The Composition of *Sir Martin Mar-all*', *Essays in English Literature of the Classical Period*, ed. Patterson and Strauss, pp. 27–38.

after Act II our attention shifts almost entirely to the luckless Barnaby, his scheming wife, and her insufferable, snobbish parents.[1] The importance of Betterton's play really lies, however, not in its alleged 'manners' elements, but rather in its increased emphasis on titillative sex.

Surveying this rather disparate London comedy of the late sixties, we can hazard some generalizations. First, as we have seen, most of it is adapted from French sources: plots and characters are freely lifted from Molière and made to serve very different ends. Action, farce, and the *risqué* are increased at the expense of serious satire. Second, though romantic plots are retained, serious lovers play a small role. Third, these plays are markedly low in tone: farce and knockabout are prominent; indecency is definitely on the rise; and even the characters we are meant to sympathize with—Betterton's Cuningham and Philadelphia, Lacy's Olinda and Leander, Caryll's Peregreen and Betty—are not taken very seriously. They are, rather, stock figures employed to carry out a plot whose interest lies in action and situation rather than character.

The next question is obvious: where does *She wou'd if she cou'd* (February 1668) fit in all this? It is a London play with unusually bawdy songs for its date. The intrigue is extremely slight, with no more than a pretence at maintaining the fiction of opposition to the course of true love. Two things stand out: Lady Cockwood's frantic desire for extra-marital sex (covered up by hypocrisy and tyranny over her husband), and the witty *badinage* involving Ariana and Gatty and their admirers Courtall and Freeman. Despite the bawdy talk and songs, the proprieties are carefully preserved: in the late sixties servants do not enter, 'tying up Linnen'. Courtall strings Lady Cockwood along, but arranges matters to frustrate anything coming of it. The drinking, gaming, wenching propensities of Sir Oliver and his friend Sir Joslin Jolley are amusingly satirized, though their desire considerably outruns performance. Two general

---

[1] The precise date of the first performance of this long-popular play is unknown: guesses range from 1668 to 1670. It was not printed until 1706. Another Betterton play, *The Woman Made a Justice* (February 1670), is lost; its character may be deducible from its title. Apparently it was much less popular, though Downes (p. 30) says it did well initially. For a probable source (Montfleury's *La Femme Juge et Partie*, 1669), see Montague Summers, 'The Comedies of Thomas Betterton', *Notes and Queries*, clxx (1936), 454–6.

points should be made: plot exists here for the sake of displaying character, and the language is far more refined, less colloquial and realistic, than in contemporary London comedies. The characters are from the upper middle class (Rake-hell *et al.* having only minor parts) and the plot is entirely concerned with social diversions: inexpert players of the social game are satirized, while those more polished and self-controlled enjoy success.

Kathleen Lynch (whose opinion is often echoed by later scholars) says flatly that in *She wou'd if she cou'd* 'the main course of development of Restoration comedy had been determined'.[1] But if we look for literary relationships to other plays of the time, we find some resemblances in the parts, but no parallel to the nature of the play as a whole. Wenching and gaming are common enough in London comedies right through the next decade. The witty young ladies and their lovers are part of the gay couple tradition: the refinement of the wit is anticipated in Dryden's Celadon and Florimell the previous year. Such mild horse-play as Courtall's being hidden under a table (V. i) closely recalls a scene in *Flora's Vagaries* (1663). But despite such partial resemblances, *She wou'd* is unique: its combination of refinement and a London setting, and its emphasis on wit and character instead of intrigue are unparalleled. Pepys's comment on the *première* (6 February) reflects this de-emphasis of plot: he says the audience blamed the play 'as a silly, dull thing, though there was something very roguish and witty; but the design of the play, and end, mighty insipid'. We know from Pepys, and from Shadwell's preface to *The Humorists* (pub. 1671), that, as Shadwell says, 'imperfect representation of it at first' nearly damned the play. Court favour preserved it, and gradually *She wou'd* achieved a satisfactory success. But in view of its bad start, little immediate effect could be expected. As we have seen, save for some possible influence on the character of Betterton's Lady Laycock, no significant influence had appeared in the plays staged by the end of 1670. According to most authorities, *She wou'd* was a play of a new kind, and its long-vaunted uniqueness has indeed been borne out in this detailed survey of contemporary productions. That it initiated a boom in

[1] *The Social Mode of Restoration Comedy*, p. 174.

its mode, though, is open to question: the extent to which the plays of the 1670s follow Etherege's lead, and the extent to which they develop naturally from the more established modes, remains to be seen.

To say that there is a sudden jelling or change in direction in 1668 is misleading. One can fairly claim only that between 1667 and 1669 some trends become increasingly plain and the Caroline residue greatly diminishes. The two companies compete much as before; again we can see clearly that the King's Company is fighting back more than taking the lead. Against such smash hits as *The Tempest* and *The Sullen Lovers* in the 1667–8 season, Killigrew keeps going to the older plays he controlled—*The Sea Voyage, Philaster, The Maid's Tragedy, The Goblins, The Wild Goose Chase, The Changes*. At times Killigrew tries to fight fire with fire directly, as in his disastrous revival of *Flora's Vagaries* against the *première* of *Tarugo's Wiles* (5 October 1667). Pepys comments that night that 'to see how Nell cursed, for having so few people in the pit, was pretty'. The staging of Fletcher's *The Faithful Shepherdess* against Shadwell's *The Royal Shepherdess* in February 1669 proved equally disastrous. 'Lord! what an empty house, there not being, as I could tell the people, so many as to make up above £10 in the whole house!' (Pepys, 26 February). Since basic daily expenses were at least £25, one can see why the actors would be upset. The adaptation of Fletcher's *The Island Princess* staged by Killigrew in November 1668 with fancy scenes (including a town on fire) and a lot of songs is clearly an answer to the success of *The Tempest* a year earlier: the King's Company's production of *The Sea Voyage* (September 1667) had suffered badly by direct comparison with *The Tempest* (see Pepys, 25 March 1668). Probably no play shows Killigrew fighting back more clearly than Dryden's *An Evening's Love*. Dryden's contempt for tarted-up Spanish romance is well documented, but Davenant had been making money on plays of this sort, and Killigrew plainly set his best man on this track, regardless of Dryden's personal feelings about it. The excellent commercial results are testimony to Dryden's professional skills.

Assessing the various modes so far as they are distinguishable, one sees easily that comic accretions have killed Spanish romance as a special form. Moral tone in general is sagging, and comedy has been affected by a heavy dose of French-originated farce. The gay couple, witty-conversation comedy has made a clear-cut appearance by 1667, but is almost buried in the flood of farce toward the end of the decade. The heroic play seems very much less prominent and dominant than one would anticipate. Not everyone was happy with this state of things: the next few years saw an effort, spearheaded by Dryden, to re-establish serious drama in a clearly defined heroic mode and to reverse the trend in comedy.

CHAPTER 7

SEX, HORROR, FARCE, AND THE HEROIC INCLINATION IN THE SEVENTIES

THE sixties saw the re-establishment of a vigorous theatre, the emergence of several promising playwrights, and the gradual development of new modes and vogues in the drama. The seventies were to see this new drama and its writers at their peak. Within the decade there are two broad patterns. In comedy, a great boom in sex seems to blow itself out late in the seventies. In serious drama, the rhymed heroic play enjoys its protracted vogue but gives way to other forms.

At the outset of the new decade the writers engage in deliberate and vigorous debate about what sorts of plays ought to be written. But regardless of theory and noble prescriptions, sex, horror, and spectacle flourish in the next few years: both genteel comedy and the rhymed heroic play suffer accretions. Nonetheless, in the brief period 1675–7 Carolean drama reaches its greatest heights. Dryden, Shadwell, Etherege, Wycherley, Lee, and Otway are all at or near the peak of their powers, and each of them brings out at least one major play. After 1677, however, the onset of theatrical depression is quick and ruinous: the uproar attendant upon the Popish Plot and the following Exclusion Crisis drastically thins the playgoing audience. The King's Company does not actually die until 1682, but competition and innovation had long since been stifled.

I. HEROIC INCLINATIONS AND THE CRISIS AROUND 1670

Before launching into a detailed survey of new plays in the seventies, we may find useful a brief account of the playwrights' sense of direction. To an unprecedented degree some of the Carolean writers had become self-conscious about their literary productions. The abrupt rise in literary criticism in these years reflects a determination to analyse the directions drama should take. Dryden's celebrated *Essay of Dramatick Poesie* (pub. 1668) is such a consideration. There Dryden weighs the practice of the Ancients and the French against English tradition. Perhaps as important, he inquires into the claims of 'ideal' as against 'literal' representation in drama, and comes out with the conclusion that heightened imitation ('Nature wrought up to an higher pitch'—XVII. 74) best suits the nature of a 'serious play'. In due course he reached a similar conclusion for comedy.[1]

The trends in English drama in the later sixties were profoundly unpalatable to Dryden and to those with similar élitist predispositions. Serious drama, including the rhymed heroic play, had never really taken hold. In comedy the lightened Spanish-style intrigue romances and French-style farces were dominant. Dryden had been compelled to imitate the former in *An Evening's Love*, had helped Newcastle with *Sir Martin Mar-all* in the latter—and had a vigorous contempt for both forms. Other writers evince similar feelings. The rhymed heroic play is Dryden's proffered solution; Edward Howard champions a modified form of *comédie heroique*, and Dryden (who had already tried that in *Secret Love*) follows suit; Shadwell rails at popular modes but looks to satiric theory rather than to 'raised imitation' for a solution.

According to popular belief, the rhymed heroic play blossoms in 1664, reaches its peak and maturity about 1670 with *The Conquest of Granada*, and is in decline by 1675 when Dryden brings out the last of his rhymed plays, *Aureng-Zebe*. Arthur Kirsch points out the more personal and emotional qualities of that play, which does indeed seem to serve as a kind of bridge toward later vogues in serious drama. But to focus exclusively on Dryden can give a very misleading impression. As a survey of the sixties has made clear, the number of such plays in that decade is small, and the form never really jelled or assumed a dominant position in those years. By my count, only eight plays of this type precede *Tyrannick Love* and *The Conquest of Granada*, whereas more than twenty follow them in the next decade.[2]

---

[1] These issues are discussed in a broader context in Chapters 2 and 4, above, and in detail with reference to Dryden in Chapter 6 of my *Dryden's Criticism*.

[2] Nicoll's figures (I. 100–1), 18 rhymed plays for the sixties, 24 for the seventies, are not to be trusted, since he counts such partly rhymed plays as Etherege's *Comical Revenge*, Tuke's *Adventures*, and Crowne's *Juliana*—none of them heroic.

Considering that Orrery quickly fades, Dryden does have to be seen as the popularizer of the rhymed heroic extravaganza. And despite the frequent critical objections to rhyme in the later sixties, what really sets the fashion is the success of *The Conquest of Granada* in 1670–1. Thus the work which brings the genre near exhaustion for Dryden should be seen, more broadly, as an example of early maturity for the whole form.

Tyrannick Love (June 1669), and, especially, Dryden's preface for the quarto (1670), give us a clear picture of his exalted sense of the potentialities of serious drama. Dryden writes with a self-consciously noble sense of his own purpose. 'Persons of Honour' convinced him that 'it would be of good Example to undertake a Poem of this Nature. Neither were my own inclinations wanting to second their desires.' Pleasure, he assures us primly, is 'not the only end of Poesie'; 'Precepts and Examples of Piety' are to be presented in order to 'allure the Soul' of the spectator. This explicitly exemplary theory of dramatic response is in keeping with Dryden's persistent association of serious drama with epic, discussed in Chapter 4, above. The design of *Tyrannick Love* is accordingly simple. St. Catharine is the 'pattern of piety', amply provided with the opportunity to display heroic fortitude in the process of martyrdom. The lustful tyrant Maximin is a contrasting figure of evil—'designed . . . to set off the Character of S. *Catharine*', as Dryden says exasperatedly in replying to denunciations of Maximin's blasphemy. Dryden is right: he has *not* 'proposed him as a pattern to be imitated'; Maximin is 'severely punished', and even 'the Holy Scriptures' record the words and deeds of 'wicked and prophane persons' in order to fix 'a Brand of Infamy' upon them, as he has done with Maximin here. All very true—and yet Dryden is the victim of a common paradox: Satan is attractive and exciting, God is dull. Henceforth Dryden was to keep his villains under better control, but in Maximin we see the germ and inspiration for the horror form of rhymed heroic drama which was to flourish in the seventies. That genre appealed to Dryden not at all, and it should not really be categorized with the exemplary-heroic, rhyme notwithstanding. The common association of Maximin with Almanzor is completely understandable: Dryden himself is guilty of it in later disavowing the excesses of their language.[1] But to think of them both as ranting heroes is deplorably wrong, for the proper reactions to the two should be almost diametrically opposite. The use of similar verbal puffery to build stature in both cases has led to an unfortunate confusion.

Tyrannick Love is an experiment. Alone among Dryden's heroic plays, it is a straight tragedy. Several critics have guessed, plausibly enough, that Dryden was inspired to modify the practice of *The Indian Emperour* by the King's Company revival of Dekker and Massinger's *The Virgin Martyr* in February 1668. He gets some exciting effects out of the martyrdom scenes, and, perhaps significantly, seizes on the opportunity to introduce aerial spirits (*Works*, X. 112), a part of the epic machinery after which he hankers. The love tangles and love and honour ethical dilemmas of earlier plays are present here, but the *self-control* motif is further developed. Critics differ on whether the implicit homily is sufficiently clear: I would say yes. The importance of the play, though, lies in the possibilities Dryden's experiments open up. Dryden himself goes on to explore the power of epic magnitude and near-exemplary characters, and he is occasionally imitated. More often, other writers seize on the potentialities of rant, spectacle, and the super villain, and then tend to move toward the straight horror play.

In the two parts of *The Conquest of Granada* (December 1670, January 1671) Dryden solves the problems in *Tyrannick Love*, though at some cost in vividness and economy. Ten acts give him the scope he wants. The attractions of vice are kept under control: only the lustful female opportunist–libertine Lyndaraxa is really forceful among the negative characters. The normative heroes, Almanzor and Ozmyn, have to learn from experience before appropriate distributive justice can be enacted. The resultant happy ending is a return to the epic-romance pattern. Dryden's preface, the 'Essay of Heroique Playes' (1672), is a tricky document, largely accurate but easy to misinterpret.

Dryden commences the essay by defending rhyme as a means of raising a play above the level of 'ordinary converse', the merely 'natural'. Plainly the rhyme matters less in itself than as a means to 'raised imitation'. Dryden desires the grandeur

---

[1] Preface to *The Spanish Fryar*.

and respectability of epic form, and so produces his famous definition: 'an Heroick Play ought to be an imitation, in little of an Heroick Poem: and consequently . . . Love and Valour ought to be the Subject of it.' Few critics are now prepared to take this literally. Dryden's principal models are Corneille and Fletcher. And his subject is not love and valour as abstract qualities but rather the characters who exemplify them. The point to the reference is Dryden's determination to take serious drama above the level of the ordinary and the real. To this end he sanctions the use of spirits, ghosts, and magic, all in aid of 'a freer scope for imagination'. Aiming to present 'the highest patern of humane life', Dryden has to answer the charge 'that *Almanzor* is no perfect pattern of Heroick vertue'. This he grants, pleading epic precedent.

The Conquest of Granada is finely written, and it succeeded as a grandiose spectacle. The abuse it took in the next few years helps blind us to its power as a political *exemplum* and to its attractions as a dramatized chivalric romance. Lacking the Carolean taste for the likes of Scudéry, we are impatient with such stuff; worse, we tend to impute the extravagancies of Drawcansir to the relatively blameless Almanzor. The huffery of Dryden's hero can seem absurd (and was vigorously cried down by Buckingham, Shadwell, Arrowsmith, and others), but his actions are not so very exaggerated: as Dryden points out, he is made a prisoner in Part 1 and 'defeated' in Part 2. Mrs. Evelyn's response to the play—discussed briefly in Chapter 2, above —seems highly revealing:

I have seen 'The Siege of Grenada', a play so full of ideas that the most refined romance I ever read is not to compare with it; love is made so pure, and valour so nice, that one would imagine it designed for an Utopia rather than our stage. I do not quarrel with the poet, but admire one born in the decline of morality should be able to feign such exact virtue; and as poetic fiction has been instructive in former ages, I wish this the same event in ours.[1]

This view lacks a sense of the play's political implications, but gives a good feeling for the intended admiration for exalted, out-of-this-world virtues; it also should encourage us to see *The Conquest of Granada* as it is—closer to *comédie heroique* than to tragedy.

[1] *The Diary and Correspondence of John Evelyn*, ed. Bray, IV. 25.

The inclination to raise serious drama above the level of common converse is easier to comprehend than the concomitant determination to do the same thing for comedy. In the later sixties 'French' farce and lightened Spanish romance sweep the stage, and the popularity of plays like *Sir Salomon* breeds revulsion in writers who have a serious concept of drama. What form then does their reaction take? According to the dogma of a dominant Etheregean form in comedy, in the years following *She wou'd if she cou'd* Etherege's combination of (1) a London setting, (2) wit and sex, and (3) social refinement ought to be replacing extant modes. Actually, the immediate trend is against wit and refinement: as we have seen, the new comedies of 1669 and 1670 are Shadwell's Molière translation, *The Hypocrite*; Caryll's *Sir Salomon*; Betterton's *The Woman Made a Justice*; Medbourne's *Tartuffe*; Shadwell's *The Humorists* (not farcical, but not Etheregean either); and Betterton's *The Amorous Widow*. Not everyone was pleased with the prevailing winds: the comments and productions of Dryden, Shadwell, and Wycherley will be of special interest, but we may best get a sense of the situation by examining a less well-known test case, Edward Howard.

Howard's *The Womens Conquest* (acted by November 1670) is a fascinating historical curiosity. As the lengthy preface and triple prologue show, it is a deliberate and thoughtful attempt to change the course comedy was taking. (See the analysis in Chapter 2, above.) Howard discusses various categories: tragedy, comedy, tragicomedy, farce, historical plays, and heroic drama. Comedies 'as they are corruptly understood, imply, little more then scurrility and laughter', but the form is 'of far greater dignity, if rightly apply'd'. He strongly opposes making laughter 'the chiefest end' or indulging in mere 'Mimikry and other ridiculous Gestures': such farce 'is no more of kin to a Play, then a Mule is to a Horse'. Howard comments on the evolution of the heroic play, and delivers sound arguments against the use of rhyme. With some justice he calls the works of Davenant and Orrery more '*Poems*' than '*Plays*', and so he proposes to mingle heroic elevation with less exalted concerns, the whole to be written in unrhymed verse. He calls the results tragicomedy merely to indicate that they are not 'low'. Howard sharply criticizes some current trends. He briefly objects to personal satire: presumably he had not enjoyed his role as the poet Ninny in Shadwell's *Sullen Lovers*. But he devotes far more energy to denouncing 'mean imitation of *French* Plays'. His target is of course the flood of farcical adaptations of Molière just detailed. His reasoned objection that a play cannot be 'compleated with Humours and Characters alone' is certainly another hit at Shadwell, and possibly at the rather plotless *She wou'd*. The ghost of Jonson rises in the second prologue to denounce the predominance of farce; in the third, Howard announces bluntly that he is trying to revive 'True Comedy'. His notion thereof is clearly delineated in the preface. 'The chief end of Comedy is improvement of manners'—hence 'laughter' is contemptible as a principal aim. Exemplary characters are appropriate, he insists, as having a place in a 'Heroick mixture' in which 'humour and mirth [are given] a natural rise and generous correspondency with the grandeur' of a wholly serious part. He might almost have been defining *Marriage A-la-Mode* to come.

Howard's own results are no success. *The Womens Conquest* is a near-heroic account of complexities, including intervention by the Amazons, following from an unusual divorce law in Scythia. The conception is interesting, but the results seem stiff and the tone artificial; Howard was more at ease in his less poetical *Change of Crownes*. But what seems most significant about the effort is his explicit attempt to make the concept of the heroic play conform to his notion of comic function. The play ran a respectable six nights and expired. Howard's next effort, *The Six days Adventure, or the New Utopia* (March 1671), was evidently an attempt to render his conception more accessible to the audience. The theme is again female rights; the preface is in the same vein; the prologue emphasizes that the play is more than a 'pretty farce'. But this time the work is simply 'A Comedy': Howard includes some verbal wit and an amusing Jonsonian sham marriage of the hypocrite Sir Grave Solymour to what turns out to be a blackamoor boy. Foppering and Peacock are extravagantly hyperbolical humour characters. But despite such concessions, the play failed completely, apparently damned by faction.

The play which was a roaring success, a year later, is Edward Ravenscroft's *The Citizen Turn'd Gentleman* (acted by July 1672;

analysed in Chapter 3, above), an indecorous adaptation of
Molière's *Le Bourgeois Gentilhomme*. A thunderous chorus of
sneers at 'Mamamouchi' from Dryden and others[1] is eloquent
testimony to its popularity. This play is precisely the sort that
Edward Howard was complaining about; his pessimistic assessment of audience taste seems to have been quite accurate.[2]
Downes says that 'This Comedy was look[ed] upon by the
Criticks for a Foolish Play; yet it continu'd *Acting* 9 Days with
a full House; . . . Mr. *Nokes*, in performing the *Mamamouchi*
pleas'd the King and Court, next Sir *Martin*, above all Plays.'[3]
The reference to *Sir Martin* is significant: the later play, likewise
an adaptation from Molière put into an English setting, continues and extends the emphasis on the farcical. Ravenscroft's
play represents all that those writers with heroic inclinations
despised—and it was staggeringly popular, performed more
than thirty times in its first year, according to the dedication.

Edward Howard's manifesto sheds some light on the significance of his brother-in-law's productions. Dryden too is
deliberately trying to stem the tide of London comedy and to
introduce a strong 'heroic' element. Thus *Marriage A-la-Mode*
(late November 1671 ?)[4] develops the form of *Secret Love*: a
heroic plot (unrhymed) set against a witty love plot. The
social tone is elevated; despite bawdy songs, Dryden's statement in his dedication to Rochester that he has copied the
gallantries of courts, achieved delicacy of expression, and
preserved the 'Decencies of Behaviour' is basically accurate.
The epilogue says wittily but bluntly that though 'Reformation'
has been the object, the author has refrained from crude or

[1] See, for example, Dryden's snarls at Ravenscroft in the prologue to *The Assignation*:

> Th' unnatural strain'd Buffoon is onely taking:
> No Fop can please you now of Gods own making.
> You must have Mamamouchi, such a Fop
> As would appear a Monster in a Shop.

[2] Ironically, Ravenscroft had contributed commendatory verses to the 1671
quarto of *The Six days Adventure*, saying, among other things, 'this age disesteems
true Comedy. . . . Now Comedy to Farce gives place.' Ravenscroft seems to have
known precisely what the audience *did* want.   [3] *Roscius Anglicanus*, p. 32.

[4] Date uncertain. The play was completed by July 1671 and performed some
time in the next ten months. See Charles E. Ward, 'The Date of Two Dryden
Plays', *PMLA*, li (1936), 786–92, and my 'The Date of Dryden's *Marriage A-la-
Mode*', *Harvard Library Bulletin*, xxi (1973), 161–6.

'bloudy Satyr' set in London—and he accuses the audience of wanting just such stuff. The play seems to have succeeded passably, which was far more than *The Assignation* did the following November. 'Love in a Nunnery', as the sub-title revealingly calls it, is a schizophrenic attempt to combine heroic sentiment with rousing, almost farcical action.[1]

These two plays, like Edward Howard's, show that the heroic play was still very much an influence on the direction comedy might take: clearly the heroic *inclination* is there. Dryden wrote no preface to *Marriage A-la-Mode*, but what he wrote to introduce *An Evening's Love*, published while he was writing his grander comedy, is a good clue to his thinking at the time. (For an analysis, see Chapter 2, Section I, above.) 'Low Comedy' disgusts him; he detests 'those Farces, which are now the most frequent entertainments of the Stage'. French translations are obnoxious, and he resents having had to produce work like *An Evening's Love*, which he had been in no hurry to publish. 'The natural imitation of folly' has no appeal for him: he urges 'more of the *Urbana, venusta, salsa, faceta*', more graceful conversation and genteel characters. In short, Dryden is for *courtly* comedy, and *Marriage A-la-Mode* (dubbed simply 'A Comedy') is what he had in mind. Far more than the character-oriented Edward Howard, Dryden is wrapped up in the potentialities of fine conversation. Time and again he returns to this topic, as in the dedication to Rochester, or especially in his 'Defence of the Epilogue' to Part 2 of *The Conquest of Granada*. In the latter his mania for gentility has full play, and he particularly commends (without naming the author) Buckingham's revision of Fletcher's *The Chances*: Don John 'now speaks better' than Fletcher made him do. Over all, though, Dryden's point is almost exactly Edward Howard's: low comedy must be eschewed in favour of something more akin to the heroic.

Shadwell has some similar reactions, but comes up with different solutions. Critics occasionally note with surprise that *She wou'd* found a champion in Shadwell, supposedly the leader of the humours school in opposition to Etherege's wit comedy. In the preface to *The Humorists* (pub. 1671) he calls

[1] For an excellent discussion of *The Assignation*, explaining its place in Dryden's systematic attempt to 'heighten' comedy, see Moore, *The Nobler Pleasure*, Chapter 5.

She wou'd 'the best Comedy that has been written since the Restauration of the Stage'. The inadequacy of conventional categories is apparent here. Actually, Shadwell and Etherege have much in common. Both employ London settings; both (so far) are more concerned with display of character than with plot and action. Both champion 'natural' presentation rather than the 'hyperbolical' sort favoured by Edward Howard and Dryden. Shadwell objects to putting 'Fopps into extravagant, and unnatural habits' (e.g. Howard's Foppering and Peacock). And, of course, he declaims bitterly against farce: 'The rabble of little People, are more pleas'd with *Jack-Puddings* being soundly kick'd, or having a Custard handsomely thrown in his face, than with all the wit in Plays.' The likes of Lacy did not appeal to any of these writers. We may assume that Dryden would share Shadwell's preference for Etheregean refinement over farcical city comedy, but where Shadwell upholds a Jonsonian social level, Dryden has a strong preference for the social and linguistic refinement of 'Fletcherian' characters. We can see here two markedly different concepts of non-farcical comedy.[1]

In the midst of this muddled situation Wycherley's first two plays appear. Significantly, neither seems particularly modish. *Love in a Wood* (March 1671) follows the multi-strand pattern of Etherege's first play ('Love in a Tub') and Sedley's *The Mulberry-Garden*. Wycherley wisely refrains from putting the Ranger–Lydia and Valentine–Christina plot in verse; his serious love-and-jealousy plot goes better in prose than his predecessors' do in couplets. Lydia and Ranger are half-way to the witty couple; Sir Simon Addleplot is of Sir Nicholas Cully's tribe; Alderman Gripe, his sister, and Mrs. Crossbite are low characters and sharply satirized. The range is from bawd to heroic lover; the result is no drawing-room comedy.[2] *The Gentleman Dancing-Master* (acted by February 1672)—not a

---

[1] 'Farce' is an inexact term here. For a careful analysis of the opposition to farce, see Leo Hughes, 'Attitudes of Some Restoration Dramatists Toward Farce', *Philological Quarterly*, xix (1940), 268–87; and for a general account of farce and low comedy, his *A Century of English Farce* (Princeton, N.J., 1956). In the dedication of *A True Widow* (dated 1679) Shadwell criticizes farce for its horse-play, overdrawn character, and lack of sequential motivation; this is probably a fair summation of the views of 'serious' dramatists.

[2] Sources and date of composition of this play have occasioned confusion. Wycherley's claim to Pope that he had written the play at age 19 (i.e. in 1659) is ridiculous: his source was not published until 1664. See James Urvin Rundle,

success—is likewise an imitation of popular devices. The satire on the French and Spanish affectations of 'Monsieur de Paris' and 'Don Diego' recalls both the humours characters of Shadwell and the anti-French satire of James Howard. Further, though Wycherley's setting is London, the attitude evoked toward Don Diego's Spanish outlook is anticipated in a number of the pseudo-Spanish intrigue comedies—*An Evening's Love*, for instance. Wycherley, having abandoned all pretence of a foreign setting, concentrates on affectations, a collection of farcical mishaps, and a love plot governed by the whims of a witty girl. Basically, Wycherley gives us *Flora's Vagaries* divested of still more of the Spanish romance trappings. In brief, like Dryden and Shadwell, Wycherley fails to conform to the dictates of modern Etheregean doctrine. Indeed, he starts by working in modes that were going out of fashion.

To call 1670 and 1671 years of crisis may seem fanciful. Nonetheless, we can fairly say that about this time both serious and comic drama reach a critical turning point. The former is in a depressed state: in 1670 Dryden was the only important serious dramatist still writing—Davenant was dead, Orrery and Robert Howard inactive.

The next few years were to see the possibilities of heroic romance, 'history', and horror exploited in imitation of Dryden's experiments in *Tyrannick Love* and *The Conquest of Granada* —both of them seminal plays, written with definite principles in mind. In comedy, even more clearly, a halt is called to popular trends and new theories are propounded. The conflict is not simply a matter of Etheregean 'manners' or 'wit' displacing plots of action. Rather, as we have seen, three types are being championed: heroic comedy (Dryden, Edward Howard); satiric city comedy (Shadwell, Wycherley); and farcical city comedy (e.g. Ravenscroft). There is extensive precedent for all three modes in the 1660s. For example,

---

'Wycherley and Calderón: A Source for *Love in a Wood*', *PMLA*, lxiv (1949), 701–7; and P. F. Vernon, 'Wycherley's First Comedy and Its Spanish Source', *Comparative Literature*, xviii (1966), 132–44. Rose Zimbardo has tried to prove that *Love in a Wood* is 'a close imitation of Fletcher's *The Faithful Shepherdess*' (p. 21). The attempt is ingenious, but the parallels seem forced, and Mrs. Zimbardo does not take account either of the other plays in the period or of Rundle's discovery that Summers had been right in postulating a Spanish source for the main plot. For a good account of the play, see Loftis, *The Spanish Plays of Neoclassical England*, pp. 121–5.

Secret Love and Spanish romance for the first; *The English Mounsieur, The Cheats,* and *The Sullen Lovers* for the second; the plays of Lacy and several Molière adaptations for the third. The distinction between the second and third modes is a matter of degree. Neither has the social or verbal refinement Dryden wants, but the satiric city comedy takes its characters and plot more seriously, both in making us care about the romantic part of the plot and in handling its satire for more than laughs. The developments of the succeeding decade are tribute more to the power of the box office than to the allure of literary theory, but the productions and arguments of this brief interim period are not without effect.

II. THE EARLY SEVENTIES: TOWARD SEX, HORROR, AND SPECTACLE

The fortunes and misfortunes of the two companies prove important in these years. Since Davenant's death in April 1668 the Duke's Company had been led by Thomas Betterton and Henry Harris, co-managers acting for themselves and for Lady Davenant. Performance records are exceedingly sketchy (especially in 1669–70), so we know even less than usual about what was going on. True to Davenant's heritage, however, the Duke's Company decided in the summer of 1670 to build a new theatre—one especially designed to incorporate major advances in fancy stage machinery. Dorset Garden opened on 9 November 1671. Its capacity for spectacle—the equivalent of the wide-screen, super-colour cinema attractions of today—had been eagerly awaited,[1] and evidently it gave the Duke's Company a major competitive advantage. Worse yet for their rivals, less than three months later the Bridges Street theatre was totally destroyed by fire (25 January 1672). With it went their entire stock of scenery and costumes. The King's Company reopened on 26 February in the old Lincoln's Inn Fields theatre recently vacated by the Duke's Company.[2] For the next two years they limped along, staging few new plays and poor ones

---

[1] Sober John Evelyn records the previous 26 June: 'I went home, steping in at the Theater, to see the new Machines for the intended scenes, which were indeede very costly, & magnificent.'

[2] Their choice of a play was indicative: Fletcher's *Wit Without Money*—a tired stock play which turned out to be at the end of its popularity. Dryden provided a good new prologue.

at that. When their new Drury Lane theatre finally opened (26 March 1674), Dryden felt he had to apologize in his prologue for 'a plain-built house' designed for 'bare convenience only'.[1] Trying to defend so 'homely' a place, Dryden sneers loudly at the rival company for 'their vast expense' which produces only 'excess' and a 'reign' of 'scenes, machines, and empty operas'. Dryden's epilogue for the occasion denounces French farce—always a bogey—and 'fustian stuff/Of rhyme, more nauseous than three boys in buff'. The heroic play had not turned out as Dryden had planned.

Dryden's 'barren period' after 1671 has been variously explained as a reaction caused by *The Rehearsal*, revulsion against the excesses of other writers' heroic plays, and as reflecting a new influence by Milton.[2] In fact, he was a playwright whose theatre could not mount what he then wanted to write. Heroic comedy fizzled out with the failure of *The Assignation* in November 1672. Dryden had no wish to write more low comedy; the King's Company never mounted his only serious play from these years—*The State of Innocence*. This couplet version of *Paradise Lost* demands super-spectacular scenes and machines.

The first Scene . . . from the Heavens, (which are opened) fall the rebellious Angels wheeling in the Air, and seeming transfix'd with Thunderbolts. . . . The Scene shifts, and on a sudden represents Hell: Part of the Scene is a Lake of Brimstone or rowling Fire . . . a Tune of Horrour and Lamentation is heard. (III. 425)

As Montague Summers observes, however, this rhymed extravaganza was definitely meant for stage performance—the very full and careful stage and music directions leave no doubt on the point. Whether the Drury Lane theatre was equipped to handle such a piece is questionable, and the company, increasingly wracked by dissension, probably did not want to incur the expense.

The plays they did mount while in exile at Lincoln's Inn Fields are few and poor. Dryden contributed *Amboyna*, his propaganda play on Dutch atrocities, and wrote a new scene for an old MS. play (by Brome?), *The Mistaken Husband*. Two

---

[1] Again the choice of a play is telling: Fletcher's *Beggar's Bush*.

[2] For the last, see George McFadden, 'Dryden's "Most Barren Period"—and Milton', *Huntington Library Quarterly*, xxiv (1961), 283–96.

Duffett burlesques on rival productions, three sex intrigue plays (*The Spanish Rogue, The Mall, The Amorous Old-woman*), and Shipman's indifferent rhymed melodrama, *Henry the Third of France*, complete the list. Shipman's epilogue expresses the wistful hope that the audience will 'sometimes range/Fro' th' *other House*'. It had little reason to do so. Against this scanty display of mediocrity and rehash, the Duke's Company mounted a series of block-busting successes, including *The Citizen Turn'd Gentleman, Epsom-Wells*, and *The Empress of Morocco*. The ability of the King's Company to produce spectacular mountings of plays like *The Conquest of Granada* was not regained even with the building of the Drury Lane playhouse. Worse yet, the company was ageing, its members and proprietor bickering—problems which came to a head in 1676. Meanwhile the Duke's Company was being skilfully run by the highly professional Betterton, and it was making good its losses in personnel. Around the middle of the decade, Downes observes, 'the Company was very much Recruited'[1]—the additions including such stalwarts-to-be as Anthony Leigh, Jevon, and Mrs. Barry. Over all in this half-decade, the Duke's Company has only about a 5 : 4 ratio advantage in the number of new plays produced, but the real disparity in the fortunes of the two groups is far greater than that.

For two key years, then, the Duke's Company was without serious competition, and its productions set current modes. Were writers affected by the Third Dutch War during this period? Pierre Danchin hypothesizes a crucial swing toward cit taste in 1672 while the gentry are away fighting.[2] The prologues to *Charles the Eighth, Marriage A-la-Mode*, and *The Gentleman Dancing-Master* refer to the absence of gallants and the players' reliance on 'men of the city' to fill theatres. But I doubt that this change greatly affected theatrical fads and fashion. The popular plays—*The Citizen Turn'd Gentleman, Epsom-Wells, Charles the Eighth, The Empress of Morocco, The Tempest*—seem no more than extensions of forms already proven popular before the war—in *Sir Salomon, The Conquest of Granada, The Amorous Widow*, and *Sir Martin Mar-all*. Sex, spectacle, and horror become more prominent elements in many plays, but there is ample precedent for such attractions.

[1] *Roscius Anglicanus*, p. 35.   [2] Danchin, 'Le Public des théatres londoniens . . .'.

Music and fancier staging are on the rise in these years, again simply extending progressions well established in the sixties. The sudden boom in music was indicated in Chapter 5, above. Suffice it to say that the first new production at Drury Lane was Pierre Perrin's French opera *Ariadne* (March 1674); within a month Shadwell's operatic revamping of *The Tempest* was mounted at Dorset Garden. *The Triumphant Widow* that year verges on the ballad opera genre. The audience was running mad after music, dancing, and scenery. Worse yet, in the actors' view, a steady stream of foreign players were acting in London (by special licence), stealing patrons the playhouses could ill spare.[1] Regardless of the alleged prevalence of cits in 1672 and 1673, Dorset Garden had already been designed for dazzling show, and that was what Betterton produced. He could mount heroic spectacle, as in *Charles the Eighth* and *The Empress of Morocco*, with the King's Company helpless to reply. With glossy new productions he could get more mileage out of popular old shows like Davenant's *Macbeth*, which was revived early in 1673, 'drest in all it's Finery, as new Cloath's, new Scenes, Machines, as flyings for the Witches', and with 'all the Singing and Dancing' revised and probably enlarged (Downes). To find Betterton staging *Hamlet* 'adorned and embellished with very curious dances between the acts'[2] is no surprise. Over all, however, we know painfully little about the productions of these years. With Pepys silent, no newspapers, and a terrible dearth of other theatrical gossip, much depends on inference. Nonetheless, the outlines are perfectly clear.

At the end of the 1660s four semi-distinct dramatic modes were conspicuous in the theatres. (1) The heroic play—few in number but much discussed. (2) Heroically inclined comedy, partly in the form of two plot tragicomedy. (3) Intrigue comedy: generally set abroad, originally quite serious, but often (as in

---

[1] See Sybil Rosenfeld, *Foreign Theatrical Companies in Great Britain in the 17th and 18th Centuries* (London, 1955). Such visitors appeared in 1672; one group was active from December 1672 to May 1673, another from April to September 1673 (at Yorke House); another in 1674 (details vague). In June 1675 an Italian Scaramuchio was allowed to give performances at the King's theatre in Whitehall and to charge admission to the general public—which naturally outraged the two domestic companies (see *The London Stage*, Part 1, p. 234).

[2] December 1674. Newsletter cited in *The London Stage*, Part 1, p. 225.

the popular 'Spanish' plays) lightened with a humorous admixture. (4) Low comedy set in London—much of it translated
or adapted from French, and farcically inclined. The greatest
successes of the preceding decade had been Etherege's *The
Comical Revenge* and the Newcastle–Dryden *Sir Martin Mar-all*.[1]
Dryden had opened up new possibilities with *Tyrannick Love*
and *The Conquest of Granada*, and like Edward Howard had tried
to establish an improved pattern for comedy. What followed
was not precisely what Dryden had in mind.

A striking index to changes of taste during the seventies
can be found in the comedies of Aphra Behn. As a versatile
professional catering to popular taste, she stands almost as
a paradigm for the pattern of development we will see in
surveying this decade. She starts with two rather old-fashioned
tragicomedies, *The Forc'd Marriage* (1670) and *The Amorous
Prince* (February 1671), serious intrigue plays which enjoyed
no great success. She does better with *The Dutch Lover* (February
1673), another such mishmash of sword-play, love and honour,
and mistaken identity in the Spanish–Italian principality mode,
but this time the intrigue is leavened with the buffooneries of a
Dutch fop, Haunce van Ezel, and his servant Gload. (Falatius,
the 'fantastick Courtier' of the first play, is much less prominent.) *The Town-Fop* (1676) takes a half-serious love plot, again
on the theme of enforced marriage, and sets it in London,
integrating it with a less serious plot involving a fop. The pattern
and structure are precisely that of *The Dutch Lover*, but the social
level is lowered, the scene made more realistic, and the humorous element increased. With *The Rover* (1677) we are again
abroad, but love and honour conventions serve principally to
occasion extensive sword-play. The audience is entertained with
a gay couple and rapid-paced intrigue. The romance, tragicomic element has been reduced, though its conventions are still
visible. With *Sir Patient Fancy* (1678) Mrs. Behn is *à la mode*: the
play is a low London comedy of cuckoldry—vigorous, farcical,
and dirty. Thus in eight years she covers the full span from the

---

[1] So says Downes (p. 28), and *The London Stage* seems to bear him out. When the
Duke's Company opened the fancy Dorset Garden theatre (9 November 1671),
Sir Martin was acted the first three nights, 'notwithstanding', Downes says, 'it had
been *Acted* 30 Days before in Lincolns-Inn-Fields, and above 4 times at Court'
(p. 31). Interestingly, the next two or three nights were devoted to *The Comical
Revenge*.

pseudo-heroic to the London farce, stopping along the way at various degenerate varieties of 'Spanish' romance. This progression gives us a microcosmic version of the history of comedy from *The Adventures of Five Hours* to *The Country-Wife* and Dryden's roistering *Limberham*.

The serious drama cannot be as tidily traced, though the basic developments are clear enough. Heroic drama proper (e.g. *The Empress of Morocco*, *Aureng-Zebe*) moves decisively away from the romance modes. The horror element is cultivated, leading toward *Nero*, *Abdelazer*, and *The Conquest of China*; concomitantly hints of the pathos to come appear. While a flood of sterile imitations of *The Conquest of Granada* (the Conquest–Siege mode) fills the theatres quite late in the decade (1675–7), *avant-garde* theory and practice swing back to the character-oriented catastrophe type of the early seventeenth century. In 1677 and 1678 the great debate reaches its peak, one of the key questions being 'how far we ought to imitate Shakespeare and Fletcher', as Dryden poses it. Thus late in the decade heroic dinosaurs are numerous (*The Destruction of Troy*, *The Siege of Babylon*, *The Destruction of Jerusalem*—in two parts), but at the same time in *The Rival Queens*, *All for Love*, and *Oedipus* serious drama is being steered back toward tragedy proper.

The serious productions at the beginning of the decade have attracted little study. A survey of the directions they indicate yields some surprises. If we consider *Tyrannick Love* and *The Conquest of Granada* as a pair of models with inherently different potentialities—horror versus grandeur—the greater appeal of the villain-oriented play in the next years is obvious. The later play is often referred to, but rather little copied except in incidentals—scenic extravagance, rant, and huffing hero. The moral design, the *pattern* of action and character so crucial to Dryden's purposes, made little impact on other playwrights. Ironically, Dryden was to spend the rest of the decade jealously denouncing the element that really did catch on—fancy scenery. Evidently what Evelyn calls 'very glorious scenes & perspectives, the work of Mr Streeter' (10 February 1671) made quite an impression.

The one play in the next few years which clearly seems an imitation of Dryden's *Conquest* in design is Crowne's *The History of Charles the Eighth of France, or The Invasion of Naples by the French*—according to Downes, the first new play staged at Dorset Garden (late November 1671). Complications of love, politics, and war are well juggled, and distributive justice is effected: Charles marries Julia, sister of the Neopolitan Prince, Ferdinand, who is allowed to inherit his father Alphonso's crown and happily marries Cornelia, the Cyprian Queen. The plotting princess Isabella is wounded in a mêlée and dies, fulfilling the prophecy of the ghost of her husband. The valiant rebel prince of Salerne, who disclaims loyalty, holding that 'Natures dictates are the highest Law' (10) is properly bested by Ferdinand: he then 'Tears his wounds, and dyes' (72), remaining adamant to the last. The treacherous general Trivultio is killed and Crowne discreetly reports the exhibition of his head to the mob. Love tangles are numerous, valour 'nice' indeed. When Trivultio leads his troops over to the French, Charles flatly rejects the deed:

> Thy Treason I'le reward, and send thy head
> To *Ferdinand,*—unless thou dost from hence
> Withdraw thy Troops, and fight in his defence. (26)

The results are good imitation Dryden, though lacking flair. Crowne displays some ambivalence towards his mode, ironically apologizing in the epilogue for 'the whining noise of a dull Rhiming Play'. A fair verdict would give him credit for a workmanlike job.

To think of Carolean heroic plays in our usual comedy-versus-tragedy terms obscures their nature. The common but often absurd term 'heroic tragedy' describes the chivalric romance plays very badly indeed. The tragicomedy pattern of *The Conquest of Granada* and *Charles the Eighth* is susceptible of development in various directions. The horror and villain plays so common in the next ten years are one possibility; heroic comedy, pattern tragicomedy, and mixed tragicomedy are others. Mrs. Behn's *Forc'd Marriage* and *Amorous Prince* are old-fashioned intrigue tragicomedies which lack rhyme and the grandiosity of Dryden's conception. *Marriage A-la-Mode*, in its high plot, is an experiment in heroic comedy. Crowne's little-noticed *Juliana; or The Princess of Poland* (*c.* June 1671) makes partly humorous use of romance materials. The Harbage–Schoenbaum *Annals* very oddly designate this play a 'tragedy';

actually, it is a happy-ending tragicomedy, and an exceptionally lively and cheerful one at that. Unrhymed verse and prose
are interspersed with occasional couplet passages. Romantic
posturing of the wildest sort is freely mixed with low and
humorous commentary. At the dénouement, the Russian
Prince Demetrius 'proffers to fall on his sword', but is prevented,
whereupon his supposedly dead wife, Paulina (who has faithfully followed him in male attire) begs him to live. The Landlord of the lodging the Duke of Curland has occupied incognito
then remarks: 'sure my house was inchanted to day, lodg'd
Princes, and Dukes, like Mummers and Masqueraders, and
Women and Wenches in mens cloathes, and Cloakbags, and
scufflings, and they kill one another, and they'r alive again, and
this, and that, and I know not what; here's work indeed' (61).
Political intrigue, love and honour complications, secret
marriage, ghosts, and Russian–Polish international friction are
served up in liberal portions. Presumably we rejoice at the final
marriage of Juliana to Duke Ladislaus and his becoming King
of Poland. But the extreme conspicuousness of the Landlord
drastically reduces the heroic exaltation of the play. He directly
and grossly mocks the serious characters, particularly Ladislaus
(e.g. 8); when the intriguing Cardinal's schemes go awry and
he has to commit suicide with a poisoned handkerchief, the
Landlord (of all people) delivers reflections over his dead body
—reflections mostly on what a souse the Cardinal had been
(42–5). To inject the Landlord into the midst of the play's best
romantic agonies yields a strange effect. Nicoll characterizes
this play as dull and ranting (I. 140); artistically it is indeed
imperfectly integrated. The play was no success, but its strong
satirical element should not be ignored. As an unsuccessful
experiment, *Juliana* prefigures such neglected satirical tragedies
as *The Libertine* and *Timon* later in the decade.

Crowne's combination of serious romance and satirical
commentary works poorly: it is far better to overinflate and
exaggerate a mode, as Shadwell was to do in *The Libertine*. The
mode Shadwell had in view there was the villain–horror play,
which was the most popular form of serious drama in the early
seventies. Settle's very successful *Cambyses* (January 1671) is
first in a considerable series, and a good example of what is
to come. The resources of Dorset Garden were a year away,

but even so the Duke's Company managed a spectacular production—the sort of thing Hollywood was later to do with
exotic setting and a cast of thousands. In ringing rhyme we get
court intrigue and rebellion, love complications, the pathos of
the captive princess Mandana (who escapes the horrid death
Cambyses orders), prison scenes, the ghosts of the murdered
Cambyses and the 'real' Smerdis, and even 'a bloody Cloud' (75).
The prologue description ('a damn'd dull serious Play') mockingly underestimates the fascinations of unstinted blood-and-
thunder. Settle's sheer energy makes *Cambyses* work as a crowd-
pleaser. Shipman's *Henry the Third* (Spring 1672) is a similarly
bloody melodrama, but it lacks the excitement even of such
spurious intensity. The spectacle (unlike Settle's dazzling oracle
scene—74) seems inorganic, and even the 'two *grand Scenes* of
horrour and blisse' late in the play fall a bit flat. Shipman's
mediocre couplets are no support for his prefatory argument for
rhyme: writing in 1678, he denounces Dryden's backsliding and
'inconstancy', and asserts that *Paradise Lost* would have been
much better in rhyme.

   The greatest success among serious plays from these years
was Settle's *The Empress of Morocco* (acted by July 1673)—a
gorgeous and spectacular 'Rapsody of non-sense' as Dryden
angrily called it. The recipe: to blood, thunder, rhyme, and
rant, add villainous intrigue, the spectacular execution of
Crimalhaz, an elaborate masque, and a fine battle scene—and
conclude with Prince Muly Hamet appropriately rewarded
with kingdom and the beauteous Mariamne. Settle's great
success roused bitter jealousy: Dryden, Shadwell, and Crowne
banded together to produce an abusive anonymous booklet
denouncing the play—*Notes and Observations on the Empress of
Morocco* (1674). Settle's pamphlet reply at the end of that year
was called 'equal to the censure' by Samuel Johnson.[1] Settle
defends his extravagant language with skill—the whole controversy is a major step forward in the practice of English textual
criticism—and he indulges in a highly embarrassing examination of extravagancies in *The Conquest of Granada*. Settle's own
exuberance and indeed deliberately absurd exaggerations put
his play in the silly thriller realm. Novak accurately compares it to a 'horror movie'. But when the 'commentators'

---

[1] *Lives of the English Poets*, ed. George Birkbeck Hill, 3 vols. (Oxford, 1905), I. 350.

slung mud at it, Settle made similar charges against Dryden's plays—and made them stick. The result certainly diminished Dryden's enthusiasm for the heroic play: the whole mode comes out of the controversy looking thoroughly ridiculous. *The Empress of Morocco*'s success was great enough to attract a King's Company burlesque by Duffett, an enjoyable travesty which probably did Settle's play no harm.[1]

The Settle recipe is exploited under his patronage by Samuel Pordage in *Herod and Mariamne*.[2] The couplet rants are even sillier than usual in this kind of shilling shocker. Herod, fatally wounded, kills his rival Tyridates and then is sorry: 'Hee'l be my Rival in the other World' (64). Mariamne refuses a blindfold as she is led to execution, then 'appears laid on a Couch as Beheaded' when the 'scene opens' (59, 61). Salome stabs herself, but expires only after she 'Tares open her Bosom and stabs agen' (65). Nat Lee's first effort, *Nero* (acted by May 1674), is another such piece, analysed briefly in Chapter 5, above. It was popular enough to encourage the Duke's Company, in the following year, to mount *Piso's Conspiracy* (*c.* August), an undistinguished adaptation of an anonymous *Nero* (pub. 1624). Mostly in couplets, Lee's play is full of 'heroic' inflation and sentiment. Super rant; Caligula's ghost; the fifth-act stabbing of the lustful queen, Poppea (now conscience stricken) by her real husband Otho; and the deaths of the true heir Britannicus, Nero, and his favourite Petronius, all combine to give the audience a jolly good time. A similar but more serious play, in verse but not in rhyme, is Nevil Payne's *The Siege of Constantinople* (acted by November 1674). Its exciting intrigue and bloody horror-ending make a good complement

---

[1] On the controversy see Frank C. Brown, *Elkanah Settle: His Life and Works* (Chicago, Ill., 1910), pp. 51–61. Settle's play, the two pamphlets, and the Duffett farce are collected in *The Empress of Morocco and Its Critics*, ed. Maximillian E. Novak (Los Angeles, Calif., 1968). Dryden's participation in the attack was denied by Charles E. Ward, *The Life of John Dryden* (Chapel Hill, N.C., 1961), Appendix D, but Novak's case (expanded in Dryden's *Works*, XVII. 387–400 nn.) seems solid. Evidently Dryden designed the attack and got most of the actual details written by his cohorts—jealous fellows of Settle in the Duke's Company. We may also note that Bentley and Magnes, Dryden's publishers in the later seventies, advertise 'Notes of *Morockor*' as 'by John Dryden Esq.' with several of his other works in the 1680 quarto of Durfey's *The Virtuous Wife*.

[2] Published in late 1673 with a dedication by Settle. The date is either *c.* September 1671, or more probably *c.* September 1673, acted at the old Lincoln's Inn Fields theatre.

to a highly effective savaging of Shaftesbury, presented as the scheming Chancellor. Here the gothicky fun does not really disguise a serious moral and political purpose. Payne's excellence might be predicted from his fine first effort, *The Fatal Jealousie* (acted by August 1672), a more strictly domestic bloodbath, also unrhymed (discussed in Chapter 5, above). Payne had real talent and with practice might have joined the first rank of playwrights.

One of the most interesting and little-noticed tragedies of these years is William Joyner's sole effort, *The Roman Empress* (*c.* August 1670), a play with a powerful catastrophe and genuinely affecting pathos. Joyner achieves what is truly rare in tragedies of these years—a sense of sadness. The execution is not up to the author's design: the diction is stiff, and perhaps through inexperience Joyner does not sufficiently animate his characters. But the preface makes clear the author's desire to cultivate an English form of classical tragedy, and the affecting, suspenseful results are an impressive first effort. The model is Sophocles's *Oedipus*. The principle is events grounded in character. The action is simple ('nothing Episodical'): the emperor kills his son, denounced by the empress—a passionate, evil queen figure. But like Oedipus, the emperor 'incurs those very misfortunes, which with all imaginable care he shun'd'. Joyner has no use for 'the gingling Antitheses of Love and Honor, and such like petty wares': he aims 'to raise Terror and Compassion' while retaining seriousness, dignity, and 'the Majestique Grace of a Tragique Theater'. Joyner was about a decade ahead of his time, and his play made no impact on theatrical trends.

The dominant serious type in the early seventies is the horror play. Not all are rhymed. Dryden's pot-boiler *Amboyna* (*c.* May 1672), with its rape and torture scenes, is simply Dutch War propaganda, but such wallowing in atrocities was popular anyway. The scenes and flyings of Dorset Garden encourage show, while a taste for grisly endings encourages growing doses of horror. As of 1674, spectacle, atrocity, and even rhyme are doing very nicely. Whatever is responsible for changing theatrical directions thereafter, it is not Buckingham's *The Rehearsal* (December 1671). Scholars have known for more than fifty years that *The Rehearsal* did nothing to diminish the popularity of rhymed plays—most of which are subsequent to it. Buckingham's parodic farce was a great success, but nonetheless, as Gildon noted in 1718, those very plays, or others full 'of all the absurdities exploded in that pleasant Criticism', were not less thronged.[1] Lacy's take-off of Dryden in the role of Bayes probably stung, but Dryden was willing to pay Buckingham's version of *The Chances* a high compliment in the criticism attached to *The Conquest of Granada* when it was published in 1672. And plainly the actors did not think that they would damage Dryden or his heroic plays. *The Rehearsal* was, after all, put on by Dryden's own company: would the King's Company actors deliberately undercut their principal writer and some of their own most popular plays? The satire is very funny indeed, but it does almost nothing toward embarrassing us out of our enjoyment of the originals. *The Rehearsal* has usually been read as a specific (hence quickly dated) literary burlesque, and is well analysed in such terms by P. E. Lewis. Sheridan Baker has recently called attention to the broader aspects of the farce, while George McFadden has proposed a political reading, tying the two Kings of Brentford to Charles II and the Duke of York, Bayes's nose to Lord Arlington. Plainly Buckingham's farce works to some degree on all three levels.[2] Duffett's burlesques, more specific literary travesties, are spoofs which likewise capitalize on the popularity of other plays but do not really try to damage them.

Tragedy was running to shock and show rather than to the 'raised imitation' and pattern characters Dryden had proposed, but comedy was no better. The heroic—often two plot—comedy championed by Dryden and exemplified in *Marriage A-la-Mode* does not hold its own after the failure of *The Assignation* (*c.* November 1672)—a play which is itself, like Edward Howard's *The Six days Adventure* before it, a reluctant compromise. Worse yet, Dryden found that he had unwittingly contributed to a growing vogue for sex comedy that he must have detested.

Dryden's heroic plays, especially *The Conquest of Granada*,

---

[1] *The Complete Art of Poetry*, 2 vols. (London, 1718), I. 203.
[2] See Peter Lewis, '*The Rehearsal*: A Study of its Satirical Methods', *Durham University Journal*, n.s. xxxi (1970), 96–113; Sheridan Baker, 'Buckingham's Permanent *Rehearsal*', *Michigan Quarterly Review*, xii (1973), 160–71; George McFadden, 'Political Satire in *The Rehearsal*', *Yearbook of English Studies*, iv (1974), 120–8.

had roused clamorous detraction from Buckingham, Richard Leigh (*The Censure of the Rota*, 1673), and others.[1] Few contributions to the ensuing debate are so entertaining as Joseph Arrowsmith's *The Reformation: A Comedy*.[2] The play's pointed cracks at Dryden's heroic formula have long been enjoyed, but the degree to which the whole play is a systematic debunking of Dryden, and of *Marriage A-la-Mode* in particular, seems not to have been noticed. Indeed J. H. Smith claims, astonishingly and incomprehensibly, that Arrowsmith was attacking Wycherley in the playwriting Tutor.[3] The title takes off from Dryden's epilogue: 'Thus have my Spouse and I . . . led you all the way to Reformation.' The Rev. Mr. Arrowsmith finds Dryden's morals obnoxious and proposes to see the Tutor 'reform'd', as he says very explicitly at the end of the play (79). The prologue is clever and complicated. The audience, it sneers, must think it is at the other house (i.e. the King's), and will expect to see Tartuffe or Scrupple (the latter in Wilson's *Cheats*; neither a promising candidate for reformation). Here the audience will find no 'Drum nor Trumpet, though so much in Fashion', 'Non-sence . . . in Rime', or hero huffing the gods. Nor will it find comedy with songs and bawdy. Arrowsmith's play itself is too verbose— good brisk dialogue but too little plot. The piece turns on a clever conceit, a Society for the Reformation of Male–Female Relations, dedicated to greater sexual freedom. As J. H. Smith accurately observes, the result is a vigorous satire on the gay couple mode. To be sure, the attack is on what Dryden shows and hints toward, not on what he concludes, but Arrowsmith confirms what we might guess, that *Marriage A-la-Mode* was seen more as a contribution to sexual innuendo than to morality. Arrowsmith's constant two-edged comments on England and English customs (though the play is technically set in Venice) systematically establish a double frame of reference: the result is good social satire. But the heart of the play is the Tutor, an English playwright. His prescriptions are worth quoting.

[1] For a summary of the pamphlet controversy, from which Dryden wisely stood aloof, see Hugh Macdonald, *John Dryden: A Bibliography* (Oxford, 1939), pp. 193 ff.

[2] It must have been acted by August 1673, when Philip Cademan (who played Pedro) was injured. A *première* anything up to fifteen months earlier seems likely, given the play's topical nature.

[3] J. H. Smith, p. 139, n. 13.

Take a subject, as suppose the Siege of *Candy*, or the conquest of *Flanders* . . . let it alwayes be some war-like action: you can't imagine what a grace a Drum and Trumpet give a Play. Then Sir I take you some three or four or half a dozen Kings. . . . You must alwayes have two Ladies in Love with one man, or two men in love with one woman; if you make them the Father and the Son, or two Brothers, or two Friends, 'twill do the better. There you know is opportunity for love and honour and Fighting, and all that. . . . Then Sir you must have a Hero that shall fight with all the world; yes i' gad, and beat them too, and half the gods into the bargain. . . . In all you write reflect upon religion and the clergy . . . be sure to raise a dancing singing ghost or two, court the Players for half a dozen new scenes and fine cloaths . . . put your story into rime, and kill enough at the end of the Play, and *Probatum est* your business is done for Tragedy. (47–8)

Comedy is even simpler: 'Then as for Comedy, which I was saying my Genius does not lead me to' (very Drydenesque), you must write 'with double sence and brisk meaning Songs. . . . The Ladies laugh at a little bawdy jest as if they would bepiss themselves.' For plot, 'love and honour will do here agen . . . 'tis but saving alive and marrying those that you would kill in Tragedy' (48–9). At the end of the play Arrowsmith announces that the Tutor must 'reform' and gives him three months 'to produce a Play which shall have nothing in't borrow'd, nor improbable, nor prophane, nor bawdy' (79). Reflecting on this reaction to *Marriage A-la-Mode*, one realizes that Dryden's ironic complexities must have passed right over the heads of most of the audience. Conveniently, an anonymous contemporary charges his fellow play-goers with exactly this failure in understanding.[1] Intending to capitalize on the growing vogue for bawdy, Dryden wound up contributing to it. Examining the various sorts of comedy written in the early seventies, one cannot miss the fascinations of sex comedy.

The intrigue comedy with heavy additional doses of humour continues to appear, sometimes still recognizably in the guise of debased Spanish romance, as in John Corye's *The Generous Enemies, or the Ridiculous Lovers* (June? 1671), a pastiche from several sources. Sword-play and sentiment are appropriate to the Seville setting. (Flaminio: 'Honour defend me, what/Was

---

[1] See *Marriage Asserted* (London, 1674), pp. 74–6, cited by Harold Brooks, 'Some Notes on Dryden, Cowley, and Shadwell', *Notes and Queries*, clxviii (1935), 94–5·

I about to do, give her the Hand that must/Her brother slay'
—66.) But the sick old moneybags, Don Bertran of Seggaral, a
ridiculous lover indeed, and his humorous servant Addibar
rather detract from noble clichés ('Him that love wounds, no
other wounds can fear'—69). The tidy ending turns on the
discovery of hidden relationships, but these matters barely
hold our attention. The epilogue pertinently argues that "Tis
worth your Money that such Legs appear;/These are not to be
seen so cheap elsewhere.' Dryden's *Assignation* comes close to
this mode (intrigue with humour, usually set abroad); so does
The Reformation, commentary upon Dryden aside, whose tone
is often as light as that of Wycherley's *Gentleman Dancing-Master*,
where the sword-play conventions are overtly mocked (e.g. 225).
A curious effort of this sort is Duffett's *The Spanish Rogue* (*c.*
March 1673), a comedy in couplets resting on the conventions
of serious Spanish romance, but often verging on farce, as in
the use of a supposed ghost (64). Bad rhyme and an over-
complex plot too dependent on an elaborate past history
detract heavily from an otherwise competent comedy of
romantic confusion. With this sort of new production, no
wonder the King's Company was sagging. Duffett's prologue
bewails 'Our poor forsaken Stage' and likens the company to a
cast mistress.

The craze for 'French farce' at the end of the sixties burns
out temporarily. The wildly popular *Citizen Turn'd Gentleman*
(analysed at length in Chapter 3, above) attracted no further
imitation, unless its date is as early as Downes implies.[1] One
possible argument in favour of the early date is the sudden
appearance of Shadwell's *The Miser* (late January 1672),
acted by the King's Company. This astonishing anomaly in
Shadwell's career has excited no remark, but never before or
after did he forsake the Duke's Company. His preface tells us
that *The Miser*, an adaptation of Molière's *L'Avare*, was done
hastily, 'wrote in less than a moneth', and at first was left
anonymous. The haste and anonymity are comprehensible if

[1] The first recorded performance is 4 July 1672, and a flurry of list entries in the
Lord Chamberlain's warrants that summer suggests a summer *première*. But
Downes (p. 32) says that it was the second new play acted at Dorset Garden—
which would date it *c.* December 1671. If it did thus run more or less opposite
Marriage A-la-Mode, we might better understand Dryden's real venom about the
play in the prologue to his next comedy—*The Assignation*.

Killigrew, frightened by the success of Ravenscroft's Molière-pastiche, hurriedly suborned Shadwell—a practised plunderer of Molière, but a stalwart of the other house—to produce a counter-attraction. The results are competent hackwork: Shadwell stays pretty close to his original, padding the work out with a sub-plot full of low characters. Technically, *The Miser* is translated into the popular 'London' mode of low comedy, as is Ravenscroft's play. The considerable variety in London comedies and the elements they comprise makes the category something of a holdall. The difference in tone between foreign- and domestic-set comedies was diminishing rapidly: *The Cheats* and *The Adventures of Five Hours* are at opposite poles, while *The Virtuoso* and *The Rover* (in 1676 and 1677) are quite similar in tone. But even so, in the early seventies a London setting is almost always a hint at the nature of the play.

In these years we find again the straight romantic plot, the chatty display of manners, and the multi-plot play with several social levels. Edward Revet's *The Town-Shifts, or, The Suburb-Justice* (acted by March 1671) is a straightforward case of boy gets girl in spite of parental opposition, with some passing satire on Justice Frump and on Leftwell, a cowardly gull. The romantic plot is decidedly serious and moral; no love game here—the hero Lovewell has an almost Steele-ish conscience (37). Other such plots appear occasionally in plays of the seventies, but usually in conjunction with a contrasting plot line or two. Nevil Payne's *The Morning Ramble* (acted by November 1672), in contrast, is a cheerful trifle. It contains far more talk than action, being simply a representation of an all-night frolic by young men about town. The Hyde Park duel scene and other local references suggest a topical and topographical appeal, but the piece is very slight. The familiar multi-level play we saw in Wycherley's *Love in a Wood* (1671), and will see again in Shadwell's *Epsom-Wells* the following year.

In several of these plays, as in the rest about to be discussed, a trend is clear: romantic and satiric elements are increasingly vitiated by a taste for sex and farce. The power of the vogue must have been great: we have noted the sexual appeal of *Marriage A-la-Mode*, and can see it again in *Epsom* (December 1672). This play appears within a year of Shadwell's preface for *The Humorists* (a strenuous denunciation of the gay couple mode), but theory be damned: Shadwell's play is a substantial jump ahead in the type he had condemned, falling half-way between Wycherley's *Love in a Wood* and *The Country-Wife*. Shadwell here employs the witty and 'indecent' lead characters of whom he had been complaining so loudly. Like Dryden, he makes moral claims in his epilogue, and perhaps with almost equal justice. But whether the 'satire' outweighed the appeal of the behaviour satirized we may wonder. The over-all design, with its multiple plot lines, is rather old-fashioned, reminiscent of *The Mulberry-Garden* and *Love in a Wood*. The two couples in the top plot (Rains and Lucia, Bevil and Carolina) put up a graceful, romantic show of wit. A step down are the Woodlys, who occupy the position of Etherege's Cockwoods, but end up in divorce. A second step down come the luckless cuckold cits, Bisket and Fribble; like Justice Clodpate (whose marriage to a prostitute turns out to be invalid—luckily for him), they are brutally satirized. And finally we reach the scum—Kick, Cuff ('cheating, sharking, cowardly Bullies') and Mrs. Jilt ('A silly, affected Whore'). Shadwell manages the tangle beautifully: the play is quite lively and entertaining. *The Miser* had been a decidedly moral play, taking its love seriously and teaching by direct example. (The play is well analysed by J. H. Smith.) But *The Miser* fared indifferently, and Shadwell, always a sensitive weather-vane, promptly turned to the gay couple and lots of adultery, titillatingly represented: his reward was a great popular success. Note a progression: Courtall in *She wou'd* (1668) avoids illicit sex when it is thrust upon him; Shadwell's Rains (1672) indulges but makes excuses for himself; Dorimant in *The Man of Mode* (1676) leaps to it without a qualm.

Another Duke's Company gay couple play, rather more decorous, is Ravenscroft's *The Careless Lovers* (March 1673). J. H. Smith is almost alone in admiring this engaging trifle. Careless and Hillaria enact a wild romp of a love game, ending with an impudent imitation of the proviso scene in *Secret Love* (76–7), including provision for joint adultery. A more serious couple (Lovell and Jacinta) is used as a contrasting plot; a conceited Lord, De Boastado, is a rival for Jacinta's hand. He is liberally mocked and then married off to Beatrice—the girls' scheming maid. At this her friend Toby is upset, and he pretends to stab himself—with a candle (74). As always, Ravenscroft has a good eye for chances to mock conventions: as much as any writer in the period, he deliberately jokes about the cliché elements of which he makes such effective use. The prefatory matter blasts Dryden, whose nastiness had invited the attack. The prologue compares Almanzor and Mama-mouchi and asks whether '*Fool* or *Hero* makes the better Farce'. Ravenscroft's Epistle to the Reader mocks Dryden's pretentious dedications to patrons and his critical essays, twits coffeehouse pundits, and asks 'why there are such continual Picques amongst the *Poets*'. The acid answer strikes home: 'I can give you no other Reason than what one Whore told the other—*Two of a Trade can seldome agree.*'

The difference between the decorum of *She wou'd* and the blatantly suggestive sex scenes in *The Country-Wife* only seven years later can seem startling. But the change comes strictly by degrees. Two key but little studied links are *The Mall: or The Modish Lovers* (*c.* February 1674), probably by John Dover, and *The Amorous Old-woman: or 'Tis Well if it Take* (*c.* March 1674), possibly by Duffett.[1] Both are King's Company productions, dating from near the end of their unhappy tenancy of the old Lincoln's Inn Fields theatre. *The Amorous Old-woman* presents love complications in the old Spanish-style mode, with honourable posturing and serious duelling. Mixed into this intrigue mode (in which the affairs of three romantic couples are disentangled) is a huge dose of farce and degraded sex. The blind old Senator Cicco (who 'pretends to see') is tricked by the servant Furfante, 'drest like a Woman on one side, and like himself on the other' (33). Cicco's brother Riccamare courts the widowed Strega, 'an old Rich deformed Lady' who wants to be had for her 'well-favouredness', not her money. Riccamare feels, with the money in prospect, that he 'can Digest a few imperfections'. The lady admits to five of them. After she removes her eyebrows, an eye, her teeth, and her hair, the suitor is discouraged but game. However he quits when she takes off a leg (40–3). The lying romancer Buggio tells Cicco the lady is lovely—and in due course he

---

[1] The attribution is made hesitatingly by Langbaine: Duffett was not quite the 'Person of Honour', specified on the title-page.

and Strega gambol onstage, just married. This sardonic brutality accords oddly with the romantic plot.

Dover's *The Mall* is an even more strident sex comedy. Young Lovechange has secretly married rich Widow Woodbee. He pursues young Mrs. Easy, whose maid Peg (dressed as Mrs. Easy while the lady gallivants) is bedded by Mr. Easy in that role—undressed on stage and hauled off, helpless (34–5). Mrs. Woodbee presents herself at one of her husband's assignations, and is swived in the dark by the gallant Courtwell, thinking he is her husband. Learning of this, Lovechange brutally blackmails his wife into hushing up their marriage and handing over half her fortune (61–2), whereupon he demands that Easy yield his young wife, which that gentleman does, saying 'live—and lye—and be hang'd—together if you please, with all my heart' (71). To this are added two lesser plots: one a standard London marriage story, the other an incongruous romance story in which a Spanish lady pursues Courtwell to England in disguise and finally marries him. *The Mall* apparently failed—indeed its construction is pretty indifferent—but its large dose of raw sex is symptomatic of a developing mode.

At the end of March 1674 the King's Company finally moved into its replacement theatre and reassumed something like a competitive position, mounting Lee's *Nero* and Pierre Perrin's opera, *Ariadne*. In his prologue for the opening, Dryden complains that 'scenes, machines, and empty operas reign': four days later the King's Company mounted *Ariadne*. The craze for music (detailed in Chapter 5, above) is reflected in the Duke's Company production of the revised *Tempest* that spring, and the long delayed *Psyche* the next year. Duffett's brilliant travesties of both productions (only shadows of themselves on the printed page) were the King's Company's way of capitalizing on their rivals' vast but expensive successes.[1] Another play with a lot of music is Newcastle's *The Triumphant Widow* (acted by November 1674), a proto-ballad-opera with some surprising resemblances to *The Beggar's Opera*. Over all,

---

[1] *The Empress of Morocco* (c. August 1673), which includes a fine epilogue take-off of the new Dorset Garden production of *Macbeth*; *The Mock-Tempest* (c. August 1674); and *Psyche Debauch'd* (c. August 1675). For an account of Duffett's rapid improvements in technique, see Peter Elvet Lewis, 'The Three Dramatic Burlesques of Thomas Duffett', *Durham University Journal*, n.s. xxvii (1966), 149–56.

the play is too much a rag-bag of disparate elements, loosely stitched together. But the whole thing has bounce, the songs have a delightfully earthy vigour, and satire on the fop Codshead and the heroic poet Crambo is brilliant if unsubtle.[1]

By 1674 spectacle and horror have become major ingredients in most serious plays. Music, always popular, has quite suddenly become more than an incidental attraction. The taste for French farce had abated slightly after 1672, but in its place in comedy we find rapid growth in ever more explicit sexual scenes and innuendo. Looking back, J. H. Smith rightly points to Betterton's *The Amorous Widow* as the seminal play in the development of sex comedy.[2] Betterton's ploy was quickly picked up and is used with increasing bluntness in half a dozen important plays prior to *The Country-Wife* in 1675. To observe that sex, spectacle, and horror are rampant in the early seventies may suggest (as it did to Dryden) that the drama was degenerating. Curiously enough, however, the Carolean theatre was on the eve of its greatest triumphs.

III. THE CAROLEAN SUMMIT 1675–1677

Precisely why the next few years were so fruitful one can only speculate. The trends and omens of the early seventies mostly seem unpropitious, yet somehow the lull between the end of the Dutch War and the onset of the Popish Plot yields some singularly happy results. In just three seasons we find an astonishing concentration of fine plays, both comic and tragic. The first Carolean decade was spent in breaking away from imitative modes and establishing a drama of the

---

[1] At least part of the play is by Shadwell. See Albert S. Borgman, *Thomas Shadwell* (1928; rpt. New York, 1969), pp. 27–8. In his preface to *Ibrahim* (pub. 1677) Settle says angrily of Shadwell: 'Having a Play, call'd the *Triumphant Widdow*, given him to bring into the Duke's Play-house, he spitefully foists in a Scene of his own into the Play, and makes a silly Heroick Poet in it, speak the very words he had heard me say.' (A rather ingenuous complaint!) Here again we see Shadwell's special association with personal satire. The connection appears too in a letter by John Aubrey to Anthony à Wood (26 October 1671): 'I am writing a comedy for Thomas Shadwell. . . . And I shall fit him with another, The Country Revell, . . . but of this, mum! for 'tis very satyricall against some of my mischievous enemies.' *Brief Lives*, ed. Andrew Clark (Oxford, 1898), I. 52 n. Only a fragment of the proposed comedy was completed.

[2] J. H. Smith, p. 85. Lady Cockwood of *She wou'd* is of course a much imitated character. But plenty of earlier plays have similar characters (e.g. Lady Love-all in *The Parsons Wedding*), and Etherege carefully preserves the decencies. *She wou'd* is merely a significant landmark in the development toward comedy of cuckoldry.

time. The early seventies fail to see the development of the potentialities apparent at the end of the sixties. Despite isolated high spots (e.g. *Epsom-Wells, Marriage A-la-Mode*), the drama seems to be sliding into the cheap tricks and crowd-pleasing mediocrity Dryden so loudly bewails. Unpredictably, however, things are about to change for the better. Peace, prosperity, and a new theatre contribute to a jump in new play productions. In 1676 the number is more than double the total for 1673, and the increase comes at just the right time. The veteran professional playwrights, Dryden and Shadwell, have arrived at the peak of their powers. Etherege is ready to speak again. Wycherley, Behn, and Crowne pass out of apprenticeship toward full stature. Lee and Otway make rapid strides toward maturity. Comedy is in its period of glory. Serious drama is in a state of transition between the rhymed heroic play and a less extravagant, unrhymed form of tragedy, but we will see some fine plays of both types.

Yet not everything is sunny. In 1674–5 the King's Company were genuinely competitive for the first time in four seasons. But with the 'plain built' Drury Lane theatre, they still felt disadvantaged.[1] Worse, the troupe was increasingly wracked by bitter internal dissension. In February 1676 the King had to order his players to act:

His Ma[jesty] understanding That His Company of Comoedians have left off acting upon private differences and disagreements betweene themselues is very much displeased thereat And hath commanded mee to require and order the said Company forthwith to act and play as formerly And that none of the said Company presume to leave off Acting.[2]

The players were feuding with Killigrew, who started to turn his interest over to his son Charles, and then reneged. A violent altercation between father and son ensued. Multiple lawsuits produced only chaos, expense, and occasional cessation

---

[1] The disadvantage was less than they imagined. Dorset Garden reigned unchallenged for spectacle-oriented plays and operas, but Drury Lane actually proved more satisfactory for ordinary plays and had a more convenient location for most of the audience. The United Company was to use both houses in the eighties, but preferred Drury Lane. See *The London Stage*, Part 1, pp. xli–xliii.

[2] P.R.O. L.C. 7/1. The controversies are summarized and extracts of relevant documents printed by Nicoll, in his Appendix A.

of acting in the next three years.[1] As we shall see in the next section, Dryden finally decamped in disgust to the Duke's Company, taking Lee with him. One marvels that the King's Company was producing great plays in the midst of these sordid squabbles—including *The Plain-Dealer*, *All for Love*, and *The Rival Queens*. Some shifting of allegiances takes place in these years. Most professional playwrights worked under contract to one house or the other (Durfey is a prominent exception), and a company's security depended on such allegiance. The rather pitiful complaint against Dryden and Lee written (but probably never filed) by the managers of the King's Company makes plain the desperate importance of having working agreements with front-rank writers.[2] Their defection ('almost undoing . . . the Company, They being the onely Poets remaining to us') was prefigured in reverse a year earlier when Crowne and Ravenscroft transferred allegiance to the King's Company—a move probably engineered by Charles Killigrew. Crowne apparently cost the company a £112 penalty: why Dryden was not in turn subject to legal restraint no one has been able to determine. All these imbroglios foreshadow the collapse of the King's Company, which was extremely shaky even in these boom years.

The most conspicuous trend in comedy continues a familiar pattern: romantic elements are increasingly subordinated to rogue plots and ever-more-suggestive sex scenes. The flood of sex was predictable; what genius could do with stereotyped popular modes was not.

Debased Spanish romance still makes half-hearted appearances. Ravenscroft's *The Wrangling Lovers* (July 1676), for him a stiff and awkward effort, provides the usual light-hearted treatment of the honour conventions, interspersed with mild foolery, especially from the valet, Sanco. A much better comedy is Thomas Porter's *The French Conjurer* (*c.* June 1677), set in Seville. It has two plot lines. In one Dorido wins Clorinia, despite his false friend Horatio, who frames him by stabbing the girl (fairly harmlessly) and planting the bloody

<hr/>

[1] For the best account of the last years of the King's Company, see John Harold Wilson, *Mr. Goodman the Player* (Pittsburgh, Pa., 1964).

[2] The document is printed and analysed, with an account of Dryden's defection, by James M. Osborn, *John Dryden: Some Biographical Facts and Problems*, rev. edn. (Gainesville, Fla., 1965), pp. 200–7.

dagger on Dorido. In the other, gallant young Claudio seduces Pedro's wife Leonora, with the help of Monsieur, a French astrologer–crook. In their first encounter the lady is reluctant. But told that 'your sweetness has so transported me, that if you cannot yield, I must force you' (29), she agrees cheerfully enough. At their next encounter, Monsieur makes her 'invisible' by sending her down a trapdoor, and he holds Pedro's attention while Claudio joins her. Pressed for details of her experience by her husband, she gives a two-edged allegorical account of a 'Devil' who has (the audience realizes) satisfied her *twice* (oh bliss!) in quick succession (42–4). Despite such concessions to the times, Porter seems rather indifferent to his bawdy stuff. The play as a whole is a bit simplistic, and quite lacks the genius and charm of *The Carnival* (1664). Porter's epilogue, in Monsieur's broken English, grumpily derides 'de *French* Troop at toder end o' Town'—a reminder that competition from touring foreign companies continued to plague the English actors. The most interesting direct effect of such counter-attractions is Ravenscroft's experiment in *commedia dell'arte*: *Scaramouch a Philosopher, Harlequin a School-Boy, Bravo, Merchant, and Magician. A Comedy After the Italian manner* (acted by May 1677). The inspiration probably came from Fiorilli's second visit (Summer 1675): Ravenscroft complains bitterly about a long delay in production—probably aggravated by Otway's successful afterpiece, *The Cheats of Scapin* (*c*. December 1676). Ravenscroft's experiment in turning the Molière-adaptation type of play toward pantomimic farce did not catch on at the time. His concept though, bespeaks an impressive (if 'unliterary') dramatic imagination, and the play deserves serious study in the history of English farce.

The intrigue comedy mode, in its 1660s manifestations often closely related to Spanish romance, has by now suffered so much comic accretion as properly to approach the designation 'intrigue farce'. The relevant plays are mostly of poor quality. Peter Belon's *The Mock-Duellist* (*c*. May 1675) is a very indifferent piece of hackwork, though it offered someone, probably John Lacy, an amusing vehicle in the French valet, Champagne. Sir Francis Fane's *Love in the Dark* (May 1675), set in Venice at Carnival time, is at least lively and high-spirited. But despite a dedication to Rochester, praising his conversation, the contents are routine fare. Good ideas are inexpertly developed, especially Intrigo, a potentially amusing Marplot character. Neither Carnival frolics nor a supposed plot against the state really capture the attention. The same holds for the heavy, blustering humour of Ravenscroft's *The English Lawyer* (*c.* December 1677), an adaptation of Ruggle's Latin *Ignoramus* (1615). Its only real virtue is being less heavy and verbose than Robert Codrington's translation (pub. 1662). These three intrigue farces were all King's Company plays. A pair of Duke's Company productions are altogether better. The anonymous *The Woman turn'd Bully* (March 1675) seems to have found no champion save Summers, despite Langbaine's praise of it. Vivid characters, lively intrigue, and repartee make the piece enjoyable if unremarkable. The title character, Betty Goodfeild, comes to London in male attire, and as 'Sir Thomas Whimsey' she swaggers about, issues challenges, and finally drops her disguise to marry Jack Truman. Mrs. Behn's *The Town-Fop* (September 1676) is a more complex play, and a splendid example of the domestication of what ten years earlier was almost always a foreign intrigue plot. The scene here is Covent Garden, but there is plenty of serious melodrama and sword-play, and even a genuine offer to fall on a sword. Behn makes sober use of the theme of her source, George Wilkins's *The Miseries of Enforced Marriage* (1607). Bellmour is forced to marry Diana, but he cannot love her and leaves the union unconsummated. He loves Celinda, whose brother Friendlove wants Diana. Finally the tangle is sorted out. In the meantime the fop Sir Timothy, deprived of Celinda, woos Bellmour's sister Phillis and traps her in a mock marriage which promptly turns out to be real. The multiple plots are well integrated, despite the gap between romance elements and the low scenes involving Sir Timothy, his whore Betty Flauntit, and his hirelings Sham and Sharp. Here we see Mrs. Behn in midflight between the Italian intrigue romance and the London sex comedy.

Examination of two major plays, *The Rover* and *The Plain-Dealer*, shows the way sex was being added to the old swordplay and intrigue forms. *The Plain-Dealer* (December 1676) is a very strange play. Unquestionably, parts of it are brilliant— but what do they add up to? Savage, sardonic social commentary gives the play life and impact: the author's seething indignation cannot be missed. Precisely how we should respond to the characters and situations, however, remains problematical. Is Manly to be considered an *alter ego* and spokesman for Wycherley? Or is he a vigorously satirized humour character? Chorney made the latter view popular, but critical opinion has veered back to the former in recent years.[1] K. M. Rogers suggests acutely that the play suffers from a 'fatal inconsistency' in the presence of Manly as both comic misanthropist and serious satiric spokesman. Wycherley both denounces society and shows the folly of refusing to accept society's compromises. Whether Freeman's triumphant bilking of the litigious Widow Blackacre was meant to seem a happy case of decent expediency, or something worse, is arguable.[2] Despite the brilliance of the parts, the play's aim and focus seem indistinct. Its elements are an interesting mingling of 'domestic' social satire and 'foreign' intrigue and sword-play. The rape and sex motifs are a sign of the times. The introduction of Fidelia, an escapee from romantic tragicomedy, rings oddly against the gritty, vivid 'London' elements. Into this jumble of standard parts Wycherley's satiric fervour, however muddled, infuses exceptional vitality.[3]

[1] See Alexander H. Chorney, 'Wycherley's Manly Reinterpreted', *Essays Critical and Historical Dedicated to Lily B. Campbell* (Berkeley, Calif., 1950), pp. 161–9. Zimbardo feels that Manly degenerates. Birdsall says that we pity his inability to cope with a despicable society—hence he is *not* satirized. A. M. Friedson, 'Wycherley and Molière: Satirical Point of View in *The Plain Dealer*', *Modern Philology*, lxiv (1967), 189–97, argues (to me convincingly) that Manly is not much satirized, which is also Craik's opinion. J. M. Auffret, in '*The Man of Mode* & *The Plain Dealer*: Common Origin & Parallels', *Études anglaises*, xix (1966), 209–22, suggests that Manly is 'an idealized portraiture of John Sheffield, Earl of Mulgrave', an *à clef* character constituting an 'answer' to the picture of Rochester in *The Man of Mode*. The case is provocative, but highly speculative.

[2] See K. M. Rogers, 'Fatal Inconsistency: Wycherley and *The Plain-Dealer*', *ELH*, xxviii (1961), 148–62, and *William Wycherley* (New York, 1972), Chapter 4; and Vernon, *Wycherley*, pp. 29–33. The possibility that Wycherley is deliberately creating satiric overtones is explored by Cynthia Matlack, 'Parody and Burlesque of Heroic Ideals in Wycherley's Comedies: A Critical Reinterpretation of Contemporary Evidence', *Papers on Language and Literature*, viii (1972), 273–86, who suggests reading Manly as a sardonic parody of Almanzor. For a 'straight' reading of some of the same elements, see B. Eugene McCarthy, 'Wycherley's "The Plain-Dealer" and the Limits of Wit', *English Miscellany*, xxii (1971), 47–92.

[3] Critics have long wondered if *The Plain-Dealer*, the last-produced of Wycherley's plays, was perhaps written between *The Gentleman Dancing-Master* and *The Country-Wife*. The intrigue and sword-play and setting in the time of 'the Dutch War' have fed such speculation. The indifferent success of Wycherley's second play, and the King's Company's hard times, might conceivably have kept an early version of

Almost as vital, if less serious, is Aphra Behn's delightful *The Rover* (Part 1, March 1677). The scene is Naples in Carnival time, a setting taken over from Killigrew's unperformed *Thomaso* (written 1654) and demanded by the honour and sword-play conventions which are central to the plot. Behn's mastery of rollicking razzle-dazzle never appears to better advantage. A serious romantic couple (Belvile and Florinda) is balanced against a really attractive gay couple (Willmore and Hellena). A friend, Blunt, is royally duped by a jilting whore, Lucetta, who drops him through a trap into the sewer to return home in his underwear. In vengeful mood Blunt finds a strange female in the men's quarters and prepares to rape her with help from a friend, but Florinda is spared by the timely arrival of others. An unusual element in the plot is the courtesan Angelica Bianca, who falls seriously for Willmore. Behn's treatment of her verges on the tragic; but leaving her dangling in mid air at the end of the play is a major blemish on the plot. Despite the forced marriage theme and the acute and sympathetic psychological treatment of several main characters, *The Rover* remains a joyous caper, a light-hearted but not farcical intrigue comedy leavened with sex. In fairness, one must add that Mrs. Behn actually reduces Killigrew's bawdy.[1]

London sex comedy achieves its finest form in three comedies from these years—*The Country-Wife* (January 1675), *The Man of Mode* (March 1676), and *The Virtuoso* (May 1676). The first two are analysed in detail in Chapter 3, above. The heart of Wycherley's play is a rogue's intrigue, with cuckoldry as its object. From comments in *The Plain-Dealer* one can deduce

---

The Plain-Dealer off the stage in 1673 or 1674. The schizophrenic picture of Manly plus the greater artistic control of *The Country-Wife* can be adduced for such a theory; against it is the apparent progression toward more serious morality, culminating in the indignation of *The Plain-Dealer* (see Rogers, *Wycherley*, p. 149, n. 40). The only non-intuitive evidence for an earlier version is distinctly suspect—a Pope anecdote: 'The chronology of Wycherley's plays I am well acquainted with, for he has told it me, over and over. *Love in a Wood* he wrote when he was but nineteen, the *Gentleman Dancing-Master* at twenty-one, the *Plain Dealer* at twenty-five, and the *Country Wife* at one or two and thirty.' Spence, *Anecdotes*, ed. Osborn, no. 78, dated 1735. The dates thus implied are of course impossible, but why should Wycherley falsify the *order* of composition? Lacking hard evidence, however, the earlier dating must be judged unlikely.

[1] The best critical account of the play is Frederick M. Link's Introduction to his Regents Restoration Drama Series edition (1967).

that at least part of the audience was shocked, though the play succeeded. Etherege's last play, as J. H. Smith observes, represents a further step in the abandonment of moral propriety. Dorimant does succeed in his sex intrigues. And unlike Horner, Dorimant is a glamorous upper-class character, ultimately rewarded with the hand of the lovely, wealthy Harriet. In their presentation of sex these plays imply a philosophical libertinism far removed from the satirical morality which a careful reading should derive from *Epsom-Wells* or *Marriage A-la-Mode*.

Shadwell's *Virtuoso* can justly stand in this rarefied if indecorous company. Shadwell's plot is once again multi-lined; his view of his material is more overtly and simply satiric; his interest lies more in fools than wits. He balances a serious romantic plot involving two pairs of lovers (Longvil and Clarinda, Bruce and Miranda) against a series of satiric plot elements—Sir Nicholas Gimcrack (the ludicrous scientist of the title), his wife (a Lady Cockwood figure), and three brilliantly drawn butts: Sir Formal Trifle, Snarl, and Sir Samuel Hearty. Shadwell was never to write a more perfectly controlled play. Not even the romantic lovers escape his mockery: the gentlemen bestow their affections the wrong way round, and after nearly fighting a duel have to be induced to transfer their allegiance. Says Bruce: 'Since our affections will not thrive in the soil we had plac'd them in, we must transplant them' (III. 177). Shadwell's satire on science is brilliant, especially the famous swimming scene (125–7): Sir Nicholas does his practising on a table without water, for he is 'content . . . with the speculative part'. Ruined at the end of the play, the foolish Virtuoso laments his failure to realize that the proper study of mankind is man—not spiders and insects.[1] Throughout the work Shadwell plays beautifully with a mousetrap motif, especially in Act III. Clarinda drops Sir Formal into a vault, and then adds Sir Samuel (who is disguised as a woman). The homosexual encounter which

[1] For an account of the satire on science, see the Regents Restoration Drama Series edition by Marjorie Hope Nicolson and David Stuart Rodes (1966). Joseph M. Gilde, in 'Shadwell and the Royal Society: Satire in *The Virtuoso*', *Studies in English Literature*, x (1970), 469–90, points out that the Royal Society is very little satirized; rather, it 'provides a standard for judging the follies of the two principal fools.'

follows is wildly funny, and makes a good introduction to the triple discovery scene. Snarl and Mrs. Figgup retire to a hired room for their delights—whipping in this case—only to have to hide when they are interrupted by Lady Gimcrack and her hired lover, Hazard. They too pile into the woodhole when Sir Nicholas turns up with a whore, Mrs. Flirt. Round-robin recriminations are complicated by the discovery that Hazard and Mrs. Flirt have been copulating in their spare time. In due course Lady Gimcrack casually grants Longvil all liberties during a masked ball; Sir Formal marries the chambermaid Betty, masked in place of Clarinda; Snarl marries his whore, for 'better marry my own, than another mans'; Sir Samuel's matrimonial schemes come to naught, and he learns that he has 'been kick'd, beaten, pumpt, and toss'd in a blanket, &c. to no purpose'. Shadwell supplies plenty of titillating sex, though always as part of a satiric debunking of the participants. This vigorous comedy is no angry satire, but neither does it make much concession to the libertine ethic.

Lesser plays with a marked sex component foreshadow and swell the flood. One of the most enjoyable is Crowne's *The Countrey Wit* (March 1675?), which approaches farce. Sir Mannerly Shallow is the country gull to end all gulls, and is finally married off to Winnifrid Rash, a porter's daughter. The heiress Christina falls for the wild Ramble. His wildness is more in the telling than in anything he is allowed to do, and even more important, he is forced to beg forgiveness on his knees before he is actually accepted. J. H. Smith rightly sees him as part of the move toward Dorimant, and simultaneously as a premonitory symptom of the moral sentimentalism so prominent in a later play like *The Squire of Alsatia* (1688)— which is to say that Shadwell and Cibber did not invent the penitent rake. Crowne uses sex and basks in morality and seems not a whit uncomfortable. His attention is mostly on gulling: Ramble's servant Merry successfully schemes to marry Sir Mannerly's aunt, Lady Faddle, while Sir Mannerly makes his much-mistaken marriage, and his servant Booby gets landed with responsibility for a bastard not of his own making. This crude, good-humoured, easy-going farce seems to have been a favourite of Charles II.

The plays following *The Man of Mode* tend to be blunter

than Crowne's. Thus *Tom Essence: or, The Modish Wife* (c. August 1676), probably by one 'Rawlins', opens with a smutty prologue, and shows us Mrs. Moneylove coolly defying her cuckolded husband when he discovers her adultery with Stanly. Dressed as her own brother, she visits her husband, who then beds 'him' with Stanly in a fit of parsimony. (Similar devices are used in *A Fond Husband* and *Sir Patient Fancy*.) Most of the play's intrigue is derived from the jealous misunderstandings of a serious couple (Courtly and Theodocia), who get entangled with Tom Essence (a seller of gloves, ribbons, and perfume) and his crabby wife. In a lesser action, Loveall, 'a wilde Debaucht Blade', repents and marries a wealthy widow, Luce. Mrs. Behn's (?) *The Debauchee: or the Credulous Cuckold* (c. February 1677), an alteration of *A Mad Couple Well Matched*, employs a similar mixture of elements: (a) Clara, once seduced by Lord Loveless, follows him in male attire and claims his vows—to which he replies 'You melt my soul' (62) and yields. (b) Young Lady Thrivewell is forgiving about her husband's amorous proclivities; clears herself of slander; and virtuously refuses the advances of her husband's nephew Careless. (c) Careless, loved by the rich young widow Mrs. Crostill, reforms to marry her (63), giving up his mistress Phebe Gimcrack, who marries his servant Watt. The intrigue is well managed, the sex interests titillating but really fairly pure.

The jumble of elements in these plays serves as an important caution against easy assumptions. One can find exemplary moral reformation by a rake right in the midst of a successful cuckoldry action, as in *Tom Essence*. With that play, as with *The Amorous Widow* and some of Shadwell's, J. H. Smith is forced to discuss one part of the plot in the chapter on 'Cynical Comedy', other parts in the chapter on 'Forces in Opposition'. Yet the Carolean authors do not seem to have been bothered by what seems to us moral schizophrenia in their plays. Audiences could enjoy the love game and cuckoldry; they seem also to have been partial to perfectly moral romance plots and displays of ethical niceties. The critics who once saw *Love's Last Shift* (1696) as a sudden turning point simply had not read enough of the earlier plays. Sex comedy is in the ascendant in 1677, but even so, a piece like *The Debauchee* can, while playing with sex, give us a more serious moral show than Cibber saw fit to do twenty years later.

Two Durfey plays from November 1676, one for the King's Company, one for the Duke's, illustrate the possibilities of largely moral romance right in the middle of the sex boom. *The Fool Turn'd Critick* is careless patchwork, a slack piece with slight intrigue. Durfey spices it with sexy talk, but keeps solid morals in view: Penelope likes Frank Amorous, but will be cautious, for 'The choice of prudent Judgments I approve;/ Honour and virtue must obtain my Love' (11). *Madam Fickle: or The Witty False One* adapts Rowley's *A Match at Midnight* (1622). Interest centres on the supposed widow's vengeful tricks on her suitors. But the supposedly dead husband who abandoned her returns and indicates his remorse in blank verse soliloquies, whereupon we are treated to a very romantic reconciliation scene.

Despite the viability of such pieces, the trend was toward explicit sex, and more of it. Durfey joins the bandwagon with *A Fond Husband* (May 1677), a brilliantly plotted and very influential sex intrigue comedy. Charles II loved it and attended three of the first five performances. Durfey outdoes previous sex plays: *A Fond Husband* is the first Carolean comedy to focus almost exclusively on a cuckolding action. Betterton, Wycherley, and Dover all include standard romantic plots; Durfey adds only a very minor secondary action, and leaves it dangling at the end. The story is simple. Rashley and Ranger are rivals for Emilia, the wife of Peregrine Bubble, a credulous, fond cuckold. Rashley is conscience-less, Emilia faithless. Together they thoroughly abuse the luckless Bubble, despite his sister Maria's attempts (aided by the jealous Ranger) to undeceive him. Plot and counter-plot follow in dazzling succession as the adulterers escape exposure by the barest of margins. Finally they are caught *in flagrante delicto*: we wait for an explosion, but none comes. The brazen Rashley says coolly: 'Well, Sir, if I have injur'd you, I wear a Sword, Sir,—and so—Farewel' (60–1). J. H. Smith is nauseated by this 'cynical study', being especially offended by what he calls glamorization of adultery. This seems too severe a view of a boisterous and farcically inclined play. I think we care too little about any of the characters to take a serious view of the events. The spoilsports Maria and Ranger are selfish and jealous. Bubble is too fatuous to be pitied. The minor characters are strictly butts: old Alderman Fumble, almost deaf and blind, dotes on black women; Sir Roger Petulant is a womanizing knight 'of the last age'; his loathsome nephew Sneak undergoes the sweating treatment for his clap.

Kind words for *A Fond Husband* are hard to find from modern critics. Yet Langbaine's praise in his *Account of the English Dramatick Poets* is fully justified: unedifying the play may be, but the exciting plot construction and vivid pillorying of the characters make the piece highly enjoyable. The results are curiously amoral: Durfey cheerfully capitalizes on sex without particularly approving or disapproving of it. The use of sex is almost incidental: as the prologue says, 'Plot' is emphasized, and since a 'Smutty Tale' will please the town, that is made the subject of the plot. But whether the critic likes or dislikes *A Fond Husband*, its historical importance should be recognized: it is a key play in determining the directions taken in comedy at the end of the seventies. Its great success (and popularity at court) in Spring 1677 had a clear influence—explicitly admitted by Dryden—on *Limberham, Sir Patient Fancy*, and *Friendship in Fashion* in 1678. To treat Durfey's play with indifference or distaste is to miss the impact of an especially popular work. Durfey furthers the adultery mode Wycherley had popularized: 1678 was to see both the culmination and the disintegration of the sex comedy type founded by Betterton in *The Amorous Widow*.

The years of the Carolean summit thus see in comedy the extension and advancement of trends well established early in the decade. Concurrently in the serious drama we will find the rhymed heroic type petering out, while experiments in new types give promise of better things to come. 'Petering out' is perhaps a misleading phrase: the rhymed play (contrary to myth) is actually numerically dominant in these years, but from prologues and prefaces one easily sees the writers' realization that a change is due. Settle, Durfey, Otway, and Crowne go on writing in the old fashion, without pretending to much conviction—almost as if they were waiting for someone to show the way elsewhere, as Dryden and Lee were to do.

Of the sixteen serious plays which fall into the period under consideration (1675–7), twelve are rhymed. Of the other four, one is satirical (Shadwell's *Libertine*), and another, *Abdelazer* (acted by July 1676), is a wild flood of butchery and sex adapted by Mrs. Behn from an Elizabethan play. With the exception then of *All for Love* and *The Rival Queens* (both of 1677), the rhymed heroic play goes unchallenged. Dryden, weary of being 'condemn'd to Rhyme', announced his discontent in the preface and prologue to *Aureng-Zebe* (1675). In the preface to *Ibrahim* Settle says—rather misleadingly—that his play suffered the 'misfortune' of being 'written in Rhime, a way of writing very much out of Fashion'. Crowne's epilogue to *1 Destruction of Jerusalem* (January 1677) says: 'for his Rhime he pardon does implore,/And promises to ring those Chimes no more.' Thus by 1677 rhyme had lost its attractions, but by no means was it visibly being supplanted.

Rhymed plays appear (1) in the well-established horror mode, (2) in more serious heroic vein, (3) in would-be high heroic strain, and (4) in tragical form which suggests the advent of the unrhymed tragedies at the end of the decade. Two of the horror plays pick up parts of the Alexander the Great tale made popular by Lee's unrhymed *Rival Queens*. John Banks's *The Rival Kings: or the Loves of Oroondates and Statira* (June 1677) has the vigour of poetic youth and little else to recommend it. The temple scene with its human sacrifice, and the falling statue of Jupiter killing the priests have a rude effectiveness. The dying Alexander, 'discover'd in torment', maintains his noble character: 'Lives 'e ye Gods? Go fetch him instantly,/ Let me the pleasure have to see him dy,/Then let my soul with satisfaction fly' (45). Such awkward lines and ringing triplets are entirely characteristic. By Banks's own later standards, this is poor stuff. Worse may be said of Pordage's *The Siege of Babylon* (*c*. September 1677), which concerns Statira and Roxana, Alexander's widows. The love-and-honour posturing is about as silly as these plays get, and it goes unredeemed by imagination or vigour. Predictable changes are rung on three princes and three queens (including Thalestris, Queen of the Amazons), a prison scene, and madness: Roxana is 'carried off the Stage Raveing' (61). An altogether better horror play, analysed in Chapter 5, above, is Otway's *Alcibiades* (September 1675). Every predictable device is introduced and milked for all it is worth—

poison, ghost, rape, lustful villainess, etc.—but even in this first effort Otway's genius is apparent.

Equal genius of a different sort produced the exuberant bloodbath in Shadwell's *The Libertine* (June 1675), a work 'As wild, and as extravagant as th' Age', the prologue tells us. This version of the Don Juan story has attracted almost no critical discussion. Nicoll says only (I. 205) that the play is in blank verse—which it is not, save for isolated passages. Atrocities abound. Don John has killed his own father (among some thirty murders), and specializes in raping nuns. His friends are Lopez and Antonio: the former has killed his elder brother to acquire an estate; the latter has impregnated his own sisters. The three of them roar through the play, butchering, plundering, and raping. Shadwell points out in his preface that for these crimes 'a dreadful punishment [is] inflicted'. Is *The Libertine* then (a) horror tragedy with a tidy moral ending? (b) A serious questioning of the social and ethical values of civilization by 'a tragic rake'?[1] (c) A sardonic comment upon both horror tragedy and the ethic of libertine comedy? Alssid is certainly right in denying that the play is a simple moral tale of crime and punishment. But I cannot take it quite as he does. What we find here are the form and devices but not the tone of a serious horror play. As in *Timon* (discussed in the next section), Shadwell imports the moral code of contemporary libertine comedy into a tragic structure, and the result is a sober-faced burlesque. In these satirical tragedies Shadwell hits at the values of comedy and the devices of tragedy. Especially in *The Libertine* (as Langbaine noted) the results are highly diverting.

By far the most ambitious effort in the serious heroic vein is Crowne's two-part *The Destruction of Jerusalem* (January 1677), a considerable success. *The Conquest of Granada* obviously served as the model: Crowne works up cultural differentiation in his Jews and Romans, uses the popular 'siege' setting, and establishes Phraartes as an Almanzor figure. At the end of Part 1 Phraartes is hailed as king. Part 2, however, follows a different pattern from Dryden's. The love of Titus and Berenice largely displaces the love of Phraartes and the maiden Queen Clarona

---

[1] This position is argued by Michael W. Alssid, *Thomas Shadwell*, pp. 107–10. For a subtler view, see Loftis, *The Spanish Plays of Neoclassical England*, pp. 172–7.

as the centre of attention, and the work moves to an unhappy ending: Clarona is murdered, Titus and Berenice are separated; Phraartes escapes and resumes the Parthian throne. Part 2 is full of the sensational. The battle scene in Act V is dazzling, as is Crowne's grand 'Scene, the Temple burning, fill'd with *Jews* lamenting'. *The Destruction of Jerusalem* is a *lush* work, nothing stinted. Heroes, heroines, villains (more believable than usual), and ghost (of Herod) are all in place and functioning smoothly. The results are certainly highly competent, though lacking the inspiration which could infuse some life into the proceedings. Crowne's play has no significant intellectual or political design, and hence cannot begin to stand comparison with Dryden's. For a play with this subject and scope, it is remarkably lacking in *intérêt d'état*. Instead, Crowne stresses personal feeling. His conclusion, contrasting Phraartes's wild sorrow at Clarona's death with the parting of Titus and Berenice, is a well-wrought experiment in a kind of pathos that was becoming increasingly fashionable.

Otway's *Titus and Berenice* (*c.* December 1676) at almost the same time is simply an indifferent couplet recension of Racine's tragedy. Its interest lies largely in a historical freak. Otway left the play at three acts, rather than fill it out to full length as was usual in such English versions of French or classical plays (cf. the Dryden–Lee *Oedipus*). As filler, he added an adaptation of Molière material, *The Cheats of Scapin*, thus anticipating the tragedy with farcical afterpiece pattern which becomes so common in the eighteenth century.

Lee's *Sophonisba, or Hannibal's Overthrow* (April 1675) shows him moving from his beginnings in *Nero* and the horror mode toward lofty heroism and the straight heroic. Its surging vigour and good suspense compensate fairly well for slovenly construction and vague motivation. Lee has trouble connecting the Sophonisba plot to the Hannibal plot, and the latter trails away weakly. He does a fine job with Sophonisba and her second husband, Massinissa, who finally drink poison together; Hannibal's Roman mistress Rosalinda is handled with skill, discounting the conceit of her being wounded by two cupids. Political implications are somewhat underplayed, tending simply to get lost in elaborate spectacle, fancy language, and overheated emotion. Grand but sloppy is a fair verdict.

Gloriana (January 1676), though better held together, reverts in the direction of *Nero*. Augustus Caesar is made a lustful tyrant who forces Gloriana to be his mistress, and kills her true love, Caesario, whereupon she stabs herself and dies. Lee injects intensity into an otherwise routine affair with copious supplies of rant: basically, the play shows him marking time. It failed on the stage—its troubles perhaps augmented by strife among the King's Company actors, who could not agree well enough to act at all in early February.

Gloriana is at least enlivened by Lee's erratic genius for language and passion. Two other failed attempts at high heroic drama have even less to recommend them. Durfey's first play, *The Siege of Memphis* (*c*. September 1676), is a dismal affair, as even the dedication admits. Standard devices (siege, love triangle, and so forth) are badly imitated. Durfey did at least wisely avoid trying to concoct a grand hero. Sir Charles Sedley's *Antony and Cleopatra* (February 1677) presents the story after Actium. Sedley could write good comic prose, but his couplets are execrable. Cleopatra enters and announces: 'The Captain of my Gallies I have try'd,/And for his cowardice the Villain di'd' (8). His notions of psychology and passions are if anything worse: the scene between Antony and Cleopatra after Antony has stabbed himself is especially feeble. No doubt the play suffers unfairly from inevitable comparisons, but awful is the word for it.

Another such curiosity in the late rhymed mode is Charles Davenant's opera *Circe* (May 1677), a peculiar redaction of the Iphigenia in Tauris story. Style and handling have little to recommend them. We should note, though, that *Circe* is the only opera from the entire decade between *Psyche* and *Albion and Albanius*. The reason for this sudden cooling of enthusiasm for musicals was probably expense and risk. *Psyche* made money, but evidently gave no great return on what Settle calls 'prodigious expence'. *Circe* too did adequately; however, after 1677 hard times and decreased competition gave little impetus for such ventures.[1]

---

[1] See Downes, pp. 35–7. Settle's comments on the expense are suggestive but plainly over-abusive: 'I have often heard the Players cursing at their oversight in laying out so much on so misliked a Play' (preface to *Ibrahim*). However, prologues and epilogues throughout the middle seventies do suggest that operas were considered a frighteningly high-priced gamble.

While the rhymed play is trailing off into such sorry stuff, signs of change and vitality begin to appear even in some late rhymed pieces. Settle's *Ibrahim the Illustrious Bassa* (*c.* March 1676) indulges in many of the usual devices, but here the psychology seems much better than usual; Roxolana's nobility on her deathbed is more than pure trumpery; and the muted conclusion helps make the play seem more than a commonplace exercise in love, honour, and political intrigue. Settle remains a strictly journeyman writer, but here he shows some good instincts. A play even more suggestive of coming fashion is Otway's *Don Carlos* (June 1676), discussed briefly in Chapter 5, above. Jealousy, lust, and court intrigue, served up with authorial relish, make a very exciting play. The blood-and-thunder elements and rant are much as usual, but even amidst the couplets, Otway's characters come out as real individuals, however stereotyped their roles. Again Otway takes us into a bloodbath, but here the sense of tragedy is far greater than in *Alcibiades*: King Philip II discovers his mistake too late, and there is real pathos at the end when Don Carlos and the Queen forgive him as they die. The play 'never fail'd to draw Tears', says the preface; Downes informs us that it 'got more Money than any preceding Modern Tragedy'. *Don Carlos* has a court setting and political intrigue, yet its attention centres on individuals and psychology, and its conclusion has genuine tragic impact. The great popularity of this formula is a strong hint of future directions—especially the noble pathos.

The key role of Dryden's *Aureng-Zebe* (November 1675) as a transitional play has been well analysed by Kirsch. Dryden's dissatisfaction with rhyme is announced; *intérêt d'état* is lessened in favour of more attention to domestic situations and individual psychology; emotion and pity come more to the fore than admiration for honour. I think we can accept this analysis without having to deny Waith's contention that the 'heroic ethos' is being changed rather than actively subverted.[1]

---

[1] Arthur C. Kirsch, 'The Importance of Dryden's *Aureng-Zebe*', *ELH*, xxix (1962), 160–74; Waith, *Ideas of Greatness*, pp. 223–31. Leslie Howard Martin, 'The Consistency of Dryden's *Aureng-Zebe*', *Studies in Philology*, lxx (1973), 306–28, notes the play's epic affinities and argues for its essential continuity with Dryden's earlier dramatic practice. See also Chapter 5, above.

Dryden gets plenty of shock value out of his ending, with Nourmahal's delirium and death, Morat's death, and Melesinda's insistence on immolating herself on his funeral pyre. The central issues of the play, however, concern even more clearly than before self-control in the face of temptation and provocation. The scale of the heroics diminishes: *Aureng-Zebe* gives us the image of a 'practicable virtue' as Dryden says in the preface. He has by no means abandoned positive example, however: both Aureng-Zebe and Melesinda (Morat's wife) are basically exemplary characters, though Dryden refrains from exalting them into figures of romance. Despite the violent ending, distributive justice is for the most part maintained. The results approximate more to heroic romance than to tragedy, though the signs of Dryden's changing directions are unmistakable. The nature of this change is well analysed in an important study by Harold F. Brooks,[1] who shows in detail that Dryden borrows ideas, characters, and details from five different French plays in the course of concocting a 'regular' play which nonetheless possesses the fuller plot demanded by an English audience. As Dryden's critical essays suggest, especially 'The Grounds of Criticism in Tragedy' (1679), by the later seventies he was trying to mediate between French and English practice. Brooks shows more clearly than any critic heretofore the close relationship between *Aureng-Zebe* and Dryden's next tragedy, *All for Love*, in which he turned to the freedom of Shakespearean blank verse but 'like Corneille and Racine . . . contented himself with few principal persons and a single plot'.

The honour of abandoning rhyme, however, belongs to Nat Lee. *The Rival Queens* (March 1677), despite its blank verse, retains the exaltation and ethos of heroic drama, and Lee's rhapsodic style is little changed. Nevertheless this play marks a considerable jump in new directions. Lee is maturing: one might surmise that he had been studying Dryden's schematic psychological contrasts to good effect. He has his usual problem of focus (we lose track of Alexander too often); even so, the basic juxtapositions work well—the mild Statira against violent Roxana, steady Clytus against fiery Alexander. The

---

[1] 'Dryden's *Aureng-Zebe*: Debts to Corneille and Racine', *Revue de littérature comparée*, xlvi (1972), 5–34.

fast pace, the exuberant bombast, the exhilarating release of passions entitle the play to its tremendous and lasting success. Lee's ability to make violent passion seem vivid and genuine is his greatest virtue. The achingly real feelings of Statira and Roxana are only a little undercut by Lee's enthusiastic excursions into rant, spectacle (e.g. the battle of the birds in mid air—I. 238), and ghosts. The ghost of King Philip is routine flummery; the singing ghosts which appear to Statira just before Roxana knifes her are notorious, though rather enjoyable. This florid production is a seventeenth-century form of *La Forza del destino*. But Lee here builds on his development in *Sophonisba* to diminish the ritual heroic exaltation while emphasizing tragic pathos.

The emphasis here on pathos in what may properly be called a heroic tragedy should serve to remind us that pity is not associated solely with pathetic drama. (This problem is discussed in Chapter 4, Section III, above.) To dwell solely upon suffering quickly produces bathos, but in the plays of the later seventies, pathos is a highly desirable element. It helps move serious drama from the heroic back toward tragedy, and it helps reduce the frigid romance models to more human dimensions. The change comes by degrees. Thus Dryden's *All for Love* (December 1677) can be discussed as a heroic play by Waith, but in its pathos-oriented emotionalism, we definitely see the softening of the once remote and grandiose heroic ethos. *All for Love* is a blank-verse *tragedy*: here Dryden has finally not only abandoned rhyme but turned to a catastrophe ending. The love and honour conflict remains, but *intérêt d'état* loses more ground. Despite some weaknesses in the play's construction (discussed in Chapter 5, above), it presents its protagonists with a powerful imaginative sympathy and invests them with a personality far superior to anything in Dryden's earlier plays. This is not to claim that *All for Love* is necessarily a 'better' play than the heroic romances; rather, the emphasis on imaginative sympathy signals a major generic change: for the first time, Dryden is trying to write tragedy of character. The result, by Jacobean standards, is no great success. Here, as later, concern with the affective impact of the play seems to interfere with its internal design. The play's reputation enjoys a curious duality: Shakespearean scholars very unfairly dismiss the piece out of hand, while most Dryden scholars seem to me to overrate it.[1]

The new tragedy was to reach no great heights. In *The Rival Queens* and *All for Love* we see, however, the potential for a new wave in serious drama. By 1678 the rhymed heroic play is clearly a spent force, and the new possibilities are eagerly explored. Two factors weigh heavily as influences in the next few years: a new set of critical hypotheses, and the Popish Plot.

IV. THE ONSET OF DEPRESSION 1677–1679

Like the stock market crash of 1929, the Popish Plot had effects which developed only over a period of years. The long-term results will be one of the major subjects of Chapter 8, below. The radical insecurity engendered by the Plot and the following Exclusion Crisis had a catastrophic effect on theatrical prosperity. The weaker King's Company, managing ill in boom times, struggled on for four years until the inevitable amalgamation occurred in 1682. The already unhappy state of the King's Company is clear from the box-office receipts for a performance of *All for Love* on 12 December 1677, shortly after its *première*. The total takings were only £28. 4s. (representing an attendance of 249), or only about half what a passably full house would bring.[2] To find Dryden's next new play at the Duke's House the following March can come as no surprise. The Popish Plot proper begins in September 1678 and its impact is immediate. In the 1676–7 and 1677–8 seasons we find eighteen new plays each year; for 1678–9 we find only

---

[1] Frank J. Kearful, ' "'Tis past recovery": Tragic Consciousness in *All for Love*', *Modern Language Quarterly*, xxxiv (1973), 227–46, makes as good a case as is possible for the affective power of the characters.

[2] Box-office receipts from this decade are otherwise unknown. See *The London Stage*, Part 1, p. 265 for details of these figures. Cf. those for *The Rival Queens*, 26 December. I have some qualms about the authenticity of these documents. *The London Stage* prints them from Percy Fitzgerald's unreliable *A New History of the English Stage* (1882). Fitzgerald took them from *The Theatrical Inquisitor* (1816), a periodical of no great scholarly reputation. They were contributed anonymously by someone claiming that 'a friend' found them 'among some waste-paper'. Curiously enough, they were allegedly offered for publication in response to the printing (in the previous number) of the 'First Play-Bill of Drury-Lane Theatre'. That this is none other than the celebrated *Humorous Lieutenant* forgery ('Thursday April 8th, 1663') does not increase my faith in the box-office receipts, though they appear plausible.

six. Naturally the King's Company, already beset by dissension, fared worse. A lawsuit tells us that during a considerable period in 1678 and 1679 the Drury Lane 'Playhouse was shut up and no Plays were acted'[1]—apparently on account of squabbles over management and money. Performance records are very sparse for these years: we have no play-loving diarist to help us, and the King was otherwise occupied—hence entries in the Lord Chamberlain's warrants shrink to almost nothing for three years.

Comparing the lists of new productions between 1675 and 1679, a pattern is plain.[2] After opening its new Drury Lane house in 1674 the King's Company comes to life and out-produces its rival in 1675 (6 : 5). Management troubles become serious in the latter half of the 1675–6 season, and so Killigrew's troupe manages only 4 new productions (versus 10) in 1676. Enough stability was regained in the compromises of Autumn 1676 for competitiveness to be partly regained under Charles Killigrew's direction: the proportion for 1677 is 8 : 9. With internal uproar on the rise again in the 1677–8 season conditions worsen: for 1678 the proportion is 4 : 11. All four King's Company plays come in the spring—i.e. the company has *no* new plays that autumn. In 1679 the proportion is a dismal 2 : 8. In short, after replacing its burned playhouse, the King's Company regains something like parity, fades, revives, fades—and then is crushed by the effects of the Popish Plot. In the meantime (Spring 1678) Dryden and Lee had prudently deserted the sinking ship. The Duke's Company, better led and with most of the best writers, seems to have operated normally throughout this period, though new productions are fewer, and audiences were apparently sparse. The prologue to Behn's *Feign'd Curtezans* (March 1679) complains that 'this cursed plotting Age' is wrecking the stage. The epilogue warns, during one of Drury Lane's periods of darkness, that Dorset Garden too is feeling the pinch: 'So hard the times are, and so thin the Town,/Though but one Playhouse, that must too lie down.' The only surprise about the demise of the King's Company is the slowness with which it arrived.

---

[1] Cited and discussed by Hotson, p. 262.

[2] For simplicity, I am using calendar years rather than seasons: the over-all proportions are of course the same.

Unlike the 1929 stock market crash, the Popish Plot did not really come as a surprise to anyone. Titus Oates could not have been predicted, but as most historians observe, England was ripe for a plot in 1678. The nagging, dangling succession question could not be suppressed forever: Oates's imagination simply provided the spark for an inevitable explosion. As early as January 1674 Shaftesbury had tried to rouse popular hysteria with claims about a bloody papist plot (and was pilloried as the evil Chancellor in Payne's *Siege of Constantinople* the following autumn). In March of 1678 the Commons were worriedly sniffing out papist schemes. Portentous events were sensed in the offing—perhaps representing a realization that a fragile *status quo* could not last forever.[1] As Andrew Marvell remarks in a letter to the Hull Corporation, 'there seems a more than usuall concernment among all men as if some great and I hope good thing were to be expected.'[2] Shaftesbury was waiting his chance, and people knew it. Nearly a year before the Popish Plot Marvell writes to Sir Edward Harley: 'To day is acted the first time Sir Popular Wisdome or the Politician where my Lord Shaftsbury and all his gang are sufficiently personated. I conceiue the King will be there.'[3] Marvell was right: *Sr Popler Wisdome* appears in a Lord Chamberlain's warrant—17 November 1677, at Dorset Garden. The author is unknown and the text is lost, but the political purpose remains crystal clear.

The obsession with politics after 1678 is evident. A flurry of dramatic comment is what one would expect. Not surprisingly, most of it takes the form of serious drama—safer than comedy when the outcome is still in doubt. A play like *City Politiques* (1683) is a phenomenon of the aftermath. The relative proportions of comedy and tragedy always fluctuate, but in 1679 and 1680 the swing to tragedy is heavy indeed.[4]

The completeness and abruptness with which the rhymed play went out of fashion is striking. In the last three-year

---

[1] For a summary of matters leading toward the Popish Plot, see Ogg, Vol. II, Chapters 15 and 16.

[2] *Poems and Letters*, 2 vols., ed. H. M. Margoliouth, 2nd edn. (Oxford, 1963), II. 226.

[3] *Poems and Letters*, II. 330 (17 November 1677).

[4] The proportion of tragedy to comedy each year runs as follows: (1) 1675—6 : 3; (2) 1676—5 : 9; (3) 1677—9 : 7; (4) 1678—4 : 10; (5) 1679—7 : 3; (6) 1680—9 : 2.

period considered, more than three-quarters of the new serious plays were rhymed: in these years not a single new rhymed play is produced. The quasi-heroic play continues its somewhat discouraged course, but now in blank verse. Nahum Tate's first effort, *Brutus of Alba* (*c.* June 1678), represents this type. Ghost, witches, poisoned bracelet, exit tearing hair, free use of the 'stabs self and dies' formula, an abundance of alarms and passionate statements—the result of this awkward compound of clichés is a very dead play. A failure in the theatre, the play's only importance is its evidence of influence by *All for Love*.[1] A distinctly better example of the late quasi-heroic play is Banks's *The Destruction of Troy* (acted by November 1678). Banks has not yet found his mode, but the improvement over *The Rival Kings* is great. The opportunities for pathos with the Trojan women are exploited with enthusiasm, though here with a melodramatic swagger that Banks was later to eschew. When 'The *Scene* draws, and discovers *Polyxena* weeping over the dragg'd Body of *Troilus*, her Hair and Garments disorder'd, a Dagger in her hand', Achilles is terribly remorseful, and delivers a storm of rant against himself. Indeed he is ready to go over to the Trojans, and has to be tricked by Ulysses into preoccupation with his marriage while the horse scheme is worked (54–9). A rousing Act V gives us Andromache mourning and Cassandra distracted. Paris kills Achilles with a poisoned dart—shot from behind the altar during Achilles's wedding. 'The great Horse is discover'd' (64), and at the end the '*Scene* opens, and discovers *Troy* Burning' (73). The play is a pleasant spectacular, though the scale is larger than Banks can handle comfortably.

Once the Popish Plot is launched the political note in drama increases sharply. John Bancroft's *The Tragedy of Sertorius* (*c.* March 1679), a rather dull, heavily rhetorical blank-verse exercise, gives us an appropriate piece of Roman history. The importance of treasonable letters, in particular, suggests one of those oblique comments of which Carolean dramatists are so fond. This failure was, we may recall, one of only two new plays staged by the King's Company during the whole of 1679. Otway's *The History and Fall of Caius Marius* (*c.* October 1679) grafts the Romeo and Juliet story onto Roman history. The

[1] Discussed by Christopher Spencer, *Nahum Tate* (New York, 1972), pp. 55–60,

results are a queer mixture—a salutary account of the misfortunes of an ambitious tyrant into which is worked a pathetic tale of young lovers. Otway's growing skill makes for some fine things: the mob scenes, the pendular changes of fortune, the combination of arrogance and growing insecurity in the political leaders, all come across beautifully. The pathetic story is tidily integrated into a broader historical framework. Unhappily, the direct use of Shakespeare only seems ridiculous to a modern reader. When Lavinia exclaims, 'O *Marius, Marius*! wherefore art thou *Marius*?' in the balcony scene (I. 461), or the dying Sulpitius (Caius Marius's other son) gives us the 'not so deep as a Well' speech on the last page of the play, one is inclined, however unfairly, to laugh. As was his custom, Otway mocked 'This Drumming, Trumpetting, and Fighting Play' in his epilogue. The work shows him mid-way between his origins in the rhymed heroic form and his ultimate destination in pathetically inclined tales of individuals.

Possibly one indication of the changing theatrical climate is the appearance of two tragicomedies, both claiming to be long delayed. Ravenscroft's *King Edgar and Alfreda* (*c*. October 1677), discussed above in Chapter 5, 'at least Ten Years ago was writt' —or so the author claims. It lacks rhyme and heroic puffery, but is put forward now, since 'Heroes . . . that are no more than men,/May be allow'd to tread the Stage agen.' Similarly Mrs. Behn's *The Young King* (*c*. March? 1679) is a romantic intrigue tragicomedy of the sort popular in the sixties. Her dedication says it was her first effort, long held back—a claim which seems very plausible if we view it against the progression in her plays described earlier. The piece is a competent reprise of bits from La Calprenède and Calderón, a tidy collection of love, politics, war, and disguise. Its unremittingly elevated tone does seem logically to place it as a forerunner of *The Forc'd Marriage* and *The Amorous Prince*. Presumably it was tidied up for performance in 1679. Summers claims that remnants of an early version in couplets can be discerned, but the evidence is slight. In any case, the belated appearance of these plays suggests that the era of rhyme and show was fading.

As before, the most interesting experimental plays are those of Dryden and Lee—together and separately. Their association is worth more notice than critics have yet given it. They wrote

two plays together, and they seem to have had a warm personal
relationship. But even R. G. Ham[1] fails to see just how much
influence Dryden exerts on his young colleague. In 1675
Dryden tires of rhyme, and a year later Lee (the greatest
ranter in rhyme) proceeds to write *The Rival Queens* in blank
verse—published with commendatory verses by Dryden. In
1677 the older poet starts to worry about the uses of English
dramatic tradition and its relevance in the Carolean theatre.
A few months later Lee comes out with a dedication to
Mithridates, propounding some of the ideas basic to Dryden's
'Grounds of Criticism in Tragedy', published in 1679. Lee
remains always pre-eminently a writer of passion, while Dryden,
a vastly cooler writer, concerns himself with design, thought,
and precise expression. I think, though, that close study would
reveal profound influence on Lee—in style, design, and
politics.

Mithridates (*c.* February 1678), Lee's last effort for the
King's Company and a popular one, has much to recommend
it, but is somewhat spoiled by the author's inability to refrain
from emotional exaggeration and purple passages. The plot is
better worked out than usual for Lee; the blank verse is often
thrilling; the passions are made searingly vivid. The picture of a
grandiose tyrant destroyed by incestuous passion and the
weaknesses of his own character has an enthusiastic force
which perhaps a cooler head could not have produced, but
which suffers from lack of artistic restraint. Lee gets splendid
pathetic mileage from Monima and Semandra. Even his
exuberant blood-thirstiness suits the play's rather Byzantine
flavour. (For example, the Roman captive Aquilius enters in
golden chains and Mithridates orders them melted and
poured down his throat—I. 303.) Lee explains his models:

I have endeavour'd in this Tragedy to mix Shakespear with Fletcher;
the thoughts of the former, for Majesty and true Roman Greatness,
and the softness and passionate expressions of the latter, which
makes up half the Beauties, are never to be match'd. . . . I desire
to be so found a Refiner on those admirable Writers; the Ground is
theirs . . . [but] I have disguiz'd it into another fashion more suitable
to the Age we live in. (I. 292)

---

[1] *Otway and Lee* (New Haven, Conn., 1931), Chapter 13.

Alas, he cannot resist pumping the majesty too hard and swooning too lyrically over the passionate beauties, thus dehumanizing his characters. Lee comes so close to being a great tragic writer that his failures are somewhat infuriating.

The collaborative *Oedipus* (September 1678) was long a stock play. Dryden produced the outline and wrote Acts I and III; Lee filled in the rest.[1] Few critics have cared much for this 'curious medley of Sophoclean, Senecan, Elizabethan, and heroic tragedy'.[2] The added sub-plot is right out of rhymed heroic clichés: the noble prisoner Adrastus loves Eurydice, as does Creon—who is made into a dangerous republican agitator. The dramatic irony of the original is greatly increased: from the outset Dryden and Lee lay it on with a trowel: for example, 'He much resembles/Her former Husband too. . . . When twenty Winters more have grizzl'd his black Locks/He will be very *Lajus*' (IV. 356–7). Oedipus's sleep-walking vision, the repeated use of the ghost of Lajus, and the bloody ending give the play a macabre Jacobean air. The major characters are all wiped out. Creon kills Eurydice and is killed by Adrastus, who is then killed by Creon's soldiers (424). Jocasta—still alive —is discovered 'stabb'd in many places of her bosom, her hair dishevel'd, her Children slain upon the Bed' (425). She expires only after seeing Oedipus prepare his suicide: the play ends as he defenestrates himself. To judge the results by Sophocles can only make the play seem a travesty. However, the aesthetic bases of the Dryden–Lee version are quite different, and are carefully calculated. Dryden's preface explains the collaborators' admiration for Sophocles, and their realization that 'the *Athenian* Theater . . . had a perfection differing from ours.' The 'variety' of the sub-plot is a necessity, and the whole must be made *affecting*. Dryden comments on other versions. Corneille 'miserably fail'd in the Character of his Hero: if he desir'd that *Oedipus* should be pitied, he shou'd have made him a better man'. Seneca 'is always running after pompous expression, pointed sentences, and Philosophical notions, more proper for the Study than the Stage'. Dryden

---

[1] Dryden tells us this in *The Vindication of the Duke of Guise*, *Dramatic Works*, V. 327. Downes wrongly ascribes I and II to Dryden (p. 37), adding that *Oedipus* 'took prodigiously'.

[2] William Van Lennep, unpub. diss. (Harvard, 1933), cited in Lee, *Works*, I. 370.

and Lee push the play rather far toward the horror mode, but undeniably they make it theatrically gripping. *Terror* and *pity*, the epilogue says, are the engines which work upon the audience (we might rather say *horror* and pity)—and indeed they do. Had we not Sophocles's version to compare, this play would be accounted far better than it has been: in its day, *Oedipus* was considered one of the major monuments of Carolean tragedy.

Oedipus is important historically as a step away from the popularity of 'admiration' and toward a pitying 'concernment' in tragedy. *All for Love* balances admiration and pathos fairly equally; here pathos and horror assume a more prominent position. Lee's participation is probably responsible for some of the play's excesses, but also for its high emotional temperature. By himself, Dryden tends to be slightly frigid, his designedly emotional scenes too obviously calculated. This problem plagues both *All for Love* and his adaptation of *Troilus and Cressida* (acted by April 1679), also a popular play. This work is a routine and tidy tragedy: Cressida is merely thought false—she dissembles with Diomedes on her father's orders, and stabs herself in vindication. Hector's death occurs offstage and is barely mentioned. Troilus kills Diomedes and is killed by Achilles in a mêlée at the end. Dryden regularizes and tidies.

[Shakespeare's] Tragedy is nothing but a confusion of Drums and Trumpets, Excursions and Alarms. The chief persons, who give name to the Tragedy, are left alive: *Cressida* is false, and is not punish'd. Yet after all, because the Play was *Shakespear's*, and that there appear'd in some places of it, the admirable Genius of the Author; I undertook to remove that heap of Rubbish, under which many excellent thoughts lay wholly bury'd. Accordingly, I new model'd the Plot; threw out many unnecessary persons; improv'd those Characters which were begun, and left unfinish'd: as *Hector*, *Troilus*, *Pandarus* and *Thersites*; and added that of *Andromache*. After this, I made with no small trouble, an Order and Connection of all the Scenes; removing them from the places where they were inartificially set. . . . (preface)

In so doing, Dryden spoils an excitedly complex play, and tacks onto it a relevant moral: 'since from homebred Factions ruine springs,/Let Subjects learn obedience to their Kings.'

For reasons one can only speculate about, tragic theory takes a fairly sharp turn in the later seventies. The false lead of the heroic play fizzles out, while criticism has an increasing influence. Rymer's translation of Rapin's *Reflections on the Poetics* and Boileau's French version of Longinus's *On the Sublime* appear in 1674, Rymer's *The Tragedies of the Last Age* in 1677. In *All for Love*, *Troilus and Cressida*, and *Oedipus* we can see simultaneously the oft-noted 'classicizing' influence of Rymer in a concern for regularity and tragic structure, and also a growing interest in the *affective* power of drama. Part of the latter seems to come from Le Bossu (Dryden cites him), part perhaps from the proven effectiveness of horror plays in the earlier seventies. To play upon the emotions increasingly becomes the preoccupation of serious dramatists. Naturally they look to English models. Dryden's 'The Grounds of Criticism in Tragedy' appended to his preface for *Troilus* is a theoretical consideration of how Shakespeare (a mover of terror) and Fletcher (a mover of compassion) may be conjoined for maximum impact while still being reconciled with Rymer's demands for decorum, poetic justice, and design. The synthesis which emerges is discussed above in Chapter 4; let it suffice here to recollect that the formulas of 1679 are a long way from those of 1672.

Affective power was to be a lasting preoccupation; for the moment, politics loomed large. In *Sertorius* and *Caius Marius* we have seen the stirrings. A milestone in the move toward the politically oriented plays of the eighties is Crowne's *The Ambitious Statesman* (*c.* March 1679). This play, a good one which failed to succeed (perhaps let down by the dilapidated King's Company), deals in the vague parallels so popular in these years. The Constable of France wants power; his virtuous son the Duke of Vendosme (the King's favourite) loves and is loved by Louize, who is treacherously married off to the Dauphin. Quasi-heroic love complications are woven into politics. Louize is killed; the good Duke is 'shew'd wrack't'— still alive—and then expires. Finally the Constable, a most unnatural father, is unmasked, but as in Dryden's *Troilus*, truth is found too late. *The Ambitious Statesman* is a good play of its sort. Probably Crowne was quite conscious of its formula: prologue and preface note that the times are bad for plays, while the epilogue comments at length on the vogue for sad endings.

By mid-1679 the move toward affective tragedy was strongly launched. The sense of a mode worn out, so strong in the late rhymed plays of 1676 and 1677, is past: an era has been left behind, and astonishingly quickly another, radically different type is in full flower. Waith rightly reminds us of the degree to which such a play as *All for Love* has affinities with the old heroic 'admiration' mode, and certainly the love and honour clichés (among others) persist almost indefinitely. But the *kind of impact* sought changes drastically when admiration gives way to pity and concernment.

Tragedy has made strong new beginnings. Comedy, in these years, is reaching a point of diminishing returns. The great Carolean show-piece mode, the social sex comedy, loses its momentum, and comedy writers flounder for several years, relying on tried formulas most of the time. Genial libertine displays are exaggerated into something else, fail, and are supplanted by farce, intrigue, and politics. A fascinating sample of values in the drama of the late seventies is Shadwell's maverick adaptation, *The History of Timon of Athens* (*c.* January 1678), a 'satyrical' tragedy. Comparison with Shakespeare is simply a needless distraction. As several critics have recently seen, *Timon* is genuinely a 'play of ideas'—in at least three distinct realms, we should observe. First, Shadwell vigorously attacks a money-ethic, both in society and in personal relationships. Second, in a play dedicated to Buckingham, Shadwell introduces a character parallel to Alcibiades while making a prudently guarded political comment on the Duke's behalf. Third, and perhaps most important, Shadwell deliberately recalls the themes of *Le Misanthrope* and *The Plain-Dealer*. Timon is made a test case for the libertine ethic, with two women to choose between: the good Evandra and the hypocritical Melissa. Thus into a tragedy Shadwell introduces the kinds of characters, situations, and ethics belonging to sex comedy. Juxtaposing the comic values with an essentially exemplary code (in Evandra and Alcibiades) Shadwell 'compelled his unsuspecting audience to develop a gradual but unequivocal revulsion for the Hobbesian principles of conduct which they approved in comedy'.[1] The tragic structure makes

[1] John Edmunds, ' "Timon of Athens" Blended with "Le Misanthrope": Shadwell's Recipe for Satirical Tragedy', *Modern Language Review*, lxiv (1969), 500–

Shadwell's sharp social and ethical criticisms highly effective, though he softens what Edmunds calls a 'nihilistic mood' by the faithfulness of Evandra. Downes praises the play for its 'Excellent Moral', and he is right. *Timon* should be seen together with *The Libertine* as part of a serious, consistent, and brilliantly effective attack on the moral code approved—or at least enjoyed—in Carolean comedy. The great popularity of *Timon* helps confirm a point I shall make in analysing comedy in the late seventies: the spring of 1678 marks a definite turning point in audience taste.

The tremendous success of Durfey's *A Fond Husband* in the spring of 1677 bred vigorous imitation. In *Sir Patient Fancy* (acted by January 1678) Mrs. Behn serves up a bawdy farce into which are mixed bits of *Le Malade imaginaire*. The results are engagingly vigorous, dirty, and fast paced. The preface says that the author is forced to write for bread, and hence will give what is wanted—smut. The prologue complains that authors write

> . . . like good Tradesmen, what's in fashion vent,
> And cozen you, to give ye all content.
> True Comedy, writ even in *Dryden's* Style,
> Will hardly raise your Humours to a Smile.

Mrs. Behn's preface bitterly protests against objections to bawdy coming from a woman—especially objections from 'the Ladies'. Bawdy there is aplenty: it is, however, all in good fun. Lodwick is introduced by mistake into Lucia's chamber and swives her, thus cuckolding Sir Patient; meanwhile Wittmore pursues Isabella—thinking her to be Lucia. Sir Patient finds Lodwick in his wife's bed—a contretemps easily explained away—but Lucia is thoroughly astonished at the identity of her bedmate. Mrs. Behn makes good use of Wycherley's device of a love letter with a misattributed signature; lashes out at puritan cant via Sir Patient; employs young Fanny as 'a bawd at seven years'. Following Molière, Sir Patient feigns death and catches his wife with Wittmore.

---

507. See also P. F. Vernon, 'Social Satire in Shadwell's *Timon*', *Studia Neophilologica*, xxxv (1963), 221–6; Gunnar Sorelius, 'Shadwell Deviating into Sense: *Timon of Athens* and the Duke of Buckingham', *Studia Neophilologica*, xxxvi (1964), 232–44; and Alssid, pp. 110–14.

Mrs. Behn proceeds with marvellous gusto. Hearing of the 'death' Lucia says cheerfully, well, there is 'no more to do, but to bury the stinking Corps of my quandom Cuckold' (IV. 112). The much abused Sir Patient (whom we have seen drunk and importuning his wife for sex) finally decides to drop his puritan cant and turn town gallant—upon which Mrs. Behn has him invite the audience to 'take example by my Reformation'. *Sir Patient Fancy* is one of Mrs. Behn's most delightful plays, but apparently it did not flourish, even though she regarded it as a concession to town taste. Her next comedy, *The Feign'd Curtezans* (acted by March 1679), returns to a rollicking 'Spanish' romance mode reminiscent of *The Rover*. This comedy of intricate, bustling intrigue (set in Rome) did as well as hard times would allow. Wild but chaste girls, Marcella and Cornelia, run off to Rome and marry two English gentlemen. The girls' brother Julio, Marcella's fiancé Octavio, and his sister Laura Lucretia provide complications, while Sir Signal Buffoon and his puritan tutor Mr. Tickletext are pleasantly mocked. As J. H. Smith says, *The Feign'd Curtezans* reverts successfully to the mode of *An Evening's Love* a decade earlier. Such a turning away from London sex comedy is part of a pattern.

Dryden's notorious, neglected *The Kind Keeper; or Mr. Limberham* (March 1678) is called his best comedy by Langbaine, but has struck most twentieth-century critics with poorly disguised horror. The piece is a roaring, dirty farce. Whether we should accept Dryden's claim that it is also a highly moral satire critics have not seriously tried to determine. A letter to Lord Latimer explains the play's genesis.

The Kings Comedy lyes in the Sudds till you please to send me into Northamptonshyre: it will be almost such another piece of businesse as the fond Husband, for such the King will have it, who is parcell poet with me in the plott; one of the designes being a story he was pleasd formerly to tell me; and therefore I hope he will keep the jeast in countenance by laughing at it.[1]

As before, Dryden is able to do a superb job with a mode he obviously does not care for. 'Woodall', a Horner figure, comes to London and lodges with the hypocritical Mrs.

---

[1] *Letters*, ed. Ward, no. 5 (*c.* July 1677).

Saintly, a brothel keeper. Also in residence is his father, Aldo, a whoremonger of decayed capacity who fails to recognize him. Woodall pursues every woman in sight, and copulation follows copulation with discovery always a hair's-breadth away. The keeper Limberham is savaged: we see him apologizing to his whore, Tricksy, for premature ejaculation; too scared to prevent other men from using the hot-crotched Tricksy; and generally cheated and abused on all sides. Woodall starts to mount Tricksy (with Mrs. Brainsick hidden under the bed, indignantly pinching him): they are interrupted by Mrs. Saintly (who wants Woodall herself), and so forth. Mr. Brainsick is tricked into standing guard while Woodall sports with his wife. At the end of the play Woodall marries Mrs. Pleasance, an heiress, and browbeats the luckless Limberham into marrying Tricksy. The piece closes as Woodall hails 'A most excellent Reformation. . . . The Moral on't is pleasant, if well consider'd.'

What are we to make of this? The energy and high spirits Dryden infuses into the play make it great fun.[1] Is there any moral indignation here, or do we find only a cold-blooded attempt to outdo *A Fond Husband*? In the dedication Dryden vehemently denies 'particular *Satyre* . . . whatsoever may have been pretended by some Criticks in the Town'. He avers that

'Twas intended for an honest *Satyre* against our crying sin of *Keeping*; . . . [but] was permitted to be acted only thrice. The Crime for which it suffer'd, was that which is objected against the *Satyres* of *Juvenal*, and the *Epigrams* of *Catullus*, that it express'd too much of the Vice which it decry'd.

Of course the reader may ask wherein lies the decrying.[2] Dryden adds that he has 'taken a becoming care, that those things which offended on the Stage, might be either alter'd, or omitted in the Press'. Possibly the cuts were in 'personal' material; one wonders how the piece could have been much

---

[1] Limberham (self-pityingly): '*Tricksy* has murder'd Sleep' (IV. 323). Woodall (pleased with his tactics); 'that *Fe-fa-fum* of a Keeper wou'd have smelt the blood of a Cuckold-maker' (327).

[2] Van R. Baker, 'Heroic Posturing Satirized: Dryden's *Mr. Limberham*', *Papers on Language and Literature*, viii (1972), 370–9, is accurate in pointing out the many satiric deflations in the play, but I cannot agree with him in finding Woodall's servant Gervase an effective 'moral norm'.

gamier.[1] Clearly the play is one of Dryden's most brilliant efforts, and its place in Carolean sex comedy is as central as that of *The Country-Wife* and *The Man of Mode*. To see those plays, as critics usually do, as the end of a 'wit' type picked up again only in the nineties completely ignores their place in the sex comedy boom, which goes right on escalating until 1678. Dryden blatantly imitates Wycherley's 'china' scene and presents far more sex in a blunter way than Wycherley ever attempted. Woodall's 'Reformation', however loudly trumpeted, makes that at the end of *Love's Last Shift* seem serious and convincing. *Limberham* is—designedly or not—perhaps the most cheerfully indecent of all Carolean comedies, and it was found objectionable.[2]

Not surprisingly, similar charges of personal satire and filth were brought against Otway's first comedy, *Friendship in Fashion* (April 1678). This great play has attracted no critical attention at all. If one is looking for bitter, angry social satire in Carolean comedy, here it is. The play's evil flavour provoked a hysterical denunciation from J. C. Ghosh, its last editor.[3] The friendship-theme so pervasive in Otway's tragedies is a hint of what he will do here. The truly ugly picture of broken friendship is reinforced in all possible ways. The lead male Goodvile chases Camillia (engaged to his good friend Valentine), while trying to palm off his cast mistress Victoria as a wife for his best friend, Truman. Goodvile lays the hypocritical Lady Squeamish in the dark, thinking her to be Camillia, while Mrs. Goodvile commits adultery with Truman. Intrigue, confusion, narrow escapes galore are served up here with none of the lively cheer we are accustomed to. Otway makes the whole crew range from indifferent to nauseating. Even the minor fools are made thoroughly objectionable. Malagene, for instance, who likes to 'act *Punchinello*, *Scaramouchio*, *Harlequin*, Prince *Prettyman*, or any

---

[1] Montague Summers, *A Bibliography of the Restoration Drama* (London, n.d. [1935]), p. 58, records Malone's report that he had seen (*c.* 1785) an unaltered MS., but what became of it is unknown.

[2] Later that month Dryden complains bitterly in the prologue to Shadwell's *A True Widow*:

> Fools you will have, and rais'd at vast expence,
> And yet as soon as seen, they give offence.
> Time was, when none would cry, that Oaf was mee. . . .

[3] *Works*, I. 44.

thing' boasts happily of knocking over a legless cripple in the street (I. 371). The mutual loathing of the Goodvifes is made vivid: 'I will sooner return to my Vomit' than to her, he says (408). At the end, however, Otway patches up at least a pretence of both marriage and friendships in a ghastly parody of the usual comedy conclusion. Unlike Wycherley at the end of *The Country-Wife*, Otway slams home a realization of just how nasty these ugly relations will continue to be. *Friendship in Fashion* is brilliant, but not fun. Neglect of it is astonishing: critics are forever worrying about the attractiveness of vice in Carolean comedy, and here for once the characters are made contemptible beyond question. How the play was viewed by its original audience we can only guess. Langbaine says 'acted with general applause', but lack of evidence of any revival, or reprinting, and a rather defensive dedication suggest mediocre success.

A worse fate—flat failure—met Shadwell's *A True Widow* (March? 1678). The author complains bitterly in his dedication to Sedley that the satire sat ill with the audience, and that the public has run mad over farce—'the putting out of Candles, kicking down of Tables, falling over Joynt-stools, impossible accidents, and unnatural mistakes'. One gathers that he did not care for *A Fond Husband*. Here as in his recent 'tragedies' Shadwell is remarkably innovative and experimental. In a note to the reader he says, 'I had rather suffer, by venturing to bring new things upon the Stage, than go on like a Mill-Horse in the same Round.' As in *The Virtuoso* Shadwell's action uses a routine double romantic plot and subsidiary satiric objects, but emphasizes a parent-figure as a special focal point. Rakish Bellamour reforms and wins Isabella; Carlos and Theodosia provide a mild gay couple contrast. The butts—Selfish, Old and Young Maggot, Prig, and Lump—help establish the play's air of teeming folly. The whorish Gartrude and hedonist Stanmore are made vivid types. But the successful rogueries of Lady Cheatly (an expert in disappearing ink) bear the most interest. The mixture of attitudes evoked by these characters allows for genuine complexity of perspective: Shadwell gives us a representative cross-section, from the exemplary and the reformed down to neatly assorted specimens of roguery and folly. The result is a beautiful play. Its high point is the burlesque of a farce in Act IV, where Shadwell produces a brilliant satirical representation of the Carolean audience mooning over a dead pan travesty of *A Fond Husband*. Shadwell fretfully allows that his design failed: 'For some, I believe, wish'd all the Play like that part of a Farce in it; others knew not my intention in it, which was to expose the Style and Plot of Farce-Writers, to the utter confusion of damnable Farce, and all its wicked and foolish Adherents' (III. 288). Shadwell's response to the failure of *A True Widow* was practical: he follows it with *The Woman-Captain* (*c*. September 1679), little more than a straight farce. The epilogue grumbles 'Remembring how you used that last he writ,/He made this Low.' Tone and characters are indeed lower. The abused Mrs. Gripe assumes male attire, and gains the upper hand over her usurer husband with joyous Amazonian trumpery. The idiotic Sir Humphrey represents absurd libertinism and is appropriately chastised—a reprise of Shadwell's pervasive education theme. The play is entertaining, but definitely light-weight.

Just as Mrs. Behn backed off to *The Feign'd Curtezans* after the failure of *Sir Patient Fancy*, so Shadwell retreats toward a sure-fire formula in *The Woman-Captain*. The tide of sex plays which rises during 1675 and 1676 and seems to be carrying on suddenly slackens. Probably the concatenation of failures in Spring 1678 is coincidence, but it is a sign of a trend played out. Just as theatre audiences of the 1960s were for a time titillated by ever more explicit sex and nudity, until finally they wearied of such stuff, so in the 1670s the audience finally seems to have reached satiety. Sex comedy continues to appear in the eighties, but no longer after 1678 do the new comedies seem as a group to be moving in so clearly definable a direction.

As was observed in the last section, moral comedy continues to appear right through the seventies, as in Durfey's first efforts. A strong moral bent, temporarily shaken by fashion, is evident in the three plays of John Leanerd. *The Country Innocence: or The Chamber-Maid Turn'd Quaker* (*c*. March 1677) is largely a close rendering of Brewer's (?) *Country Girl* (*c*. 1632; pub. 1647). Its light-hearted intrigue and fake puritan canting do not disguise considerable emphasis on the purity of Margaret, who flatly refuses to be seduced by Sir Robert Malory, though she is his tenants' daughter. The wife reclaiming a wandering husband is seriously treated here. *The Rambling Justice* (late February 1678) is more *à la mode*: J. H. Smith calls it an unpleasant cuckolding play. Much of it is from Middleton. Lascivious Sir Arthur Twilight and horn-mad Contentious Surly are well cuckolded by Sir Generall Amorous. Sir Arthur finally catches his wife in the act with Sir Generall, but apologizes profusely for interrupting after he is threatened with a sword (65–7). Sir Generall thereupon marries Flora, Sir Arthur's daughter by a previous marriage, and at the end of the play he announces (in verse) his reformation: his 'Licentious Youth' is now 'past', and he will be a good husband. At any rate Leanerd contrives to sound pious. He returns to markedly moral comedy in *The Counterfeits* (*c.* May 1678),[1] a Spanish romance of impersonation, confusion, seduction, and disguise, with marriages finally sorted out. The moral intention is loudly announced in the prologue—interestingly, in view of the date: 'Ladies, for you he writ, much griev'd to see . . . harmless Comedy,/Made Bawd to such mean durty Ribaldry.' Overlong speeches make the play's texture too heavy, but its good points may have been observed by Colley Cibber, who plundered its Spanish source more skilfully for *She wou'd and She wou'd not* (1702).

Whatever audiences did or did not want in the puzzling spring of 1678, 'slight plays' relying on 'a little tattle sort of Conversation' fared poorly. *Tunbridge-Wells* (*c.* March 1678)[2] is a frothy non-satiric bagatelle with a near-cuckolding, two false marriages, and a strictly predictable romance plot. The dialogue is pleasant, the action too slight. Edward Howard breaks a seven-year silence with *The Man of Newmarket* (*c.* March 1678), the last and weakest of his plays. This piece is a horsy humours comedy (jockeys abound) in which little occurs beyond a demonstration of the author's lack of flair for comic dialogue.

One might expect the stuff of *Limberham* from Durfey after *A Fond Husband*, but in what Nicoll dubs his 'second period' Durfey moves tentatively in a rather different direction.

---

[1] If the play is his: Langbaine offers the suggestion, but finds the piece 'too good to be his Writing'. For an analysis, see Loftis, *The Spanish Plays of Neoclassical England*, pp. 163–6.
[2] Variously ascribed to 'Rawlins', 'L. Baker', and 'anonymous'.

Trick for Trick (*c.* March 1678) is only a new recension of Fletcher's *Monsieur Thomas*, a classic love-duel play. *Squire Oldsapp* (*c.* June 1678) is a routine smorgasbord of stale humours, intrigue, and a bit of sex. Oldsapp gets tied to a tree while wild young Welford uses Mme Tricklove, his deceitful mistress. But despite that scene, this is not really a sex play, Pimpo and the hapless Oldsapp's potency aids notwithstanding. Durfey mocks his characters, but without a satirist's conviction. *The Virtuous Wife; or, Good Luck at Last* (September or October 1679) is the first play in which we definitely begin to see the real Durfey. The piece is light-hearted, often verging on the farcical, but the serious presentation of female virtue looks forward to Durfey's later proto-'sentimental' plays. Here the hero Beauford remains a long way from the exemplary protagonist: a would-be Horner, he fails twice but finally manages to bed another man's wife before he acquires Lidia and her £10,000 for his own—'good luck at last'. Durfey muddles with female rights and marital discord: here the serious characters come more to life, and for the first time his peripheral humours characters have real vividness, especially old Lady Beardly (played by James Nokes!).

Looking back over Carolean comedy, we may well want to ask what has become of the 'comedy of manners' mode in the midst of all this. Nicoll's definition, still widely cited, is worth quoting and considering again at this point.

Genteel comedy—to employ Addison's phrase—is this late seventeenth century drama. . . . The manners school, after all, depends rather on an atmosphere which cannot be precisely analysed than on outstanding characteristics. . . . In the main, we may say, the invariable elements of the comedy of manners are the presence of at least one pair of witty lovers, the woman as emancipated as the man, their dialogue free and graceful, an air of refined cynicism over the whole production, the plot of less consequence than the wit, an absence of crude realism, a total lack of any emotion whatsoever.[1]

By the terms of this definition, the plays of 1677 and 1678 are not comedies of manners, but then neither are *The Country-Wife* and *The Plain-Dealer*. Wycherley's plays are emotional, lacking in refinement, plot- rather than wit-oriented, and distinctly

[1] Nicoll, I. 196–7. This definition seems representative of the sort of assumptions which have long underlain critical views of Carolean comedy.

short on witty lovers. The *social* element in many Carolean comedies is indisputable, but this is not to say that there was a distinct and discrete manners mode. I cannot comfortably lump *The Amorous Widow, Marriage A-la-Mode*, and *Love in a Wood* together with *The Man of Mode*, as Scouten does. I would call the first an intrigue-farce, the second a double plot tragi-comedy, the third a jumble of elements ranging from the serio-romantic to the humorous and farcical. Certainly Wycherley's Alderman Gripe and Mrs. Crossbite do not inhabit the 'polished and sophisticated society' of which makers of literary glossaries speak, and the 'wit and sparkle' the glossarists emphasize is more prominent in *The School for Scandal* and *The Importance of Being Earnest* than in any seven-teenth-century play. In fact, if we stop to ask what plays Nicoll's definition really *does* fit, the answer is—none of these.

What constitutes a category? If definitions such as Nicoll's fit only two or three plays before Congreve's—and some of those imperfectly—we should not be surprised to find some illogicalities in their application. Thus Scouten, one of the most acute of recent critics, treats *Marriage A-la-Mode* as comedy of manners while excluding *The Rover* on the grounds that 'the scene is not set in a London drawing room, as a comedy of manners must be.' Both works possess elements which appear in contemporary London plays, but both are set in Italy. And is *The Plain-Dealer* a 'drawing-room' comedy? Actually it has much of the adventure and intrigue of *The Rover*. Similarly *The Country-Wife* engages us not with witty conversation but with a rogue's intrigue. Shadwell comes closer to Etherege than do Dryden, Wycherley, or Behn, especially in *Epsom-Wells*, though he never utilizes Etherege's narrow social focus. Nonetheless, that play, like *The Virtuoso* in its sharp satire and romantic intrigue, is a long way from Etherege's slight plot, character display, and witty exchanges. Poor Shadwell has been very oddly treated by modern critics. To a majority, he has seemed a humble Son of Ben. To mongers of wit comedy he is the pitiable proponent of an opposing (and inferior) humours comedy. To critics with monolithic tendencies, contrarily, he is a humble imitator of Etherege! 'Throughout a long career, with patient, plodding devotion,

Shadwell revived in comedy after comedy the dramatic scheme of *She Would if She Could.*[1]

This peculiar view is based on the postulates that 'with the conspicuous exception of Wycherley, Restoration dramatists accepted the leadership of Etherege', and that 'by 1676 the dramatic mode of Restoration comedy of manners had become so authoritative that all comic dramatists felt the pressure of its unwritten laws.'[2] This kind of thinking has continued right up to the present, and is clearly visible in Anne Righter's assertion (discussed earlier) that 'Etherege . . . charted the basic dimensions of Restoration comedy in *She Wou'd if She Cou'd.*' The fallaciousness of such a view has already been amply demonstrated. Clearly Etherege is not a norm for his time. His narrow social focus and emphasis on character rather than action sharply differentiate his plays even from other London comedies. If we must identify a prototype for the comedy of the 1670s, Betterton's *Amorous Widow* probably gives us a more typical combination of the elements popular at that time—romantic plot cuckoldry (not quite consummated in this instance), satire on cits and pretenders to gentility, borrowing from Molière, and a good bit of farce. The combination of romance action and satire can be traced right back to *The English Mounsieur*, *The Committee*, and Cowley's *Cutter*.

According to long-standing dogma, the manners mode appeared full blown in a few plays and then ceased abruptly in 1676, reappearing only in the 1690s.[3] This supposition makes no sense at all. It depends on the questionable hypothecation that there was such a thing as manners comedy. But were such plays as *The Country-Wife*, *The Plain-Dealer*, *The Man of Mode*, and *The Virtuoso* considered manifestations of a special mode when they were first produced? And are not such later plays as *Limberham*, *Sir Patient Fancy*, *A True Widow*, and *Friendship in Fashion* a continuation of the sort of London comedy Wycherley and Etherege contribute to? Looking broadly at the comedy of the 1670s I am disinclined to see 'wit' or 'manners' comedy as a discrete entity. What stopped in 1676 was the play-

---

[1] Lynch, p. 162.

[2] Lynch, pp. 174, 182. Wycherley is explained away as not a born gentleman.

[3] Scouten, 'Notes Toward a History of Restoration Comedy', p. 64. If we must have a terminal date, 1679 is preferable to 1676: not only are changes in taste obvious by then, but the political influences alter the whole state of the drama.

writing of George Etherege. Wycherley's plays—certainly brilliant satiric pictures of society—belong to a sex and intrigue form which continues. The elements of this form as it appears early in the decade are originally drawn from disparate backgrounds: the rogues' intrigues and satiric bite of the low London comedy of the 1660s are joined with the romance and higher social tone of romantic and even heroic tragicomedies. *Marriage A-la-Mode* is no drawing-room comedy, but it does make a contribution to sex comedy. The developments of the later seventies reflect the steady inroads of farce. The popularity of the farcewrights—Ravenscroft, Duffett, and Co.— as an influence on 'serious' comedy has been underestimated. Scouten rightly calls attention to the flood of farce in the later 1670s, suggesting that it crowded 'wit comedy' out. But though the serious writers bemoan the popularity of the *Citizen Turn'd Gentleman* and Duffett's burlesques, these works were not without direct effect. Such writers as Dryden, Shadwell, and Behn write increasingly farcical plays, a fact probably responsible for critics' unwillingness to see them as a continuation of the so-called manners mode. We should remember, however, that Dryden himself chose to defend his *Limberham* in precisely the moral and satiric terms with which he praised Wycherley. Modern critics have been oddly ready to accept Dryden's word on the latter case but not on the former. Need farcical additions destroy satiric purpose? Not if we consider Molière a standard of judgement. The whole tangle here is the result of long-standing confusions about manners comedy: all comedies present manners, but the term is usually employed to mean 'genteel' manners 'realistically' portrayed.[1] In truth though, little Carolean comedy is either realistic or genteel. Certainly Wycherley's plays seem neither realistic nor refined. And ironically enough, Shadwell's *A True Widow* is probably a more literal portrayal of London society than any of Etherege's plays.

To sum up the state and achievement of Carolean comedy as it enters the eighties is properly a task for the next chapter, but the crucial conclusions may be stated very briefly. (1) Carolean comedy continues to comprise a considerable variety

---

[1] For a useful discussion see F. W. Bateson, 'Contributions to a Dictionary of Critical Terms: I. Comedy of Manners', *Essays in Criticism*, i (1951), 88–93.

of types. The heroic play, the Italian court tragicomedy and Spanish romance, romantic and satiric London comedies, and farce do not exist in different worlds. And as plays in this period are not composed according to abstract principles, they tend to reflect interactions among a number of competing modes. (2) The myth of a dominant Etheregean mode is unsound. Etherege himself drew on existing types and found no close imitators. Few plays are devoted to 'representing the life of a small, brilliant, aristocratic society'.[1] The serious dramatists felt themselves fighting a losing battle against the incursions of farce. Dryden's heroic prescriptions and the satire of Shadwell and Wycherley are markedly different from each other and from Etherege. (3) To look for drawing-room comedy is misguided, but certainly we may agree that there is a good deal of *social* comedy in these plays. The opening of *The Plain-Dealer*, for instance, strikingly introduces thematic questions about behaviour in society and social codes. Otway's *Friendship in Fashion* is an angry comment on social codes. And when in the 1690s Congreve and others (advised by Dryden) look to Carolean comedy for models, they seize on such social elements and develop them. We must recognize, however, that Congreve and Southerne were not continuing an already distinct mode. During the Carolean period no such social comedy form ever quite jelled, and in 1679 the development of comedy in which the social element was predominant could not have been predicted. (4) Most broadly, we can now see that Carolean comedy, comprising a variety of types, develops in a coherent pattern from post-Caroline beginnings to the works we commonly read. At any one time two or three strikingly different sorts of comedy are being produced, and in their successes, failures, and interactions we can see the influence of changing audience taste. The over-all pattern of development involves the combinations and permutations of many types produced by many playwrights, and indeed it would almost undoubtedly have been much the same had Etherege never lived.

[1] From a definition of 'comedy of manners' by V. de S. Pinto, *Sedley*, p. 257.

CHAPTER 8

THE POLITICAL EIGHTIES

THE eighties are a watershed. The Exclusion Crisis, the death of Charles, and the ousting of James contribute to drastic changes in theatrical conditions. The drama was changing its character anyway: signs of the disintegration of the Carolean synthesis in heroic drama and social sex comedy are plain by the later seventies. But extrinsic factors, especially the end of playhouse competition, help cause rapid shifts in play fashions, followed by stagnation. A flood of political drama (1680–2) is succeeded by the virtual cessation of playwriting. Even with the King's Company very shaky, the first three years of the decade average twelve new plays a year; the next six produce only four per annum—almost all of them from established authors, or actors. Play types change quickly at the beginning of the decade: tragedy, so dominant initially, soon almost disappears. Apart from the end of competition, there is never any sharp discontinuity: Court interest continues even after Charles's death—James and Mary were both play-goers. But the Court focus of the theatre world is waning, and, to an increasingly obvious extent, new pressures of audience taste are being felt. 'The Ladies' turn up more and more often in prologues and epilogues. Theatre audiences change constantly of course; by the later eighties a full generation has passed since the reopening of the theatres; and after a decade of upheaval, distraction, and stasis, new directions had to be sought. There is a false dawn of sorts in the spring of 1688, culminating in *The Squire of Alsatia*, a play remarkably prophetic of the new wave. And when the theatre revives a year later, following the Revolution, the play types—considered against those of the mid-seventies—turn out to have altered to a surprising degree.

I. POLITICAL DRAMA AND THE DEATH OF THE KING'S COMPANY 1679–1682

The King's Company was already in dire straits at the start of the Popish Plot, and matters rapidly worsened. In the 1679–80 season they produced but two new plays, only one successful; part of the company defected temporarily to Scotland, and reconciliation proved difficult; quarrels over alleged theft of scenes, costumes, and properties by company members divided the remaining actors.[1] New Articles of Agreement drawn in July 1680 made little difference: the 1680–1 season was another disaster. Hotson prints details of a lawsuit for default of rent against the King's Company in the spring of 1681: theatre 'rent' alone was £5. 14s. per acting day, but several times the takings fell below £4—less than 20 per cent of the amount needed for bare subsistence. The theatre was closed from late spring into October 1681. Several new plays were mounted in the 1681–2 season in a last-gasp effort at survival, but the death warrant was signed on 14 October when Hart and Kynaston concluded an agreement with Charles Davenant, Betterton, and William Smith (of the Duke's Company) promising (1) not to act for the King's troupe, and to switch companies if legally possible; (2) to assign their rights in King's Company plays and properties to the Duke's Company; (3) to promote a union; and (4) to sue Killigrew if it proved necessary. In return for their collusion in this subversion, Hart and Kynaston were promised attractive pensions—5s. per acting day for no work.[2] The King's Company struggled on until 21 March, when 'there happened a difference between the Senior and Young men belonging to the King's play house which grew to such a height that they all drew their swords which occasioned the wounding of severall.'[3] Lawsuits commenced; the theatre closed; and the process of amalgamation ensued.

The Duke's Company, meanwhile, was doing passably well. And in these last years of competition, a surprising number

---

[1] *The London Stage*, Part 1, p. 279; Nicoll, I. 327–30; Hotson, pp. 262–77; Wilson, *Mr. Goodman*, Chapter 5.

[2] Gildon reprints the agreement in *The Life of Mr. Thomas Betterton* (London, 1710), pp. 8–9.

[3] Newdigate Newsletters, cited in *The London Stage*, Part 1, p. 307.

of new plays got produced, including a fair proportion of really fine ones—*The Spanish Fryar, Lucius Junius Brutus, Venice Preserv'd,* and *The Souldiers Fortune.* Indeed, political upheaval, however bad for business, stimulated both a burst of topical relevance and some display of seriousness and vitality in English playwriting.

Especially in 1679 and 1680, tragedy is heavily predominant, and it remains so until 1683. Among some twenty-four serious plays we find the usual types represented: (1) horror tragedy (*Thyestes, Caesar Borgia*); (2) heroically inclined unrhymed tragedy (*Theodosius, Fatal Love*); (3) the growing pathetic tragedy (*The Orphan, Anna Bullen*). But the dominant type, comprising almost half of the new serious plays, may be dubbed political tragedy. This category is of course compounded of very different sorts of plays with radically diverse objects. And naturally the centrality of the political concern varies. *Lucius Junius Brutus* and *The Ingratitude of a Common-Wealth* are conceived almost as propaganda fables, while *The Conspiracy* and *Henry the Sixth* seem more designed to batten upon topical concerns than to contribute seriously to popular opinion. In 1679 and 1680 anti-Catholic hysteria is happily exploited by both Whig and Tory partisans: only later are cracks at priests taken as whiggish sentiment. We will find some strongly ideological plays, but to see these works in tidy subdivisions distorts most of them.[1] Among these pieces are horror and pathetic plays, pattern tragicomedy, and semi-heroic plays. Politically speaking, they can be broken down into three general types: Tory moral, Whig moral, and general-warning plays.

In view of its chequered later history, Dryden's *The Spanish Fryar* (November 1680) can seem an odd contribution to the

---

[1] George W. Whiting, 'Political Satire in London Stage Plays, 1680–83', *Modern Philology*, xxviii (1930), 29–43, gets over-schematic, speaking of 'the Whig offensive' of 1680 and 'the Tory offensive' of 1681 and 1682. Nicoll, using such terminology, is led to discuss Dryden's strongly Tory *Spanish Fryar* as part of the 'Whig offensive' (I. 79). A more sensible brief account is John Loftis's *The Politics of Drama in Augustan England* (Oxford, 1963), Chapter 2. The production circumstances of the major political plays are analysed by Arthur F. White, 'The Office of Revels and Dramatic Censorship During the Restoration Period', *Western Reserve University Bulletin*, n.s. xxxiv (1931), 5–45. See also George W. Whiting, 'The Condition of the London Theaters, 1679–83: A Reflection of the Political Situation', *Modern Philology*, xxv (1927), 195–206.

Tory cause: the sub-plot's satire on Father Dominic comes across with savage gusto.[1] But the serious plot's Tory fable cannot be missed: conspiracy and usurpation fail. Dryden slams home this moral at the end: 'let the bold Conspirator beware,/For Heaven makes Princes its peculiar Care.' The play is an unusually impressive example of split plot tragicomedy. (For a brief analysis see Chapter 5, above.) Dryden uses the split both for thematic reinforcements and ironic commentary, and also for pragmatic reasons—he writes in support of the King, while appealing to popular anti-Catholic mania. Another Tory fable with a happy ending is Thomas Southerne's first effort, *The Loyal Brother* (February 1682), a more single-minded play which comes closer to a parallel of the contemporary scene. The plot turns on a love tangle: both Seliman (Sophy of Persia) and his faithful brother Tachmas adore Semanthe. Complications involve Ismael, 'a Villanous favourite', and Arbanes, 'a disaffected General'. The results are—in slightly silly guise—'a thinly disguised political allegory which exalted James Duke of York at the expense of Shaftesbury and even of Charles'.[2] The scene with Tachmas on the scaffold (31) shows pathetic leanings; the misdirected poison at the end and all the mouthing of noble sentiment are, as Rothstein says dismissively, 'standard stuff'. The play's considerable success is probably the result of its politics, though Tachmas is a relatively human and thoughtful hero, and Ismael is an enjoyably vigorous villain:

> Vertue avaunt! . . .
> Ambition is our Idol, on whose wings
> Great minds are carried only to extreams;
> To be sublimely great, or to be nothing. (12–13)

Standard stuff this is—but Southerne's language is remarkably spare and clear, and gives promise of the mature dramatist to come.

[1] On 8 December 1686 James II ordered 'that yᵉ play called yᵉ Spanish Friar should bee noe more Acted' (*The London Stage*, Part 1, p. 354). It was the first play attended by Queen Mary (28 May 1689), a choice which occasioned much scandalized comment and greatly embarrassed her. A daughter usurping a banished father's throne was a theme with parallels impossible to ignore. (See ibid., p. 371.) Nonetheless, the play continued to be a stock piece.

[2] Clifford Leech, 'The Political "Disloyalty" of Thomas Southerne', *Modern Language Review*, xxviii (1933), 421–30.

At the opposite end of the political spectrum comes Lee's powerful *Lucius Junius Brutus* (December 1680). It was banned within a few days by the Lord Chamberlain, supposedly for its 'very Scandalous Expressions & Reflections upon ye Government'.[1] In fact, this order is misleading. The play is neither satire nor parallel, but rather a fiercely ideological play, vehemently upholding constitutional principles which the Stuarts considered inimical at best. The criticisms of Tarquin may or may not be meant to refer to Charles II—but in any case a celebration of the establishment of a republic was not acceptable to the authorities at this juncture. Politics aside, the play is a fine one. Some of the speeches are too long, and the motivation occasionally goes awry, but as an example of the heroic–stoic mode it entirely surpasses an arid exercise like Addison's *Cato* (1713). Brutus's iron self-control is perhaps excessive (e.g. II. 373), but his chilliness is offset by Lee's characteristic exuberance, as in a famous scene in Act IV: 'The Scene draws, showing the Sacrifice; One Burning, and another Crucify'd: the Priests coming forward with Goblets in their hands, fill'd with human blood' (363). The blood is then drunk.

Few plays are so centrally ideological, but many of them capitalize on politics. Tate's *Ingratitude of a Common-Wealth* (*c.* December 1681), an adaptation of *Coriolanus*, shows how Carolean playwrights find and develop political relevance in rather distant material. The play is mostly pretty close to Shakespeare—though reversing his practice in *Lear*, Tate arranges a wholesale slaughter at the end. Melodrama and sentiment are heightened: Virgilia stabs herself to avoid rape by Aufidius, who ultimately dies of a wound inflicted by Coriolanus. In the midst of such love and honour broils, however, Tate saw 'no small Resemblance with the busie *Faction* of our own time. And I confess, I chose rather to set the *Parallel* nearer to Sight, than to throw it off at further Distance' (dedication). The attack, he assures us, is on types, not persons, showing 'what Miseries *Common-Wealths* have been involv'd in, by a blind Compliance with their popular Misleaders'. In case we are in any doubt, matters are spelled out: 'The Moral . . . [is] Submission and Adherence to Establisht Lawful Power',

[1] L.C. 5/144, p. 28.

and 'LOYALTY'. Tate had good reason to make this crystal clear—a year earlier, his *The History of King Richard the Second* had been banned (14 December 1680). Acted the next month in disguised form, it was promptly suppressed, and the luckless King's Company shut down for ten days.[1] Of course the reason is simple: the deposition of an English King was not a tolerable subject. Curiously, Tate was astonished and indignant. He had raised and ennobled Richard, while worsening Bullingbrook, making him a rabble-rousing preacher of sedition, especially in a scene added to Act II. Tate's 'Design was to engage the pitty of the Audience' for a 'Wise, Active and Just Prince' whose 'heroick Vertues' should 'draw Tears'. This design is lamely carried out, and Tate certainly picked the wrong time for it. Charles II did not want pity; he wanted to retain his throne.

The uses and dangers of English history are likewise demonstrated in Crowne's *The Misery of Civil-War* (*c.* February 1680) and *Henry the Sixth*, Part 1 (Autumn 1680 or Spring 1681)—a pair of Shakespeare adaptations, though Crowne vigorously and disingenuously denies his debt. *The Misery* is a general warning about the results of religious faction, showing the 'scurvy Joys . . . Fools take in pelting out each others Brains' (prologue). The play was allowed, even though King Henry is killed—perhaps because Crowne insists (via Richard II's ghost) so loudly that this is what happens when true Kings are deposed. The later 'first' part, 'With the Murder of Humphrey Duke of Glocester', is an even cruder and coarser job, emphasizing horror. Humphrey is strangled in full view; Suffolk's bloody head is displayed on stage. In the prologue Crowne laments that '*Play-Houses* like forsaken Barns are grown', and hopes that his 'Vineger against the Pope' will please the audience. Indeed the play is liberally doused with anti-popish vinegar. Crowne's dedication hints that it proved 'scandalous' and he touts the play as anti-Catholic satire. Ten years later, in the dedication to *The English Frier* (1690), he says that 'e're it liv'd long, it was stifled by command' on account of its

---

[1] The 1681 title-page says 'Acted at the Theatre Royal under the Name of the *Sicilian Usurper*'. Richard was dubbed Oswald, Gaunt became Alcidore, Bullingbrook appears as Vortiger, and so forth. The play was prohibited before it could be acted in December: the performances recorded in *The London Stage* for December are a misconstruction from confusing evidence. For a brief account of this play, see above, Chapter 5.

honest exposure of 'Popery and Popish Courts'. This may not be the whole truth: other vitriolically anti-Catholic plays were left alone, but this one's depiction of successful rebellion against an incumbent King cannot have been welcome. The most extreme anti-Catholic play is Settle's *The Female Prelate* (May 1680), a wild and woolly account of 'The Life and Death of Pope Joan' dedicated to Shaftesbury. Joanna Angelica's story is retailed, suitably adorned with fiendish plots, poison, ghost, lots of macabre sex, and gruesome death. Otway attests to its success, and, though silly, the piece is exuberant. The Duke of Saxony and his wife Angeline are potentially strongly pathetic characters, but Settle concentrates on comic-book horrors.

All of these plays, save possibly *Richard the Second*, are deliberate contributions to contemporary politics. William Whitaker's *The Conspiracy* (*c.* March 1680) is more distant from reality. Whitaker does a bad job with an untidy intrigue plot, getting what mileage he can out of a 'Turkish' setting and paraphernalia. The play is not improved by being in bad rhyme. Such power as it has comes from the ambitious Flatra, who wants her husband Meleck Hamet to kill her brother and take the throne, and from neo-Fordian claptrap: in 'a Room hung all with black' we find coffins and mutes; people drink (poisoned) wine from skulls; the Sultan's ghost leads in *Death* —and so forth (51 ff.). Political relevance, such as it is, comes from the nature of the plot, and from a law-and-order prologue touting a moral: 'Forget not what is *Due* to *Majesty*.'

Undoubtedly the finest of these plays is the one in which politics are basically an incidental attraction—*Venice Preserv'd* (February 1682). Otway's tragedy is one of the few, apart from Dryden's, that have aroused markedly different readings. The critical divergencies depend largely on whether one stresses the politics, the pathetic element, the quasi-heroic parts, or the sense of tragic meaning implied by the play's events. (See the brief analysis in Chapter 5, above.) Dobrée dislikes the addition of sentiment and pathos; Aline Taylor finds the balance effective.[1] Several recent critics, from differing per-

---

[1] Dobrée, *Restoration Tragedy*, pp. 141–8; Aline Mackenzie Taylor, *Next to Shakespeare: Otway's 'Venice Preserv'd' and 'The Orphan' and Their History on the London Stage* (Durham, N.C., 1950), Chapter 2.

spectives, agree substantially that the power of the tragedy stems from a sense of man's inability to control himself.[1] As tragedy, the play's power certainly rests on its communication of man's agonizing inadequacies—not that Otway has abandoned his craving for inaccessible heroic ideals. In 1682 *Venice Preserv'd* had not only its emotional appeal, but a potent political message. Where Dryden and Southerne give us Tory fables, Otway bitterly denounces plots and conspiracies, savaging Shaftesbury as both Renault and Antonio, and achieving in the sexual slurs of the nicky-nacky scenes the nastiest and funniest personal debunking of the whole period. Not many critics have had the stomach to relish it. The play is a brilliant anti-Whig fable—and, happily, a tragedy which transcends such particulars.[2]

Other sorts of serious plays are likely to have peripheral political references in these years—especially anti-Catholic material. Thus both Lee's *Caesar Borgia* and Crowne's *Thyestes*, horror tragedies, take an aggressively hostile view of priests. Critics usually assume that a similar horror play, Banks's *Cyrus the Great* (performed in 1695), was banned on political grounds. Banks's preface calls it 'A banish'd Play that tedious Years had mourn'd . . . Writ and design'd . . . E're my then happier *Favourite*'—i.e. before *c.* May 1681. Given the quasi-heroic style (atypical of Banks's later pathetic bent) the early date may be correct. However, there is in the play no apparent reason for political banning—and in such cases the reason is almost always obvious. Banks may have been fudging an excuse: *A*

---

[1] See William H. McBurney, 'Otway's Tragic Muse Debauched: Sensuality in *Venice Preserv'd*', *Journal of English and Germanic Philology*, lviii (1959), 380–99; Ronald Berman, 'Nature in *Venice Preserv'd*', *ELH*, xxxvi (1969), 529–43; Derek W. Hughes, 'A New Look at *Venice Preserv'd*', *Studies in English Literature*, xi (1971), 437–57—who sees the play as an attack upon 'Restoration heroic ideals' set against man's animal and sexual nature; and Bessie Proffitt, 'Religious Symbolism in Otway's *Venice Preserv'd*', *Papers on Language and Literature*, vii (1971), 26–37— stressing man's fallen nature. A consonant, less negative view is presented in David R. Hauser's 'Otway Preserved: Theme and Form in *Venice Preserv'd*', *Studies in Philology*, lv (1958), 481–93.

[2] W. Van Voris, in 'Tragedy through Restoration eyes: *Venice preserv'd* in its own theatre', *Hermathena*, no. xcix (1964), 55–65, finds the play 'a tragic satire against all parties and plotting rulers', Charles II included. From our perspective, perhaps it is. However, Van Voris offers no evidence that the original audience felt so, or that the King—as he asserts—disliked the play. For contrary evidence, see *The London Stage*, Part 1, pp. 306–9.

Comparison Between the Two Stages calls it a play 'which the
Players damn'd and wou'd not Act of a great while'.[1]

Horror tragedy remains a viable mode. Lee's *Caesar Borgia*
(late 1679?) is, as critics complain, a *mélange* of atrocities. It is
discussed briefly in Chapter 5, above. The strangling of
Bellamira, the disposal of the Duke of Gandia's body, the
poisoning of Ascanio ('I burn, I burn, I toste, I roste, and my
Guts fry,/They blaze, they snap, they bounce like Squibs/And
Crackers: I am all fire . . .'), and the cutting out of the child
Seraphino's eyes (II. 132, 141) are but passing items in the
ghastly catalogue. Yet in the midst of all this, the characters
of Borgia and Machiavel are real and interesting. Crowne's
Thyestes (*c.* March 1680), partly based on Seneca, is a more
focused and cohesive play, though a rather dispassionate one
for the subject. Crowne gets effective results out of the dramatic
ironies of the situation, and milks the obvious: the Queen is
shown in chains on the ground, in hair-cloth, following her
rape by Thyestes; Philisthenes, in raptures over his marriage,
finds himself headed for the pot; his mangled remains are
displayed after the banquet; Antigone (his fiancée) enters raving and stabs herself. Over all, however, the piece is flaccid
—for once, a subject really demands the high emotional
temperature of Lee.

Two lesser examples of the horror mode are Ravenscroft's
adaptation of *Titus Andronicus* (1678–9?) and Settle's *Heir of
Morocco* (March 1682). Like *Thyestes*, both were King's Company efforts. *Titus* is little changed. Ravenscroft revels in the
bloodbath ending, enjoying Aron on the rack (on stage, at
length), the display of Tamora's sons' heads and hands hung
on a wall, and finally ending with Aron on fire. *The Heir of
Morocco* is a feeble example of the *Son of Dracula* mode. Settle
—who could see which way the wind was blowing—calls it
'a Tory Play' in the prologue, but really it is a straight love
and horror play: the true heir Altomar has 'His manly Flesh
torn off with burning Pincers' (44), while his beloved is
forced to watch. A very flat moral—'See here the dire Effects
of unkind Parents'—concludes an uninspired effort. At this
point the horror tragedy falls into abeyance for most of a
decade. In part, its attractions get subsumed into pathetic plays.

---

[1] *A Comparison*, p. 16. *Cyrus* is discussed in Chapter 9, below, in the context of 1695.

Both pathetic and political tinges appear in the routine quasi-heroic blank-verse plays of these years. Settle's *Fatal Love* (*c*. September 1680) shows a strong pathetic inclination (sub-title: 'The Forc'd Inconstancy'), but is finished off with a bloody massacre, Lysandra alone remaining alive. This formula should have pleased the audience, but the piece failed, perhaps let down by the 'feeble Fragment of a Company' at Drury Lane, as Settle intimates in his preface, while complaining that a highly politicized atmosphere is inimical to the theatres. Lee's *Theodosius* (Spring 1680?), set in Constantinople, is a similar piece of work, with its affecting nobility and pathos. Still in a heroic setting, Lee here emphasizes love and sensibility: this is a softer play than his earlier efforts. Distributive justice is effected; the dedication shows that Lee himself was aware of a new sense of restraint in his writing. R. G. Ham finds the play political,[1] but it seems only peripherally so, raising succession questions and discussing Salic law (II. 255). Here the issues are topical, but we find neither parallel of events and persons, nor ideological fable. *Theodosius* is not a partisan document. Neither is Charles Saunders's *Tamerlane the Great* (March 1681), a respectable first (and only) effort at the heroic manner. Love, intrigue, reversals, and discoveries are briskly handled, and a happy ending achieved: Arsanes marries Asteria (Bajaset's daughter) with Tamerlane's blessing. Dryden's epilogue, very complimentary to the beardless author, has some foundation for its praise. Saunders (who does not follow Marlowe) handles the usual tragic high jinks with verve, especially when Ispatia is poisoned by kissing a copy of the 'Sacred Alcoran' in pledge of love. Tate's *The Loyal General* (*c*. December 1679) has only the vaguest of political parallels. A weak king, scheming queen, a faithful daughter, and the clever villian Escalus are tied into a love-misunderstandings-plus-villainy catastrophe-plot. The quick twists and turns are good, but dialogue is wooden and the characters fail to live. The piece is of interest mostly as a sample of the kind of Carolean dramaturgy Tate was shortly to be foisting on Shakespeare. Tate's dedication is a significant critical document, drawing on and paralleling Dryden's view of Shakespeare in the later seventies.

[1] *Otway and Lee*, p. 130.

The serious plays discussed so far are mostly either topically oriented or routine developments of well-established types. The five pathetic plays from these years mark an important step in new directions. They are foreshadowed by such works as *Oedipus* and *Mithridates*, but they are the one important new mode established in the early eighties. Some of their elements, of course, have appeared all along in horror tragedy and pattern tragicomedy, but a new sub-genre is emerging.

Otway's *The Orphan* (February 1680), analysed above in Chapter 5, is a landmark. In its context, the piece is startlingly domestic and personal. With no basis in evil, the tragedy has to stem, as Rothstein observes, from corrupt nature and ground-less mistrust. The lack of probability and the questionable motivations are shortcomings which an appeal to seventeenth-century viewpoints can mitigate but not wholly remove.[1] Yet despite its numerous problems, *The Orphan*, as a stage vehicle, has tremendous power. One could not begin to say the same for Tate's *History of King Lear* (Autumn 1680). Tate's dedication quotes Dryden, and obviously he had Dryden's criticism in view. The play is shortened and tidied up; love, sex, and espec-ially 'distress' are increased. Some contemporary touches are introduced: Edmund, becoming the Carolean villain, plots the rape of Cordelia; and the succession question, with the sup-pression of rebellion by an illegitimate son, is deftly (and safely) commented upon. Tate creates a pattern tragicomedy, though plainly his concoction of a happy ending (Lear retiring gracefully in favour of Edgar, who marries Cordelia) repre-sents a deliberate choice, and not a concession to audience taste: Shakespeare's horrors were tame stuff by Lee's standards. Tate tries to arouse pity for misfortune, and minimizes the horrors. The result is wretchedly mangled Shakespeare, but in its own right a good melodrama whose long success is entirely comprehensible. And Tate's *Lear* does not seem so bad when considered against Durfey's version of *Cymbeline*, *The Injured Princess* (*c.* March 1682), discussed briefly above in Chapter 5. This, or possibly Settle's *The Heir of Morocco*, was the last new King's Company production—a feeble end in either case. Durfey's adaptation is ungainly—Genest says 'vile'—and apart from some nice songs, the play has few

[1] See Taylor, *Next to Shakespeare*, Chapter 1.

attractions. Acts III and IV see the addition of strong pathetic touches: this is what Durfey chooses to stress in what is already a pattern tragicomedy. The epilogue's claim that 'this Play was writ nine years ago' seems unconvincing in light of the pathos, and since the implied date would be before Durfey was active and before the boom in Shakespeare adaptation.

The real champion of the pathetic is Banks, who there found his *métier*. *The Unhappy Favourite* (*c.* May 1681) shows him feeling his way toward the she-tragedies of Anne Boleyn, Mary Queen of Scots, and Jane Grey. Essex is, Rothstein remarks, 'the stupid hero' Banks favours, but even here he is well nigh buried under feminine schemes and sentiment. The situation is almost static: the play lives on whopping infusions of emotion. Elizabeth is furious to learn of Essex's marriage (his farewell scene with his wife is a Banks special—70 ff.), but he gets executed only because the jealous Countess of Nottingham suppresses the ring which would have granted Essex any boon. (Here history prefigures Banks!) The letter explaining everything arrives—of course—just an instant too late, a device of which Banks is overfond. Banks's intended prologue calls the piece a 'Ladies Play', a fair hint of the vein he was cultivating. *Vertue Betray'd: or Anna Bullen* (March 1682), discussed above in Chapter 5, gives us full-blown she-tragedy. Moving to the Duke's Company and writing for Mrs. Barry must have been a help. Here Banks increases his action and intrigue, but the crucial component is pathos, unstinted, and the result is a bathetic tearjerker.

The early eighties are not a vintage period for serious drama, though in 1682 one certainly could not predict the virtual hiatus in its production, especially with the pathetic mode seemingly ready to flower. The comedies of these years are on the average somewhat better, but show little movement in any particular generic direction. Three principal varieties appear between 1680 and mid-1682, two of them carryovers and one topical: (1) romantic intrigue plays; (2) sex comedy; (3) political comedy.

The remnants of the old Spanish romance mode had showed new life in the later seventies as the sex boom began to fade. Thus such plays as *The Feign'd Curtezans* and *The Counterfeits*

are a prefiguring of further efforts along these lines, especially
by Mrs. Behn. Lewis Maidwell's *The Loving Enemies* (January
1680) is another such piece. Maidwell runs serious and light
romantic plots in an Italian setting, handling the romance
commonplaces with enjoyable verve. The high plot retails love
complications in a family feud, with a night-time duel, girls
in male attire, and so forth. Fortune is explicitly treated as
less important than virtue and beauty (25). In the lighter
plot we get humorous courtships, an attempted elopement
which goes awry, and amusing use of a mock ghost (54).
Circumstantio, the over-rhetorical valet, must have made a
fine vehicle for Underhill, especially in his wooing of Nuarcha,
a frantic old maid. The piece is an entertaining romance in
contrasting semi-serious and light veins. Three plays by Behn
stray further from romance norms, but all have a serious
romantic element. *The Revenge: or A Match in Newgate* (*c.* June
1680) is simply an adaptation of Marston's *The Dutch Courtezan*
—but with some very revealing changes.[1] As in other of her
plays, Behn's treatment of the prostitute is serious and unusual.
Marston dispatches his whore to whip and jail; Behn reclaims
her. Wellman has ruined Corina (played—significantly—by
Mrs. Barry), but pities her, 'that forsaken Beauty I have
ruin'd' (52). He really loves Marinda, who is gracious to the
poor whore. Responding, Corina says, 'Madam, the Generous
Pattern that you have set me, I shall be proud to follow.'
Wellman, instead of abandoning her, arranges to marry her
off to Sir John Empty: 'This Knight, *Corina*, then resolve to
marry, I'll make thy Fortune equal to his Quality. . . . He
thinks thou art my Sister—nor will I ever undeceive him' (62).
With this romantic strain goes Behn's usual lively intrigue and
fun—for example, Nan, displaying true conjugal constancy,
is loyally determined to hang with her husband (63). *The
Rover*, Part 2 (*c.* January 1681), is a good play which cannot
quite match its predecessor. Hellena has died at sea, so rover
Willmore is unattached in Madrid. He is one of three suitors
to the courtesan La Nuche (again Mrs. Barry), who loves him
despite his poverty, and finally abandons prudence and gives

---

[1] For an analysis, see Leo Hughes and Arthur H. Scouten, 'Some Theatrical
Adaptations of a Picaresque Tale', *University of Texas Studies in English* (1945–6),
pp. 98–114.

herself to him—without marriage. In part the play is dead serious: Frederick M. Link points out the careful development of disguise and deception themes, and a deliberate contrasting of value systems.[1] Here the problem of the whore, left dangling so badly in Part 1, is fully developed, albeit to an end which is romantically satisfying but simply seems a flight from reality. The intrigues are very complicated, replete with brawls, fisticuffs, and night-time confusions. The main romantic tangle is five-sided. There are two other major levels in the play. Shift and Hunt, the Rover's officers, win and marry a pair of wealthy Jewish heiresses—a giant and a dwarf respectively. And in addition, Harlequin (the Rover's servant) and Scaramouche appear prominently, their part in the Rover's masquerade as a mountebank (I. 142) being particularly effective. The total effect of this combination of serious themes with wild farce is a little dizzying. Considered analytically, the play flies apart in all directions, but its tremendous vitality should not be slighted. Finally, in *The False Count* (acted by November 1681) Behn produces a romantic farce. There are two romantic plots and an associated light one. First, old Francisco marries Julia, but they are captured 'by the Turks'—actually by her true love Don Carlos, Governor of Cadiz—and Francisco is amusingly bullied into yielding her. Second, Carlos's friend Antonio is enabled to marry Julia's sister Clara. Third, Francisco's obnoxiously arrogant daughter Isabella is humbled: she jumps at the chance to marry a 'Count', who is actually Guiliom, a chimney sweep. The fancy of capture by the Turks, and the way Francisco *begs* Julia to yield her virtue to the grand Turk, are enjoyably preposterous. J. H. Smith is appalled by the play, finding it 'considerably more "immoral" than all Wycherley's plays put together'.[2] This view oddly exaggerates the moral impact of a gay farce—light, very funny, and not really obscene at all.

For genuine sex comedy, one can turn to Otway's highly successful *The Souldiers Fortune* (June 1680). The prologue, referring sadly to 'our abandon'd Stage', testifies to the popularity of 'Pope Joan' at Drury Lane—one of the King's Company's last successes. In a dedication to Bentley (the publisher) Otway wittily refutes complaints about obscenity:

[1] *Aphra Behn* (New York, 1968), pp. 62–6. [2] J. H. Smith, pp. 102–3.

no true lady, he announces, would know enough about it to be able to recognize the stuff. Construction is better than in *Friendship in Fashion*: the plot moves well and the dialogue is lighter and brisker. The violent satire of his first comedy gives way to a bitter, sardonic cynicism which pervades this play, creating a brilliantly effective and quite unattractive atmosphere.[1] Captain Beaugard, disbanded and penniless, cuckolds Sir Davy Dunce, a rich old cit who has married Beaugard's true love in his absence. J. H. Smith, as usual, finds this 'true love' idea merely an obnoxious glamorization of adultery. But in a society in which women often did have to marry for money, Otway's presentation of the problem could be seen as more than a specious excuse for adultery. Sir Davy's ineffectual attempts to get Beaugard murdered allow the couple to blackmail him into accepting his horns. The second plot has Beaugard's friend Courtine woo and win the witty Sylvia. Smith calls it a 'feeble' example of the gay couple love game, but is perhaps too influenced by the sequel (discussed below in Section II). Here they are made an attractive and sympathetic couple as they try to work out a basis for marriage, ending with a good proviso scene (II. 175–6). Otway's dissection of this marriage in *The Atheist* is beautifully set up by this apparently happy romantic ending. The play's most memorable character is Sir Jolly Jumble, an old whoremaster-pimp (a voyeur and homosexual) exhibited with his girls (106). That he turns out to be one of the more decent and humane people in the play is surely a very blunt authorial comment.

Otway's comedy is amusing, unpleasant, and serious; Ravenscroft's *The London Cuckolds* (October 1681) is amusing, pleasant, and frivolous—a sex comedy more in the spirit of *A Fond Husband*. The central device is simplicity itself. Three old cits have married young wives, and each is convinced that he has chosen wisely. Wiseacre has opted for a foolish country girl; Doodle for a witty woman; Dashwell for a pious one. Add Messrs. Ramble, Townly, and Loveday, two maids, one guardian aunt, darkness, a loaded chamberpot, etc.—and we have wild confusion, concluding with three triumphant cuckoldings. The whole play is sheer farce: some memorable bits

---

[1] See Thomas B. Stroup, 'Otway's Bitter Pessimism', *Essays on English Literature of the Classical Period*, ed. Patterson and Strauss, pp. 54–75.

are Loveday's 'conjuring trick' (18); his slipping Ramble away as a 'spirit'; and Wiseacre teaching young Peggy worship-ful obedience to his nightcap to occupy her during his absence (41). Of its kind, *The London Cuckolds* is certainly the master-piece that J. H. Smith calls it, and is rollicking good fun with no ulterior point whatever. It is often considered a 'political' play because city Whigs are made fools of. Possibly this added a fillip in 1682, but there is no serious attack on the cuckolds, and indeed the play was staged annually on the Lord Mayor's Day especially for the cits until David Garrick halted the practice in 1751. Ravenscroft's prologue to *Dame Dobson* tells us that 'the Ladies' were outraged by the former play, and even made special trips to the theatre to decry it! The men of the pit evidently felt otherwise.

The point of these two plays—or lack thereof, for Ravens-croft's—is obvious enough. Lee's *The Princess of Cleve* (September 1680 or later)[1] is a puzzling case: even its genre is wildly disputed. Nicoll and the *Annals* term it a tragedy; Thomas B. Stroup considers it a prototype for sentimental comedy.[2] Lee himself calls it a 'Farce, Comedy, Tragedy or meer Play' in the dedication, and indeed it is a bewildering amalgam of elements. The heroic Prince of Cleve dies of love for his wife, while his false friend Nemours busily pursues her. Half the story is thus tragedy (in verse); the other half, in prose, is termed by J. H. Smith one of the most 'brutal' displays of 'free gallantry' in the whole period. Half of the Countess de La Fayette's sentimental romantic novel (1678; trans. 1679) is retailed straight; the other half, concerning Nemours, is de-graded into a display of treachery, debauchery, and hypocrisy. The audience 'expected the most polish'd Hero in Nemours, I gave 'em a Ruffian reeking from Whetstone's-Park' (a whores' hangout) says Lee, adding that the exposures in *The Chances*, *Marriage A-la-Mode*, *The Libertine*, and *Epsom-Wells* are 'but Copies of his Villany'. The combination of serious romantic sentiment in the prince and the nasty character of Nemours is

---

[1] The date is frustratingly vague. A tribute to 'Count Rosidore' (Rochester) now 'dead' (II. 162) places the play after 26 July 1680. The B.M. MS. of the play's music is dated December 1682. The play was not published until 1689—astonish-ingly late.

[2] 'The Princess of Cleve and Sentimental Comedy', *Review of English Studies*, xi (1935), 200–3.

disconcerting. Nemours's spirit pervades the play, and the evil atmosphere has repelled modern critics. Ham says simply that the piece has 'nothing' to recommend it. Nicoll calls it ineffectual and worthless, chaotic, corrupt, without true dramatic sentiment—and likens it to 'a rotting dung-heap' (I. 147).

How can this nauseating piece be a sentimental comedy? Stroup points to the last speech in the play.

Nemours: For my part, the Death of the Prince of Cleve, upon second thoughts, has so truly wrought a change in me, as nothing else but a Miracle cou'd—For first I see, and loath my Debaucheries—Next, while I am in Health, I am resolv'd to give satisfaction to all I have wrong'd; and first to this Lady, whom I will make my Wife before all this Company e'er we part—This, I hope, whenever I dye, will convince the World of the Ingenuity of my Repentance, because I had the power to go on.

> He well Repents that will not Sin, yet can,
> But Death-bed Sorrow rarely shews the Man. (II. 226)

What are we to make of this? Forty lines earlier Nemours bets that he will 'Bed her [the widowed Princess] eighteen months three weeks hence, at half an hour past two in the Morning', and we have no prior hint of his final 'repentance'. J. H. Smith is surely right in calling this reform perfunctory and unconvincing, and in objecting to Stroup's contention that it shows Lee preaching 'the natural goodness of man in the character of Nemours'. James Sutherland very plausibly sees 'disgust' as the reaction Lee sought over all; and he suggests that Lee is debunking the Dorimant-style hero. I agree, and would go farther. Lee ridicules the ineffectuality of the whining heroic ethos in the Prince; shows us the true worth of the Carolean rake in Nemours, and in the marital-discord sub-plot; and in the 'reform' I suspect that he is taking a cut at Rochester. Montague Summers was the first to show that despite the compliment to Rochester in Nemours's 'Count Rosidore' speech (162), Nemours's whole character can very plausibly be read as a mixed but profoundly hostile depiction of that noble rake. Sutherland endorses this reading, but without noting the 'scorpion sting' Summers sees in Nemours's closing couplet: 'He well Repents that will not Sin, yet can,/But Death-bed Sorrow rarely shews the Man.'[1] This icy judgement of Roches-

---

[1] Summers, *Playhouse of Pepys*, p. 301; Sutherland, pp. 143–4.

ter's famous deathbed conversion really hits home. The contradictory compliments, the 'mixed' picture, and the lack of open identification are all comprehensible. At one time, 'to Lee the name of Rochester was almost beyond praise.'[1] He had felt Rochester's attractions; he had perhaps suffered second thoughts; and he may well have sensed the dangers in too plain an attack—dangers which Crowne was to learn, to his cost, after *City Politiques* (see Section II, below). In sum, *The Princess of Cleve* is a great play, a savage and sardonic attack on the heroic ethos, the sex comedy ethos, and on Rochester—a satire that deserves to stand with Otway's bitter comedies.

Not surprisingly, the largest group of comedies in these years is political. Some marked differences from the serious political plays should be noted. The genres are suited to different endeavours. Instead of Whig and Tory fable, anti-Catholic, and general-warning plays, we find in comedy a single anti-Catholic (hence Whiggish) play, and a series of debunkings of Whigs. These attacks divide into plays which focus centrally on political matters (*The Roundheads, The Royalist*), and those which simply include incidental political satire on an appropriate cit figure (*Sir Barnaby Whigg, The City Heiress*). As a group, the comedies start rather late. Political tragedy flourishes in 1679 and 1680; political comedy begins to appear in the autumn of 1681. After the Oxford Parliament, writers start to turn on the Whigs; after the tide had definitely turned (by around December 1681), they hasten to rub in the Tory triumph.

Shadwell's *The Lancashire Witches, and Tegue O Divelly the Irish Priest* (*c.* September 1681), the sole Whig play, was 'Printed as it was intended (but not allowed) to be acted' (*Term Catalogues*, November). Shadwell indignantly had the disallowed passages printed in italics: the Master of the Revels did indeed cut the play to ribbons. It has three major elements. (1) A routine, moral, double romance plot; (2) savage satire on Tegue O Divelly, a knavish Irish priest (with appropriate accent), and secondarily on Smerk, a crooked Anglican chaplain: the censor had fits over both; (3) a liberal display of music and machines. Shadwell's witches scenes are spectacular—for example, when they tear a black lamb to bits

---

[1] Ham, p. 49.

and pour its blood into a hole (IV. 116), or when 'All kiss the Devil's Arse' and 'Their Brooms all march off and fetch Bottles' of wine (131). Dorset Garden's dazzling machines were employed to full advantage, especially for the flyings. Shadwell was evidently proud of his witchcraft lore, and includes elaborate footnotes and citations explaining it after each act. He has a flair for such incidentals, demonstrated again in the colloquial cant (with glossary) in *The Squire of Alsatia*. As in that play, however, Shadwell's satirical points get rather muddled. Here Sir Edward Hartfort is an exemplary model of the true gentleman, representing the virtues of good old England and country purity. And his rationalistic philosophy is firmly endorsed. It comes out principally, however, in his vigorous scoffing at the existence of witches—which turn out to be real, and like to gather in his house! Sir Edward is never disillusioned, and the incongruous irony has to bother even a casual viewer. As a whole, *The Lancashire Witches* is quite farcical and adds a fair dose of sex (for example, Tegue copulates with one of the witches, under a slight misapprehension of identity). Downes calls the piece 'a kind of Opera', and probably music and flyings are the key to its long success and great profits. The play is spirited: the epilogue justly compares its anti-Catholic satire to that in *The Spanish Fryar*. The censor's wrath may represent the darker political climate of 1681, or may indicate suspicions about Shadwell's intentions.

The best known of the Tory comedies is Behn's *The Round-heads* (*c.* December 1681), a revision of Tatham's *The Rump* (1660). The savaging of the puritan leaders is once again timely; into this Behn works, incongruously, a double romantic plot in which Loveless and his friend Freeman, a pair of noble cavaliers, woo Lady Lambert and Lady Desbro, wives of puritan politicians. The results are boisterous but hopelessly disjointed: political hits mingle with routine adultery-farce tricks, but to no joint end. Lambert's willingness to whore his wife for political advantage (I. 403) is as close a connection as Behn makes. The pious pimping preacher, Ananias Gogle, is an isolated high point in one of her weakest mature efforts. That she could do much better with a combination of sex and politics is proved in *The City Heiress; or Sir Timothy Treat-all* (early May 1682). Sir Timothy is a brilliant domestic travesty of Shaftesbury, perfectly integrated into a double marriage plot. Sir Timothy, a seditious old knight and Commonwealth supporter, is begulled with a fake 'offer of the crown of Poland' and married off to his nephew's mistress, Diana, thinking her the city heiress. Meanwhile his disinherited nephew, Tom Wilding, first seduces Lady Galliard, and then marries his faithful city heiress, Charlot. His friend Sir Charles Meriwill finally gets to marry the wealthy Lady Galliard, urged on by his roistering old Tory uncle, Sir Anthony. Wilding's forceful seduction of Lady Galliard is good sex comedy fare, but Behn is careful to end more primly. Lightning fast dialogue and deft handling of intrigue make the piece entertaining, and the smear on Shaftesbury is highly effective. A 'burglary' gives the young couples the material to blackmail Sir Timothy into silence. Thus the formula is standard: wild and sober protagonists; witty and romantic heroine (pairing opposites for once), tricking an obnoxious father-figure. But in Diana, sorry to have to marry an old man, though accepting the necessity; in the wild *old* man, Sir Anthony; and in attaching political significance to a private citizen, Mrs. Behn goes beyond the ordinary.

Durfey's *Sir Barnaby Whigg* (*c.* October 1681) incorporates a similar pattern, mixing a romantic plot (Tory Wilding gets the witty Gratiana), and a cuckolding plot (Tory Townly cuckolds Captain Porpuss and Sir Walter Wiseacre), with incidental satire on Sir Barnaby Whigg, 'A Phanatical Rascal, one of *Oliver's* Knights'.[1] In a minor plot Wilding's friend Benedick pursues the Welsh jilt Winifrid, to no end. The results are pleasant routine entertainment. Captain Porpuss's 'blunt Tarpawlin' jargon is sometimes funny, but the high point of the play is a song, 'Farewell my Lov'd Science, my former delight,/*Moliere* is quite rifled, then how should I write?' The answer is—turn musician, and the song goes on: 'I got Fame by filching from Poems and Plays,/Like a Fury I rail'd, like a Satyr I writ,/*Thersites* my Humour, and *Fleckno* my Wit' (28). Durfey is a splendid song writer. *The Royalist* (January 1682)

---

[1] The popularity of this formula is obvious. Another instance around this time is the anonymous *Mr. Turbulent* (January 1682), a rather turgid humours comedy with a romantic plot and some political hits at the title cit and his creature, Rabsheka Sly. The fifth act makes amusing use of madmen in a lively chaos.

is much poorer stuff, an inferior imitation of *The Committee*, offering only mechanical lampoonery of the sequestration committee. Sir Charles Kinglove lays siege to the Chairman's wife, while his friend Heartall copulates with the Chairman's niece, Aurelia, before and also after her marriage to Sir Paul Eitherside, a J.P. ready to take anybody's bribe. The anti-Whig satire is effective in a crude way: 'Here ye shall see a Butcher, a great Common-wealths Man, bloated with Brewis, and fatned with the grease of his own Tripes, railing against the Succession' (preface). Indeed we do. The bawdy cavalier loyalists rather scandalize Nicoll (I. 274), but really only add sexual farce to a political lampoon. The end turns on a silly kind of *deus ex machina*: Cromwell returns Sir Charles's estate, because he is about to die and is looking to his salvation (63).

To pause here suggests, appropriately, an end with a whimper rather than a bang. With the exception of *The Lancashire Witches* and *The City Heiress*, these political comedies do not have a great deal to recommend them. Indeed the drama generally seems to be marking time. To pin down the *malaise* which afflicts writers in these years is hard, beyond recognizing the obvious: the state of the theatres has a demoralizing effect. The excitement, experimentation, and new directions which so enliven the plays of the sixties and seventies largely disappear, and in their place one gets a sense of grim commercial determination. Political preoccupations temporarily change and animate the character of the drama, but do nothing to improve it.

II. THE THEATRE QUIESCENT 1682–1688

The collapse of the King's Company and the consequent end of competition changes the whole theatrical situation. Play production falls off drastically as management policy becomes acutely conservative. Emphasis is naturally on the revival of 'safe' old plays, and the few new ones are markedly unventuresome. These are not years for new writers to emerge and flourish. Southerne is the only important young playwright, and he produces only a single new play in the years 1683–9. Actors could get some consideration: hence we find dramatic carpentry from Lacy, Jevon, and Mountfort. Basically, the established professional writers—Durfey, Ravenscroft, Behn—

have a tight grip on what market there is for new plays. Crowne is at the peak of his powers in *City Politiques* and *Sir Courtly Nice*. But the major Carolean authors contribute little. Etherege and Wycherley have stopped writing; Dryden has lost interest in the theatre. Otway and Lee, though still young, are already at the end of their careers. Shadwell, an unpenitent Whig, finds the theatre temporarily closed to him and is silent until 1688. Downes reports (pp. 39–40) that upon the union 'The mixt Company then Reviv'd the several old and Modern Plays, that were the Propriety [*sic*] of Mr. *Killigrew*.' Downes names *Rule a Wife*, *The Scornful Lady*, *The Plain-Dealer*, *An Evening's Love*, *The Jovial Crew*, *The Beggar's Bush*, *Bartholomew Fair*, *Othello*, *Rollo*, *The Humorous Lieutenant*, and *The Double Marriage*, along 'with divers others'. Most of these are pre-Restoration plays, old favourites. With all these sure-fire pieces to produce anew, and a monopoly, why risk money on untried new plays? As George Powell accurately complained in 1690: 'upon the uniting of the two *Theatres* . . . the reviveing of the old stock of Plays, so ingrost the study of the House, that the Poets lay dorment; and a new Play cou'd hardly get admittance, amongst the more precious pieces of Antiquity, that then waited to walk the Stage' (preface to *The Treacherous Brothers*).

In the spring of 1682 both the political and the theatrical situations are highly unsettled. By December a new equilibrium has been found in both realms. Plays banned during the summer (*City Politiques* and *The Duke of Guise*) are allowed on stage, and the theatrical union takes the form that was to last until Betterton's breakaway in 1695. The precise details of the union remain hazy: from 7 May Betterton and Smith were paid for managing both Dorset Garden and Drury Lane, but remnants of the King's Company seem to have tried their luck in Oxford during July, and the union became complete only about the fifteenth of November, following the lease of Drury Lane to Charles Davenant and his company on 9 November. At any rate, after mid-November the new arrangement is set.[1] The history of the play types in the next few years is eloquent testimony to the benefits of competition. Singularly little

---

[1] See Edward A. Langhans, 'New Restoration Theatre Accounts, 1682–1692' *Theatre Notebook*, xvii (1963), 118–34.

happens: most of the new plays are derivative samples of tried and true modes. Indeed, the most conspicuous generic development is a small boom in magic-and-machinery farce: *The Devil of a Wife*, *The Emperor of the Moon*, and *The Life and Death of Doctor Faustus*.

Serious drama almost vanishes between 1682 and 1688. We will find only a couple of political plays; a few pathos-directed efforts; and some pattern tragicomedies. The most important political play is Dryden and Lee's *The Duke of Guise* (analysed in Chapter 5, above). Disguise of topical relevance is very thin, and its import was crystal clear to contemporaries. John Drummond says in a letter that Monmouth himself protested to his father about allowing the piece to be acted. A newsletter (29 July) reports that 'A play by Mr Dryden . . . wherein the Duke of Monmouth was vilified . . . coming to His Majesty's knowledge is forbid, for though His Majesty be displeased with the Duke yet he will not suffer others to abuse him.'[1] The play is no more or less than a Tory fable, giving an account of the Exclusion Crisis and ending with the King's asserting his authority and having the insurgent Duke killed. The ban was lifted in November.[2]

Lee's rather astonishing political about turn is continued in his last play, *Constantine the Great* (November 1683). Lee's editors read the piece, plausibly, as a vague parallel to the Rye House plot (June 1683). Clearly the villain Arius represents Shaftesbury (already dead), and Dalmatius is a compliment to the Duke of York. Crispus might be a version of Monmouth; Lycinius has been read as Algernon Sidney (executed in December). Lee's exposition is sloppy, the characters' motivation erratic. (Why does Constantine tolerate Arius, whom he knows from the outset to be a traitor?) The plot turns on having father and son love the same woman,

[1] Both documents are cited in *The London Stage*, Part 1, p. 310.

[2] Monmouth was a touchy subject, and an attack on him brought Mrs. Behn to grief in August 1682. Her epilogue to the anonymous *Romulus and Hersilia; or The Sabine War* suggests that death is too good a fate for one who rebels against a king and father. Having thus 'reflected on yᵉ Duke of Monmouth' both Behn and Lady Slingsby, who spoke the piece, were thrown in jail (Newdigate Newsletters). The play itself, though dubbed 'a swinging Tory Play' in Mrs. Behn's prologue, is routine love and honour posturing, in prose and discouraged semi-verse, and is political only by a strong effort of imaginative extrapolation.

Fausta. A happy ending is worked out, with the heroes saved and Arius deposited in the poisoned bath he had prepared for others. But the play deserved its quick extinction.

The last of these political plays is Dryden's opera-masque, *Albion and Albanius* (analysed above in Chapter 5). Dryden supplies in allegory a Tory history of the Restoration period, an elaborate compliment designed for Charles II and finally publicly presented for James II. The piece was in preparation in the summer of 1684; had been rehearsed by 1 January 1685; was delayed by Charles's death in February; and was pre-mièred on 3 June—'a very Unlucky Day', Downes observes, 'being the Day the *Duke* of *Monmouth*, Landed in the *West*: The Nation being in a great Consternation, it was perform'd but Six times, which not Answering half the Charge they were at, Involv'd the Company very much in Debt' (p. 40). Edward Bedingfield says in a letter that the United Company 'advance 4,000 *l.* on the opera'—a mind-boggling sum—and hence had 'set the boxes at a guyny a place, and the Pitt at halfe'.[1] This was more than double the usual prices. The fiasco helps explain the rarity of operas in the eighties.

The pathetically inclined specimens of these years include two banned plays by Banks. *The Island Queens* (described above in Chapter 5), on the death of Mary Queen of Scots, was pub-lished in 1684 'in Defence of the Author and the Play . . . occasion'd by its being prohibited the Stage'. It was finally acted (with changes) in 1704. Another such example of female pathos is Banks's Jane Grey tragedy, *The Innocent Usurper* (see Chapter 5), never performed at all.[2] Crowne's *Darius* (April 1688) was barely acted: Mrs Barry fell ill the first day, and left after the third act. In his dedication Crowne laments this misfortune, and expresses his regret that he 'medled with Tragedy; for there is nothing more plain, than that the humor of the present Age runs quite to another extreme'. The play is a feeble reflection of the old heroic mode, with strong

[1] Cited in *The London Stage*, Part 1, p. 334.

[2] Its date of composition is questionable. Banned in April 1692, it was published in the spring of 1694, with a dedication dated 5 October 1693 in which Banks com-plains of the prohibition; claims that 'it was written Ten Years since, just as it is now, without one tittle of Alteration'; and denies any 'intent to pattern with these Times'. The style does not belie the claim for composition *c.* 1683, but where the claim is an attempt to evade political charges, it must be considered suspect.

pathetic leanings. It verges on the topic of Lee's *The Rival Queens*, and the contrast in handling is telling. We begin with Darius defeated and his family captured: following treason and misfortune he is murdered. However his ghost is pleased to see 'the Carcasses of *Bessus* and *Nabarzanes* [his murderers]... hung in Chains, and stuck with Darts' (69). The main story is rather flat. In a more powerful sub-plot we are given a standard triangle: father kills son; gets killed himself; girl kills herself. Crowne wrote while sick, and the play seems weary.

Mountfort's *The Injur'd Lovers* (February 1688), his first effort, is a much more vigorous piece of work. (See above Chapter 5.) Gildon tells us it was no great success, but as a sample of the bloodbath and pity mode it is lively enough. Mountfort was unlucky in being a few years ahead of audience taste, for this sort of thing flourished anew in the mid-nineties: *The Royal Mischief* and *Cyrus the Great* are examples already noted. Love and friendship complications (including a Steeleish reconciliation of friends—29), the King's rape of Antelina (37–8), and the eventual slaughter of all the principal characters allow for a mingling of horror and pathos highly characteristic of the vogue to come. The way in which the heroic pathos plays of the nineties represent an outgrowth of the old Carolean heroic mode is interestingly demonstrated in Rochester's adaptation of Fletcher's *Valentinian* (staged by February 1684).[1] J. H. Wilson has shown that the alterations represent a desire for tighter focus and unity, but also a marked heightening of heroic sentiment and the kind of love interest common in rhymed heroic plays.[2] But the treatment of the rape of the virtuous Lucina by Valentinian gives the

---

[1] The date of composition is uncertain, but is plainly much earlier than this The B.M. MS. (Add. MS. 28,692, ff. 3a—59a) gives an intended cast for a King's Company production *c.* 1675–6. See *The London Stage*, Part 1, p. 238.

[2] 'Rochester's *Valentinian* and Heroic Sentiment', *ELH*, iv (1937), 265–73. Wilson's further suggestion ('Satiric Elements in Rochester's *Valentinian*', *Philological Quarterly*, xvi (1937), 41–8) that Rochester 'intended Valentinian as a portrait of Charles II, and that his own personality was reflected in the character of Maximus, the philosophical-minded favorite of the Roman emperor' seems no more than a speculative hypothesis. The satire—if any—cannot have been too disturbing, since Charles had the piece played at court. For an excellent discussion of Rochester's attack on popular concepts of kingship and social order, see Carole Fabricant, 'Rochester's *Valentinian* and the Subversion of the Augustan Hierarchy', forthcoming.

play obvious affinities with a piece like *The Injur'd Lovers*, despite Rochester's heroic inclinations.

Pattern tragicomedy is a mode related to, and often partaking of, the pathetic. Hence to find some examples of that form in the mid-eighties is no surprise. Southerne's second play, *The Disappointment* (April 1684), dubbed only 'A Play', is of this sort. Dodds calls it a sentimental problem drama.[1] Alphonso is jealous of Alberto's attention to his wife, Erminia; his sensible friend Lorenzo averts a bloody dénouement. In a related sub-plot Alberto pursues Angelline (daughter of humorous old Rogero), but he is finally induced to marry his slighted mistress Juliana, and Angelline is left for Lorenzo. In form, this plot might suit a comedy, but the handling is serious. Southerne gives us blank verse and no wit. Lorenzo and Angelline are exemplary characters; Erminia, wronged but noble, faithful, and patient is an almost heroic heroine. The social scale is decidedly domestic, rather than heroic, but the serious morality is reminiscent of the early Spanish romance, or of bourgeois tragedy like *The Orphan*. The virtuous characters and near approaches to death would make the piece very sombre, were it not for Rogero's appalling concubine, supposedly his wife and Angelline's mother. The sardonic picture of her attempt to bewhore her 'daughter' has seemed discordant to some critics: Dodds finds the piece 'a *pot-pourri* of widely diverse elements'. Such combinations are, however, to become a habit with Southerne, and he comes to use them with increasing thematic skill.

Durfey's *The Banditti, or A Ladies Distress. A Play* (c. January 1686) and Tate's adaptation of *The Island-Princess* (April 1687) are similar stuff. Durfey's play, much more high-flown than his norm, was a complete failure and is dedicated 'To the extream Witty and Judicious Gentleman, Sir *Critick-Cat-call*'. The mode is Spanish intrigue comedy, here focusing on the ultimate reclamation of a strayed gallant, Don Diego, who designs to turn bandit in order to rob his supposed father. Despite the play's miscarriage, Durfey had a very precise audience in mind. The prologue appeals to the Ladies (in the boxes) to support a non-smutty play against the gallants (in the pit).

[1] John Wendell Dodds, *Thomas Southerne, Dramatist* (New Haven, Conn., 1933), pp. 48–9.

But in this instance, smarmy sentiment could not save a dud. Tate's reprise of Fletcher's play, an Italian court tragicomedy, is an exemplary-minded romantic melodrama. Tate's changes in this hardy perennial (to be picked up by Motteux a decade later) are designed to shorten, simplify, and especially to purify—clearly a sign of the times, as is the dedicatory assertion that 'the design of my Authors . . . was to shew transcendent Vertue, Piety and Constancy successful.' The adaptation, as Christopher Spencer points out, is actually wrought upon the anonymous 1668 version (pub. 1669), and so makes an especially interesting example of updating.[1] Perhaps another sign of times to come is the publisher's inclusion of an advertisement for a miracle face cream (p. 56), a touch which looks toward the increasing hucksterism associated with the drama around the end of the century.

The serious drama, in brief, is in none too healthy a state in the mid-eighties. Comedy is doing better, though not flourishing. Little experimental work is done: we will find a stray political comedy; some isolated sex comedies; some routine intrigue pieces and adaptations. The rise of farce is the most striking development of the mid-eighties. Still, the increasingly 'pure' tone of several of the adaptations and intrigue plays foreshadows the exemplary trend which becomes more explicit after *The Squire of Alsatia*.

Crowne's *City Politiques* falls into this period only by virtue of political interference. Banned in June 1682, it was allowed the following January after the Tory triumph was secure. The piece is a sex farce designed, through a thin Neopolitan disguise, as a personal satire and political comment. In my opinion, this gay, racy, biting romp is Crowne's finest play, good though *Sir Courtly Nice* is. Titus Oates is delightfully savaged as Dr. Sanchy, as is Stephen College in the Bricklayer. Other identifications are more questionable. Bartoline and Lucinda have been taken (perhaps wrongly) as Sir John Maynard and his young wife. The poetical fop Craffy, busy writing answers to *Absalom and Achitophel* and *The Medal*, is perhaps Samuel Pordage.[2] Wilson feels that Rochester is

---

[1] *Nahum Tate*, pp. 108–9.

[2] John Harold Wilson has a good discussion of these problems in his Regents Restoration Drama edition (1967).

depicted in the debauched Artall; I would opt for Florio, the 'penitent' who pretends to be dying of the diseases contracted in his career as a debauchee. Whichever is the case, 'Libels may prove costly things' as Crowne's note to the reader ruefully observes. A contemporary report tells us that 'Mr Crowne was cudgled on Wednesday last in St Martin's Lane and hee that beat him said hee did it at the suite of [i.e. on behalf of] the Earle of Rochester some time since deceased who was greatly abused in the play for his penetency &c.'[1] The whole piece has a driving energy nowhere else present in Crowne's work.

The Newdigate Newsletters describe the play perfectly:

a Lᵈ Mayor Sheriffs & some Aldermen with their wives in yʳ usuall formalityes buffoond & Reviled a great Lawyer with his young Lady Jeared and Intreagued Dr Oates pfectly represented berogued & beslaved the papist plott Egregiously Rediculed the Irish Testemonyes Contradictiorily disproved & befoold the Whiggs totally vanquished & undon Law and property men oreruld & there wanted nothing of Artifice in behaviour and discourse to render all those obnoxious & dispised.

John Dennis tells us that even in 1683 the play was performed only after the King intervened personally.[2] As pure sex farce the play would be good fun: the political meanings add vastly to both bite and amusement. Without doubt this is the most effective political comedy of the period. Crowne balances the 'plots' of the Whigs against the courtiers' plots on Whig wives. But despite two cuckoldings and Craffy's failed seduction of his stepmother, the play is not really very bawdy. Plot mania is well debunked. Florio reports that 'There's a *French* Fleet upon the Coast, and six of the principal Commanders lurk in the Disguise of *Pilgrims* about Mount *Vesuvio*, to burn the Town by night, and let in their Friends.' The fatuous Podesta hastily announces 'I knew all this several Hours ago', whereat Florio mutters, aside, 'I'm sure 'tis not half an Hour since I invented it'. So off the Podesta hastens, 'he knows not whether, to catch he knows not whom' (33, 35). At the end, as usual in such Tory manifestos, Charles II (represented as the Viceroy)

---

[1] Morrice Entry Book, cited in *The London Stage*, Part 1, p. 318.
[2] See *The London Stage*, Part 1, p. 318, and Dennis, *Critical Works*, II. 404-6.

asserts his authority and sweeps aside the follies of the London politicians.

Crowne's play is a sex comedy of sorts, and to find a smattering of others is no surprise. The pit still approved, whatever the Ladies might think. Otway very naturally produced a sequel to *The Souldiers Fortune*—*The Atheist* (*c.* May? 1683). In the main plot Beaugard is finally attached to the merry widow Porcia, despite frantic opposition by her brother-in-law Theodoret, and by his friend Gratian, who wants her himself. Beaugard has inherited money from an uncle; hence his father, a merry old gamester, sponges on him in a tidy reversal of common patterns. The secondary interest is a marital discord plot involving Courtine and Sylvia, whose courtship, proviso scene, and agreement to marry we follow with pleasure and approbation in the earlier play. Courtine now finds his wife nauseating and associates matrimony with impotence (II. 312). She in turn is bored with him and angry at his neglect. Otway offers no reconciliation whatever, and the profoundly ugly picture of what happens 'after' the romantic marriage with which these comedies customarily conclude has revolted most commentators on the play. Withal, the piece is tremendously energetic, full of intrigue, sword-play, and slapstick farce. The title character, Daredevil, is a blustering fake, a good humour character used too often and too long. J. H. Smith finds *The Atheist* an 'aggregate of cheap romance and cheap farce', and probably the farce is indeed excessive, especially in the conceit of the 'enchanted castle' near the end. But Otway makes an effective comment on the exaggerated romance plot by juxtaposing it as he does with the Courtine-Sylvia plot. And onto the gritty reality of a bleakly nasty world he foists a harsh, macabre gaiety which scarcely for an instant distracts one from the savage picture of reality. *The Atheist* is not as well integrated and controlled as its predecessor, but it is by no means negligible. The Courtine–Sylvia plot especially, however unpleasant, is the work of genius.

Increasing disapproval of sex comedy is manifest in the defensive epistles which preface Behn's *The Lucky Chance* (April 1686) and Sedley's *Bellamira* (May 1687). Mrs. Behn's dedication loudly trumpets the idea that plays are schools of virtue, but the preface is a noisy vindication against the charge 'That 'tis not fit for the Ladys'. Citing *City Politiques*, *The London Cuckolds*, *The Man of Mode*, *Valentinian*, and others does not, however, alter the gamey character of the play. In the main plot two young men win their ladies from the old knights they have married—the kind of romanticizing of sex that J. H. Smith so hates. Gayman gambles with Sir Cautious Fulbank: £300 against a night with Sir Cautious's new wife, Julia. Gayman wins; Sir Cautious consents to his horning, and the sex is accomplished in the dark, just offstage and with the lady unaware of the substitution (III. 270–2): she is very upset when she learns the truth. For the most part, *The Lucky Chance* is a cheerful city marriage farce, full of tricks, intrigue, and mock ghosts. But betting—successfully—on a night with a still-virgin wife is decidedly *risqué*, and the Ladies seem to have raised quite a fuss over it. Sedley's play (a development from *The Eunuch*) provoked a similar storm, and little wonder. Terence's Thais is turned into the wanton Bellamira, whose wit and infidelity has been taken by Summers as a reminiscence of the Duchess of Cleveland.[1] Her abuse of her credulous keeper, Keepwell, is a more brazen and dashing reprise of the similar situation in *Limberham*. In the notorious part of the plot, the witty Lionel wins Isabella via rape: to accept his rapturous account of his successful assault (34–5), without serious and evidently inappropriate distaste, requires a firm sense of the distinction between dramatic artifice and reality. In a third plot line, bright young Thisbe winds up marrying her guardian, Merryman, a fat, elderly, hard-drinking old Falstaff whose wit proves equal to her own in an amusing Act III proviso scene. *Bellamira* is easily Sedley's best play, but it failed to hold the stage. The flat ending aside, the piece bounces and sparkles, yet there is felt throughout the hard edge of a court wit's cynical view of human nature. This is not an angry play after the fashion of *The Plain-Dealer*, nor a bitter one like *Friendship in Fashion* or *The Atheist*. The view of man is more akin to that found in Southerne and Congreve during the next decade. But the more overtly cynical tone of *Bellamira* apparently contributed to its lack of success.

The pressures toward overt purity are evident too in some of the intrigue plays and adaptations of these years, especially

[1] *The Playhouse of Pepys*, pp. 305–6.

Ravenscroft's *Dame Dobson* (May 1683). This piece is a one-woman equivalent of *The Alchemist*, a good-humoured play in which we enjoy all the deceit and counter-plots. Dame Dobson is a quack and conjurer: finally exposed and caught, she is forgiven on account of all the genuine good she has done. Some of the scenes are highly effective—especially the famous one in which after thunder and lightning a 'body' falls down the chimney (50). Unfortunately, long, sodden speeches undercut the play's liveliness. Ravenscroft also has some trouble juggling the large number of characters.[1] In the prologue, he makes the play's basic premiss plain: no smut. *The London Cuckolds* pleased the pit, but 'some squeamish Females of renown/Made visits with design to cry it down.' Annoyed, the author has made this pure and dull. 'Chast Ladies' are informed that this is 'the Poets *Recantation* Play . . . Stick by him now, for if he finds you falter,/He quickly will his way of writing alter'.[2]

Two Durfey adaptations from Fletcher show him, as ever, trying to sniff out popular taste. *A Common-Wealth of Women* (August 1685), from *The Sea Voyage*, adds farce and foolery at the expense of serious elements in a romantic tragicomedy. A fine romance becomes a rather odd jumble. Durfey's Amazons are incongruously sex mad ('Would I were a Whore'—25), so mildly smutty references are tumbled in with the tale of kidnapping and marooning by pirates. La Mure, the 'Vilainous' French pirate, is entertainingly presented, in predictable dialect, and the Amazons' unruly Commonwealth is made amusing. Altogether the plot is patchy, the characters feeble, the bits of satire lacking in conviction. In parts, Durfey makes the play work effectively (e.g. the 'cannibal' scene—30–3), but the lack of any over-all sense of purpose, or even outlook, robs

---

[1] *Dame Dobson* has nineteen named characters. One effect of the Union in 1682 is to increase cast size. Several of the last King's Company productions (e.g. *Thyestes*) seem almost desperately spare, written for an absolute minimum of persons. After the Union the desire to employ a maximum number of actors produces both some examples of overstuffing (*Dame Dobson* is one) and some rich panoramas (e.g. *The Squire of Alsatia*).

[2] Perhaps a sense of the demand for this sort of 'pure' intrigue comedy accounts for the revival (c. September 1684) of *The Mistaken Beauty*, an anonymous translation from Corneille put on by the King's Company in the sixties. Steele later used the same source to good effect in his severely moral *Lying Lover* (1703), but as it stands the earlier translation seems an odd choice for a revival by the United Company.

the play of the cohesion which its pretensions to satire seem to demand. *A Fool's Preferment* (April 1688) follows the failure of *The Banditti* and tries to have things both ways. Sprague is much offended by the 'consistent and deliberate addition of filth',[1] yet at the end Durfey introduces exaggerated, almost ridiculous repentance and morality. The central device is simple: Cocklebrain, a foolish country gentleman, is kept in town by the stratagems of his dissipated wife Aurelia, a jilt and basset player. (The satire on card sharping in Act II is excellent.) Finally Aurelia runs out of the tricks and stunts which give the play its substance, and at the end she kneels to her husband, promises to be a good wife, and returns to the country. A reader can hardly help thinking ahead to the design of the Vanbrugh–Cibber *Provok'd Husband* (1728). From the defensive dedication, tender about charges of obscenity, we can deduce that the final moral flourish was not enough.

To understand why one somewhat smutty play passes without apparent objection while another rouses a storm of criticism appears to be impossible. Clearly chronology makes a difference: audiences get a lot fussier between the time of *The Souldiers Fortune* or *The London Cuckolds* and *The Lucky Chance* or *Bellamira* later in the decade. Curiously enough, audiences both in the eighties and later in the period are much more tolerant of the *risqué* in an older play than in a new one. Thus in the mid- and later eighties *The Amorous Widow*, *The Rover*, *The Souldiers Fortune*, and *City Politiques* are stock plays, performed with every evidence of continuing success, at the very time that racy *new* plays are running into increasingly heated opposition. The same odd double standard is even clearer around 1700.

The popularity of Crowne's *Sir Courtly Nice* (May 1685), quite a chaste play, is clearly a sign of the times. It is light-hearted Spanish romance, adapted from the same original as *Tarugo's Wiles* at the suggestion of Charles II. Crowne's epilogue makes explicit his decision to abandon 'all that lewdness' found in recent plays. His handling of a classic plot is neat and economical. Jealous Lord Belguard employs Hothead, Testimony, and an amorous old aunt to guard his sister Leonora, who is designed for Sir Courtly, but manages to

---

[1] *Beaumont and Fletcher*, pp. 238–44.

marry the wealthy Farewel. Belguard is united with Violante (also courted by the churlish Surly); the aunt (masked) is mistakenly carried off by Sir Courtly. Crack, the Tarugo-figure, a dizzy schemer, provides chaos and passes himself off as a crazy foreign heir. Thus every detail is tried and true, yet the results are a delight. Sir Courtly is the most pleasing fop since Sir Fopling Flutter: significantly, he is an amiable fool, quite unlike the Foppington breed. Sir Courtly sends his linen to Holland to be washed and cannot stand the thought of wine —made, after all, from grapes squashed by the naked feet of clowns. But he is ineffectual, and so harmless. The whole play bubbles with good humour. Crowne manages to ring fine changes on standard devices. The juxtaposition of Sir Courtly with Surly is especially effective. When Sir Courtly is finally goaded to challenge his tormenter, Surly promptly exercises his choice of weapons—a squirt (40). The intrigue is routine but brisk, the fop scenes superb. The play has, however, a vein of serious romance. Farewel and Leonora are no gay couple: the romantic purity of their discussion of a possible elopement (42–3) is to be taken at face value. In its balance of elements, *Sir Courtly Nice* might almost be a throwback to the sixties. In this, it is atypical, but certainly it does signal a move away from the tastes of the seventies.

The principal and most conspicuous development in comic play types is the farce boom. Of the half-dozen plays involved, the later trio are the real indication of a trend, but their predecessors are a good hint of the direction in which audience taste was felt to be swinging. Lacy's *Sir Hercules Buffoon* (June 1684), though decidedly *sui generis*, belongs in this progression if anywhere. Lacy, a King's Company man, died on 17 September 1681, and the play has no logical chronological place in terms of events at that time. The decision to mount it in 1684 makes sense on two counts: exemplary morals and riotous farce are, incongruously, the main features of the work, and both are coming into vogue. The weirdly melodramatic main plot line has Sir Marmaduke Seldin persuade his daughters (Mariana and Fidelia) to connive at the marooning of his wealthy wards (Belmaria and Innocentia, heirs to £300,000) so that the daughters can pass as the heiresses. But the virtuous daughters work secretly to save their cousins. Most of the action, however, turns on the silly frolics of Sir Hercules, a lover of wit and lying, and his uncle and son. Mariana is married to the wealthy Lord Arminger, who becomes the new guardian to the wards; Fidelia is contracted to Squire Buffoon, thus uniting the plots after a fashion. But the combination of cheap farce humour (e.g. 7–8) with melodrama (Mariana is stabbed by her irritated father—43) is too disjunct to let the play work.

Two farcical adaptations by Tate point the way toward the later Jevon, Behn, and Mountfort farces. *A Duke and no Duke* (August 1684), from Cokain's *Trappolin Suppos'd a Prince* (1658), was a great success and can be considered the seminal work in the new farce genre. In the second edition of the play, following Dryden's protests against farce in the preface to *Cleomenes*, Tate added 'A Preface concerning *Farce*', largely borrowed without acknowledgement from Mariscotti.[1] However unoriginal the facts and arguments, Tate's aim is clear. As Scouten observes, he badly wants to justify the form against charges that it is 'new', and hence piles up page after page on the 'classical descent' of farce, with special reference to Aristophanes and Plautus. Like Edward Howard, Tate is glad to be able to cite Jonson's extravagances. He realizes very clearly that the defining basis of farce is an anti-realistic element with which most moderns are uncomfortable. 'Comedy properly so called, is an Imitation of Humane Life . . . and subsists upon Nature; . . . whereas the business of Farce extends beyond Nature and Probability.' Hence the 'nicest Judgment' is needed, since 'Extravagant and monstrous Fancies are but sick Dreams'. The *farceur*, he argues, must employ moderate improbabilities, which surprise and please the audience while establishing a view of the subjects which provokes fresh thought about them. *A Duke and no Duke*, with its mocking references to *A King and No King* and take-offs of the heroic, is a careless but highly entertaining play. The central conceit is simple: Trappolin is magically transformed to look like the absent Duke, imprisons the Duke's advisers, and so forth. Finally the two 'Dukes' meet, and after the predictable contretemps, the magician tidies matters up. Dryden's *Amphitryon* is a comparable, if more sophisticated fantasy. Tate's second adaptation, also

[1] Quarto of 1693. See Arthur H. Scouten, 'An Italian Source for Nahum Tate's Defence of Farce', *Italica*, xxvii (1950), 238–40.

openly designated 'A Farce', is *Cuckolds-Haven* (July 1685), from *Eastward Ho!*, plus bits of *The Devil is an Ass*. The piece is amusing, superficial, and mildly bawdy. Here Tate remains closer to the form and concerns of Carolean comedy: hence the complete lack of any resolution is more bothersome. Isolated passages are extremely funny, especially the final prison scene (an excellent parody) and the exposure of Security's apparatus for foaming at the mouth. The piece failed, however. Tate complained about the unavailability of Nokes to play Alderman Touchstone, a part written for him. We may guess too that the sexual bent of the plot was unseasonable.

The form of *A Duke and no Duke* is picked up in Jevon's *The Devil of a Wife, or a Comical Transformation* (March 1686), a highly successful and influential play.[1] The central device is simple: Sir Richard Lovemore's wife is a ghastly shrew; by enchantment she is made to change places with the cobbler Jobson's wife; after she has been sufficiently humbled, the charm is undone, she confesses her former ill ways, and all propose to live happily ever after. The contrast between the two women in their unaccustomed circumstances is made pointed and amusing, but the whole piece is extremely light. As the mocking preface, addressed to 'the Grave, Learned, Judicious, and Deliberate', makes plain, Jevon did not take himself seriously: the wild frolic he concocts (e.g. 21–2, 44) is played only for laughs. The magic element, however, seems to have been a pleasant and popular device. Peregrine Bertie's reaction is revealing: 'To day is acted Jevarns' new farse; Thursday was the first day. I must confess it is the strangest thinge I ever saw; 'twas mighty full the last time, and to day there is noe getting in.'[2]

Mrs. Behn's *The Emperor of the Moon: A Farce* (March 1687) gives the form another major boost. In mode, the play is a crossing of Ravenscroft's *The Citizen Turn'd Gentleman* and *Scaramouch a Philosopher* with Behn's own *2 Rover* and the more strictly farce type cultivated in *A Duke and no Duke* and *The Devil of a Wife*. Behn's dedication directly challenges objections to farce, without ever quite explaining its virtues

---

[1] It serves as the basis for *The Devil to Pay* (1731), which held the stage into the middle of the nineteenth century and was reprinted in more than fifty editions.

[2] Letter of 6 March 1686, cited in *The London Stage*, Part 1, p. 348.

beyond light amusement. Here, as in *2 Rover*, we see the new 'Italian-style' farce, a dazzling mixture of knockabout, fantasy, pageantry, romance, song and show. The more traditional sort of 'French' or 'English' farce, never a respectable form and never advertised openly as a form, we have seen in *The Old Troop*, *The Woman-Captain*, and Behn's own *False Count*. Despite the diversity of elements in *The Emperor of the Moon*, Behn achieves excellent over-all unity. The daughter and niece of the moon-mad Dr. Baliardo are courted by two gentlemen, who have to pretend to be Emperor of the Moon and Prince of Thunderland, respectively. Scaramouch and Harlequin are servants involved in the plotting, and both court the duenna Mopsophil. The operatic spectacle demands extremely fancy staging: we see the moon shift from new to full (III. 457); Emperor and Prince appear in a flying chariot—the Emperor's train held by four cupids (458). Such Dorset Garden spectacle is mixed with simpler fare: Harlequin in female dress (430), the famous trick cart (436–7), Harlequin tossed in a blanket (448), and the grand duel for Mopsophil (460). The play has more dazzle than substance, but is great fun and well deserved its long success.

The final document in this progress of farce is Mountfort's adaptation, *The Life and Death of Doctor Faustus, Made into a Farce* (*c.* March 1688).[1] The title-page adds: 'With the Humours of *Harlequin* and *Scaramouche*'. In his hands, the work becomes a catalogue of foolery. We are offered thunder and lightning (2); a giant who flies into pieces (13–14);[2] a flying table (14); Harlequin using 'a Chamber-pot of Piss, and a Lamp of Oyl' to make a salad dressing (15); the pantomimers caught in trick chairs and squirted with milk by devils (16; cf. *The Citizen Turn'd Gentleman*); the horse-courser pulling Faustus's leg off (17); a magic wand; horns grown on Benoolio's head (20)—and so forth. At the end, Faustus's limbs are torn asunder, but in Hell they rejoin, and Mountfort concludes with 'A Dance, and Song' (26). The staging tricks put even *The Lancashire Witches* to shame. Mountfort's *Faustus* is the grand culmination of the farce boom, neatly combining magic, machinery, pantomime, and horseplay: what it aims to do, it does well.

[1] See my 'The Date of Mountfort's *The Life and Death of Doctor Faustus*', forthcoming in *Archiv*.   [2] Reused from *2 Rover* and *Dame Dobson*.

III. THE PASSING OF THE CAROLEAN PERIOD

Because there is no sharp break in continuity, one may easily underestimate the drastic changes in drama and the theatrical climate during the eighties. Many of the same writers continue active (Dryden, Shadwell, Crowne, Durfey, Ravenscroft), and the plays of the seventies continue to be popular. But the character of the new plays changes greatly. Generic trends are harder to follow here than in the seventies: the fact that there are fewer plays makes the trends seem more tenuous. The full extent of the change during the eighties is apparent only when the plays of 1678 are set against those of 1688. One can, of course, similarly contrast the plays of 1668 with those of 1678, but with this difference: in the seventies the drama seems to be fulfilling an inherent potential, working in a natural direction from the potentialities developed in the sixties. In the eighties a reversal of direction is obvious: new types are being tentatively explored while the achievements of the seventies are suffering rejection.

Amidst the welter of particular plays, two generic modes stand out as quintessentially Carolean: the heroic play and the social sex comedy. Neither form is anything like monolithic, yet during the seventies both seem, in retrospect, to represent a special synthesis, achievement, and outlook characteristic of the time. Spanish romance, 'French' farce, horror tragedy, and other types are popular, but none seems so specially related to the period of Charles II. By the later seventies, however, both heroic drama and sex comedy were dying a natural death. The uproar of the Popish Plot and the flurry of political plays temporarily mask movements in generic type, and the quiet eighties produce deceptively sparse evidence. Nonetheless, two basic developments are unmistakably plain. (1) Serious drama becomes increasingly *affective*, though during the eighties one gets only a limited sense of the full potentialities of pathos. The move into the pathetic is clearly signalled in the later seventies. (2) In comedy, a gradual move toward a new, purer type is evident.

The development of a pathetic drama after 1675 has long been recognized, albeit in over-simplified terms. An understanding of the major trends in comedy has been much slower

to develop, largely on account of assumptions about a dominant and monolithic comedy of manners. The first major
step toward clarifying exactly what does happen was taken by
J. H. Smith in his 'Shadwell, the Ladies, and the Change in
Comedy' (1948), an article drawing on his work on the gay
couple. Much can be added to the picture Smith gives, but his
basic conclusion is entirely sound: during the eighties one can
see the beginning of what ultimately becomes defined as
'exemplary' comedy. And what we see is not the replacement
of social sex comedy by a new mode, but rather the establishment of a new comic method as a 'rival' form. Smith is perhaps
inclined to overstate the 'newness' of exemplary method, for as
we have seen, it was already popular and viable in the early
sixties; and in Spanish romance, heroic comedy, and pattern
tragicomedy it had continued popular ever since. But we do
see both the domestication of exemplary method in an imposing
number of London comedies, and growing restiveness about
the *risqué*. *The Squire of Alsatia* (May 1688), as Smith rightly
saw, is one of the most crucial plays in the whole period for
an understanding of generic developments. (It is analysed in
detail in Chapter 3, above.) Shadwell's play is a long way
from Steele's notion of exemplary method: Belfond jun.'s
seducing, paying off, and abandoning an innocent bourgeois
girl would be unthinkable in an exemplary model of reformation a few years later. But Shadwell's fiercely didactic point, and
the play's fantastic popularity, certainly tell us a lot about
generic directions.

The appearance of a viable 'London' comedy with an exemplary bent should not blind us to either the tentativeness
of the new type, or to the continuing power of the older social
sex comedy. The growing audience objection to sex in plays
like *The Lucky Chance* or *Bellamira* can be overstressed: numerous
sex comedies flourish in the nineties, and a quasi-exemplary
play like *The Banditti* could get cat-called off the stage in
1686. Sex comedy takes several forms: cynical libertine display
(*The Man of Mode*); satire (*Friendship in Fashion, The Princess
of Cleve*); sex farce (*A Fond Husband*). During the eighties
objections to what J. H. Smith calls brutal free gallantry
change the formula for 'acceptable' new sex comedies: sex in the
form of farce (*The London Cuckolds*) or satire (*The Atheist*) was

generally more acceptable than libertine sex of the sort portrayed in *Bellamira*.

Comedy with a healthy dose of sex was far from dead, as the nineties were to prove. The immense success of *Sir Courtly Nice* and *The Squire of Alsatia* is, however, clear proof of a growing vogue for pure comedy, and in particular for 'London' comedy which displays purity in a noble and admirable way that was once largely the province of Spanish romance and pattern tragicomedy. Plainly the audience was changing: thirty years had passed since the Restoration, and the political upheavals of the eighties contributed to the rapid dissolution of whatever remained of the old 'coterie', such as it was.

Shadwell's comment in the prologue to *The Squire of Alsatia* is extremely telling:

> Our Poet found your gentle Fathers kind,
> And now some of his works your favour find.
> He'll treat you still with somewhat that is new,
> But whether good or bad, he leaves to you.
> Baudy the nicest Ladies need not fear,
> The quickest fancy shall extract none here.

Shadwell's sense of addressing a *new* audience is plain. (This is his first play in seven years.) He is glad that his older plays still please—*The Virtuoso* and *Epsom-Wells* had recently been revived—but hastens to assure the Ladies of his consideration for their preferences. Given the Belfond jun.–Lucia plot, the disavowal of bawdy may seem disingenuous. It indicates, probably, the degree to which 'bawdy' was thought of in purely verbal terms—and of course Shadwell can feel virtuous about his explicitly didactic reclamation of a sower of wild oats. Shadwell is always a bell-wether, and hence *The Squire* is a striking indication of his sense of trends. Starting out with what seems designed as a satiric comedy of sex and gulling, Shadwell twists his materials into an avowedly exemplary display.

> He to correct, and to inform did write:
> If Poets aim at naught but to delight,
> Fidlers have to the Bays an equal right.

Shadwell complains bitterly about the popularity of Farce, Machines, and Decoration: as at the beginning of the seventies, we will soon find a reaction, a move to re-establish and develop 'true' comedy.

During the middle eighties one gets a remarkable sense of indirection in the theatre. The conservative stance of the United Company contributes greatly to this drift. Scanty as the new offerings are, though, two varieties of social comedy are increasingly discernible. One we may call *hard* comedy, a continuation of the satiric and sex comedy types popular in the seventies; the other may be dubbed *humane* comedy, and rests on a much more sympathetic view of its subjects. The result of this dichotomy is the dual comic tradition of the nineties.

CHAPTER 9

THE DOUBLE TRADITION
OF THE NINETIES

EMERGING from virtual paralysis in the later 1680s, the
theatre strikes out vigorously in contradictory directions
during the busy and increasingly stormy nineties. In play
types two trends are obvious: (1) initially the comedy splits
sharply between the hard and humane schools; (2) simultaneously, serious drama enjoys a considerable resurgence—in
quantity if not in quality. After 1688 the United Company
doubles, trebles, and once nearly quadruples its annual quota
of new plays, which had been averaging only about three per
year. Following the Lincoln's Inn Fields breakaway in 1695
the total soars. In 1695 (a partial year, owing to Queen Mary's
death) there are 15 new plays; in 1696 and 1697 we will find
21 each year.

Despite this tremendous activity the theatre is far from
healthy. Management problems and internal dissension are
part of the trouble. Alexander Davenant (a crook) partially
supplanted the stable, competent, and successful Betterton–
Smith management in 1687, ran himself and the company
into financial trouble, and fled the country in 1693, leaving
the actors to the tender mercies of his money-lender, Christopher
Rich. Rich's attempt to squeeze out expensive star actors and
replace them with inexpensive beginners was one of the major
causes of the Lincoln's Inn Fields secession.[1] The competition
which followed was bitter and cut-throat in a fashion never
before experienced in this period. There was genuine ill will
between the two houses, and neither was ever secure and
profitable.

The principal problem for the theatres (other than mismanagement and theatrical warfare) seems to have been
finding and holding an audience. The Carolean theatres had

---

[1] See the 'Petition of the Players' (c. November 1694) against Rich and his partner Skipwith, L.C. 7/3, rpt. (in part) by Nicoll, I. 368–70.

relied on an audience that was far more than a coterie, but was definitely Court-oriented. Dramatists looked to Court patronage and interest for support. James II was less help than Charles II, and Queen Mary provided still less assistance.[1] After her death in December 1694, Court interest in the drama was essentially nil. The old audience was dying off, and the 'court wit' circle was gone. As we will see very clearly at the end of the decade, the theatres were floundering as they tried to find an audience—changing curtain-time, offering variety shows and double bills, experimenting with singers, dancers, and jugglers as entr'acte attractions.

Even the spate of new plays after 1689 is more a hectic flush than a sign of a vigorous theatre. As the prologue to Mountfort's *Greenwich-Park* (April 1691) remarks, unsettled conditions had the United Company scrambling just to survive:

> Hard have we toil'd this Winter for new Plays,
> That we might live in these Tumultuous Days.

In the new comedy we can see an effort to please an audience which did not care for the libertine ethic of Carolean sex comedy. This shift in sensibility is symptomatic of a change in general moral climate. The rise of the S.P.C.K., and the outcry of 'the Ladies' against smut, are warnings of the coming storm. The thunderclap provided by Jeremy Collier did not come out of the blue. Withal, even in these troubled circumstances, we will find an abundance of fine plays.

I. THE NEW COMEDY AND THE OLD 1689–1694

This half-decade is a good period for comedy, and a most interesting one. In these years come the last comedies of Dryden and Shadwell, Southerne at his peak, and the first plays of the young Congreve, as well as solidly competent work from Durfey and Crowne. For the first time in a decade the new comedies display a clear sense of possible purposes and directions. The chaotic indirection of the comic types after the

---

[1] Habits die hard. Twice in the nineties Dryden, discussing the possibility of competing with French drama, says wistfully that it could be done if a really fancy theatre were built and maintained 'at a King's charges' (*Critical Essays*, II. 161, 200). This was wishful thinking, of course: William III had not even a tepid interest in English drama.

collapse of the sex boom *c.* 1678 gives way to an almost schematically neat division between the 'new' humane comedy and the 'old' hard comedy. As we have seen in the eighties, quasi-exemplary comedy is a long time developing. Its roots are in the tragicomedies and Spanish romances of the sixties; signs of the coming change are all over relatively 'pure' plays like *Sir Courtly Nice* (1685) or *The Banditti* (1686), and the moral trumpetings of *The Squire of Alsatia* (1688). But the old comedy is not dead yet. Indeed, it is just beginning its second great period, a resurgence which carries it at least to the heights attained in the seventies. For a number of years, then, two quite distinct concepts of comedy compete, and most playwrights seem to feel the attractions of both.

The crucial distinction between the two turns on an intangible factor—the attitude of the playwright towards his material, especially his lead characters. Admiration, sympathy, and respect for a comic protagonist produce a remarkably different work than do detachment, scepticism, and irony—not to mention hostility and contempt. *Hard comedy* may be cutting, cynical, and libertine (*The Old Batchelour*), or more engaged with and concerned for the subjects (*The Wives Excuse*)—but whether contemptuous, sardonic, bitter, or merely condescendingly amused, the ways of the world are accepted as inevitable. *Humane comedy* is much more sympathetic. Faults are less harshly judged; and without often going to the extreme of maintaining that uncorrupted human nature is intrinsically good, writers are able to acknowledge a basic goodness in individuals—as even Vanbrugh does, so surprisingly, in *The Relapse*. Humane comedy is much more tolerant, less critical. And obviously it is easily extended into the overtly exemplary. Indeed, after 1700 we will find it sorting itself out into three groups, ordinary 'soft' intrigue comedy, the more didactic 'reform' comedy, and Steele's truly exemplary comedy—the last always a rarity.

The old comedy exists both as a carryover and as a deliberate attempt under Dryden's sponsorship to revive and advance the Carolean mode. Southerne and Congreve were his instruments, but they are best approached through Dryden himself and some miscellaneous throwbacks.

Dryden's delightful *Amphitryon* (October 1690) is a greatly underrated play. The reasons for its neglect are several. First, it is a farce. Second, it draws heavily on Molière and Plautus, and the dependency is often overestimated. Third, it is a distinctly unrefined play: the indelicacy is not extraordinary, but the speech is racy, coarse, and colloquial: Dryden eschews the courtly polish which so pleases manners-comedy critics. And fourth, the play is flippantly cynical, right through to its concluding 'moral':

> In fine, the Man, who weighs the matter fully,
> Wou'd rather be the Cuckold, than the Cully.

Amphitryon is too uncomplicated to need critical explication. It is, however, one of the most entertaining farces of the whole period.

Amphitryon draws heavily on machines. As the play opens, '*Mercury* and *Phœbus* descend in several Machines.' And Purcell's fine songs (the music is printed with the play) give it a charming extra dimension. But the use of the supernatural, of magic transformations, and of impersonation is irresistibly reminiscent of the magic-and-machine farce boom of the later eighties. *Amphitryon* is written with a lighter touch, finer wit, and vastly more appreciation of implicit issues, but it belongs to the genre of *A Duke and no Duke* and *The Devil of a Wife*. Dryden makes the play low, often verging on pure burlesque. The action is racy and farcical, with sex chat among the gods made prominent. Thus Mercury to Phœbus:

There has been a devillish Quarrel, I can tell you, betwixt *Jupiter* and *Juno*: She threaten'd to sue him in the Spiritual Court, for some Matrimonial Omissions; and he stood upon his Prerogative. Then she hit him on the Teeth of all his Bastards; and your Name and mine were us'd with less reverence than became our Godships. They were both in their Cups. . . . (VI. 153)

Or Mercury to Jupiter:

I was considering into what form your Almighty-ship would be pleas'd to transform your self to night. Whether you wou'd fornicate in the Shape of a Bull, or a Ram, or an Eagle, or a Swan . . . in short, whether you wou'd recreate your self in Feathers, or in Leather? (154–5)

Phœbus grumbles, and Mercury advises him to leave off: 'No more of your Grumbletonian Morals Brother; there's Preferment coming, be advis'd and Pimp dutifully.'

As John Loftis observes, Dryden willingly exploits the eroticism in his chosen plot, but without the deliberate grossness of *Limberham*.[1] Behind the easy ironic jokes and knockabout lurks an unmistakable theme: the abuse of power. Whether Jupiter represents Charles II (as has been suggested) scarcely matters. But in the midst of a pungent, high-spirited play Dryden introduces an astonishingly mordant view of his gods. The fantasy quality to which Loftis calls attention lightens what would otherwise seem rather nasty. So leavened, *Amphitryon* is tremendously lively and amusing, full of brilliant imaginative flights and witty satire—the mock-proviso scene being especially good. Phædra bargains 'that my Eldest Son shall be a Hero, and my Eldest Daughter a King's Mistress'. Mercury rejoins—'That is to say, a Blockhead, and a Harlot.' 'True', she says, 'but who dares call 'em so?' They proceed to provision for 'Pin-money, and Ali-money' and 'a thousand things more' (216). Cynicism lightened with high spirits give the play its unusual tone.

A much more routine example of the old comedy is John Smyth's *Win her and Take her*, produced some time in 1691—a boisterous low comedy in which people frolic and storm their way through routine antics and forced stage hilarity. The characters are reliable stand-bys. Sir John Oldfop, an ageing coxcomb; old Waspish, courting a young coquette; two young gentlemen; Dulhead, a country fool; two young women; and Lady Fancifull—a stale old maid with designs on Dulhead. Strain Conscience (a lawyer) and Donnell (a foolish Irish servant) are promising minor characters poorly handled. Here the formula never comes to life. Devices such as Oldfop and Fancifull conducting a mistaken-identity love scene in the dark (56), or Toby's easy management of his master Dulhead, are mediocre not because they are derivative, but because they are unskilfully handled. The play has more noise than comic spirit.

Durfey's *The Comical History of Don Quixote*[2] is worth a lot

---

[1] 'Dryden's Comedies', in *John Dryden*, ed. Earl Miner (London, 1972), pp. 27–57, esp. 51–6.

[2] Parts 1 and 2, May 1694; Part 3 produced by Rich's Company in November 1695.

more attention than it has received. To find Durfey with a foot
in this camp is surprising: he was a prompt imitator of
Shadwell's new comedy, as we shall see. But unlike Shadwell,
Durfey wrote without any special personal convictions. Here
he reverses the direction he had just taken in *Love for Money*
and *The Richmond Heiress*. Don Quixote is 'shown'—played
with, his 'humour' milked for all it is worth. The result is a
roistering low comedy, but one with all the vitality, bite, and
humour that *Win her* so badly lacks. Sutherland finds it
'vulgarly effective' and he is right.[1] The *Gentleman's Journal*
calls the first two parts very entertaining and reports that they
were exceptionally well received. Part III, even racier, drew a
storm of protest from the Ladies. Nicoll is certainly correct in
saying that the novel is impossible to dramatize—but Durfey
was simply in search of 'humour', as his first preface says, and
he found it. The 'indecent ditties' that outrage Nicoll I find
delightful. Clearly the low life exhibited in Part III went a lot
further than the audience would stand. Sancho's daughter,
Mary the Buxome, speaks rough, coarse comic dialogue as she
prepares for marriage, and her joyously dirty song, 'The old
Wife she sent to the Miller her Daughter . . .' (29), was unacceptable to the audience of 1695. The indecent puppet show
in Act IV was similarly beyond the pale. The whole trilogy is
vividly crude, but it teems with life, and Purcell's songs are
lovely. If we can ignore the random plot and accept the
conception of Don Quixote as a travelling freak show, there is a
lot to enjoy.

Southerne remains the most neglected of the major writers
in this period. He alone has never had a modern edition, a
desideratum soon to be supplied. With his plays readily
available, he should certainly take his place with Wycherley,
Etherege, and Congreve. The three plays to be considered
here bring Southerne to his comic peak. In *Sir Anthony Love*
(October 1690) he is finding his bearings. The piece is a jumble
of romance, adventure, and intrigue. Written for Mrs.
Mountfort, it turns on the title character, a breeches part.
Much of the appeal lies in the young woman strutting through
the play as a libertine and talking like a rakehell. In the main
action Lucia (Sir Anthony), having robbed her keeper, Sir

---

[1] Sutherland, p. 140.

Gentle Golding, chases off to France in pursuit of Valentine. With their friend Ilford, these 'rakes' pursue three French females. Sir Anthony actually 'marries' Volante—and then sends Ilford to bed with the bride. In secondary plots 'Sir Anthony' cheats her keeper out of £500 a year for life; and Palmer, a thief and pretended pilgrim, is shown up. Langbaine particularly commends the satire on religious hypocrisy. The plot is dazzlingly energetic; lusty and vivacious action combines with a fine display of wit. Morality is just not an issue. Tremendous energy and headlong pace compensate for frequent patches of over-clever wit strung out too long. Numerous sources testify to the play's 'extraordinary' success. The action is too farcical for the taste of most modern critics, and the play does go on too long. The dedication points out that it was cut for performance—one of the omissions being the scene in which an old abbé makes homosexual advances to Sir Anthony and is greatly disappointed at the discovery of her true sex. Without this scene the play is *risqué* but not particularly smutty.

Southerne was especially known in his own day for his 'language', and this reiterated comment has distracted some modern critics from the greatest virtues of his plays.[1] In *The Wives Excuse: or, Cuckolds make Themselves* (December 1691) we have a truly serious satire. The town did not care for it, the *Gentleman's Journal* tells us—but then *The Way of the World* was not popular either, so contemporary indifference is scarcely a good justification for continuing neglect. J. H. Smith calls it one of the five most considerable comedies of the whole period; Scouten and Sutherland concur; yet the piece does not appear in collections for students, and is seldom referred to by critics. This is a shame, for it is a brilliant play.[2]

As Sutherland observes, Southerne's genius lies in 'unusually acute observation of human behaviour and human motives'. In *The Wives Excuse* he 'puts the whole business of cuckolding on a psychological basis', and accounts for it, instead of just displaying it for our entertainment. Marital

---

[1] See, for example, Anthony Kaufman, ' "This Hard Condition of a Woman's Fate": Southerne's *The Wives' Excuse*', *Modern Language Quarterly*, xxxiv (1973), 36–47.

[2] See J. H. Smith, pp. 144–8; Scouten, 'Notes Toward a History of Restoration Comedy'; Sutherland, pp. 144–6. A stop-gap edition has been supplied by Ralph R. Thornton (Wynnewood, Pa., 1973).

discord is the heart of the action. Mrs. Friendall finds that she has married a coward and philanderer; and then she gets importuned by a somewhat better man. She resists Lovemore's wooing, but we are left to suppose that she will succumb and duly be abandoned. Ugly cuckolding, seduction, and intrigue plots are masked by a surface civility whose urbanity well emphasizes the hollowness of the pretence. Southerne's social satire is nastily effective, the opening scene being one of the finest in the period. We see a crowd of servants waiting outside for a concert to end; when it does they scatter and the gentry enter—saying almost exactly what the servants have been saying. In the climax of the play Friendall, a truly contemptible character, commits adultery with Mrs. Wittwoud (under the impression that she is Mrs. Sightly)—and in the middle of the proceeding he is caught *in flagrante delicto* by the whole company, including his wife: '*Scene* draws, shows *Friendall* and *Wittwoud* upon a Couch' (53). Mrs. Friendall has just been struggling to obey the demands of honour and resist Lovemore's blandishments. At the end the Friendalls agree to separate: he can philander, but she is miserably stuck in a hopeless position— and Lovemore hopes this will help him seduce her.

Only Otway and Wycherley, among Southerne's predecessors, had produced anything like so angry, ugly, and effective a satire. But the consistent satire and the acute psychology scarcely disguise the fact that it is an exceedingly disagreeable play. Southerne actually wrote himself in—as Wellvile, a sardonic, unhappy observer who is writing a play with this title. This touch aids a strong sense of the author's unhappy entrapment in a degraded society. Nicoll saw no virtues in the play, and Dodds calls it 'fetid', a 'dreary cuckolding' action marred by the presence of a 'sentimental' character in Mrs. Friendall—'sentimental', presumably, because she does not yield during the play! But here the display of free gallantry is used to attack immorality and hypocrisy—and a passage like Wilding's talk of letting Fanny leave 'Lighter by a Maidenhead', though Dorimantish, is ugly and quite without attraction or glamour.

The Maids last Prayer: or, Any, rather than Fail (February 1693) is a similar play, and a very fine one. Again, free gallantry is displayed only to be blasted. However, Nicoll says that

'Southerne sinks below even the level of *The Wives Excuse*';
Dodds agrees, complaining bitterly about this 'graceless lot of
rogues'.[1] Southerne gives us an amorous old woman in Lady
Susan Malepert; marital discord between Mrs. Siam and
Captain Drydrubb; a society whore in Lady Trickitt. The
main action is remarkably ugly. Mrs. Wishwell is prostituting
young Lady Malepert, whose husband is a vacuous cuckold.
Lady Malepert fancies Gayman, but she is given to Sir Ruff
Rancounter. Gayman takes Sir Ruff's place in a night assignation—which is quite all right with the lady when she discovers
it, since she was trying to imagine it was he anyway. The play
is splendidly brisk, an icy account of corruption, and a beautiful
example of hard comedy at its best. The dedication hints at a
so-so reception. The *Gentleman's Journal* admired the purity of
diction (of all things), but this was comedy too hard-bitten
for the mid-nineties.

Dryden had admired these plays and encouraged his
protégé, contributing ringing commendatory verses to *The
Wives Excuse*. The two of them proceeded to take Congreve
under a joint wing. *The Old Batchelour* (March 1693) may have
been written as early as 1689 and clearly shows that the young
author had done plenty of reading in Carolean comedy. As
Maximillian E. Novak suggests, he took the standard formulas
and breathed life into them—and his genius was obvious.
Southerne stood godfather; Dryden himself 'putt it in the order
it was playd', according to Southerne.[2] Thus Congreve
immediately became the protégé of the leading proponents
of hard comedy. His first play was published with a commendatory poem by Southerne explicitly hailing Congreve as the
successor to Dryden, who 'grown old in Pow'r . . . Can wish
for nothing, but a Successor'. Wycherley and Etherege have
withdrawn; Lee and Otway are dead—but 'CONGREVE
appears'. Bevill Higgons adds a poem to precisely the same
effect. Thus Congreve was immediately viewed as the great
hope of the Carolean tradition.

'The Baudy Batchelour', as the envious Henry Higden called

---

[1] Nicoll, I. 241; Dodds, pp. 77–92.

[2] See B.M. Add. MS. 4221 (341), cited in *The London Stage*, Part 1, p. 419. For an
analysis of the play, see Maximillian E. Novak, 'Congreve's *The Old Bachelor*:
From Formula to Art', *Essays in Criticism*, xx (1970), 182–99.

it, was a tremendous success. Congreve provides a Carolean-style sex comedy turned into a highly formulaic game—even the sex scenes, though beautifully done, smell of the lamp. Around themes of deception and self-delusion Congreve contrives a vigorous romp. The characters are sharply drawn, especially the old bachelor, Heartwell, who secretly loves Silvia and is dreadfully deluded in doing so: indeed he becomes an almost tragic character. The foolish cuckold Fondlewife is humanized (especially in his baby talk with his wife in Act IV) and made funny. Even Bellmour's successful seduction of Mrs. Fondlewife is taken lightly. The sceptical attitude toward love and marriage, the wry view of the whole sordid mess of characters, somehow lightened the play enough for the audience (or much of it) to be able to accept what it objected to in Southerne's nastier plays.

Congreve was not so lucky with *The Double-Dealer* (November 1693), which was coolly received. It had a respectable initial run (at least eight nights) and stayed in the repertory, but better had been expected. Dryden's verses 'To my Dear Friend Mr. Congreve', prefaced to the play, call him above Fletcher and Jonson, combining the best of Etherege, Southerne, and Wycherley: 'Heav'n that but once was Prodigal before,/To *Shakespeare* gave as much; she cou'd not give him more.' In short, Congreve is the new Shakespeare, and Dryden passes on his own 'Lawrels'. The play is no less than a deliberate resurrection of Wycherley, with obvious reference to *The Plain-Dealer*. The butts are brilliantly drawn, but as Novak observes, they do not exist just to be amusing, they are more than a Durfey-style gallery of fools.[1] The central character is the villain Maskwell, not the romantic lead Mellefont: the play is an analysis of villainy. It is actually much more moral than Congreve's first. Mellefont and Cynthia are decidedly 'good' characters, and Mellefont is kept clear of the two cuckolding plots, which are carried out by his friend Careless and a fop. Even the cuckoldings have moral import, particularly that of the foolish Sir Paul Plyant (cuckolds make themselves). The play offers a serious moral commentary on a serious theme—but it failed to take well. Dryden explained to Walsh: 'The women thinke he has exposd their Bitchery too much; & the

[1] See Novak, *William Congreve*, p. 97.

Gentlemen, are offended with him, for the discovery of their follyes: & the way of their Intrigues.'[1] This explanation seems too facile, or at least incomplete. The Ladies presumably objected to *what* was shown; the men of the pit probably objected to the negative *way* it was shown. From the high-spirited and coolly contemptuous acceptance of the world's faults and follies in *The Old Batchelour*, Congreve has moved into a decidedly more negative attitude. In the relatively realistic satire the actions are no more acceptable to the Ladies, and the Gentlemen are offered a lot less fun. Probably the play is too icily contrived: it has none of the energetic high spirits or romantic charm of *The Old Batchelour* or *Love for Love* respectively. But in any case the hard comedy attitude was proving increasingly unpalatable to the audience.

Comedies in the 'new' style are almost as numerous as those in the 'hard' style. Following *The Squire of Alsatia*, Shadwell got his exemplary formula under better control in *Bury-Fair* (*c.* April 1689). Here he uses two couples, one serious, romantic, and exemplary (Lord Bellamy and Philadelphia), one a discreetly moral gesture in the direction of the old love game (Wildish and Gertrude). Wildish talks libertinism, but is not shown indulging in it; Lord Bellamy is cultured and moral, an upholder of simple country virtues against city corruption. Philadelphia has a breeches part in the Fidelia tradition, but as J. H. Smith observes, we see here the man and woman of good sense: morals and rationality are of crucial importance in determining their actions and feelings. Withal, the play is full of bustling good humour and lots of satire, despite its exemplary bent. The country setting is refreshing. As in Jonson's *Bartholomew Fair* the central metaphor is skilfully handled, and Shadwell brings his usual verve to such ridiculous characters as Trim, the Fantasts, and the false count, La Roch.

Shadwell's last two plays do not reach this level. *The Scowrers* (*c.* December 1690) gives a lively picture of scowring rakehells, but its point is the reformation wrought in Sir William Rant by his wise and benevolent father (a believer in 'a sober Country Life'—V. 147) and the severely virtuous Eugenia, who announces bluntly that she will never take him

---

[1] *Letters*, no. 28.

'till I see a full Reformation in his Life, and Manners', advising her friend Clara: 'If they think us worth that, they will soon shew the change, if they do not, sure we shall have the sense to think them not worthy of us' (121). Dorimant would have been out of luck here. *The Volunteers, or the Stock-Jobbers* (November 1692) has some good topical satire on war-profiteering, and benefits from a lively design: its spirit however is so serious as to make it 'resemble a tract rather than a play'.[1] There is a cuckolding action, but Mrs. Hackwell is an obviously negative example, and her lover Nickum is a 'Sharper', while her husband, though more amiable, is a 'somewhat Immoral' hypocritical Anabaptist who is busy stock-jobbing. The two serious couples are sincere, impeccable in conduct, mindful of their duty to their elders—in short, people of exemplary good sense. I count nine satiric butts in the play (including a beau, Sir Nicholas Dainty; an 'ugly Sub-Beau', Sir Timothy Kastril; Nickum; the dancing-master Hop, *et al.*). Shadwell sets up a rigorously schematic contrast of positive and negative examples. Serious commitment is displayed against idle humour: thus the silly Winifred is rewarded with her ideal, the dancing-master Hop. The soldiers in the play are stoutly loyal to King William, and Shadwell goes out of his way to tout the sobriety of Williamite England against the gaiety of the Carolean cavaliers. The play came off posthumously with 'reasonable success', the *Gentleman's Journal* tells us.

Shadwell was not mounting a single-handed campaign: plays by James Carlile, Henry Higden, and Durfey follow the path he charted. Carlile's *The Fortune-Hunters* (*c.* March 1689) is called by Smith 'indicative of the arrival of a turning point'.[2] It is cheerful, reasonably moral, and a bit weighed down by heavy dialogue. Heiresses Sophia and Maria are pursued by Shamtown and Littlegad; two well-mocked beaux. The girls, despite the heavy guardian figure of Sir William Wealthy, wind up marrying sober Tom and wild Frank Wealthy. Madcap Maria traps and tames the rakish Frank (who has been 'kept by the Widdow *Sly*'); but the serious couple is given just as much prominence in the plot. Frank and Sophia could step right into Spanish romance. The play seems to have had no particular success. Higden's *The Wary Widdow: or, Sir*

---

[1] J. H. Smith, p. 142.   [2] J. H. Smith, pp. 127–8.

Noisy Parrat (March 1693) miscarried badly, and in his preface Higden storms at the 'Camelion Ladies' who went and supported the 'success of the Baudy Batchelour' and left his play in the lurch. His angry complaint that 'there cannot be a taking Play without some Limberham or fumbling Alderman, or keeper to expose' is greatly exaggerated, but is a good hint that sex comedy was not dead yet. Higden's play is a ham-handed imitation of late Shadwell. The ideas are not bad, but the execution is poor: speeches are much too long and heavy, and the play quickly sinks under them. The plot is simple: rich, spritely Lady Wary likes the rakish Frank Fox, tests his claim to honour, and rewards him when he passes the test.[1]

Durfey's exemplary comedies did better. *Love for Money* (January 1691) is a strenuously energetic play: Durfey carefully leavened his exemplary characters with boisterous low-life characters and scoundrels. Like Shadwell, he makes this formula work. Young Merriton sees Mirtilla's virtues; she refuses him because she is poor—but she turns out to be an heiress, so all ends well. Old Merriton, 'honest, religious, conscientious', is one of the exemplary fathers who are becoming so common. In a contrasting plot line the mercenary Betty Jiltall (whose motto is the play's title) does a thorough job of cheating Jack Amorous, who comes to see the error of his womanizing ways. Betty, as an 'heiress', marries Sir Rowland Rakehell, a vicious old man who has made £3,000 a year by cheating an infant orphan. Thus poetic justice is served. *The Richmond Heiress* (April 1693) is a much preachier and less entertaining play.[2] For once there are no marriages. Fulvia (heiress to £50,000) is pursued by Frederick, who has been courting Sophronia but abandons her for wealthier prey. Shown his inconstancy, Fulvia refuses him, and renounces marriage.

---

[1] In an oft-quoted anecdote 'Whincop' says that by the end of the third act of this play the actors were too drunk to continue and had to dismiss the audience. (*Scanderbeg* (London, 1747), p. 247.) Nothing in the quarto supports this tale. Higden damns an unruly audience, and complains bitterly of the actors' parsimony in producing the play ('not a farthing expended') and their mangling it with cuts—but he never mentions drunkenness, and he was certainly angry enough to do so if it were true.

[2] Durfey's place in the 'sentimental heroine' tradition, especially in these two plays, is discussed by Kathleen M. Lynch, 'Thomas D'Urfey's Contribution to Sentimental Comedy', *Philological Quarterly*, ix (1930), 249–59.

Since such a general defect of honesty corrupts the Age, I'll no more trust Mankind, but lay my Fortune out upon my self, and flourish in contempt of humane Falshood. . . . My eyes . . . have ever (scorning Interest) fix'd on Merit. . . . But, oh! the Race of Men are all Deceivers, and my relief, is my resolve to shun 'em. (63–4)

The minor characters are vigorous, low, and colloquial. Dick Stockjobb is effectively satirized. Durfey's satire on fortune hunters is sharp: Tom Romance, Sir Quibble Qyere, and the Welsh fop Rice ap Shinkin are all after Fulvia too. Perhaps Mrs. Barry (Sophronia) and Mrs. Bracegirdle (Fulvia) could make the romantic pathos in this play affecting; on the printed page it comes out sickly-sweet. Both women truly love the worthless Frederick, and are profoundly wounded by his faithlessness. Dryden calls the scene in Act II in which Fulvia feigns madness to escape her importunate suitors 'wonderfully diverting', but notes that the rest was 'woefull stuff, & concluded with Catcalls'.[1] Revived with alterations the following October the play seems to have been adequately popular.

Naturally there are a number of comedies which fall somewhere between the extreme groups. Some of them are basically old-style hard comedy toned down to suit the Williamite audience; others display a more positive inclination toward the humane, and even the exemplary.

Shadwell's *The Amorous Bigotte* (Spring 1690), a frantic-paced intrigue and confusion comedy, is lively but mechanical. Set in Madrid, the play nonetheless passes for a sequel to *The Lancashire Witches* by importing Tegue O Divelly, the rogue priest. Satire on priests was again timely: predictably, Tegue tries to rape Rosania. Searching hopefully for 'significance', Alssid calls the play a farcical treatment of Shadwell's education theme. Belliza, the title character, is a widow torn between worldly and churchly inclinations, and certainly she is a bad guide for her daughter and niece—women of sense. The play efficiently mocks its predictable butts without much subtlety and with little of the didactic fervour of Shadwell's other late plays. The best thing about the piece was probably the vehicle it offered Leigh as Father O Divelly, and Nokes (in petticoats) as Gremia, aunt to a 'fine Courtezan'.

[1] *Letters*, no. 24.

An even clearer case of old-style comedy toned down is Durfey's interesting, much neglected, *The Marriage-Hater Match'd* (January 1692). 'The taming of the rake' sums it up. Sir Philip Freewit, wild and witty, has been jilted by Lady Subtle and avows libertine principles. He has seduced, impregnated, and abandoned Phæbe, who truly loves him and to whom he promised marriage. As 'Lovewel' she follows him in breeches—fully aware of her own guilt in consenting to the seduction (42). She is able to blackmail him with important papers, and in a kind of skit on the proviso scene they argue. (He: '*Imprimis*, to Marry ones Stale Mistress, ridiculous!'— 43.) He finally agrees to see justice done—and arranges to have the marriage performed by his Irish valet, MacBuffle. She announces the marriage; he announces the trick; but the marriage turns out to be legitimate, since the service was read by MacBuffle's brother, a priest (51–2). At the end Phæbe says it 'was just . . . a special Act of Providence befriended me'. But she will be a good wife, and Sir Philip admits the justice of Providence (53–4). This romanticized ending greatly softens the libertine side of the play. For the rest, Durfey gives us his usual well-wrought assortment of knaves and fools: Myn Here Van Grin, a clown role for Leigh; Captain Darewell, a nautical-jargon humour who wins a good wife in the witty, practical-joking Berenice; and the prating, hoggish Lady Bum-fiddle are the best of an enjoyable crew.

Ravenscroft's *The Canterbury Guests* (October 1694) is another slightly pale example of the old love game. Three couples are followed: the 'serious' Lovell and Jacinta; the mildly frolic-some Durzo (yet another 'blunt Sea-Captain' overflowing with nautical jargon) and Arabella; and a gay couple, Careless and Hillaria. Yet even the 'airy' Careless is passionately in love: warning off a rival (actually Hillaria in breeches) he announces, 'Look you Sir, tho' I scorn to tell her so, or any of her Sex, yet I do Love her, will Love her, must Love her, and no body else shall Love her' (38). At the end of the play Careless and Hillaria settle down, but announce: 'Whil'st other Wives and Husbands Scold and Rant,/We two will live like Mistress and Gallant.' The piece is a pleasant, light intrigue comedy carefully balancing a 'sensible' couple against a prudently laundered gay couple.

Two plays by Crowne show his sense of the changing times. *The English Frier* (March 1690) combines lively satire on town sparks with ethical preachment. Bellamour and Julia are a serious and sensible romantic couple. Lord Wiseman, a reformed libertine, courts the 'gay' Laura, who gets severely punished for her teasing ways: a rake assaults her, and she renounces the coquette's role after Wiseman rescues her. The title character, Father Finicall, is a sex-mongering hypocrite: anti-Catholic satire was good box office immediately after the Revolution. Despite some good satirical ideas, the play comes out rather heavy handed. *The Married Beau* (April 1694) has an even stronger new-comedy component. Mr. Lovely asks his friend Polidor to test Mrs. Lovely—a coquette. She yields to him and then bitterly repents. In a second plot Polidor makes a serious and romantic marriage, winning Camilla, who is virtuous, devout, and beautiful, but also poor. Crowne's preface defends the morals of the piece, 'some Ladies' having taken offence at the seduction. J. H. Smith reads this as evidence that the Ladies 'were now beginning to get the better of the male faction in the battle of taste'.[1] Their power is increasingly obvious, but we should note both the strong romantic and moral bent of the play (libertinism is *not* endorsed) and a simple fact—the play was a success. The *Gentleman's Journal* notes that it had been 'already acted many Times' within a month.

The softening in comic attitudes is apparent even in a routine Molière-hash like Thomas Wright's *The Female Vertuoso's* (May 1693). Bouncy, light, easy-going, and low, the play still retains—seriously—Molière's test of love: does it withstand a report of the woman's losing her fortune? Clerimont loves Mariana for herself alone, so all is well. Wright tacks on a secondary plot competently enough, and Wittless, the Cambridge-scholar role he added for Doggett, is quite amusing.[2] A much more important 'soft' comedy is Mountfort's *Greenwich-Park* (April 1691). Its similarity to Carlile's *The Fortune-Hunters* is often noted. Two breeches parts (a speciality with Mrs. Mountfort), light sexual intrigue, and crisp wit

---

[1] J. H. Smith, p. 152.
[2] *The Female Vertuoso's* is fairly short, but was evidently a single-bill show. Nicoll's assertion that Molière's five acts are reduced to three (I. 260), is incorrect.

make a pleasant show which would be no discredit to the
young Farquhar. Mountfort follows the increasingly common
formula of a witty couple (Young Reveller and Florella)
balanced against a more serious one. Lord Worthy is forgiven
his past and accepted by Violante after a penitent confession
(55–6). For contrast we are given comic marital discord
between the henpecked grocer Raison and his wife, who are
finally reconciled.[1] Another play with a marked 'soft' inclination is George Powell's imitative *A Very Good Wife* (April 1693),
acted with some success. Here Courtwitt and his wife unite
against two would-be seducers. Busy intrigue and light satire
on obvious humours make the piece a routine city comedy—
but to find hard-drinking actor and man-about-town George
Powell, of all people, following this quasi-exemplary formula
certainly argues a trend.

Mountfort's comedy is a good example of the changing
times. The morality is there, but not to a Shadwellian degree.
The play remains airy, brisk, and amusing. But can one
imagine Dorimant confessing his sins to Harriet and being
accepted on the basis of his reform? In the early nineties hard
and humane comedy are both in vogue. The trend toward
exemplary morals is unmistakable, and pressures from 'the
Ladies' are well documented by J. H. Smith. We would be
foolish not to observe, however, that the really great comic
successes of these years are *Amphitryon*, *Sir Anthony Love*, and
The Old Batchelour—all hard comedies. The exemplary wave
is by no means yet dominant.

II. THE RESURGENCE OF SERIOUS DRAMA 1689–1694

Serious plays are few and far between in the mid- and later
eighties. A bare half-dozen plays, including pattern tragicomedies, follow the political dramas of the early eighties.
After 1688 there is a tremendous upsurge: in the five and a half
seasons covered here, there are more than twenty new serious
plays. Unhappily, the upsurge is more in quantity than
quality. The majority of these plays are fairly dismal. The
types represented, however, make an interesting study: the

---

[1] On the social implications of the play and its pro-citizen stand, see Martin W.
Walsh, 'The Significance of William Mountfort's *Greenwich-Park*', *Restoration and
18th Century Theatre Research*, xii (November 1973), 35–40.

pathetic is much less dominant than one would expect from clichés about nineties tragedy. We will find four semi-distinct groups. (1) Various sorts of tragicomedies; (2) revisions of old tragedies—the flurry of which is testimony to the sudden rise of interest in tragedy; (3) tragedy proper, comprising three basic tendencies—the pathetic, the heroic, and the classic–stoic; and (4) opera, in which we see the beginnings of a major vogue.

The four tragicomedies comprise a pair of Spanish romances from actors, and a pair of split plot plays from distinguished senior authors—Behn and Dryden. Mountfort's *The Successful Straingers: A Trage-Comedy* (*c.* January 1690) is so light as to be nearly straight comedy. A Scarron novel is given numerous comic additions and changes (principally, Dom Manuel becomes the lewd Don Lopez, a lively vehicle for Nokes). Mountfort contrives bustling action and good humours characters, and he uses the 'Sevill' setting for all the intrigue and sword-play it is worth. The garden scenes especially are straight farce, but Mountfort keeps up a pretence of seriousness: parts of the play are set as verse, and the sentiments are appropriately dignified. Mountfort contributed a scene to a very similar effort by a fellow actor—Joseph Harris's *The Mistakes* (December 1690), set in Naples with Spanish characters and employing verse of a sort at times. Harris concocts a routine romantic melodrama with lots of intrigue, sword-play, and a serious offer of suicide (57). The servant Lopez adds a bit of humour, but the play is distinctly more serious in tone than Mountfort's. It survived on the stage, but did less well.

The double plot plays are considerably more impressive. Mrs. Behn's posthumous *The Widow Ranter: or, The History of Bacon in Virginia* (November 1689) is discussed briefly above in Chapter 5.[1] General Bacon's heroic love for an Indian princess and their deaths are serious romantic tragedy. Satire on the corrupt rogues in the government council makes a good political and ethical contrast to Bacon. The series of couples (from General Daring and the Widow down to Parson Dunce and the tapstress, Mrs. Flirt) provides a whole spectrum of

---

[1] For an account of the play see Anne Witmer and John Freehafer, 'Aphra Behn's Strange News From Virgina', *Library Chronicle*, xxxiv (1968), 7–23.

types of 'love' as a contrast to Bacon's heroic love. Complex ironies and counter-ironies emerge from these juxtapositions, which are perhaps at once too extreme and too subtle to work effectively in the theatre. The play failed, hurt by heavy cuts and bad casting: Sandford, a specialist in villains, was a decidedly peculiar choice for Lieutenant-General Daring, a noble and valiant officer and a romantic lead.

Dryden is the great exponent of the split plot play in this period, so for him to end his play-writing with such a work is appropriate. *Love Triumphant, or Nature will Prevail* (January 1694) was a failure and has attracted almost no attention subsequently. The serious plot drags, and the sentimental conversion of the tyrant Veramond by his exemplary daughter Celidea is implausible; worse, it leaves the audience indifferent. The comic plot is mechanically seamy, and the marriage of the stupid Sancho to Dalinda, a previously unwed mother of two, is neither pleasing nor amusing. Among its other problems, the play is certainly too long. Its interest lies in its design. Dryden starts with a play 'of the nature of the Spanish Fryar', as the *Gentleman's Journal* describes it, a split plot quasi-heroic play set in Spain, and looks beyond the story to essentially philosophical issues. Dryden sets up a question: what is nature? He then proceeds to unfold an elaborate affirmation of faith in Divine Providence. Both prologue and epilogue point loudly to this 'Moral'. Thus *Love Triumphant* is unworkable drama, but a most significant document in Dryden's intellectual development.

The revival of interest in tragedy is indicated by the appearance of four refurbishments of old plays in these years. Chapman's *Bussy D'Ambois* was acted in March 1691 and published that spring, 'Newly Revised by Mr. D'Urfey'. The changes were designed first to remove 'obsolete Phrases and intolerable Fustian',[1] and second, to 'mend' the character of Tamira, reducing her 'lewdness' and introducing 'a former Contract between her and *D'Ambois*, which gives some Excuse for her Love afterwards, and renders the Distress in the last Act to be much more lyable to Pity', as Durfey explains in his

---

[1] Cf. Dryden's criticisms of the play in his preface to *The Spanish Fryar* a decade earlier.

dedication. In short, purity, pathos, and modern language were wanted. A much less altered play is *The Traytor* (March 1692), published that year 'With Alterations, Amendments, and Additions'; the unsigned dedication asserts that the play was by 'Mr Rivers'. The *Gentleman's Journal* calls it an old tragedy now revived and reprinted with alterations and amendments, and states that it is by 'one Mr. *Rivers* a Jesuite', not by Shirley. Actually, this is simply Shirley's well-known tragedy of 1631, popular in the sixties and seventies, reprinted in slightly cut form, presumably as the United Company was now acting it. As with the 'Betterton' *Henry IV* of 1700 we have not an original play or even an adaptation, but an acting text.

The two historical plays generally assigned to Bancroft are problematical. *King Edward the Third . . . An Historicall Play* (November 1690) was politically apropos and did well. The style and tone have a decidedly pre-Restoration flavour; the comic scenes may well be a contemporary addition. Some internal inconsistencies suggest a slightly imperfect patchwork.[1] Possibly Mountfort, who signed the dedication but disclaimed authorship, made the revisions. *Henry the Second* (November 1692) is a similar piece of work, also brought to the stage by Mountfort. Alfred Harbage suggests that both plays are reworkings of old MSS.—Davenport's *The Politick Queen* and *Henry the Second* respectively.[2] This hypothesis is quite plausible. Both are good historical tragedy, though *Henry* is distinctly the better of the two. 'A Tragedy with a mixture of Comedy' is the *Gentleman's Journal's* description. Satire on priests is still timely; the Abbot (Sandford) is a fine villain. The sub-title— *The Death of Rosamond*—is an indication of the strong pathetic element. The jealous Queen and the enforced drinking of poison are effectively handled, as is the parting of Henry and Rosamond (41). The use of historical themes mingled with pathos was a favourite pattern in the nineties. The plays, whoever wrote or altered them, are stimulating historical tragedy.

The new tragedies of these years tend to wobble uncertainly between the tired old heroic mode and the newer pathetic

---

[1] See the edition by John Cadwalader (Philadelphia, Pa., 1949), Introduction pp. 8–15.   [2] 'Elizabethan–Restoration Palimpsest', pp. 310–18.

one, though the trend of the future is discernible in such works as *Cleomenes* and *Regulus*, which have heroic and pathetic elements, but which also emphasize a classic–stoic subject and treatment to be popular later in the decade, appearing in such plays as *Pausanias, The Roman Brides Revenge, Pyrrhus, Caligula,* and *The Fate of Capua*—and ultimately culminating in Addison's *Cato* (1713).

Two plays by the actor George Powell illustrate the continuation of the heroic and pathetic modes. *The Treacherous Brothers* (c. January 1690) is a nineties-style *Empress of Morocco* with pretentious verse, romantic love, poisoning, impaling, and a happy ending. The plot, turning on confusion and jealousy, is messily handled, and the horrors (particularly Menaphon shown impaled on spikes—61) are done without gusto. *Alphonso King of Naples* (c. December 1690) relies more on pathos. Cesario (a conquering general soon disgraced—a numerous tribe in plays of this sort) and Prince Ferdinand both want the King's daughter Urania. The unhappy rivals kill each other (45), and Urania, after stabbing herself in the breast, enters 'bleeding, her hair hanging loose' to die. Powell works in the mandatory rape threat along the way. Cesario finds her 'ty'd to a Tree by the Hair, the *Banditti's* on each side of her' (21), and rescues her for a fate that is mere suicide. There is no real villain in the tragic dénouement; Urania's father is duly sorry for his obduracy; and we are supposed to be very touched by these unlucky misfortunes. Again, Powell has all the elements correct, but writes without conviction.

Heroic pathos is the keynote to Settle's *Distress'd Innocence: or, the Princess of Persia* (October 1690). Hormidas and Cleomira mingle pathos and nobility, and Settle indulges in a fair amount of bloodshed in an effort to drum up sympathy. Mrs. Barry exults in vengeance; Mrs. Bracegirdle suffers. That the play succeeded is testimony to their skill. Nothing could save Settle's *The Ambitious Slave* (March 1694). Originally written in 1682, it is a blank verse exercise in a heroic mode last popular about 1677, and a pretty poor one at that. A contemporary letter notes that the United Company refused the play, whereupon Settle 'made a present of it to the women in the house'.[1] Celestina (Mrs. Barry) has sold her soul to the

---

[1] Anonymous; cited in *The London Stage*, Part 1, p. 433.

devil for beauty; seduces the King of Persia; and encourages him to have his wife and his brother Tygranes (another conquering hero) sent to the block. The emotional blather before the execution is even worse than usual (48); afterwards 'The Ghosts of *Herminia* and *Tygranes* ascend in Glory' (54). The play's failure was richly deserved. Presumably the continued presence of such nonsense on the stage had inspired Jo Hayns's sole play, *A Fatal Mistake*, printed in 1692 and probably not meant to be acted. A wild burlesque of the heroic warrior ethos in deliberately vile couplets, it ends up with butchery *à la Tom Thumb*, and makes an entertaining spoof.

Not all of the pathetically inclined plays are contemptible. Dryden's *Don Sebastian* (December 1689) is a very considerable play indeed. It functions on at least three distinct planes. In its full printed form (some 1,200 lines were cut in performance) it is a forceful political tract which only just misses being open Jacobite propaganda.[1] Second, as a pathetic tragedy it is a moving story of the accidental incest of Sebastian and Almeyda with butchery artfully avoided. Sutherland finds it 'more painful than tragic',[2] but from a modern perspective one might say the same of Sophocles' *Oedipus*. Third, it is a complexly interwoven split plot tragicomedy, well analysed as such by Rothstein. Questions of justice, reward, and will run parallel in both plots, and the contrasting moralities developed make this a shrewd and thoughtful play. Don Antonio's sex sub-plot is vivid, vigorous, and funny, a superb counter-balance to the heavy pathos of the top plot. The excellence of the complex and contradictory observations of motive in Dryden's play is all the more evident in comparison with other specimens of the pathetic.

Lee's *The Massacre of Paris*, Popish Plot agit-prop finally staged in November 1689 (see above, Chapter 5), is lurid, bloody, and bathetic—but evidently proved effective, since according to *The Reasons of Mr. Joseph Hains Conversion* (anon., 1690) it drew floods of tears from the audience. Nicholas Brady's *The Rape* (February 1692) is historical, tragical pathetic. The politics of the Goths and Vandals are thrown in; the play is serious, pretentious, and over-inflated, but passably lively even

---

[1] See John Robert Moore, 'Political Allusions in Dryden's Later Plays', *PMLA*, lxxiii (1958), 36–42.   [2] Sutherland, p. 69.

so. Genselaric's musings preparatory to rape have some force (23). The Princess Eurione is discovered 'in an Arbour, gagg'd and bound to a Tree, her hair dishevel'd as newly Ravish'd' (25). She is prevented from stabbing herself on page 26, but succeeds thirty pages later. After Rodoric says (on the rack) who performed the rape, the rapist is stabbed on the spot (54). The emotional temperature in Banks's *The Innocent Usurper, or the Death of the Lady Jane Grey*, ready in April 1692 but banned (see Chapter 5, above), is much higher, and Banks has a much better sense of theatrical effect. But in both cases the invitation to tearful empathy is too simple, obvious, and unrelieved.

A much more successful variety of pathos is found in Southerne's *The Fatal Marriage: or, the Innocent Adultery, A Play* (February 1694), already discussed in Chapter 5. This 'hip-hop' play was popular in various forms for 150 years. Downes (p. 38) mentions it with *The Orphan* and *Venice Preserv'd* as among the most successful of all 'modern' plays. In all three Mrs. Barry 'forc'd Tears from the Eyes of her Auditory'. In the dedication Southerne says, 'I made the Play for her part, and her part has made the Play for me.' The plot is from a Behn novel. Isabella, her husband missing for nearly seven years, is in financial distress and finally agrees to marry Villeroy. Her first husband's return drives her to madness and suicide. He had been caught by pirates, and his brother Carlos has destroyed his letters, hoping to claim the inheritance for himself. Carlos finally kills his brother, and his accomplice Pedro is shown on the rack (74). But the heart of the play is the character of the luckless Isabella, her wild display of misery and passion (e.g. 70), and finally her suicide. There is almost no internal conflict; this is tragedy almost entirely of circumstances, and Southerne supercharges the pathos. Into this bloody tale of crime and wretchedness he interpolates a brisk comedy. Frederick wins Victoria, despite her father's opposition —the father's young wife gives him a sleeping potion before the elopement, convinces him he died and was restored to life, and he forgives everyone very nicely. This sub-plot is handled with excellent comic verve. A parallel between the plots is obvious: in each a scheming brother tries to marry a sister or in-law out of the family to clear the way to an inheritance. Southerne thus indulges his penchant for psychological observations and study of motivation with parallel tales told in different keys. Striking language, vivid characters, and expert construction help the play: Southerne has become an extremely polished playwright. *The Fatal Marriage* has everything a play needs to be great—except internal *raison d'être* for the tragedy. The pain we feel is that elicited by a gruesomely enacted accident —and so we may be left tearful, but we are never deeply moved.

Southerne's play is as fine as pathetic drama gets. Not only is its construction beautifully done, but the comic variety is both welcome and thematically pointed. Too often the pathetic plays have on one the effect of watching a dog die by inches after being run over in the street. Pathetic plays may be roughly categorized as (1) heroics and horrors style, as in Mountfort's *The Injur'd Lovers;* (2) pure female distress, as in *The Innocent Usurper;* (3) half of a split plot, a Dryden and Southerne speciality; (4) the classic–stoic plays. We often think of pathetic drama as 'she-tragedy', but obviously the two are not synonymous. Eugene Waith has issued valuable reminders (see Chapters 4 and 5, above) that heroic and pathetic drama can intersect, and indeed they often do. The stoic nobly suffering is a kind of male analogue to Banksian she-tragedy.

As so often, Dryden was the pioneer. *Cleomenes, the Spartan-Hero* (April 1692) is an exceedingly sober play. The preface defines Dryden's endeavour: 'I thought I was capable of moving Compassion'; he has left his tragedy 'unmix'd with *Comedy*', and even more radical he has left the plot 'single'. Cleomenes' spartan stoicism is tempered by 'love': his beloved wife Cleora is not in Dryden's source, and adds greatly to the pathos, as does the use of a child dying of starvation. The icy Cleomenes is well contrasted with an evil ruler, the degenerate Ptolomy. The heroic ethos is maintained, including triple suicide at the end—noble suicide; but the clear, striking language is utterly free of rant, and almost of passion. Lack of incident and severe repression of emotional expression leaves the work impressive but a little frigid. Even so, the stern but humane figure of Cleomenes is decidedly imposing.

Much less can be said for Crowne's *Regulus* (June 1692), which has some similar leanings. Crowne throws in an irrelevant vein of comedy, with much prosy, unwitty dialogue. And he heightens the pathos still further, having Regulus' wife go mad in the usual fashion. But Regulus himself is massively calm, an absolute model of *pietas*, as Rothstein remarks. His fortitude is the point of the play. He goes off to be tortured with aplomb; discovered after the procedure is well under way he calmly talks with his wife, dismisses his discomforts with the explanation 'My Soul's all over pleasure' (61), and expires. This formula —stoicism and a classical story—was soon to be popular.

To inflate three examples into a trend may seem an exaggeration, but 'operas' were rare and expensive, and the flock of them to come perhaps justifies seeing these three as a sign of the approaching vogue. *The Prophetess* (June 1690), 'Written by Francis Beaumont [actually, Massinger] and John Fletcher With Alterations and Additions, After the Manner of an OPERA' according to the title-page, was exceptionally popular throughout the decade. Downes calls Betterton the author, but 'producer' would be a more accurate term. Basically 'Fletcher's' *The History of Dioclesian* was cut a bit to accommodate song, dance, and a lavish use of Dorset Garden's machines. We are offered 'a Chariot drawn by Dragons', 'A dreadful Monster', a building collapsing at the wave of a wand, characters 'turn'd into a Dance of Butterflies', figures emerging from a tapestry to dance while other figures slip into their places in the tapestry from behind—and so forth. What Betterton provides is spectacular variety entertainment with a *deus ex machina* happy moral ending. Sympathetically, one can admit that all the falderal is good fun, especially the fancy masque at the end. Contrariwise, one can say that Betterton was tarting up Fletcher to appeal to popular taste.

Dryden's *King Arthur* (June 1691) is a much more serious effort. (See Chapter 5, below.) Purcell's marvellous music forms a major part of the entertainment. Though the principal characters do not sing, the songs are for once well integrated into the play. In genre the piece seems to consist of equal parts of the operatic *Tempest*,[1] *Amboyna*, *The State of Innocence*, and *Albion and Albanius*. Blunt and mildly rakehell dialogue ('Yes,

---

[1] The play on Emmeline's sexual innocence is highly reminiscent of Miranda, and Philidel and Grimbald are obviously Ariel and Caliban refurbished.

he's a valiant Dog, Pox on him'—VI. 248) is combined with lush fantasy, as in the Bower of Bliss episode (276, 279). Rival magicians, cupids, Saxons 'led off by the Priests, in Order to be Sacrific'd' (253), the magic restoration of blind Emmeline's sight, Osmond's attempted rape of her, are all stirred together in a peculiar potpourri. The work was a tremendous success, 'very Gainful' according to Downes, and ran well throughout the decade. As a play it is patchy, especially for reading. With music and a production artfully employing Dorset Garden's wonders, it might have seemed the *Fantasia* of its day.

An even fancier show is *The Fairy-Queen: An Opera* (May 1692), an adaptation of *A Midsummer Night's Dream* possibly by Settle. Here the United Company overreached itself. Downes reports that 'This in Ornaments was Superior to the other Two; especially in Cloaths.' But though 'The Court and Town were wonderfully satisfy'd with it . . . the Expences in setting it out being so great, the Company got very little by it' (42–3). Prologue, epilogue, and preface make a big point of the high cost. As usual with opera, production was slow: the piece appears in the *Stationer's Register* 2 November 1691. Basically, the adapter simply trimmed Shakespeare's text to make room for song, dance, and machine play. There is a twelve-foot-high working fountain (40); Juno appears in a machine drawn by peacocks, which spread their tails (47); the dance of six monkeys near the end is notorious (50). As a sample of the elaborate show, consider this: 'While a Symphany's Playing, the two Swans come Swimming on through the Arches to the bank of the River, as if they would Land; there turn themselves into *Fairies*, and Dance' (30). Such transformations obviously fascinated the audience.

The popularity of operatic show led to an increase in the interpolation of masques into plays. We will observe the practice in the late nineties: an example to hand is *The Rape of Europa by Jupiter: A Masque* (by William Ranson?), evidently performed in early 1694. As it is only 8 pages long, we may presume that it was added to something staged at Dorset Garden (the title-page specifies the locale). The cast is brilliant; the songs attractive;[1] the rape motif *à la mode*. Europa is shown

[1] An interpolated (sung) dialogue by Doggett adds interesting variety: 'At *London* che've been'. It describes (in dialect) picking up a whore in Cheapside.

'her Hair loose about her, as just Ravish'd' (7), her rapist lolling beside her. The combination of ethereal beauty, light bawdy, and ugly bawdy is startling but effective. In a little masque like this, as in the 'operas' just discussed, we see the audience proclivity for what would today be termed multi-media attractions.

III. THE DILUTION OF THE CAROLEAN TRADITION
1695–1697

In the years immediately following 1695 the Carolean norms are rapidly left behind. One reason for this is moral pressure brought to bear by reformers, but just as important, the revival of theatrical competition creates opportunities for a large number of young writers, who bring new attitudes and values into the theatre. In both comedy and serious drama we will continue to see a double tradition. But hard and humane comedy represent opposite poles: increasingly in these years a given play will be a muddled combination of the two. In serious drama the poles are less clear. The old heroic style is still very much alive (albeit unrhymed), now often blended with the inheritance of the pathetic drama developed in the eighties. Against this background is developing the new classic–stoic mode, consciously cooler, calmer, less emotionally overwrought. For whatever reasons, these years do see several great new comedies, while little among the tragedies is even tolerable. By this time the Carolean tradition is clearly losing its special identity, although the nature of the new directions to be taken remains unclear in the late nineties. The greatest influence on drama in these years is extrinsic—the re-establishment of a second theatre.

Betterton versus Rich: The Revival of Competition 1695–1697

The basic reason for the Lincoln's Inn Fields breakaway is simple: the actors refused to tolerate Rich's pinchpenny tyranny. The United Company had not been prospering. Between May 1682 and August 1692 the operation showed 'Clear Profits' of £18,594, or some £1,800 per year. Even split into 23 shares, this was a tidy profit. By the 1691–2 season, however, the company was running at a loss; the actors were protesting about cuts in their salaries; and Betterton prudently altered his status from shareholder to salaried actor.[1]

---

[1] For details of the lawsuits which supply these figures, see Hotson, pp. 288–90.

We have already noted Mountfort's comment on the flurry of new plays at this time—the fruit of alarm, not prosperity. As Cibber informs us, the managers adopted the expedient of gambling huge sums on the mounting of operas, hoping to recoup all losses by bringing home 'the *Indies*'.[1] Luttrell tells us that *The Fairy-Queen* in May 1692 cost £3,000, and even the loyal Downes admits it failed to pay. The company did better in 1692–3, but Alexander Davenant's flight left Rich in control of the company by December 1693, and within a year he had unwittingly induced a successful mutiny.

The players' petition of complaint (*c.* November 1694) and the patentees' pettifogging reply (10 December) are summarized and largely reprinted by Nicoll (I. 368–79): in essence the actors were being squeezed financially. But the star actors' outrage and alarm had more solid ground. Cibber reports that the patentees 'under Pretence of bringing younger Actors forward, order'd several of *Betterton*'s, and Mrs. *Barry*'s chief Parts to be given to young *Powel*, and Mrs. *Bracegirdle*'. (The latter wisely refused to co-operate.) But the patentees would not compromise. 'The Actors offer'd a Treaty of Peace; but their Masters . . . refus'd all Terms of Accommodation.'[2] The patentees' obduracy was probably founded on two premises: first, that they had a monopoly; and second, that consequently they could make money no matter who was acting. They had some promising evidence. According to Skipwith's affidavit, 'ye Young People Acted ye last vacacon [July 1694] near 30 Days without Mr Betterton . . . [*et al.* and] by this means got enough to keep them over the vacation' (Nicoll, I. 374). The aggrieved actors, however, had friends in high places, and after three months of fruitless arbitration King William granted the actors a separate licence (25 March 1695). Reconverting Lisle's Tennis Court for use as a theatre, 'Betterton's' Company opened at Lincoln's Inn Fields on 30 April.

Both sides enjoyed advantages. Rich had control of two fine theatres and almost a monopoly on the possibilities of spectacle. His actors were relatively young, and the operation was run with firm central authority—in contrast to the chaotic prima donnaism at Lincoln's Inn Fields. But Rich had to double wages to keep the actors he did, and few of them had any pull with

---

[1] Cibber, p. 105. [2] Cibber, pp. 106–7.

the public.[1] Betterton's Company certainly suffered from having to use a cramped theatre abandoned by the Duke's Company in 1671 and last used in 1674. But the group comprised most of the star actors of the day—and popular feeling was on their side. As Gildon reports, at the opening of Lincoln's Inn Fields 'the Town was so prepossess'd in Favour of the very Actors, that before a Word was spoke, each Actor was Clapt for a considerable Time.'[2]

One major difference between this competition and the old King's–Duke's competition should be emphasized: neither company had exclusive rights to the old repertory, or to any part of it. They could offer the same play on the same night and both suffer, if they chose to be so stupid. The advantage here lay with the veteran actors, already popular in all the repertory roles. But in the initial, very bitter phase of competition, Rich's Company seems deliberately to have tried to play the role of spoiler. Thus Cibber reports that Drury Lane, hearing that Lincoln's Inn Fields was to act *Hamlet* on a Tuesday, promptly announced it for Monday at Drury Lane; Betterton's Company rejoined by cancelling *The Old Batchelour* and moving *Hamlet* back to Monday—at which Drury Lane promptly shifted over to *The Old Batchelour* for Monday, with Powell 'to mimic Betterton'.[3] Such games would profit no one: to succeed, a company would have to find successful new plays, and both groups set about it at once—with more haste than judgement. In the first two seasons of competition nearly fifty new plays were mounted. Of these only eight achieved substantial success: a large majority were flat failures.

All the evidence suggests that (initially at least) competition between the two houses was bitter and destructive. As the prologue to *Bonduca* (Drury Lane) declares in September 1695, 'Between us and the other Theatre/There is proclaim'd, and still maintain'd a War.' The author suggests that the audience should prefer 'Our Growing Spring' to 'Fading Autumn there'. He boasts of 'Our Nobler Theatre's', which provide 'Machines, Scenes, Opera's, Musick, Dancing, Singing'—as against Lincoln's Inn Fields' age and antiquity. Faced with a rebellion, Rich decided to fight it out, relying on his good theatres and financial resources. He was willing to run at a loss

1 Cibber, p. 108.   2 *Lives and Characters*, p. 22.   3 Cibber, pp. 113–14.

temporarily if need be: 'we were assur'd', says Cibber, 'that let the Audiences be never so low, our Masters would make good all Deficiencies.'[1] The 'Second Part' of Vanbrugh's *Æsop* (*c.* March 1697) argues Rich's case: the Lincoln's Inn Fields Company are 'mutineers' who should return to their lawful monarch. But the patentees were having their troubles. They had even considered giving up and letting the patent company fold.[2] The going proved hard, and by the autumn of 1696 we find rumours of their collapse. Reporting a successful double bill at Lincoln's Inn Fields, Robert Jennens writes: 'The other house has no company at all, and unless a new play comes out on Saturday revives their reputation, they must break.'[3] The new play was *The Relapse* and it did give the company a major boost.

Competition was eventually to induce the importation of expensive foreign singers and dancers, extravagant extras who cost far more than they were worth. But right away we see a competitive scramble. Congreve's prologue to Hopkins's *Pyrrhus* (August 1695) likens the theatrical competition to war and says 'That Stage will win, which longest keeps the Field', a reference to an unusual August production in which we see the Lincoln's Inn Fields Company 'forrage for an Audience out of Season'.[4] A popular in-season device was the addition of a musical entertainment. Motteux's *The Taking of Namur and His Majesty's Safe Return* was evidently such a throw-in at Lincoln's Inn Fields in the autumn of 1695. Namur fell on 26 August 1695 and the 'entertainment', with music by Eccles, is strictly topical. A year later Motteux wrote *The Loves of Mars and Venus. A Play Set to Music* (November 1696), a short masque played with Ravenscroft's *Anatomist* in a double bill. Two contemporary observers aver that Motteux's musical was a

---

[1] Cibber, p. 109.   [2] Legal deposition cited by Hotson, pp. 299–300.

[3] Cited in *The London Stage*, Part 1, p. 470.

[4] This desire to act without competition may explain an apparently anomalous record of a performance of *Love for Love* on Christmas Day 1700. See P.R.O. Coram Rege Roll 27/2147, Rex Roll no. 9, an indictment of Doggett and others for profanity 'on the five and twentieth day of December'. Quotations identify the play. Avery refused to enter this performance in *The London Stage* on the ground that Christmas performance was implausible. There is no other record of such a practice in this period. Pepys went out to see a play on Christmas Day 1666 and found none acted—a suggestion perhaps that there was no actual prohibition. I suspect that Betterton was glad to find a day on which his offering went unopposed, and hence that the record is accurate—especially as the date is repeated three times in the indictment.

great 'advantage'.[1] It was printed and sold at the theatre, and is one of the earliest preserved librettos.

Two plays deserve special notice as competitive endeavours. Motteux's *The Novelty: Every Act a Play* (May 1697) is a confection reminiscent of Davenant's *The Play-house to be Let* (1662). Motteux strung together a pastoral by Oldmixon, a short comedy, a masque, and a farce 'after the *Italian* Manner' by himself, and a one-act version ('the most moving Part') of Filmer's failed tragedy, *The Unnatural Brother*. The masque was printed and the libretto distributed at the *première*. All five of the one-act plays are poor stuff, but the conglomerate caught the town's fancy, and gave Motteux two benefit nights.

A much more impressive specimen is *The Female Wits: or, the Triumvirate of Poets at Rehearsal* (anonymous), staged at Drury Lane in mid-1696,[2] and a fascinating example of personal satire and the rehearsal play genre. Mrs. Manley, Mrs. Pix, and Mrs. Trotter are very effectively brutalized. Mrs. Manley had a comedy fail at Drury Lane that spring; she then transferred her tragedy, *The Royal Mischief*, to Lincoln's Inn Fields, which rushed it into production. *The Female Wits* presents the Drury Lane view of the tragedy, a piece of bloated heroic nonsense which fairly begs for burlesque. It got what it deserved (although it had succeeded on stage, further annoying Drury Lane, no doubt). Frame and mock play are better integrated than in either *The Rehearsal* or Sheridan's *The Critic*. The actors play themselves—cheerfully including personal characteristics like George Powell's early-morning drinking (13). The styles of Mrs. Barry and Betterton are effectively travestied (32, 51, 57). At the end Mrs. Manley storms out, vowing to take her bathetic masterpiece to the other house—precisely as she had done. This delightful spoof and smear, too little known today, seems to have enjoyed the topical popularity it sought.

For the first time since the burning of the Bridges Street theatre in January 1672 we find really vigorous theatrical competition, carried on with unprecedented ill will. Both houses hastily mount all the new plays they can: unhappily they do not have much to choose from. Dryden has stopped

---

[1] *A Comparison* and Gildon, *Lives and Characters*.

[2] Probably it was a committee enterprise managed by Jo Hayns. See Lucyle Hook's helpful Introduction to the Augustan Reprint Society facsimile (1967).

writing plays; Southerne is about to follow suit; Shadwell, Lee, Otway, Behn, and Mountfort are dead. Congreve is approaching his best; Vanbrugh makes his brief appearance—but the flood of plays is by Dilke, Gould, Granville, Hopkins, Scott, Gildon, the 'Female Wits', Richard Norton, James Drake, and others of their ilk. Settle and Durfey remain fitfully active; Cibber is actually one of the better practising playwrights. Unlike the mid-1670s, when the last boom in new plays had occurred, there are simply not many experienced professional playwrights at work.

The Mixing of the Comic Modes

Love for Love (April 1695), the play with which Lincoln's Inn Fields opened, is a good example of the mixing of the old and new comedy. (The play is analysed at length in Chapter 3, above.) Congreve has prudently softened his attitude on a number of key points. The cuckolding and seduction do not involve the 'hero' Valentine, who has produced bastards but is now a sincere and honourable lover. Valentine is a sentimental but not a mawkish protagonist who undergoes and passes a test. His sincerity proved by his generous renunciation, he can be awarded Angelica. The prologue is accurate in claiming that humour, plot, and satire are presented, and explicitly claims to be carrying on the Wycherley tradition:

> Since the *Plain-Dealers* Scenes of Manly Rage,
> Not one has dar'd to lash this Crying Age.
> This time, the Poet owns the bold Essay,
> Yet hopes there's no ill-manners in his play.

In short, Congreve waves the flag for hard comedy in the old Carolean tradition, but after the reception of *The Double-Dealer* he is going to be prudently discreet about it.

Cibber's *Love's Last Shift* (January 1696), ostensibly on the other side of the fence, similarly mingles elements of the old and the new comedy.[1] There are three couples. Young Worthy (no cuckolder) and Narcissa play out a pale imitation of the old love game. The Elder Worthy, a reformed rake and now a man of sense, tames the teasing, jilting humour of Hillaria.

---

[1] For an excellent account of the play's 'mixed' outlook, see Paul E. Parnell, 'Equivocation in Cibber's *Love's Last Shift*', *Studies in Philology*, lvii (1960), 519–34.

In the famous plot Loveless returns to England in debt. Amanda, the wife he abandoned ten years earlier, has inherited money and remained strictly virtuous: she wins him back by allowing him to 'seduce' her and then revealing her identity. Shocked by 'horrour and remorse' (91) the rake endorses 'the chast Rapture of a Vertuous Love'. This ending, done in romantic tragicomedy style with semi-verse, brought floods of tears from the audience, and the play proved one of the major props of the shaky young Drury Lane company.

Obviously Cibber was trying to provide something for everyone in his potpourri. The epilogue pointedly reminds the Ladies that 'There's not one Cuckold made', while begging the 'rakes' to excuse the conclusion, since 'He's Lewd for above four Acts, Gentlemen!' Loveless is indeed a hard-nosed rake for above four acts—making his reversal implausible, but all the more effectively emotional. Much of the conversation in the play is suggestive of the hard school, and certainly some incidental elements belong to the old comedy. Loveless's servant Snap makes a parallel seduction move against Amanda's maid; she drops him through a trap-door to get rid of him, but he grabs her and drags her down (81)—the resulting copulation is atoned for with enforced matrimony (97). Sir Novelty Fashion, the fop played by Cibber, would be a peculiar part in a genuinely humane comedy. He is a nasty and unpleasant character (e.g. 29), conscienceless, selfish, and brutal. He is a world away from such good-humoured, ineffectual, and unthreatening predecessors as Sir Fopling Flutter and Sir Courtly Nice.

Cibber's play, far from being a 'sentimental' tract, or noticeably different in kind from contemporary plays, exhibits an indifferently ambiguous and quite normal mixture of hard and humane elements. So, in fact, does Vanbrugh's sequel and 'answer', *The Relapse* (November 1696). The strange popular reputation of these two plays suggests that they epitomize a clash—the first great 'sentimental' comedy debunked by one of the last true 'Restoration' comedies. Later derogation of Cibber undoubtedly has contributed to the myth that Vanbrugh was attacking him. But consider the facts: *The Relapse* was a Drury Lane production, and the company would scarcely have mounted a destructive satire on one of its few popular successes. Furthermore, Cibber himself played the newly ennobled Lord Foppington, and was hugely delighted with the part and the play.

Vanbrugh proceeds to cast doubt on the durability of Loveless's reform. While Loveless pursues Berinthia, Amanda finds herself greatly attracted to Worthy. On the verge of adultery they stop: Amanda expresses her chaste love, and Worthy is converted.

> *Worthy* (Solus.) Sure there's Divinity about her; and sh'as dispens'd some portion on't to me. For what but now was the wild flame of Love, or (to dissect that specious term) the vile, the gross desires of Flesh and Blood, is in a moment turn'd to Adoration. The Coarser Appetite of Nature's gone, and 'tis, methinks the Food of Angels I require. (I. 93)

Worthy himself wonders 'how long this influence may last', but in fact Vanbrugh has played for very much the kind of emotional response Cibber looked for. When Amanda bursts into semi-verse, or exclaims 'Protect me Heav'n' when she meets her tempter, we are in the raised and artificial world of romantic tragicomedy.

Most of the elements in *The Relapse* are of the old school. Young Fashion tricks his brother, Lord Foppington, out of the stupid, over-sexed Hoyden (the most memorable *ingénue* of the period, save Margery Pinchwife) with the help of the homosexual pimp, Coupler. Foppington is the greatest fop conceived in this period—brutal, evil, and smart. His sardonic comment to his brother at the end of the play effectively reminds us that Young Fashion has got his money at a price.

> Dear *Tam*, since Things are thus fallen aut, prithee give me leave to wish thee Jay. I do it *de bon Cœur*, strike me dumb; you have Marry'd a Woman Beautiful in her Person, Charming in her Ayrs, Prudent in her Canduct, Canstant in her Inclinations, and of a nice Marality, split my Wind-pipe. (99–100)

Like Foppington, Hoyden's father, Sir Tunbelly Clumsey is harshly viewed: indeed, beyond Amanda and Worthy none of the characters is sympathetically treated. But just as there is a significant 'hard' element in Cibber's play, so there is a definite 'humane' touch in Vanbrugh's. This qualifying softness leads

Mrs. Birdsall to dismiss Vanbrugh as a dishonest romantic—
too unsympathetic a view.[1]

Vanbrugh's only other original play, *The Provok'd Wife*
(April 1697), is a good index to his outlook. It is one of the
harshest marital discord plays in the whole period. Constant,
an admirable gentleman, loves Lady Brute, who is married
to a sot, Sir John Brute. She cannot get free, and there is no
prospect of change at the end of the play. The really ugly
picture of marriage is balanced against a romantic plot, in
which Bellinda (Lady Brute's niece) decides to marry Heartfree
because she likes him, rather than look for a wealthier suitor.
Thus Vanbrugh is not against marriage. Indeed he supports it,
but with a profoundly unsettling awareness of how badly it
can go wrong. Any affirmation of love, marriage, or honour is
greatly qualified by realism and pessimism. Like Southerne
and Congreve, Vanbrugh is a thoughtful writer: he does not
preach, he does not extract morals, but the plays reflect a keen
observation of life—and any positivism is muted by scepticism
and irony.

In attitude, Vanbrugh is largely of the hard comedy per-
suasion, and most of his materials are in that tradition. The
female fop Lady Fancyfull (who wants Heartfree) mounts a
plot with Rasor and her French maid, and is sharply satirized;
so is Sir John Brute, especially in his scowring scenes (e.g.
I. 151-3). Vanbrugh's witty conversation is truly of the
Etherege style. Indeed, for my taste, Vanbrugh writes the finest
comic prose of the age, Congreve not excepted. The conversation
is witty, supple, and toughly colloquial—more natural, less
obviously contrived, less polished and precious than Congreve's.
Vanbrugh does not, however, allow himself the blunt sex
characteristic of Carolean comedy. There are no seductions
and no cuckoldings in these two plays. In both Amanda and
Worthy, Constant and Lady Brute, virtue is at least temporarily
upheld. Vanbrugh constantly verges on the sex he refuses to
bring to fruition. And he can use some of the devices of the old
sex comedy. For example, Constant—caught in a compromising
position—faces down Sir John Brute with an ominous assertion

---

[1] *Wild Civility*, p. 22. For an important account of Vanbrugh's thematic concerns and his place between the old and new comedy, see Paul Mueschke and
Jeannette Fleisher, 'A Re-evaluation of Vanbrugh', *PMLA*, xlix (1934), 848-89.

of fact: 'I wear a Sword, Sir' (168), reminiscent of the style of *The Mall* (1674). The softening of the hard comedy in Vanbrugh should not be regarded as a bad thing. The sensitivity of his perceptions, the acuteness with which he analyses his characters' predicaments, is founded on the very sensibility which may seem to betray the school of Wycherley to which Vanbrugh by direct descent belongs.

With the exception of the plays just noted, the descendants of the hard comedy style are a fairly sorry lot, though in a numerical sense such comedy remains at least as popular as the soft style. George Granville's *The She-Gallants* (January 1696) is representative. The author states that it was written in the mid-eighties (the source, Campistron's *L'Amante Amant*, was acted in 1684), which may explain the relatively *risqué* style. In breeches, the heroine pursues the inconstant hero. Along the way we meet Toby Cusifle, knight and pimp; a pair of fops, and amorous old Lady Dorimen, who attempts to get seduced by the disguised heroine in a lively boudoir scene (50–3). At the end, Bellamour romantically repents—on his knees (68–9). This concession to the new style was not enough: Downes notes that the play offended 'some Ladies' and 'made its Exit'. Mrs. Behn's *The Younger Brother; or The Amorous Jilt* (February 1696) has even less of the soft style, and got hissed. The play is complicated and a bit tired. That it waited until the resumption of competition to see the stage is not surprising, though by that time it was badly dated. In one plot Mirtilla, the amorous jilt, is followed to England by the besotted Prince Frederick. Her husband, the stupid Sir Morgan Blunder, is no impediment to her scheming ways. The prince's true love Olivia is disguised as his page, and finally gets her man. In the second plot Sir Rowland Marteen's two sons vie for Teresia, the younger and more deserving son getting her. Sir Rowland gives way easily and weepily. But the sexual attitudes in the play are those in vogue a decade earlier.

Comedies with substantial doses of sex tend to be light and farcical by this time. Joseph Harris's *The City Bride: or, The Merry Cuckold* (March 1696), from Webster's *A Cure for a Cuckold*, is a gay trifle. The double romantic plot has only token seriousness, though the male leads come to the point of a duel. Captain Compasse returns home (after being supposed

dead for three years) to find that his wife Peg has added to the
family—and proceeds to treat it as a great joke. Their 'divorce'
and reconciliation (34–7) make a good spoof on contemporary
marital discord plots. Doggett's *The Country-Wake* (April 1696)
is even more just a farcical romp. Its trio of couples arrive at
the predictable conclusion, though along the way Woodvill
manages to debauch the young wife of an old man.[1] He gets
rebuked by a man of sense (40–1), and again we see a mixing
of the old and new styles. The rustic humour and Gloucester
setting contribute to a genial tone. As an afterpiece, *Hob* (1711),
it held the stage throughout the eighteenth century. At the
end of the one-act version Doggett cleverly chose to fracture
the romantic convention he had originally upheld.

Dick: Come, Sir, don't be as obstinate as an old Father at the
   latter end of a Comedy; you see the main Action is over; you had
   as good be reconcil'd.
Sir Thomas: Zoons, Sir, I can't be reconcil'd, nor I won't be
   reconcil'd.
Dick: Won't you? Why then, Mr. Pack give out the Play, and Mr.
   Newman let down the Curtain.

The difference between the two versions illustrates well the
shift from light comedy to afterpiece farce. A much more
entertaining play than *The Country-Wake*, a straight farce, is
Ravenscroft's *The Anatomist: or, The Sham Doctor* (November
1696), played in a double bill as already noted. It is largely
unoriginal (an adaptation of Hauteroche's *Crispin médecin*), a
confection of obvious horse-play, but done with panache.
Crispin has to pose as a cadaver and listen to the surgeon's
discussion of what he proposes to do. Ravenscroft later arranges
a scene (not in the source) in which Crispin poses as the doctor
while old Gerald (a heavy father) is forced to take the role of
cadaver. The repetition, and Crispin's medical errors, are
highly effective. The piece is certainly trivial, but also very
funny. As an afterpiece, it was a lasting success.

   To find a straight farce discussed in this company should
suggest the breakdown of the old divisions. Scarcely any of the
comedies after 1694 carry on the Carolean tradition cham-

---

[1] J. H. Smith (p. 167) reports that *The Country-Wake* is the last comedy in the
period in which a 'hero' is 'permitted to make a cuckold in the progess of the play,
and win the heroine also'.

pioned by Dryden, Southerne, and Congreve. The bulk of what are (relatively speaking) hard style comedies are but shadows or dilutions of the old form. The previous dividing lines fade, and the key criterion in placing a comedy becomes its relative position in the hard-to-humane-to-exemplary continuum. Congreve and Vanbrugh gain thereby some strange bedfellows, but perhaps the couplings are instructive. Some feeble plays lay claim to hard comedy status. John Dryden jun.'s *The Husband His own Cuckold* (June 1696) has two cuckolding actions, but frustrates both. In one the husband takes the gallant's place and reforms his wife with a lesson; in the other the rake Feewell is denied his success with young Mrs. Lurch by the cautious author. The intrigues are standard; the reproach of the rake (12) draws on the new style; the heavy, ponderously 'funny' speeches drag, and the whole enterprise lacks either energy or sparkle. 'Poetical Cookery' the dedication calls it.

If sex comedy was taboo, what would entertain? Dryden's son tried applying the concept of *coitus interruptus* to cuckoldry. Durfey makes a stab at wit comedy; John Dennis tries realistic humours. Durfey's *The Intrigues at Versailles* (May 1697) comes very oddly from him. He attempts to produce an Etherege- or Southerne-style comedy of manners, emphasizing witty conversation among upper-class French characters. He flirts discreetly with the patterns of sex comedy, but talk and intrigue outweigh titillation. Unfortunately the *soufflé* obstinately refuses to rise, and we are left with a watery version of the usual Durfey humours.[1] Dennis's *A Plot and no Plot* (May 1697) is a sodden humours comedy, neatly designed but 'laboriously Writ'.[2] Act II, 'Scene: *The Playhouse*', is a sad disappointment compared to Shadwell's *A True Widow*. The play 'did pretty well', perhaps because of an extra-literary device: Jo Hayns, who plays the plot-monger Rumour, announces in the prologue that *he* is impersonated in the play. So he is—by Penkethman as the trickster Baldernoe, 'A Player in Disguise'. As schemer, fake parson, sham magistrate, and

---

[1] For an account of the disputes about comic theory in the nineties which constitute the background for this play, see Harold Love, 'Dryden, Durfey, and the Standard of Comedy', *Studies in English Literature*, xiii (1973), 422–36.

[2] *A Comparison*, pp. 18–19.

architect of the *deus ex machina* solution, he is the one bright spot in the play. To an audience which revelled in Hayns's antics, the device must have been appealing.[1]

The hard comedy has turned fairly mushy. In a number of cases the inclusion of assumptions and elements from the new comedy alters the whole character of the play. Thus Mary Pix's *The Spanish Wives: A Farce* (August 1696) has—like some of the plays just discussed—a sex comedy plot design, but carefully 'baulks' the action. In one plot line the wife of the merry and trusting Governor of Barcellona flirts with Colonel Peregrine, but comes to realize the attractions of virtue. In a second plot 'love' and a prior engagement are used to excuse Elenora's eloping with Count Camillus, abandoning her marriage to the jealous Marquess of Moncada. But a Cardinal has promised the lady a divorce (46), and she virtuously goes to a monastery to await it (48), so the whole business is made as moral as possible. Compared to Mrs. Behn's somewhat similar *The False Count*, this is wishy-washy stuff indeed.

The 'mixing' at work is evident in Thomas Dilke's *The Lover's Luck* (December 1695), which ran profitably for eight days. Nicoll calls it rich, rough, realistic, coarse, a comedy in the old style.[2] This is true, but it is only half the truth. As in *Love for Love* an ex-libertine must prove that the leopard has changed his spots. Colonel Bellair is seriously in love (21), and his faithful passion is rewarded in romantic style. The action is vigorous; the use of street bullies is reminiscent of Shadwell. There are contradictions everywhere. A 'little girl' epilogue rings oddly against the serious view of love in the play. Mrs. Purflew is right in insisting on a reformation in Bellair, but she is sharply rebuked for capriciousness in playing coy (27): Dilke sees no charms in the love game, and yet he is not really the exponent of the new comedy that J. H. Smith's criteria would make him. James Drake's *The Sham-Lawyer* (May 1697) has a similar balance, and is quite reminiscent of Dennis's *A Plot and no Plot*. Long, heavy speeches completely ruin intrigue, which drags anyway.[3] A nasty old miser, Wrangle,

---

[1] See Tobyas Thomas's *The Life of Jo Hayns* (1701) for a miscellaneous assortment of the kind of pranks and scandals associated with Hayns. This is the tradition on which Dennis is drawing.   [2] Nicoll, I. 217.

[3] The best thing about this comedy is the description on the title-page: 'As it was DAMNABLY Acted at the Theatre-Royal in Drury-Lane'.

mistreats his young wife, who nobly refuses the advances of Friendly, an attractive gentleman posing as a law-student. Wrangle is finally blackmailed into treating his wife better, and Friendly promises to respect her virtue. In a feeble imitation of the love game Careless (a witty, extravagant gentleman) wins Olympia, a wealthy young widow of exemplary honour.

The considerable vogue for 'country' comedy continues with *The Cornish Comedy* (July 1696),[1] a confection of light romantic intrigue filled out with 'dialogues' inserted after the second and third acts, miscellaneous knockabout, and obvious padding. Squire Swash, a great hunter, is a good character; however, the play as a whole fails to cohere. Such potpourris seem occasionally to have caught the audience's fancy, as Motteux's *Love's a Jest* (June 1696) did. Set in Hertfordshire, the play has numerous songs, good-humoured country clowning, gipsy pickpockets, and lots of interpolations (e.g. a dialogue between a little boy and a little girl, 78–9). Sir Topewel Clownish and his nephew Squire Illbred, Frankly (a young gentleman masquerading as a chambermaid), and others romp airily through predictable nonsense. In the midst of this, however, we find Francelia, a serious heroine, firmly disciplining the ex-libertine Lord Lovewel. (The ranks of the libertines were being rapidly depleted by 1696, and the supply was about to give out.) Truly, when the 'man of sense' stereotype appears in *this* context, we may say that it has become the norm. By the mid-nineties the 'libertine approved' pattern is dead.

A unique but revealing indication of the direction comedy was taking is Vanbrugh's *Æsop* (January 1697), a reworking of material from Boursault. Critics have made little of it. Dobrée calls it dreary, written in the interest of a morality Vanbrugh accepted but was not interested in. Nicoll calls it rather poor, and dull, and finds Æsop 'very objectionable and cynical'.[2] Possibly he did not read to the end, in which the cynicism is dramatically reversed. The plot is largely incidental: ugly old Æsop is apparently willing to let Learchus force his daughter Euphronia to marry him, though she loves Oronces. The play rambles along its ill-focused way in a series of tableaux

---

[1] Gildon, in his *Lives and Characters*, states that the author was 'a Cornish attorney'. Powell brought the play to the stage.

[2] Dobrée, *History*, p. 232. Nicoll, I. 244.

which allow Æsop to present his fables. Some of them are acute and funny, and some of the incidental humours are well done (e.g. Sir Polidorus Hogstye, of Beast-Hall, in Swine County—II. 47). At the dénouement in Act V Æsop joins the lovers' hands and preaches the obvious moral. The substance of the play is the character of Æsop: little wonder that Cibber delighted in the role.[1] Little as the moralizing style appeals to us now, we have to recognize that the original audience loved it. '*Oronoko*, *Æsop*, and *Relapse* are Masterpieces, and subsisted *Drury-lane* House, the first two or three Years.'[2] The 'Second Part', added about March, is simply an addendum, not a separate play. It is original to Vanbrugh, and quite without focus. Its point is to give the patentees' views on the Lincoln's Inn Fields breakaway, satirizing Betterton's crew as foolish, wrangling mutineers. Æsop's fable tells them to rejoin and obey. From there (without any transition) Vanbrugh wanders on to consider the state of the nation, a foolish beau, and so forth. Part II does not even pretend to be drama in any formal, generic sense.

Naturally these years produce several specimens of the new comedy. I use this phrase advisedly: they are poor stuff. *She Ventures and He Wins* (September 1695), written by 'a Young Lady', is advertised in the prologue as 'a Woman's Treat'. Despite vigorous use of breeches and a mildly smutty epilogue about the writer's maidenhead, the design is rigorously moral. One couple (Sir Charles Frankford and Juliana) is romantically serious, the woman 'diffident, delicate, and modest'. In the second plot the heiress Charlot Frankford devises an elaborate sincerity test for the impecunious Lovewell: even the 'lively' heroine has very rigid standards of love and truth indeed. In contrast we are shown Squire Wouldbe attempting the virtue of Urania; she indignantly tells her husband, who punishes the would-be rake and delivers him up to his shrewish wife.

The attitudes behind this 'comedy' of example are repeated in a flock of contemporary plays. Thomas Scott's *The Mock-Marriage* (September 1695) has a livelier action, the same heavy speeches, and a very similar point. The man of sense, Fairly, fairly exudes conscious self-rectitude (about which J. H. Smith grumbles loudly) and wins Marina; along the way he

---

[1] Cibber, p. 121.   [2] *A Comparison*, pp. 20–1.

rebukes the 'rakish' Willmot (5), who is being tamed by the virtuous Clarinda. The love-duel is passably lively, but it ends with Willmot's romantic renunciation speech (43). Smith compares the love game to that in *Secret Love*, but what a world of difference in the upshot![1] Dilke's *The City Lady: or, Folly Reclaim'd* (December 1696) uses a little girl epilogue, and is full of boisterious city comedy and light intrigue—but the point of it all is the reform and reclamation of Lady Grumble, a 'City Lady lately remov'd into *Covent-Garden,* in all things affecting Quality'. The two romantic couples remain distinctly subsidiary. Cibber's *Womans Wit* (*c.* January 1697) is a busy play, but not a lively one. Here the coquette is the villainess. Lovemore, a man of sense, loves the insincere Leonora, and has to be brought to value the true love of Emilia. Ashley's verdict —frigidly tidy—sums it up.[2] The one mildly amusing part is Mass Johnny, a frivolous role added for Doggett after the play —designed for the Lincoln's Inn Fields actors—was shifted to Drury Lane. Cibber later extracted the part for an afterpiece, *The School-Boy* (1702).

To find women writers working in the new comedy style is to be expected. Mrs. Manley's *The Lost Lover* (March 1696) is trivial and mechanical, and deservedly failed to last three days. The story is exemplary. Olivia has been forced to marry Smyrna (a rich old merchant) despite her passionate love for Wildman. That gentleman tries every trick to get to her and seduce her: she refuses him flat, and he learns to admire and respect her virtue (30, 33-4). In Belira (seduced and now ill-treated by Wilmore) we are shown the evil effects of yielding. Mrs. Pix's *The Innocent Mistress* (June 1697) relies even more heavily on preachy righteousness. Sir Charles Beauclair has to renounce his true (platonic) love, Mariamne, and she him, until we find that the wife he was forced to marry is a bigamist, leaving him free. His friend Beaumont, an honest country gentleman and man of sense, is made intolerably complacent. Beaumont's smug lectures are a major feature of the play, which, Gildon tells us, enjoyed good success.

Surveying the state of comedy in the mid-nineties, we find that the average quality is the worst yet in the period—partly

---

[1] J. H. Smith, pp. 161-4.
[2] Leonard R. N. Ashley, *Colley Cibber* (New York, 1965), pp. 45-6.

as a result of exemplary moral demonstrations, partly just as the result of a lot of heavy and inexpert writing. In 'kinds' we have seen a rapid collapse of distinctions. Even the descendants of hard comedy—*Love for Love, The Relapse, The Provok'd Wife*— have significant concessions to the 'humane' outlook. A majority of the plays just surveyed actually include overtly exemplary characters, even where there is also vigorous comic satire and humour—as in *The Sham-Lawyer* or *The Spanish Wives*, the latter openly designated 'A Farce'! By the late eighties two parallel schools of comedy had developed, and both flourish in the early nineties. By 1695–7 the old comedy has wasted away to a shadow. Its elements and stock characters are retained, but the attitudes involved have changed drastically. The 'hard' view has given way to the 'humane' outlook, positive example is enjoying a rapid rise, and the old comedy is dead.

Directionless Tragedy

Unlike the comedy, tragedy shows no clear change in these years. The older modes, derived from heroic and pathetic drama, continue, as does the newer classic–stoic mode. Tragedy is numerically flourishing, but is largely marking time in respect to types. The best and most successful plays, *Oroonoko* and *The Mourning Bride*, are both decidedly backward-looking, skilful reprises of established forms.

The worst of the late heroic love-and-drivel mode is well represented by Banks's *Cyrus the Great* (December 1695). *A Comparison* reports that the players had previously refused it; only the urgent need for new plays brought it to the stage. Shock and horror seem to be Banks's principal objects. The play opens on a battlefield 'almost cover'd with dead Bodies'— Cyrus has just defeated Crœsus. On page 5 'A dead Carkass of one of the slain rises' and speaks oracles. Ghosts, thunder and lightning, a witches' song (in imitation of the Davenant *Macbeth*), threatened executions, female insanity, and Panthea's reconstruction of the mangled remains of Abradatas ('whose Limbs she had seemingly fix'd to his Body'—53) go along with the usual love complications and heroic verbiage, badly done. Mrs. Manley's *The Royal Mischief* (May 1696) is extremely similar, but carried out with more vigour. The lustful princess

Homais precipitates a bloodfest. In the notorious part of the play the virtuous Osman is shot out of a cannon (alive at the start), and the loving Selima faithfully collects the 'smoking Relicks' and covers them with 'burning Kisses' (44, 46). The near-Eastern setting, the inflated sentiment, the attempt at fancy scenic effect,[1] all speak of the spirit of 1675 *redivivus*. The 'little girl' epilogue is one of a number at about this time, and is a reminder that the audience had by no means eschewed all titillation.

Female writers, especially, seem consistently to have favoured the heroic mode. Catharine Trotter's *Agnes de Castro* (December 1695) is a standard mixture of court intrigue, heated heroic sentiment in blank verse, and fairly limited pathos. Something of the stoic mode appears at the end when the Prince, preparing to fall on his sword after Agnes's death, is persuaded by his father that his duty is to remain alive and govern. Mary Pix's *Ibrahim the Thirteenth Emperour of the Turks* (May 1696) is an obvious imitation of Lincoln's Inn Fields' Barry and Bracegirdle pattern in tragedy. The Sultan's mistress, Sheker Para, wants young Amurat, who refuses her because he loves Morena. Annoyed, Sheker Para persuades the Sultan to rape Morena (who returns to her father with her 'hair down' and takes poison). Practically everyone gets killed in the ensuing complications. The short verse lines contribute to a vigorous melodrama. Lust and the macabre fascinate Mrs. Pix; in this instance Amurat and Morena give the play a considerable pathetic interest.

The one reasonably impressive 'heroic' play from these years is Congreve's *The Mourning Bride* (February 1697), a tragicomedy which rewards virtue and punishes vice. (It is analysed above in Chapter 5.) Herbert Davis rightly reminds us that as Dryden's protégé and heir Congreve was more or less bound to enter the heroic field.[2] The result is a beautifully modelled melodrama which takes the virtue, heroism, and setting of *The Conquest of Granada* and puts it on a more human scale. Congreve's single plot (possibly modelled on *Cleomenes*) and irregular blank verse reflect the experience of the mature Dryden. Into the clichés of court intrigue and lust Congreve

---

[1] For example, the river (27)—quite ambitious for Lincoln's Inn Fields, if they did indeed display it.   [2] *Complete Plays*, ed. Davis, pp. 317–19.

reads a high, even religious moral. The dedication to Princess Anne says that the play is 'constituted on a Moral'—to wit, that 'The just Decrees of Heav'n' will see that 'Blessings ever wait on vertuous Deeds;/And tho' a late, a sure Reward succeeds' (321, 383–4). Thus the 'End is to recommend and to encourage Vertue'. Many of the nineties writers could make such a claim. What made *The Mourning Bride* a huge success[1] was less the moral trimmings than its slick, professional construction. The lovely precision of its language, the skilful and economical exposition, the sure handling of the cliché situations[2] place the play a world away from the butcherly dramaturgy of the Female Wits, Gould, Scott, Hopkins, Gildon, and Filmer, who are writing 'tragedy' at the same time. Against this smash hit at Lincoln's Inn Fields Rich chose to run *The Triumphs of Virtue: A Tragi-Comedy* (anonymous; February–March 1697), morally a somewhat similar play. In a court setting (more domestic than Congreve's) we are given intrigue and love triangles. The Duke pursues Bellamira, but is talked round and winds up admiring her virtue (32). This play gives us on a raised and romanticized level the kind of thing a 'new' comedy is putting into a London setting.

The standard formula for a serious play in these years is simple: graft pathos and sentiment onto an old play. Gould's *The Rival Sisters* (October 1695) works from Shirley's *The Maid's Revenge* (and directly from its source). Forced marriages yield five deaths, the ambitious father being preserved to speak the Moral:

> And O! hereafter may all Parents see
> This Story, and Example take by me;
> That to each Child they may alike be kind;
> Nor rashly part what Heav'n and Love has joyn'd.

The play ('moral' aside) is vivid, forceful, and natural—despite some rhyme. As a domestic tragedy it has force, not-

---

[1] Its popularity continued well into the eighteenth century. See Emmett L. Avery, *Congreve on the Eighteenth-Century Stage* (New York, 1951).

[2] For example, the noble prisoner in disguise, secretly married to the princess, who is designed for a favourite's son by a tyrannical father. A captive queen, wanted by the King but preferring the prisoner. The King killed by mistake. A headless corpse misidentified. Mistaken suicide averted by a whisker. The like is to be found in thirty other plays.

withstanding the too-obvious striving for pathetic effect.[1] Thomas Scott's *The Unhappy Kindness* (Summer 1696) is Fletcher's *A Wife for a Month* made into straight tragedy. The low comedy is dropped, the action pulled together, sentiment and moral platitudes poured in. Thus a pleasant, rambling tragicomedy becomes a stodgy tragedy. The liveliest thing about the play is the epilogue, spoken by Jo Hayns mounted on an ass. Fletcher's *Bonduca* (October 1695), with anonymous alterations, was printed 'With a New Entertainment of Musick, *Vocal* and *Instrumental*' by Purcell. The alterations consist of a bit of sentimentalizing for pathetic effect, and the interpolation of a good deal of music. The epilogue, spoken by 'Miss Denny Chock, but Six Years Old', is mildly smutty. Settle's revision of *Philaster* (Spring 1696) cuts references to usurpation and somewhat tidies up the morality.

All four of these adaptations are Patent Company shows— acquired and mounted on the cheap, evidently. So was *Neglected Virtue* (February 1696), perhaps by Charles Hopkins. This plodding bloodbath gives us the forced marriage theme; love triangles; court intrigues; and a rescue from the scaffold. Alinda enters poisoned and raving, and expires, whereupon Artaban falls on his sword—finis.

The one good pathetic tragedy in these years (also a Rich production) is Southerne's *Oroonoko* (November 1695), discussed briefly above in Chapter 5 as a split plot tragicomedy. All sources agree that the play was a tremendous success. Southerne uses Behn's novel with great skill, giving us an affecting picture of Oroonoko—a noble savage, but preeminently a heroic figure trapped by fate, and (like Cleomenes) meeting it with a granitic firmness made human by love. The treacherous governor who tricks him into surrender (and tries to rape his beloved wife, Imoinda) can destroy but cannot diminish him. The sub-plot—involving the husband-hunting Welldon sisters—provides a necessary distraction from the throbbing pathos of the central plot and gives us, once again, an example of Southerne's acute psychological perception and his ability to clarify by contrast. Oroonoko's stature, the evil governor, and the planters' avarice are simply part of a

[1] For example, Miss Cross (then aged 13) enters 'mad, stab'd in many places' (53); she then tears her wound and dies.

pathetic fairy story unless some very everyday spectators are introduced for contrast. The widow Lackitt, the Welldons, the virtuous Blanford have their own plots and schemes, and provide parallel themes and motives. But above all they return Oroonoko to the real world. Sutherland complains that as in *The Fatal Marriage* Southerne pours on too much in Act V. The long scene between Oroonoko and Imoinda in which they decide there is no hope drips with hyper-intense emotion. And to have Oroonoko manage to stab the governor before throwing himself on Imoinda's body to die (84) is perhaps too tidily satisfying. Act V does not read well; but it might play very effectively indeed in the theatre.

The classic–stoic plays make an almost startling contrast to the flaming emotion of *Oroonoko*. Hopkins's *Pyrrhus* (August 1695) is yet another instance of a play written years earlier suddenly brought to the stage after the Lincoln's Inn Fields breakaway. There are heroic tinges—the ghost of Alexander the Great, love tangles, a siege, drums, and reported fighting. Like Cleomenes, Pyrrhus is an example of the humanized hero, his faithful love for his wife softening the icy firmness of his character. Unhappily, the stiff and formal writing makes the play over all more frigid than stoic. *Pausanias, the Betrayer of His Country* (April 1696), probably by Richard Norton, is commended in Garth's *Dispensary* for its classicism. In the dedication (signed by Southerne) the author is highly praised: 'he built for the Experiment, upon the Model of the Antients, and according to the reformation of the *French* Stage.' As Rothstein acidly observes, all Southerne's praise of the 'single action' is inaccurate—Norton threw in a fop and an *ingénue* hoyden named Mawkine who are ludicrously irrelevant to the main action. The play's obvious moral is brought home with tedious clarity. The prose passages are competent; the verse portions come out flat. The importance of this unexciting play is in the deliberate 'classicizing' and the support such a venture found. Another attempt at the 'French' style is Edward Filmer's *The Unnatural Brother* (January 1697). The preface complains that 'the Play was too grave for the Age' and contained 'too few Persons'—seven named characters, put on stage very sparingly. Most of the play is a chilly series of conversations. The relatively rousing catastrophe was turned into a one-act tragedy for Motteux's *Novelty* later in the spring, after this play's 'very cold reception'. In the finale, Elvira proves her innocence to her husband Grammount by stabbing herself, whereupon he stabs himself. Both die, and the villain Dampierre, condemned to death by fiendish tortures, merely laughs. But by the time we get to this, we are in no condition to be moved by it.

Gildon's *The Roman Brides Revenge* (November 1696) deserves notice for its attempt to graft the classic–stoic code onto the somewhat more vigorous and stimulating heroic mode. The emperor wants Martian's wife Portia, which does not please the empress. After the usual intrigues and heroic clutter, Portia, thinking Martian dead, poisons herself and the emperor. Martian, disabused of the notion that she is polluted, stabs himself and dies. The play is pretty turgid stuff, but the underlying concept is sensible. There is more life, motion, and feeling in this plot than in the Hopkins, Norton, and Filmer plays, yet the sense of love and duty is present in 'classical' rather than 'pathetic' terms. We are spared the emotional bath that Banks or the Female Wits would give us. Unfortunately, Gildon is too poor a playwright to make the formula work.

Operatic productions continue in these years, but without any clear sense of form or direction. There are two standard formulas for the construction of operas—one a descendant from the masque tradition, the other amounting to the interpolation of music, fancy scenes, and machine business into an old play. To find a work, like *King Arthur*, in which there is full integration of the musical and scenic elements with a story is a real rarity.

The masque tradition is represented by Durfey's *A New Opera, call'd Cinthia and Endimion* (January 1697). The piece benefits from Durfey's usual lovely songs. The moral message concerning chastity is reminiscent of Crowne's *Calisto* (1675). As the dramatis personae states, in case the message should be vague, the characters are conceived as 'morally fashioning the Vertues and Vices of Human Nature'. Thus Daphne is pride and ill nature; Endimion is modesty, integrity, and good nature; and so forth.[1]

---

[1] Scholars have sometimes been sceptical of Durfey's claim that it was originally designed for presentation at Court before Queen Mary. But Rich's choosing to

The habit of vamping up old plays as operas appears in *The Indian Queen* (anonymous), and the Powell–Verbruggen *A New Opera; called Brutus of Alba* (October 1696). The former was supposed to be mounted at the United Company by Betterton, who specialized in such productions, but was delayed, probably until autumn 1695. According to Gildon, Rich's production did well: certainly we find a surprising number of performances in the next two years.[1] *Brutus of Alba* is of the 'semi-opera' genre about which Roger North complains so bitterly.[2] The text of Tate's play is cut to make room for one big musical number in each act, reusing the effects designed for *Albion and Albanius* and *The Fairy-Queen*. Fame, Augusta, airy spirits, a scaramouche and harlequin dance, a dialogue between an old man and a young girl—all are tossed in at random. This vulgar mishmash brings opera to a new low.

The one interesting operatic piece from these years is Settle's *The World in the Moon* (June 1697). Gildon calls it a 'comical opera'. The piece is a hybrid: Settle sets up an ordinary London romance comedy (with both serious and farcical elements), but lets part of the action take place in the Dorset Garden theatre, where Rich's company is rehearsing a new opera called *The World in the Moon*. Thus in Act II Wildblood, Stanmore, and the country gull Tom Dawkins sit on stage with Jo Hayns watching the rehearsal. Hayns manages to convince Tom that the Fairy Queen has fallen in love with him, and dresses him up as a beau (21). Tom's mother has a fit over the transformation and spoils the romance, much to Tom's disgust. Along the way Settle gets in some good bits of humour. Arriving in London, Tom marvels: 'Here's a whole thousand of Houses, and not one Barn among them all' (1). Asked why he has no part, Jo inquires if he looks like a cupid (13). The romantic plot has Palmerin Worthy—a grave and

---

mount it at Drury Lane rather than Dorset Garden reinforces an obvious point—the staging is unusually simple for this kind of show, and could well have been planned with the limited resources of the Whitehall stage in mind.

[1] This version is unpublished. See B.M. Add. MS. 31,499. It is discussed in Dryden's *Works*, VIII. 325–30. The performances noted in *The London Stage*, Part 1 (pp. 461, 476, 480, 489) are almost without question of this adaptation, not of the original, as the entries there imply.

[2] Roger North, *The Musical Grammarian*, ed. Hilda Andrews (London, 1925), p. 34.

moral male virgin of 26—win Jacintha. Her brother Ned
Stanmore champions Palmerin's deserving poverty against the
claims of wealthy old Sir Dottrell Fondlove (30). Tinges of the
new comedy are evident here. The piece is pleasant if strictly
ordinary, but Settle manages to make the show a pleasure by
so cleverly working in the fancy 'operatic' entertainment
without making it seem contrived and disjunct. The operatic
portions remain essentially separate, but Settle had an excellent
idea in trying a low London backdrop. English opera never did
jell as a form, but this is one of the cleverest experiments.

Surveying the first two years of competition, a few general
conclusions are evident. The Lincoln's Inn Fields breakaway
brought on a great flood of new plays, most of them bad, and
the majority immediate failures. The rate at which audiences
damned plays appalled both writers and the managers;
prologue after prologue notes the harshness or captiousness of
the audience and begs indulgence, as in Congreve's prologue
for *The Husband His own Cuckold*, where he notes worriedly that
the year is remarkable for 'Blasted Plays'. Most of them, to be
sure, were pretty dreadful. The scarcity of solidly professional
writers and well-to-do amateurs contributes to a sharp decline
in the quality of new plays, which are nothing like as good
(even in purely technical terms of writing and construction)
as the average twenty years earlier.

Rich had to mount new plays: his actors could not compete
with the older stars in those stars' own repertory. Betterton's
retaliation with nearly as many new plays is somewhat surprising. Probably, though, he remembered that Killigrew had
failed to hold the audience with experienced actors and
exclusive claim to the classic repertory back in the sixties, and
was determined not to stand pat on the past. Betterton also
had the advantage of Congreve's services, and he got hold of
Vanbrugh's second original play. In repertory, both houses
put on heroic, pathetic, and classic–stoic dramas, and do so in
the same proportions. Similarly they perform the new and the
mixed forms of comedy pretty equally. Betterton, however, has
a near-monopoly on such remnants of the old comedy as can
be found (e.g. *Love for Love, The Provok'd Wife, The City Bride,
The Country-Wake, The Intriguos at Versailles*). Plainly he has a

strong inclination that way. To offset this preponderance, Rich has essentially a monopoly on opera. Lincoln's Inn Fields was not equipped for such display, and Rich uses his control of Dorset Garden to some advantage. The other Rich speciality is cheap revisions of old plays (*The Rival Sisters*, *The Unhappy Kindness*, *Bonduca*—with operatic leanings, and *Philaster*). The first round was clearly Betterton's, but the Patent Company, having survived two seasons, had achieved stability and was about to become a more formidable antagonist.

Surveying the state of the dramatic types is a somewhat dismal business. In tragedy neither the heroic nor the pathetic form was flourishing. The new classic–stoic type had produced a long series of frigid and dull failures after *Cleomenes*, the seminal work in this mode. The popularity of mixed-bag 'opera' is a clear hint of the audience's increasing taste for multi-media entertainments. In comedy, the mid-nineties witness the collapse of the hard comedy revival carried on so promisingly under Dryden's sponsorship at the beginning of the decade. The 'soft' view becomes widely prevalent, and in a long series of plays (*She Ventures*, *The Mock-Marriage*, *The Innocent Mistress*, *et al.*) we find rapidly increasing doses of overtly exemplary didacticism.

The theatres were about to find themselves in deep trouble. The dearth of major writers—even just competent writers— was a large part of the difficulty. Possibly the best of them felt that the climate was unpropitious, the audience unreceptive to what they wanted to write. At any rate Southerne (who lived to 1746) and Congreve (d. 1729) wrote exactly one more play apiece in this period; Vanbrugh never again wrote an original play. Of the other writers active in 1697, Colley Cibber was clearly the best—no great recommendation for the state of English drama.

In the spring of 1697 both companies had some reason for optimism. The Drury Lane company had stabilized; Betterton's Company had enjoyed a string of considerable successes, of which *The Mourning Bride* was the latest. Yet the storm clouds of the coming Collier crisis were plainly to be seen, if anyone wanted to look. Defensive remarks about morality are legion in prefaces and prologues. And though audiences cannot have suddenly become rigidly prudish—as the flood of 'little girl' epilogues attests—somewhere among the public, pressure to clean up the drama was obviously gathering strength. In January 1696 Dorset, the Lord Chamberlain, issued an order demanding that the players faithfully submit all MSS. to the Master of the Revels, and directed that officer 'to be very Carfull in Correcting all Obsenityes & other Scandalous Matters & such as any wayes Offend against ye laws of God Good manners or the knowne Statutes of this Kingdom'.[1] On 4 June 1697 Sunderland, the new Lord Chamberlain, repeated the injunction, with an angry complaint that 'many of the new Plays Acted by both Companys of his Mat^s Comedians are Scandalously lewd and Prophane.'[2] Already faced with the problems of destructive competition, a shortage of good writers, and a sparse and captious audience, the two companies were about to find themselves in an unpleasant mess.

[1] P.R.O. L.C. 7/1.   [2] P.R.O. L.C. 5/152, p. 19.

CHAPTER 10

THE EMERGENCE OF
AUGUSTAN DRAMA 1697–1710

THE double tradition of the 1690s keeps the Carolean play types alive, and for a time obscures the decisive swing toward new kinds of drama. By the late nineties, however, Carolean drama is definitely a thing of the past: the new era dawns early in the decade, and by the time of the theatrical union of 1708 the transition is complete. In this chapter we will see the final breakdown of the old types and the establishment of a new synthesis. Defining it, however, poses considerable problems.

Within the 1660–1800 period in drama there seem to me to be four overlapping and connected but essentially distinct centre-points: Carolean drama (*fl.* 1665–85), Augustan drama (dominant in the first quarter of the eighteenth century), the experimental drama of the 1730s, and Georgian drama (*fl.* 1760–80). The designation 'Augustan drama' will certainly annoy at least one group of contemporary scholars, but *faute de mieux* it will serve. Whatever the name applied to the new agglomeration, I hope that its essentially different character will be granted. The new Augustan drama is of course no more homogeneous than the old Carolean drama. Just as the basically Tory Carolean drama encompasses some Whig zealots, so the 'Whig drama' of Cibber, Centlivre, Steele, and Addison has its Tory stalwarts. The factors contributing to the shift, including political, religious, and social matters, defy tidy definition. In the broadest sense, the change is ideological.

Study of the transition is complicated by the heated competition between Drury Lane and Lincoln's Inn Fields, which produces an unprecedented number of new plays—fully 170 in the years covered here. Most of them are very poor stuff, and need detain us only briefly. Basically, we will find two phases in this period. The first (1697–1702) represents a desperate attempt on the part of the two companies simply to stay alive, to survive hard times and the Collier crisis. Both groups do weather the storm, shakily, and proceed (1702–7) with experiments designed to restore prosperity and establish a new equilibrium. Singers, dancers, jugglers, animal acts, and double bills are all tried with varying success. The construction of the Haymarket theatre (opened in April 1705) coincides with and then fuels the Italian opera boom which does so much to change the theatrical situation in London. The new union of 1708 reflects the failure of all these efforts, and signals the onset of a stasis in the drama and in the theatres which was not really to be broken for fully two decades.

I. THE STRUGGLE FOR SURVIVAL 1697–1702

In these years the history of the drama is increasingly affected by the state of the theatres.[1] Now in hard times, Lincoln's Inn Fields found that it had a serious fight on its hands. Rich's ragtag and bob-tail company barely survived its first two seasons, losing a lot of money and subsisting on a few lucky hits—*Oroonoko*, *The Relapse*, and *Æsop*, as *A Comparison Between the Two Stages* tells us, to which we may add *Love's Last Shift*. Having survived, the Patent Company had some significant advantages: youth, vigour, strong centralized management, and a monopoly on the only two good theatre buildings in London. By contrast, the Lincoln's Inn Fields group was old, and suffered from its cramped and inadequate theatre—'*Betterton's* Booth', as Powell caustically calls it in the prologue to *The Fatal Discovery* (February 1698), applying the advertising terminology of Bartholomew Fair. As Milhous observes, the seceders probably anticipated the failure of their leavings, and so made no effort to recruit or to arrange for better quarters, expecting to regain Drury Lane and Dorset Garden by default. Worse, the company itself fell into serious disarray. An under-capitalized co-operative venture, Lincoln's Inn Fields suffered the ill effects of management by a committee of *prima donna* actors. David Crauford's much-quoted account of the chaos, inefficiency, and incompetence which caused him to withdraw *Courtship A-la-mode* and take it to Drury Lane (July 1700) definitely represents

---

[1] For my knowledge of the theatrical competition in these years I am much indebted to Judith Milhous, 'Thomas Betterton at Lincoln's Inn Fields', unpub. diss. (Cornell University, 1974).

an extreme. But the seriousness of the situation is made plain in the Lord Chamberlain's order of 11 November 1700.[1] By the 1699–1700 season Lincoln's Inn Fields is clearly in dire straits. Vanbrugh wrote, 25 December 1699: 'Matters [are] running very low with 'em this Winter; if Congreve's Play don't help 'em they are undone.'[2] *The Way of the World* achieved only an adequate run the following March, but Betterton's Falstaff in *King Henry IV* had 'drawn all the town' in January. Prior notes that 'to encourage that poor house' the Kit-Cat Club took a special box at the *première*.[3] But the situation remained desperate.

Both houses were suffering from the efforts of the moral reformers. Talk of closing the theatres down altogether was in the air.[4] More immediately damaging was legal harassment from the zealots. Luttrell (12 May 1698) reports an attempt to get an indictment not only against the actors, but also against 'Mr Congreve for writing the "Double Dealer"; Durfey, for "Don Quixot"; and Tonson and Brisco, booksellers, for printing them'. There are rumours of prosecutions of actors in 1699, but our first hard evidence comes from 1701, when Betterton, Doggett, Bowman, Underhill, Barry, *et al.* were convicted and fined for profanely and jestingly using the sacred name of God upon the public stage. *The Provok'd Wife*, *The Anatomist*, and *Love for Love* were complained of: from the quotations of Ben's speeches in the last play, we can deduce that Doggett added a good bit of profanity not in Congreve's printed text.[5] Rich's actors, indicted about the same time for *Volpone*, *The Humour of the Age*, and *Sir Courtly Nice*, escaped on a technicality. Two loose documents in L.C. 7/3 (printed by Krutch) give an idea of the players' line of

---

[1] 'Whereas I am informed there are frequent disorders among ye Actors [at Lincoln's Inn Fields] ... for want of sufficient Authority to keep them to their Duty: for ye better Government thereof ... I do hereby appoint Mr Thomas Betterton to take upon him ye sole management thereof, with power to reward those who are diligent, and to punish such as he finds negligent.' P.R.O. L.C. 5/153, f. 23.

[2] *Works*, IV. 4.

[3] Letters by Villiers Bathurst and Prior, cited in *The London Stage*, Part 1, pp. 522–3.

[4] See Joseph Wood Krutch, *Comedy and Conscience after the Restoration* (1924; 2nd edn. [1949] rpt. New York, 1961), p. 178.

[5] P.R.O. K.B. 27/2147, Rex Roll no. 9. On these prosecutions in general, see Krutch, pp. 167–85.

defence. George Bright petitioned against a conviction (based on an informer's sworn evidence) for having played Old Bellair in *The Man of Mode*—on the grounds (1) that his superiors at Lincoln's Inn Fields had ordered him to speak the part, and (2) that the Lord Chamberlain had licensed the play. Similarly an undated petition from the Lincoln's Inn Fields actors to Queen Anne argues that they should be free from prosecution for acting licensed plays. The net result, apart from a long series of expensive legal hassles, seems to have been a considerable tightening up of licensing procedures.

The general trends in comedy clearly reflect these pressures. Contrary to myth, the old comedy is not pushed out by the new. Rather, a new synthesis emerges, a median comedy which is neither 'hard' nor truly sentimental–exemplary. In the five years to be surveyed here there are a few works clearly belonging to the hard and the new comedy schools, and a few outright farces. But more than half the new comedies from these years seem to represent a compromise of sorts. One could call it half-heartedly sentimental; from another angle one could call it a laundered form of the old comedy. Neither description is quite right. The cutting edge and cynicism of satiric Carolean comedy are gone, but most of these plays are not especially emotional or exemplary in bent. Humane comedy (Shirley Kenny's phrase) is probably the best general descriptive term for the kinds of comedy characteristic after 1700. (A play like *The Beaux Stratagem* can be denounced for dishonest romanticism by a proponent of hard comedy, but it is scarcely very Steele-ish.) 'Exemplary comedy', J. H. Smith's preferred term, is too restrictive, and hence misleading. The term 'sentimental' should likewise be avoided, both because it is hopelessly hazy and because it sets up an opposition between old and new which does not really hold true. In the early nineties there is a relatively sharp contrast, but then the two start to meld and converge—a process which encourages the 'equivocation' in new comedy noted by Paul E. Parnell.[1]

Only four genuine hard comedies are to be found in these years. Farquhar's first play, *Love and a Bottle* (December 1698), is racy, bawdy, and coarse. Roebuck, the wild Irish

---

[1] 'The Sentimental Mask', *PMLA*, lxxviii (1963), 529–35.

rover, finally does 'reform' (I. 73) to marry Leanthe, who
has been disguised as page to Lucinda—who gets Leanthe's
sober brother Lovewell, friend to the rakish hero. The friends
share in paying for Roebuck's bastard by Mrs. Trudge—
expressing satisfaction that the female twin luckily died (16,
18). Thinking of the horrors of marriage, Roebuck reflects 'Ay,
but there's Money.—Oh but there are Children; squawling
Children. Ay but then there are *Rickets* and *Small-Pox*, which
perhaps may carry them all away' (64). Roebuck is no platitudinous man of sense. Farquhar makes lively use of conventions
—libertine talk; a breeches part; mock marriage; good jokes
about the formulas for comedy and tragedy (51); the foolish
poet Lyrick; a smutty epilogue by Jo Hayns snarling at Collier.
Rather like *The Old Batchelour*, the concatenation suggests
wide reading in earlier comedies. So exuberantly does Farquhar
deploy his clichés that one critic has even been misled into
supposing that the play (in the fashion of *Three Hours After
Marriage*) is a burlesque debunking of its type.[1] We may find
satiric overtones, but in both the bawdy libertine and the serio-
romantic heroine (quite capable of breaking into verse—61)
Farquhar is within the limits of convention.

Farquhar's first play seems even cruder by the side of
Congreve's last. *The Way of the World* (March 1700) needs no
critical analysis here. Contrary to a durable myth, the play
did not fail: rather, it had a respectable success, though
nothing like what was hoped. And instead of vanishing from
the stage, thus signalling the end of wit comedy, it seems to
have been revived within two years.[2] Downes says that the
play 'being too Keen a Satyr, had not the Success the Company Expected' (p. 45). Critics have quibbled with this statement, feeling that the comedy (despite its ironical denial of
satire in the prologue) is not especially satiric. We can grant
this, without necessarily agreeing with Jean Gagen that the
protagonists are in essence exemplary. Congreve, says Clifford
Leech, 'lacks the animus of the satirist. . . . There is appraisal
in his mind, but acceptance too.' The hard comedy views are

---

[1] Eugene Nelson James, 'The Burlesque of Restoration Comedy in *Love and a
Bottle*', *Studies in English Literature*, v (1965), 469–90.

[2] Dryden (*Letters*, no. 74) attests to 'moderate success'. See also my 'A Revival of
The Way of the World in December 1701 or January 1702', *Theatre Notebook*, xxvi
(1971), 30–6.

softened only a bit, yet (in Leech's words) 'the final impression the play leaves is perhaps one of suppressed melancholy.' The problem Downes senses is perhaps less the keenness of the satire than the coldness of the presentation. In places the play is remarkably sensitive (the proviso scene), or contrariwise boisterously amusing (Lady Wishfort's cracking, peeling face, or the drunk scenes). But over all it is neither particularly lively nor especially amusing.[1]

The brilliance of the construction and dialogue have fascinated critics. What they are in aid of remains vague. The themes and serious tone lead Alan Roper to find it a kind of tract: '*The Way of the World* is about the difficulty of identifying and following a decent private life while still participating fully in the public life of society.' Novak (rightly, I think) reads it more in terms of our response to character, especially to Millamant. Almost without question, Congreve was responding to Collier in the *design* of the play, seeking to construct a serious comedy in the old mode which yet remained beyond moral reproach.

The old mode found one last disciple in William Burnaby. *The Ladies Visiting-Day* (*c.* January 1701) is beautifully modelled, even over-wrought. In the main plot, jealous old Sir Testy Dolt—no fool—trusts his spritely wife with young Polidore, who has supposedly been castrated by an irate Italian husband. Polidore uses his status in the family to get at Sir Testy's ward, Fulvia, and we know that he has no interest in Lady Dolt. Sir Testy, however, goes through agonies when he learns the truth about Polidore. In a second (title) plot, the social pretensions of Lady Lovetoy are vigorously ridiculed. She rejects the plain country gentleman Courtine, but disguised as a Russian prince he wins her. Burnaby's dedication says that he had thought the play would be inoffensive to the Ladies. It is a good, second-rate hard comedy, and at this date its failure comes as no surprise. *The Modish Husband* (*c.* January 1702) contains

---

[1] On this play see Novak, *Congreve*, Chapter 8, and 'The Artist and the Clergyman: Congreve, Collier and the World of the Play', *College English*, xxx (1969), 555–61; Holland, *The First Modern Comedies*; Paul and Miriam Mueschke, *A New View of Congreve's Way of the World* (Ann Arbor, Mich., 1958); Clifford Leech, 'Congreve and the Century's End'; Jean Gagen, 'Congreve's Mirabell and the Ideal of the Gentleman'; Alan Roper, 'Language and Action in *The Way of the World*, *Love's Last Shift*, and *The Relapse*', *ELH*, xl (1973), 44–69.

a good deal more cynical libertinism. Into a single plot Burnaby works a lot of complicated intrigue. Lord Promise, an unpleasant fop (Cibber), intrigues with Lady Cringe, while getting his friend Lionel to court his own wife (Lady Promise) to keep her distracted. The foolish Sir Lively Cringe is no threat. Both wives, however, prefer Lionel. The play suffered the flat failure one might anticipate. Burnaby is a competent minor playwright, but was writing twenty-five years past his time.

The 'new' comedies of these years are few and for the most part equally unsuccessful. *Love without Interest* (*c.* April 1699), an anonymous play evidently sponsored by Penkethman for the third-night profits, is representative. A lively couple (Wildman and Letitia) are pretty well smothered by a serious one (Trulove and Honoria). Trulove's fortune is 'slender', so Honoria at first miserably refuses him, unwilling to be a burden. They do get engaged, but when Honoria is found to be an heiress, Trulove (unwilling to take advantage of her) breaks off the engagement and has to be talked round. Other elements in the play are distinctly brisker—amorous old Sir Fickle Cheat, news-mad malaprop Wrangle, the cunning jilt Eugenia, who has been kept by Wildman. The elements are standard, and routinely handled, but as J. H. Smith notes, heavy emphasis is given to the things which will appeal to the Ladies. Another such anonymous effort, just as unsuccessful, is *Feign'd Friendship* (May 1699). Three couples are followed. Sabina tests the virtue and constancy of Townley. Eugenia, in male attire, reforms Lord Frolicksome, making him ashamed of his 'wildness', such as it is. In her spare time, Eugenia lectures the wealthy widow, Lady Generous, a pale imitation of the gay heroine, who then gives herself to Mr. Truelove. The title comes from Richley, a pretended friend of the heroes who also wants the widow. Complications are introduced by the wealthy fop No Wit, an overdone caricature. The play is cheerful but preachy, as is Thomas Baker's *The Humour of the Age* (March 1701). In form, this play exhibits many of the characteristics of the older comedy. Wilson wins the airy Lucia; his rival Quibble is married to the maid Pert, masked as her mistress; the extortionist Justice Goose marries Miranda, cast mistress of the malcontent Railton. But in the central action the virtuous Freeman falls in love with Tremilia, who turns out to be no Quaker after all: she has pretended to be poor in order to find a man uninterested in her fortune. Miranda, struck with admiration for this paragon, vows to lead a virtuous life henceforth. The play suffers from long, ponderously 'humorous' speeches, which are witty but too effortful. The prologue calls the play a moral satire, but its firm ethical basis did not save it from the reformers. One of the legal actions against the players cites this work—clear proof that the S.P.C.K. and its allies represent a force outside the theatres, not the 'new comedy' party.[1]

The one successful 'new' comedy is Steele's *The Funeral: or, Grief A-la-Mode* (December 1701). It combines humour and satire with exemplary characters: one can fairly call it a mixed comedy. Yet as Kenny says, 'several playwrights consciously cleaned up their bawdry, but only Steele actively campaigned for a new kind of drama.'[2] This is 'no amusing game; the stakes are too high.' Lord Brumpton, supposedly dead, discovers that his second wife is a hypocritical monster— and a bigamist. His virtuous, persecuted son Lord Hardy wins the exemplary Lady Sharlot, while Campley wins Lady Harriot in a discreet version of the gay couple game. The serious lovers and the steward Trusty are straight exemplary characters. Lord Brumpton and the spritely lovers are noble, generous, and warm-hearted, needing only to overcome minor flaws. Against these six are set the villainess, Lady Brumpton; her confidante-maid Tattleaid; her husband Cabinet; and the undertaker, Mr. Sable. Steele injects enough high spirits and foolery (e.g. Sharlot jumping out of the coffin—90) for the play almost never to seem ponderous or over-didactic. Indeed the author of *A Comparison* objects strenuously to lack of probability and decorum, concluding that the comedy is reduced to the indignity of the vilest farce.[3] Yet even this author concedes that 'it's fit every Gentleman shou'd be

---

[1] For an important elucidation of this point, see Calhoun Winton, 'Sentimentalism and Theater Reform in the Early Eighteenth Century', *Quick Springs of Sense: Studies in the Eighteenth Century*, ed. Larry S. Champion (Athens, Ga., 1974), pp. 97–112.

[2] Shirley Strum Kenny, 'Richard Steele and the "Pattern of Genteel Comedy" ', *Modern Philology*, lxx (1972), 22–37.

[3] *A Comparison Between the Two Stages*, pp. 78–92.

incourag'd that writes with so good an Intention.' Steele is experimenting, applying new techniques and meanings to old materials. In doing so he brought a sense of high purpose and clear direction to the tradition founded by Shadwell in his last plays. Despite the serious moral and the benevolist didacticism, *The Funeral* long remained a stock play, and I suspect that it was one of the really seminal works in the turn-of-the-century period. It represents only a tentative groping after the theory and pattern toward which Steele was working: Kenny is surely right in seeing *The Conscious Lovers*, two decades later, as the embodiment of Steele's philosophy of comedy. And yet this earlier play, at a time when the theatre was in low water, does much to suggest a viable popular formula: intrigue, humour, satire, and farce jollity do much to leaven the virtuous characters and didactic preachments imposed by moral theory. Doubtless many readers of *The Conscious Lovers* wish Steele had learned his own lesson.

Considering the attempt to appeal to a lower-class audience in these years, there are surprisingly few farces. Vanbrugh's *The Country House* (acted by January 1698) is a cheerful trifle translated from Dancourt. Almost certainly it was designed and played as an afterpiece. What it was played with initially we do not know, but in January 1703 it served as a finale for a concert and exhibition of dancing (a fact not made plain in *The London Stage*—cf. the *Daily Courant* playbill). Barnard is driven mad by uninvited guests, so finally decides to turn his expensive status symbol into an inn and charge 'friends' and relatives for room and board. In the course of the two brief acts Barnard's daughter Mariane is won by Erast. The piece long remained popular. Crowne's *Justice Busy, or the Gentleman Quack* (Spring 1700?) was not printed. We may guess that it was a farcical intrigue main piece; Downes implies that it expired after a short run.[1] Joseph Harris's *Love's a Lottery* (*c.* April 1699) consists of good-humoured foolery, to which a fancy masque and music were added. Lotteries were a craze of the time.[2] Clytander gets Amaranta, daughter of the

---

[1] See Arthur Franklin White, *John Crowne: His Life and Dramatic Works* (Cleveland, O., 1922), p. 177.

[2] For example in October 1698 the Dorset Garden theatre was used as the site of a huge public lottery draw, which was advertised in theatrical terms: 'There is now Acting at the Theatre Royal in Dorset Garden a Tragy-Comedy called The Wheel

Lottery-master, plus dowry; along the way some obvious butts are rallied: Brush-beard the philosopher, the mountebank Dr. Non-such, the author Mr. Scribble.

The median humane comedy must itself be roughly subdivided. A flock of translations and adaptations range from near-farce to almost pure Shakespeare. The standard comedies, most of them relying heavily on intrigue, tend to reflect old-comedy or new-comedy sympathies, without managing quite to belong to either camp: the extremes were doing badly, so writers took a middle way.

Two Shakespeare adaptations display heavy injections of farce. Granville's *The Jew of Venice* (December 1700) is a nasty, garbled mess. Crudities are interpolated (Portia's German suitor becomes a Dutchman, Myn Heer van Gutts—4); a musical masque including Prometheus chained to a rock with a vulture at his breast is added, and so forth. No major changes are made in Shylock's part, but the use of Thomas Doggett in that role suggests a clownish conception—borne out by Rowe's complaints in his edition that the real import of the part is tragic. Nonetheless, this version held the stage until Macklin restored Shakespeare's original in the 1740s. John Dennis's *The Comical Gallant: or the Amours of Sir John Falstaffe* (May 1702) is a cloddish and sodden vulgarization. Evidently it was an appeal to popular taste—quite a condescension from Dennis—but it was a flat failure.

Dennis had probably hoped to follow up the success of 'Betterton's' *King Henry IV* (January 1700). This is actually not an adaptation at all—merely a players' quarto with some cuts, and to call it a play by Betterton (as scholars usually do) is extremely misleading. Milhous points out that the cuts are politically motivated: the rebels are made unattractive; Henry the Fourth is whitewashed and his status as usurper played down; the churchmen are cut out of the rebels' plot; profanity is deleted. Betterton—if he was indeed responsible for this production version—wanted to anticipate political and moral objections.[1]

---

of Fortune, or The Fool's Expectation' (*Post Boy*, 18–20 October). *London Stage*, Part 1, p. 504.

[1] See Judith Milhous, 'Thomas Betterton's Playwriting', *The Bulletin of the New York Public Library*, lxxvii (1974), 375–92.

A Comparison Between the Two Stages (pp. 25–7) tells us that
Lincoln's Inn Fields scored a great success with *King Henry IV*
and other Shakespeare plays; Drury Lane riposted with a
Ben Jonson revival. Lincoln's Inn Fields brought out an
altered *Measure for Measure* (traditionally ascribed to Gildon),
whereupon Drury Lane got Vanbrugh to update Fletcher's
The Pilgrim. The adapter of *Measure for Measure* (*c.* February
1700) draws without acknowledgement on the Davenant version, though Mariana is restored. The result is a routine
tragicomedy with four major musical entertainments interpolated—making ample use of thunder machine, dancing
furies, and masque machinery ('*Phæbus* Rises in his Chariot
over the Sea. The *Nereides* out of the Sea'—45). *The Pilgrim*
(29 April) was a great success for more than thirty years. Vanbrugh turns Fletcher's blank verse into brisk prose, greatly
reducing the flowery beauty of a rather high-flown romance.
To this was added Dryden's *Secular Masque*, a reply, evidently,
to Lincoln's Inn Fields' musical additions to *Measure for Measure*.

    In rough outline, Vanbrugh's *Pilgrim* represents the English
notion of Spanish romance, which undergoes a revival about
this time. To this trend Vanbrugh also contributed *The False
Friend* (January 1702), a failure, though occasionally played
in later years. A translation of Le Sage's *Le Traître puni* (itself
founded on a Spanish play), the piece is a tense intrigue
melodrama. Guzman and Don John both pursue Leonora,
wife to Don Pedro. The treacherous Don John is stabbed,
confesses, and dies begging forgiveness; whether Guzman will
ultimately succeed with the lady is left unclear. The author of
A Comparison (pp. 95–6) complains that principal characters
cannot properly be killed in a comedy. Perhaps the audience
was uncomfortable with the conclusion, and certainly the play
suffered initially from Cibber's getting hurt after the third
night. Francis Manning's *The Generous Choice* (February 1700)
is another unsuccessful pseudo-Spanish play, though of a much
more standard design. Don Philip is finally united to Olivia
(who has pursued him in breeches); Frederick takes Cornelia;
the scheming Eleonora is dispatched to a nunnery. Serio-
romantic intrigue and sword-play (even the two heroines, in
breeches, have to draw and 'Fight awkerdly'—45) are lightened
by the addition of *Comedy of Errors* material, the reuniting of

long-lost twins, the 'Anthonys'. The one 'Spanish romance' which does succeed is Cibber's *Love makes a Man* (December 1700), a cleaned-up prose amalgam of *The Elder Brother* and *The Custom of the Country*. After a halting start, it ran steadily for the next two decades. Two sets of tragicomic intrigues are followed: Cibber enjoys swooping up to romantic precipices (e.g. the near strangling of Angellina—64), but generally keeps his tone light. Intrigue weighs more heavily here than sentiment, reversing Manning's balance.

Intrigue is indeed featured by a lot of authors in these years, even in those comedies with rather strong 'moral' tendencies. Mrs. Trotter's *Love at a Loss, or Most Votes carry it* (November 1700) is a good example of the 'mixed' intrigue play with new comedy leanings. Lesbia has contracted herself to the gay spark Beaumine, partly to spite Grandfoy. Now she thinks him honest and believes she loves him. The two men almost fight, but eventually all the characters *vote* on who should have her! Beaumine 'reforms', however, and wins her; Grandfoy announces that he will be their friend. In another action Constant wins Miranda—a gay couple reduced to moral circumstances; and on the fringes of the plot a variety of old-fashioned humours characters are routinely satirized. In Burnaby's first play, *The Reform'd Wife* (March 1700), Astrea, the young wife of old Sir Solomon Empty (an obnoxious *nouveau riche* ass, a bungling intriguer and adviser of playwrights) falls in love with Freeman, but the lady finally resigns herself to her unsatisfactory married life, and Freeman marries Sir Solomon's daughter, Clarinda. Lady Dainty, a super-fop, and Sir Solomon are excellent characters; the intrigues are well conducted; the serious issues in Astrea's position are sympathetically—not pathetically—handled; the minor humours characters are well mocked. Nonetheless, the play failed, hurt perhaps by its sharp but over-fussy and bookish dialogue. A similar effort the same month, also a failure, is Mary Pix's *The Beau Defeated*, from Dancourt's *Le Chevalier à la mode*. The key scene is the testing of young Clerimont (42–3): what ten years earlier had been the stamp of 'new comedy' ideology is by now simply part of the standard arsenal of comedy plot lines.

A better play, though little more successful, is Mrs. Centlivre's

The Beau's Duel (June 1702). Brisk, amusing, and good-humoured, it is nonetheless strictly moral. (A maid is turned away for taking money!—53–4.) Old Careful 'marries' the whore, Mrs. Plotwell, thinking her a Quaker, and settles his estate on her. She promptly refuses to go to bed with the old fool, and after he is thoroughly tormented, Captain Bellmein admits that he served as parson, thus dissolving the marriage. Colonel Manly is thereupon given Careful's daughter Clarinda and Bellmein her cousin Emilia. Sir William Mode and Ogle are the beaux, Manly's rivals for Clarinda—rather pallid stock figures. Durfey's *The Bath* (May 1701) is altogether finer. Brisk, serious, and moral, it supplies the humane comedy answer to the marital discord problem. Sophronia (who likes the witty and amorous Transport) has had to marry Lord Lovechace, a blunt country foxhunter who is intriguing with Lydia, wife of Sir Oliver Oldgame, a rich old cit. The situation is saved by Sophronia's brother, Colonel Philip, a worthy man of sober virtue (e.g. 46), who lies to protect his sister, but gives her a 'timely caution'. Transport is shamed into leaving town (50), and even Lydia embraces virtue. In a sub-plot Gillian Homebred, an awkward heiress with a heavy Somersetshire accent, marries Crab, witty servant to Lord Lovechace. Despite the heavy emphasis on virtue, the boisterous humours (especially Sir Carolus Codshead and Sir Sackfull Simile) and high spirits keep the play lively.

A slightly earlier Durfey play illustrates the normally lighter side of humane comedy. In *The Campaigners* (June 1698), set in Brussels, Durfey follows up his experiments in *The Intrigues at Versailles* a year earlier. The curious mixture which results is evident in Nicoll's reaction. He finds the play 'immoral, indecent, vulgar'—but admits that 'even here the author has had to succumb to the new forces at work' (I. 277). The central plot line is indeed rather bathetic. Angellica has had an illegitimate child by Colonel Dorange. He comes to realize (while paying Madam la Marquise) that a wife is cheaper than a whore (52). In a fight with Angellica's brother, Don Leon, Dorange is wounded slightly, but gets his opponent's sword and returns it, whereupon the two of them fall into each other's arms (58). Dorange then kneels to Angellica and begs .forgiveness. At the end of the play he is kissing the baby, looking forward happily to marriage, and announcing his pleasure in the prospect of trying to beget another son. Despite such comments, Kathleen Lynch calls this 'sentimental',[1] which it is. However, the cynical, satirical view of high life, and the genuine rakishness of Dorange, prevent the play from approaching Steele's form of the new comedy. It is more akin to such earlier, 'mixed' new comedies as *The Squire of Alsatia* and *Love's Last Shift*.

Other such plays are numerous. Mrs. Pix's *The Deceiver Deceived* (November 1697 at Lincoln's Inn Fields) is full of brisk intrigue, and allows an unfortunate wife one bout of adultery before she repents and sends her gallant on his way. Old Melito Bondi, a Senator of Venice, feigns blindness to avoid foreign service. Count Andrea is gallant to Bondi's wife; Count Insulls is the favoured suitor to his daughter, who finally marries Fidelio, a nobleman of decayed fortune. (Insulls gets fobbed off with Lucinda, a pretended heiress.) Gervatio is a good version of the tricky servant, here playing a double game. Bondi's wife sensibly parts with her lover (37), and despite the sex this remains a fairly moral play, as well as a lively one. George Powell seems to have recognized its merits when it was originally offered to Drury Lane, for he stole the Bondi story and worked it into a *mélange* of farce and music called *Imposture Defeated* (September 1697 at Drury Lane). The results are crude and coarse, stressing debauchery and drunkenness amidst the intrigue. The introduction of an *Endimion* masque seems singularly inappropriate; another obvious inspiration seems to have been the Lincoln's Inn Fields revival of Mountfort's *Faustus* the preceding spring. Dilke's *The Pretenders: or, The Town Unmaskt* (March 1698) is a much better play than these, or indeed than its own reputation would suggest. The design and handling are reminiscent of late Shadwell, but with a delightful injection of joking high spirits. (In his report of widespread raping, Dilke notes happily that at least the women were left precisely as found—non-virgin.) In a world of pretenders, hypocrites, whores and knaves (all shown up with zest) Sir Bellamour Blunt, a plain and sensible country gentleman, wins the virtuous Ophelia. Dilke eschews sickly sentiment and moral platitudes; the play did not deserve its flat failure.

[1] Lynch, 'Thomas D'Urfey's Contribution to Sentimental Comedy'.

By far the greatest comic success of these years is Farquhar's *The Constant Couple; or a Trip to the Jubilee* (November 1699; Drury Lane). The triumph of this play—some fifty performances in five months—'dealt a devastating blow' to the Lincoln's Inn Fields company, already weakened by internal dissent.[1] Racy in style, this light and cheerful play is in fact fairly moral. There are two main plot lines. Angelica falls in love with Sir Harry Wildair, a rake (I. 106). He takes her for a whore, and the mistake lands him in a position where he must marry or fight; he decides that marriage is the more daring, and the play concludes with a verse encomium on the reforming powers of a virtuous woman. In the second plot Lurewell, a jilting Madam Fickle type, is romantically reunited to her true love, Colonel Standard (150), whose seeming abandonment of her some years before had been, we find, unintentional. The play is slight but entertaining. Farquhar's sequel, *Sir Harry Wildair* (April 1701), is altogether weaker. Angelica, supposedly dead, disguises herself as Beau-Banter, Sir Harry's younger brother. In that role she is dispatched to pimp for Sir Harry ('like a dutiful Brother'—191) in his attempt on Lady Lurewell. Her appearance as her own ghost shocks the others into reform. (We gather that Sir Harry truly loves his wife, for on hearing of her supposed death in France he has roared through the country impregnating nuns in revenge—173.) Despite some good ideas and situations, the play is flat and its structure decidedly weak.[2]

Middle-of-the-road comedies of this sort were the norm by 1700. John Corye's *A Cure for Jealousie* (c. December 1699) attempts the witty style of Carolean comedy, but its libertinism is mostly talk. Old Scrapeall regrets having married a young wife, Arabella, and considers getting her killed (27)—inquiring if ten shillings would be sufficient payment. His distress at seeing her 'ghost' paves the way to forgiveness and reconcili-

---

[1] On the tremendous impact of this play see Shirley Strum Kenny, 'Theatrical Warfare, 1695–1710', *Theatre Notebook*, xxvii (1973), 130–45.

[2] *Sir Harry Wildair* is quite short. W. J. Lawrence offers the hypothesis, on this and other grounds, that it was played with *The Stage-Coach* (printed in 1704) added as an afterpiece. ('The Mystery of "The Stage Coach" ', *Modern Language Review*, xxvii (1932), 392–7.) On that farce, see Section II, below. The hypothesis seems to me implausible, since it would require a transfer of the farce from Drury Lane to Lincoln's Inn Fields, and no other such transfer is known.

ation (56). Colonel Blunt and his servant Pimpwell, the gay
Wildish (who wins Scrapeall's daughter Olinda), the beau
Sparkish, Loveday and Bellinda belong to a rather middle-class
beau-monde. Scrapeall, the clerk Dash, the grocer Prunello
and his wife, and the whore Peggy occupy a distinctly lower
social level. The whole amounts to a brisk, farcical, city
intrigue comedy. David Crauford's *Courtship A-la-mode* (July
1700) similarly attempts to suggest the dashing libertine style
(especially in Sir John Winmore) while keeping matters clean
enough and farcical enough to avoid reproach. Charles Johnson's (?) *The Gentleman-Cully* (c. August 1701) uses the brisk
elements of old comedy to amuse, without rewarding the
libertine. Airy young Flash, amorous old Lady Rakelove, the
bawd Mrs. Twist, and the debauchee Townlove make for a lot
of low and bawdy talk. But in the main action the wealthy
Sophia catches her suitor Faithless out, refuses him (cf. *The
Richmond Heiress*), and announces that he must marry the maid
Grace or pay a heavy fine.

A clear sign of the times, albeit an unsuccessful play, is
The Inconstant (February 1702). Farquhar took Fletcher's *The
Wild Goose Chase*, focused it more fully on Oriana's attempts
to tame the wild Mirabel, and produced a new fifth act. As
Cibber once said of Loveless, he's wild for above four acts:
well into Act V, Wilks, as Mirabel, is allowed to act the libertine. Trapped by the whore Lamorce in a den of bravoes, he is
rescued by the efforts of Oriana, disguised as a page (I. 266–74),
whereupon he begs her pardon on his knees and they plan to
marry. With its dashing hero, traps, disguises, love game,
and witty heroine in breeches, *The Inconstant* is a fine play which
deserved more success than it initially met. Farquhar complains angrily about '*Gallick* Heels' in his preface—Mme Subligny was dancing at Lincoln's Inn Fields, and as *A Comparison*
indicates, the audience was flocking to admire her. The play
finally did take its place in the repertory.

Surveying the 34 comedies from these years, we find only
half a dozen which proved what Downes likes to term 'living
plays'. None of the hard comedies really did well, though
Love and a Bottle and *The Way of the World* had adequate initial
runs. The successes represented various forms: quasi-exemplary
comedy (*The Funeral*); farce (*The Country House*); adaptation

(*The Pilgrim,* and *King Henry IV*); middle-of-the-road humane comedy (*The Constant Couple*). The sub-group which consistently runs most poorly is that of the very moral humane comedies, those with strong new-comedy leanings. Hard comedy is rapidly disappearing, to be sure, but the new comedy is faring little better. The most common type in these years is the relatively flippant humane comedy represented by plays like *The Pretenders, The Constant Couple,* and *The Inconstant.* These works are not sex comedies, and they give a distinctly softened, even a sentimental view of the rakish heroes who figure so prominently in them. But they remain a far cry from the principles now touted by Steele; they represent a compromise with the new comedy tradition, not a development of it.

In these years, while comedy is settling down to something like an adjusted set of norms, the new tragedies are numerous, remarkably variegated in type, and even less successful than the comedies. The pathetic and classic–stoic modes are well represented, but (surprisingly) a majority of the new tragedies are in types descended from the old heroic and horror modes of the 1670s. The beginnings of this revival were obvious in the mid-1690s in *Cyrus the Great, The Royal Mischief, Agnes de Castro,* and *Ibrahim.* These plays are not rhymed, but they turn on love and honour, spectacle, and inflated nobility quite in the style of early Settle and Lee. Like the Carolean heroic play, they range from shilling shocker to happy-ending tragicomedy. In this third mode the types represented, roughly speaking, are (1) the heroic–horror play; (2) the virtue-rewarded thriller; (3) the love tragedy—usually with pathetic elements; (4) the domestic shocker; (5) straight tragicomedy.

The bloodbath has the virtue of being easy to concoct. 'A Young Lady' produced *The Unnatural Mother* (October 1697), set in Siam. It encompasses attempted rape, death in torment by poison (together with semi-comic dialogue—15), a wife attempting to perform suttee, a ghost, and a lively villainess who stabs herself before she can be burned at the stake (51–2). William Philips's *The Revengeful Queen* (June 1698) is similarly forceful, vigorous, and crude. The rash, cruel King Alboino is killed; his nasty Queen, Rosamund, drinks poison, and the crown is inherited by the sensible general Aistolfus. Secondary love plots, most of them involving unattractive characters coming to bloody endings, fill out the action. Even greater heights of melodramatic bombast are achieved by Cibber in *Xerxes* (March 1699), a failure. Cibber indulges in pathos as well as sadism, having the virtuous Tamira (Mrs. Barry) enter 'Plunder'd, her Hair and Cloaths disorder'd; the Rabble with her child, she striving to recover it', after which she is dragged about by the hair (41–2). Xerxes gloatingly tells her husband Artabanus that he has whored and killed her; they mortally wound each other—at which point Artabanus learns that his wife is alive, and she enters to stab herself. Cibber did far better with *The Tragical History of King Richard III* (*c.* February 1700). It failed initially, cut to bits by the censor, but survived to become the standard version, played even in the twentieth century. Cibber actually draws on six different Shakespeare history plays: what he produces is a superb vehicle for himself as Richard III. Indeed it is Cibber's version of Richard Crookback that fired the popular imagination and reinforced the Tudor myth about him. Richard is greatly built up and becomes a compelling monster. 'Off with his head. So much for *Buckingham*' (45) is Cibber's memorable contribution. Naturally he has the little princes butchered on stage (38 ff.) Odell delivered the startling judgement that Cibber improved on Shakespeare.[1] The complexities and nuances disappear: what remains is a compelling melodrama, highly effective in the theatre.

Some writers were of the opinion that an eleventh-hour rescue was even better than a consummated bloodbath. William Walker's *Victorious Love* (June 1698) is an instance. The wicked Emperor Jamoan lusts for Zaraida, who loves Barnagasso.

> *Emperor:*
> Think, Can you bear to see him piece-meal torn?
> His angry flesh wrench'd from th' unwilling bones?
> His Bowels ript, while Life yet shivers there?
> His big heart, dancing in a Sea of Blood,
> Shall first be mash'd, then thrown into his Face. (37)

Zaraida promptly swoons, whereupon the Emperor orders *him*

[1] George C. D. Odell, *Shakespeare from Betterton to Irving*, 2 vols. (1920; rpt. New York, 1963), II. 153.

borne to death, *her* to the royal bed. A convenient rebellion
produces a happy ending and due thanks to providential justice.
Another such distributive justice piece, this time in rhyme, is
Charles Hopkins's *Friendship Improv'd* (November 1699). The
author says in his dedication, 'it grates me to delineate a
Villain': he prefers to show honesty and virtue. The usurper
Zoilus stabs his wife and falls on his sword (52); the loyal
general Maherbal turns out to be the true heir to the throne
and wins the usurper's lovely daughter Locris, brought up in
men's clothes and educated as a male. Hopkins gets good mileage with the Ladies in this 'Female Warriour', especially in her
effective 'farewell' scene, in which Othello-like she renounces
her soldierly occupation (46–7). With such stuff returning to
the stage, we should not be surprised to find a revival of
Orrery's *The Generall* (1664)—the first of the rhymed heroic
breed—brought out as *Altemira* (November 1701), with alterations by Orrery's grandson Charles Boyle. The play remains
an uninspiring display of rhymed love-and-honour heroics.

The revival of these two branches of the heroic school
is evident in Nicholas Rowe's first plays. The great she-
tragedizer of the early eighteenth century starts out writing
Settle-style oriental palace intrigue tragedy in *The Ambitious
Step-mother* (*c.* December 1700). The dedication stresses the
charms of pathos, explaining that to have kept hero and heroine
(Artaxerxes and Amestris) alive would have diminished audience
compassion. The wicked Queen Artemisa gets deposed and the
villainous courtier Mirza killed, producing the author's boasted
poetical justice, at least to the extent of punishing the evil.
The verse is competent, the design and characters stock and
uninspired. The noble general disgraced (Memnon), the evil
priest, and the love triangle, are handled in the usual ways.[1]
Tamerlane (December 1701) preserves the heroic setting and
elements, while working in more pathos. The structure is less
smoothly handled than in the earlier play, but Rowe brings
more individuality and imagination to his standard elements,
and the play long remained immensely popular. Rowe revels
equally in the insipid love of Bajazet's daughter Selima and

---

[1] On this and other Rowe tragedies see Malcolm Goldstein, 'Pathos and Personality in the Tragedies of Nicholas Rowe', *English Writers of the Eighteenth Century*, ed.
John H. Middendorf (New York, 1971), pp. 172–85.

Tamerlane's favourite, Axalla, and in the doomed love of Moneses (strangled by mutes—66) and Arpasia, who is also wanted by Bajazet. The dedication says outright that Tamerlane is a representation of William III (on whose birthday the play was acted until the middle of the century). To realize that the contrasting picture of Bajazet is a hit at Louis XIV requires no great perspicuity. The comparison between the two kings lies at the heart of the play. Indeed, a strong case can be made for systematic political allegory involving several characters.[1] This very Whiggish play ends with Tamerlane sentencing Bajazet to the cage, Omar and the 'Dervise' ('Tory' figures) to a death fit for traitors.

The third variety of heroic play is the love tragedy, which allows still more emphasis on the pathetic. All four of the plays discussed in this category were Barry and Bracegirdle specials at Lincoln's Inn Fields. Mrs. Pix's *Queen Catharine: or, the Ruines of Love* (June 1698) is a historical tearjerker. (It is analysed briefly in Chapter 5, above.) Owen Tudor, beloved husband of Queen Catharine, among assorted misfortunes, is foully murdered by Gloucester (Richard III to be). Charles Hopkins's successful *Boadicea* (November 1697) is less mawkish, fairly animated despite its rhyme. Boadicea has two daughters, Camilla (raped by a Roman general, Decius) and Venutia; after a variety of revenge complications we are treated to a wild mass suicide scene, completed by the British Prince Cassibelan falling on his sword.[2] Gildon's *Love's Victim* (April 1701) similarly uses ancient British heroic colour (Druids in this case), but belongs to what may be called the school of gasps and sighs. Gildon compensates for temperamental frigidity with pants, groans, fainting, and exclamatory rhetoric. The wicked Queen of Bayonne gets Queen Guinoenda to drink poison as a means of 'saving' her husband Rhesus, King of Wales. When he rejects her, she stabs herself, after which we wallow in a bathetic farewell scene between Rhesus and Guinoenda (and their children). At length she dies; he faints. Gildon

---

[1] See Willard Thorp, 'A Key to Rowe's *Tamerlane*', *Journal of English and Germanic Philology*, xxxix (1940), 124–7, who suggests that Axalla is Hans William Bentinck, First Earl of Portland (William's favourite), and that the Tartar [Tory] general Omar represents Godolphin.

[2] On Hopkins's debt to *Bonduca* see Baldwin Maxwell, 'Notes on Charles Hopkins' *Boadicea*', *Review of English Studies*, iv (1928), 79–83.

explains in his preface that terror is more important than poetic justice, and then notes that Guinoenda is punished for her parents' misdeeds, her father having been a tyrant! Jane Wiseman's *Antiochus the Great* (November 1701) uses good themes vigorously. Nicoll calls it dull, bloody, Elizabethan, heroic, and classic—an ill-fitting description. A Babylonian setting allows heroic decoration, but the centre of the play lies in love and the ethics of forced marriage. Antiochus has had to abandon his mistress Leodice to marry Berenice, who loves Ormades. In the ensuing complications only Berenice remains alive at the end, and she admits her guilty love: "'Twas a hard Case: yet I am justly punish'd ... For Heaven its severest Justice shows/On lawless Love, and violated Vows.' None of these plays has much tragic merit, yet excepting Gildon's, they offer fine vehicles for the sort of histrionic emotional bath in which Barry and Bracegirdle specialized.

Pathetic tragedy proper is no great distance from the heroic-love type, the principal difference being more emphasis on the domestic. The examples from these years are both un-distinguished and unsuccessful. Motteux's *Beauty in Distress* (May 1698), analysed briefly above in Chapter 5, 'had the honour of forcing Tears from the fairest Eyes', though it suffered the disadvantage of having 'no Singing, no Dancing, no mixture of Comedy, no Mirth, no change of Scene, no rich Dresses, no Show, no Rants, no Similies, no Battle, no Killing on the Stage, no Ghost, no Prodigy ... *no Smut, no Profaneness, nor Immorality*' (preface). Nicoll credits the play with 'classical restraint' (I. 170), but the text does not bear out the preface in all respects: the play is a cliff-hanging tearjerker, full of heated rhetoric, attempted rape, incest-threat, and poisoning. Two brothers, Vincentio (disguised as a blackamoor) and Ricardo, love Placentia (Mrs. Bracegirdle), as does Fabiano, who finally gets her after a wild series of intrigues and quarrels. In the course of these Ricardo regretfully poisons his mistress Laura (42), and after a suitably bathetic scene with her children she expires in agony (57). Despite rigid imposition of the unities (scene: an ante-chamber; time: 5–8 p.m.), Motteux contrives a lively if trashy version of the Barry and Bracegirdle special.

Other pathetic specimens have even less merit. Trotter's *Fatal Friendship* (June 1698) is exceedingly tearful. Gramont, fearing that his infant son by Felicia will starve, commits mercenary bigamy with Lamira, which is sexually unconsummated. Gramont finally stabs himself, thus ending a domestic-intrigue melodrama whose principal interest lies in the psychology of characters plunged into intolerable situations. As drama, the results are weak, especially in the too-predictable use of obvious devices—thus the little son is captured by pirates (47), and we too easily foresee that Gramont will accidentally kill his friend Castalio (who loved Lamira) and have to commit suicide. Pix's *The False Friend* (June 1699) has tinges of heroic inflation—a Viceroy of Sardinia, a villainous general, the Indian female slave Zelide—but gets its effect out of over-exclamatory synthetic passion. Good and bad characters are slaughtered impartially. The heroine Lovisa, poisoned, is led on mad, with her hair down (always a bad sign), and wounded in the breast, having maimed herself. Her faithful lover Emilius stabs himself, and they die, giving rise to the 'moral' the prologue makes much of: children should obey their parents. Trotter's *The Unhappy Penitent* (February 1701) shows a similar balance: a technically heroic setting (the court of Charles VIII of France), but a focus on essentially personal love-and-honour misunderstandings. The pathetic parting of the Duke of Lorrain and Margarite of Flanders (43–7) in Act V is the emotional centre of the play—sentimental mush of the most contrived sort. In *The Double Distress* (March 1701) Mrs. Pix eschews both butchery and sweet sorrow to try a happy ending after revelling in distress. In a grand setting (the court of Darius, King of Persia) we follow all kinds of twists and tricks, wallow in 'horrid' discoveries, and finally applaud a smugly satisfactory ending: 'The Good have Heav'n their sure and certain Guard,/And Virtue always meets a just Reward.'

The classic–stoic mode produces mostly failures, and exhibits a split between plays with classical subjects or rules-conscious form versus those following the *Cleomenes* tradition. The one fair success was George Granville's *Heroick Love* (January 1698), a Trojan-war love tragedy. The preface touts the single action; Dryden adds a commendatory poem, bestowing his laurels (or a third set thereof) upon Granville. Agamemnon (Betterton) wants Chruseis—and is even willing to become a shepherd if that will help. At the (revised) end he is left lying on the ground in a swoon, while Ulysses delivers homilies about the evils of love. But the parting scene (70–1) is quite cool as such things go (cf. *The Unhappy Penitent*), and Granville's first concern seems to be with full, clear presentation of character. Gildon's *Phaeton* (March 1698), written 'In Imitation of the ANTIENTS', is classical only in form (borrowed from Quinault). Relatively fancy scenery (imported from France) and music contribute to a heroic air: we are treated to ghosts, groves, love scenes, a mob, a gruesome poisoning, and madness.

The classic mode derived no advantage from the collision of two 'Iphigenia' plays in December 1699. Dennis's *Iphigenia* failed to make its expenses, Downes tells us, and little wonder. It is a turgid, sententious exercise in providence-mongering, and not even Bracegirdle was able to disguise the insipidity of the title character. Dennis's blustering preface denounces the degeneracy of the English theatre, and offers to lead the age to true classic excellence. Dryden says dryly that Dennis cried the play up at an excessive rate—a kindly understatement.[1] 'Euripidean' tragedy made no headway under this sponsorship. Against Dennis's play Drury Lane mounted Boyer's *Achilles: or Iphigenia in Aulis*, translated from Racine. A fancy production with machine spectacle (e.g. 47–8) was not enough to save a rather understated play, and the opposition of the two helped spoil the success of both.[2]

The old stoic mode proper is represented by Crowne's *Caligula* (February 1698) and Southerne's *The Fate of Capua* (April 1700). Crowne, by now a sick old man, put his play mostly in couplets. Bits of rant are served up as compensation for static presentation. The work is not frigid, despite the coolness of the presentation; short lines help keep it moving, averting stiffness. But Crowne gets no imaginative spark out of stock characters: the weak king (Caligula), the general noble (Valerius), the romantic heroine (Cesonia). Southerne's play is altogether

[1] *Letters*, no. 70.
[2] For a very full account of this contretemps, see *A Comparison*, pp. 23–5.

finer. Decius Magius, a supporter of alliance with Rome, is offered his life but commits suicide with the other senators— a true patriot and stoic *exemplum*. The self-seeking, perfidious Pacuvius makes a good foil. He is a complex figure (which upsets Dodds): his scenes with his son Perolla are warmly human, and he is capable of brave and effective action. In the subsidiary love plot Favonia loves her husband Virginius's best friend Junius, but being honourable they try to repress their passion. Southerne handles the ensuing deaths well, and his use of the Capua mob is masterly. There are many fine things in the play, and though over all it is too full of talk, it deserved better than its complete failure.

Beyond the major modes (heroic, pathetic, and classic) fall a few plays of divers types: the shocker, the straight tragicomedy, and the experimental prose tragedy. The shocker is closely related to the heroic–horror play, but here the butchery is restricted to a more domestic setting. *The Fatal Discovery* (February 1698), brought to the stage by George Powell, sets an ugly incest plot against a comic triangle plot, with jealous husband, clever wife, and lover. The bloody violence of the main plot is, as Rothstein observes, seriously subverted by superficial parallelisms in the comic part.[1] The spectacle of men crawling about the stage in dresses lends the proceedings a tawdriness which ill accords with the attempted seriousness in the incest plot. Ravenscroft's *The Italian Husband* (November 1697) is short, brutal, and effective. Duke Frederico strangles his wife Alouisia (after having her lover killed), puts her body to bed, and placidly awaits the arrival of her father— who will approve the deed, we are assured. Ravenscroft's 'Prælude' explains that he designed 'to bring a guilty person to be pity'd in her circumstances', rather than to rouse pity for distressed innocence. Plain language contributes to a powerful impact.

Tragicomedy, out of fashion, appears in various guises. Henry Smith's *The Princess of Parma* (April 1699) is a traditional triumph of virtue play, set in Genoa. Admiral Doria, restorer of his country's liberty, marries Almira, despite the machinations of the villainess, Julia, and an apparent poisoning (42–7).

---

[1] *Restoration Tragedy*, p. 146.

Mrs. Centlivre's *The Perjur'd Husband* (September 1700) is a slovenly split plot play. In a serious plot line Count Bassino kills his wife Placentia, who has killed Aurelia (with whom he was intriguing); Bassino is then killed by Aurelia's fiancé Alonzo. In a comic sub-plot we are given standard assignations and contretemps. Bevill Higgons's *The Generous Conquerour* (December 1701) is a stiff, turgid, unoriginal, distributive-justice tragicomedy, interesting principally for its political references. (See Chapter 5, above.) The Jacobite implications are impossible to miss: Higgons enacts a wish-fulfilment fantasy in which (roughly speaking) William III moves to restore the Stuart line. The only lively character in this dreary exercise is Malespine, the evil minister of state, a mouther of Hobbesian truisms.

Prose tragedy is so unusual that two cases almost constitute a group to themselves. Pix's *The Czar of Muscovy* (March 1701) is really only a heroic melodrama, with its usurping tyrant, forced marriage, attempted rape, good and bad generals, and so forth. Durfey's *The Famous History of the Rise and Fall of Massaniello* (2 parts; c. May 1699) is another matter. This brilliant play failed, and only Eric Rothstein seems ever to have recognized its power.[1] The fisherman Massaniello (who enters crying 'Buy my Flounders, come buy my Flounders'—4) leads a rebellion, becomes dictator of Naples, and is bloodily overthrown. Part II ends with 'the Trunk of *Massaniello* Headless and Handless, dragg'd by Horses, his Head and Hands fastned to a Pole'. He has been a cruel and lustful tyrant, and we do not lament him. His wife Blowzabella is drawn with a crude, nasty verisimilitude just about unique in this period. The display of the raped and bloody Fellicia (Part II, p. 43) uses a stock situation not for pathos or titillation, but to rouse a more serious response. Durfey succeeds marvellously in showing the horrifying bestiality of the mob. *Massaniello* is a fiery Tory play, taking a bitterly contemptuous view of vulgar workers and tradesmen who meddle in politics. The flat, harsh prose is tremendously effective in communicating Durfey's ugly, realistic picture of the lower orders, foolish and cruel, raised to power. The mob scenes have astonishing impact, and the play seethes with contempt—as in Durfey's icy exposure of

[1] See his analysis, *Restoration Tragedy*, pp. 170–3.

the upstarts mimicking their betters' ways in a banquet scene (Part I, p. 44). *Massaniello* is an isolated freak, an experiment not repeated. Yet in its coarse mimetic realism and ideological commitment there is a seriousness nowhere else to be found in these years. Here in a forgotten failure we have a hint that Durfey, given his head, had the makings of a major playwright.

Operas and added attractions are tried by both houses in these years, though mostly without much success.[1] Oldmixon's *Amintas* (1698) is a namby-pamby pastoral; his *The Grove* (February 1700) is a pastorally inclined tragicomedy with music added. Both failed, as did *The Virgin Prophetess* (May 1701), Settle's fancy Trojan opera. Spectacular staging (e.g. when the city burns we see flames breaking through the windows—40) could not save the piece. We are treated to transformation scenes at the wave of a wand (25, 27–8); flying cupids; and Helen leaping off a tower into the flames, all to no avail.

Only once does Lincoln's Inn Fields mount an opera— Dennis's *Rinaldo and Armida* (late November 1698). *A Comparison* says 'this surpriz'd not only *Drury-lane*, but indeed all the Town, no body ever dreaming of an *Opera* there ... [though] they had heard of *Homer*'s Illiads in a Nut-shel' (p. 22). In this pocket-opera Dennis endeavours to be both sublime and pathetic, and proudly tells us so. He considered the work a tragedy, though Eccles's music makes it a Purcell-style opera, and quite a good one.[2] Drury Lane managed to spoil Lincoln's Inn Fields' success by rushing out *The Island Princess ... Made into an OPERA* (early February 1699). Motteux handled this re-working of two earlier alterations of the Fletcher play. The

---

[1] Motteux's little musical masque, *Europe's Revels for the Peace* (played at Court in November 1697) was, I would conjecture, designed to complement Ravenscroft's *Italian Husband* that month, just as his *Loves of Mars and Venus* had been run with Ravenscroft's *Anatomist* a year earlier. Dryden's *Secular Masque* (April 1700) was added to Vanbrugh's revamping of *The Pilgrim*. Congreve's *The Judgment of Paris: A Masque* (March 1701) is unique—a text initially used in a composers' prize contest, but later played in concerts and used by both houses as an afterpiece.

[2] For a discussion of Dennis's theory and a reprint of the libretto of the musical parts evidently distributed at the theatre, see Herbert Davis, 'Musical Entertainments in *Rinaldo and Armida*: by John Dennis', *Theatre Miscellany: Six Pieces connected with the Seventeenth-Century Stage*, Luttrell Society Reprints, no. 14 (Oxford, 1953), pp. 99–115.

result is a thundering melodrama, trashy but effective, and certainly successful.[1]

The dismal state of serious drama is obvious. In the next few years we will find 'tragedies' few in number, and going from bad to worse. Not much more can be said for the state of the theatres. The balance of power shifts, rather mysteriously, during the 1698–9 season. Neither company had any real successes the preceding year, but it is Rich's group that seems to be in trouble.[2] A year later, however, Lincoln's Inn Fields is on the verge of collapse. The smashing success of *The Constant Couple* (familiarly known by its sub-title as *A Trip to the Jubilee*) had given Drury Lane a tremendous boost. Motteux's epilogue to *The Princess of Parma* reports a nightmare vision: Lincoln's Inn Fields, for want of support, once more turned into a tennis court; stage wars ceased, with Drury Lane in control. Outright failure is envisaged ('if we go down'), and support begged. That very month, in desperation, Betterton had imported Balon, the famous French dancing-master. Luttrell marvels at the outlandish price: 400 guineas for five weeks—this at a time when only four actors in the company made anything like that much in a year. Audiences did turn out for such extras. But Downes's terse summation is telling:

Mr. *Betterton* to gratify the desires and Fancies of the Nobility and Gentry; procur'd from Abroad the best Dances and Singers, as, Monsieur *L'Abbe*, Madam *Sublini*, Monsieur *Balon*, *Margarita Delpine*, *Maria Gallia* and divers others; who being Exorbitantly Expensive, produc'd small Profit to him and his Company. (46)

Rich riposted with animal acts and jugglers. By the season of 1701–2 Betterton is reduced to mounting *The Country-Wife* with the addition of 'that delightful Exercise of Vaulting on the Manag'd Horse, according to the Italian manner' (21

---

[1] See Haun, *But Hark! More Harmony*, pp. 171–4; Sprague, *Beaumont and Fletcher*, pp. 147–54; and Roger Fiske, *English Theatre Music in the Eighteenth Century* (London, 1973), pp. 11–12. On the date see Judith Milhous and Robert D. Hume, 'Dating Play Premières from Publication Data, 1660–1700', *Harvard Library Bulletin*, xxii (1974), 374–405.

[2] Powell's prologue to *The Fatal Discovery* (February 1698) suggests that the house may fold; Walker's preface to *Victorious Love* the following June speaks of the 'Declining Fabrick' of Drury Lane, and says that the company is discountenanced by the town.

October), and reviving *The Way of the World*, with Mme Subligny, a sexy French ballerina, put on between the acts. By March the prologue to *The Double Distress* is groaning that tumblers and monkeys are not enough, that Lincoln's Inn Fields will soon have to revert to tennis. No doubt there is some pathetic exaggeration here. Nonetheless almost every new play fails during a period of two years, and by the spring of 1702 an absolute low point is reached in the fortunes of the theatres in England.

II. THE SEARCH FOR A NEW EQUILIBRIUM 1702–1707

Information about the theatres and their offerings is infuriatingly scanty for the years just after 1700. The establishment of the *Daily Courant* in the spring of 1702 is a great help, though Lincoln's Inn Fields buys advertisements only sporadically during the next three seasons. Only after 1705 can we begin to feel at all confident about our knowledge of repertory and competition. All the signs, however, point to a state of near-collapse at the end of the 1701–2 season. Rumours of a new union are in the air: the author of *A Comparison Between the Two Stages* (published in April 1702) actually wrote with the express intention of promoting a union.

I have been very free with the *Theatres*, but I don't at all repent it: Their Distempers wanted the *Incision Knife*, and I have given it them. . . . *Our present Poetry* . . . never was at so low an Ebb, and yet the Stages were never so delug'd: I am sure you can't name me five Plays that have indur'd six Days acting, for fifty that were damn'd in three [a mild exaggeration]. . . . The division of *the Houses* made way for a multitude of young Writers, some of whom had nothing else to subsist on but their Pens; and I despair of seeing our *Poetry* restor'd, till I see the *Houses* united; for then the bad Plays may be shut out. (2–3)

Remembering the stagnant days of the United Company, we may differ from this splenetic gentleman about the desirability of a monopoly, but certainly new plays are failing at an appalling rate. No one knew what would succeed, and the two houses flounder about, experimenting with a variety of expedients. Comedy limps on and tragedy dwindles while the managers search frantically for anything that will attract paying customers.

Two outgrowths of the competitive situation are the after-piece tradition and the benefit system. The rise in double bills is evident in the number of short new farces (discussed below), though masques, musical attractions, and excerpts also serve as afterpieces.[1] The tremendous upsurge in benefit performances for single actors and actresses remains a some-what murky matter.[2] A series of benefits in the late spring was a tradition by the end of the seventeenth century. The practice seems to have expanded greatly by the 1702–3 season, and more after that. The anonymous author (William Walker?) of *Marry, or do Worse* (October 1703) complains that his piece 'was so hem'd in between the *Benefits,* that it seem'd meerly Confin'd to the Limits of a Single *Night* before hand'. Declaring benefits was evidently a means both of pleasing favoured actors at a time when full salaries were seldom being paid, and also of getting the actors actively involved in selling tickets.

Certain kinds of added attractions become increasingly conspicuous. The playbills constantly stress extraneous music and dancing. Thus with *The Maid's Tragedy* (4 February 1704) Drury Lane offered dancing by du Ruel and Mrs. Mayers, plus 'A Masque set to Musick by the late Mr Henry Purcell, per-form'd by Mr Leveridge and others. And a piece of Instru-mental Musick composed by the great Arcangelo Corelli for a Flute and Violin, perform'd by Signior Gasperini and Mr Paisible.' Stranger additions are common. Drury Lane played *Oroonoko* (27 April 1703) adding music, dancing, and vaulting 'By Evans, lately arrived from Vienna, who will Vault on the manag'd Horse, where he lyes with his Body extended on one Hand in which posture he drinks several Glasses of Wine with the other, and from that throws himself a Sommerset over the Horses Head, to Admiration.'[3] With *Love's Last Shift* (18 June) they tried music, dancing, and imitations: 'The Famous Mr Clynch will for this once . . . perform his Imitation of an Organ, with 3 Voices, the Double Curtel, and the Bells, the Hunts-

---

[1] Thus the last act of Centlivre's *Le Medecin Malgre Luy* (i.e. *Love's Contrivance*) was played as an afterpiece for *Æsop*, 21 January 1704.

[2] Some facts and hypotheses are gathered by David Edward McKenty in 'The Benefit System in Augustan Drama', unpub. diss. (University of Pennsylvania, 1966), but this study is inadequate in many respects.

[3] In October 1705 (with *City Politiques*) Lincoln's Inn Fields uses the same performer, specifying the drinking of *nine* glasses of wine in that posture.

man with his Horn and Pack of Dogs; All which he performs
with his Mouth on the open Stage.' Drury Lane was also fond
of throwing in fancy scenes from old spectaculars—for example,
the 'Dome scene' from *The Virgin Prophetess* (27 December
1703) or machine scenes from *The Prophetess* (31 December).

The circus atmosphere in which plays were produced in these
years is sufficiently indicated in the advertisement for *King
Lear* (Tate version) at the Haymarket, 30 April 1706.

Singing. Comical Songs and Dialogues from *Wonders in the Sun*, particularly a Song by Mrs Willis representing one of Queen Elizabeth's
Dames of Honour; and a Comical Dialogue perform'd by Pack
and Bowman, representing a vain promising Courtier and a Syco-
phant, a Comical Dialogue by Dogget and Cook, representing a
Widdow in Tears for the Loss of her Husband and a Town Rake
making Love to her.
Dancing. A new *Entry* by de Barques and Mrs Elford. *French Peasant*
by Firbank and Mrs Bicknell. The famous *Italian Scaramouch* by
Layfield.

All this is promised 'without any Omission at common Prices'.
Medleys were tried, somewhat in the fashion of *The Novelty*.
Thus on 24 October 1702 Drury Lane offered *The Death of King
Henry VI*, 'a Tragical Interlude of one Act only'; 'several
select Scenes' from *Æsop*; and the *première* of *The School-Boy*,
an afterpiece by Cibber. The following 1 February they tried
one act from *The Fairy-Queen* plus a two-act version of *Marriage
A-la-Mode*. Simply reading the new plays from these years gives
little hint of the true state of the theatres. To appreciate the
struggle to attract an audience, any audience, one must read
the newspaper advertisements: even the summaries in *The
London Stage* give an inadequate idea of the extent of the theatrical degradation.

The one major new factor in the situation is Vanbrugh's
construction of the 'Queen's' or Haymarket theatre. Designed
as an opera house, it contributes to the reorganization of 1708
discussed at the end of this Section. It was less help to the
Lincoln's Inn Fields company (which moved into it) than
anticipated, for its acoustics were so bad that plays were
practically unintelligible there.[1] Betterton's troupe returned

[1] See Cibber's caustic account, *Apology*, pp. 172–4. Donald C. Mullin dismisses
these criticisms ('The Queen's Theatre, Haymarket: Vanbrugh's Opera House',

to Lincoln's Inn Fields in July 1705, three months after the
grand opening—presumably to allow some hasty revamping.
The Haymarket never did prove fully satisfactory for plays,
and the operatic competition it fostered was a contributing
factor to the new union, long delayed, which took place in
January 1708.

Surveying the types in comedy, we will see a tidy continuation of established trends. Pseudo-Spanish intrigue comedies flourish (numerically at least); farce exhibits an anticipated upsurge. The dominant modes, however, are settling down
into consistent patterns for the first time since the early 1690s.
The extremes of hard and soft comedy wither, and the median
group sorts itself out into two basic varieties, ordinary *humane*
comedy and *reform* comedy.

Durfey's *The Old Mode and the New* (March 1703) failed,
but typifies the tempered outlook of humane comedy. Full of
farcical humours (Sir Fumbler Oldmode, M. de Pistole,
Misterious Maggothead—Mayor of Coventry), the play mockingly contrasts Sir Fumbler (a Queen Elizabeth crank) with
his son Frederick, who loves new-style court modes. Despite
sharp intrigue and such elements as the hoyden Smicket and a
Spanish-humoured fop played by Cibber, the play is quite 'soft'
in its final reconciliations, and in its overt approval of Will
Queenlove, an honest country gentleman rewarded with the
heiress Lucia. The piece would be better if it were shorter
and less schematic. Walker's (?) *Marry, or do Worse* (October
1703) is similar but livelier. The intrigues between Freewit
and Trapum's young wife Athelia border on old comedy, but
are frustrated. Freewit marries Silvia; his servant Snap marries
the maid Betty (masked), thinking her wealthy. Again we are
given a plain, blunt country gentleman to approve—Manly.
Two efforts from Thomas Baker are exactly of this school.
The popular *Tunbridge-Walks*, usually known as *The Yeoman of
Kent* (January 1703), is a good-humoured romance comedy
with spirit but no bite. Woodcock (the yeoman) marries his
daughter Belinda to the clever Reynard, who has pretended to
be a sober country gentleman in order to get his girl. In a second

---

Theatre Survey, viii (1967), 84–105), but the lack of later confirmation I would
explain as the result of major alterations carried out in 1709.

plot Hillaria makes a lively heroine, calling the solemn Love-worth a fawning spaniel (56) and shaking him up a bit before they finally agree to marry. Maiden, an effeminate fop, Mrs. Goodfellow ('A Lady that loves her Bottle'), and Penelope, a forerunner of Lydia Languish, make pleasant diversions. *An Act at Oxford* (1704) is a racy intrigue play, and highly enter-taining. Banned on account of absurd protests from the Uni-versity, the piece was reworked as *Hampstead Heath* (October 1705), which is altogether inferior. The central action holds: Captain Smart, slighted by Berynthia, has his cohort Chum court her as a rich young Jew. She 'marries' Chum (Smart performing the ceremony in disguise); Chum treats her to spectacular ill usage; and finally she is glad to accept Smart. In a second action a marital reconciliation is effected, and in a third the fortune-hunter Squire Calf marries Miss ap Shin-ken, thinking her a woman of fortune. But in the revision action is curtailed, too much time is spent on talk, and the brilliant theatre scene (48–52 of the original) disappears en-tirely.

Middle-of-the-road comedies of this sort are numerous. Rowe's one essay at comedy, *The Biter* (November 1704), has more than the usual satiric leanings. Despite Nicoll's contempt, it is an amusing, farcical piece. A biter is a kind of humbugging practical joker. Genest (II. 328) cites the *Spectator*'s biter story: a condemned felon sells his body to a surgeon, pockets the cash, and announces: 'Bite! I am to be hanged in chains.' Here Sir Timothy engages his daughter Angelica to Pinch, a biting squire—without the couple having met. Pinch bites Sir Timothy and gets thrashed for his pains. When he identifies himself he gets locked up as an impostor—Sir Timothy is quite sure that no old friend of his could have a son like that! By the standards of 1704 the play is decidedly tart. Downes tells us that it ran six nights and died. David Crauford's *Love at first Sight* (March 1704) evidently died the first night, and deserved to. Frigid characters spoil routine intrigues, and pathetically inept attempts at a witty Congrevean mode (e.g. 62) are not helped by platitudinous virtue. *The Fashionable Lover* (*c.* April 1706—anonymous), largely from *The Bride* (1640), combines ungenteel humours and intrigue, with undistinguished results. Centlivre's *The Platonick Lady* (November 1706) has a romantic tragicomedy strain (e.g. 69); its intrigue is less lively than in most of her plays. Mrs. Dowdy, a Somersetshire widow come to town to learn breeding, is a crude but effective character. On the whole, the piece deserved its oblivion after four performances.

Two pieces based on Dancourt's *Les Bourgeoises à la mode* exhibit the old-comedy new-comedy duality common in these middle-of-the-road plays. Estcourt's *The Fair Example* (April 1703) contains a successful in-play seduction (a real rarity by this time), but in the main plot Lucia, though married to the silly Sir Rice-ap-Adam, virtuously rejects the advances of Springlove. Short, flippant speeches keep the play lively, and the contrast between old style and new is striking. The epilogue notes the sickly condition of the stage, and expresses the hope that this 'refin'd' treat will suit the taste of the town. Estcourt was hedging his bets. Vanbrugh's *The Confederacy* (October 1705) is very different—racy, realistic, urban, and with the air of hard comedy (e.g. III. 26—on husbands). Moneylenders Gripe and Moneytrap, and their pretentious wives Clarissa and Araminta, are boisterously satirized. Mrs. Amlet, a purveyor of necessaries to society ladies, is a brilliantly vivid and most unusual character; her son Dick, a sharping rogue pretending to be a colonel, wins Gripe's daughter Corinna, a woman of fortune. The intrigues are farcical and silly, but the whole is handled with the panache and wit of Vanbrugh at his best (e.g. 33, 58-9). After a shaky start—the play apparently suffered from the Haymarket's bad acoustics—it ran well for a century. So different is it from Estcourt's version that one might scarcely notice the common source.

Farquhar is the greatest writer of these years, and the most successful writer of humane comedies. Starting out in 1698 as a hard comedy man, he soon had to reckon with the changing theatrical climate. In a similar position Congreve retired and Vanbrugh betook himself to architecture and opera, with occasional forays back into translation. Of the major writers, Farquhar alone adapts to the changing times—and he does so triumphantly. *The Twin-Rivals* (December 1702) is a strange, experimental play. Nicoll supposes its important preface to be cynically satiric; Rothstein takes it literally to mean that Farquhar was trying to put the principles of Jeremy Collier into practice.[1] Farquhar claims that the work can 'Answer the strictness of Poetical Justice' (I. 286), but, despite the benevolist tinge in Richmore's late conversion, the tone and satire are extremely harsh. In a younger-brother older-brother confrontation Farquhar is wholly against the scheming younger twin. Here the younger brother is a rake and a hunchback, not the usual sympathetic underdog. He attempts to dispossess his elder brother, suborning a lawyer and witnesses and forging a will. The elder brother is an overtly exemplary character, and Farquhar casts a very unusual light on a stock situation (cf. *The Relapse*). The villainous machinations of Young Wou'dbee loom large in the play, but we do follow three couples: the Elder Wou'dbee wins Constance; his friend Trueman wins Aurelia; and the rakish Richmore, a harshly presented Dorimant, is forced to marry Clelia, whom he has impregnated and abandoned. Young Wou'dbee's confederate, the bawd and midwife Mrs. Mandrake (played in transvestite style by Bullock), is effectively loathsome. Farquhar's construction is tight and sharply focused, his outlook bluntly radical, as in the depiction of an exemplary tradesman (323). *The Twin-Rivals* is an angrily moral play, presenting a spectrum of characters rather like that in Steele's *The Funeral* a year earlier. Farquhar's play, though less preachy, proved too starkly harsh to be popular, and he was to find a more genial formula. The work was revived, though never popular. Nonetheless it possesses a splendid design, and a blunt fierceness reminiscent of Otway, Southerne, and early Vanbrugh. Farquhar attacks rakes and legal jiggery-pokery with savage gusto, and the humour is often brilliant. J. H. Smith can see this work as old comedy, but Farquhar really seems to be trying to adapt the bite of hard comedy to the moral purpose of the new. He does experiment half-heartedly with 'reform' in Richmore (346), but the idea of the play is profoundly original.

After a long silence, Farquhar produced *The Recruiting Officer* (April 1706). Here harsh moral melodrama gives way to genial realism. According to taste, one may call the results

---

[1] Nicoll, II. 148. Eric Rothstein, 'Farquhar's *Twin-Rivals* and the Reform of Comedy', *PMLA*, lxxix (1964), 33–41, and *George Farquhar* (New York, 1967), Chapter 3. Neither view seems to me to do justice to the complex ironies in the prefatory essay.

dishonest romanticism or engaging decency. All critics comment on the country 'freshness' of Farquhar's last two plays. Here the Shrewsbury air contrasts sharply with the 'London' ways of Melinda. The characters are stock types, as are the plot lines. Justice Ballance's daughter Silvia marries Captain Plume; Melinda takes Mr. Worthy; Captain Brazen almost marries the maid Lucy masked. Farquhar provides his usual good hits at the law in amusing courtroom scenes (II. 102–3), and plenty of rapid, light intrigue. The army officers are patriotic, but not idealized; Farquhar knew the army and the recruiting business from the inside, and gives an affectionate but tartly realistic picture of them. In *The Beaux Stratagem* (March 1707) he mixes the cynical and the sentimental even more strikingly. Archer tries to seduce Mrs. Sullen, but is interrupted, and then is given the lady in marriage via a spectacularly unrealistic divorce proceeding, achieved by blackmail. The innkeeper's daughter Cherry is a luscious figure, swept conveniently aside in the flurry of the ending. Aimwell, pretending to be his wealthy elder brother, courts Dorinda for her fortune, planning to split the takings with his fellow-conspirator Archer. But at the crucial moment his natural virtue surfaces, brought out by her virtue, and he exclaims:

Such Goodness who cou'd injure; I find my self unequal to the Task of Villain; she has gain'd my Soul, and made it honest like her own;—I cannot, cannot hurt her. [He tells the priest to withdraw and continues.] Madam, behold your Lover and your Proselite, and judge of my Passion by my Conversion.—I'm all a Lie, nor dare I give a Fiction to your Arms; I'm all Counterfeit except my Passion. . . . I am no Lord, but a poor needy Man, come with a mean, a scandalous Design to prey upon your Fortune:—But the Beauties of your Mind and Person have so won me from my self, that like a trusty Servant, I prefer the Interest of my Mistress to my own. (II. 185)

Dorinda exclaims 'Matchless Honesty' and announces her readiness to marry him. By a singularly fortunate coincidence Sir Charles Freeman then enters to inform him that his brother has died and Aimwell is now the Viscount he pretended to be. The Irish priest Foigard makes a fine butt; Lady Bountiful represents the growing tribe of benevolent parents; the Sullenses marriage gives us marital discord miraculously ended. One may easily forget just how improbable and farcical this all is. These plays are escapist, but delightfully so. They represent humane comedy at its finest. The sense of human nature which emerges is benevolently sceptical, neither cynical nor saccharine. Farquhar indulges himself and us in the possibility of virtue, but without blinding himself to reality.

Even at his most escapist, Farquhar retains the saving grace of clear sight. The school of 'reform' comedies which flourishes in these years relies on reversals and assumptions not much removed from the conclusion of *The Beaux Stratagem*, but almost never exhibits that all-important sceptical tinge, an awareness of self-indulgence. Instead of being realistic but genial, these plays tend simply to be blindly and delusively benevolist in their assumptions.

As You Find it (April 1703) is typical of the hybrid reform comedy, grafting reformation on to an old-style marital discord plot. Charles Boyle's inclination is evidently to follow Congreve and Burnaby. Jack Single and Chloris are of the old mode, but Bevil, Orinda, and Eugenia are quasi-exemplary. The rakish Hartley declaims against husbandly drudgery (1), and keeps a mistress (Lucy), but his friends send him off to an assignation with his wife, and when he discovers who she is, he announces that this will bring him to his senses—he will reform (66–7). The results are more sentimental–exemplary than Nicoll allows, and are the worse for long and sodden speeches. Richard Wilkinson's *Vice Reclaim'd* (June 1703), though more overtly didactic, is considerably livelier. There are three main plot lines. Merry old Sir Feeble Goodwill marries the widow Purelight, a rich Quaker. The rakish Wilding falls for Annabella (in breeches) and reforms to win her (55)—so drastic a change as almost to appear a satiric joke. And finally Fondle, the rich old keeper of Mrs. Haughty, marries her under the impression that she is Annabella veiled. After he discovers the truth she makes a serious, romantic appeal (in verse) promising to be a good wife, and he accepts her (60–1). Despite lively handling and gay elements, this is quite a serious play, and not a bad one. A very similar formula is employed in Mrs. Pix's *The Different Widows* (November 1703). Sir James Bellmont, on the verge of raping Angelica (45), winds up marrying her as a reformed character.[1]

Steele is naturally the great exponent of 'reform comedy', with Cibber and Centlivre right behind him. *The Lying Lover* (December 1703) is an extreme example, not well done, and it deserved its quick demise. Young Bookwit, the liar and braggart, thinks he has killed the jealous Lovemore in a duel. His remorse, his good old father's anguish, the noble generosity of his friend Latine in trying to take the blame on himself are all rather undercut by our knowing that Lovemore is really perfectly all right. Steele works in a predictable sermon about the evils of duelling; the epilogue rejects the pride and scorn of laughter in favour of pity; the preface stresses strict morality and the propriety of such comedy as entertainment for a Christian Commonwealth. Compared to his source, Corneille's *Le Menteur*, Steele works in a remarkable amount of ponderous, pseudo-tragic didacticism.[2] *The Tender Husband* (April 1705) is lighter-hearted and was much more successful. Clerimont Senior is being ruined by his extravagant wife: finally he catches her with her 'lover', Lucy disguised as 'Fainlove', and in a sentimental reform scene she weeps, kneels, and is forgiven (263–5). Captain Clerimont woos and wins the romance-mad Biddy, destined for a country booby, Humphry Gubbin. This is Steele's most Shadwellian play, and a fine one. For once he indulges the audience with humours and classic intrigues. Some of the incidental wit is very fine, as in Humphry's reverse proviso scene (249–50). Mrs. Clerimont's reform is exaggerated, but mercifully unpreachy.

Steele complained that *The Lying Lover* was 'damn'd for its Piety', but Mrs. Centlivre's tremendous success with *The Gamester* (February 1705) suggests audience receptivity to a

---

[1] The prologue to this play comments on the bad state of Lincoln's Inn Fields. 'What Arts have we not try'd? What Labour ta'en,/To Reconcile You to Our House again?' Tragedy is unpopular, we are told; even '*Irish Farce*' has palled, and 'That Lure grown stale, we since are forc'd to fill,/With Supplemental *Epilogue*, our *Bill*.' Unlike Rich, Betterton apparently found incidental attractions intensely distasteful.

[2] For analyses see Kenny's Introduction, and Susan Staves, 'Liars and Lying in Alarcón, Corneille, and Steele', *Revue de littérature comparée*, xlvi (1972), 514–27. On Steele's *humanitas* in general see Malcolm Kelsall, 'Terence and Steele', *Essays on the Eighteenth-Century English Stage*, ed. Kenneth Richards and Peter Thomson (London, 1972), pp. 11–27.

well-handled didactic play. Young Valere keeps promising Angelica that he will quit gambling, but does not do so. In male attire she wins all his money; his father disinherits him; he says he will repent and be good, whereupon she reveals that *she* has won his money, and they can marry. Secondary characters and intrigue are well handled in lively prose, off-setting the author's determination to eschew 'that Vicious Strain which usually attends the Comick Muse'. The result is a highly competent if entirely implausible exercise in reform and reclamation. *The Basset-Table* (November 1705) inverts the formula. Here Lord Worthy cannot get Lady Reveller to stop gaming: he reforms her by staging a rape-attempt and rescuing her. Centlivre does more here with sensibility, and Loftis notes the careful social distinctions between merchants and tradesmen (Sir Richard Plainman versus Sago).[1] The piece is more thoughtful but less focused than *The Gamester*, and did not do as well.

Colley Cibber's first play had been a great hit in the im-plausible reform mode, so his later indulgences in it are no surprise. *The Careless Husband* (December 1704) is a verbose, patchy play. Lord Foppington reappears, and though always a good character, he is not employed to advantage here. Lord Morelove, serious and sober, tames Lady Betty Modish. In the main action the good-hearted Sir Charles Easy intrigues with Lady Graveairs, and is found by his wife asleep with her maid Edging. Lady Easy discreetly leaves a scarf over his head; waking, he takes the hint, and in a reconciliation scene he repents and reforms (54–60). The tremendous popularity of the scarf ('Steinkirk') scene seems to have made the play. Its appeal lies both in sentimental reform, and in the air of genteel high life Cibber is so good at conveying. His dedication decries coarseness; he wants to appeal to people of quality, and so he avoids boisterous low humours and city intrigue devices. Instead he relies on conversation to fill out his play—and unhappily only the skill of a Vanbrugh can really support such a balance. *The Lady's last Stake* (December 1707) is much more serious. The proud, virtuous Lady Wronglove is maddened by her husband's amours, and they are saved from divorce only by the kindly intervention of Sir Friendly Moral, a sententious

---

[1] *Comedy and Society from Congreve to Fielding*, p. 66.

guide, philosopher, and friend. Cibber attempts a dead-serious treatment of marital discord, showing a keen sense of the way in which small, everyday irritants work in marriage (e.g. 48). This wife, as the prologue warns us, is altogether tougher than Lady Easy, and the slick solutions of *The Careless Husband* are explicitly rejected (44). One realizes, studying this ponderous effort, that there are virtues to implausible reform.

Some of these reform comedies are pleasant enough— especially *The Gamester*, *The Careless Husband*, and *The Tender Husband*. Modern critics tend to find them self-delusory, or even dishonest. Few of us can muster much faith in a Shaftesburyan view of human nature, and we may often suspect that Cibber and Centlivre, if not Steele, were indulging in sentimentally satisfactory solutions they did not believe in. This may well be true, but the reform plays rely on a convention, we should remember, which is really little more delusory or escapist than that to be found in *The Beaux Stratagem*, or even in the marriage convention which ends *The Man of Mode*. And certainly the reform pattern solves moral problems which seemed very important in the years of the Collier controversy, and satisfied a genuine taste for didacticism without forcing authors into the sterility of exemplary comedy.

The Spanish romance mode proved serviceably moral, and continued in popularity. Francis Manning's *All for the Better* (October 1702), from 'Fletcher's' *The Spanish Gypsy*, is full of light-hearted intrigue and sword-play, rather in the old *An Evening's Love* style, with two English gentlemen taking major parts. But along with the intrigue pattern we are shown reform: wild young Alphonso has to beg pardon on his knees (50) before Isabella will accept him. In *She wou'd and She wou'd not* (November 1702) Cibber stresses the light, bright, and sparkling. The wild Hypolita 'spurns' Don Philip, but follows him in breeches when he goes off to Madrid to woo Rosara. Hypolita claims to be Don Philip, duels with the real one, and 'marries' Rosara. Finally they are united ('They Advance slowly, and at last Rush into one anothers Arms'—71). Hypolita is one of the best madcap heroines of the *post*-1700 era; and the piece, fast-moving and well constructed, deserved its steady popularity through the century. The tone is light, but decidedly romantic. Centlivre's *The Stolen Heiress* (December 1702) is essentially a split plot tragicomedy, heavily dependent on complicated intrigue. The elopement of Palante and Lucasia is handled with romantic and pathetic fervour, including a verse prison scene, Palante's preparations for death, and his poor old father pleading for his son's life (44, 57, 59, 61, 63). Against this is balanced a farcical romance plot involving Sancho and Lavinia. The conclusion trumpets Providential Justice, but fails to redeem a rather mechanical exercise.[1] *Gibraltar* (February 1705) finds John Dennis contriving to stoop without conquering. Two English colonels, Wilmot and Vincent, are taken by the French to Gibraltar, pay their ransom, and then linger in a nearby village, attracted by Don Diego's nieces. Dennis does passably in this mode, but the results are a bit heavy for so trivial a confection. A. Chaves's *The Cares of Love* (August 1705) is a sodden exercise which proved equally unsuccessful. Lisena follows Florencio to Toledo, and they are routinely reconciled after the standard repentance. Vanbrugh's *The Mistake* (December 1705) is a vigorous, colloquial prose translation of Molière's *Le Dépit amoureux* with the scene shifted to Spain. Even John Wilcox, usually grudging, admits that Vanbrugh may have improved the original.[2] Love quarrels, intrigue, and confusion contribute to a sound if not especially witty play. *The Adventures in Madrid* (*c.* June 1706), possibly by Mrs. Pix, provides breezy treatment of semi-serious intrigues. As is so common in these 'Spanish' plays, the principal male leads (here Gaylove and Bellmour) are English, following a pattern set by Dryden in 1668 and exploited successfully ever since.

Three adaptations with a similar middle-of-the-road appeal may be mentioned at this point.[3] Burnaby's *Love Betray'd*

---

[1] *Love the Leveller*, by 'G. B. Gent.' (January 1704) is not even technically Spanish, but may be mentioned as another example of the now rare split plot tragicomedy. Set in Crete, it balances a dreary pseudo-heroic serious plot full of intrigue and attempted poisoning against a better comic plot in which Sordico tries to prostitute his wife to Dewcraft, but is foiled when her virtue converts her would-be seducer.

[2] *The Relation of Molière to Restoration Comedy*, pp. 169–74.

[3] An apparent fourth, *The Royal Merchant*, described in *The London Stage* (Part 2, p. 96) as an adaptation of Beaumont and Fletcher's *The Beggar's Bush*, is actually simply a revival of the original. Nicoll's account follows Genest's (II. 322), which is based on alterations printed in the 1761 quarto, a copy of which was owned by Genest and is now in the Yale Library.

(January 1703) is a dismal mess made out of *Twelfth Night*, jumbling social comedy and the romance world in a thoroughly inept way. The preface complains of the House's failure to get the masque in Act V set to music—testimony to Lincoln's Inn Fields' corner-cutting in hard times. Cibber's *The Comical Lovers* (February 1707) is simply the comic sub-plots of Dryden's *Secret Love* and *Marriage A-la-Mode* grafted together. All the serious point of the latter is lost, and Celadon and Florimell are reduced to a sad shadow of the old gay couple. The hybrid is brisk and cheerful; Cibber creates a good contrast between Melantha (Mrs. Bracegirdle) and Florimell (Mrs. Oldfield). In *The Double Gallant* (November 1707) he contrives a passable amalgam from bits of dead plays, lifting plot lines out of Centlivre's *Love at a Venture*,[1] and Burnaby's *The Ladies Visiting-Day* and *The Reform'd Wife*. As usual, Cibber does a slick job of piecing together standard elements: the results are good theatre entertainment but indifferent drama.

The upsurge in farce is surprising only in that it did not start earlier. Most of these works are afterpieces, confections of slapstick and foolery often worked up from French sources, especially Molière. The best of them is Farquhar's *The Stage-Coach*.[2] Basically Farquhar translated De la Chapelle's *Les Carosses d'Orleans*. Captain Basil hopes to save Isabella from a forced marriage to a Lancashire booby, Squire Somebody. A chance meeting at an inn and a night's contretemps supply a conclusion. Farquhar did choose to rewrite the ending: instead of fleeing from the inn and vanishing, Captain Basil and Isabella find themselves locked in—but spying 'a Light in the Parsons Chamber . . . we went up, found him smoking his Pipe. He first gave us his Blessing, and then lent us his Bed' (II. 28). The conclusiveness of this ending is decidedly more satisfying than the open-endedness of the original. This fizzy bagatelle was long a great success: it is a miniature comedy of the sort Garrick was to cultivate so successfully.

Cibber's *The School-Boy* (October 1702) is simply the enter-

---

[1] Performed at Bath and printed in 1706. It is one of her poorer efforts (taken from Thomas Corneille), but Cibber saw the possibilities in one man playing two gallants.

[2] By 2 February 1704. (See p. 446, note 2, above.) For an analysis see Jonathan E. Deitz, 'Farquhar and De la Chapelle: *The Stage Coach* and Distinctions Between Farces', forthcoming in *Révue de littérature comparée*.

taining Mass Johnny parts salvaged from his *Womans Wit.*
Walker's (?) *The Wit of a Woman* (June 1704) is more routine
stuff: Aurelia elopes with Gayford, despite her father Boastwit's
best efforts, and in one final page of wild reversals and sentimental forgiveness all are reconciled. Motteux's *Farewel Folly;
or The Younger the Wiser* (January 1705) is similar stuff at main-
piece length.[1] Owen Swiny's *The Quacks* (March 1705) is a
three-act trifle derived from Molière's *L'Amour médecin.* The 'fake
marriage' conducted by a 'footman' turns out to be real, having
been performed by Father Nicholas. The preface makes much
of the satire on doctors, though it is no more than plain foolery.
The author complains bitterly about the Lord Chamberlain's
delaying the *première* 'because the other House were to Act one
upon the same Subject'. This was evidently *The Consultation*
(anonymous, not printed), acted with *The Loves of Ergasto* in
April 1705. In fact, the real reason that the farce was first
banned, and then censored before it was allowed on the stage, is
more interesting. *The Quacks* contains a sharp satiric attack on
the Kit-Cat Club—which had helped underwrite Vanbrugh's
new theatre—and in particular on Jacob Tonson ('Stationer
Freckle').[2]

The low literary value placed on such bits of stage carpentry is reflected in unusually slow publication, or even
non-publication. Cibber's farce waited five years to see print;
Motteux's two. In March 1704 Congreve, Vanbrugh, and
Walsh collaborated on a translation of *Monsieur de Psource-
augnac,* Englished as *Squire Trelooby.* First played at a sub-
scription concert, it was later used as a main piece at the Haymarket, and seems to have been mildly popular, but the authors
declined to publish.[3] Similarly Vanbrugh never printed his

---

[1] This piece, printed in 1707, has become entangled with *The Amorous Miser: or
The Younger the Wiser* (4to, 1705), which is evidently a piracy of Motteux's farce.
For a summation of the controversy over the relation of the two plays, see Robert
Newton Cunningham, *Peter Anthony Motteux* (Oxford, 1933), pp. 137–42.

[2] See Albert Rosenberg, 'A New Move [error for 'Motive'] for the Censorship of
Owen Swiney's "The Quacks" ', *Notes and Queries*, cciii (1958), 393–6.

[3] Another translation was rushed into print in the spring of 1704, with a title-page
stating falsely that it had been performed at Lincoln's Inn Fields. For a sensible
analysis of the controversy surrounding the alleged use of the 'Congreve' version in
The Cornish Squire (1731), see Graham D. Harley, '*Squire Trelooby* and *The Cornish
Squire*: A Reconsideration', *Philological Quarterly*, xlix (1970), 520–9, who denies the
claim.

The Cuckold in Conceit (March 1707), an afterpiece concocted from Molière's *Sganarelle ou le cocu imaginaire*. A pair of main-piece farces can be noted briefly. Centlivre's *Love's Contrivance* (June 1703) is a light and cheerful Molière hash, later canni-balized as an afterpiece. John Corye's *The Metamorphosis* (Octo-ber 1704) is another such production (actually taken from *Albumazar*, 1615, despite a title-page acknowledgement to Molière), relying on magical transformations used for more than they are worth (e.g. 33).

Surveying the state of comedy, one must be struck by the increasing predominance of intrigue. Most comedies in all periods employ intrigue, but in these years it becomes an end in itself. Where once sex, cuckoldry, the love game, satire on cits and fops, social display, humours, and conversation occupied a major place, now authors rely on plot for plot's sake. The other elements do not disappear, but they pale and recede. Farce is safe, Spanish romance pure, and the upsurge in these forms is part of a retreat into safe and non-controversial formulas.

Turning to tragedy, one finds mostly stasis and decay. Discounting operas, comedies outnumber tragedies nearly three to one in these years. Prologue plaints about the rejection of tragedy have some basis in fact. Of the 26 'serious' works, 10 are operas, and 9 belong to the late heroic school. The latter figure is astonishing, since it strikingly contradicts the usual assumptions about the rise and dominance of pathetic and classic tragedy after 1700. *The Fair Penitent* (1703), often reprinted, did indeed become popular in the 1720s, but it is one of only two genuine pathetic tragedies to appear in this five-year span. Not one of the four classical plays was at all successful. Indeed, of the 16 serious plays only two proved 'living plays'—the second being Trapp's *Abra-Mule*. Of the 9 heroic plays, 8 turn out to be L.I.F.–Haymarket shows: Better-ton stubbornly stuck with a genre he believed in, long after Rich had given it up as hopeless. Five of them were mounted after the move to the Haymarket: we should recollect that this sort of noisy showpiece would suffer less than other play types from bad acoustics.

Joseph Trapp's (?) *Abra-Mule* (January 1704), set in Constantinople, typifies the slack and slushy form of heroic play predominant in these years. Abra-Mule (Mrs. Bracegirdle) is sold to the Emperor Mahomet. She loves the Grand Vizier Pyrrhus; however, the emperor's brother Solyman also falls in love with her. Pyrrhus, disguised as a blackamoor, is caught visiting her and sent off to be racked; the emperor is deposed by a convenient rebellion, and Solyman takes over. He addresses her; she stabs herself—but recovers, and Solyman resigns her to Pyrrhus, who turns out not to have been racked after all. The prologue emphasizes the lack of ghosts, rant, lightning and thunder: the new heroic formulas turn more on sentiment than on noise. Trapp exemplifies the dominant pattern of 'soft' tragedy, relying on pathetic sensibility and a happy ending, in which, as he complacently tells us, mankind can learn that 'Villany at last shall mourn/And injur'd Virtue Triumph in its Turn'. *The Faithful Bride of Granada* (*c.* May 1704), possibly by Taverner, is more pathetic and exclamatory, though the villain Oliman finally stabs himself (58), and the distressed hero and heroine, Abinomin and Zelinda, live happily ever after. *Zelmane* (November 1704)[1] is less turgid, and benefits from a better villain (Pirotto).

This sort of play was a speciality of the women writers. Pix's *The Conquest of Spain* (May 1705), founded on *All's Lost by Lust*, goes right back to battles, love and honour dilemmas, and so forth. Julianus is an effective character—an old Spanish general who comes out of retirement to fight the Moors, remaining a pattern of loyalty and helping his king escape, even after the king has raped Julianus's daughter. Mrs. Trotter's *The Revolution of Sweden* (February 1706) mixes love complications and treachery with politics. Gustavus becomes the King of Sweden, and his friend Count Arwide, almost executed for apparent treachery, is saved at the last instant: Christina, wife of the evil Beron, swoons before she can explain the count's innocence, but revives just in time to clear him. Despite a good deal of turgidity, this is not a bad play of its kind. *Almyna* (December 1706), possibly by Mrs. Manley, is an Arabian Nights melodrama. Caliph Almanzor puts

[1] According to the *Diverting Post*, Mrs. Pix was the author. The common ascription to Mountfort is highly implausible. See Albert S. Borgman, *The Life and Death of William Mountfort* (Cambridge, Mass., 1935), pp. 176–7.

his wives to death after the first night. Almyna wants to marry him, hoping to end this practice. Needless to say, she succeeds, after we are treated to her preparations for death (59). *The Faithful General* (January 1706), by 'A Young Lady', is no more than a hideously mangled, sentimentalized recension of Fletcher's *The Loyal Subject*. Drury Lane mounted the original against this abortion, and drove it off the boards.

Two male exercises in the heroic mode are a bit more interesting. Dennis's *Liberty Asserted* (February 1704) concerns love and honour heroics amidst French and Indian wars in Canada, complete with the obligatory Indian princess. The Indian general Ulamar turns out to be the long-lost son of the French Governor, Frontenac, who is then persuaded to break with France and found an independent country. The preface makes a major point of the political import. Dennis claims merely to be denouncing treachery and arbitrary power; in fact, his blast at the French was extremely topical in the year climaxed by Blenheim, and undoubtedly helped his play to achieve its run of eleven nights over a five-week span. Rowe's *The Royal Convert* (November 1707) is set in Kent twenty years after the Saxon invasion, mixing pagan rites and Old English colour with love and honour complications. It is a rather frigid exercise: Rowe's evil characters (Hengist, Rodogune) seem absolutely vapid even when in blind rages. Nicoll exaggerates in saying that we are out of the heroic style here, but Rowe certainly is not very comfortable in it. The happy ending for Aribert and Ethelinda, and the triumph of Christianity, are thoroughly predictable.

Comparing this dismal set of heroic plays with those written in the preceding five years, the decline in horror plays and love tragedy is obvious—the norm is now very definitely virtue rewarded. Possibly this shift reflects a belated reaction to widespread demands for providential, or at least poetical justice. At any rate, the habit of mangling innocents to move compassion falls off sharply—indeed to the point at which pathetic drama proper almost disappears. Oldmixon's *The Governour of Cyprus* (December 1702) is a stiff verse excursion into old-fashioned pathos. Issamenea marries Phorsano (the governor), presuming her husband Iopano dead. Phorsano starts to pursue her sister-in-law Lucinda. Iopano returns in disguise and is stabbed by his wife, who does not realize that his addresses are merely meant to test her virtue. She drinks poison and they die agonizing over the pity of it all (41–5). Phorsano is killed as he attempts to rape Lucinda—saying wistfully that he would have died happy had he accomplished the rape (46). Other writers, notably Southerne, made better capital out of returned husbands. Rowe's *The Fair Penitent* (May 1703), in contrast, is highly effective theatre. (It is analysed above in Chapter 5.) Gentle rant, melodious verse, and a weepy celebration of friendship contribute to this 'melancholy Tale of private Woes'. Note, though, that Rowe depicts the wretchedness of guilt, not the tribulations of innocence. The guilty die, the hero faints—like a drooping flower to earth, his friend notes—and the audience retires well satisfied with its vicarious trip through a carnival of emotions. Rowe's slick manipulation of sensibility should not blind us, however, to the heavy didactic overlay in his tragedies. The day of pity for pity's sake is past, and, unlike Otway or Banks, Rowe insists on giving us sermons along with bathos. In this respect, *Jane Shore* (1714) is the summit of his art.

The classic–stoic mode, like the pathetic, almost vanishes in this half-decade. Gildon's *The Patriot* (November 1702) may be assigned to this group. It is no more than a stiffened, regularized revamping of Lee's *Lucius Junius Brutus*. Even with the anti-monarchical reflections cut out, the Master of the Revels refused the play a licence, necessitating a shift of scene to Florence and the substitution of Cosmo di Medici for Brutus. Gildon allows more open pathos, but mostly works to make the play conform, dispiritedly, to French rules. Rowe's *Ulysses* (November 1705) is neither fish nor fowl, and suffers from weak construction. Ulysses returns to Ithaca and regains his throne after much intrigue. Telemachus' wife Semanthe parts from him after he has to kill her father Eurymachus, King of Samos (who is pursuing Penelope)—but Rowe handles the parting with surprising restraint. He indulges, feebly, in more heroic clutter than one would expect from him, and the whole work seems tentative and ill planned. According to Downes, a fancy production, 'new Cloath'd', allowed it a decent initial run. Almost as awkward is Cibber's *Perolla and*

Izadora (December 1705), a solemn lecture packaged as a distributive justice tragicomedy. Roman–Carthaginian conflict provides a background for love complications and family feuds. Pacuvius commits suicide; Hannibal unites the young lovers. Cibber manages a vigorous and effective plot, but the language is woefully ponderous. Dennis (who was in no position to talk) calls it 'stiff, awkward Stuff', full of 'Lines that make as hideous a Noise, as if they were compos'd in an Itinerant Wheel-Barrow'.[1]

The one genuinely classic-style play from these years is Edmund Smith's insipid *Phædra and Hippolitus* (April 1707), founded on Racine's *Phèdre*. Distributive justice is effected: Phædra declares Hippolitus' innocence and commits suicide, leaving him to marry the captive princess Ismena. It ran for four nights in 1707: Addison comments with disgust on the indifference of the audience (*Spectator*, 18). Regular reprints and occasional revivals testify to determined support for the play's type—rather, one suspects, than to any particular pleasure in the play itself.

In light of the prominence of opera in the London theatre world after 1705, the years 1702–4 seem to mark a kind of lull. Apart from short musical masques (Motteux's *Britain's Happiness*, February 1704, is an example), only one new work is tried prior to 1705 after the failure of *The Virgin Prophetess*. *The Fickle Shepherdess* (*c.* March 1703) is an anonymous re-working of Randolph's *Amyntas* (1630),[2] staged with an all female cast in imitation of an old King's Company device. As such things go, it is reasonably lively, with a good mad-song by Mrs. Bracegirdle (18–19) and a striking sacrifice scene (41).

Ironically, the first shot in the great opera war was Rich's production of *Arsinoe, Queen of Cyprus* (January 1705), which achieved a success not soon repeated. Thomas Clayton provided music for a translation of Stanzani's *Arsinoe*. The result is a curious hybrid, an 'Italian' opera sung entirely in English, but the piece achieved a considerable popularity and was performed regularly for several years. The Haymarket opened

[1] *Critical Works*, II. 407.
[2] Apparently it was not related to Mrs. Behn's lost adaptation of the same work (1684), of which only two songs are extant.

on 9 April 1705 with a dreary and unsuccessful pastoral called *The Loves of Ergasto*, sung by specially imported Italian singers. Some patriotic opposition sprang up (cf. the epilogue to *The Tender Husband*). The great question at this point was which sort of opera would flourish—English, Italian, anglicized Italian, or some variety of hybrid. Rich had won the first round, but the Haymarket had been built specifically for opera, and its managers were determined to plunge heavily on some major productions.

In the spring of 1706 they mounted three such efforts. George Granville's *The British Enchanters* (February), with music by Corbett, is a fancy Purcell-style opera reminiscent of *King Arthur*. Elaborate scenery and occasional musical interludes are interlarded with spoken dialogue in rhymed couplets. Hero and heroine are saved by good enchanters from the evil wizard, Arcalaus. Downes tells us that the piece did well. Motteux's translation, *The Temple of Love* (March), did not: 'it lasted but Six Days, and answer'd not their Expectation', Downes reports (p. 49). The work consists 'all of Singing and Dancing'. 'Fedelli' provided Italian-style music; French dancers were imported; the singers were English. April brought Durfey's weird extravaganza, *Wonders in the Sun, or The Kingdom of the Birds, A Comick Opera*. This piece mingles low humour and trick staging with *Erewhon*-style satire (in the world of the sun, riches accrue to the unworthy and punches are a sign of friendliness), and with some fairly serious political commentary on the proposed union with Scotland, and on Whigs (low-flyers) and Tories (high-flyers). Music comes mostly at the end of acts in what amount to masques, and the plot appears and disappears. Many of the tunes are popular or traditional: Fiske comments on the 'music-hall flavour' of the production. Downes notes mournfully that it lasted only six days and lost a distressing amount of money. Its failure, and the baffling complexities of the fantastic allegories in this peculiar farrago, should not be allowed to deprive Durfey of credit for a truly brilliant production.[1] As in *Massaniello* he entirely transcends his reputation.

[1] The work was reprinted in facsimile in 1964 by the Augustan Reprint Society, with a brief introduction by William W. Appleton. For an analysis, see Fiske, pp. 41–4.

Rich replied with *Camilla* (March 1706), an Italian-style adaptation from Bononcini done by Swiny and Haym. Genest calls it 'contemptible', and I would agree, but it remained popular for twenty-five years. Thus, ironically it is Rich and the Drury Lane company who profit from Italian opera! So traumatized were the Haymarket managers—or perhaps so much out of pocket—that they did not mount another opera before the union. During the 1706–7 season Rich tried two. *Rosamond* (March 1707), with a good libretto by Addison, died after three nights, undone by Clayton's 'cretinous' music— according to Fiske 'the most notable and influential operatic failure of the century'. *Thomyris Queen of Scythia* (April 1707) is a hybrid. Pepusch arranged the music, mostly taken from Scarlatti and Bononcini, while Motteux rigged out a story and lyrics to fit the tunes. The piece was all-sung, in a mixture of Italian and English. It profited initially from being the first opera with an Italian castrato, but continued to be performed into the 1720s on its own merits.

The opening of the Haymarket and the rise of opera— however unexpected the beneficiary of its success—gave rise to some considerable reorganization in the theatre world. Following the operatic disasters at the Haymarket in the spring of 1706 the whole competitive situation altered. Rich allowed most of the best Drury Lane actors—including Cibber, Wilks, Johnson, Mills, Bullock, and Mrs. Oldfield—to decamp to the Haymarket company, which in return seems to have agreed to present plays alone—shorn of the now customary entr'acte entertainments. Rich, Cibber explains, had decided that 'Singing, and Dancing, or any sort of Exotick Entertainments, would make an ordinary Company of Actors too hard, for the best Set, who had only plain Plays to subsist on.'[1] The season and a half which followed saw straight plays pitted against variety entertainments. Cibber, by now thoroughly disgusted with Rich, reports that the Haymarket venture flourished, but other evidence suggests that neither group was doing especially well. On 31 December 1707 the Lord Chamberlain issued an order for a new union. Noting that 'by reason of the Division of her Majestys Comedians into two distinct houses or Companys the Players have not been able to gaine a

[1] *Apology*, p. 180.

reasonable Subsistence for their Encouragement in either company', that plays cannot 'always be Acted to the best Advantage', and that the cost of opera is prohibitive, he restricts plays to Drury Lane and operas to the Haymarket—which made good acoustical sense—and authorized an appropriate redistribution of performers, regardless of current contracts.[1] The order undoubtedly made sense in the circumstances, but the immediate result, predictably, was stagnation.

III. THE THEATRICAL SITUATION *circa* 1710

The dismal state of English drama at this time is in part simply a reflection of the condition of the theatres. This is not the place for a full account of theatrical vicissitudes in the chaotic years after 1708, but clearly the lack of competition was stultifying. By the terms of the new union Drury Lane acted plays (shorn of music) six nights a week, leaving the Haymarket to mount operas on Wednesday and Saturday. Returning all the actors to Rich's mercies soon produced the predictable result: financial disputes, followed by the Lord Chamberlain's silencing of the house on 6 June 1709, and the return of the actors, *en masse*, to the Haymarket for the 1709–10 season. During this year William Collier and Aaron Hill got permission to reopen Drury Lane with a second company, and did so.[2] In the autumn of 1710 Swiny, Wilks, Cibber, and Doggett led the actors back to Drury Lane (Rich having been manœuvred out of the way), leaving the Haymarket to put on its operas twice a week. This monopoly arrangement worked quite profitably until 1714, when John Rich re-established competition by opening a new Lincoln's Inn Fields theatre. But as in the profitable days of the first united company, the result was that the new plays that were produced were exceedingly cautious and unimaginative offerings.

In popular myth, the year 1700 marks a last hurrah for 'Restoration' drama, after which a flood of dismal sentimental drama sweeps all before it. The pernicious tendency to see *The Way of the World* as a culmination, and its appearance and 'failure' as a simultaneous triumph and tragedy, suggests that

---

[1] A complete transcription of the order appears in B.M. Add. MS. 20,726, f. 36.
[2] For documents related to these broils, see B.M. Add. MS. 20,726.

the transition had the abruptness of an earthquake. Thus Nicoll can tell us that 'the comedy of manners was in the full flush of its highest bloom . . . when the year 1700 came' (II. 125). Actually, as we have seen, the transition from hard comedy toward the new had been in progress for more than a decade; hard comedy was a dying mode by the middle 1690s; and Congreve's play clearly reflects these major changes in theatrical and moral climate. Easy dichotomies are treacherous, and even the most learned scholars sometimes indulge in them. Thus John Harold Wilson helps perpetuate the reductive formulas still deeply ingrained in most students of this drama. Surveying types of comedy, he observes: 'it ran the gamut from broad, vulgar farce, through burlesque and intrigue comedy, humours and satiric comedy, to the comedy of wit. At the close of the century it turned, like a penitent prodigal, to the comedy of tears.' Concluding a survey of tragedy, Wilson notes plays by Banks, Southerne, and Motteux, and suggests that they 'prepared the way for the "she-tragedy" of the eighteenth century, as it was developed by "soft, complaining" Rowe in *The Fair Penitent* (1703) and *Jane Shore* (1714). The age of sentiment and tears was ushered in with showers.'[1] Most thundering clichés have some basis in fact—and the replacement of 'Restoration' by 'sentimental' drama is no exception. But the reader will, I trust, have noted in the last two chapters of this study some evidence contrary to the replacement cliché. The number of pathetic tragedies in recent seasons had been negligible, the number of weepy comedies *à la* Cumberland just about nil.[2]

Carolean drama does indeed gradually give way to something else in the years between 1685 and 1705. The problem is to define the new drama. If we examine the new plays in the years just after the second union, what do we find? Operas are in good supply, at first in bilingual form,[3] but the tremendous success of Mancini's *Hydaspes* (March 1710) prefigures the triumph of Handel's *Rinaldo* a year later—and the

---

[1] *Preface to Restoration Drama*, pp. 118, 129.

[2] Steele's *The Lying Lover* (1703) is as weepy a play as we have found—a flat failure.

[3] Motteux's *Love's Triumph* (February 1708), Swiny and Haym's popular *Pyrrhus and Demetrius* (December 1708), and the anonymous *Almahide* (January 1710).

dominance of the Italian mode was assured.[1] Tragedy, meanwhile, is in a deplorable condition. The predominant type, numerically, is a sterile and imitative form of the late heroic mode. Charles Goring's *Irene* (February 1708), set in a Constantinople harem, and Lewis Theobald's *The Persian Princess* (May 1708) are rubbishy exercises in balderdash, as is Aaron Hill's *Elfrid* (January 1710)—this time in an Old English setting. Charles Johnson's *The Force of Friendship* (April 1710) is at least in concept something like a real tragedy, despite its ludicrous honour conventions, but is ruined by hopelessly stilted language. All four failed.

The most astonishing thing about tragedy in these years is the scarcity of plays in the 'new' modes—pathetic and classic–stoic. One finds pathetic tinges here and there, and with *Jane Shore* in 1714 we encounter Rowe's heavily moralized she-tragedy, but in the Otway and Banks sense of the form it has pretty well died out. The classic–stoic form does retain its identity, such as that is. It is an untidy grouping, and perhaps ought to be subdivided. But as with Gothic and historical novels a century later, disentanglement proves difficult. Dennis's *Appius and Virginia* (February 1709) has a good design, but the author's attempts to inject passion into a 'classic' treatment vary from frigid (14) to incredible (32) to ludicrous (36). Ambrose Philips's *The Distrest Mother* (March 1712), Scriblerian contempt aside, is a competent adaptation of Racine's *Andromaque*. Sublimity is the aim—but held within a sharply limited concept of propriety. Steele's prologue criticizes Shakespeare for breaking the rules, and expresses the hope that '*French* Correctness' can be joined to '*British* Fire'. Addison may or may not have written the epilogue 'by Mr. Budgell': in any case, the play is part of the campaign which culminates in *Cato* (April 1713), the epitome of the classic–stoic mode. There stoicism and reason entirely outweigh love and passion. In the character of Cato, Addison embodies some real imaginative sympathy and nobility, but the results,

---

[1] A single countervailing burlesque was tried, to no avail. Estcourt's *Prunella* (February 1708), mounted at Drury Lane right after the union, is a clever take-off, but evidently met with no approval. It was acted only once, apparently serving as an entr'acte for *The Rehearsal*. Estcourt sends low London characters prancing through a nonsensical plot, singing incongruous words to tunes from popular operas—*Arsinoe*, *Thomyris*, and *Camilla*.

as a stage play, are remarkably frigid—helped not at all by excessively long speeches and pseudo-archaism. Nicoll tells us that 'the most important movement of the time was that to which has been given the name of pseudo-classical' (II. 51). In the realm of literary theory he is right, but in dramatic practice 'classical' plays are few in number and—*Cato* notwithstanding—not particularly successful.

In comedy, the play types continue to exhibit the pattern we have seen established: (1) humane intrigue comedy; (2) moral comedy, stressing repentance, reform, and forgiveness; and (3) farces designed as afterpieces.[1] There is naturally a strong temptation to see the humane comedy as a gutted, laundered descendant of 'Restoration' comedy, reform comedy as the offspring of Shadwell's 'new' comedy. In fact, this formula is misleadingly simple. The shift which has taken place is more a matter of amalgamation and sideways slippage than tidy lineal descent. The humane comedy of these years should be seen as an outgrowth of the 'median' comedy which emerges in the late 1690s. Basically, in its outlook and value-system, humane comedy is 'soft' and hence belongs to the 'new' comedy camp. The old 'hard' comedy simply withers away, while some of its plots and devices are subsumed into a new tradition.[2]

The Augustan comedy is probably best conceived as a set of types which emerge from the mixing process of the late 1690s. 'New' comedy—in the early 1690s sense—does not remain pure: as all comedy shifts uncomfortably away from the 1670s norms we find some very disconcerting mixtures of values and attitudes—as in *The Relapse*, which both satirizes and relies on Cibberian assumptions. The evaporation of the hard-comedy outlook leaves comedy in the difficult position of having to treat its principal characters sympathetically. Within the resulting 'soft' comedy we find three distinct modes: *humane* comedy, *reform* comedy, and *exemplary* comedy. Full-dress exemplary comedy is a rarity. When in 1722 Steele touts *The*

---

[1] For example, Aaron Hill's *Squire Brainless* (not printed) and *The Walking Statue*, Centlivre's amusing *A Bickerstaff's Burying*, and Charles Johnson's *Love in a Chest*, all from 1710.

[2] Only occasionally does an overt satire appear after 1707—for example, Baker's *The Fine Lady's Airs* (December 1708) and Durfey's topical *The Modern Prophets* (May 1709), both failures.

Conscious Lovers as a revolutionary theoretical innovation, he is indulging in no more than a little exaggeration. The usual formula for authors who hope with Taverner to make the theatre 'A moral School'[1] is reform, not flawless example. Genuinely exemplary comedy is about as rare in Augustan drama as genuine hard-line satire is in Carolean drama. It represents an ideal and an aspiration, not the norm.

The mainstream of Augustan comedy is well represented by Mrs. Centlivre's *The Busie Body* (May 1709), analysed at length in Chapter 3, above. It possesses the form but not the spirit of Carolean social comedy; its analogue in the 1670s would be a play like Wycherley's vapid *The Gentleman Dancing-Master*. Plot and humours make the substance of the play: there are no serious attitudes or issues beneath the surface. The complete triviality of the concoction is evident in comparison with Howard's *The Committee*, another intrigue comedy with a prominent lovable, bungling servant. There is no toughness in Centlivre's play, no strong feeling, no anger, no willingness to shock, offend, or disturb. Plot exists for the sake of plot. In her sequel, *Mar-plot* (December 1710), the action is moved to Spain, continuing the pseudo-Spanish mode. In *The Man's Bewitch'd* (December 1709), from Thomas Corneille's *Le Deuil*, she produces another such farcical romance. Similar formulas appear in such plays as Cibber's *The Rival Fools* (1709), an alteration of Fletcher's *Wit at Several Weapons*, and Gay's indifferent *The Wife of Bath* (1713). As a rule, such plays are cautiously genteel, eschewing crudity, coarseness, and low characters. In this respect Charles Shadwell's *The Fair Quaker of Deal, or The Humours of the Navy* (1710) is a welcome variation. It is strictly 'soft' and moral, and Shadwell jun. carefully 'reforms' even the whores, Jenny Private and Jiltup; but he follows his father's recipe and gives us plenty of boisterous low life along with our lesson.

The alternative to humane intrigue comedy—reform comedy —is different more in the elements it stresses than in its underlying assumptions. Charles Johnson's popular *The Wife's Relief: or, The Husband's Cure* (November 1711) is typical. It falls in the now familiar gambler-reclaimed mode (and is in fact an unacknowledged adaptation of Shirley's *The Gamester*,

[1] Prologue to *The Maid the Mistress* (1708).

1637). We are encouraged to sympathize with Cynthia, virtuous wife of the wastrel gambler and debauchee Riot, before a solution is provided. Johnson's *The Generous Husband* earlier the same year uses marital discord between Lucia and rich old Carizales in a common variant of the reform pattern. Taverner's (?) *The Maid the Mistress* (1708) serves to show how fundamentally akin the reform mode is to the plain intrigue type. In the main plot Beauford loves Harriot, designed by her father for Squire Empty—so she and her 'maid' Charlot exchange clothes and bamboozle the booby. In the sub-plot Gaylove pursues Sir David Fancy's wife, but reforms to marry Charlot, who turns out to be the sister of James Constant, a friend of Gaylove's who died in a duel as his second. The intrigues are amusing, but the author's moral trumpetings do affect the tone and impact of the play.

By 1710 tragedy is essentially dead. Even distributive justice tragicomedies have lost their pull; opera has usurped the appeal of serious drama with music and spectacle. Addison touts the classic–stoic mode, but it never achieves the sort of flowering that the rhymed heroic drama did a generation earlier. In comedy we find Steele the prophet of the exemplary mode. *The Conscious Lovers* does not appear for more than a decade, but as John Loftis has shown, Steele was planning the play by 1710,[1] and it is entirely consistent with the barrage of periodical criticism he started laying down at that time. Nonetheless, in practice Augustan comedy consists mostly of routine, formulaic plays from cautious professionals like Cibber, Centlivre, and Charles Johnson. In the course of this chapter we have seen an astonishing stasis set in: new play types are simply not being tried. Writers seem to have lost their sense of direction, and even the clarion calls of Addison and Steele fall on deaf ears. Augustan drama is *cautious* drama: traumatized by a decade of theatrical disintegration, its authors seem to fear failure more than they hope for success. Augustan comedy is not especially 'sentimental', and truly exemplary plays are quite rare, but authors are very concerned indeed that their work prove unobjectionable. They dedicate their efforts to the great god of

---

[1] 'The Genesis of Steele's *The Conscious Lovers*', *Essays Critical and Historical Dedicated to Lily B. Campbell* (Berkeley, Calif., 1950), pp. 173–82.

inoffensiveness, and we can scarcely be surprised that the results range from bland to preachy.

IV. EPILOGUE: THE NEW ERA AND THE OLD

By 1710 the Carolean tradition (*fl.* 1665–85) is a thing of the past. What remains of it has been assimilated into a new synthesis, one suited to a different age. The transition occurs gradually over a period of roughly twenty years (1685–1705), but by the end of that time the change is decisive: the rival tradition which arose in the 1690s has achieved dominance, and the era with which we have been concerned has drawn to an end. At this point we may look back and try briefly to decide what characterizes the Augustan drama, as against the Carolean drama which it both draws upon and reacts against. The changing taste of the audience is obviously a crucial determinant of the differences—and one often misunderstood.

Carolean drama is Court-oriented; Augustan drama is not. This point requires clarification, especially since it is often over-simplified into a stale and misleading cliché. Carolean drama is not, for the most part, by or about courtiers, and numerically speaking the bulk of its audience consists of lawyers, cits, army officers, government clerks, wives, young men-about-town, whores, and rabble. Charles II, however, is the drama's protector and patron, and exalted members of the Court circle regularly attend the theatre and write plays—among them Buckingham, Robert Howard, Tuke, Orrery, and Sedley. Several of the major playwrights are closely associated with the Court group, including Etherege, Wycherley, and Dryden. When I say that Carolean drama is Court-oriented, I do *not* mean to imply either that it is a coterie drama like that of the Court of Louis XIV, or that it reflects actual life in English Court circles. Rather, I mean that the Carolean drama derives conspicuous and trend-setting support from the Court circle, and that many of the plays very naturally express the tastes, values, and prejudices of this group.

Charles's intense personal interest in the theatre is clearly reflected in the Lord Chamberlain's books (which concern the theatre only peripherally as part of the King's 'household' affairs). These books also chronicle beautifully the drama's loss of status under succeeding monarchs. James II does usually see a play once a week, but the attention which Charles devoted to drama and bedroom furnishings William diverts to courtiers' trips to Holland and Anne lavishes on concerts, apothecaries, and preachers. Command performances and regular attendance at the public theatres by royalty produce a substantial income before 1688, as well as being wonderful advertisements.[1] After that we may find the Kit-Catters or the Knights of the Toast taking a box, but grand patronage is a thing of the past.[2] In the same period the theatres lose their status as *the* entertainment for the gentry. By the late 1690s concerts are diverting a significant part of the potential audience. Opera appealed to that group, but proved horrendously expensive to produce.

The loss of the Court circle is clearly less damaging numerically than in terms of lost protection, attention, and prestige. For most of a century the theatre had been a special preserve and playground for Stuart monarchs: the resultant association of King and playhouse is evident in puritan attacks on the stage. Indeed, there is reason to believe that Queen Anne's stubborn refusal to close the theatres is founded on a conviction that to do so would be disloyal to her father and uncle. They had seen fit to reopen and maintain the theatre: so be it, and no one was going to tell a Stuart Queen otherwise. The habit of looking to the monarch for support died hard. Rather than make a pitch to the merchants, writers keep hoping that Queen Anne will come to love them. In this respect, prologues, prefaces, and dedications in the decade after 1700 are rather pathetic.

When the Carolean audience dies off and Court attention shifts elsewhere, writers have to attract and educate a new audience. In this task they prove reluctant and inept. The *post*-1688 audience is patently more bourgeois and Whiggish, as one would expect after the accession of William and Mary. Authors adapt politically, but only with painful slowness do

---

[1] Charles's theatre-going was erratic, dropping off to almost nothing during the Popish Plot. For reprints of the accounts rendered complete with plays and dates, see Nicoll, I. 343–52. Nicoll does not record the many extant lump sum warrants— for example, £540 for plays put on by the King's Company between March 1662 and March 1663 (L.C. 5/137, p. 421). Command performances in particular, yielding £20 pure profit, represent a tremendous boon to the Carolean companies.

[2] Downes (pp. 46–7) goes out of his way to comment on four performances commanded by Queen Anne—over a period of three years.

they learn to modify the social prejudices by then traditional in English drama.[1] Play types in a healthy theatre reflect the preferences of the trend-setting part of the audience: the sense of confusion and indirection evident at the end of the century suggests that deprived of the influential Court circle, writers simply did not know where to look for guidance or approval. The result is failure and gnawing insecurity.

Where Carolean drama is above all ambitious and confident, Augustan drama is cripplingly defensive. A key to the whole character of the Augustan drama lies in its emergence out of a period of theatrical retrenchment and reform. The 1660s and 1670s are a time of hope: playwrights are boisterously insistent that a golden age is at hand, that English drama is about to surpass all previous ages, if indeed it has not already done so. The confident aspiration evident in Dryden's *Essay of Dramatick Poesie* (for example) translates in practice into fervent experimentation. The flaming excesses of heroic and horror plays, like the exuberant energy of the comedies, reflect a prosperous theatre. All this exhilaration and rugged confidence starts to evaporate at the end of the 1670s when hard times set in. Dryden is the inspiration for a second effort in the nineties, but the times prove unpropitious. By the late 1690s the very existence of the theatres is in doubt: they may collapse, even if they are not outlawed. Despite the rising tide of literary criticism at the end of the century, Augustan drama seems less responsive to theoretical speculation than Carolean. Dryden and Shadwell are two writers among many who are constantly asking what drama *should* be, and how it may be improved. They simply assume that drama is valuable, that it can and should be morally beneficial. In contrast, Augustan criticism is full of apologies and justifications, arguments that drama is not so very wicked, or need not be, and ought not to be suppressed. The prescriptions of Dennis, Addison, and Steele are in fact a reaction to outside pressures. For them, the critic's job is to rescue drama from collapse and moral turpitude. Dryden and Wycherley respond to moral criticism with contempt; in the 1680s wounded indignation is a common reaction; by the later 1690s cringing apology is the norm, and

[1] See Loftis, *Comedy and Society*, for a lucid demonstration.

writers no longer dare shock, attack, and experiment. The problem is not a rage for 'sentimental' drama so much as lack of
support for any drama.

In the mid-1670s, the heyday of the Carolean period, two
strong theatre companies do a booming business, producing a
luxuriant profusion of play types and a long series of plays
from major writers near the peak of their powers. We find
rhymed heroic tragedy (*Aureng-Zebe*), musical spectacular (the
1674 *Tempest*), villain–horror tragedy (*Nero*), high tragedy (*All
for Love*), two plot tragicomedy (*Marriage A-la-Mode*), satiric
tragedy (*The Libertine*), sex comedy (*The Country-Wife*), libertine
wit-comedy (*The Man of Mode*), humours satire (*The Virtuoso*),
intrigue romance (*The Rover*), satire (*The Plain-Dealer*), farcical
comedy (*The Countrey Wit*). Against this dazzling array the
Augustan drama makes a very poor showing. The quarter-
century or so in which it holds sway seems by contrast to be a
prolonged dead spot, a lull between 'Restoration' drama and
Fielding. Probably the best reason for seeking a serious understanding of Augustan drama is its relation to the transitional,
post-Carolean phase which does produce such major authors as
Southerne, Congreve, Vanbrugh, and Farquhar. Of those four,
Farquhar alone makes the jump and does important original
work in an Augustan mode. One cannot read his late plays
without wondering whether, had he lived, he might have led his
age to something better.

Augustan drama can scarcely be said to have a heyday.
Indeed, as we follow the survey just completed into the
eighteenth century, it increasingly becomes a tediously descriptive account of static play types, and ever fewer of them.
Until *The Beggar's Opera* revives real theatrical competition
in 1728 by successfully tapping a huge and unsuspected potential
audience, the history of eighteenth-century drama is largely a
depressing series of variations upon shrunken and derivative
formulas. The regularized 'classical' tragedy sponsored by
Addison (*The Distrest Mother*, *Cato*), the occasional specimen
of moralized pathos (*Jane Shore*), and watery remnants of the
late heroic mode (*The Persian Princess*) constitute tragedy.
Comedy comprises sterile intrigue comedy, with no sex, little
passion, and little satire (*The Busie Body*); moral reform comedy
(*The Wife's Relief*); and afterpiece farce (*The Walking Statue*).

Contemplating the relative scantiness and poverty of the Augustan play types, we must remember that Augustan plays generally represent not an evening's entertainment, but merely the bulk filler in a variety show. Obviously the writers do not like to consider or describe their work in this light, but the playbills tell a damning story. And occasionally a writer will be blunt, as in Cibber's admission that *Love makes a Man* 'only held up its Head by the Heels of the *French Tumblers*'.[1] Rich's allowing his principal actors to decamp to the Haymarket in 1706 is clear proof of his conviction that plays were the least important part of the evening's entertainment.

The collapse of tragedy is largely attributable to two factors: the usurpation of much of its appeal by opera, and the rising demand for poetic or providential justice. The clamour from Dennis and others for Christian tragedy (a contradiction in terms, as he describes it) and a reaction against the easy pathos of 'murdering innocents to move compassion' combine to produce a dreary flock of distributive justice tragicomedies in the years after 1700.[2] Addison did see how silly and restrictive poetic justice was proving, and his ringing denunciation of it in *Spectator*, 40, does him credit. The classical mode he championed, however, proves no answer: disdaining 'Enthusiasm' (as Nicoll writes), one cannot introduce much passion. The result is almost invariably shallow, frigid characters, even where the puerilities of providential justice do not make 'tragedy' a simple display of stick and carrot.

The diminished state of comedy is attributable more to theatrical depression than to philosophical necessity. The best Carolean comedies mock and question; the best Augustan comedies preach or reassure. But though we may prefer hard comedy to soft, there is no actual bar to excellence in the latter mode, as Farquhar proves, and Goldsmith and Sheridan demonstrate again in a later period. The customary blanket condemnation of eighteenth-century comedy, and the tendency to explain the writers we like as noble upholders of the true Restoration way amidst darkness, simply ignore the diversity of the 'soft' comedy. The Farquhar of 1707 is not Steele—he

---

[1] Preface to *Ximena* (1719).
[2] For example, *Abra-Mule*, *The Faithful Bride of Granada*, *The Revolution of Sweden*.

does not adopt the exemplary method—but neither is he Wycherley *manqué*.

The soft Augustan comedy is in a sense founded in Shadwell's last plays.[1] There admirable *old* characters,[2] 'reform', and a quasi-exemplary bent are usually offset by boisterous low life and unreclaimed sinners. This formula, however moral, gets amended in the midst of the ethical broils a decade later. Augustan writers are forever harping on the goodness and reason in man—largely, one may suspect, from fear of the dangers of exhibiting the bad, rather than from passionate proto-Shaftesburyite convictions. Writers feel that they ought to display man as he should be, not as he is—or at least that this is the safest thing to do. Shrinking from the coarse, low, and crude, writers turn to 'genteel' comedy. This should be understood not as a sub-genre but rather as a self-conscious avoidance of the indecorous. In Cibber's hands especially the results are 'nice' drama—with all the worst connotations of false refinement implicit in that adjective. This is what makes a boisterous low play like *The Fair Quaker of Deal* so refreshing, even though it is an intensely moral piece of work. The popularity of that play suggests that authors may have been misgauging their audience.

The fussy propriety customary in Augustan comedy contrasts most unfavourably with the aggressive energy of Carolean comedy. The tremendous moral pressure on writers after about 1695 is obvious enough, and yet one cannot simply say that a stuffy bourgeois audience demanded nothing but tediously pure plays after 1700—for the simple reason that the audience continued to attend such plays as *The Country-Wife*, *The Rover*, *The Old Batchelour*, *The Plain-Dealer*, *Amphitryon*, *City Politiques*, and *The London Cuckolds*. The days of bowdlerizations like Garrick's *The Country Girl* and Sheridan's *A Trip to Scarborough* are still two generations away.[3] How audiences could cheerfully

---

[1] For an important discussion of Whig ideology in drama, see Alan S. Fisher, 'The Significance of Thomas Shadwell', *Studies in Philology*, lxxi (1974), 225–46.

[2] Not unknown in Carolean comedy (e.g. Sir Richard Plainbred in *The Country Gentleman*), but certainly rare. See Elizabeth Mignon, *Crabbed Age and Youth* (Durham, N.C., 1947).

[3] One might anticipate wholesale excisions from the old plays. Words and phrases—basically blasphemy—do get cut (e.g. from *The Double-Dealer*, 4 March 1699), and occasional scenes are dropped or replaced (a well-known instance is the 1726

swallow camels by the herd in old plays while choking over the veriest gnats in new ones remains a mystery.

Carolean audiences obviously revelled in both rogues and villains, feasting alike on gritty low life, epic heroes, and bloodbaths. The Carolean drama is fiercely opinionated: personal, literary, and political satire abound; the resultant controversies and feuds are fought with vim, whether the grounds of dispute are *The Empress of Morocco* or anti-Whig allegory during the Exclusion Crisis. By contrast the Augustan dramatists seem stodgy and careful, always fearful of offending. Literary disputants are sometimes (like Dennis) pettifoggingly quarrelsome, but more often they seem principally concerned to cover themselves against reproach. Their pervasive sense of insecurity and defensiveness is acutely aggravated by Collier-era attacks, but the change from hard comedy toward soft was well advanced long before Collier, and would plainly have occurred without the reformers' campaign. Collier and his angry fellows created a lot of heat and noise, and they probably made some Londoners uncomfortable about attending the theatre—but the reformers were for the most part not play-goers, and the change in drama reflects audience preferences, not puritan dogma. The reformers gave the dramatists and players a bad scare, and the Anglican bishops might actually have got the theatres closed again. But these external pressures merely complicate and confuse what was an inevitable transition.

How the Augustan drama unfolds, and the new boom of the 1730s, cut so unhappily short by the Licensing Act, are fascinating subjects, but as Kipling likes to say, they belong to another story. This survey has taken us to the end of the Carolean tradition and into the Augustan period, and is therefore complete. Looking back, one sees that underlying the obvious diminution of smut and cynicism is a more profound change in the whole philosophy reflected in the plays. At the extremes, the difference is easy to see: Steele's outlook is not Etherege's, and the value-systems implicit in their plays naturally differ. Similarly if less spectacularly Cibber refines upon

---

production of *The Provok'd Wife*), but neither printed quartos nor contemporary comment yield much evidence of significant tampering in the years of the Collier controversy—which is rather astonishing.

DED—R

Shadwell's reform pattern, Centlivre moralizes Behn's racy intrigues, Addison regularizes and democratizes Dryden's classic–stoic mode. Translating such particulars into broadly ideological terms, one may say that we have seen what is, philosophically speaking, an aristocratic Tory drama give way to one which is increasingly bourgeois and Whig.

INDEX OF NAMES AND TOPICS

Some incidental names and references are omitted. Entries under a playwright's name do *not* include pages where a play of his is mentioned, unless the writer himself is referred to more generally.

INDEX OF PLAYS

The following bibliographical list indicates modern editions where I have used them. In the index the edition of late seventeenth-century plays quoted is specified in parentheses. In the majority of instances a plain date indicates the first quarto. For plays in one of the modern editions an appropriate short title (e.g. *Works*) or editor's name (e.g. Nahm) is given. Where authorship or the version referred to might be the subject of confusion (e.g. the 'Davenant' *Macbeth*), the author's name is supplied in square brackets. Principal discussions are indicated by bold-face type.

I *Collected Editions*

The Works of Aphra Behn, 6 vols., ed. Montague Summers (1915; repr. New York, 1967).
The Complete Plays of William Congreve, ed. Herbert Davis (Chicago, 1967).
The Works of John Dryden. Vol. viii, ed. John Harrington Smith, Dougald Mac-Millan, and Vinton A. Dearing (Berkeley, Calif., 1965). Vol. ix, ed. John Loftis and Vinton A. Dearing (Berkeley, Calif., 1966). Vol. x, ed. Maximillian E. Novak and George R. Guffey (Berkeley, Calif., 1970).
Dryden: The Dramatic Works, 6 vols., ed. Montague Summers (1931–2; repr. New York, 1968).
The Dramatic Works of Sir George Etherege, 2 vols., ed. H. F. B. Brett-Smith (Oxford, 1927).
The Complete Works of George Farquhar, 2 vols., ed. Charles Stonehill (1930; repr. New York, 1967).
The Works of Nathaniel Lee, 2 vols., ed. Thomas B. Stroup and Arthur L. Cooke (1954–5; repr. Metuchen, N.J., 1968).
The Dramatic Works of Roger Boyle, Earl of Orrery, 2 vols., ed. William Smith Clark, II (Cambridge, Mass., 1937).
The Complete Works of Thomas Shadwell, 5 vols., ed. Montague Summers (1927; repr. New York, 1968).
The Plays of Richard Steele, ed. Shirley Strum Kenny (Oxford, 1971).
The Complete Works of Sir John Vanbrugh, 4 vols., ed. Bonamy Dobrée and Geoffrey Webb (1927–8; repr. New York, 1967).
The Complete Plays of William Wycherley, ed. Gerald Weales (Garden City, New York, 1966).

II In addition to these collected editions, the following modern editions have been consulted, usually in addition to the original quarto. In the index the edition given first has been quoted except where specified in the text.

John Aubrey, *The Country Revell* (fragment), in *Brief Lives*, 2 vols., ed. Andrew Clark (Oxford, 1898).
The Dramatic Works of William Burnaby, ed. F. E. Budd (London, 1931).
Colley Cibber: Three Sentimental Comedies [*Love's Last Shift, The Careless Husband, The Lady's last Stake*], ed. Maureen Sullivan (New Haven, Conn., 1973).
Davenant's 'Macbeth' from the Yale Manuscript, ed. Christopher Spencer (New Haven, Conn., 1961).
Three Burlesque Plays of Thomas Duffett, ed. Ronald Eugene DiLorenzo (Iowa City, 1972).

Edward Howard, *The Change of Crownes*, ed. Frederick S. Boas (London, 1949).
Sir Samuel Tuke, *The Adventures of Five Hours*, ed. B. van Thal, Introduction by Montague Summers (London, 1927).
George Villiers, Second Duke of Buckingham, *et al.*, *The Rehearsal*, ed. Montague Summers (Stratford-upon-Avon, 1914).
John Wilson's The Cheats, ed. Milton C. Nahm (Oxford, 1935).